PREDICTING AND CHANGING BEHAVIOR

PREDICTING AND CHANGING BEHAVIOR

The Reasoned Action Approach

Martin Fishbein
Icek Ajzen

Psychology Press
Taylor & Francis Group

New York   Hove

Psychology Press
Taylor & Francis Group
270 Madison Avenue
New York, NY 10016

Psychology Press
Taylor & Francis Group
27 Church Road
Hove, East Sussex BN3 2FA

© 2010 by Taylor and Francis Group, LLC
Psychology Press is an imprint of Taylor & Francis Group, an Informa business

Printed in the United States of America on acid-free paper
10 9 8 7 6 5 4 3

International Standard Book Number: 978-0-8058-5924-9 (Hardback)

Library of Congress Cataloging-in-Publication Data

Fishbein, Martin.
 Predicting and changing behavior : the reasoned action approach / Martin Fishbein and Icek Ajzen.
  p. cm.
 Includes bibliographical references and index.
 ISBN 978-0-8058-5924-9 (hard back : alk. paper)
 1. Behavior modification. 2. Expectation (Psychology) 3. Human behavior. I. Ajzen, Icek. II. Title.

BF637.B4F57 2010
153.8'5--dc22   2009020871

Visit the Taylor & Francis Web site at
http://www.taylorandfrancis.com

and the Psychology Press Web site at
http://www.psypress.com

This book is dedicated to:

My wife, Deborah, for making the impossible, possible

The memory of my parents—Gloria and Sydney Fishbein

Les Squier, Bert Raven, and Irv Maltzman for teaching me what it means to be a psychologist and teacher.

And to Rachela, for being there when I need her, and to Ron and Jonathan, for just being there.

CONTENTS

PREFACE

It has been almost 30 years since we published our previous joint book, *Understanding Attitudes and Predicting Social Behavior*. In that book we tried to familiarize the reader with our theoretical approach and show how the small number of constructs comprising our original theory of reasoned action—attitudes, subjective norms, and intentions—can be used to predict and explain human social behavior in a variety of applied settings. Since then our theoretical framework has stimulated a great deal of empirical research; at last count, well over 1,000 empirical papers based on our reasoned action approach have appeared in professional journals. In the course of this period the theory has undergone several modifications, notably the addition of perceived behavioral control and of descriptive norms, and a number of theoretical and methodological concerns have emerged. In this book we describe the current status of our theoretical approach to the prediction and change of human behavior.

We begin by offering our theory as a conceptual framework that holds out the promise of accommodating the multitude of theoretical constructs currently used to account for behaviors related to health and safety, politics, marketing, the environment, the workplace, and many other domains in which social scientists are active. The introduction to our approach is followed, in Chapter 2, by an in-depth analysis of behavior, its measurement, and prediction. We discuss critical issues concerning the effect of intention on behavior and the moderation of this effect by actual and perceived control over the behavior. Chapters 3 through 5 deal, respectively, with the three major predictors in our model: attitude toward the behavior, perceived normative pressure, and perceived behavioral control. We define each concept, describe its measurement, and review research relevant to a number of important conceptual issues. We also explain the role of salient behavioral, normative, and control beliefs as the foundations of attitudes, perceived norms, and perceived behavioral control.

In Chapter 6 we provide empirical evidence for our model of behavioral prediction, and in Chapter 7 we show how variables of interest to social scientists, from demographic characteristics to individual difference and social structure variables, can be accommodated in our conceptual framework. Generally speaking, we see most of these variables as background factors that can influence salient behavioral, normative, and control beliefs and thus, indirectly, have an impact on intentions and actions. Given their central role in most social psychological attempts to predict and explain behavior, we devote Chapter 8 to a consideration of general attitudes toward objects, issues, and events. These general attitudes are undoubtedly the most prominent type of background factor studied by social scientists.

In Chapter 9 we take up a number of important challenges to our theoretical framework. In particular we consider questions concerning the theory's sufficiency and the degree to which it can be viewed as a rational model of behavior. Finally, in Chapters 10 and 11 we deal with the application of our theoretical approach to the design of behavior change interventions. In the first of these two chapters we provide a general overview of considerations guiding the development of behavior change interventions, and in the second we illustrate our reasoned action approach to behavior change by describing a few select intervention studies. We conclude this book with a final chapter in which we discuss some of the implications of our approach as well as directions for future research.

The theory and research covered in this book should be of interest to any student of human social behavior. Readers unfamiliar with our reasoned action approach will obtain a thorough introduction to its rationale and methods. Those who have some familiarity with our approach will find in this book an up-to-date account of the theory's current status, outstanding issues, and what we believe is still needed research. This book will perhaps be of greatest value to graduate students, academic researchers, and practitioners who are trying to understand or modify human social behavior in a given domain. As such, it should benefit social and clinical psychologists, sociologists, public health professionals, political scientists, economists, marketing researchers, organizational psychologists, and others who are interested in the social and behavioral sciences.

When we first started developing our model of behavioral prediction, there was general agreement that social behaviors were very difficult, if not impossible, to predict, and serious reservations were being voiced about the utility of the attitude construct as a basis for predicting and understanding social behavior. Today there is little doubt that social behaviors can indeed be predicted, often with considerable accuracy, and there is even less doubt about the importance and utility of the attitude construct. We like to think that the theory and research described in this book have contributed to this progress.

Although the empirical literature provides considerable support for our approach, work on our theory is far from complete. We both intend to continue working on the many unresolved issues, but it is unlikely that we will be the ones to find most of the answers. We are therefore delighted to see that there are many talented investigators as interested in predicting, understanding, and changing human social behavior as are we. It would give us a great deal of satisfaction if the issues and questions raised in this book keep these investigators busy in the years to come.

As was the case in our previous two books, the order of authorship for this book does not reflect our contributions, but for this volume it is simply an acknowledgment of seniority. We contributed in equal measure to the current volume, which we wrote together in the course of many meetings in Philadelphia and Amherst. We therefore take equal credit, and equal blame, for the contents of this book.

We would like to acknowledge the students in Communications 577 at the Annenberg School for Communication at the University of Pennsylvania, who read and commented on drafts of all of the chapters. Fishbein's work on this book was supported in part by the National Institute of Child Health and Human Development (NICHD) Grant 5 R01 HD044136 and by the National Cancer Institute (NCI) Grant 5 P50 CA095856. Neither NICHD nor NCI are responsible for, nor do they necessarily endorse, the contents of this book. We would also like to thank Mario Giorno, Hyun Suk Kim, and Sarah Parvanta for their help in developing the subject index. We are grateful to the Annenberg School for Communication, and the Annenberg Public Policy Center at the University of Pennsylvania, as well as the Department of Psychology at the University of Massachusetts for providing a supportive and encouraging environment in which to work.

Introduction

The behaviors people perform in their daily lives can have profound effects on their own health and well-being, on the health and well-being of other individuals, groups, and organizations to which they belong, and on society at large. There is a growing awareness that human behavior can both cause and alleviate social problems in a variety of domains such as health, safety, the environment, racism and intergroup relations, work motivation, and productivity. If people engaged in safer sex and safer drug injection practices they would be less likely to contract or to spread AIDS. The decision to get an advanced education influences employment opportunities and determines whether a skilled workforce, essential in an increasingly technological society, will be available. Cigarette smoking, unhealthy diets, and lack of physical activity have all been linked to numerous medical problems, including heart disease, obesity, and various types of cancer. Clearly, we cannot design effective interventions to address social problems without a thorough understanding of the factors that determine human behavior.

The great number and variety of behaviors implicated in the multitude of social problems facing both the developed and the developing world makes explanation of behavior a daunting task. Each class of behaviors seems to require a different set of explanatory constructs. To account for low voter turnout in elections and low participation in other political activities, theorists have relied on such constructs as alienation, (lack of) political involvement, and (low) political efficacy; to encourage people to get screening for various medical conditions, investigators have turned to perceived susceptibility or risk of contracting a particular illness and the severity of the illness; with respect to discrimination in housing, employment, or health care, explanations have focused on stereotyping and prejudice based on race or ethnicity, gender, age, and sexual orientation; to increase productivity or performance in the workplace and to reduce absenteeism and turnover, investigators have measured job satisfaction, organizational climate, and commitment to the organization; and to deal with such issues as energy or water conservation, pollution, and recycling, much of the interest has centered on ecological knowledge and concern for the environment. Each set of explanatory constructs was developed specifically to deal with behaviors in a given domain, and these constructs cannot easily be applied or generalized to other domains. Thus, severity of illness or job satisfaction have little value in trying to account for such newly emerging issues as bioterrorism or violations of intellectual property rights, and attempts to understand these emerging issues will most likely lead to the development of additional domain-specific constructs.

To complicate matters further, in addition to domain-specific factors, investigators typically invoke a variety of demographic variables, personality characteristics, and situational factors that must also be taken into consideration when attempting to explain a specific behavior. It may thus appear that human social behavior is extremely complex, with each behavior being determined by a large number of unique factors, and with each class of behaviors requiring its own set of explanatory constructs. By way of contrast, we argue that human social behavior is really not that complicated, that people approach different kinds of behavior in much the same way, and that the same limited set of constructs can be applied to predict and understand any behavior of interest. This is not to say that the explanatory factors that have been identified in different behavioral domains are unimportant. On the contrary, we recognize that domain-specific constructs are both useful and important for gaining a complete understanding of any behavior. In this book we therefore offer our reasoned action approach as a unifying conceptual framework that encourages the incorporation of unique constructs from divergent disciplinary perspectives.

☐ Approaches and Explanatory Constructs

The need for an integrative conceptual framework is perhaps best illustrated by reviewing some of the work that has attempted to explain behaviors in different domains, with an emphasis on the constructs that have been used to explain these behaviors. Although many different domains could be considered, we restrict our review to organizational behavior, political behavior, and prejudice and discriminatory behaviors.

Organizational Behavior

Of paramount concern for any business enterprise is the productivity of its employees. A great deal of research has therefore focused on job performance and such related behaviors as tardiness, absenteeism, and voluntary turnover. Two complementary approaches have been brought to bear in attempts to understand and influence these behaviors. One approach focuses on promoting a supportive work environment to increase productivity and reduce absenteeism and other negative behaviors. This strategy is directed primarily at existing employees. The second approach concentrates on personnel selection with the aim of hiring new employees who will be maximally productive and who will stay with the company. Although these two approaches are concerned with predicting and understanding the same set of organizational behaviors, each has come up with its own unique set of explanatory variables, and we were unable to find any attempts to integrate the two approaches. In the following brief overview we focus primarily on explaining the organizational behaviors of current employees.

Job Performance

With respect to the existing workforce, job satisfaction was proposed to be the primary determinant of job performance and of most other job-related behaviors. The assumption was made that a happy worker was a productive worker; indeed, the assumed relation between job satisfaction and job performance has been described as the "Holy Grail" of organizational behavior (Landy, 1989). Over the years, efforts have been made to develop valid measures of both job satisfaction (e.g., Smith, 1974) and job performance (see Viswesvaran & Ones, 2000), and virtually hundreds of studies have examined the relation between these variables.

To give just one example, Birnbaum and Somers (1993) used supervisor ratings on nine job-related dimensions to assess the performance of 142 staff nurses. Job satisfaction among the nurses was measured by means of a five-item self-report scale. The correlation between self-ratings of job satisfaction and the supervisor's ratings of job performance was a nonsignificant –.03. Although higher correlations have been reported, most correlations associating job satisfaction with job performance have been quite low. A meta-analysis of 312 data sets (Judge, Thoresen, Bono, & Patton, 2001) reported a mean correlation of .18 between these two measures.

In addition to assessing overall job satisfaction, investigators have also developed measures of satisfaction with different elements of the work environment: the work itself, pay, coworkers, supervision, and opportunities for promotion (see Kinicki, McKee-Ryan, Schriesheim, & Carson, 2002; Smith, Kendall, & Hulin, 1969). Unfortunately, the predictive validity of these facets of job satisfaction was found to be no better than that of overall job satisfaction. Across a wide range of studies, the mean correlations between facets of job satisfaction and performance was found to range from .13 (satisfaction with pay) to .21 (satisfaction with supervision) (Kinicki et al.), and the simultaneous consideration of all five facets produced little if any improvement in prediction.

It should be noted that the correlations reported here and in subsequent discussions are the mean correlations weighted for sample size but uncorrected for attenuation due to unreliability. Meta analyses often report corrected correlations as well, but these corrected correlations tell us only how strong the correlation would be if we had perfectly reliable measures. The uncorrected correlations provide an estimate of how well we can actually predict the criterion with the measures that are currently available.

Turnover and Other Withdrawal Behaviors

Because of the high costs associated with recruiting and training new employees, a great deal of research has been devoted to trying to understand the determinants of voluntary employee turnover. Job satisfaction again serves as the major explanatory construct, with results similar to those obtained for the prediction of job performance. In a meta-analysis based on 67 data sets (Griffeth, Hom, & Gaertner, 2000), the mean correlation between overall job satisfaction and voluntary turnover was −.17, and prediction of turnover from the different facets of job satisfaction produced correlations ranging from −.12 (satisfaction with pay) to −.24 (satisfaction with work). Simultaneous consideration of all facets again did little to improve prediction. Finally, job satisfaction measures have also been used in attempts to predict tardiness and absenteeism, with meta-analyses again showing low mean correlations of −.09 for both behaviors (Hackett & Guion, 1985; Koslowsky, Sagie, Krausz, & Singer, 1997).

A variety of other variables have been considered in the search for antecedents of voluntary turnover. Unfortunately, none of these variables have been found to account for much of the variance in this behavior. A comprehensive meta-analysis (Griffeth et al., 2000) revealed that among the most frequently studied factors are length of tenure (mean correlation of −.20 with turnover), age (mean $r = −.09$), education (mean $r = .05$), marital status (mean $r = −.05$), gender (mean $r = −.03$), alternative job opportunities (mean $r = .11$), organizational commitment (mean $r = −.22$), intention to search for another job (mean $r = .26$), and intention to quit (mean $r = .35$).

Attempts have also been made to link negative behaviors in the workplace to personality characteristics, with equally disappointing results. In a meta-analysis (Salgado, 2002), the "big five" personality traits (emotional stability, extraversion, agreeableness, conscientiousness, and openness to experience) were found to correlate, on average, in the range of .03 to .05

with being late or absent from work, .00 to .05 with work-related accidents, and .01 to .16 with measures of theft, disciplinary problems, substance abuse, and other deviant behaviors. The strongest correlations between personality traits and behavior were found with respect to turnover, but here too the correlations were of modest magnitude, ranging from −.11 for openness to experience to −.25 for emotional stability.

In addition to measuring the big five personality factors, investigators have also used integrity tests to predict various counterproductive behaviors, including disciplinary problems, violence on the job, excessive absenteeism and tardiness, drug abuse, and theft. A meta-analysis based on 138 data sets (Ones, Viswesvaran, & Schmidt, 1993) found a mean correlation of .22 between personality measures of integrity and performance of negative work-related behaviors. A subsequent meta-analysis (Ones, Viswesvaran, & Schmidt, 2003) focusing exclusively on absenteeism reported a correlation of .25 with personality-based measures of integrity.

In this brief review of organizational behavior we have seen that attempts to predict and explain such varied behavioral criteria as job performance, voluntary turnover, absenteeism, and tardiness have largely relied on broad dispositional constructs, primarily job satisfaction, organizational commitment, and personality characteristics. The results of these efforts have been disappointing. Although correlations between the broad dispositions and specific behaviors are often found to be statistically significant, the amount of variance accounted for is usually very low.

Political Behavior

Of crucial importance for a well-functioning democracy is active participation of its citizens in the political process. By this measure, the American democracy does not fare well. Even if we consider only the act of voting in an election, perhaps the prime indicator of political participation, large segments of the U.S. population fail to participate. According to the best available estimates (McDonald & Popkin, 2001), the percentage of eligible citizens who cast a vote in U.S. presidential elections between 1948 and 2000 ranged from 52.2% in 1948 to 63.8% in 1960. In midterm congressional elections, voter turnout was even lower, ranging from 39.0% in the 1978, 1986, and 1998 elections to 48.7% in 1966. And in primary elections, voter turnout is usually close to 20%. With such figures, the United States has what is probably the lowest rate of voting among the world's stable democracies.

Considerable effort has been devoted to trying to understand why so many American citizens choose not to cast a vote, with much of the research focused on presidential elections. At the same time, much time, effort, and money has also been invested in attempts to predict the outcomes of our elections, with major emphasis again on presidential contests. A whole industry has grown up around opinion polling that is designed to determine the preferences of the voting public, and considerable research explores why people vote the way they do. Although focused on different behaviors, prediction of voting participation and of voting choice are intertwined because accurate prediction of election outcomes depends on our ability to identify likely voters.

Voting Participation

Participation in the political process can take many different forms, such as acquiring information about the candidates, attending political rallies, and donating money to a campaign. However, as indicated already, casting a ballot on Election Day is often considered to be the single most important act of political participation. The fact that voter turnout is relatively low even in presidential elections has been of great concern to both academic researchers trying to understand the voting process and to survey researchers interested in identifying likely voters. Over the years, investigators have examined a large number of variables that may influence voter turnout. These variables are often organized under three major headings: legal factors, personal or demographic factors, and psychological factors. Historically, legal barriers such as the poll tax and denying the vote to women prevented many people from voting, but legislation has removed most of these barriers. Unfortunately, new obstacles have emerged. For example, Indiana's voter ID law bans anyone from voting who doesn't have a government-issued identity card. This law tends to disenfranchise poor people, minorities, and the elderly because these groups disproportionately tend not to have drivers' licenses—the most common form of government-issued ID. To make matters worse, the Supreme Court appears to have abandoned its role of protecting voting rights by recently rejecting a challenge to this law, and it is now likely that other states will pass similar legislation. Sadly, shortly after the court's ruling, 12 nuns in their 80s and 90s were not permitted to vote in Indiana's 2008 presidential primary because they did not have proper ID. Thus, although almost every American citizen over 18 years of age is eligible to vote, there are still legal means to make voting difficult for some segments of the U.S. population. In addition to these new legal barriers, other structural factors such as one's distance from the poll (Gimpel & Schuknecht, 2003) can also make it difficult for people to vote.

Personal or Demographic Variables and Voter Turnout

Among the personal and demographic factors considered in relation to voter turnout are education, income, type of occupation, age, gender, ethnicity, geographic location, and religious affiliation. None of these factors is found to account for much variance in voting participation. For example, based on data from the 1988 National Election Survey, Chen (1992, p. 158) reported that participation in the presidential election was correlated .18 with age, .12 with race or ethnicity, .28 with family income, and .31 with education.

Psychological Factors as Explanations of Voter Turnout

In the first systematic investigation of voting behavior (Lazarsfeld, Berelson, & Gaudet, 1944), turnout in the 1940 presidential election was found to be related to interest in the upcoming election. Among respondents who expressed a great deal of interest, 96% voted in the election, compared with 78% who expressed medium interest and 27% who expressed no interest. Note, however, that the majority of participants (55%) expressed medium interest, and the behavior of these individuals is most uncertain. Similarly, in the seminal study of *The American Voter* (Campbell, Converse, Miller, & Stokes, 1960), strong interest in the 1956 presidential campaign produced a turnout of 87%, moderate interest a participation rate of 72%, and low interest a rate of 58%. Again, the largest group of participants fell into the moderate category. This study also showed an association of voter turnout with such other related psychological variables as intensity of partisan preference, concern over the election outcome, sense of political efficacy, and sense of citizen duty. An index of political involvement based on all of these factors was then used to predict voting participation. Only 22% of respondents at the lowest level of involvement participated in the election compared with 96% at the highest level of involvement. Once again, the large majority of respondents fell into the intermediate categories of involvement.

Unfortunately, but consistent with the finding that most individuals fall into the intermediate categories of interest and involvement, this impressive association at the aggregate level was not reflected at the level of the individual. A secondary analysis of the data presented by Campbell, Converse, Miller, and Stokes (1960) in which the sample was split as close to median involvement as possible revealed that voting turnout could be predicted accurately for 59% of the participants. This compares with a 50% accuracy rate by chance alone and to a 76% base-rate level of accuracy if it is assumed that everybody turned out for the election. The correlation between level of involvement and voter participation was .27. Subsequent studies have reported very similar results for individual-level prediction of election turnout from these types of psychological factors (see Gant & Luttbeg, 1991).

In conclusion, attempts to identify specific factors that influence voter turnout have been quite successful at the aggregate level, pointing to the importance of such personal and demographic characteristics as race, age, and education and of such aspects of political involvement as concern about the election outcome, a sense of political efficacy, and a sense of civic responsibility. However, these types of demographic and psychological factors often have much less value for explaining voting participation at the individual level. Many demographic classifications do not produce differential predictions for voting turnout, and, at least at the individual level, reliance on measures such as political involvement can actually reduce predictive accuracy compared with predictions that everybody or nobody will vote (i.e., a prediction reflecting the base rate).

Voting Choice

Beyond a basic interest in the dynamics of the political process, a prime motivation for research on political behavior is the desire to predict and understand election outcomes. A great deal of research has been devoted to examining how voters make their voting decisions, with a major emphasis again on presidential elections.

Demographic Variables

Early work (Lazarsfeld et al., 1944) discovered that voting choice was strongly influenced by three demographic characteristics: religion, socioeconomic status, and urban versus rural residence. Based on these factors, an index was constructed in which a predisposition to vote for Democratic candidates was indicated by being a Catholic, of relatively low socioeconomic status, and urban residence and a predisposition to vote Republican was indicated by being a Protestant, of higher socioeconomic status, and rural residence. This index showed good prediction at the aggregate level. For example, of respondents with strong Republican predispositions, 74% voted for the Republican candidate in the 1940 presidential election, whereas among respondents with strong Democratic predispositions, 83% voted for the Democratic candidate. At the individual level, a multiple correlation of .50 was obtained for the prediction of voting choice from the three demographic variables. Subsequent research has shown that the influence of specific demographic characteristics tends to shift over time. For example, whereas Campbell et al. (1960) found that Catholic voters were significantly more likely to support the Democratic than the Republican candidate in the 1948 presidential election, in the 2000 election Catholics were as likely to vote for the Republican as for the Democratic candidate (CNN News exit poll). Generally speaking, at least at the aggregate level, in any given election some demographic variables are found to be predictive of voting choice, while others are not.

Partisan Attitudes

In contrast to demographic characteristics, certain psychological factors are found to have a consistent effect on voting choice. Work on this topic relies heavily on the social psychological approach developed by investigators at the University of Michigan's Center for Political Studies (CPS, originally known as the Survey Research Center; see Campbell et al., 1960; Campbell, Gurin, & Miller, 1954), and on the election survey data the center makes available to researchers in the field. The Michigan model focuses on social psychological antecedents of voting choice. In a nutshell, it posits that the most basic determinant of voting for a certain candidate is identification with the candidate's party. Party identification is assumed to remain relatively stable over time and to influence partisan attitudes, that is, attitudes toward the candidates, toward the parties, and toward specific issues prominent in the campaign. These partisan attitudes are considered to be more variable from election to election and to constitute the most proximal determinants of voting choice.

In support of the Michigan model, measures of partisan attitudes are found to be strong predictors of voting choice at the aggregate as well as the individual level. For example, in the 1956 contest between Dwight Eisenhower and Adlai Stevenson, 94% of respondents who held extremely favorable attitudes toward Eisenhower voted for this candidate as opposed to only 2% of respondents who held extremely unfavorable attitudes toward him (Campbell et al., 1960). This strong relation was also confirmed in an individual-level analysis, which showed a correlation of .52 between attitude toward Eisenhower and voting choice. A total of 75% of voting choices could be predicted correctly from attitudes toward this candidate, which compares with a 59% base-rate vote in favor of Eisenhower. Considering all six partisan attitudes assessed in the survey (attitudes toward the two candidates, toward the two parties, and toward the parties' stands on issues), voting choice was predicted with a multiple correlation of .71 (and an 86% hit rate).

As to party identification, beginning with the original studies of the 1952 and 1956 presidential elections and continuing to recent contests, this variable is also found to be a strong predictor of voting choice. More than 90% of participants in the 1956 presidential election who strongly identified with either the Republican or the Democratic Party voted for their party's candidate, and even among respondents who only weakly identified with one of the parties, about 75% voted for their party's standard bearer (Campbell et al., 1960). Respondents who considered themselves independents were, in this election, more likely to vote for the Republican candidate (73%). (Although there has been somewhat of a decline in strong party identification, virtually identical results were obtained in the 1988 presidential election that pitted George H. W. Bush against Michael

Dukakis; CPS election survey, 1988; see Gant & Luttbeg, 1991). In terms of predictive accuracy at the individual level, Campbell et al. reported that adding party identification to the regression equation containing the six partisan attitudes raised the multiple correlation from .71 to .73 and increased the hit rate by about 2%.

To summarize briefly, we have seen that at least at the aggregate level, a number of demographic and psychological factors influence voter participation as well as choice among candidates. For some purposes, however, the aggregate level of analysis is not sufficient. To identify likely voters or voters who are undecided, for example, we must have data at the individual level. Unfortunately, we have seen that relations established at the aggregate level of analysis do not always translate to the individual level. Indeed, with respect to voting participation, most of the strong effects observed at the aggregate level do not hold at the level of the individual. In contrast, with respect to voting choice, partisan attitudes and party identification seem to affect behavior at both the aggregate and the individual level.

In our review we have focused on the two major actions of interest to students of political behavior: voting participation and voting choice. Although some attention is always paid to demographic factors, the main variables of interest are of a psychological nature, and here we saw that very different kinds of variables are needed to explain the two behaviors. Attempts to predict voter participation have focused on strength of partisanship, interest in the election, concern over the election outcome, political efficacy, alienation and cynicism, a sense of civic responsibility, and perceived closeness of the election outcome. In contrast, analyses of voting choice have relied on party identification; attitudes toward candidates, parties, and issues; perceptions of candidates' stands on the issues; and the influence of the social environment and of persuasive campaigns. If we were to examine additional behaviors in the political domain, such as attending rallies, watching televised debates, contacting a representative, or contributing time or money to a campaign, still other variables would probably be invoked to predict and explain these behaviors. For example, party identification, which predicts voting choice quite well, does not play much of a role in determining voter participation, and it would in all likelihood also have little effect on watching televised debates.

Interestingly, in contrast to researchers trying to explain voting behavior, opinion pollsters who attempt to predict the outcome of the election often rely on measures of intentions: the intention to participate in the election as well as the intention to vote for one candidate or another. As noted earlier, to accurately predict election outcomes, it is important to know who will participate in the election. Thus, representative samples of respondents are frequently asked to indicate how likely it is that they will vote in the election, and their responses to this question are one of the variables used to identify likely voters. The respondents are also asked, "If the election were held today, for whom would you vote?" The election outcome is projected largely on the basis of these two intentions.

This practice of course implies that intentions should provide a good basis for predicting voting participation as well as choice among candidates. Evidence for a strong correlation between intentions to vote for one candidate or another and actual voting choice can be found in a study of the 1976 U.S. presidential election, which pitted Jimmy Carter, the Democratic candidate, against Gerald Ford, the Republican candidate (Fishbein, Ajzen, & Hinkle, 1980). The difference between the intentions to vote for the two major candidates predicted actual voting choice with a correlation of .80. Despite its high degree of predictive validity, investigators in this domain usually do not view the construct of intention as a primary determinant of voting behavior. Instead, they treat intentions as proxies for actual behavior and rely on a number of broad dispositions such as partisan attitudes, political inclinations based on demographic characteristics, and party identification to predict and explain voting participation and election outcomes.

Discriminatory Behavior

Our final area of consideration concerns discriminatory behavior. Discrimination against members of various social groupings produces some of the most severe and vexing social problems facing many countries. It can deprive people of access to medical care, education, affordable housing, and job opportunities, and it can adversely affect mental health, motivation, and self-esteem or have other detrimental consequences for individuals. It is thus not surprising that considerable effort has been invested in attempts to understand and prevent discriminatory behavior. In most discussions, discrimination is intimately tied to the concepts of stereotyping and prejudice, and prejudice and discrimination are often used in conjunction. Stereotypes are commonly shared beliefs about the attributes of a group of people, and prejudice refers to negative attitudes toward the group in question. Just as job satisfaction is assumed to underlie job performance, it is an article of faith that discriminatory behavior is caused by stereotypic beliefs and prejudicial attitudes. This implies that we should find strong correlations between measures of prejudice and measures of discrimination.

Empirical Findings

There is little in the existing empirical literature to support the proposition that prejudicial attitudes are responsible for discriminatory behavior.

In most studies, the correlation between prejudice and discrimination is found to be weak or nonexistent. Prejudice is usually assessed by means of standard attitude scales with respect to such groups as African Americans, gays, or the elderly. No standard measures of discriminatory behavior are available. Instead, investigators typically assess one or more of an individual's behaviors with respect to members of the group in question, behaviors that they believe to be indicative of discrimination. Thus, measures of discrimination have included such behaviors as signing a petition for open housing, agreeing to have one's picture taken with a member of another race, administering shocks in a learning task, deciding to hire a member of a certain ethnic or religious group, agreeing to accompany a minority group member to a restaurant, and providing accommodation to members of a minority group.

For example, in a study of racial prejudice and discrimination (Himelstein & Moore, 1963), attitudes of White students toward African Americans were assessed by means of a standard attitude scale. On a later occasion the White students came to the laboratory to participate in an ostensibly unrelated experiment. Seated in the waiting room was a confederate, either Black or White. As they were waiting for the experiment to begin, a third person (an assistant) entered the laboratory with a petition that asked the university to extend library hours on Saturday night. The Black or White confederate either agreed or refused to sign the petition, and then it was the naive participant's turn. According to the investigators, discrimination would be indicated if the behavior of the White confederate had a stronger influence on the participants than did the behavior of the Black confederate. Results showed no effect of prejudice on this presumed indicator of discriminatory behavior.

Two recent meta-analyses (Schütz & Six, 1996; Talaska, Fiske, & Chaiken, 2004) suggest at best a very limited role for prejudice as a determinant of discriminatory behaviors. The average correlation between measures of prejudice and discrimination was .29 in the first analysis (based on 46 effect sizes) and .26 in the second (based on 136 effect sizes). One reaction to this weak association between racial prejudice and discriminatory behavior was to question the validity of the measures of prejudicial attitudes (e.g., Crosby, Bromley, & Saxe, 1980; McConahay, Hardee, & Batts, 1981). Specifically, it was argued that people are reluctant to express their true (negative) feelings because of self-presentation concerns, and, for this reason, measures of prejudice fail to predict discriminatory behavior.

The disappointing correlations between prejudicial attitudes and discriminatory behavior are accompanied by another seeming disparity. Although stereotypical beliefs and prejudicial attitudes are found to have declined markedly over the past decades (e.g., Dovidio, 2001; Schuman, Steeh, Bobo, & Krysan, 1997), discrimination against historically disadvantaged racial and ethnic groups continues to be evident in employment, education, housing, health care, and criminal justice (e.g., Bushway & Piehl, 2001; Crosby et al., 1980; Daniels, 2001; Hacker, 1995; Landrine, Klonoff, & Alcaraz, 1997; Myers & Chan, 1995). To account for this disconnect, it was suggested that the nature of racial prejudice has changed to become more subtle and nuanced, that prejudice is now milder than the blatant racism of the past (McConahay, 1986). That is, prejudice might be expressed indirectly and symbolically, for example as opposition to preferential treatment for minorities (Sears, 1988). Other theorists proposed that racial attitudes had become ambiguous or aversive, containing explicit egalitarian elements as well as more subtle and unacknowledged negative beliefs and feelings (Gaertner & Dovidio, 1986). In addition, it was argued that people may not be fully aware of their prejudicial attitudes and thus cannot express them on an explicit attitude measure.

These ideas led to the conclusion that prejudice was still present but that standard attitude scales—which measure *explicit* stereotypes and prejudice—were incapable of capturing the subtle and *implicit* nature of contemporary prejudice. Investigators therefore turned to implicit measures of prejudice under the assumption that such measures are not subject to social desirability biases and can capture unacknowledged negative sentiments. They should therefore be good predictors of discriminatory behavior.

Most popular among the measures of implicit attitudes are the Implicit Association Test (IAT; Greenwald, McGhee, & Schwartz, 1998) and evaluative priming (Dovidio, Evans, & Tyler, 1986; Fazio, Jackson, Dunton, & Williams, 1995; see Fazio & Olson, 2003). The IAT in particular has been widely used to assess implicit attitudes toward various racial and ethnic groups, toward gays, toward women, and toward other social categories. Because of its popularity, we focus our discussion on the IAT as a measure of implicit attitudes. Relying on reaction times, the IAT assesses the relative strength of the association between an attitude object and positively versus negatively valenced concepts. Thus, participants seated in front of a computer may be asked to press, as quickly as possible, a certain key when the photo of a Black person's face appears on the screen or when a positive word (e.g., *party, love*) appears on it (*Black + good*), and another key for photos of White faces or negative words (e.g., *poison, trash; White + bad*). The combinations of racial categories and positive or negative concepts are reversed on other trials of the measurement session such that the first key is used for Black faces or negative words (*Black + bad*) and the other key for White faces or positive words (*White + good*). Racial prejudice with respect to Blacks is inferred when participants take less time to respond in the *Black + bad* condition than in the *Black + good* condition, indicating stronger associations between Black faces and negative valence than between Black faces and positive valence. Of course, because on each trial participants have to choose between pressing one key for Black faces and another for White faces, this measure can also reflect a stronger association between White faces and positive valence than between White faces and negative valence. In fact, the IAT has been criticized on the grounds that it compares two attitude measures, and thus it is not clear whether the "prejudicial attitudes" identified by means of this instrument reflect relatively negative attitudes toward Blacks or relatively positive attitudes toward Whites. Questions have also been raised as to whether the IAT does, in fact, assess attitudes or whether it reflects other meaningful phenomena such as similarity or familiarity between concepts (see, e.g., Blanton, Jaccard, Gonzales, & Christie, 2006; Jaccard & Blanton, 2007).

Implicit Versus Explicit Measures of Prejudice

In any event, the implicit attitudes assessed by the IAT appear to fare no better as predictors of behavior than do measures of explicit attitudes. Perhaps the best evidence regarding the relative predictive validity of explicit and implicit global attitude measures comes from a meta-analysis of the IAT literature (Greenwald, Poehlman, Uhlmann, & Banaji, in press). This analysis was based on 122 studies that reported data for 184 independent samples. The meta-analysis went beyond prejudice and discrimination to include data regarding a variety of other attitudinal and behavioral domains (e.g., food choice, achievement, condom use, self-esteem, smoking, political behavior). Overall, the mean correlation between explicit attitude measures and various behavioral criteria, weighted for sample size, was .36 compared with a significantly lower mean correlation of .27 for implicit attitude measures. Considering only the 32 studies in the domain of racial attitudes and behavior, the mean correlation for the prediction of discriminatory responses was significantly higher when implicit ($r = .24$) rather than explicit ($r = .12$) measures of prejudice were obtained, even though the correlations were rather low in either case.

Investigators quickly realized, however, that just as people may misrepresent their true prejudice on an explicit attitude measure, so too could they behave in socially desirable ways that may be at odds with their true attitudes. In other words, measures of overt behavior may be just as susceptible to social desirability biases as are verbal measures of prejudice. In Devine's (1989; Devine, Monteith, Zuwerink, & Elliot, 1991) dissociation model, prejudiced and nonprejudiced individuals are assumed to be equally familiar with prevailing cultural stereotypes. These stereotypes are activated automatically in the actual or symbolic presence of stereotyped group members. Nonprejudiced individuals are assumed to differ from prejudiced individuals in their explicit rejection of the cultural stereotypes and their greater motivation to inhibit the influence of automatically activated stereotypes on judgments, feelings, and actions. Thus, in this model, the explicit attitude actually controls behavior and is, in a sense, the "true" attitude.

A different view emerges from application of Fazio's (Fazio & Dunton, 1997; Fazio & Towles-Schwen, 1999) MODE model to the relation between prejudice and discrimination. Whereas in Devine's (1989; Devine et al., 1991) dissociation model what is automatically activated are culturally shared stereotypes, in the MODE model the individual's own attitude is assumed to be automatically activated. In this sense, implicit measures may provide a "bona fide pipeline" (Fazio et al., 1995) to the person's true attitude. As in Devine's model, however, whether this implicit attitude affects judgments and behavior depends on the individual's motivation to control seemingly prejudiced reactions (Dunton & Fazio, 1997; see also Devine & Monteith, 1999).

These models of prejudice are perhaps consistent with the proposition that people can hold two attitudes at the same time: one an implicit and often unrecognized prejudicial attitude and the other an explicit egalitarian attitude that is under conscious control (Wilson, Lindsey, & Schooler, 2000). The implicit attitude (or stereotype) is assumed to be automatically activated, whereas activation of the explicit attitude is said to require cognitive effort. In this view, the implicit as well as the explicit attitude may be considered to reflect "true" attitudes. The implicit prejudicial attitude is activated automatically, but, as in the models previously described, given sufficient motivation and cognitive resources the explicit egalitarian attitude can be retrieved and override the effect of the implicit prejudicial attitude.

Despite the differences between theorists regarding the nature of implicit and explicit prejudice, their various views have basically the same implications for the prediction of behavior. Specifically, it is expected that implicit measures of prejudicial attitudes are valuable predictors of discriminatory behaviors that are not consciously monitored or that are difficult to control (e.g., facial expressions, eye contact, blushing, and other nonverbal behaviors) as well as of behaviors that people have little motivation to control because they do not view them as indicative of prejudice. Implicit measures should be less predictive of behaviors that are under conscious control. With respect to explicit attitude measures the opposite pattern is expected. These measures should be predictive of behaviors that are under volitional control and whose implications for prejudice are apparent but less predictive of spontaneously emitted reactions that are not consciously monitored (see Dovidio, Brigham, Johnson, & Gaertner, 1996).

Empirical Evidence

Thus far, only a small number of studies have directly tested these hypotheses. Consistent with expectations, some studies have found that implicit measures of prejudice are superior to explicit measures for the prediction of various nonverbal behaviors such as blinking and eye contact, smiling, and spacial distance (e.g., Dovidio, Kawakami, Johnson, Johnson, & Howard, 1997; Fazio, Jackson, Dunton, & Williams, 1995; Wilson et al., 2000; see Fazio & Olson, 2003 for a review. However, even the implicit attitude measures in these studies did not do very well, with correlations rarely exceeding the .30 level observed in earlier research with explicit measures.

There is also some evidence for the advantage of explicit over implicit measures in the prediction of controlled behaviors. Thus, it has been found that, in comparison with implicit measures of prejudice, explicit measures are better predictors of judgments concerning interracial situations. Note that the criterion measures in these studies were verbal judgments, not overt behaviors. For example, judgments concerning the verdict in the Rodney King trial involving police brutality were better predicted by explicit than by implicit measures (Fazio et al., 1995; see also Dovidio et al., 1997). But even in these studies, the predictive accuracy of the explicit measures was inconsistent and usually quite low, with correlations ranging from .24 to .54.

Given that implicit measures seem to fare no better than explicit measures, why do we see the continuing interest in measures of implicit prejudice? It seems to us that there may be two major reasons. First, many investigators are convinced that high levels of prejudicial attitudes continue to exist in contemporary society. In contrast to explicit measures of prejudice that suggest a decline in prejudice over time, measures that rely on the IAT have found that high levels of prejudice continue to exist. Second, the recognition that implicit attitudes are unlikely to predict controlled behavior was accompanied by the realization that implicit attitudes should have good predictive validity with respect to behaviors that are either not under volitional control or are not typically viewed as indicators of prejudice (e.g., eye contact, blinking, personal space, orientation). While such spontaneous (uncontrolled) behaviors may initially seem relatively trivial compared with behaviors such as hiring, working with, or dating a member of a racial, religious, or ethnic group, it can be argued that these nonverbal behaviors serve as cues to a person's true prejudicial feelings that are recognized by members of a minority or other outgroup and that this can lead to discomfort, distrust, and possibly hostility and aggression.

Note that in contrast to the political domain where multiple constructs are used to explain a given behavior, in the area of discrimination, a single construct is used to explain multiple behaviors; almost all explanations rely on the construct of prejudice to predict a large number of behaviors, each of which is taken to be indicative of discrimination. It is widely accepted that prejudicial attitudes are responsible for discriminatory behavior, and, consistent with this view, most current research in this domain is concerned with identifying the determinants of prejudice and with developing methods to reduce prejudice. Unfortunately, the fundamental assumption linking discrimination to prejudice is not well supported by empirical research, and this has led to various theories concerning the nuances of prejudice as revealed in implicit as well as explicit measures. Generally speaking, correlations between prejudice and discriminatory behaviors are quite low, irrespective of whether the measure of prejudice is explicit or implicit.

☐ Discussion

Even this cursory review of research in three behavioral domains shows that neither demographic characteristics nor general personality traits account for much variance in any particular behavior, and the same can be said to a large extent about general attitudinal dispositions such as job satisfaction or prejudice. As we will see in Chapter 8, research over the past 40 years has shown conclusively that although broad dispositions, such as personality traits and general attitudes, can explain broad patterns or aggregates of behavior, they are generally very poor predictors of the specific actions that are investigated in different domains (Ajzen, 2005; Epstein, 1979; Fishbein & Ajzen, 1974; Weigel & Newman, 1976). We can also see that the focus on domain-specific constructs has led to the development of different models and minitheories designed to account for a particular behavior or a small class of behaviors. By its very nature, this approach has not led to the development of a general theory that could be used to predict, explain, and influence behavior in any domain. As we noted at the beginning of this chapter, it is our contention that at the core, the processes underlying all human social behavior are essentially the same and can be described by reference to a small set of constructs. We will try to show that our conceptual framework can be used to account for any social behavior of current interest and that it can be applied directly to deal with new issues and behaviors as they arise. Moreover, the framework allows us to understand and appreciate the role played by the domain-specific attitudes, personality characteristics, or other factors that have been used to explain behaviors in different substantive domains.

We have been working on our approach to the prediction and change of behavior both jointly and individually for more than 45 years, modifying and refining its theoretical constructs and their measures. In the original formulation, largely adapted from Dulany's (1968) theory of propositional control, Fishbein (1967a) proposed that intentions are the immediate antecedents of behavior and that intentions, in turn, are a function of attitude toward the behavior and the sum of normative beliefs weighted by motivation to comply. Based on Fishbein's (1963) expectancy-value model, the attitude was assumed to be determined by beliefs about the likely outcomes of performing the behavior (behavioral beliefs or outcome expectancies) weighted by the evaluations of these outcomes. Given that behavioral beliefs weighted by outcome evaluations are theoretically at the same level of explanation as normative beliefs weighted by motivation to comply, we recognized that the theory lacked a normative construct comparable to the attitude construct. Thus, the concept of subjective norm was introduced to represent perceived social pressure, and we argued that, analogous to the attitude construct, this higher-order normative construct was determined by underlying beliefs (i.e., by the sum of normative beliefs weighted by motivation to comply; Fishbein & Ajzen, 1975).

In our second joint book (Ajzen & Fishbein, 1980) we began to refer to our theory as a theory of reasoned action (TRA). By that time we had developed a standard set of procedures to elicit salient behavioral and normative beliefs and to measure the theory's constructs. In addition, we explicitly included background factors such as demographic, personality and other individual difference variables in the presentation of the theory. We argued that a wide range of background factors can influence behavior indirectly by influencing the behavioral and normative beliefs that a person might hold.

Shortly after the completion of our 1980 book, our career paths diverged. While Fishbein became involved in applying the theory to HIV prevention research, Ajzen continued to focus on refining and testing the theory, primarily in laboratory settings. Recognizing that many goals and behaviors are not under complete volitional control, Ajzen (1985, 1988) introduced the construct of perceived behavioral control as an additional predictor of both intention and behavior. Consistent with the TRA's other two components, perceived behavioral control was assumed to be a function of underlying beliefs, specifically, control beliefs weighted by the power of control factors. Ajzen called his extension of the TRA the theory of planned behavior (TPB).

In the late 1980s, the National Institute of Mental Health (NIMH) asked five theorists—Albert Bandura, Marshall Becker, Martin Fishbein, Frederick Kanfer, and Harry Triandis—to clarify the similarities and differences among their theories. Concerned that HIV prevention research was not being guided by a unified theory, NIMH asked these theorists to try to come up with a "finite set of variables that could be used in any behavioral analysis." Toward this end, a three-day theorists' workshop was held at NIMH in spring 1991, and although there was no agreement on a theoretical structure, there was agreement on a set of key variables that were assumed to underlie behavior. More specifically the theorists agreed that for a person to perform a given behavior, one or more of the following must be true:

1. The person has formed a strong positive intention (or made a commitment) to perform the behavior.
2. There are no environmental constraints that make it impossible for the behavior to occur.
3. The person has the skills necessary to perform the behavior.
4. The person believes that the advantages (benefits, anticipated positive outcomes) of performing the behavior outweigh the disadvantages (costs, anticipated negative outcomes); in other words, the person has a positive attitude toward performing the behavior.
5. The person perceives more social (normative) pressure to perform the behavior than to not perform the behavior.
6. The person perceives that performance of the behavior is more consistent than inconsistent with his or her self-image or that its performance does not violate personal standards that activate negative self-sanctions.
7. The person's emotional reaction to performing the behavior is more positive than negative.
8. The person perceives that he or she has the capabilities to perform the behavior under a number of different circumstances; in other words, the person has perceived self-efficacy to execute the behavior in question.

A majority of the theorists also felt that the first three variables were necessary and sufficient to produce behavior, whereas the remaining five variables could best be viewed as serving primarily as determinants of intention. This model was presented in 1997 as part of an NIMH consensus conference to evaluate the effectiveness of HIV prevention research. In 1999, Fishbein presented a reduced version of this model at the International AIDS Impact conference, and he called it the Integrative Model (IM; see Fishbein, 2000). In this version, both emotion and self-image were dropped as immediate determinants of intention. Emotion was treated as a background variable and consistency or inconsistency with one's self-image, and concern with violations of one's self-standards were viewed as possible advantages or disadvantages of performing the behavior in question. In this reduced form, the integrative model was almost identical to Ajzen's TPB, but it added the concept of descriptive norms in recognition of the fact that perceived normative pressure can reflect not only what others think we should do but also what they themselves are perceived to be doing; in addition, given its origins in the theorists' workshop, it incorporated Bandura's (1977) notion of self-efficacy rather than Ajzen's more recent concept of perceived behavior control. Thus, even though we were at that time working quite independently, we were moving in similar directions, albeit from very different perspectives. Fortunately, a move by Fishbein allowed us to again start working together in 2001, when we began to reconcile the differences between our models.

☐ The Reasoned Action Approach

We are now ready to provide an outline of our theory of behavioral prediction in its most current form. The starting point of our analysis is a particular behavior of interest to the investigator. It is therefore of utmost importance that the behavior under consideration be clearly identified and properly operationalized. This is not as easy as it might at first appear. We will discuss some of the problems associated with definition and measurement of behavior in Chapter 2.

Once the behavior of interest is clearly identified we can begin to examine its determinants. Basically, we assume that human social behavior follows reasonably and often spontaneously from the information or beliefs people possess about the behavior under consideration. These beliefs originate in a variety of sources, such as personal experiences, formal education, radio, newspapers, TV, the Internet and other media, and interactions with family and friends. Individual differences (e.g., demographic characteristics, personality) can influence not only the experiences people have and the sources of information to which they are exposed but also the ways they interpret and remember this information. Consequently, individuals from different social backgrounds or with different personality traits are also likely to differ in the beliefs they hold.

No matter how beliefs associated with a given behavior are acquired, they serve to guide the decision to perform or not perform the behavior in question. Specifically, three kinds of beliefs are distinguished. First, people hold beliefs about the positive or negative consequences they might experience if they performed the behavior. These outcome expectancies or *behavioral beliefs* are assumed to determine people's *attitude toward personally performing the behavior*—that is, their positive or negative evaluation of their performing the behavior in question. In general, to the extent that their performance of the behavior is perceived to result in more positive than negative outcomes, the attitude toward the behavior will be favorable. Second, people form beliefs that important individuals or groups in their lives would approve or disapprove of their performing the behavior as well as beliefs that these referents themselves perform or don't perform the behavior in question. In their totality, these *injunctive and descriptive normative beliefs* produce a *perceived norm*, that is, perceived social pressure to engage or not engage in the behavior. If more important others are believed to approve than disapprove, and if the majority of important others perform the behavior, people are likely to perceive social pressure to engage in the behavior. Finally, people also form beliefs about personal and environmental factors that can help or impede their attempts to carry out the behavior. In their aggregate, these *control beliefs* result in a sense of high or low self-efficacy (Bandura, 1986, 1997) or *perceived behavioral control* with regard to the behavior. If control beliefs identify more facilitating than inhibiting factors, perceived behavioral control should be high.

Once attitudes, perceived norms, and perceived behavioral control have been formed they are directly accessible and available to guide intentions and behavior. Specifically, in combination, attitude toward the behavior, perceived norm, and perception of behavioral control lead to the formation of a *behavioral intention*, or a *readiness to perform the behavior*. As a general rule, the more favorable the attitude and perceived norm, and the greater the perceived behavioral control, the stronger should be the person's intention to perform the behavior in question. However, the relative importance or weight of these three determinants of intentions is expected to vary from one behavior to another and from one population to another.

The intention formed in this fashion is now available to determine performance of the behavior. The stronger the intention, the more likely it is that the behavior will be carried out. It is well recognized, however, that lack of requisite skills and abilities, or presence of environmental constraints, can prevent people from acting on their intentions. That is, they may lack *actual control* over performance of the behavior. It is only when people do have control over behavioral performance that intention is expected to be a good predictor of behavior. Actual behavioral control thus moderates the effect of intentions on behavior. To predict and understand behavior fully, we therefore have to assess not only intentions but also actual behavioral control (i.e., relevant skills and abilities as well as barriers to and facilitators of behavioral performance). For most behaviors, however, measures of actual control are not available. In those instances, we can use our measures of perceived behavioral control as a proxy. To the extent that perceived behavioral control accurately reflects actual control, it can be used to improve behavioral prediction.

Figure 1.1 is a schematic representation of our reasoned action framework. The theory suggests that intention is the best single predictor of behavior but that it is also important to take skills and abilities as well as environmental factors (i.e., behavioral control) into account. At the lowest level of explanation, therefore, people are said to perform a behavior because they intend to do so, they have the requisite skills and abilities, and there are no environmental constraints to prevent them from carrying out their intentions (i.e., they have favorable intentions and actual behavioral control). At the next level we achieve a deeper understanding by considering the determinants of intentions. We now learn that people will intend to (and thus will) perform a behavior if they have positive

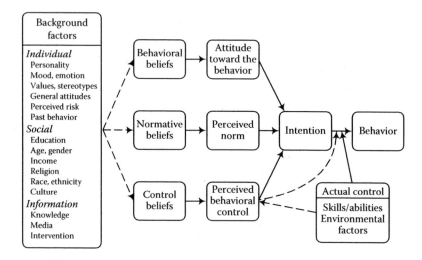

FIGURE 1.1 Schematic presentation of the reasoned action model.

attitudes toward personally performing the behavior and if they perceive normative pressure to do so. However, even under these circumstances they may not form an intention to perform the behavior if they believe that they lack control over performing the behavior. Consider, for example, the decision faced by academics or other professionals to attend or not attend a professional conference or meeting. They may favorably evaluate attending the conference and experience social pressure to attend, but if they have made prior commitments they cannot break, or if they lack the financial resources to cover the cost of registration, transportation, food, and lodging, they will perceive that they cannot attend the meeting and thus may form an intention to not attend the conference.

The fact that the three predictors of intentions can take on different weights tells us that the intention to perform a given behavior is based on a particular combination of attitudinal, normative, and control considerations. Thus, some people may attend a professional conference because they have positive attitudes toward this behavior, whereas other may do so because of perceived social pressure. The relative importance of the different predictors can vary from one population to another. Thus, at one university some professors may fail to attend a professional conference because of control issues, but at another they may not attend the conference because they perceive social pressure against this behavior, that is, because their colleagues and other important referents don't approve of their going to this particular conference.

This level of analysis can also help explain why people with similar attitudes, perceived norms, and perceptions of control behave in different ways. Consider two professors at a given university, one male the other female, who both value attending a conference and believe that they could do so but at the same time perceive social pressure not to attend. If among males the intention to attend the conference is primarily influenced by perceived norms whereas among females this intention is largely controlled by attitudes, we would expect that the female professor will attend the conference whereas the male professor will not.

It is at the next level, the level of beliefs, that we gain most of the concrete information unique to a given behavior. At this level we learn about the substantive considerations that guide people's decisions to perform or not to perform the behavior of interest. This level of analysis offers insight into the ways people think about the behavior: about its likely consequences, the demands placed on them by others, as well as the required resources, possible barriers, and other issues of control. Thus, we may learn that many professors believe that attending a particular conference will enable them to acquire important information and to make new professional connections (behavioral beliefs), that their spouses and department chairs approve and most of their colleagues plan to attend (normative beliefs), and that they have the required time and financial resources (control beliefs). This pattern of beliefs would reasonably lead to a decision to attend the professional meeting. Other individuals, however, may be found to hold a different set of beliefs. Although they may also believe that they have the time and resources to attend the conference, they may believe that they would learn very little of professional value and that there is very little support among professional friends and colleagues for attending this meeting. Clearly, these individuals would be much less likely to attend.

It should also be clear that information of this kind can be used to design effective behavior change interventions. By identifying behavioral, normative, and control beliefs that discriminate between individuals who perform the behavior of interest and individuals who do not, we can design properly targeted behavioral interventions.

Note that Figure 1.1 provides an oversimplified representation of our theoretical framework, a representation that lacks important conceptual distinctions as well as feedback loops and other relations among the constructs. Throughout this book we will expand on our theory, address a variety of issues raised by our earlier work, and fill in missing details.

The Nature of Reasoned Action

At this point we must address a common misconception regarding our reasoned action approach. Because we have used the terms *reasoned action* and *planned behavior* in our past work, many investigators mistakenly believe that we consider people to be rational and to deliberate at length before engaging in any behavior. This has never been our position. As we shall see in subsequent chapters, our theoretical framework does not assume rationality, and it encompasses both deliberative and spontaneous decision making. The processes previously described whereby people arrive at their intentions represents a "reasoned" approach to the explanation and prediction of social behavior only in the sense that people's behavioral intentions are assumed to follow in a reasonable, consistent, and often automatic fashion from their beliefs about performing the behavior. This does not mean that people are assumed to be always logical or rational. The beliefs they hold need not be veridical; they may be inaccurate, biased, or even irrational. However, once a set of beliefs is formed it provides the cognitive foundation from which attitudes, perceived norms, and perceptions of control—and ultimately intentions and behaviors—are assumed to follow in a reasonable and consistent fashion. Moreover, the formation of attitudes, perceived norms, and perceptions of control—and the intentions they produce—do not have to involve a great deal of deliberation but can follow spontaneously and automatically from the underlying cognitive foundation of beliefs. As a general rule, people are likely to engage in careful deliberation when they are confronted with a novel situation or when they confront an important decision. Under these conditions they may well evaluate the likely consequences of the behavioral options, imagine what other people would want them to do or what important others would do themselves and consider the factors that may make it easy or difficult for them to perform the behavior in question. Such elaborate information processing is much less likely when people are confronted with performing a familiar behavior or when they make a relatively unimportant behavioral decision. These issues are discussed in greater detail in Chapters 8 and 9.

Background Factors

We saw that according to our reasoned action approach the major predictors of intentions and actions follow reasonably from—and can be understood in terms of—behavioral, normative, and control beliefs. This approach, however, does not address the origins of these beliefs. Clearly, a multitude of variables could potentially influence the beliefs people hold: age, gender, ethnicity, socioeconomic status, education, nationality, religious affiliation, personality, mood, emotion, general attitudes and values, intelligence, group membership, past experiences, exposure to information, social support, and coping skills. Our model of behavioral prediction recognizes the potential importance of such background factors. However, the dotted arrows in Figure 1.1 indicate that, although a given background factor may in fact influence behavioral, normative, or control beliefs, there is no necessary connection between background factors and beliefs. Whether a given belief is or is not affected by a particular background factor is an empirical question. In light of the vast number of potentially relevant background factors, it is difficult to know which ones should be considered without a theory to guide selection in the behavioral domain of interest. Theories of this kind are not part of our conceptual framework but can complement it by identifying relevant background factors and thereby deepen our understanding of a behavior's determinants (see Petraitis, Flay, & Miller, 1995).

In fact, we saw earlier that research in different behavioral domains has focused primarily on what we would now call background factors: general attitudinal and personality dispositions as well as demographic characteristics. The findings obtained in this research can serve as a guide for the kinds of background factors that are relevant for understanding the likely origins of behavioral, normative, and control beliefs concerning a given behavior. For example, it has been found that the decision to hire a member of a minority group is, to some extent, influenced by prejudice toward the group in question (e.g., Dovidio & Gaertner, 2000). Given this finding, it is reasonable to expect that prejudiced individuals will hold different beliefs about hiring the minority applicant than will nonprejudiced individuals. For example, in comparison with nonprejudiced individuals, people prejudiced toward African Americans may be more likely to believe that hiring an African American applicant would adversely affect productivity and create interpersonal problems in the workplace. They may also be more likely to believe that friends and current employees would disapprove of such a hiring decision. However, as we noted in our review of research on discriminatory behavior, most studies report little or no relation between prejudice and many specific behaviors directed at minority group members. Such negative findings are explained if it is found that people high and low in prejudice do not differ in their behavioral, normative, or control beliefs regarding the particular behaviors investigated. We have more to say about the role of background factors in Chapters 7 and 8.

Related Reasoned Action Models

The notion that behavior follows reasonably from information or beliefs about the behavior is not unique to our model (see Fishbein et al., 2001). For example, Bandura's (1986; 1997) well-known social cognitive theory relies in part on outcome expectancies or behavioral beliefs and, more importantly, on the construct of self-efficacy (or perceived behavioral control) to explain behavior. In the theory of subjective culture and interpersonal relations, Triandis (1972; 1977) includes intentions, facilitating factors, perceived consequences of performing a behavior, and perceived social influences as important determinants of behavior. According to the health belief model (Rosenstock, Strecher, & Becker, 1994; Strecher, Champion, & Rosenstock, 1997), decisions to engage in health-related behaviors take into account one's susceptibility or perceived risk of contracting an illness, perceptions of the severity of the illness, beliefs about the costs and benefits of performing the recommended health behavior (behavioral beliefs), as well as perceived self-efficacy in relation to the behavior. Other models of this kind include the information-motivation-behavioral skills model (Fisher & Fisher, 1992), the AIDS risk reduction model (Catania, Kegeles, & Coates, 1990), and the theory of trying (Bagozzi & Warshaw, 1990). Like our own reasoned action approach, all of these models assign a central role to behavioral beliefs or outcome expectancies. Most models also include variables dealing with control or self-efficacy and normative influences. Beyond these basic constructs, some models suggest consideration of additional factors, such as habit and emotion (Triandis, 1977), knowledge (Fisher & Fisher, 1992), and motivation and goal pursuit (Bagozzi & Warshaw, 1990). We will encounter some of these additional factors in Chapter 9. We will also try to cover recent developments in the field that have potential implications for our approach. Among these developments are the distinction, already alluded to, between implicit and explicit attitudes; the role of mood, emotions, anticipated affect, and self-identity; the distinction between injunctive and descriptive norms; attitudinal ambivalence; framing; and a variety of other factors. These discussions address some of the issues that have been raised in relation to our approach and spell out our current position on these issues.

Following this introductory chapter, we begin an in-depth consideration of our approach in Chapter 2 with a discussion of behavior, how it is defined and measured, and how it can be predicted from intentions and perceived behavioral control. Chapters 3 through 5 deal with the three major influences on intentions: attitudes toward a behavior, perceived norms, and perceived behavioral control, as well as with the behavioral, normative, and control beliefs that are assumed to determine these factors. In Chapter 6 we combine all the elements in our model of behavioral prediction and consider its empirical support.

The following two chapters deal with the role of background factors. Chapter 7 provides a general discussion of various kinds of background factors, including demographic characteristics and personality traits, while Chapter 8 focuses on one particular background factor that plays a prominent role in the social and behavioral sciences, namely, general attitudes toward objects, issues, and events. In Chapter 9 we take up challenges and issues raised by both supporters and opponents of our reasoned action approach. Finally, in Chapters 10 and 11 we discuss the implications of our theory for developing and evaluating behavior change interventions, and we describe a few sample interventions as illustrations. The last chapter, Chapter 12, summarizes the current state of our approach and draws out some of its implications.

☐ Conclusion

Ideally, a theory of human social behavior is general enough to permit us to predict and explain various kinds of behaviors in different domains. We have seen, however, that attempts to explain behavior often originate in the context of a single behavioral domain and potential determinants that are specific to that domain are identified. Not only have these attempts met with rather mixed success, but they also have done little to advance the development of a general theory of behavior. We have presented the outline of our reasoned action approach that we believe provides a unifying framework to account for any social behavior. At the same time, this framework allows us to include and examine the role of domain-specific factors that have previously been investigated or identified as possible determinants of specific behaviors. It is our hope that application of our theory will aid communication among investigators in different domains, will further the accumulation of general knowledge about the determinants of human behavior, and ultimately will contribute to the solution of personal and social problems caused by human behavior.

Defining and Predicting Behavior

Because our concern is with predicting and understanding human social behavior, the first and in some ways the most crucial step is to clearly define the behavior of interest, a task that is much more complex than it might at first appear. The definition of the behavior will guide not only how the behavior is assessed but also the way we conceptualize and measure all other constructs in our model of behavioral prediction. Unlike beliefs, attitudes, and intentions, behaviors are observable events. Any observation of such an event must take place in a certain context and at a given point in time. In addition, most behaviors are also directed at some target. It is therefore useful to think of a behavior as composed of four elements: the *action* performed, the *target* at which the action is directed, the *context* in which it is performed, and the *time* at which it is performed. A simple example is buying (action element) a General Electric (GE) dishwasher (target) at a Sears Department Store (context) in the past 30 days (time). Sometimes there is more ambiguity in defining a behavior's elements. Consider attending an aerobics class at the University of Pennsylvania Fitness Center on a particular Thursday night at 6 p.m. Table 2.1 presents several possibilities. We could identify *attending* as the action element, the *aerobics class* as the target, the *University of Pennsylvania Fitness Center* as the context, and *Thursday night at 6 p.m.* as the time element. Alternatively, we might define the action as *attending an aerobics class*, the target as the *Fitness Center*, the context as the *University of Pennsylvania*, and the time again as *Thursday night at 6 p.m.* A third alternative might not specify a target element at all. *Attending an aerobics class* would be the action, the *University of Pennsylvania's Fitness Center* would be the context, and the time element would remain the same.

Clearly, how we parse the behavior into action, target, context, and time elements is to some extent arbitrary. It is up to investigators to define the

TABLE 2.1 Parsing of Action, Target, Context, and Time Elements of a Behavior: Attending an Aerobics Class at the University of Pennsylvania Fitness Center

Possible parsing	Action	Target	Context	Time
A	Attending	Aerobics class	University of Pennsylvania Fitness Center	Thursday night, 6 p.m.
B	Attending an aerobics class	Fitness center	University of Pennsylvania	Thursday night, 6 p.m.
C	Attending an aerobics class	—	University of Pennsylvania Fitness Center	Thursday night, 6 p.m.

behavioral criterion as it best fits their research purposes. Once the elements are specified, however, the behavior is defined. A change in any one of the elements constitutes a change in the behavior under consideration. It is self-evident that buying a GE dishwasher is not the same behavior as renting a GE dishwasher (change in action element). It is also obvious that buying a GE dishwasher and buying a GE refrigerator (change in target) are not the same behaviors. Perhaps less obvious, buying a GE dishwasher at Sears is a different behavior from buying a GE dishwasher at Best Buy. By our definition of behavior in terms of four elements, this change in the context element constitutes a change in the behavior itself. This means that we cannot perform the same behavior in two different contexts. Instead, from our perspective, two different behaviors are being performed as we move from one context to another, even if the other elements remain the same. Finally, and again not readily apparent, modification of the time element also changes the definition of the behavior. Thus, buying a dishwasher within a 30-day period is not the same behavior as buying it with in a 6-month period.

☐ Levels of Generality

Each of a behavior's four elements—action, target, context, and time—can be defined at various levels of generality or specificity. The first row of Table 2.2 shows that at the most specific level is a single action (attending an aerobics class), directed at a specific target (Fitness Center), performed in a given context (University of Pennsylvania), and at a specified point

TABLE 2.2 Defining Behavior at Varying Levels of Generality: Attending an Aerobics Class at the University of Pennsylvania Fitness Center

Level of generality	Action	Target	Context	Time
Specific	Attending an aerobics class	Fitness center	University of Pennsylvania	Past Thursday night, 6 p.m.
Intermediate-low	Attending an aerobics class	Fitness centers and sports facilities	Universities	Past 30 days
Intermediate-high	Exercising	Fitness centers and sports facilities	Educational institutions	Past 6 months
High	Exercising	—	—	Past 12 months

in time (last Thursday at 6 p.m.). In Row 4 of the table we see that at the most general level the action element is defined as a category of behaviors (exercising) whereas the target and context elements are left unspecified. For practical purposes we usually place some limit on the time element; in Table 2.2, the time element is set to the past 12 months. Between these extremes, we can define behaviors at intermediate levels of generality. In the second row of Table 2.2, we broadened the action element from a specific aerobics class to any aerobics class, we generalized the target element from the fitness center to other sports facilities, we expanded the context element from a particular university to all universities, and we broadened the time element from a specific point in time to the past 30 days. Finally, at the next intermediate level of generality (Row 3), the action element has changed from a single physical activity to a behavioral category (exercising), the target has changed from universities to all educational institutions, the context has remained the same, and the time period has increased from the past 30 days to the past 6 months.

Behaviors can be defined so narrowly as to be of little theoretical or practical significance. Consider, again, attending an aerobics class at the University of Pennsylvania Fitness Center on a particular Thursday night at 6 p.m. No matter how we parse the elements of this behavior, it is so narrowly defined as to be of little value to anybody save perhaps the instructor of the particular class given on the day in question. This limitation raises questions about the value of direct observation, often considered the gold standard of behavioral assessment. When a single action is directly observed on a particular occasion, the measure of behavior obtained is very specific in all its elements and therefore of limited utility. This, unfortunately, is often the case in laboratory experiments in which a specific behavior performed in a particular context is directly observed. We will discuss some of the problems associated with this practice in Chapter 8.

☐ Direct Observation Versus Self-Reports of Behavior

Returning to the physical activity example, from a theoretical perspective, it is more valuable to know why people attend aerobics classes in general than why they attend a particular aerobics class in a specific fitness center on a given day and at a particular time. To move toward a more general and more meaningful behavioral criterion, we could broaden the time and context elements. Thus, we might decide to assess attendance at aerobics classes over the course of a semester or a whole year by means of direct observation. To do justice to this behavioral criterion, however, we would have to observe attendance (or obtain attendance records) for each and every aerobics class offered by the fitness center in the course of the specified time period. Moreover, the broadened behavioral criterion of interest (i.e., attending aerobics classes in the course of a semester or year) also generalizes across the locations at which the aerobics classes take place. We would thus have to first identify all nearby locations, including private homes, in which aerobics classes are offered and then observe attendance or nonattendance at each of these locations over the course of the specified time period.

To make matters worse, public health professionals are usually not concerned with a particular kind of exercise, such as aerobics, but with the behavioral category of exercising in general as a means to improve physical health and fitness. This behavioral criterion requires that we expand the action element to include all possible forms of exercise. We would first have to identify the different kinds of exercise (e.g., walking, jogging, swimming, climbing stairs, lifting weights, doing push-ups) in which the research participants can engage as well as the locations in which these activities can take place. Measuring the behavioral criterion would be a formidable task as it would require that we observe, over the course of a semester or year, whether each participant performs or does not perform the different physical activities in each location. In other words, we would have to observe each of the research participants 24 hours a day, 7 days a week, for the specified time period. Needless to say, this is not realistic.

It is, however, possible to take a simpler route. Thus far we have assumed that the behavior of interest is directly observed (or that a record of the directly observed behavior is obtained). We saw that although it is usually quite easy to observe a single behavior performed on a given occasion, conducting direct observations for a behavioral category is virtually impossible. It is often for this reason that much social science research relies on *self-reports* of behavior rather than on direct observation. We can simply ask people whether they attended an aerobics class, or whether they exercised, in the course of a given time period. Note, however, that whereas there is general agreement about what it means to attend an aerobics class, this is not the case when asking about a broad behavioral category, such as exercising, dieting, or studying. To assess a category of behaviors via self-report, therefore, we must provide a clear definition of the category in question. For instance, we might tell respondents that by exercising we mean participation "in active sports or vigorous physical activities long enough to get sweaty at least twice a week" (Godin, Valois, Shephard, & Desharnais, 1987, p. 150). With this definition in mind, we can ask respondents whether, within the past 2 months, they exercised, or we can include the definition of the behavior in the question and ask, "Did you participate in active sports or vigorous physical activities long enough to get sweaty at least twice a week in the past 2 months?"

For other behavioral categories, such as political participation, it may be necessary to list representative examples of the specific activities that define the category. Thus, we could make it clear that by political participation we refer to such activities as canvassing a neighborhood, stuffing envelopes, contributing money to a campaign, running for office, writing to public officials or to the editors of newspapers or magazines, attending political rallies, meetings of school boards, or city councils, and other forms of political participation. We could then ask respondents to indicate which of these activities they have performed over a specified period of time and construct an index to represent the behavioral category. This issue and other measurement concerns are discussed in greater detail herein and in subsequent chapters.

It is evident that developing good measures of behavioral categories, even when using self-reports, is a complex task, much more difficult than assessing performance of a single behavior. The challenge is to ensure that all participants have the same definition and understanding of the behavioral category and that their definition matches that of the investigator.

☐ Varieties of Behavioral Criteria

Dichotomies, Frequencies, and Magnitudes

No matter how broadly or narrowly a behavior is defined in terms of its target, action, context, and time elements, the most fundamental question we are trying to answer is why people do or do not perform the behavior of interest. To answer this question, we must be able to assess whether the behavior was or was not performed. Consider, for example, charitable donations to Doctors Without Borders. To obtain a suitable measure, we could assess whether a person did or did not make a contribution to this organization within a given time period (*dichotomous criterion*). This information can be obtained by means of a self-report or by inspecting the organization's records.

In addition to the primary dichotomous criterion, we could be interested in the amount of money that was donated to Doctors Without Borders within a given period of time (*magnitude criterion*), or we could measure how often a monetary contribution was made (*frequency criterion*). Frequency measures sometimes take the form of numerical estimates that correspond to the actual number of times a donation was made, but at other times, a verbal scale might be used, perhaps ranging from *never* to *many times*. In addition, frequency can be quantified as a *proportion*, either the proportion of occasions on which a person made a donation in response to a solicitation from Doctors Without Borders or the proportion of donations that went to this charity as opposed to all other charitable organizations.

Note that behavioral frequencies generalize one or more of the behavior's elements. Consider, for example, the behavior of watching the news on television. A dichotomous behavioral observation might assess whether individuals watched (action element) the evening news (target) on CBS (context) on a given day (time). The frequency with which this behavior was performed might be assessed by observing how often the participants watched the CBS evening news in a 2-month time interval. In this case, the frequency count has the effect of broadening the time element. Alternatively, we could assess how often our participants watched any news program on CBS within a 2-month period, which generalizes the target as well as the time elements. Or we could measure how often they watched any news program on television in a 2-month period. Here, the frequency measure produces a criterion that generalizes the context, target, and time elements.

A behavioral criterion that is quantified in terms of magnitude, frequency, or proportion poses serious challenges when we try to understand the behavior's determinants. It is not inconceivable that different factors must be invoked to explain performance of varying behavioral quantities. Donating $1,000 to Doctors Without Borders may be motivated by different factors than donating $5 to this organization, and jogging every day may require a different explanation than jogging once a week. In fact, strictly speaking, different quantities of a behavior define different action elements and, in this sense, constitute different behaviors. For practical reasons, we cannot provide a separate explanation for each and every behavioral frequency or magnitude. However, it is often the case that even though a frequency or magnitude measure is available, the investigator has a special interest in a particular behavioral quantity, and this quantity can be used to redefine the behavior in terms of a dichotomy. For example, as we noted earlier, the basic question may be why people do or do not donate money to a particular charity, irrespective of the amount they donate. In that case, the behavioral criterion will be a dichotomy created by classifying participants as donors or nondonors. Alternatively, we may want to understand why people join the group of supporters known as the "Fellows Circle," whose members donate at least $500. In this case, we could classify participants in terms of whether they did or did not donate at least $500. Note that this criterion defines a different behavior from the original dichotomy, which divided participants into donors and nondonors. Earlier we mentioned an exercise criterion that took the form of participating in active sports or vigorous physical activities long enough to get sweaty at least twice a week. This is an example of a behavioral criterion involving a specific magnitude and frequency that produces a dichotomous criterion. It can thus be seen that when quantitative measures focus on a specific frequency or magnitude they are basically reduced to dichotomous measures. It is, of course, also possible to have an interest in more than two points on a behavioral continuum (e.g., donating no money vs. less than $500 vs. $500 or more), resulting in a trichotomy.

The important point to be made is that attempts to understand behavior require careful attention to the exact nature of the behavioral criterion. The most fundamental questions revolve around dichotomous criteria that can help us understand why some people perform a given behavior while others do not. It is for this reason that it is usually desirable to think of our behavioral criterion in terms of whether the behavior, as defined, was or was not performed. Nevertheless, in some cases, a continuous measure representing behavioral magnitude or frequency is of interest to the investigator and thus serves as the behavioral criterion.

Behavioral Categories

Somewhat different though related considerations apply to behavioral categories. Clearly, the discrete actions that make up a category constitute different behaviors. In the case of studying, for example, the category contains such diverse activities as attending classes, reading assigned books or papers, searching the Web for relevant information, taking notes, and memorizing materials. Each of these activities is a behavior in its own right, and, as we have seen, each can be assessed in terms of specific, discrete quantities or in terms of continuous frequencies or magnitudes. In addition, we can aggregate the individual actions into a general measure that represents the category as a whole (see Ajzen & Fishbein, 1980; Fishbein & Ajzen, 1975; see also Chapter 8 in this volume). How this aggregation is accomplished will depend on the nature of the behavioral category and on the objectives of the investigation.

We can aggregate individual actions in several ways. We can simply count the number of actions that have been performed, can examine how frequently they have been performed, or can determine how much (e.g., amount of time) each action has been performed. These measures can then be used to construct an index that reflects the extent to which a person engaged in the behavioral category under consideration. For some behavioral categories, all actions may become part of the aggregate index, but for other categories, different combination schemes may be appropriate. For example, a dieting regimen to reduce weight may involve three actions: avoiding sugar, eating a variety of fruits and vegetables, and avoiding snacks of any kind. An investigator may decide that people will be classified as engaging in this dieting behavior if, and only if, they perform all three actions. It would still be possible, of course, to quantify the behavior by, for example, aggregating the proportion of days on which the diet was maintained. Other behavioral categories may require only that at least one of the actions in the category be performed. Engaging in any vigorous physical activity to the point of building up a sweat is an example of such a criterion.

As in the case of individual behaviors, magnitude or frequency measures of behavioral categories may present problems when we try to explain the behavior. Studying or exercising a great deal may require a different explanation than engaging in these behaviors only a little. Here, too, it may therefore be preferable to define a dichotomous criterion instead of focusing on the whole continuum (i.e., it may be preferable to define a criterion that allows us to say whether a person did or did not engage in the category of behaviors). The exercise example used earlier illustrates this possibility. Instead of trying to find an explanation for the extent to which a person "exercises," Godin et al. (1987) focused on trying to understand why people do or do not participate "in active sports or vigorous physical activities long enough to get sweaty at least twice a week."

☐ Validity of Self-Reports

We have highlighted the practical advantages of self-reports compared with direct observations of behavior. However, questions have often been raised about the validity of self-reports (Jaccard, McDonald, Wan, Dittus, & Quinlan, 2002; Schwarz, Groves, & Schuman, 1998; see Tourangeau & Yan, 2007, for a review). People may not be able to accurately recall their past behavior, or, usually due to self-presentation concerns, they may choose not to report it accurately. Thus, people tend to overreport medication adherence (Wagner & Rabkin, 2000) but to underreport drug use (Lapham, C'de Baca, Chang, Hunt, & Berger, 2002). Whether we have to be concerned about these kinds of issues depends on the nature of the behavioral criterion. Generally speaking, it is more difficult to recall behaviors that were performed a long time ago than recently performed behaviors. However, it has also been found that infrequent behaviors, especially if they are of personal significance, are well recalled even after an extended period of time (Schwarz, Groves, & Schuman, 1998). When we are studying a behavior that we suspect may not be accurately recalled, we can employ methods to improve recall accuracy. For example, we can ask participants to keep a daily or weekly diary, or we can provide them with cues to aid recall. Thus, if people find it difficult to recall what they did several months ago, we can specify a significant event that occurred around that time (perhaps a birthday, holiday, or anniversary) and ask respondents to recall their behavior close to that event.

The possibility of self-presentation biases is of concern primarily when dealing with behaviors that are socially desirable (e.g., using condoms, voting) or undesirable (e.g., using drugs, cheating). We can reduce or eliminate these kinds of biases by motivating people to tell the truth (see Jaccard & Blanton, 2005). For example, we can assure them of confidentiality or anonymity, we can ask them to sign a declaration or contract that they will tell the truth, we can try to impress them with the importance of providing accurate data for scientific purposes, or we can convince them that the accuracy of their self-reports can be verified (e.g., by checking with others knowledgeable about their behavior).

In sum, it is important to be aware of the potential threats to validity posed by use of behavioral self-reports, and it is incumbent upon the investigator to employ methods that will maximize their accuracy. When proper precautions are taken, self-reports of behavior can be quite reliable and valid—perhaps no less so than direct observation of behavior. In fact, direct behavioral observations have their own problems. First, it can often be difficult to assess with direct observation whether a particular behavior was performed. If we observe people at the opera or a lecture we can say that they were present, but we cannot be sure that they were actually listening. Second, we sometimes don't have the access required to observe performance of a behavior. For instance, neither sexual behavior nor voting choice can be directly observed. Finally, as noted earlier, direct observation is extremely difficult, time-consuming, and expensive if we want to generalize across context, action, and time elements or if we want to know whether people perform a category of behaviors such as exercising, studying, or participating in the political process. For these reasons, the vast majority of empirical investigations rely on self-reports rather than direct observations of behavior.

☐ Behaviors Versus Goals

The examples in Table 2.2 show that it is possible to generalize target and context to the point where these elements are left unspecified, and the time element can also be left unspecified by considering, for example, whether a person ever performed the action under consideration. However, although we can move from single acts to behavioral categories, we cannot define a behavior without specifying the action element at some level of generality or specificity. That is, a behavioral criterion always involves an action. This stipulation allows us to deal with an issue that has caused some confusion. Investigators often try to predict such criteria as losing weight or getting a high grade in a course and have sometimes treated these criteria as behaviors (e.g., Ajzen & Madden, 1986; Netemeyer, Burton, & Johnston, 1991; Perugini & Bagozzi, 2001; Schifter & Ajzen, 1985). Clearly, however, losing weight is not a behavior but a *goal* that can perhaps be achieved by performing behaviors associated with dieting or exercising. Similarly, getting a high grade on an exam is a goal students can set for themselves and that they can try to achieve by attending classes regularly and reading assigned materials.

It may appear that goals differ from behaviors in that they depend, at least in part, on performing one or more preceding actions. However, performing a behavior, such as participating in an aerobics class, is also preceded by, and dependent upon, other activities, such as changing clothes and getting to the building where the class is held. Indeed, most human social behavior involves a sequence of actions, not a single act. The phrase *participating in an aerobics class* is shorthand for the total sequence involved. Similarly, *going to the movies* is shorthand for a sequence of activities that includes finding out where a movie of interest is playing and its starting times, getting to the theater on time, purchasing tickets, and taking a seat. However, in the case of a behavioral sequence, the ultimate step (e.g., participating in an aerobics class or watching a movie) is itself an action whereas in the case of a goal, such as losing weight, the final step in the sequence no longer has an action element. Instead, losing weight is an event that either may or may not follow from the behaviors performed previously.

☐ Predicting Behavior

It is an article of faith among behavioral and social scientists that human behavior is complex, multiply determined, and can be understood only by considering a large number of interacting causal antecedents. In contrast to this view, we suggested over 30 years ago (Fishbein & Ajzen, 1975) that human social behavior is determined by a relatively small number of factors, and these factors form the basis of our reasoned action approach. Based on this approach, we concluded that prediction of behavior is not that difficult after all. Within our theory, behavioral intentions are the most important immediate antecedents of behavior, although control over performance of the behavior also has to be taken into account. We therefore first examine the proposition that an appropriate measure of intention will be a good predictor of the behavior under consideration.

The Concept of Intention

Behavioral intentions are indications of a person's readiness to perform a behavior. The readiness to act, represented by an intention, can find expression in such statements as the following:

- I will engage in the behavior.
- I intend to engage in the behavior.
- I expect to engage in the behavior.
- I plan to engage in the behavior.
- I will try to engage in the behavior.

In other words, as is true of any hypothetical construct, different indicators can be used to assess intention or readiness to perform a given behavior. The essential underlying dimension characterizing an intention is the person's estimate of the likelihood or perceived probability of performing a given behavior. We expect that the higher this subjective probability, the more likely it is that the behavior will in fact be performed.

Although we define intentions in terms of a subjective probability dimension, it is also possible to consider additional characteristics associated with behavioral intentions. Analogous to work on the attitude construct, intentions can vary in terms of such characteristics as their accessibility in memory, the confidence with which they are held, and the personal relevance or importance of the behavior to the individual. In work on attitudes, characteristics of this kind—as well as the attitude's polarity or extremity—are often considered indicators of attitude strength (see Petty & Krosnick, 1995). As we will see in Chapter 8, attempts have been made to show that taking these characteristics into account can improve prediction of behavior from attitudes. It stands to reason that the predictive validity of intentions may also improve if other characteristics are considered, but as of this writing, there is only very limited empirical evidence relevant to this proposition.

Some support for the importance of an intention's accessibility in memory comes from a study on voting in the 1990 Ontario provincial election (Bassili, 1995). During the 3 weeks that preceded the election, voters were interviewed by telephone, were asked to indicate, among other things, for which party they intended to vote, and the latency of their responses to this question was recorded. Response latency is assumed to reflect the construct's accessibility in memory (see Fazio, 1996b), and thus intentions produced relatively fast are, by definition, more accessible. In addition, the participants were asked whether their choices were final or if they might still change their minds (voting certainty). At each level of voting certainty, the investigator divided the sample at the median latency score into high and low accessibility subgroups. Immediately following the election, participants were contacted and asked whether they had voted and, if so, for which party. For the total sample of participants, there was a very high correlation between voting intention and behavior. Nevertheless, this correlation was, as expected, significantly stronger in the high accessibility group ($r = .87$) than in the low accessibility group ($r = .74$). This moderating effect of accessibility on the intention–behavior relation was also confirmed in a meta-analysis (Cooke & Sheeran, 2004) that included Bassili's investigation and four additional studies.

Although characteristics of an intention other than subjective probability are worth exploring, research on the intention–behavior relation has focused almost exclusively on the subjective probability dimension. Unless otherwise noted, our use of the term *intention* in this book therefore refers to the subjective probability of performing a behavior.

Behavioral Expectations and Willingness

We have noted that various indicators can be used to assess intentions. Examples are statements that I intend to engage in the behavior, I expect to engage in the behavior, I plan to engage in the behavior, I will try to engage in the behavior, and so on. Some investigators, however, have proposed that rather than being indicators of a single construct, these varied measures are better viewed as indicators of different constructs. Thus, for example, a distinction has been made between behavioral intention and behavioral expectation (Warshaw & Davis, 1985) and, more recently, it has also been suggested that intention to perform a behavior differs in important ways from willingness to perform the behavior (Gibbons, Gerrard, Blanton, & Russell, 1998). Although it may be of interest to consider differences of this kind, the utility of such distinctions for the prediction of behavior is ultimately an empirical question. As we show next, available evidence to date suggests that there is little to be gained by the proposed distinctions.

Behavioral Expectation

Most research on this issue has been devoted to the distinction between behavioral intention and behavioral expectation or self-prediction. It was hypothesized that behavioral expectations are better predictors of behavior than behavioral intentions because the former are more likely to take into account possible impediments to performance of the behavior (Sheppard, Hartwick, & Warshaw, 1988; Warshaw & Davis, 1985). In this research, such items as "I intend to ...," "I will try to ...," and "I plan to..." are said to assess intentions whereas such items as "I expect to..." and "I will..." are said to assess behavioral expectations (Warshaw & Davis).

The hypothesized advantage of behavioral expectations over intentions was supported in an initial meta-analysis (Sheppard et al., 1988). The mean correlation between intentions and behavior was .49 compared with a correlation of .57 between expectations and behavior. Subsequent research, however, has often reported little difference, or even a difference in the opposite direction. For example, in a study of participation in a gubernatorial primary election (Netemeyer & Burton, 1990), college students expressed their intentions and behavioral expectations 1 week prior to the election and, immediately following the election, reported whether they had or had not voted. Behavioral intentions were assessed on a seven-point scale: "Please indicate whether you presently intend to vote in the October 24th governor's primary," *no, definitely not* to *yes, definitely intend to.* A second seven-point scale assessed behavioral expectations: "All things considered, how likely is it that you will actually vote in the October 24th governor's primary," *extremely unlikely* to *extremely likely.* Responses to these two items were highly correlated ($r = .64$), but intentions predicted actual voting participation better ($r = .59$) than did behavioral expectations ($r = .38$).

Recent meta-analyses have also failed to provide support for the superiority of behavioral expectation measures over measures of behavioral intention. In a synthesis of studies concerned with the prediction of condom use, Sheeran and Orbell (1998) found no difference in the mean amount of variance accounted for by behavioral expectation (18%) and by behavioral intention (19%), and a meta-analysis of a much broader set of behaviors (Armitage & Conner, 2001) also found no difference between the predictive validity of expectations and intentions (see also Randall & Wolff, 1994).

Willingness

Only a limited amount of research has been conducted on willingness to perform a behavior. In their analysis of willingness, Gibbons et al. (1998) proposed that unlike measures of intentions or behavioral expectations, a measure of willingness is somehow capable of capturing nonintentional, irrational influences on behavior. They did not assume that willingness is a better predictor than behavioral intention or behavioral expectation, only that a measure of willingness adds a significant amount of unique variance to the prediction of behavior. In one of their three studies, willingness to engage in unprotected sex was assessed by asking participants to "imagine being with their boyfriend or girlfriend who wanted to have sex but with no birth control available" and to indicate how likely it was that they would do each of the following: have sex but use withdrawal, not have sex, and have sex without any birth control. As a measure of behavioral intention (or more precisely, behavioral expectation), participants were asked to rate the likelihood that they will have sex in the next year without using birth control and the likelihood that if they were to have sex in the next year they would use no birth control. The behavioral criterion was a measure of behavior obtained 6 months after questionnaire administration. Participants indicated how often, in the past 6 months, they had had sexual intercourse without using any kind of birth control and what kinds of birth control, if any, they had used. Correlations were computed among the latent constructs as assessed by the multiple indicators of willingness, behavioral expectation, and behavior.

The results confirmed the investigators' expectations. Willingness to engage in unprotected sex and behavioral expectation correlated significantly ($r = .60$), but behavioral expectation was a slightly better predictor of behavior than was willingness ($r = .73$ vs. $r = .65$, respectively). More important, a secondary analysis showed that considering the measures of willingness and behavioral expectation simultaneously significantly improved prediction of reported behavior from $R = .73$ to $R = .78$. Similar results were obtained in a second study that dealt with adolescent smoking behavior, but here the willingness measure was a slightly better predictor of smoking than was the measure of behavioral expectation.

Gibbons et al. (1998) interpreted these findings to mean that willingness to engage in a behavior differs substantively from behavioral expectation or intention. Note, however, that the obtained pattern of results is also consistent with the idea that willingness and behavioral expectation (or intention) are expressions of the same underlying construct, namely, readiness to engage in the behavior. Indeed, in a more recent study on smoking, drinking, and drug use among adolescents (Gibbons, Gerrard, Cleveland, Wills, & Brody, 2004), measures of intention, expectation, and willingness were combined to yield a single index, a procedure consistent with this interpretation. Moreover, a closer look at the measure of willingness further supports the idea that we are not really dealing with a new construct. For example, it is not at all clear why a measure of willingness to engage in a behavior is assumed to reflect the influence of nonrational, intuitive, or reactive factors. Asking people whether they would or would not engage in unprotected sex or smoke *under certain circumstances* may simply measure a more specific intention than the intention to perform these behaviors in general. The obtained results can then be interpreted to mean that specifying a context can add unique variance to a measure of behavioral intention or expectation. (A more detailed discussion of this issue can be found in Chapter 9.)

Clearly, more research is needed to clarify these issues, but in this book we use the term *intention* to refer to readiness to engage in a behavior, a construct that incorporates such concepts as willingness, behavioral expectation, and trying.

Using Intentions to Predict Behavior

At the most fundamental level we are trying to understand why people do or do not perform a given behavior. A dichotomous behavioral measure is most suitable to answer questions of this kind, and it is indeed a very common behavioral criterion in empirical investigations. Among other things, investigators have measured whether people do or do not donate blood; get a diagnostic test such as a mammogram, a prostate-specific antigen (PSA) test, or a test for HIV or other sexually transmitted diseases; vote in a presidential election; donate money to a charity; and buy an automobile, household appliance, or life insurance policy. To predict a behavioral criterion of this kind, we need a measure of intention that captures the essentially dichotomous character of the behavior. Thus, we could ask participants whether they do or do not intend to perform the behavior in question. A more sensitive measure, however, can be obtained by asking people how strongly they intend to perform the behavior or how likely they are to do so, as illustrated in the following example from a study on blood donation on a university campus (Giles & Cairns, 1995).

I intend to give blood at the university on Monday.

      extremely likely | ___ | ___ | ___ | ___ | ___ | ___ | ___ | extremely unlikely

This intention measure correlated .75 with whether students did or did not donate blood, as reported by the students 1 week later.

As we illustrate later, the scales used to assess the subjective probability of engaging in a behavior can take many forms. In addition to *extremely likely–extremely unlikely*, we could use such adjectives as *probable–improbable*, *not at all–definitely*, *agree–disagree*, or *true–false*. For greater reliability, investigators often use two or more intention items, as was done in a study that applied our theory to hunting (Hrubes, Ajzen, & Daigle, 2001). The following two items, appearing at different points in the questionnaire, constituted the measure of intention.

1. I intend to go hunting in the next 12 months.

   extremely unlikely | 1 | 2 | 3 | 4 | 5 | 6 | 7 | extremely likely

2. I am planning to go hunting in the next 12 months.

   definitely no | 1 | 2 | 3 | 4 | 5 | 6 | 7 | definitely yes

The participants were asked to circle the number that best described their intentions. Scores on the two items correlated very highly with each other ($r = .99$). Consequently, scores for the two items were averaged to yield a measure of hunting intention, which correlated .62 with actual hunting behavior as reported 12 months later.

The Principle of Compatibility

Perhaps the most important prerequisite for predictive validity is that the measure of intention be compatible with the behavioral criterion in term of its level of generality or specificity. We saw earlier that any behavior is defined by four elements: action, target, context, and time. According to the *principle of compatibility* (Ajzen & Fishbein, 1980; Fishbein & Ajzen, 1975), an intention is compatible with a behavior if both are measured at the same level of generality or specificity—that is, if the measure of intention involves exactly the same action, target, context, and time elements as the measure of behavior.

Single-Act Dichotomous Criteria

Consider first how we would have to assess intentions to make the measure compatible with a single behavioral dichotomy. For example, we may be interested in predicting whether people will or will not enroll (action) in a continuing education course (target) at a local community college (context) the next time it is offered (time). To maintain strict intention–behavior compatibility, we would assess intention to enroll in a continuing education course at a local community college the next time it is offered. Alternatively, we may not care whether people enroll in a continuing education course at a local college the next time it is offered but only whether they enroll in any continuing education course sometime in the next 12 months. In this case, the target and action elements are clearly specified as before, the time element has been expanded, and the context is undefined. A measure of intention compatible with this new criterion is the intention to enroll in a continuing education course in the next 12 months. This example illustrates that changing one or more elements produces a different behavior, and people may intend to perform the more general behavior even if they do not intend to perform the specific behavior.

Single-Act Continuous Criteria

Even at the level of a single act, when we are dealing with continuous measures that involve behavioral frequency or magnitude, we must consider an aspect of compatibility that goes beyond generality or specificity of target, action, context, and time elements. For instance, it stands to reason that asking people how likely it is that they will go to the movies in the next month (intention) will not necessarily predict how many movies they will see (behavioral frequency criterion). Similarly, the strength of people's intentions to donate money to the American Red Cross in the course of a year may not accurately predict how much money they donate (magnitude criterion). These are examples of *scale incompatibility* (Courneya, 1994; Courneya & McAuley, 1994) where the intention refers to a dichotomy (i.e., the likelihood that the person will or will not perform a behavior) whereas the behavioral criterion is a continuous measure of frequency or magnitude. To secure both scale and behavioral compatibility, we would have to formulate intention questions such as the following:

1. In the next month, how many times will you go to the movies?
2. How much money do you intend to donate to the American Red Cross in the next 12 months?

An actual research example can be found in a study of marijuana use among college students (Conner & McMillan, 1999). The behavioral criterion in this study was self-reported use of marijuana in a 3-month period. Specifically, the following four items inquired into frequency and quantity of use:

1. Over the last 3-month period how often have you been using cannabis/marijuana?

   never / only once / more than once / every few months / every month / every week / more than weekly / most days (scored 0 to 7)

2. How often would you say that you have been using cannabis over the last 3 months?

never |___|___|___|___|___|___|___| very frequently (scored 1 to 7)

3. How would you rate the amount of cannabis/marijuana you have been using over the last 3 months?

non-existent |___|___|___|___|___|___| very high (scored 0 to 5)

4. How much cannabis/marijuana would you say you have been using over the last 3-month period?

none |___|___|___|___|___|___| a lot (scored 0 to 5)

Scores on these four items were standardized and then averaged, producing a highly reliable measure of behavior (alpha = .97).

Three months earlier, participants had expressed their intentions to use marijuana by responding to the following two items:

1. Please indicate how often you intend to use cannabis/marijuana over the next 3-month period.

   never / only once / more than once / every few months / every month / every week / more than weekly / most days

2. How often do you feel it is likely that you will use cannabis/marijuana over the next 3-month period?

   never / only once / more than once / every few months / every month / every week / more than weekly / most days

Responses to both items were scored 0 to 7, and the two item scores were averaged to produce a measure of intention with a reliability coefficient alpha of .98.[1]

Whereas the two intention items dealt only with frequency, the measure of behavior included items that referred to frequency as well as magnitude of the behavior. Nevertheless, because the behavioral measure had high internal consistency, intentions to use marijuana were found to predict self-reported use of the drug very well; the correlation between intentions and behavior was .84.

This discussion shows that when the behavioral criterion is a continuous measure of frequency or magnitude, we can develop compatible quantitative intention measures that do a good job of predicting the behavior. This should not be taken to mean, however, that *explanation* of the behavior will be accomplished as easily. Recall that the different quantities (frequencies or magnitudes) of a continuous behavioral criterion constitute different behaviors, and we may thus be faced with the difficult task of providing different explanations for varying quantities. For instance, the factors that explain use of marijuana once a month may differ considerably from the factors that explain daily use of the drug.

Behavioral Categories

When dealing with a behavioral category, the problem of compatibility is compounded because in addition to frequency and magnitude of individual behaviors, we now also have to consider the occurrence and frequency of different behaviors that comprise the category. Earlier in this chapter we noted that the different behaviors comprising a category can be aggregated in various ways into an overall index that represents the degree to which participants engaged in the category of behaviors. However, as in the case of single behaviors, it is also possible to score the behavioral category in such a way as to produce a dichotomous score, which indicates whether participants did or did not perform the behavioral category.

To ensure that measures of intention are completely compatible with complex criteria of this kind, we could assess the intention in exactly the same way as the behavior. Suppose an investigator asked students how many hours in the past week they had engaged in each of five different studying activities (e.g., reading assigned materials, attending classes) and, as a measure of studying behavior, simply averaged the responses. A perfectly compatible measure of intention is obtained by listing the five studying behaviors and asking respondents to indicate how many hours they intended to spend on each in the following week. However, this is a fairly simple case, and it would be possible to employ a different procedure that relies on providing participants with a clear definition of the category. They might be told that what the investigator means by studying is the total number of hours spent on performing the five studying behaviors. With this definition, they could then be asked how many hours they intend to study in the following week. However, as the combination rule used to construct a behavioral criterion becomes more complicated, it becomes increasingly difficult to communicate it to participants. If there is any concern that participants' understanding of the behavioral criterion may differ from that of the investigator, the best procedure for obtaining a compatible measure of intention is to construct it in the same way the behavioral index is constructed.

Empirical Support for Prediction of Behavior From Intentions

To the extent that the indicators used to assess intention and behavior comply with the principle of compatibility, it should be possible to use intentions to predict behavior. Previously we saw that intentions to donate blood (Giles & Cairns, 1995), to go hunting (Hrubes et al., 2001), and to use marijuana (Conner & McMillan, 1999) predicted compatible behaviors with considerable accuracy. Many other studies have substantiated the predictive validity of behavioral intentions. Indeed, when appropriately measured, behavioral intentions account for an appreciable proportion of variance in actual behavior. This conclusion is supported by several systematic reviews and meta-analyses of empirical findings. For example, in an extensive review of research based on our reasoned action approach, Armitage and Conner (2001) examined the intention–behavior correlation in 48 independent studies covering such diverse behavioral domains as physical activity, smoking cessation, use of public transportation, recycling, leisure activities, living kidney donation, condom use, breast self-examination, fruit and vegetable consumption, use of illicit drugs, health screening, playing video games, donating blood, and many more. A meta-analysis of the findings revealed a mean intention–behavior correlation of .47. Mean intention–behavior correlations of comparable magnitude, ranging from .45 to .62, were reported in several other meta-analyses of diverse behavioral domains (Notani, 1998; Randall & Wolff, 1994; Sheppard et al., 1988; van den Putte, 1993). Studies in specific behavioral domains, such as condom use and exercise, have produced similar results, with intention–behavior correlations ranging from .44 to .56 (Albarracín, Johnson, Fishbein, & Muellerleile, 2001; Godin, & Kok, 1996; Hagger, Chatzisarantis, & Biddle, 2002; Hausenblas, Carron, & Mack, 1997; Sheeran & Orbell, 1998). In a meta-analysis of most of these and of other meta-analyses, Sheeran (2002) reported an overall correlation of .53 between intention and behavior.

It is worth noting that degree of intention–behavior compatibility was not taken into account in these meta-analyses, although compatibility undoubtedly varied considerably across studies. Despite this problem, the results show that intentions can indeed be used to predict behavior with a considerable degree of accuracy.

Self-Reports Versus Objective Measures of Behavior

In our discussion of the validity of behavioral self-reports, we noted the possibility that such reports may be distorted or biased in a socially desirable direction. It is also possible that self-reports of behavior are biased to be consistent with previously expressed intentions or that self-reports of behavior are erroneously recalled to have been consistent with present intentions. These kinds of biases would produce an inflated estimate of the correlation between intentions and self-reported behavior compared with the correlation of intentions with objective measures of behavior. To investigate this issue, Armitage & Conner (2001) compared the prediction of objective as opposed to self-report measures of behavior. The investigators conducted a meta-analysis of 63 prospective studies that were based on our reasoned action approach, 44 that used self-reports of behavior, and 19 that used objective measures. In line with our theory, perceived behavioral control as well as intentions were used to predict behavior. Consistent with the idea that there may be more bias associated with self-reports than with objective measures of behavior, the meta-analysis showed a significantly higher mean multiple correlation of .55 with self-reports compared with a mean multiple correlation of .44 for objective measures.[2]

Prospective Versus Retrospective Measures of Behavior

Conceptually, we want to use intentions to predict behavior at some future point in time. However, investigators frequently assess intentions and, on the same occasion, also ask for a self-report of past or current behavior. Because present intentions are likely to reflect past experience, it is often assumed that they correlate better with a retrospective measure of past behavior than with a prospective measure of behavior obtained at a future point in time. Also, we saw previously that intentions correlate better with self-reports than with objective measures of behavior. Because retrospective measures of past behavior virtually always rely on self-reports whereas measures of future behavior can be either self-reports or objective, this too suggest that intentions should predict measures of past behavior better than measures of future behavior.

Consistent with these considerations, in the Albarracín et al. (2001) meta-analysis of research on condom use mentioned earlier, the correlation between intentions to use condoms and reported condom use was .57 for past behavior and .45 for future behavior. However, other meta-analyses that included a variety of different behaviors suggest that there may be little difference in correlations of intentions with future as opposed to past behavior. In their meta-analysis of research based on our theory, Armitage and Conner (2001) identified 48 prospective studies in which intentions were used to predict future behavior, either self-reported or observed. The mean intention–behavior correlation in this meta-analysis was found to be .47. In a prior publication (Conner & Armitage, 1998), these investigators reported the results of a meta-analysis based on 16 data sets in which intentions were found to correlate, on average, .51 with past behavior, not much higher than the .47 correlation with future behavior.

Indeed, examination of individual studies often reveals little difference in, or even an advantage for, the prediction of later as opposed to prior behavior. For example, in three studies of alcohol consumption among college students (Conner, Warren, Close, & Sparks, 1999), correlations between intentions and past behavior were .35, .50, and .37. The correlations between intentions and later behavior were virtually identical, at .35, .48, and .35, respectively. Similar results were reported in another study of drinking in college (O'Callaghan, Chant, Callan, & Baglioni, 1997). Here, intentions to drink alcohol correlated .69 with past drinking and .63 with later drinking. With respect to a different kind of behavior, exercising, Sheeran and Orbell (2000a) reported the identical correlation of .63 between exercise intention and past behavior and between exercise intention and later behavior.

In a study dealing with breast self-examination among female employees in a British telemarketing company (Norman & Hoyle, 2004), intentions to perform breast self-examinations actually correlated better with later than with past behavior. Participants in this study reported how often they were currently performing breast self-examinations, and they were classified as doing so at least once a month or less than once a month (*past behavior*). In addition, they expressed their intentions to perform breast self-examinations in the next month on three seven-point scales and, 1 month later, they reported whether they had or had not performed the examination in the previous month (*later behavior*). The intention–behavior correlation was .32 for past behavior and .51 for later behavior. Very similar results were reported in an investigation that dealt with the studying behavior of college students (Sheeran, Orbell, & Trafimow, 1999). Intention to study a certain number of days over the winter break correlated .58 with the reported number of days studied but only .32 with the number of days per week studied in the past.

At least one meta-analysis (Ouellette & Wood, 1998) also showed results consistent with this trend, that is, stronger intention–behavior correlations for future than past behavior. This meta-analysis, covering a broad range of behaviors, examined the correlations of intentions with prior behavior in 33 independent data sets and the correlations of intentions with future behavior in 19 data sets. The mean correlation between intentions and past behavior was found to be .43 compared with a mean correlation of .54 when intentions were used to predict future behavior.

To the best of our knowledge, there has been little systematic research designed to explain why intentions sometimes predict past behavior better than future behavior but at other times predict future behavior better than past behavior. It is possible that reviewing and reporting past behavior, or other processes that make past behavior more accessible, influence, at least temporarily, the intentions participants express with respect to future behavior such as to make these intentions conform more closely with the past behavior (Albarracín & Wyer, 2000). Similarly, expressing an intention conceivably influences recall of past behavior in a way that makes the past behavior appear more consistent with the intention. Both of these effects would tend to increase the correlation between intentions and previous behavior. Conversely, when intentions change, they will not correlate well with past behavior, but they would be expected to predict future behavior. Further research is needed to examine these different possibilities.

In sum, on average, intentions are found to predict behavior quite well even when intention–behavior compatibility varies across studies and irrespective of whether the study is prospective or retrospective. While there is some evidence that self-reported behavior can be predicted somewhat better than objective measures, it is important to note that even with respect to the latter, intentions account for a considerable proportion of variance (Armitage & Conner, 2001).

Prediction of Routine Behaviors

Our emphasis on intentions as the immediate antecedent of behavior has often been misinterpreted as implying that people form a conscious intention prior to carrying out each and every behavior. This has never been our position. To be sure, we assume that for at least some relatively novel and important behaviors, people engage in deliberation and form a conscious decision (i.e., form an intention) to perform or not perform the behavior under consideration. After repeated opportunities for performance, however, deliberation is no longer required because the intention is activated spontaneously in a behavior-relevant situation (see Ajzen & Fishbein, 2000). In other words, the behavior has become so routine that it is initiated with minimal conscious effort or attention. Many behaviors in everyday life are of this kind: We brush our teeth, leave the house for work, put on a seat belt, walk up stairs, and so forth without first forming conscious intentions to enact these behaviors.

Automaticity

Some theorists (e.g., Aarts & Dijksterhuis, 2000; Gollwitzer, 1999; Ouellette & Wood, 1998) go one step further in their analysis of routine behavior. They argue that habits are established when people have frequent opportunities to perform a behavior under identical or very similar circumstances. Once a habit has been established under these conditions, initiation of the behavior is said to come under the direct control of external or internal stimulus cues. In the presence of these cues, the behavior is automatically activated without cognitive intervention. Consider, for example, people's early morning routines of brushing their teeth in their bathrooms. The situational cues present in the bathroom (e.g., sink, faucet, mirror) are assumed to automatically elicit the toothbrushing practice without the intervention of a behavioral intention, even a spontaneously activated one. This analysis implies that intentions become increasingly irrelevant as a behavior habituates. In other words, a measure of intention should be a good predictor of relatively novel or unpracticed behaviors, but it should lose its predictive validity when it comes to routine or habitual responses in familiar situations.

Empirical findings lend little support to this hypothesis. Ouellette and Wood (1998) performed a meta-analysis on 15 data sets from studies that reported intention–behavior correlations. They classified each data set as dealing with a behavior that can be performed frequently (e.g., seat belt use, coffee drinking, class attendance) or infrequently (e.g., flu shots, blood donation, nuclear protest). Contrary to the automatic habit hypothesis, prediction of behavior from intentions was found to be quite accurate for both types of behavior (mean $r = .59$ and $r = .67$ for high- and low-opportunity behaviors, respectively). The difference between these two correlations was not statistically significant. The same conclusion arose from a similar meta-analysis based on 51 data sets (Sheeran & Sutton, unpublished data).[3] The mean intention–behavior correlation across all 51 studies was .53; for behaviors that could be performed infrequently (once or twice a year; 7 data sets) it was .51, and it was .53 for high-opportunity behaviors that could be performed daily or once a week (44 data sets).

A different way of looking at the effect of habit on the predictive validity of intentions is to compare behaviors performed in a stable context with behaviors performed in an unstable context. Because habit formation depends on stable stimulus cues, the intention–behavior correlation would be expected to decline for behaviors performed in a stable context. The meta-analysis by Sheeran and Sutton (unpublished data) examined this possibility as well. The investigators rated the behaviors in the 51 data sets as being performed either in a relatively stable context (e.g., study at home) or an unstable context (e.g., get immunized). The results of the meta-analysis showed differences contrary to what would be predicted by the habit hypothesis. For behaviors performed in unstable contexts (where intentions should be most relevant), the mean intention–behavior correlation was .40 compared with a mean intention–behavior correlation of .56 for behaviors performed in a stable context.

It is impossible, however, to derive any definite conclusions from these kinds of meta-analyses because the high-opportunity behaviors examined in the various studies differed in substance from the low-opportunity behaviors, as did the behaviors performed in stable and unstable contexts. The behaviors that were compared may thus have differed not only in performance opportunities or context stability but also in degree of importance, familiarity, or other properties that could affect the results.

To address this problem, Ouellette and Wood (1998) conducted an original study that was designed to demonstrate the moderating effect of contextual stability on the prediction of a target behavior from intentions. The behaviors selected were two high-opportunity activities: watching TV and recycling. To estimate stability of the supporting context, participants were asked to list the activities (if any) they always performed prior to engaging in each of the two behaviors. On the basis of these responses, participants were divided—for each behavior—into groups of high- and low-context stability. For these two high-opportunity behaviors, a stable context should allow strong habits to be formed, whereas an unstable context should not. The automatic habit perspective predicts that intentions will be relatively good predictors of behavior in an unstable context. In a stable context, however, where the behavior is presumably under direct control of stimulus cues, the predictive validity of intentions should be lower. The results of the study did not support these predictions. With respect to watching TV, the intention–behavior correlation was, as expected, higher in the unstable context ($r = .63$) than in the stable context ($r = .46$), but a reanalysis showed that the difference between these two correlations was not statistically significant ($z = .96$). Moreover, there was little difference with respect to the second behavior, recycling. Here, the prediction of later behavior from intentions was actually slightly better in the stable context ($r = .48$) than in the unstable context ($r = .43$). Thus, neither the meta-analyses described earlier nor this primary research provides support for the idea that habitual behavior is activated automatically, that it is unmediated by a spontaneously activated behavioral intention, or that the predictive validity of intentions declines for routine behaviors.

In sum, it seems clear that behavior can become routine with repeated performance, but there is no evidence to suggest that intentions are irrelevant when behavior becomes routine. On the contrary, the existing evidence shows that intentions can predict routine as well as relatively novel behaviors.

Factors Influencing the Predictive Validity of Intentions

Although, overall, intentions are found to be good predictors of behavior, in the following sections we consider factors that may influence the magnitude of the observed intention–behavior relation.

Compatibility

As we have previously noted, the most fundamental requirement for a strong relation between intentions and behavior is a high degree of compatibility in our measures. This is usually not a serious problem because in most investigations intentions directly address the behavior of interest. Nevertheless, compatibility issues can arise even here.

Behavioral Incompatibility

A classic study on racial discrimination illustrates lack of compatibility between the elements defining the behavior and the elements involved in the measure of intention (behavioral incompatibility). In the early 1930s, LaPiere (1934) accompanied a young Chinese couple in their travels across the United States and recorded whether they received service in restaurants and overnight accommodation in motels, hotels, and inns. Following their travel, LaPiere mailed a letter to each establishment they had visited, asking whether the establishment would "accept members of the Chinese race as guests." As LaPiere had anticipated, there was no consistency between responses to the letter (intention) and actual behavior. The Chinese couple received courteous service in virtually every establishment, but responses to the letter were almost universally negative.

It can be seen that the target element of the intention in this study differed greatly from the target element of the behavior. Whereas intentions dealt with providing service to members of the Chinese race (a very general target), the actual service was given to a specific Chinese couple, a target that differed in many important ways from the stereotype of the Chinese in those years. Not surprisingly, the well-dressed, well-spoken, well-to-do couple received service without difficulty, but the image of the poor, uneducated Chinese conjured up by the phrase *members of the Chinese race* produced rejection in response to the mailed inquiry.

LaPiere's (1934) study has also been criticized on methodological grounds (see Ajzen, Darroch, Fishbein, & Hornik, 1970). For example, the person replying to the letter may not have been the same person who admitted the Chinese couple, and in their travels LaPiere often entered the various establishments together with his Chinese friends. We consider another issue related to this study in our discussion of literal inconsistency later in this chapter.

Scale Incompatibility

Earlier we discussed the problem of scale incompatibility in relation to the measurement of continuous behavioral criteria involving frequency or magnitude. Use of different scales for measures of intentions and behaviors is likely to lower observed correlations. An empirical study of exercise behavior (Courneya, 1994) confirmed the importance of scale compatibility for accurate prediction. In this study, participants indicated their intentions to engage in vigorous physical activity in the forthcoming month of October. These intentions were assessed in several different ways. Of interest for present purposes, one item asked the student participants to indicate whether they intended to engage in vigorous physical activity during the month of October on a seven-point scale with *definitely* and *definitely not* as its endpoints (*dichotomous graded intention*). In response to another item, participants listed the number of times they intended to engage in vigorous physical activity during the month of October (*intention frequency*). Comparable measures were obtained for actual behavior. Early in November, participants were contacted and asked to report whether they had engaged in vigorous physical activity in the month of October, again on a seven-point *definitely–definitely not* scale (*dichotomous graded behavior*) and to list the number of times they had done so (*behavior frequency*).

Clearly, the intended frequency of physical activity was more scale compatible with the frequency measure of behavior than was the dichotomous graded measure of intention to engage or not engage in physical activity. Consistent with this difference in scale compatibility, the intention frequency measure predicted the behavioral frequency criterion better ($r = .87$) than did the dichotomous graded intention measure ($r = .51$). Conversely, as would also be expected, when the behavioral score was a dichotomy, the dichotomous intention predicted the behavioral criterion better ($r = .71$) than did the intention frequency measure ($r = .52$).

Category Incompatibility

Low compatibility can also easily occur in the case of criteria that constitute behavioral categories. For example, in a study of managers who were enrolled in a physical exercise program for health reasons (Kerner & Grossman, 1998), the frequency with which participants performed a specific prescribed exercise behavior (e.g., climbing stairs or lifting weights) over a 5-month period was only weakly ($r = .21$) related to their intentions to exercise in the next 12 months. Clearly, intentions with respect to a behavioral category such as exercise cannot be expected to be good predictors of a single instance of the category. A more compatible measure of intentions in this study would have asked participants to indicate the extent to which they intended to climb stairs or lift weights (i.e., to engage in the particular prescribed exercise behaviors).

In sum, degree of compatibility can greatly impact the predictive validity of intentions. To ensure a strong intention–behavior relation, the measure of intention must be compatible with the measure of behavior in terms of the target, action, context, and time elements as well as in terms of the measurement scale. This is largely a methodological problem, and it is incumbent upon investigators to devise measures of intention that are fully compatible with the behavioral criteria they are trying to predict.

Temporal Stability of Intentions

Even when an intention is fully compatible with the behavioral criterion, its predictive validity will decline if the intention changes after it was assessed but prior to performance of the behavior. Thus, intentions that remain stable over time should predict behavior better than intentions that are unstable. The time interval between measurement of intention and assessment of behavior is often taken as a proxy for temporal stability because it is assumed that with the passage of time, an increasing number of events may cause intentions to change. Meta-analyses of intention–behavior correlations show the expected temporal pattern, although the effect is not always statistically significant. For example, in the area of condom use, prediction of behavior from intention was found to become significantly less accurate with the passage of time (see Albarracín et al., 2001; Sheeran & Orbell, 1998). The correlation between effect size and amount of time in weeks between assessment of intention and behavior was –.59 in the Sheeran and Orbell analysis. In a review covering a broader range of behaviors (Randall & Wolff, 1994), the intention–behavior correlation declined from .65 for short time intervals (less than a day) to .40 for long intervals (1 or more years). This difference, however, was not statistically significant.

Instead of relying on the time interval as an indication of stability, some investigators have assessed stability of intentions directly, and these studies have consistently found that the intention–behavior correlation declines substantially when intentions are unstable. In one of these investigations (Sheeran, Orbell, & Trafimow, 1999) undergraduate college students indicated twice, 5 weeks apart, how many days they intended to study over the winter vacation. After returning from the winter vacation, they reported on how many days they had actually studied during the vacation. For participants whose intentions remained relatively stable during the 5-week period prior to the vacation, the correlation between the second intention measure and behavior was .58, whereas for participants with relatively unstable intentions it was .08. Similar results were reported with respect to attending a health screening appointment and eating a low-fat diet (Conner, Sheeran, Norman, & Armitage, 2000).

Sequential Hurdles

As we noted earlier, performance of most behaviors requires a sequence of prior actions. A person who intends to buy a house, for example, might first contact a real-estate agent, then visit available homes, make an offer on a house, secure a mortgage at the bank, and so forth. The greater the number of intervening steps, the lower the intention–behavior correlation is likely to be. Note that the problem may largely be related to the stability of the intention. At any step in the sequence—whether successfully completed or not—new information may become available that produces a change in the individual's intention to perform the behavior.

Volitional Control

Even assuming a measure of intention that is stable and compatible with the behavior, performance of the behavior may be thwarted by factors beyond a person's control. It stands to reason that people cannot act on their intentions if they lack the skills or resources required to perform the behavior or if external factors prevent them from doing so. Note that lack of measurement compatibility or of temporal stability can reduce the correlation between intentions and behavior, but neither incompatibility nor instability of intentions has a *causal* effect on behavior. In contrast, lack of volitional control can be causally implicated because it can prevent performance of a behavior. For example, people may intend to move a piece of furniture but cannot do so because they underestimated its weight and are physically incapable of performing the task (a factor internal to the person). Similarly, a person who intends to go to the opera may be unable to do so because the performance is sold out and no tickets are available (an external factor). We return to the question of volitional control and its effects on behavior later in this chapter.

Behaviors Versus Goals

Earlier in this chapter we noted that it is important to distinguish between behaviors and goals. Attainment of a goal depends not only on the person's behavior but also on other factors over which the person may have little or no control. For example, prospective college students who plan to attend a given university may perform all required behaviors: complete an application, write an essay, take the SAT, obtain letters of recommendation, and submit the application. At this point, whether they are admitted is beyond their control. The final step toward goal attainment depends, in this case, on the actions of other people.

Interestingly, similar considerations apply to the performance of a behavior that requires a sequence of prior actions. Earlier we suggested that information obtained at each stage of the sequence may produce a change in intentions to carry out the behavior under scrutiny. We can now see that a failure to perform the behavior may also be due to a lack of control at one or more of the behavioral steps. For example, your intention to apply for a new job may be based, among other things, on the assumption that you will get a required letter of recommendation from your current supervisor—an event over which you have no direct control. If the supervisor refuses or otherwise fails to provide this letter, you cannot complete your application. The ability to reach the final step in the behavioral sequence thus depends on the actions of another person at an earlier point in time.

These examples illustrate the important role of volitional control in the performance of a behavior and in the attainment of behavioral goals. A person who has little or no volitional control may not be able to carry out an intended behavior or to achieve a desired goal. As previously illustrated, the factors that determine the extent to which a person has control in a given situation can be classified into internal and external factors. The internal factors are mainly concerned with motivation, skills, and abilities, whereas external factors include resources (time, money, tools, and equipment), dependence on other people or events, and laws, rules, and regulations. It should be noted, however, that just because a person has volitional control does not mean that this will lead the person to form a favorable intention to perform a behavior or to attain a behavioral goal. While lack of control has a causal effect in that it prevents performance of a behavior, the presence of control over the behavior does not in and of itself cause the person to perform the behavior.

In conclusion, we would argue that, as a general rule, if individuals who intend to perform a behavior have the necessary skills and ability, and if there are no external factors to prevent the behavior, it is likely that they will act on their intentions. Similarly, individuals who intend to reach a certain goal are likely to form intentions to perform behaviors they believe will help them attain the goal. If these behaviors are indeed effective determinants of goal attainment, then the intention to reach the goal will have good predictive validity. However, if goal attainment depends not only on the individual's behavior but also on factors beyond his or her control, then the person may not be able to attain the intended goal. Thus, as a general rule, intentions will usually be better predictors of behaviors than of goal attainment.[4]

Memory for Intentions

Assume that our measure of intention is compatible with the behavioral criterion, it is stable over time, and the behavior of interest is under volitional control. Even under these favorable conditions, the measure of intention will fail to predict behavior unless it is activated on the appropriate occasion. Indeed, when asked to explain why they failed to act on their intentions, people often mention that they simply forgot or that it slipped their minds (Orbell, Hodgkins, & Sheeran, 1997; Sheeran & Orbell, 1999b). The processes involved in the encoding and activation of behavioral intentions is the focus of research on *prospective memory* (Brandimante, Einstein, & McDaniel, 1996). Although a thorough review of work on prospective memory is beyond the scope of this book, several ideas and findings are relevant to our present discussion and are worth noting. First, it is assumed that aspects of newly formed intentions, such as what to do and when and where to do it, are encoded in memory. Second, there seems to be good evidence that memory for encoded intentions decays at a slower rate than memory for other kinds of material. Third, the presence of situational cues that match one or more of the encoded aspects of the intention prompts its activation. Finally, formation of intentions is found to sensitize people to intention-relevant cues. (see Ellis, 1996; Goschke & Kuhl, 1996). These observations imply that intentions with specified context and time elements are more likely to be activated and acted upon than intentions that generalize across these two elements. Without specific context and time elements, there are fewer situational cues to which individuals could be sensitive and whose presence could activate the intention.[5]

Intention–Behavior Gap: Literal Inconsistency

Up to this point we have reviewed various factors that can influence the correlation between intentions and behavior. Inconsistency between intentions and behavior can, however, not only can be evidenced by low correlations but can also be observed in a more literal sense. In this second type of inconsistency, the predictor and criterion are identical, both dealing with the same specific action, but there is a contradiction between what people say they will do and what they actually do. Generally speaking, the pattern of literal inconsistency is asymmetrical such that people who do not intend to engage in a socially desirable behavior tend to act in accordance with their negative intentions but people who do intend to perform the behavior may or may not do so.[6] For example, in a study of racial prejudice (Linn, 1965), female students were asked to indicate whether they would be willing to release photos of themselves with an

African American male for a variety of purposes related to improving race relations. Almost without exception, those who were unwilling to do so later signed very few releases. Among the participants who indicated a high level of willingness to release their photographs, however, only about one half actually followed through on their intentions. Similarly, research in the health domain has found that participants who do not intend to use condoms, to undergo a cancer screening, or to exercise rarely if ever do so, but of those who intend to engage in these health-protective behaviors, between 26% and 57% fail to carry out their intentions (Sheeran, 2002).

Pseudo-Inconsistency: An Explanation of Literal Inconsistency

Perhaps the most ingenious explanation for literal inconsistency was offered by Donald Campbell (1963), who suggested that observed discrepancies between words and deeds may often be more apparent than real. He argued that verbal and overt responses to a psychological object are both indicators of an underlying hypothetical disposition and that one of these responses may be more difficult to perform than the other. Campbell used LaPiere's (1934) study of racial discrimination described earlier to illustrate his argument.

Campbell (1963) assumed that rejecting the Chinese couple in the face-to-face situation (overt behavior) would have been more difficult than rejecting a symbolic representation of "members of the Chinese race" in response to a written inquiry. Individuals strongly prejudiced toward the Chinese would be expected to give a negative response in both situations, whereas individuals who are not at all prejudiced should provide a positive response in both. The apparent inconsistency in the LaPiere (1934) study reflects, according to Campbell, a moderate degree of prejudice toward the Chinese, sufficiently strong to produce the relatively easy verbal rejection in a letter (negative intention) but not strong enough to generate the more difficult overt rejection in a face-to-face encounter (overt behavior) (Figure 2.1).

Campbell (1963) argued that literal inconsistency arises because people with moderate dispositions tend to display behaviors consistent with the disposition when the behaviors are easy to perform (e.g., express willingness to perform a behavior) but not when they are difficult to perform (e.g., actually carry out the intention). Although this argument is intuitively compelling, it has rarely been put to empirical test. Contrary to Campbell's thesis, recent research has found that participants who display literal inconsistency do not necessarily hold the expected moderate dispositions. In one experiment (Ajzen, Brown, & Carvajal, 2004), college students in small groups voted for or against making an $8 contribution to a scholarship fund under hypothetical as well as under real payment conditions. Literal inconsistency was shown by participants who voted to make a

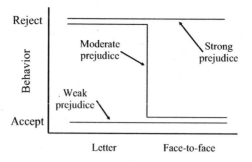

FIGURE 2.1   Campbell's conception of literal inconsistency.

contribution when the question was hypothetical (i.e., intention) but chose not to make a contribution in the real payment situation, a discrepancy known as *hypothetical bias*. This hypothetical bias emerged despite the fact that, in the hypothetical payment condition, participants were asked to vote as if they really would have to pay $8. To test Campbell's hypothesis, a measure of the underlying disposition to vote yes was obtained by asking participants, prior to casting their votes, to indicate their attitudes toward voting yes. If Campbell's hypothesis is correct, participants with strong positive attitudes should vote yes in both conditions whereas those with strong negative attitudes should vote no in both conditions. Hypothetical bias should be displayed by participants with intermediate attitudes who would be expected to vote yes in the hypothetical situation but not in the real payment situation. This pattern of results, however, was not obtained. Instead, attitudes to vote to contribute $8 to the scholarship fund among participants toward voting hypothetical bias were no less positive than among participants who voted to make a contribution under both payment conditions. Similar results were reported by Sheeran (2002) in a reanalysis of data from an earlier study (Sheeran & Orbell, 2000a) on the prediction of physical exercise.

In contrast to these negative findings, a secondary analysis of data from a study on smoking marijuana among adolescents obtained findings consistent with Campbell's (1963) predictions. As part of the evaluation of the National Youth Anti-Drug Campaign (see, e.g., Hornik et al., 2002), adolescents were asked to indicate their intentions to smoke marijuana regularly in the next 12 months. At the same time, they were also asked to indicate their attitudes toward this behavior. Approximately 1 year later, the same set of adolescents provided self-reports on the frequency with which they had smoked marijuana over the past 12 months. Most participants (83%) did not intend to smoke marijuana and in fact did not do so (no–no); a small subsample (2%) of participants intended to and did smoke marijuana (yes–yes); and the remaining participants (15%) said they did not intend to smoke but did report smoking (no–yes). Consistent with Campbell's proposition, the attitudes of this last group were more favorable than those of the no–no group but less favorable than the attitudes in the yes–yes group.

Thus, the empirical findings at this point are inconsistent. Despite its elegance, the jury is still out on Campbell's (1963) pseudo-inconsistency hypothesis. It is already clear, however, that this hypothesis cannot explain all cases of literal inconsistency.

Hypothetical Versus Real Situations

People sometimes seem to act irrationally in the sense that they fail to carry out an intended behavior that is in their best interest. For example, people may realize the benefits of staying calm in the face of provocation yet "in the heat of a confrontation" lash out verbally or physically. Similarly, despite realizing the benefits of consistent condom use, and in spite of their best intentions to use condoms regularly, "in the heat of the moment" both men and women all too often engage in unprotected sex. To account for such apparent irrationality, it is important to make a distinction between contemplating performance of a behavior when filling out a questionnaire and facing its actual performance in a real-life context. Clearly, the information considered while filling out a questionnaire may differ from the information that is available during behavioral performance (Ajzen & Sexton, 1999; Gold, 1993). As a result, the intentions expressed in response to the questionnaire may differ from the intentions that are present in the real-life context and thus may turn out to be poor predictors of actual behavior. What's more, when filling out a questionnaire people may find it virtually impossible to correctly anticipate the strong drives and emotions that may influence their behavior in real life. Thus, new Army recruits may intend to stay calm under fire and to go fearlessly into battle, but their actual conduct may differ greatly from this imagined scenario when bombs begin to explode. It is for this reason that the military conducts training exercises with live ammunition. If sufficiently true to life, such exercises will not only help soldiers adapt to battlefield conditions but will also lead to the formation of more realistic behavioral intentions.

The potential discrepancy between responses provided on a questionnaire and responses in a behavioral context can be viewed as largely a question of proper measurement. If, when filling out a questionnaire about behavioral performance, respondents could be induced to be realistic in their expectations, the intentions assessed should permit better prediction of actual behavior in the performance context. However, this can be quite difficult, as is illustrated by the results of a follow-up[7] to Ajzen et al.'s (2004) study on hypothetical bias in willingness to contribute to a scholarship fund. In addition to the usual real and hypothetical payment conditions, participants in several additional hypothetical conditions of this follow-up experiment were given different kinds of instructions designed to make their hypothetical votes more realistic, thereby reducing hypothetical bias. In one of these conditions, they were instructed to vote yes only if they were absolutely certain that they would do so in a real payment situation, otherwise to vote no. In another condition, prior to casting their votes, they were asked to list the advantages and disadvantages of voting yes. Participants in a third condition went through a *process simulation* (Taylor & Pham, 1996) in which they were asked to visualize the process of voting yes and then actually paying the $8 prior to casting their votes. In a fourth condition, participants were asked to list 10 reasons why they should vote yes. Because most people find it very difficult to come up with so many supportive arguments, this task is expected to lead to an inference that voting yes may not be such a good idea after all (Sanna & Schwarz, 2004). Finally, prior to indicating how they actually intended to vote, participants in a fifth condition were instructed to first indicate how they would vote in an ideal world. This was supposed to make more salient potential limitations in the real world in which their vote took place (see Carlson & Tanner, 2006). None of these manipulations had an appreciable impact on hypothetical bias. In the standard hypothetical payment condition, 63% of the participants voted yes compared with 39% in the real payment condition, a finding consistent with the typical pattern of hypothetical bias. Attempts to reduce this hypothetical bias in the additional five hypothetical payment conditions were not successful. The percentages of yes votes in these conditions ranged from 59% to 73%—none significantly different from the 63% yes vote in the standard hypothetical payment condition.

To summarize briefly, literal inconsistency between stated intentions and actual behavior can be explained in two ways. First, as suggested by Campbell (1963), intentions are verbal responses to a psychological object that are often more easily performed than are compatible overt responses, but both are a function of the same underlying disposition. Viewed in this way, performing the easy response but not the difficult one is consistent with a moderate disposition. Limited empirical research suggests that this explanation may be viable in some instances but not in others. An alternative, though not incompatible, explanation attributes literal inconsistency to instability in intentions brought about by accessibility of different cognitions in hypothetical and real situations. Thus, on a questionnaire, people may express an intention to engage in a given behavior, but when they enter the real situation, their perceptions may change, producing a different intention.

☐ Perceived Behavioral Control

We noted previously that individuals can successfully carry out their intentions only if they have sufficient volitional control over the behavior. This implies that we should be able to improve prediction of behavior if we consider not only intention but also the degree to which an individual actually has control over performing the behavior. Volitional control is expected to moderate the intention–behavior relation such that the effect of intention on behavior is stronger when actual control is high rather than low. In fact, when most people actually have control over performance of a behavior, intention by itself should permit good prediction. Only when people vary in the degree to which they have control can we expect that taking control into account will improve behavioral prediction (Ajzen, 1985).

Unfortunately, it is not at all clear what constitutes actual control over a behavior or how to assess it. Although we may be able to measure some aspects of actual control, in most instances we lack sufficient information about all the relevant internal and external factors that may facilitate or impede performance of the behavior. However, it is possible that people's *perceptions* of their control over a behavior accurately reflect their actual control. To the extent that perceived behavioral control is indeed veridical, it can serve as a proxy for actual control and be used to improve prediction of behavior.

Definition and Measurement of Perceived Behavioral Control

We define perceived behavioral control as people's perceptions of the degree to which they are capable of, or have control over, performing a given behavior. (An in-depth discussion of this construct is reserved for Chapter 5.) This definition of perceived behavioral control is conceptually very similar to Bandura's (1977; 1997) *perceived self-efficacy* construct. As is true of intentions, the construct of perceived behavioral control can find expression in different statements such as, "Performing this behavior is up to me," "I can perform this behavior if I really want to," or "I have the necessary skills and abilities to perform this behavior." The definition and measurement of perceived behavioral control are discussed in greater detail in Chapter 5, where we consider its role as a determinant of behavioral intentions.

Empirical Support for the Predictive Validity of Perceived Behavioral Control

Moderating Effects of Perceived Behavioral Control

As noted earlier, according to our reasoned action approach, perceived behavioral control acts as a moderator of the intention–behavior relation such that intentions will predict behavior better when perceived control is high rather than low. Relatively few studies have submitted this hypothesis to empirical test. In those studies that have tried to examine whether perceived control acts as a moderator of the intention–behavior relationship, investigators typically use hierarchical regression analyses in which they enter intentions and perceptions of behavioral control on the first step followed by the interaction term, i.e., by the product of intention × perceived control on the second step. Results indicate that the interaction term is often not significant, and even when it does have a significant regression coefficient it tends to accounts for little or no additional variance in the prediction of behavior (see Ajzen, 1991; Armitage & Conner, 2001; Yang-Wallentin, Schmidt, Davidov, & Bamberg, 2004). Perhaps it is for this reason that most investigators examine the direct effect of perceived behavioral control on behavior rather than its role as a moderator of the intention–behavior relation.

Before we dismiss the idea that perceived behavioral control moderates the effect of intention on behavior, it is instructive to examine the implications of using hierarchical regression analyses to test for an interaction between intention and perceived behavioral control. An important aspect of such analyses is the fact that intention and perceived behavioral control are first entered into the regression equation as main effects. Now, it seems perfectly reasonable to expect a significant positive correlation between intention and behavior such that, as a general rule, the stronger the intention, the more likely it is that the behavior will be performed. The same cannot be said for control. To be sure, when people lack control (i.e., when they are incapable of performing the behavior), it is unlikely that the behavior will be carried out. However, knowing that individuals have a high level of control by itself does not tell us whether the behavior will or will not be performed (Eagly & Chaiken, 1993).

Nevertheless, there is reason to expect that, under certain conditions, a measure of perceived behavioral control will correlate with behavior. In fact, in the meta-analysis by Armitage & Conner (2001) mentioned earlier, across 40 data sets, the mean correlation between perceived behavioral control and behavior was found to be .40. How can we account for this relatively high correlation? Having control simply means that people can act on their intentions; that is, they can perform the behavior when they intend to do so, and they can refrain from performing the behavior when their intentions are negative. Thus, if in a given population most people intend to perform a behavior, the greater their control the more likely it is that the behavior will be performed (i.e., there will be a strong *positive* correlation between perceived control and behavioral performance). Conversely, if most people in the population intend not to perform the behavior, the more control they have, the less likely it is that the behavior will be performed, resulting in a strong *negative* correlation between perceived control and behavior. Thus, when we correlate perceived behavioral control with behavior, the correlation takes account of the direction of the predominant intention; that is, to a large extent it captures the interaction between perceived behavioral control and intention. It follows that little can be gained by explicitly entering the interaction term into the regression equation. We would expect a low correlation between perceived control and behavior only when there is a fairly equal distribution of positive and negative intentions in the research population. When this is the case, the interaction of perceived control and intention is more likely to be significant. That is, perceived control is more likely to be seen as a moderator of the intention–behavior relation.

In subsequent chapters, we will often report studies that tested only for main effects of intentions and perceptions of control on behavior. The finding of a significant main effect for perceived control should not be taken to mean that control did not in fact moderate the intention–behavior relation. We return to this issue in Chapter 3 where we consider the difficulty of demonstrating an interaction between two predictors in our discussion of the expectancy-value model of attitudes (see Fishbein, 1963; Fishbein & Ajzen, 1975).

Additive Effects of Intentions and Perceived Behavioral Control

Although, conceptually, perceived control is expected to moderate the intention–behavior relation, in practice most investigators have looked at the additive effects of intention and perceptions of control on behavior. Numerous studies have shown that taking perceived behavioral control into account in this manner can improve prediction of behavior. Meta-analyses that have examined the contribution of perceived behavioral control for a wide variety of behaviors have found that, on average, perceived behavioral control explains approximately an additional 2% of the variance in behavior (Armitage & Conner, 2001; Cheung & Chan, 2000). Of course, we would not expect perceived behavioral control to be an important predictor for every type of behavior. When volitional control is high, intentions are good predictors of behavior, and including a measure of perceived behavioral control accounts for little if any additional variance. When behavior is not under complete volitional control, however, measuring perceptions of control can make a valuable contribution.

Support for this expectation was provided in a study by Madden, Ellen, and Ajzen (1992) in which college students' intentions and perceptions of behavioral control were assessed with respect to the performance of 10 common behaviors in the next two weeks: exercising regularly, getting a good night's sleep, talking to a close friend, doing laundry, avoiding caffeine, going shopping with a friend, renting a video, taking vitamin supplements, listening to an album, and washing your car. Two weeks later, the participants were asked to report how often they had performed each of the 10 behaviors in the preceding 2 weeks.

Within-subjects regression analyses across the 10 behaviors showed, as expected, that intentions were good predictors of behavior (mean $r = .53$) and that adding perceived behavioral control to the equation significantly improved prediction to an average multiple correlation of .62. However, examination of the individual behaviors showed an improvement in prediction primarily for behaviors that were perceived to be relatively low in volitional control. When a behavior was perceived to be high in control, there was virtually no change in explained variance. For example, with respect to taking vitamin supplements (over which the participants believed they had a high degree of control) prediction of behavior from intention alone was .76, and the multiple correlation increased only to .77 when perceived behavioral control was added to the prediction equation. In contrast, participants believed that they had much less control over getting a good night's sleep, and with respect to this behavior, the addition of perceived behavioral control to the prediction equation raised the correlation with behavior significantly, from .36 to .64. Over all 10 behaviors, a correlation of −.63 was obtained between the mean level of perceived behavioral control and the increase in explained variance due to inclusion of this variable in the prediction equation.

Consistent with the same argument, it is found that the amount of additional variance in behavior explained by perceived behavioral control varies significantly across different behavioral domains (Cheung & Chan, 2000; Notani, 1998). For example, in the case of regularly attending an exercise class (Courneya & McAuley, 1995), the mean level of perceived behavioral control was relatively high, and it explained only 1% of additional variance in behavior beyond a measure of intention. In contrast, in a sample of smokers who, on average, perceived that they had relatively little control over not smoking, the measure of perceived behavioral control accounted for an additional 12% of the variance in smoking behavior (Godin, Valois, Lepage, & Desharnais, 1992; see also Madden, Ellen, & Ajzen, 1992).

In a related line of reasoning, Bandura (1997) postulated that people are more likely to successfully perform an intended behavior if they have a high degree of perceived self-efficacy or perceived behavioral control. A belief in one's self-efficacy in relation to performance of a behavior is assumed to produce greater persistence in the face of difficulties or initial failures. Furthermore, this effect is assumed to be independent of actual control over the behavior. The most persuasive evidence in support of Bandura's hypothesis comes from studies in which perceived self-efficacy is manipulated experimentally and the effect of the manipulation on behavior is examined. For example, Cervone (1989) manipulated perceived self-efficacy by asking participants to focus on aspects of a problem-solving task that made the task appear troublesome (low self-efficacy) or tractable (high self-efficacy). The higher the instilled self-efficacy, the longer participants were found to persevere on the task (which was actually unsolvable). Similarly, using false normative feedback, Weinberg, Gould, and Jackson (1979) manipulated self-efficacy beliefs with respect to physical strength and showed that heightened self-efficacy raised persistence as well as performance on a competitive task.

To summarize briefly, we have seen that, as a general rule, when people have control over performance of a behavior they tend to act in accordance with their intentions. When the behavior is not under complete volitional control and objective measures of actual control are unavailable, assessing perceptions of behavioral control can help improve prediction. Finally, when people intend to perform a behavior, they are more likely to persist when they believe that they are capable of doing so.

☐ Methodological Considerations in the Prediction of Behavior

We have considered a variety of factors that can influence the relation between intentions and behavior. Although many of these factors are indeed found to have a significant impact, it is fair to say that, overall, intentions have considerable predictive validity. The conclusion emerging from meta-analyses of this literature is that, without controlling for any of the potential moderators reviewed thus far, intentions have a correlation of about .50 with behavior. Clearly, under optimal conditions higher correlations are often obtained. Moreover, the fact that measures of intention and behavior contain an element of unreliability also suggests that the .50 intention–behavior correlation is an underestimate of the "true" relation (see Sheeran, 2002). Perhaps a more serious problem, however, occurs in studies where either the measure of intention or the measure of behavior has little or no meaningful variance.

Restriction of Range: Floor and Ceiling Effects

From our perspective, the starting point of any investigation that is focused on the prediction of a behavior is the identification (and measurement) of the behavior of interest. An immediate question to be asked is whether in the population under consideration there is sufficient variance in the behavior. If there is little or no variance in the behavior, there is nothing to be predicted. Although one may still want to explore the reasons that the behavior is or is not performed by all members of the research population, this is a different issue that we take up in Chapter 10.

Assuming there is sufficient behavioral variance, we can try to predict the behavior from a measure of intention. Clearly, if participants vary in their behavior but do not vary in their intentions, prediction from the measure of intention is impossible. Within our conceptual framework, such a state of affairs raises a red flag. Because we assume that behavior follows from intentions, if people differ in their behavior, they should also differ in their intentions. In our experience, lack of variance in intention when people vary in their behavior is often attributable to lack of behavioral or scale compatibility. A clear illustration of this problem can be found in a study of blood donation (Ferguson & Bibby, 2002). Immediately after donating blood, participants in this study were asked, "Having given blood today, to what extent do you intend to return to give blood again?" Responses were provided on a six-point scale that ranged from *not at all* (1) to *very definitely* (6). Then, 16 to 17 months later, the participants were contacted by mail and asked to report how many times they had donated blood in the intervening time period.

In our terminology, the behavioral criterion was a quantitative frequency measure of the number of times a person donated blood in the past 16 to 17 months. A simple way to obtain a compatible measure of intention would have been to ask participants, immediately after they made the original blood donation, how many times they intended to donate blood in the next 16 to 17 months. Unfortunately, the intention actually assessed was lacking both in time and scale compatibility. Whereas the behavioral criterion covered a period of 16 to 17 months, the measure of intention left the time element unspecified. More important, the behavioral criterion was a numerical frequency measure, but—although participants responded on a six-point scale—the measure of intention was essentially dichotomous in that it required a rating as to the certainty that the participant would or would not return to give blood at some point in the future. It would be perfectly reasonable for participants to indicate that they very definitely planned to return to give blood again and then to come back only once, whereas others might indicate the same intention and return to give blood several times over the 16- to 17-month period.

To make matters worse, the procedure used to assess intentions resulted in a measure with very little variance. Almost all participants (who were, after all, current blood donors) indicated that they would very definitely return to give blood again; the mean intention score on the six-point scale was 5.8 with a standard deviation of 0.5. In light of these problems, it is surprising that a statistically significant, albeit very low, intention–behavior correlation was obtained ($r = .17$, $p < .05$).

The effect of an even more extreme restriction of range on the intention–behavior relation is shown in an additional analysis reported in this study. Based on Ouellette and Wood's (1998) discussion of habitual behavior described earlier, the investigators hypothesized that intentions would be a much better predictor of behavior among occasional donors than among regular donors. To test this hypothesis, they divided their sample into participants who had previously donated blood less than four times (occasional donors) and those who had donated blood four times or more (regular donors). Consistent with expectations, the investigators did indeed find a stronger intention–behavior correlation ($r = .24$, $p < .05$) among occasional donors than among regular donors ($r = 0$). Closer examination of the data, however, reveals that this difference may have nothing to do with habituation. Among regular donors, there was virtually no variance at all in the measure of intention. That is, almost without exception, regular donors were very certain that they would donate blood again ($M = 5.9$ on the six-point scale, $SD = 0.1$). Among the occasional donors, there was at least some variance ($M = 5.7$, $SD = 0.7$), resulting in the significant intention–behavior correlation of .24.

Ceiling effects for intentions combined with scale incompatibility are also illustrated in a study that dealt with breast-feeding of newborn babies (Wambach, 1997). Women in their last 6 weeks of pregnancy indicated their feeding intentions on a seven-point scale anchored at its ends with *definitely will bottle-feed* (1) and *definitely will breast-feed* (7). At 4 to 6 weeks after giving birth, the mothers' method of feeding their babies was ascertained. The behavioral criterion was breast-feeding duration, operationally defined as the number of days of breast-feeding to time of weaning or to time of postpartum questionnaire administration. Thus, whereas intentions were assessed in terms of a dichotomous definition of the behavior (intention to breast- vs. bottle-feed), the behavioral criterion was a quantitative measure of duration. Moreover, although there was considerable variation in behavior, with breast-feeding duration ranging from 0 to 49 days, there was virtually no variance in intentions. The expectant mothers strongly intended to breast-feed their babies ($M = 6.7$ on the seven-point scale; $SD = 0.56$), and as might therefore be expected, the correlation between these intentions and the behavioral criterion, although statistically significant, was only .22. A measure of intention more compatible with the behavioral duration criterion could have been obtained by asking the participants for how many days after giving birth they intended to breast-feed their babies. The expectant mothers may have differed more meaningfully on this measure, and as a result, the assessed intentions could have provided a better basis for predicting actual breast-feeding duration. However, other factors might still prevent strong intention–behavior correlations. Many women who intend to breast-feed encounter difficulties of various kinds and are forced to turn to bottle-feeding their babies (see Duckett et al., 1998). Impaired predictive validity may therefore also be due to changes in intentions (see our earlier discussion of stability of intentions and hypothetical versus real situations).

In sum, restriction of range in measures of intention or behavior will limit the intention's predictive validity. We should note, however, that lack of variance on an intention is not necessarily an indication of a problem with the way the intention was measured. For example, very few if any children at around age 10 intend to smoke marijuana in the next 10 years, yet when they reach age 20, many will in fact have smoked marijuana. Because the children did not differ in their intentions at age 10, the measure of intention obtained at that time could not predict later behavior. The problem in this case is not related to the measure of intention as such but to the fact that intentions can change over such a long time period. Were we to measure intentions to smoke marijuana when the participants had reached age 19 or 20, these intentions might well show considerable variance and be good predictors of actual smoking behavior. In fact, in a study of illicit drug use among college students most of whom were 19 to 22 years old (McMillan & Conner, 2003), intentions to smoke marijuana showed a correlation of .84 with self-reported smoking behavior.

☐ Summary and Conclusions

In this chapter we discussed the definition and measurement of behavior and of its proximal determinants: intentions and perceived behavioral control. Because selection of the behavioral criterion is the starting point in any application of a reasoned action approach, we stressed the importance of unambiguously identifying the behavior of interest in terms of its action, target, context, and time elements. By making these elements more or less specific, the behavior can be defined at any desired level of generality. We further pointed out that, for purposes of explaining a behavior's determinants, it is usually preferable to conceive of the behavior as a dichotomous variable such that people can be classified as having or not having performed the behavior. However, for some purposes, investigators may prefer to assess behavior on a frequency or magnitude scale. Finally, we noted the practical advantages of self-reports over direct observation of behavior, but we also cautioned that it is important to consider the validity of either kind of measure.

In our discussion of intentions we tried to show that there was little empirical support for distinguishing between behavioral intentions, plans, willingness, or expectations. Instead we suggested that all of these measures are best viewed as manifest indicators of the same underlying latent construct, namely, intention. Irrespective of the particular indicators employed, however, accurate prediction of behavior from intentions requires that the measures of these two variables be compatible in terms of their action, target, context, and time elements. We noted repeatedly that lack of behavioral compatibility can greatly reduce the correlation between intentions and actions. In addition, problems can also be introduced by lack of scale compatibility, as when intentions refer to a behavioral dichotomy whereas the behavior is assessed on a scale of frequency or magnitude. In support of our reasoned action approach, empirical evidence shows that when behavioral and scale compatibility is high, strong correlations between intentions and behavior are usually obtained. This is true whether the behavior is relatively novel or infrequently performed or whether the behavior is routine and performed without much deliberation.

Apart from compatibility, the strength of intention–behavior correlations is also moderated by the degree to which people have control over performance of the behavior and by the temporal stability of the intention. Lack of internal resources (skills, abilities) and external impediments can make it difficult or impossible for people to carry out their intentions. As to the temporal stability of intentions, empirical research supports the proposition that stable intentions are better predictors of behavior than are intentions that change over time.

Changes in intentions may also be implicated when we observe literal inconsistency between intentions and actions. Clearly, when actions are inconsistent with compatible intentions, it is quite possible that the intention has changed. In addition, intentions activated when confronted with actual performance of a behavior may differ from intentions expressed in a hypothetical situation, as when completing a questionnaire. Such discrepancies will usually result in an overestimation of the intention to perform socially desirable behaviors. On a less theoretical note, we pointed out that restriction of range in either the measure of behavior or the measure of intention can have a detrimental effect on the predictive validity of intentions.

In addition to actual control over a behavior, a reasoned action approach also stresses the importance of perceived behavioral control.

When a measure of actual control is unavailable, perceived control—to the extent that it is veridical—can be used as a proxy for actual control. We reserve a full discussion of perceived behavioral control for Chapter 5. In the present chapter we saw that, consistent with our theory, perceived control can improve prediction of behavior above the level obtained on the basis of intentions alone, especially when dealing with a behavior over which many people have limited volitional control. When control is high, people can usually carry out their intentions, and thus intentions are good predictors of behavior. When volitional control is more problematic, consideration of perceived control can help improve prediction of behavior.

☐ Notes

1. Note that some investigators might consider the first item a measure of intention and the second a measure of behavioral expectation. Nevertheless, the two items were almost perfectly correlated.
2. The intention–behavior correlations should be similar in magnitude because the addition of perceived behavioral control explained, on average, only an additional 2% of the variance in behavior.
3. We are grateful to Paschal Sheeran for providing the results of these meta-analyses.
4. While a failure to predict behavior raises questions about the validity of the theory, a failure to predict goal attainment does not.
5. These considerations may help explain why forming a specific behavioral plan or implementation intention (Gollwitzer, 1999) can help people to carry out their behavioral intentions. We consider the role of implementation intentions in Chapter 10.
6. Similarly, people who intend to engage in socially undesirable behavior typically do so, but people who hold negative intentions may or may not perform the behavior.
7. Unpublished data.

Attitudes and Their Determinants

More than any other psychological construct, attitude has been at the center of attempts to predict and explain social behavior. Indeed, we saw in Chapter 1 that attitudes have been invoked to account for behavior in a broad range of domains, such as organizational behavior, political behavior, and racial discrimination. Over the years, social psychologists have devoted a great deal of effort to the definition and measurement of attitudes, to theories of attitude formation and change, and to the attitude–behavior relation. Much of this work has focused on attitudes toward physical objects (e.g., Yosemite National Park, the Empire State Building); racial, ethnic, or other groups (e.g., African Americans, Jews, gays); institutions (e.g., Congress, the Catholic Church); policies (e.g., gun control, tax cuts); events (e.g., September 11, the World Series); or other general targets. Although we agree that attitudes are among the most important determinants of intentions and behavior, a fundamental tenet of our theoretical framework requires that the measure of attitude conform to the principle of compatibility. That is, to have predictive validity, the object of the attitude must be composed of the same target, action, context, and time elements as the behavior. Put differently, we must assess attitudes toward the very behavior that we are trying to predict and understand.

☐ Definition of Attitude

Notwithstanding the fact that most research on attitudes has been concerned with attitudes toward general objects or targets, many of the lessons learned are equally applicable to attitudes toward behaviors. We therefore begin this chapter with a brief discussion of how attitudes in general are defined and measured.

We define attitude as a latent disposition or tendency to respond with some degree of favorableness or unfavorableness to a psychological object. The attitude object can be any discriminable aspect of an individual's world, including a behavior. Two features of this definition are worth noting. First, attitudes are evaluative in nature, ascribing to individuals a position on a unitary evaluative dimension with respect to an object, a dimension that ranges from negative to positive through a neutral point. There is widespread consensus among contemporary theorists and investigators engaged in basic research on attitudes that an attitude's essential characteristic is its bipolar evaluative dimension (Ajzen & Fishbein, 2005; Eagly & Chaiken, 1993; Fazio, 1990a; Fishbein & Ajzen, 1975; Krosnick, Judd, & Wittenbrink, 2005; Petty & Cacioppo, 1986). Second, although some theorists define attitude as the evaluative response itself (e.g., Kruglanski & Stroebe, 2005; Zanna & Rempel, 1988), most contemporary definitions equate attitude with the hypothetical disposition (Eagly & Chaiken, 2005; see also McGuire, 1969) and assume that evaluative responses of various kinds can be used to infer it. This view reflects current thinking in the social and behavioral sciences, which emphasizes the use of manifest responses as indicators of latent constructs. The popularity of structural equation modeling (see MacCallum & Austin, 2000) is an indication of the growing acceptance of this perspective.

As intuitively reasonable as this definition may appear, it has not emerged without considerable controversy over a long period of time. Social psychologists initially encountered great difficulty in their attempts to identify the essential characteristics of attitudes (see Allport, 1935). Early theoretical developments emphasized the complexity of attitudes. Thus, after reviewing definitions proposed by other theorists, Allport offered the following definition: "An attitude is a mental and neural state of readiness, organized through experience, exerting a directive or dynamic influence upon the individual's response to all objects and situations with which it is related" (p. 810). Similarly, in their influential social psychology textbook, Krech and Crutchfield (1948) described attitude as "an enduring organization of motivational, emotional, perceptual, and cognitive processes with respect to some aspect of the individual's world" (p. 152). These broad, all-encompassing views of attitude were widely shared among investigators who often cited Allport's definition in their writing.

In a parallel development, researchers interested in the measurement of attitudes—although acknowledging their complexity—realized that such multidimensional definitions were unworkable. Thurstone (1928), who was the first to apply psychometric methods to the measurement of attitudes, argued that in all measurement we must restrict ourselves to some specified continuum along which the measurement is to take place. In the case of attitudes, he identified the evaluative dimension as the critical continuum and thus defined attitude as "the affect for or against a psychological object" (Thurstone, 1931). On the basis of this definition, he developed—as we shall see herein—a scaling procedure that results in a single attitude score indicating the respondent's degree of favorableness or unfavorableness toward a given attitude object. While continuing to adhere to their multidimensional conceptions, most investigators welcomed the availability of a standard scaling method that permitted precise and reliable assessment of people's (unidimensional) attitudes. Thurstone's groundbreaking work stimulated the development of several other standard attitude scaling techniques (Guttman, 1944; Likert, 1932; Osgood, Suci, & Tannenbaum, 1957). Like Thurstone scaling, these techniques also result in a single score along an evaluative continuum (see Fishbein & Ajzen, 1975).

Noting the discrepancy between multidimensional conceptualizations and unidimensional measures, Triandis (1967) observed that "there is a gap between those who are primarily concerned with the *measurement* of attitudes and those who have written *theoretically* about attitudes. The former frequently rest their case after providing us with a single score whereas the latter make a large number of theoretical distinctions but do not provide us with precise and standard procedures for measurement" (p. 228). We may add that empirical researchers often adopted a complex definition of attitudes while at the same time they proceeded to assess attitudes by means of standard, unidimensional scales. This type of inconsistency is no longer an issue in basic research on attitudes because, for investigators engaged in this research, theory and measurement have converged on a unidimensional conception of attitude. At the same time, we often find that research of a more applied nature fails to show the influence of these theoretical developments. Many investigators working in applied areas continue to be guided by rather complex, multidimensional views of the attitude construct.

Attitude Versus Affect

Although there is now general agreement at the theoretical level that attitude is best considered to be a person's disposition to respond favorably or unfavorably with respect to a psychological object, certain ambiguities remain. Perhaps most conspicuous is the lack of a clear distinction between overall evaluation (or attitude) and affect. Early theorists tended to use the term *affect* to denote an attitude's valence, that is, its overall degree of favorability, as is illustrated in Thurstone's (1931) definition of attitude as affect for or against a psychological object. Consistent with this perspective, many social psychologists have employed the terms *affect* and *evaluation* interchangeably (e.g., Chen & Bargh, 1999; Fishbein & Ajzen, 1975; Murphy & Zajonc, 1993; Rosenberg, 1956). However, in a parallel development, personality and clinical psychologists applied the term *affect* to mood, emotion, and arousal (see Giner-Sorolla, 1999; Schwarz & Clore, 1983, 1996).

Despite the resulting confusion at the conceptual level, careful examination of operationalizations used in attitude research reveals that most investigators assess attitudes in terms of overall evaluation rather than affect. As we shall see, research participants are typically asked to label psychological objects as *good* or *bad* (Bargh, Chaiken, Govender, & Pratto, 1992), to judge them for degree of *liking* or *disliking* (Murphy & Zajonc, 1993), to rate them on a series of bipolar adjective scales, such as *desirable–undesirable* and *pleasant–unpleasant* (Ajzen & Fishbein, 1970), or to indicate how much they favor or oppose a certain policy (Rosenberg, 1956). Clearly, even when the term *affect* is used to describe the attitudinal response, in practice the dimension assessed is evaluative rather than emotional in nature. In contrast, affect in the contemporary use of the term tends to be assessed by means of physiological indicators, mood adjective checklists, or emotion inventories (see Giner-Sorolla, 1999; Petty & Cacioppo, 1983).

To avoid confusion, we use the term *attitude* to refer to the *evaluation* of an object, concept, or behavior along a dimension of favor or disfavor, good or bad, like or dislike. Examples of responses reflecting attitude are approval or disapproval of a policy, liking or disliking of a person or group of people, and judgments of any concept on such dimensions as *wise–foolish, enjoyable–unenjoyable, desirable–undesirable, good–bad*, or *pleasant–unpleasant*. By way of contrast, and consistent with contemporary usage, we reserve the term *affect* for a separate response system with a somatic component characterized by some degree of arousal (Crites, Fabrigar, & Petty, 1994; see Giner-Sorolla, 1999, for a discussion). Affect includes generalized mood states without a well-defined object of reference (sadness vs. happiness) as well as qualitatively different emotions (e.g., anger, fear, pride) with clear evaluative implications.

This view of affect is supported by research showing that, as a general rule, two relatively independent dimensions can parsimoniously describe self-reported affective experiences (e.g., Russell, 1980; Watson & Tellegen, 1985; but see Remington, Fabrigar, & Visser, 2000). These dimensions consistently emerge as major factors across different cultures and response formats. One dimension represents valence, (i.e., the pleasantness or unpleasantness of the mood or emotion), the other arousal or activation. The circumplex structure of affect defined by these two dimensions is shown in Figure 3.1 (after Russell, 1980).

Although we draw a clear distinction between attitude (evaluation) and affect, we recognize that attitudes may be influenced by moods and emotions. Thus, fear of flying may well predispose a negative evaluation of airplanes, independent of any other factors that influence this attitude. In our view, then, evaluation differs from affect, although affect may

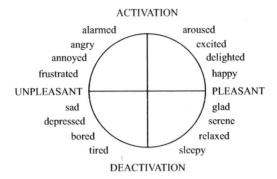

FIGURE 3.1   The two-dimensional structure of affect.

influence overall evaluation (see Eagly & Chaiken, 1993, for a similar perspective). The relation between affect and attitude is discussed in greater detail in Chapters 7 and 8.

☐ Measuring Attitudes

The Semantic Differential

The essential problem of attitude measurement, then, is reduced to obtaining a score that represents a person's position on a bipolar evaluative dimension with respect to the attitude object. A very popular and in many ways the simplest method for accomplishing this task is the semantic differential developed by Charles Osgood and his associates (1957). When the semantic differential is used to measure attitudes, respondents are asked to rate the attitude object on a set of bipolar evaluative adjective scales, usually with seven places or alternatives. To illustrate, in a study concerned with the effects of advertising on attitudes toward a fictitious brand of clothing (Coulter & Punj, 2004), brand attitudes were assessed by means of the following four seven-point evaluative semantic differential scales:

Like |___|___|___|___|___|___|___| Dislike

Bad |___|___|___|___|___|___|___| Good

Positive |___|___|___|___|___|___|___| Negative

Unfavorable |___|___|___|___|___|___|___| Favorable

Responses are usually scored from –3 on the negative side of the scale (*dislike, bad, negative, unfavorable*) to +3 on the positive side (*like, good, positive, favorable*), and the sum or mean across all scales is taken as a measure of the person's attitude. The higher the score, the more favorable the respondent's attitude toward the attitude object. Cronbach's coefficient alpha, which can range from a low of 0 to a high of 1, is usually used to measure the degree to which the items on an attitude scale are internally consistent. A coefficient of .75 or higher is generally taken as evidence of satisfactory internal consistency. The internal consistency coefficient alpha in this study was .92.

Or, to give another example, Chaiken and Yates (1985) used an evaluative semantic differential to assess attitudes toward capital punishment and toward censorship. Their measure contained the following adjective pairs placed on oppose ends of seven-point scales: *good–bad, foolish–wise, healthy–sick,* and *harmful–beneficial*.

Application of the semantic differential method to attitude measurement is, however, not quite as simple as it may at first appear. The semantic differential was originally developed not for purposes of assessing attitudes but rather as an instrument for the measurement of meaning. To obtain a representative sample of the possible dimensions of meaning along which an object can be judged, a large number of bipolar adjective scales were constructed. These adjective scales not only were evaluative in nature but also included nonevaluative adjective pairs, such as *strong–weak, fast–slow, deep–shallow, wide–narrow, large–small, sharp–dull, empty–full, wet–dry, thick–thin,* and *long–short*. Osgood and his associates (1957) performed a large number of studies in which they asked respondents from various cultures to rate several constructs on these adjective scales. For example, in one of their studies participants were asked to rate each of 20 concepts on 50 bipolar adjective scales (p. 39). The concepts were selected from different domains and included, for example, *lady, symphony, lake,* and *America*.

The investigators employed factor analytic techniques to identify the basic dimensions of meaning that underlie the multiple ratings of different constructs. Across many studies that involved different concepts and different adjective scales and that were performed in a variety of cultures, three major dimensions of meaning were consistently identified: *evaluation, potency,* and *activity*. The evaluative factor, which generally accounts for the greatest proportion of variance in a concept's meaning, is characterized by the kinds of evaluative scales mentioned earlier: for example, *good–bad, pleasant–unpleasant, harmful–beneficial*. Scales such as *large–small, strong–weak,* and *thick–thin* distinguish the potency factor, whereas *fast–slow, active–passive,* and *hot–cold* tend to load highly on the activity factor. Osgood and his associates (1957) concluded that the first factor, being evaluative in nature, reflects what is commonly considered the attitude toward the concept being rated, and they argued that it should therefore be possible to assess attitudes by means of the semantic differential.

Because attitudes are defined as evaluative dispositions, it is important to make sure that the adjective pairs used to assess attitudes do indeed represent the evaluative dimension. Unfortunately, it is often not realized that the same bipolar adjective scale may load on different factors when it is used to measure different concepts. For example, when person concepts such as *mother* or *father* are being rated, the *hard–soft* scale assesses an aspect of the concept's connotative meaning and is found to be a good indicator of the evaluative dimension. The same *hard–soft* scale may be used denotatively rather than in its evaluative sense when it is used to rate the concept *war*; here it may load on the potency factor. Similarly, when rating an institution—perhaps a local school system—the *sick–healthy* scale usually expresses evaluation, but when applied to a concept such as *disabled*, it will generally be used in its denotative sense and may load on the activity factor.

This tendency for scales to load on different factors for different concepts, termed *concept–scale interaction* (Osgood et al., 1957), has important implications for use of the semantic differential as a measure of attitude. Investigators often make the mistake of selecting a small number of adjective pairs (perhaps three to five) that were found to load highly on the evaluative factor in Osgood's original research program or that were used by another investigator. This practice can result in the selection of inappropriate scales because, in the population being considered, one or more of the selected adjective pairs may not reflect an evaluative reaction to the attitude object. For this reason, formative research should be conducted to select empirically validated evaluative scales. In this pilot work, respondents can be asked to rate the attitude object on a heterogeneous set of adjective scales representative of all three of the semantic differential's major meaning dimensions. Consistent with the approach taken by Osgood and his associates, these ratings can be submitted to a factor analysis, and only those adjective pairs that load highly on the evaluative dimension should then be used as the attitude measure in the main study.

It should be clear that the semantic differential can be used to assess attitudes toward any concept or object, including attitudes toward behaviors. In fact, this is the method by which attitudes toward behaviors are typically measured in the context of our reasoned action approach. For example, in a study on healthy eating (Conner, Norman, & Bell, 2002), attitudes toward eating a healthy diet were assessed by means of the following seven-point evaluative semantic differential scales: *bad–good*, *harmful–beneficial*, *pleasant–unpleasant*, *unenjoyable–enjoyable*, *wise–foolish*, and *unnecessary–necessary*. Consistent with the unidimensional view of attitude, the six-item scale had an alpha coefficient of .84. Similarly, studying use of cannabis (marijuana) among college students, Conner and McMillan (1999) asked participants to evaluate "using cannabis in the next 3 months" on *good–bad* and *pleasant–unpleasant* semantic differential scales, with an alpha coefficient of .81.

We saw earlier that factor analyses of a heterogeneous set of bipolar adjective scales consistently result in three major factors. The first and most important is the evaluative factor, and items from this factor can be used to assess attitudes. The aforementioned examples, however, show that investigators often use an alternative method to validate their selection of evaluative items. They start out with a set of adjective pairs that all appear to reflect evaluation and then confirm this assumption by showing that the scales selected have high internal consistency (i.e., have a high alpha coefficient). Items that lower internal consistency are usually omitted from the final instrument. It is also possible to compute correlations between scores on each individual adjective scale and the total score. Only adjective pairs with high item–total correlations are then retained for the final semantic differential attitude measure.[1]

Instrumental Versus Experiential Aspects of Attitude

Some investigators have maintained that, in contrast to the unidimensional view of evaluation, two types of attitude can be distinguished, one cognitive and the other affective in nature (e.g., Ajzen & Driver, 1991; Conner et al., 2002; Courneya, Bobick, & Schinke, 1999; Lowe, Eves, & Carroll, 2002; Wilson, Rodgers, Blanchard, & Gessell, 2003). Cognitive aspects of attitude involve such dimensions as *wise–foolish* and *harmful–beneficial*, whereas affective aspects are assumed to be reflected in such dimensions as *pleasant–unpleasant* and *boring–interesting*. This distinction can be traced to the multicomponent view of attitude (see Rosenberg, 1956; Rosenberg, Hovland, McGuire, Abelson, & Brehm, 1960), which holds that attitudes are composed of cognitive, affective, and conative or behavioral components. (We discuss this view in greater detail in Chapter 8.) From our perspective, however, the proposed distinction between cognitive and affective semantic differential items is misleading. As we saw earlier, affect involves arousal in addition to valence, but the "cognitive" and "affective" scales are all evaluative in nature and tend to form a single internally consistent scale. Nevertheless, factor analytic studies on evaluative semantic differential scales sometimes result in a two-factor solution, particularly when the attitude object is a health behavior such as going to a dentist, getting a flu shot, or always using a condom. Rather than labeling these factors *cognitive* and *affective*, we prefer the more neutral terms *instrumental* and *experiential*.

For example, in a study of adherence to a training program among adolescent competitive swimmers (Mummery & Wankel, 1999), participants were asked to rate the stem "For me to complete the assigned frequency, volume, and intensity of training during the next cycle would be ..." on a set of 12 seven-point semantic differential adjective pairs, intuitively selected to be evaluative in nature. As can be seen in Table 3.1, a factor analysis revealed an instrumental (e.g., *harmful–beneficial*) and an experiential (e.g., *painful–enjoyable*) factor, and the items loading on each factor had high internal consistency (alpha = .85 and alpha = .79, respectively). Nevertheless, the total scale composed of all 12 adjective pairs also had a high alpha coefficient of .83.

Similar results were reported in an earlier study of leisure behavior (Ajzen & Driver, 1991). College students were asked to rate each of five activities on a set of 12 seven-point semantic differential items. The five behaviors were spending time at the beach, outdoor jogging or running, mountain climbing, boating, and biking. The 12-item semantic differential scale contained 10 adjective pairs that in Osgood et al.'s (1957) work had generally been found to load highly on the evaluative factor: five with an instrumental tone (e.g., *useless–useful*) and five with an experiential tone (e.g., *unpleasant–pleasant*). The remaining two adjective pairs (*strong–weak* and *active–passive*) were included to represent the potency and activity factors of the semantic differential. A within-subjects factor analysis across the five leisure activities identified two major factors. The first seemed to capture an instrumental aspect of attitude, with such adjective

TABLE 3.1 Factor Loadings of Instrumental and Experiential Semantic Differential Adjective Pairs in Ratings of Training Regimen for Competitive Swimmers

	Factor Loading	
Adjective pair	Instrumental factor	Experiential factor
Bad–good	.76	.27
Unimportant–important	.65	.11
Useless–useful	.72	.00
Harmful–beneficial	.85	.00
Worthless–valuable	.71	.14
Unproductive–productive	.76	.30
Dull–exciting	.20	.67
Painful–enjoyable	–.15	.68
Unpleasant–pleasant	.14	.79
Aggravating–satisfying	.28	.61
Boring–fun	.18	.85
Detrimental–constructive	.34	.38

Source: Mummery, W. K., & Wankel, L. M., *Journal of Sport and Exercise Psychology, 21*, 313–328, 1999 (with permission).

pairs as *wise–foolish, harmful–beneficial,* and *useful–useless.* However, the two adjective pairs that were thought to reflect potency and activity also loaded highly on this factor. The second factor contained all of the experiential adjective pairs (*boring–interesting, enjoyable–unenjoyable, unpleasant–pleasant, attractive–unattractive,* and *ugly–beautiful*) but also two that were thought to be instrumental in nature (*good–bad, desirable–undesirable*). These findings again illustrate the phenomenon of scale–concept interactions. In this study of leisure behavior, scales that generally tend to load on the potency and activity factors were found to load on an evaluative factor, and adjective pairs that were thought to represent an instrumental type of evaluation actually merged with experiential items on the second factor. Nevertheless, the general pattern of results indicated a two-factor solution that could be interpreted as representing instrumental and experiential aspects of attitude, and both factors were found to have high internal consistency. In the within-subjects analysis across the five leisure activities, mean Cronbach's alpha coefficients were .91 for the experiential attitude measure and .79 for the instrumental measure. Note, however, that the two factors correlated highly with each other; the correlations ranged from .47 for boating to .79 for mountain climbing.

In sum, factor analyses tend to confirm the idea that in many behavioral domains it is possible to distinguish between two interrelated aspects of attitude. One aspect appears to reflect the behavior's perceived instrumentality (i.e., its anticipated positive or negative consequences), whereas the other appears to reflect the positive or negative experiences perceived to be associated with performing the behavior. However, it should be noted that another interpretation is possible. Generally speaking, the two dimensions identified in factor analyses differ not only in their instrumental versus experiential features but also in terms of valence. Many behaviors (e.g., engaging in physical exercise, getting a colonoscopy) are judged favorably in terms of their instrumentality but more negatively in terms of the experience of engaging in the behaviors. For example, in the Mummery and Wankel (1999) study, the instrumental evaluation of training for competitive swimming was extremely favorable ($M = 6.48$ on the seven-point scales), but the experiential evaluation was close to the neutral point ($M = 4.51$). It is therefore possible that the difference between the two identified dimensions has more to do with positive versus negative valence than with instrumental versus experiential types of evaluations.

Moreover, even though two factors tend to emerge in factor analyses, both factors are evaluative in nature. If items loading highly on the two factors were included among a set of more heterogeneous adjective scales (including potency and activity scales), a single evaluative factor would usually emerge. Similarly, an internal consistency analysis of instrumental and experiential items would generally show high correlations among all items and would result in a single, unidimensional evaluative scale.

Indeed, the two types of items tend to correlate highly with each other, as we saw with respect to the Ajzen and Driver (1991) study on leisure activities (see also Crites et al., 1994), and a scale composed of both types of items tends to have high internal consistency, as was shown in the training adherence study by Mummery and Wankel (1999; see also Ajzen & Driver, 1992). Perhaps the best conceptualization is a hierarchical model in which the instrumental and experiential components constitute first-order factors and the overall evaluative attitude is a second-order factor (Bagozzi, Lee, & Van Loo, 2001; Hagger & Chatzisarantis, 2005). By using appropriate analytical tools, it is possible to arrive at a single score that represents the second-order overall attitude. This measure of attitude will generally include experiential as well as instrumental evaluative items.

It is important to realize, however, that a valid semantic differential measure of attitude need not always include both instrumental and experiential items. To construct a valid attitude measure, we have to identify adjective pairs that serve as good indicators of the underlying evaluative dimension. As a starting point, it is a good idea to include both instrumental and experiential adjective pairs in formative research, but there is no assurance that both types of items will meet the criterion for inclusion on the final scale. Only adjective pairs that contribute to an internally consistent index should be selected. For attitudes toward some kinds of behavior, we may find that valid indicators consist primarily of instrumental items, whereas for other attitudes, valid items are primarily experiential in nature. For most behaviors, however, valid attitude measures will be composed of both types of items.

Belief-Based Measures of Attitude

The semantic differential is a relative newcomer to attitude measurement. Despite the ease with which an evaluative semantic differential scale can be constructed, many investigators prefer more complicated techniques developed earlier because these techniques can provide interesting information about the content of the attitude domain that is not available with the semantic differential. From a historical perspective, the major breakthrough in attitude measurement came when Thurstone (1928, 1931; Thurstone & Chave, 1929) applied psychometric methods to the problem. Based on the assumption that opinions or beliefs about an object can be viewed as verbal expressions of attitude toward the object, Thurstone proposed using opinions to assess attitudes. For example, a person who expresses the belief that "there can be no progress without war" would seem to have a more favorable attitude toward war than a person who believes that "it is hard to decide whether wars do more harm than good," and the attitudes of both individuals toward war appear to be more positive than the attitude of a person who believes that "war is a futile struggle resulting in self-destruction." Because agreement with different opinion statements expresses different degrees of favorableness or unfavorableness toward the attitude object, Thurstone argued that responses to such statements can be used to infer the underlying attitude.

It quickly became clear, however, that not only expressions of opinion but virtually all responses to the attitude object—whether opinions, feelings, intentions, or actual behaviors—can express favorable or unfavorable evaluations of the attitude object and can thus potentially be used as indicators of the latent attitude construct. Recognizing that some responses may be better indicators than others, Thurstone (1928) set out to develop a procedure to select items for inclusion in an attitude scale, items from which the attitude of interest could be validly inferred. Without going into detail, Thurstone made it clear that responses toward an object can be used to infer an underlying attitude only if two conditions are met. First, the response (e.g., agreement or disagreement with a statement of opinion or intention) must actually reflect an evaluation of the attitude object under consideration and not be a function of other kinds of factors (*criterion of irrelevance*). Clearly, if people with different attitudes are equally likely to agree with a statement, that agreement cannot be used to infer their attitudes. Second, the evaluative implication of agreement with an item has to be unambiguous (*criterion of ambiguity*). Thus, if for some individuals agreement with an item implies a positive attitude whereas for others it implies a negative attitude, knowing that a given individual agrees with the item does not enable us to infer that person's attitude.

To illustrate, consider the following statement designed to measure attitudes toward abortion: "Doctors who perform abortions should be put to death." Agreement with this statement may not meet the criterion of irrelevance because people's unwillingness to agree may not reflect a positive evaluation of abortion but instead a negative evaluation of the death penalty. Or, to take a simpler example, consider the belief statement, "President George Bush opposes gay marriage," designed to assess attitudes toward George Bush. Because President Bush clearly and frequently expressed his opposition to gay marriage, virtually all respondents— irrespective of their attitudes—are likely to agree with this statement. Consequently, agreement is irrelevant as an indicator of attitude toward Bush. In addition, this item also suffers from evaluative ambiguity. It is well known that the American public is deeply divided on the issue of gay marriage. As a result, agreement with the statement may indicate a positive attitude toward Bush for people who oppose gay marriage but a negative attitude for people who support it.

Thurstone (1928, 1931) devised different methods to select appropriate items, but the most widely used method was one that resulted in an "equal appearing interval scale." The first step involves the collection of a large pool of items related to the attitude object under consideration. A sample of judges representative of the population whose attitudes are to be assessed are asked to indicate, for each item, the degree of favorableness or unfavorableness toward the attitude object that is implied by agreement with the item. These judgments are typically made on an 11-point scale ranging from extremely unfavorable (1) through neutral (6) to extremely favorable (11). The median or mean value of these judgments is taken as the item's scale value (i.e., its location on the evaluative dimension). In accordance with the criterion of ambiguity, items are eliminated from further consideration if there is large disagreement among the judges. In addition, and consistent with the criterion of irrelevance, items are eliminated if they fail to discriminate among respondents with different attitudes.[2] The final scale is composed of a number of items that have met both criteria and whose scale values are more or less equally spaced along the entire evaluative continuum. The resulting scale is now administered to a new sample of respondents who are asked to check all items with which they agree. The attitude score is the median or mean scale value of all endorsed items.

The development of Thurstone's (1928) scaling method resulted in its widespread use as a means to assess a variety of attitudes. The amount of work involved in constructing a Thurstone scale, however, led Likert (1932) to propose a simpler procedure termed the *method of summated ratings.* This method was widely adopted since it greatly simplified matters by dispensing with the use of judges and by offering an easy test for the criterion of irrelevance, which Likert called the *criterion of internal consistency.*[3] As in Thurstone's scaling method, the starting point in Likert scaling is the construction of a large pool of items. Instead of using judges, the investigator decides for each item whether agreement implies a positive or a negative attitude toward the object in question. Neutral or ambiguous items are immediately eliminated. Participants are then asked to indicate their agreement with each of the remaining items, typically on a five-point scale, as in the following sample of statements from an early 22-item Likert scale developed to assess attitudes toward birth control (Wilke, 1934):

1. Birth control reduces the marital relation to the level of vice.
2. We should not approve of women taking the health risk involved in birth control.
3. Birth control would help to solve many of our social problems.
4. The practice of birth control evades man's duty to propagate the race.

Each item was accompanied by the following responses scale:

_____ Strongly agree
_____ Agree
_____ Undecided
_____ Disagree
_____ Strongly disagree

To be retained in the final Likert attitude scale, an item must meet the criterion of internal consistency. Like the criterion of irrelevance, the criterion of internal consistency requires that responses to the item discriminate between people with positive and negative attitudes. A preliminary estimate of each participant's attitude is obtained as follows. First, responses to each item in the original item pool are scored from 1 to 5. Strong agreements with favorable items are given a score of 5, and strong disagreements with these items are given a score of 1. Scoring is reversed for unfavorable items, such that disagreement with an unfavorable item results in a high score. Preliminary attitude scores are obtained by summing across all item scores. For a set of 100 items, the attitude scores can range from 100 to 500; the higher the score, the more favorable the attitude. In practice, an item is said to meet the criterion of internal consistency if the item score correlates strongly with the total (preliminary) attitude score. The final Likert scale is composed of the most discriminating items (i.e., of the items that have the highest correlations with the total score), usually half favorable items and half unfavorable.[4] Like the preliminary attitude score, the final attitude score is computed by summing over the retained item scores, resulting in a single overall score that represents the disposition to respond with some degree of favorableness or unfavorableness toward the attitude object. In contemporary research, Cronbach's coefficient alpha mentioned earlier is usually used as a measure of the degree to which the items on a Likert scale are internally consistent.

Factor Analysis of Attitudinal Items

Application of Likert's (1932) criterion of internal consistency ensures that the items comprising the final attitude scale are all indicators of the same underlying evaluative continuum and that a single score can represent the overall attitude. Some investigators use factor analysis to help them select items that will be representative of the attitudinal domain. For example, Brigham (1993) developed two 20-item racial attitude scales: one assessing the attitudes of Whites toward Blacks and the other assessing Blacks' attitudes toward Whites. For our discussion, we focus on the former scale. Brigham started out by identifying a large set of items on the basis of group discussions and a review of existing racial attitude scales. After eliminating redundant and ambiguous items, a set of 90 "attitude questions" were given to a sample of White undergraduates whose responses (on five-point *agree–disagree* scales) were then factor analyzed. This analysis yielded a large number of factors, and Brigham selected a subset of 20 items, each of which had a high loading on one of the first 10 factors extracted and low loadings on all other factors. This subset of 20 items was again submitted to a factor analysis, which identified three major factors. The first dealt with Whites' feelings of social distance or discomfort interacting with Blacks. A sample item on this factor is the statement, "I would rather not have Blacks live in the same apartment building I live in." The second factor is more difficult to interpret. Among the items with high loadings on this factors were, "It is likely that Blacks will bring violence to neighborhoods when they move in," "I think that Black people look more similar to each other than White people do," and "Interracial marriage should be discouraged to avoid the 'who-am-I?' confusion which the children feel." It is not clear what is common to these kinds of items or how they differ from the items on the first factor. Finally, the third factor was characterized by statements that mainly addressed issues of public policy, such as, "The Federal government should take decisive steps to override the injustices Blacks suffer at the hands of local authorities" and "Black people demand too much too fast in their push for equal rights."

By initially selecting items with high loadings on the different factors, Brigham (1993) made sure that the smaller subset of 20 items was representative of the original set of 90. Despite the fact that three factors emerged in the factor analysis of these 20 items, it was found that they nevertheless formed a scale with a high degree of internal consistency (alpha = .88). This high internal consistency indicates that the set of 20 items form a unidimensional evaluative scale and that the total score across all 20 items is a good measure of the overall attitude. It should thus be clear that although a factor analysis may identify different dimensions of belief statements, the criterion of internal consistency often suggests that these different dimensions contribute to a single, overarching, unidimensional attitude.

While accepting the basic idea that social attitudes can be assessed by means of unidimensional scales, some investigators use factor analysis not only to select items but, more important, to explore the contents of the attitude domain. For example, in preparing a study of attitudes toward condom use among Black South African university students, Madu and Peltzer (2003) relied on discussion groups as well as prior condom attitude scales to construct a set of 69 items that covered diverse aspects of this attitude domain, including inconvenience of using condoms, their potential unreliability, the perceived attitudes of important others, and the impact of condom use on the relationship with one's partner. Responses to the 69 items were submitted to factor analysis, and the results were used to reduce the initial set of items to a subset of 25 on the basis of criteria similar to those employed by Brigham (1993). This set of 25 items was found to have a high degree of internal consistency, as indicated by a coefficient alpha of .78.

The items on the final scale were once more factor analyzed, resulting in the identification of five distinguishable dimensions relevant to condom use. To illustrate, consistent with the way items were selected, the first factor had to do primarily with the perceived impact of condom use on the relationship with the partner. Among the items that loaded on this factor were, "The use of condoms makes the partner suspect that I am not faithful (that I sleep around)" and "The use of condoms is a sign of mistrust for the partner." Another factor contained items that were concerned with possible condom failure, such as "When a condom tears I have fears of many things" and "Condoms slip out during sex." The remaining factors can be interpreted as dealing with misleading beliefs about condom use, perceived attitudes and norms of important others, and possible barriers to condom use such as their unavailability.

Because Madu and Peltzer (2003) had a substantive interest in the different aspects of condom attitudes, they examined the psychometric properties of the items that comprised each of their five factors and found that each subscale had high internal consistency with alpha coefficients ranging from .77 to .88. They concluded that the five factors represent important aspects of attitudes toward condom use and that separate measures of these aspects can provide useful information that goes beyond the total attitude score. At the same time, it is also clear that each of the different subscales is itself evaluative in nature. All items, irrespective of their contents, were found to have high internal consistency, and the correlations between the subscale attitudes and the overall attitude were uniformly high, ranging from .66 to .79. Although we can compute subscale scores and use them to explore the attitudinal domain, a complete measure of attitude toward condom use requires that we combine all items into an overall score.

We noted earlier in this chapter that in contrast to basic theory-driven research on attitudes, applied research is often guided by complex, multidimensional conceptions of attitude. To deal with the complexity, investigators tend to rely on factor analytic data reduction methods. The purpose of the research is not to assess evaluation of a particular attitude object but rather to explore the multiple dimensions of complex social issues. Consider, for example, a study that was designed to "develop a set of items to tap the hypothesized multidimensionality of heterosexual attitudes" toward lesbians, gays, and bisexuals (LGBs) (Worthington, Dillon, & Becker-Schutte, 2005, p. 106). The investigators devised a large pool of items that they culled from prior research and later complemented with additional items constructed on the basis of their own information about the issue. After preliminary work, an initial set of 60 items was available for the investigation. These items represented different hypothesized aspects of attitudes toward LGBs, including violent homonegativity, positively and negatively ambivalent attitudes, civil rights, issues related to religion, and separate attitudes toward lesbians, toward gays, and toward bisexuals.

Using an Internet-based questionnaire, heterosexual college students rated, on seven-point scales, the extent to which each of the 60 items was characteristic of them or their views. For example, the item "I sometimes feel violent toward gay men/lesbian women/bisexual individuals" was included to assess violent homonegativity. To examine how well a given subset of items represented the hypothesized aspect of attitude they were supposed to measure, the investigators first computed the correlation between each item in the subset with the total score for that subset; that is, they examined each subscale's internal consistency. Eighteen items that failed to show strong correlations with the respective subset score were eliminated from further consideration. The remaining 42 items were submitted to a factor analysis, and items that failed to load clearly on one factor rather than another were deleted, leaving a total of 28 items. This final set was submitted to an exploratory factory analysis. Because of the anticipated correlations among factors, an oblique rotation was applied, and a five-factor solution was found to be most easily interpretable.

Among the six items that loaded highly on the first factor were, "It's important for me to avoid LGB individuals," "LGB people deserve the hatred they receive," and "Hearing about a hate crime against an LGB person would not bother me." This factor was labeled *hate*. Another factor had to do with issues of civil rights and contained such items as, "Health benefits should be available equally to same-sex partners as to any other couple" and "It is wrong for courts to make child custody decisions based on a parent's sexual orientation." Of the remaining three factors, one dealt with moral and religious concerns, the second with attraction and support of LBG people and activities, and the third with knowledge about LBG issues and included such items as, "I am knowledgeable about the history and mission of the PFLAG [Parents, Families, and Friends of Lesbians and Gays] organization" and "I am knowledgeable about the significance of the Stonewall Riot to the Gay Liberation Movement."

Further analyses revealed high internal consistency for each of the five subscales, with alpha coefficients ranging from .76 to .87. Because the investigators were mainly concerned with the multidimensional nature of their attitude domain (and in contrast to the two studies described earlier), no attempt was made to compute an overall attitude score. The investigators did, however, find fairly high correlations among the five factors, suggesting that we are dealing with a single underlying attitude toward LGB individuals and that it would therefore be reasonable to compute an overall attitude score (see Herek, 1994).

To summarize briefly, factor analysis is a useful tool for selecting items that are broadly representative of an attitudinal domain and for eliminating items that are irrelevant or redundant. Factor analysis can also serve to describe or identify different aspects of the attitudinal domain and to ensure that the subscales have high internal consistency. Moreover, because the subfactors typically capture the degree of favorableness or unfavorableness toward the attitude object based on some aspect of the object, it is possible to combine the subfactors to arrive at a single attitude score.

Can Items and Factors Be Used to Explain an Underlying Attitude?

When investigators use belief-based measures of attitude, such as Likert scales, they usually bring to the task an assumption that the items on the scale provide information about the beliefs, feelings, and intentions people hold with respect to the attitude object. It should be recalled, however, that the items are included on the scale only because they are found to be valid *indicators* of the underlying attitude, that is, because responses to the items correlate highly with the total evaluative score. They may not offer a good basis for learning about people's actual beliefs and intentions. Many statements of belief and intention that appear on an attitude scale may never have been considered by the respondents prior to receiving the questionnaire. Consider, for example, the following intention statement from Worthington et al.'s (2005) LGB knowledge and attitude scale previously discussed: "I would attend a demonstration to promote LGB civil rights." It is likely that most heterosexuals have never considered performing this behavior, yet when asked, they can provide an answer that reflects their attitudes toward LGB people. In other words, the expressed intention is primarily a function of the underlying attitude, and it is for this reason that it can be used as a good indicator of the attitude.

By the same token, many statements of belief contained in an attitude questionnaire address issues people have not considered before. As we saw earlier, the attitude toward Blacks scale constructed by Brigham (1993) included the statement, "Black people are demanding too much too fast in their push for equal rights." It may appear that this item captures a possible determinant of attitudes toward Blacks. That is, it makes sense intuitively that the belief that Blacks are "demanding too much too fast" is at least in part responsible for a negative attitude toward Blacks. However, it is equally plausible that although the respondents had not given this issue any thought before, their attitudes toward Blacks guide their responses to the item. Participants with positive attitudes toward Blacks would tend to disagree, whereas participants with negative attitudes would tend to agree. Responses to the item can thus be used as an indicator of the underlying attitude, but it would be a mistake to argue that these responses provide information about the causal determinants of the respondents' attitude toward Blacks.

What's more, the item selection criteria inherent in standard attitude scaling methods, such as Thurstone and Likert scaling, virtually guarantee that some of the most important determinants of an attitude are eliminated from consideration. First, if a belief statement represents a well-known fact, it will not meet standard item selection criteria. For example, because everybody is likely to agree with the statement that Adolf Hitler was responsible for the murder of millions of people, responses to this item will not correlate with the total score, and the item would not be included in the final scale. Clearly, however, this does not mean that people's attitudes toward Hitler are unaffected by their belief that he was a mass murderer.

Second, belief items are often eliminated from consideration not only because everybody agrees or disagrees but also because they are evaluatively ambiguous. Again, however, such items may be important determinants of attitude. For example, voters in an election are generally familiar with the major candidates' party affiliations as well as their stands on critical issues. Thus, in the 2004 presidential election, most voters knew that Bush was a conservative Republican who supported the war in Iraq and was opposed to gay marriage. It is likely that these beliefs served as important determinants of people's attitudes toward Bush and influenced their eventual voting choice. Nevertheless, none of these beliefs would appear on standard attitude scales because virtually all voters would agree with statements concerning these issues and because the evaluative implications of this agreement would be unclear. For example, voters would agree that Bush supports the war in Iraq, but this belief would produce a more favorable attitude toward Bush for some people and a more unfavorable attitude for others.

Similar considerations apply to the different aspects of attitude identified by factor analytic methods. Investigators who perform factor analyses on attitudinal items are often motivated by a search for explanation. In the study by Madu and Peltzer (2003) described earlier, the investigators proposed several possible reasons for people's negative dispositions toward condom use. They then proceeded to test whether the hypothesized categories of determinants would emerge in a factor analysis of items that were designed to capture these determinants. The factor analysis suggested five major reasons for unfavorable attitudes toward condom use:

1. Use of condoms could have a negative impact on the relationship.
2. It is ineffective or unnecessary.
3. Condoms are unreliable.
4. Condom use is inconvenient.
5. Important others disapprove.

At first glance, this interpretation appears eminently reasonable. A moment's reflection reveals, however, that like the original items on the scale, the factors that are derived from these items do not necessarily provide valid information about the causal determinants of an attitude. For one, given that we are dealing with correlational analyses, we cannot be sure of the causal direction. Thus, instead of causing a negative attitude toward condom use, the perceived ineffectiveness of condoms may be the consequence of a negative attitude. More important, if the scale contains, as it usually does, many items that address unfamiliar issues, factor scores based on such items are indicators of an underlying attitude, but they may tell us little about the reasons for the attitude. Similarly, because many statements that deal with potentially important determinants of the attitude are eliminated by standard scaling procedures, the factors extracted in a factor analyses cannot very well represent these determinants.

Including Factual and Ambivalent Items in Attitude Scales

The previous discussion has shown that many belief statements on an attitude scale cannot be assumed to reflect determinants of the attitude and that many important determinants are not part of the scale because items representing important determinants are eliminated by standard attitude scaling techniques. Items are eliminated for one or more of three reasons: (1) they are factual; (2) they are evaluatively ambiguous; or (3) they are irrelevant as indicated by failure to correlate with the total attitude score. However, it is possible to retain most factual and evaluatively ambiguous items by assessing not only agreement with each item but also the item's evaluative implication for the individual. Consider, for example, the statement that President Bush is a conservative. Most voters would agree with this statement, but they would vary in their favorable or unfavorable evaluation of being a conservative. If we measured this evaluation in addition to measuring agreement with the item, we could infer its contribution to each person's attitude (Fishbein, 1963, 1967b; Fishbein & Ajzen, 1975). Specifically, for people who place a positive value on being conservative, agreement with the item implies a favorable attitude toward President Bush whereas it implies an unfavorable attitude for people who place a negative value on being conservative. There would be no need to eliminate the item from consideration in attitude measurement.

To illustrate, we could ask participants to respond to the following two scales: (1) a measure of belief strength (b); and (2) a measure of the evaluative aspect of the belief, that is, the evaluation of the attribute associated with the attitude object (e):

1. George Bush is a conservative.
    _____ disagree strongly (–2)
    _____ disagree (–1)
    _____ undecided (0)
    _____ agree (+1)
    _____ agree strongly (+2)

2. Being a conservative is
    _____ very good (+2)
    _____ good (+1)
    _____ neither good nor bad (0)
    _____ bad (–1)
    _____ very bad (–2)

To arrive at a scale value for each item pair, we multiply belief strength by its evaluative aspect, using the values shown in parentheses. As in Likert scaling, agreement with a statement that has a positive evaluative aspect results in a positive scale value, as does disagreement with a statement that has a negative evaluative aspect. Conversely, disagreement with a positively valued statement and agreement with a negatively valued statement result in a negative score. In a multi-item attitude inventory, we repeat this procedure for each item pair and then sum the scale values to arrive at a preliminary attitude score. Following Likert's standard procedure, item–total correlations can be computed to select items for the final scale that display high internal consistency.

Parenthetically, investigators have sometimes pointed out that for certain attributes, it makes little sense to assess evaluations on a bipolar scale because everybody would agree that the attribute was either good or bad. For example, consider the belief statement, "George Bush is honest." Although respondents may agree or disagree with this statement, they will all judge being honest to be a positive attribute. To obtain a quantitative measure of evaluation with respect to attributes of this kind, it is possible to use a unipolar instead of a bipolar scale. Thus, participants could be asked to evaluate being honest on the following scale:

Being honest is
    _____ extremely good (+3)
    _____ quite good (+2)
    _____ slightly good (+1)
    _____ not at all good (0)

Although assessing belief strength as well as the belief's evaluative implication permits us to include factual and evaluatively ambiguous beliefs, it does not completely resolve the problem of identifying determinant beliefs.

Some important belief items may still be eliminated because they fail to meet the criterion of internal consistency. This will be the case whenever there is little variance on belief strength as well as on the belief's evaluative aspect. For example, consider again the statement that Hitler was responsible for the murder of millions of people. Because virtually everybody will agree with this statement and will also have a negative evaluation of murdering millions of people, the item scale value will have no variance and thus will not correlate with the total attitude score. The second problem that remains unresolved by the proposed scaling technique is that it will include items on the scale that refer to unfamiliar issues and that may be good indicators but may not be important determinants of the respondent's attitude.

☐ The Expectancy-Value Model of Attitude

We have, up to this point, dealt with two major issues. The first had to do with valid ways to assess attitudes defined as dispositions to respond with some degree of favorableness or unfavorableness toward a given object. We saw that the semantic differential as well as Thurstone and Likert scaling methods result in reliable and valid attitude scores. The second issue we addressed concerned the extent to which belief-based attitude measures can provide information about the determinants of attitudes. In relation to this question, we saw that items on standardized attitude scales are selected to be good indicators of the underlying attitude but that they do not necessarily provide information about the causal determinants of the attitude.

Beliefs as a Basis of Attitudes

This should not be taken to mean, however, that beliefs have no causal effect on attitudes. On the contrary, within our reasoned action framework, attitudes follow directly from beliefs about the attitude object. Generally speaking, we form beliefs about an object by associating the object with various characteristics, qualities, and attributes. In the course of their lives, people's experiences lead them to form many different beliefs about various objects, actions, and events. These beliefs may be formed as a result of direct observation; they may be acquired indirectly by accepting information from friends, teachers, the media, and other outside sources; and they may be self-generated through inference processes. Some beliefs persist over time, some are forgotten, and new beliefs are formed. More formally, we define belief as the subjective probability that an object has a certain attribute (Fishbein & Ajzen, 1975). The terms *object* and *attribute* are used in the generic sense, and they refer to any discriminable aspect of an individual's world. For example, a person may believe that physical exercise (the object) reduces the risk of heart disease (the attribute). Importantly, the subjective probability that defines a belief does not necessarily have the same properties as objective probabilities, nor need it be assessed on a 0 to 1.0 probability scale. In fact, unlike probability, belief strength is often assessed on seven-point graphic scales with such endpoints as *agree–disagree*, *likely–unlikely*, or *definitely true–definitely false*.

The way beliefs influence attitudes is described by what has become the most popular model of attitude formation and structure, the *expectancy-value model* (see Feather, 1959, 1982). One of the first and most complete statements of the model can be found in Fishbein's (1963, 1967b) summation theory of attitude, although somewhat narrower versions were proposed earlier by Peak (1955), Carlson (1956), and Rosenberg (1956). Consistent with Fishbein's expectancy-value model, we assume that attitudes toward an object are formed automatically and inevitably as new beliefs are formed about the object. Specifically, people are assumed to have preexisting evaluations of the attributes that become linked to an object in the process of belief formation. Depending on the strength of the beliefs, the attribute evaluations become associated with the attitude object and in a process of summation produce the overall attitude toward the object. Thus, on future occasions, the attitude object will automatically elicit the summated evaluative response, that is, the overall attitude toward the object. This model is shown symbolically in Equation 3.1:

$$A \propto \sum b_i e_i \qquad (3.1)$$

where A stands for attitude toward an object, b_i is the strength of the belief that the object has attribute i, and e_i is the evaluation of attribute i. It can be seen that the evaluation of each attribute contributes to the attitude in direct proportion to the person's subjective probability that the object possesses the attribute in question, that is, in direct proportion to the strength of the belief. In this fashion, people come to hold favorable attitudes toward objects they associate with positively valued attributes and unfavorable attitudes toward objects they associate with negatively valued attributes.

Consider, for example, the formation of attitudes toward a newly declared candidate for national political office. A given voter may learn that the candidate is a liberal Democrat, is married with two children, belongs to the Catholic Church, favors national health insurance, and opposes private social security accounts. Because the voter already has positive or negative evaluations of these various attributes, the new beliefs will automatically produce an attitude toward the candidate. It is assumed

TABLE 3.2 Expectancy-Value Model: Hypothetical Example of a Voter's Attitude Toward a Candidate

Attribute of candidate	Belief strength (b)	Attribute evaluation (e)	b x e
Liberal	+3	−3	−9
Democrat	+3	−2	−6
Married	+2	+3	+6
Two children	+1	+2	+2
Favors national health insurance	+1	0	0
Opposes private social security accounts	+2	−3	−6
$A \propto \sum b_i e_i$			−13

that the more strongly the voter holds a given belief, the more the attribute evaluation contributes to the attitude. The beliefs, attribute evaluations, and the resulting attitude of a hypothetical voter are shown in Table 3.2. In this example, belief strength is assessed on a three-point *slightly likely* (+1) to *extremely likely* (+3) scale and attribute evaluation on a seven-point *bad* (−3) to *good* (+3) scale. Responses to the two scales are multiplied. It can be seen that this person is expected to hold a negative attitude of −13 toward the political candidate.

Salient Beliefs

We have seen that beliefs associate the attitude object with various other objects, attributes, or events. In other words, they represent the information people have about the object, information that serves as the foundation for their attitudes. People can, of course, form many different beliefs about an object, but we assume that only a relatively small number determine the attitude at any given moment. Specifically, we have argued in the past that only salient beliefs (i.e., beliefs about the object that come readily to mind) serve as the prevailing determinants of the attitude (see Ajzen & Fishbein, 1980; Fishbein & Ajzen, 1975). The term *salience* has, in contemporary social psychology, been replaced by the notion of accessibility in memory. Accessible beliefs are activated spontaneously without much cognitive effort in the actual or symbolic presence of the attitude object. This activation may occur below conscious awareness, but accessible beliefs come readily to mind when a person has reason to retrieve them.

Research suggests that people are capable of attending to or processing about five to nine items of information at a time (Mandler, 1967; Miller, 1956; Woodworth & Schlosberg, 1954). It can therefore be argued that a person's attitude toward an object is, at any given moment, primarily determined by no more than five to nine readily accessible beliefs about the object.[5] Of course, given sufficient time and motivation, people can actively retrieve additional beliefs from memory, and these additional beliefs may also influence the attitude at that point in time. We are merely suggesting that under most circumstances a relatively small number of beliefs serve as the determinants of a person's attitude. Moreover, these determinants are subject to change; additional beliefs may be formed, and existing beliefs may be strengthened, weakened, or replaced by new beliefs. Such changes would be expected to produce corresponding changes in attitudes.[6]

We saw that attitudes are dispositions to respond in a consistently favorable or unfavorable manner to a psychological object. According to the expectancy-value model, this evaluative response tendency derives from the prevailing accessible beliefs about the attitude object. The idea that attitudes are based on relevant information accessible in memory imbues them with a degree of reasonableness. This is not to say that people form attitudes in a "rational" manner by conducting an unbiased review of all relevant information and integrating it according to formal rules of logic. On the contrary, the expectancy-value model recognizes that beliefs—although often quite accurate—can be biased by a variety of cognitive and motivational processes and that they may be based on invalid or selective information, be self-serving, or otherwise fail to correspond to reality (Allport, 1954; Eagly & Chaiken, 1993; Fishbein & Ajzen, 1975). However, once a set of beliefs is formed and is accessible in memory, it provides the cognitive foundation from which attitudes are assumed to follow automatically in a reasonable and consistent fashion.

This emphasis on a reasonable and consistent link between information about an object and attitude toward that object has often been misconstrued to imply a conscious and effortful mode of attitude formation. In reality, the expectancy-value model does *not* assume deliberate and conscious attitude construction. Instead, as noted already, attitudes are assumed to emerge automatically and spontaneously as beliefs are formed about the attitude object, and these attitudes are thought to be immediately available when a person is confronted with the attitude object. Attitudes may be based on few or many beliefs; these beliefs may or may not accurately reflect reality, but the evaluative meaning they carry is automatically activated. Just as the denotative meaning of any concept with which a person is familiar is immediately available and need not be constructed, so too is its evaluative meaning or attitude (see Osgood et al., 1957). Thus, when people are asked to indicate their attitudes regarding a social issue, such as capital punishment, they need not review their beliefs about it before they can express a position. Because of the beliefs people hold about capital punishment, this concept carries meaning for them—including evaluative meaning—which is automatically available.

It may be worth addressing a related issue that has sometimes been raised with respect to the formal structure of the expectancy-value model. The equation used to compute an attitude estimate on the basis of accessible beliefs (Equation 3.1) may seem to imply that people go through a complex calculus, involving multiplication of belief strength by attribute evaluation and summation of the resulting product terms. In actuality, although the investigator does perform these computations, people are *not* assumed to do so. We merely propose that attitude formation may be *modeled* in this fashion. The psychological processes involved in arriving at an attitude are assumed to take account of belief strength as well as attribute evaluation, roughly in the form described by the formal model: The more strongly a belief is held, and the more positive or negative the attribute evaluation, the greater is its expected contribution to the overall attitude.

Eliciting Salient Beliefs

This discussion implies that to understand why people hold certain attitudes at a given point in time, it is necessary to assess their readily accessible beliefs about the attitude object. Perhaps the simplest and most direct procedure involves asking respondents to describe the attitude object using a free-response format. For example, they could be given a few minutes to list the "characteristics, qualities, and attributes" (Zajonc, 1954) they associate with the attitude object. From this point onward, however, our discussion focuses primarily on attitudes toward behaviors because, within our theory, these are the attitudes of greatest relevance for predicting and understanding human behavior.

Personal Salient Beliefs

To identify accessible beliefs that determine attitudes toward a behavior (*behavioral beliefs*), we could ask respondents to list the advantages and disadvantages of their performing the behavior in question. In line with our earlier discussion, it can be suggested that the first five to nine beliefs emitted are readily accessible in memory and are therefore likely to serve as the primary determinants of attitudes toward the behavior under investigation. It is possible, however, that only the first two or three beliefs emitted are readily accessible for the individual and that additional beliefs emitted beyond this point are retrieved from memory in a more effortful manner. In other words, while listing beliefs about an object or behavior, a person may recall some forgotten information or make new inferences on the basis of existing information. Beliefs that were previously not readily accessible may now become part of the salient set of beliefs and, if so, they may become important determinants of the currently prevailing attitude.

Compatibility of Beliefs and Attitudes

When eliciting accessible behavioral beliefs, it is essential to ensure compatibility with respect to the action, target, context, and time elements of the behavior under investigation. For example, if we are interested in the determinants of a person's attitude toward getting a colonoscopy in the next 2 months, we would have to elicit salient beliefs about this particular behavior. Thus, we could ask participants to list the advantages and the disadvantages of their getting a colonoscopy in the next 2 months. These questions observe the principle of compatibility in that they refer to the behavior of interest in terms of the same action, target, context, and time elements. Note also that the respondents are asked about their personally performing the behavior and not about performance of the behavior in general. This is important because the consequences people expect as a result of their own performing a behavior may differ from the consequences they associate with performance of the behavior by others. For example, a woman may associate mostly favorable consequences with the use of birth control pills in general but may believe that this behavior would produce mostly negative consequences for her personally—perhaps because she is planning to get pregnant.

Once an individual's accessible behavioral beliefs are identified, we can measure belief strength and outcome evaluation in the manner described earlier (Table 3.2). Because the beliefs in this case deal with outcomes listed by the individuals themselves, we can assume that the respondents in fact expect the behavior to produce the outcomes in question. All that remains is to assess the strength of these beliefs, that is, the perceived likelihood that the outcome will occur. A unipolar likelihood scale, ranging, for example, from 1 (*slightly likely*) to 3 (*extremely likely*), can thus be used to assess belief strength. We do not need to be concerned with the possibility that a person will rate the outcome as unlikely. The outcome evaluation, however, is assessed on a bipolar scale (e.g., from –3 to +3), such as a *good–bad* scale, because each outcome can be rated as negative or positive to a certain degree. In accordance with the expectancy-value model, the measures thus obtained are used to derive an estimate of attitude toward the behavior by multiplying belief strength and outcome evaluation and then summing the resulting products (Equation 3.1).

Modal Salient Beliefs

We have up to this point dealt only with elicitation of an individual's own accessible behavioral beliefs. This approach provides insight into the basis for that person's attitude toward an object or behavior. However, the elicitation procedure usually produces sets of beliefs that differ from respondent to respondent in terms of content and number. This makes it difficult to describe or summarize the beliefs held in a population or subpopulation and therefore to compare the beliefs of different populations. For this reason, most investigators try to identify the set of beliefs held with the greatest frequency in the population of interest, that is, the *modal* set of salient or readily accessible beliefs. This can be done in formative research by asking a representative sample of individuals from the population of interest to list the advantages and disadvantages of performing the behavior under investigation.

Once the respondents have listed their individual beliefs, we have to decide which beliefs to include in the modal set. The first step essentially involves a content analysis of the beliefs emitted by different individuals. Responses are organized by grouping together beliefs that refer to similar outcomes and counting the frequency with which each outcome was listed. When differences between outcomes listed by individuals are clearly semantic, they should be considered equivalent and grouped together. For example, when eliciting beliefs about drinking alcohol, we may find that some respondents list vomiting as a possible outcome while others list throwing up. These terms clearly refer to the same outcome. Also listed may be the belief that "drinking alcohol makes me nauseous." Here we must decide whether this refers to vomiting/throwing up or to a different outcome. A useful rule of thumb is to ask whether the two outcomes in question (i.e., vomiting and being nauseous) could reasonably be emitted by the same person. If many respondents listed both outcomes, then the outcomes should be treated as separate beliefs just as one would in the case of identifying the accessible beliefs of a single individual. However, if only a few respondents listed both outcomes, we could decide that different individuals use different labels to refer to the same outcome.

We may also want to combine outcomes that are listed with low frequency but have something in common. For example, different respondents may mention weight gain, headaches, and stomachaches as outcomes of drinking. Although these are not identical outcomes, all three refer to relatively minor side effects. Despite the fact that each outcome might have been mentioned by only a few respondents, when taken together they suggest a salient belief in the population concerning minor side effects of drinking alcohol. To capture this belief, a statement such as, "My drinking alcohol leads to minor side effects (e.g., weight gain, headaches)" could be included in the modal set.

The final decision to be made is how many of the identified beliefs to include in the modal set. One possibility is to simply take the 10 or 12 most frequently mentioned outcomes. This procedure results in a modal set that is likely to include at least some of the readily accessible beliefs listed by each respondent in the sample. Another possibility is to use those beliefs that exceed a certain frequency. We might decide that we want all beliefs mentioned by at least 10% or 20% of the sample. Perhaps the most reasonable decision rule, and one that we would recommend, is to choose beliefs by their frequency of emission until we have accounted for a certain percentage, perhaps 75%, of all responses listed. For example, if the total number of responses provided by all participants in the elicitation sample was 600, a 75% decision rule would require that we select as many of the most frequently mentioned outcomes as needed to account for 450 responses.

Focus Groups

It can be seen that identification of modal salient beliefs depends on our ability to obtain a valid estimate of the frequency with which each beliefs is held in the population. We have shown that this can be done by counting the number of times a given belief or belief category is listed by different individuals in the elicitation study. In contrast to such an elicitation procedure, investigators sometimes rely on *focus groups* or group discussions to identify the set of modal accessible beliefs. Unfortunately, the beliefs that arise in the course of group discussions may differ greatly from beliefs that are held with high frequency in the population. Dominant individuals can influence the direction of the discussion and therefore make it appear that a rarely held belief is readily accessible in the population. Although focus groups may have their use in other contexts, we caution against their use for the purpose of identifying modal salient beliefs.

Empirical Support for the Expectancy-Value Model

Several meta-analyses of the empirical literature have provided correlational evidence in support of the expectancy-value model as applied to attitudes toward a behavior. Two of these analyses (Armitage & Conner, 2001; van den Putte, 1993) examined prediction across a broad range of behaviors and reported mean correlations of .53 and .50, respectively, between the expectancy-value index of beliefs ($\sum b_i e_i$) and a direct attitude measure. A meta-analysis of research on condom use (Albarracín, Johnson, Fishbein, & Muellerleile, 2001) revealed a mean correlation of .56 between the expectancy-value index and direct measures of attitudes toward this behavior. Clearly, then, assessing beliefs about a behavior's outcomes as well as evaluations of those outcomes generally affords good prediction of the overall attitude toward the behavior.

From a theoretical perspective, these findings are taken to mean that the belief composite in the expectancy-value model measures the attitude's underlying determinants. In our past publications, we have often referred to the $\Sigma b_i e_i$ index as an indirect or belief-based measure of attitude, and many other investigators have followed our lead. Consistent with this view, investigators sometimes assess attitudes toward a behavior not by means of standard scaling procedures, such as Likert or semantic differential methods, but rely instead on an expectancy-value index as their sole measure of attitude. We have now come to realize that it is misleading to view the $\Sigma b_i e_i$ index as an indirect measure of attitude. Instead, it is more appropriately considered a composite measure of beliefs that is assumed to determine the attitude. This theoretical hypothesis must of course be submitted to empirical test before it can be accepted. A high correlation between $\Sigma b_i e_i$ and a direct attitude measure confirms that the elicitation procedure identified relevant salient beliefs about the behavior and that a valid attitude measure was constructed. A low correlation, however, raises serious concerns. It is possible to question the validity of the salient belief index, the direct attitude measure, or the expectancy-value model itself. Given the strong empirical support for the model, we would be more concerned with the validity of the measures, particularly the belief-based measure. The direct measure of attitude in the expectancy-value model is typically obtained by means of a standard scaling procedure such as the semantic differential or Likert scaling. As we saw earlier in this chapter, when properly constructed, these methods provide internally consistent and valid measures of attitude. In contrast, the belief (expectancy-value) composite can be more problematic. We discuss two potential problems. First, the expectancy-value index may be based on an inappropriate set of (nonsalient) beliefs, and, second, the measure of belief strength may be scored inappropriately.

Predictive Validity of Salient Versus Nonsalient Beliefs

From a theoretical perspective, attitudes are assumed to be determined by readily accessible beliefs, and it therefore stands to reason that such beliefs should usually be better predictors of attitude than nonsalient or less readily accessible beliefs. The limited evidence available does indeed show that salient beliefs tend to correlate more highly with an independent measure of attitude than do nonsalient beliefs (Petkova, Ajzen, & Driver, 1995; van den Putte, 1993; van der Pligt & Eiser, 1984). In the belief elicitation phase of the Petkova et al. (1995) study, college students listed their beliefs about the outcomes of making abortion illegal. A total of 12 modal salient outcomes were selected as well as 12 outcomes that had been emitted with very low frequencies (nonsalient outcomes). In the main study, students provided belief strength and outcome evaluation ratings for all 24 outcomes, and they responded to a semantic differential measure that directly assessed attitudes toward making abortion illegal. Belief strength was assessed on a seven-point *unlikely* (–3) to *likely* (+3) scale and outcome evaluation on a seven-point *good* (+3) to *bad* (–3) scale. A $\sum b_i e_i$ index based on the 12 readily accessible beliefs correlated .77 with the direct attitude measure, whereas a $\sum b_i e_i$ index based on the 12 nonsalient beliefs showed a correlation of .67 with the direct measure. Although still quite strong, this latter correlation was significantly lower than the .77 correlation obtained by relying on readily accessible beliefs.[7] Comparable results were reported by Hackman and Anderson (1968).

Of course, as we saw in our discussion of Likert scaling, it is possible to use nonsalient beliefs as indicators of an underlying attitude. However, this requires that each belief item meet the criterion of internal consistency. If no measures are taken to ensure that the nonsalient beliefs included in the belief composite meet this criterion, low correlations between the composite and a direct measure of attitude may be observed. On the other hand, when the criterion of internal consistency is applied to a set of nonsalient beliefs, the result is a traditional Likert scale and, as we saw earlier, although such a scale may be a valid measure of attitude, it is unlikely to contain many of the important determinants of the attitude under investigation.

Note that when we use the expectancy-value model, we assume that *all* salient beliefs serve as determinants of attitude. We do not necessarily expect a high degree of internal consistency among salient beliefs. In fact, it is perfectly reasonable for people with positive attitudes toward a given behavior to recognize that there are also some possible disadvantages to performing the behavior in question. Conversely, people with overall negative attitudes toward performing the behavior may well associate a few positive outcomes with it. In other words, attitudes may be held with some degree of ambivalence. It would therefore be inappropriate to select or eliminate salient beliefs on the basis of internal consistency considerations.

Scoring Belief Strength

Once a modal salient set of outcomes has been identified, we can construct a standardized questionnaire in which we assess belief strength and evaluation with respect to each outcome. The principle of compatibility requires that each belief statement define the behavior in terms of the appropriate action, target, context, and time elements. Moreover, the outcome evaluated must be formulated exactly as it was identified in the elicitation procedure. For example, consider the beliefs that "my using birth control pills takes away the worry of becoming pregnant" and that "my using birth control pills increases my sexual pleasure." In these examples, the appropriate outcomes to be evaluated are "taking away the worry of becoming pregnant," not "becoming pregnant," and "increasing my sexual pleasure," not "sexual pleasure" as such.

We saw earlier that, in the case of an individual's own salient beliefs, outcome evaluations can be assessed by means of a bipolar evaluative scale, such as a *good–bad* scale, and that belief strength can be measured on a unipolar subjective probability scale, such as a scale ranging from *slightly likely* to *extremely likely*. However, when dealing with a modal set of outcomes, a particular individual may not believe that performing the behavior in question will lead to one or more of the outcomes included. For example, when—as part of a belief elicitation—a person indicates that "my drinking alcohol makes me nauseous," it is reasonable to use, for that person, a unipolar scale to assess the strength of this belief. However, when the same statement is presented to an individual who did not personally emit it, the individual may well judge it to be highly unlikely or false. To permit this kind of response, a bipolar belief scale should be used, such as a seven-point scale ranging from *unlikely* to *likely* or *false* to *true*.

Whereas most investigators would agree that evaluative scales be scored in a bipolar fashion (e.g., from –3 to +3 on a seven-point scale), questions have been raised with respect to the appropriate scoring of subjective likelihood scales (see, e.g., Ajzen, 1991; Bagozzi, 1984; Holbrook, 1977; Schmidt, 1973). A seven-point likelihood scale could be scored in a *unipolar* fashion (e.g., from 1 to 7, or from 0 to 6) or in a *bipolar* fashion (e.g., from –3 to +3). From a measurement perspective, either type of scoring could be applied with equal justification. Measures of the kind used in research with the expectancy-value model can at best be assumed to constitute equal-interval scales, not ratio scales. As such, it is permissible to apply any linear transformation to the respondents' ratings without altering the measure's scale properties (see, e.g., Dawes, 1972). Going from a bipolar to a unipolar scale, or vice versa, is of course a simple linear transformation in which we add or subtract a constant from the original values. The problem, however, is that a linear transformation on a measure of belief strength produces a *nonlinear* transformation on the $b \times e$ product term. This can be seen in the following computation where the original values of the belief strength measure (b) are transformed by the addition of a constant B. For simplicity, only one behavioral belief is entered into the expectancy-value equation:

$$A \propto (b + B)(e)$$

$$\propto be + Be$$

In this equation, A is the attitude as assessed directly, for example, by means of a semantic differential scale. Because the new term, Be, is not a constant, the transformed product term is clearly not a linear transformation of the original be term. The problem this creates is that moving from unipolar to bipolar scoring, or vice versa, can have a substantial impact on correlations involving the product term (see Orth, 1985). Thus, the way we score the belief strength scales may raise or lower the correlation between expectancy-value composites and any external criterion. Indeed, it can affect the magnitude of the correlation of the $b \times e$ composite with a direct attitude measure, a correlation that is often used to validate the expectancy-value model itself.

Disagreement With Belief Statements

Psychological Criterion

If, from a measurement perspective, there is no justification for selecting either bipolar or unipolar scoring of responses to belief statements, we may be inclined to look for a psychological justification. In our previous publications (Ajzen & Fishbein, 1980; Fishbein & Ajzen, 1975) we have argued for use of bipolar scoring. Thus, a seven-point *unlikely–likely* scale would be scored from –3 on one extreme to +3 on the other. This suggestion is consistent with Likert scaling discussed earlier where disagreement with negative statements results in a high item score and disagreement with positive statements results in a low item score.[8] This scoring scheme appears quite reasonable when we think about attitudes toward an object such as a person or group of people. For example, disagreement that a certain person is honest implies a belief that the person is dishonest and should contribute negatively to the attitude toward the person. Similarly, disagreement that the person is dishonest implies that the person is honest, making a positive contribution to the overall attitude.

In the case of attitude toward a behavior, the appropriate scoring is not as readily apparent. Consider the belief that "my drinking alcohol will lead to my gaining weight." It is unlikely that disagreement with this statement implies a belief that "my drinking alcohol will result in my losing weight" or that my drinking alcohol will prevent my gaining weight." In other words, it is not clear that denying a negative outcome necessarily implies belief in a positive outcome, nor is it clear that denying a positive outcome implies belief in a negative outcome (see Sparks, Hedderley, & Shepherd, 1991). Thus, disagreeing that "drinking makes you more sociable" does not imply a belief that "drinking makes you less sociable." In other words, when a person disagrees or rates as unlikely that a behavior will produce a certain outcome, it is not clear how the belief affects the overall attitude. We therefore cannot assume that bipolar scoring of the belief statement accurately reflects its implication for the overall attitude. If we score the measure of belief strength in a bipolar manner, disagreement with positive belief statements makes a negative contribution (e.g., $-3 \times +1 = -3$), and disagreement with negative statements makes a positive contribution (e.g., $-3 \times -1 = +3$). However, if we score the measure in a unipolar fashion, for example, from 1 (extremely unlikely) to 7 (extremely likely), disagreement with a positive statement contributes positively to the attitude ($+1 \times +3 = +3$), and disagreement with a negative statement makes a negative contribution ($+1 \times -3 = -3$).

Empirical Criterion

In the absence of an a priori basis for determining the proper scoring of belief strength measures, it has been proposed that we rely on an empirical criterion (Holbrook, 1977; Orth, 1985; Schmidt, 1973; see also Ajzen, 1991). In light of the general acceptance of the expectancy-value model, we can make its (presumed) validity the criterion of proper scaling. That is, we can examine the correlation between the belief $\times$ evaluation composite and a direct measure of attitude and adopt the scoring scheme for belief strength (unipolar or bipolar) that produces the better result. Relatively little research has examined the proper scoring of belief items empirically, but the general pattern of findings tends to support bipolar scoring (e.g., Ajzen, 1991; Gagné & Godin, 2000; Hewstone & Young, 1988; Sparks et al., 1991). In these studies, measures of outcome evaluation are scored in a bipolar fashion, whereas belief strength is scored in unipolar as well as bipolar fashion for purposes of comparison.[9] After computing $b \times e$ products and summing over the set of beliefs, the two belief composites are correlated with a direct attitude measure.

One of the first empirical comparisons of bipolar and unipolar belief scoring was reported in a study of attitudes toward the European Economic Community, the forerunner of the European Union (Hewstone & Young, 1988). With respect to both a set of belief statements constructed by the investigators and a set of modal salient beliefs elicited in a pilot study, unipolar scoring of belief strength resulted in better prediction of a direct attitude measure than did bipolar scoring. Subsequent research, however, has generally not supported the superiority of unipolar over bipolar scoring of belief strength. Ajzen (1991) reported a reanalysis of data from a study of five leisure activities: spending time at the beach, jogging or running, mountain climbing, boating, and biking (Ajzen & Driver, 1991, 1992). Based on pilot work, modal salient outcomes had been identified for each of the five behaviors. In the main study, belief strength was assessed by asking participants to rate the likelihood of each salient outcome on a seven-point *extremely unlikely–extremely likely* scale, and outcome evaluations were assessed on a seven-point *harmful–beneficial* scale. In addition, attitudes toward each leisure activity were assessed directly by means of a five-item evaluative semantic differential. With unipolar scoring of belief strength, the average correlation between the $\Sigma b_i e_i$ indices and the measures of attitude was .20 compared with an average correlation of .44 when responses to belief items were scored in a bipolar fashion.

In another comparison of unipolar and bipolar scoring of belief scales, Sparks, Hedderley, & Shepherd (1991) summarized the results of seven studies having to do with eating various foods (e.g., meat, dairy products, fried food, potato chips). Salient beliefs were elicited in pilot work or collected from the literature. Data from the seven studies permitted the investigators to conduct 13 tests that compared the correlations between belief composites and direct attitude measures for unipolar versus bipolar belief scoring. In one case (eating salt) unipolar belief scoring produced a significantly higher correlation between the belief composite and the overall attitude ($r = .73$) than did bipolar scoring ($r = .59$), and in two instances (eating fried foods and eating potato chips) there were no significant differences. A total of 10 of the 13 comparisons, however, showed an advantage for bipolar scoring, such that a significantly stronger correlation was obtained when belief strength was scored in a bipolar fashion (mean $r = .62$) as opposed to a unipolar fashion (mean $r = .50$).

Finally, Gagné and Godin (2000) summarized the results of 12 of their own studies in the health domain, dealing with such behaviors as condom use, compliance with hypertension control medication, and eating low-fat foods. Correlations between expectancy-value indices and direct attitude measures showed that for 11 of the 12 studies, bipolar scoring was superior or equal to unipolar scoring. With unipolar scoring of belief strength, correlations ranged from .02 to .53, with an average correlation of .36. When beliefs were scored in a bipolar fashion, the correlations were higher, ranging from .24 to .65, and the mean correlation was .45. In only one case (taking "universal precautions" to prevent exposure to diseases spread by blood and other body fluids) was the reverse pattern observed ($r = .33$ for unipolar scoring and $r = .24$ for bipolar scoring).

Evidence available to date, then, indicates that bipolar scoring is generally superior to unipolar scoring. However, exceptions to this rule are sometimes observed, and it therefore behooves investigators to be mindful of this issue in their own work with the expectancy-value model. It is possible that the significance of disagreement with a belief statement depends on the behavior under investigation, the nature of the belief, and the verbal labels used to identify positions and endpoints on the likelihood measure. Clearly, more research is needed to explore these issues.

Related to the question of disagreement with belief statements is whether outcomes should be presented in a positive or negative format. Instead of asking people whether they believe that performing some behavior will lead to a certain outcome, we could ask how likely it is that performance of the behavior will *not* lead to the outcome in question. For example, we could assess the strength of the belief that drinking will *not* produce nausea or that drinking will *not* make you more popular. Note that outcomes of this kind will generally not be obtained in an elicitation of readily accessible beliefs because, when asked to list what they perceive to be the outcomes of a behavior, people are unlikely to mention outcomes they do not expect to occur. Consistent with this argument, Trafimow and Finlay (2002) found that rephrasing outcomes in the negated format reduced the predictive validity of the expectancy-value formulation. Across four different behaviors (getting a tattoo, taking vitamins, dressing neatly, drinking alcoholic beverages), the median prediction of attitude from $\Sigma b_i e_i$ was .65 for beliefs framed positively and .42 for beliefs framed negatively.

Issues Related to the Expectancy-Value Model

Importance of Accessible Beliefs

Whether dealing with an individual's personal salient beliefs or with a modal salient set of beliefs that are readily accessible in a population, the expectancy-value model suggests that to understand and predict attitudes toward a behavior it is necessary to assess, with respect to each behavioral belief, the strength with which it is held and its evaluative implication for the attitude. It has sometimes been argued that some beliefs are more important determinants of attitude than are other beliefs. Consistent with this argument, it has been suggested that, in addition to obtaining measures of subjective probability and attribute or outcome evaluation, each attribute of an attitude object or perceived outcome of a behavior should also be rated for its importance (see, e.g., Hackman & Anderson, 1968; van der Pligt & de Vries, 1998a, 1998b; van der Pligt & Eiser, 1984; van Harreveld, van der Pligt, de Vries, & Andreas, 2000; Wyer, 1970).[10]

The role of importance as an additional factor in expectancy-value models has typically been examined in two ways. First, investigators have used attribute importance ratings as a third multiplicative variable; that is, they have multiplied belief strength by attribute evaluation and then multiplied this product by rated attribute importance (e.g., Hackman & Anderson, 1968; Kenski & Fishbein, 2005; Wyer, 1970a). Even though this approach is intuitively reasonable, empirical research has consistently shown that including importance ratings in this manner either has no discernible effect on the prediction of attitude or attenuates accuracy of prediction. These findings may in part be explained by the fact that outcomes judged to be important are typically evaluated more positively or negatively (i.e., their evaluations are more polarized) than are unimportant outcomes. Further, people usually have more information about issues that are important to them, and they therefore tend to be more certain and to hold stronger beliefs about important than about unimportant outcomes. As a result, probability and evaluation measures may capture enough of subjective importance to make redundant any independent assessment of belief importance.

Generally speaking, empirical evidence tends to support this view. For example, in a study of beliefs and attitudes about condom use (van Harreveld et al., 2000), participants evaluated each of 15 possible consequences of this behavior, indicated the strength of their beliefs that the behavior would lead to each of the consequences, and also rated the importance of each consequence. In a within-subject analysis across the 15 outcomes, importance ratings correlated, on average, .31 with the absolute value or polarity of the evaluations, .49 with belief polarity, and .50 with the polarity of the $b \times e$ products. These investigators reported a second study that dealt with cigarette smoking, and in this study the corresponding correlations were .29, .46, and .47. Looking at behavior in a different domain, Kenski and Fishbein (2005) assessed belief strength, outcome evaluations, and perceived importance with respect to eight possible outcomes of voting for George W. Bush and for Al Gore in the 2000 presidential elections in the United States. In this study, perceived importance did not correlate significantly with belief extremity, but it correlated quite highly ($r = .45$) with evaluation polarity. These studies thus support the idea that perceived importance may already be taken into account by belief and outcome polarity.[11]

In a series of experiments, van der Pligt and de Vries (1998a, 1998b) adopted a different approach to studying the role of belief importance. Instead of rating the perceived importance of each outcome or attribute, participants selected a small number of outcomes that they considered most important. Expectancy-value indices were computed for the subset of important beliefs thus identified, for the remaining nonselected beliefs, as well as for the total set of beliefs. For example, in a study on smoking behavior among Dutch college students (van der Pligt & de Vries, 1998a), 15 behavioral beliefs regarding the outcomes of smoking were considered. Participants rated, on nine-point scales, the likelihood that smoking produces each outcome and their evaluation of each outcome. In addition, they selected the three most important outcomes. The $\Sigma b_i e_i$ index based on the three important beliefs identified by a given participant had a correlation of .63 with a direct measure of attitude toward smoking. This compares with a correlation of .64 when the $\Sigma b_i e_i$ index was based on all 15 beliefs but to a correlation of only .15 when the index was based on the 12 beliefs that had not been selected.

The same approach was also adopted in the voting study by Kenski and Fishbein (2005) mentioned earlier. In this study, eight modal salient outcomes of voting for the two presidential candidates had been identified in a pilot study. Participants evaluated each outcome on a five-point *good–bad* scale, judged its likelihood of occurrence on a five-point *disagree–agree* scale, and rated each outcome on a four-point scale that ranged from *not important* (1) to *extremely important* (4). Expectancy-value indices were computed separately for the three to five of the eight outcomes that were given the highest importance ratings by a particular respondent and for the remainder of the outcomes (i.e., the three to five rated as least important). The variation in the number of items comprising the indices based on important and unimportant outcomes was due to ties (i.e., two or more outcomes being rated as equally important). In addition, an expectancy-value index was also computed for the total set of eight outcomes. With respect to voting for Bush, the direct attitude measure correlated .58 with the index based on the most important outcomes, .61 with the index based on all eight beliefs, and .42 with an index based on the least important outcomes. Similarly, with respect to voting for Gore, the respective correlations were .63, .66, and .41.

The results of these investigations are quite consistent, showing that an expectancy-value index based on beliefs selected as most important predicts a direct measure of attitude better than one based on nonselected (i.e., less important) beliefs. In addition, they show that prediction of attitudes based on the total set of $b \times e$ products is about as accurate as prediction based only on the beliefs rated as most important, but not more so.

In line with these findings, some scholars (e.g., Budd, 1986; van der Pligt & de Vries, 1998a; van Harreveld et al., 2000) have suggested that importance ratings contribute to the prediction of attitudes by helping to identify salient or readily accessible beliefs. As we noted earlier, salient beliefs tend to be better predictors of attitude than nonsalient beliefs. If beliefs judged as important predict attitudes better than unimportant beliefs because they are more readily accessible in memory, then we would expect that people will have lower response times for questions addressing important compared with unimportant beliefs. Support for this expectation comes from two studies conducted by van Harreveld et al. (2000). In the first study, participants were asked to select the five most important outcomes of condom use, and they judged the likelihood that each outcome will occur in a dichotomous (yes/no) as well as continuous format. The time it took participants to produce these judgments was also recorded. As expected, reaction times were significantly shorter for outcomes that had been selected as important by the participant than for the other outcomes. These results were replicated in the second study, which examined beliefs about smoking. In addition, this study showed that, as in the case of likelihood judgments, outcome evaluations were also emitted significantly faster for important than for unimportant outcomes.

This line of work, then, suggests that selection of outcomes in terms of their importance essentially serves to identify salient outcomes and it is for this reason that important beliefs are better predictors of attitude than are unimportant and relatively inaccessible beliefs. Related to this account, it is possible that outcomes selected as important are those outcomes that are associated with polarized belief strength or outcome evaluation. We noted earlier that the *rated* importance of beliefs is correlated with the polarity of belief strength and the polarity of outcome evaluation. A study by van der Pligt and de Vries (1998a) showed that this is also true for beliefs *selected* as important. In this study, expectancy-value scores based on the three beliefs about smoking selected as most important were found to be significantly more polarized in the negative direction than expectancy-value scores based on the 12 nonselected beliefs. Because polarized beliefs are known to be more salient than nonpolarized beliefs (Fishbein, 1963; Kaplan & Fishbein, 1969), this again implies that beliefs selected for their importance are likely to be more readily accessible in memory.

In sum, we have seen that weighting the expectancy-value product by perceived importance does not contribute significantly to the prediction of attitudes. On the other hand, the perceived importance of a behavior's outcomes—like the polarization of belief strength and outcome evaluation—may help to identify an individual's personal salient or readily accessible beliefs.

Multiplicative Combination Rule

In the expectancy-value model, the contribution of a behavioral belief to the overall attitude is computed by multiplying belief strength and outcome evaluation. In Chapter 2 we noted that, contrary to expectations, perceived behavioral control is rarely found to moderate the effect of intentions on behavior. Instead, intentions and perceived behavioral control tend to have additive effects, and the inclusion of the intention×control product in a multiple regression analysis usually accounts for little if any additional variance in behavior. We delayed discussion of this issue until now because the validity of a multiplicative combination rule has most frequently been questioned in the context of the expectancy-value model. Fundamentally, the issue addressed is whether the multiplicative *belief×evaluation* term adds valuable information beyond that contained in the measures of belief strength and outcome evaluation considered separately. The recommended method to examine this issue (see Bagozzi, 1984; Cohen & Cohen, 1975; Doll & Orth, 1993; Evans, 1991; Holbrook, 1977) is use of hierarchical multiple regression in which a direct measure of attitude is the dependent variable that is regressed first on belief strength (b_i) and outcome evaluation (e_i) and then on the product term (b_ie_i). It is assumed that the multiplicative combination rule in the expectancy-value model is disconfirmed if the product term fails to produce a significant increase in explained variance.

Regressing Attitudes on Individual Beliefs

Some investigators (Armitage, Conner, Loach, & Willetts, 1999; Rise, 1992; Trafimow & Finlay, 2002) have performed this analysis as follows. All of the behavioral beliefs and outcome evaluations are entered separately, followed by each of the $b \times e$ products. Thus, each belief (b) and each outcome evaluation (e) receives a separate regression weight, as does each product term. By and large it is found in these analyses that the direct attitude can be predicted from measures of belief strength and outcome evaluation considered separately and that entering the multiplicative terms into the regression equation does little to improve prediction. This finding is taken as a disconfirmation of the multiplication feature of the expectancy-value model.

For example, Armitage et al. (1999) assessed, among other things, attitudes, behavioral beliefs, and outcome evaluations with respect to using cannabis and drinking alcohol. In a pilot study the investigators had identified five salient outcomes of these behaviors, two positive (makes me more sociable, makes me feel good) and three negative (leads to me having poorer physical health, will result in my becoming dependent on it, will result in me getting into trouble with authority). Belief strength was assessed on a seven-point *unlikely* to *likely* scale (scored –3 to +3) and outcome evaluation on a seven-point *bad* (–3) to *good* (+3) scale. A four-item semantic differential scale was used to assess attitudes toward each of the two behaviors. In a hierarchical multiple regression analysis, attitudes were first regressed on the five belief strength (b) and the five outcome evaluation (e) measures, followed on the second step by the five product terms (be). The multiple correlations for the prediction of attitudes from belief strength and outcome evaluation were .77 for using cannabis and .57 for drinking alcohol. The addition of the product terms on the second step explained no more than an additional 2% of the variance, and the increases were not statistically significant. Similar results were reported by Rise (1992) and Trafimow and Finlay (2002).

A moment's reflection reveals the fallacy of this approach. The regression weights assigned by the analysis to the individual beliefs $(b's)$ take into account the beliefs' evaluative aspects: A belief linking the behavior to an outcome that most people consider to be favorable will usually receive a positive regression coefficient, whereas a belief linking the behavior to an unfavorable outcome will usually receive a negative coefficient. Consider, for example, the belief that using cannabis "makes me feel good." The hierarchical regression analysis assigns a weight to the belief strength measure in such a way as to maximize prediction of attitudes toward using cannabis. Because this particular belief links cannabis use with an outcome most people consider to be positive, the stronger the belief the more favorable the attitude will be; that is, there will be a positive correlation between degree of agreement with this item and the direct attitude measure. As a result, the regression coefficient will usually also receive a positive sign. In fact, in the Armitage et al. (1999) study, the beta coefficient for the strength of this belief was +.24 and statistically significant. Conversely, the strength of the belief that using cannabis produces a negative outcome (e.g., "will result in my becoming dependent on it") will have a negative correlation with the overall attitude and will thus usually receive a negative weight in the regression analysis. This particular belief indeed had a beta weight of −.39 ($p < .001$). In other words, the regression of attitude on belief strength takes outcome evaluations into account; it essentially multiplies belief strength by a statistically determined positive (+1) or negative (−1) evaluation. It is thus hardly surprising that, despite the theoretically expected interaction of belief strength and outcome evaluation, entering the belief by evaluation products on the next step of the analysis adds little or no predictive validity.

For regression of attitudes on belief strength to take the belief's outcome evaluation into account, the outcome of the behavior must be considered favorable or unfavorable by most respondents. Specifically, when most respondents consider an outcome to be favorable, there will be a positive correlation between belief strength and attitude, and when most participants consider an outcome to be unfavorable, there will be a negative correlation between belief strength and attitude. Although Armitage et al. (1999) did not report the means and standard deviations of the outcome evaluations in their study, inspection of the outcomes leaves little doubt that this was the case. For example, most people will assign favorable evaluations to being more sociable and unfavorable evaluations to getting in trouble with authority. As we saw already, under these conditions, when attitude is regressed on belief strength, the regression analysis assigns a positive beta weight to beliefs with favorable outcomes and a negative weight to beliefs with negative outcomes.

For other kinds of behavior, however, most people agree that an outcome is likely or that it is unlikely (i.e., there is little variance in belief strength), but they differ in their evaluations of the outcome. For instance, respondents generally agree that using oral contraceptives will prevent pregnancy even as they vary greatly in their evaluations of this outcome. Other things being equal, given the belief that oral contraceptives prevent pregnancy, the more favorably a person evaluates preventing pregnancy, the more positive will be the person's attitude toward using oral contraceptives. Thus, when attitudes are regressed on outcome evaluations under these conditions, the regression analysis assigns a positive sign to the outcome evaluation.

The situation is a bit more complicated when there is general disagreement with a belief statement. As we saw earlier, such disagreement can reflect two different reactions. First, disagreement may imply that, according to the respondent, performing the behavior will *prevent* occurrence of the outcome or that it will produce the opposite outcome. Second, it may simply mean that, because the outcome in question is considered highly unlikely, it is irrelevant to the attitude. For example, suppose most women disagree that using oral contraceptives increases sexual pleasure. If this implies a belief that using oral contraceptives reduces sexual pleasure, then the more positively the women value increasing sexual pleasure, the less favorable will be their attitudes toward using oral contraceptives. In the regression analysis, therefore, this outcome evaluation will receive a negative regression weight. However, if the disagreement simply implies a belief that sexual pleasure is unaffected by the use of oral contraceptives, then there will be no correlation between evaluations of this outcome and attitudes toward the behavior. In either case, the regression weight in a multiple regression analysis will take the proper implication of the disbelief into account, and the multiplication of outcome evaluation with belief strength on the next step of the analysis will add little to the prediction of attitude.

These considerations imply that so long as there is some agreement in the perceived likelihood of an outcome or in its valence, the regression analysis weights belief strength by taking the consensual outcome evaluation into account, or it weights outcome evaluations by taking consensual belief strength into account. As a result, computing the product of belief strength times outcome evaluation adds little unique variance in the prediction equation. Only when, with respect to each belief or at least most beliefs, there is wide variation in both belief strength and outcome evaluation can we expect the $b \times e$ product to make an appreciable difference over and above the main effects of the two component measures (see McClelland & Judd, 1993; Yzer, 2007).

We obtained support for these ideas by simulating a data set for 100 cases, each of which contained 12 randomly generated measures of belief strength and outcome evaluations as well as an attitude score based on the summed expectancy-value products plus a random error component (Ajzen & Fishbein, 2008). The belief strength and outcome evaluations took on values that covered either the full range of possible scores (–3 to +3 on a seven-point scale) or only a restricted range (+1 to +3). A hierarchical regression analysis revealed the expected pattern of results. Only when belief and evaluation scores covered the full range of the seven-point scale did the addition of the 12 belief $\times$ evaluation products make a strong and significant contribution to the prediction of attitude (over and above the prediction afforded by the separate belief and evaluation scores). When either the belief strength scores or the outcome evaluation scores covered only one side of the scale, attitudes could be well predicted from the variable that covered the full range, and adding the belief × evaluation products to the regression equation did little to improve prediction.

Regressing Attitudes on Belief Composites

Some investigators (Doll & Orth, 1993; Gagné & Godin, 2000; Sutton, McVey, & Glanz, 1999) use correlational or hierarchical regression analyses in a different way to test the multiplicative combination rule in the expectancy-value model. Rather than entering individual beliefs, evaluations, and products into the hierarchical regression analysis, these investigators enter the sum of the beliefs (Σb_i) and the sum of the evaluations (Σe_i), followed by the summed expectancy-value term ($\Sigma b_i e_i$). The assumption is again made that if the expectancy-value term does not improve prediction of attitude, the multiplicative combination rule is disconfirmed.

Two sets of investigators using this method (Gagné & Godin, 2000; Sutton, McVey, & Glanz, 1999) reached the conclusion that addition of the expectancy-value term failed to account for additional variance in attitudes, over and above the predictive validity afforded by the summed belief strength scores and the summed evaluation scores. It is important to realize, however, that prior to summing the measures of belief strength across all outcomes, the investigators reversed the scoring of negative beliefs. That is, in computing the summed measure of belief strength, they took each belief's evaluative implication for the attitude into account. In effect, they multiplied belief strength by outcome evaluation (+1 or –1) and then summed the resulting products.[12] It is thus again hardly surprising that entering the expectancy-value term at a subsequent step in the analysis provides little additional information. Consistent with this argument, in a study in which the scoring of negative beliefs was not reversed and the original measures of belief strength were summed (Doll & Orth, 1993), hierarchical regression analysis revealed strong effects of the multiplicative expectancy-value term.

In conclusion, investigators have challenged the assumption of a multiplicative combination rule for the effects of belief strength and outcome evaluation on overall attitude. On strictly theoretical grounds, there is no logic in predicting attitude from belief strength without taking the evaluative implication of the belief into account or in predicting attitude from outcome evaluation without knowing whether the outcome is considered likely or unlikely. Consider, for example, a person who believes that voting for a given political candidate will increase the likelihood that conservative judges will be appointed. Without knowing whether the person considers this consequence to be desirable or undesirable, we cannot predict the person's attitude toward voting for the candidate. Similarly, knowing that a person places positive value on the appointment of conservative judges tells us little about that person's attitude toward voting for a particular political candidate unless we also know whether the person believes it to be likely or unlikely that voting for the candidate will result in this outcome. In fact, we saw that when investigators compute a summation of different beliefs, they usually take the evaluative implication of each belief into account, thus implicitly acknowledging the importance of the multiplication rule. We thus conclude that the multiplication of belief strength and outcome evaluation, which is at the core of the expectancy-value model, is a reasonable and well-supported assumption.

Attitudinal Ambivalence

In our discussion of the attitude construct we have up to this point focused primarily on the degree of favorableness or unfavorableness of a person's reaction to an object or behavior. It is also possible, however, to consider aspects of attitude other than its valence. One of the most widely studied aspects of attitude is the concept of attitude strength (see Krosnick, Boninger, Chuang, Berent, & Carnot, 1993). In early attitude research, and in our own writing, attitude strength was identified with evaluative polarity such that extremely positive or extremely negative attitudes were considered to be strong attitudes. Contemporary usage of the term has shifted to include, in addition to attitudinal extremity, such aspects as confidence in one's attitude, involvement with the attitude object, its centrality or importance, attitudinal ambivalence, the attitude's accessibility in memory, and its temporal stability (see Krosnick et al., 1993; Krosnick & Petty, 1995; Raden, 1985). Because most research on attitude strength has dealt with attitudes toward objects rather than toward behaviors, we consider this research in Chapter 8. However, a consideration of one aspect of attitude strength, namely, attitudinal ambivalence, is relevant for the current chapter on behavioral attitudes and their determinants.

Generally speaking, ambivalence refers to the coexistence of positive and negative reactions to an attitude object. Operationalizations of this construct have, for the most part, followed Kaplan's (1972) lead. Individuals are asked to review their positive and negative thoughts about an attitude object and to rate how positively they feel toward the object and, on separate scales, how negatively they feel toward it. Different formulas have been used to compute an index of ambivalence (see Priester & Petty, 1996; Riketta, 2000; Thompson, Zanna, & Griffin,

1995, for reviews), but they tend to produce very similar results; scores based on the different methods correlate highly with each other (in the range of .70 to .90) and also significantly with subjective judgments of ambivalence provided by the participants (in the range of .40 to .50). The most popular method of computation in contemporary use was developed by Griffin (see Thompson, Zanna, & Griffin, 1995). In this model, ambivalence is estimated by adding the positive (P) and the negative (N) ratings of the object, dividing the sum by 2, and subtracting the absolute value of the difference between P and N. This computation is shown in Equation 3.2:

$$(P + N) / 2 - |P - N| \tag{3.2}$$

It is possible to assess attitudinal ambivalence in a fairly direct manner by asking people how positively and how negatively they feel about an object or by asking them to rate their own sense of ambivalence. All of the measures in current use, however, provide relatively little information about the reasons for conflicted valence. In the context of our expectancy-value model, information about the origins of ambivalence is provided by the salient beliefs that serve as the attitude's determinants. In other words, it is possible to examine an individual's personal salient beliefs, or responses to a modal salient set of beliefs, for evaluative inconsistency or ambivalence. Specifically, we could compute for each outcome the product of belief strength times outcome evaluation and then separately compute the sum of the products that have positive values (P) and the absolute sum of products that have negative values (N). Using Equation 3.2, these measures of positive and negative valence can be used to compute an index of ambivalence. Examination of the salient beliefs that enter into the positive and negative scores provides substantive information about the specific considerations that are in conflict with each other and hence offers a better understanding of the origins or basis for observed ambivalence. Consistent with this logic, in his original study of attitudinal ambivalence Kaplan (1972) did in fact examine the underlying belief structure and found that the number of positive beliefs correlated significantly with a direct measure of overall positive valence and the number of negative beliefs with overall negative valence (both correlations were .44).

   An interesting case in point noted earlier is the possibility that, with respect to certain behaviors, instrumental and experiential beliefs may be in conflict with each other. As indicated previously, this is a common experience with respect to health-related behaviors. Many people realize the health benefits of performing such behaviors as using condoms, going to the dentist, and getting a mammogram or colonoscopy (positive instrumental beliefs) but at the same time believe that performing these behaviors would be painful, embarrassing, or otherwise unpleasant (negative experiential beliefs).

The degree to which an attitude is ambivalent is assumed to have important implications for its function and predictive validity. Specifically, compared with nonambivalent attitudes, ambivalent attitudes are said to be more likely to change over time, to be less resistant to persuasive appeals, to be less likely to bias processing of attitude-relevant information, and to be less likely to influence or guide behavior (see Armitage & Conner, 2000). We take up some of these issues in our discussion of attitude strength in Chapter 8.

Illustration of the Expectancy-Value Approach to Attitude

According to the expectancy-value model, by examining the set of salient beliefs about a behavior we gain insight into the determinants of the attitude toward the behavior in question. Consider, for example, a study concerned with understanding attitudes toward hunting among hunters, wildlife viewers, and other outdoor recreationists (Daigle, Hrubes, & Ajzen, 2002; Hrubes, Ajzen, & Daigle, 2001). Based on prior studies that included belief elicitations, the investigators identified a set of 12 salient beliefs about this behavior. Examination of the list of outcomes displayed in the first column of Table 3.3 shows that in this population, people who are asked to think about the advantages and disadvantages of hunting mention that this behavior can lead to familiarity with nature and a sense of competence, to viewing scenery and enjoying nature, to observing and learning about wildlife, and to developing or maintaining significant relationships with family and friends. Additional outcomes have to do with the perception that hunting is relaxing and relieves stress and that it affords solitude and time to think. In contrast to these generally positive outcomes of hunting, members of this population also mention a few negative outcomes, including feeling tired and exhausted, getting wet or cold, and seeing wounded or dead animals.

In the expectancy-value model it is assumed that these readily accessible favorable and unfavorable outcomes represent the modal salient beliefs that underlie attitudes toward hunting in this population. If this assumption is valid, the least we would expect is that an expectancy-value estimate of attitude based on these beliefs ($\Sigma b_i e_i$) will correlate with a direct measure of the same attitude. To compute the expectancy-value index we have to obtain measures of belief strength and evaluation with respect to each of the outcomes. In the hunting study, belief strength was assessed on a seven-point *extremely unlikely* (–3) to *extremely likely* (+3) scale[13] and

TABLE 3.3 Hunting Beliefs: Belief Strength, Outcome Evaluation, Belief-Evaluation Product, and Correlations of Belief-Evaluation Product With Direct Attitude Measure ($N = 329$)

Behavioral belief	Belief strength (b_i)		Outcome evaluation (e_i)		$b_i e_i$		Correlation $b_i e_i$ with attitude
	M	SD	M	SD	M	SD	
Viewing scenery and enjoying nature	1.15	(2.35)	2.68	(0.77)	2.95	(6.68)	.61
Observing and learning about wildlife	1.49	(2.13)	2.36	(1.07)	3.89	(5.82)	.50
Feeling tired and exhausted	0.01	(2.08)	-0.01	(1.92)	-0.42	(5.13)	.11*
Creating or maintaining significant relationships with family or friends	0.62	(2.25)	2.67	(0.79)	3.16	(6.59)	.63
Relaxing and relieving stress	0.79	(2.31)	2.69	(0.72)	3.04	(6.67)	.64
Getting exercise and staying in shape	0.88	(2.18)	2.61	(0.77)	2.84	(6.52)	.62
Feeling a sense of competence	0.77	(2.15)	2.45	(0.89)	2.69	(6.38)	.61
Experiencing solitude, time to think	1.26	(2.16)	2.55	(0.85)v	2.91	(6.51)	.63
Getting dirty, wet, or cold	1.28	(1.97)	-0.02	(1.68)	-0.23	(4.39)	.03*
Feeling a sense of belonging and familiarity with nature	0.96	(2.23)	2.45	(0.96)	2.92	(6.46)	.63
Experiencing excitement	1.40	(2.22)	2.40	(0.95)	3.00	(6.30)	.68
Seeing wounded or dead animals	1.39	(2.10)	-1.35	(1.78)	-0.22	(5.78)	.26

Note. Belief strength and outcome evaluation can range from -3 to 3.

*Not significant; all other correlations significant at $p < .01$.

outcome evaluations on a seven-point *extremely undesirable* (–3) to *extremely desirable* (+3) scale. Two seven-point evaluative scales (*good–bad, pleasant–unpleasant*) were averaged to obtain a direct measure of attitude toward hunting. The summed product of the belief and evaluation scores was found to have a correlation of .76 with the direct attitude measure.

Having demonstrated a strong relation between the salient beliefs composite and the direct attitude measure we can now examine the individual beliefs in greater detail. In Columns 1 and 2 of Table 3.3 we can see the means and, in parentheses, the standard deviations of the belief strength measures and, in Columns 3 and 4, the means and standard deviations of the outcome evaluations. Note first that there is considerably more variance in belief strength than in outcome evaluations. Participants generally agreed in their evaluations of the outcomes, most of which were considered to be quite positive. Interestingly, feeling tired and exhausted and getting dirty, wet, or cold—outcomes that one would assume to be negative—received on average a neutral evaluation. Note, however, that the relatively high standard deviations indicate that participants differed in their evaluations of these outcomes. In fact, the highest standard deviations were associated with the three relatively negative outcomes.

We should not expect this pattern of findings to obtain with respect to every kind of behavior. In other behavioral domains, we sometimes find a great deal of variance in outcome evaluations but little variance in belief strength, and sometimes both elements of the expectancy-value composite contain considerable variance. For example, with respect to voting for a given candidate in an election, we often find that people agree on the candidate's policy positions, but they have very different evaluations of those positions. Thus, in a study of the 2000 presidential election in the United States (Kenski & Fishbein, 2005), voters generally agreed that Bush was in favor of making it harder for a woman to get an abortion but varied considerably in their evaluations of this policy position.

Another interesting aspect of the data displayed in Table 3.3 has to do with the belief strength measures. As we noted earlier, when people list their salient beliefs about a behavior they generally mention the outcomes they believe follow from performance of the behavior, not outcomes that they do not associate with the behavior. Because we are interested in the beliefs held by a large proportion of the population we select the most frequently mentioned beliefs for the modal set. This implies that most people should agree with the beliefs included in the model set of salient belies. This expectation is borne out by the data in Table 3.3 where it can be seen that, for each belief, the mean belief strength was on the positive side of the –3 to + 3 scale. Inspection of these values shows that the most strongly held beliefs in this population associated hunting with observing and learning about wildlife, seeing wounded or dead animals, and experiencing excitement. The outcome evaluations in Column 3 show that two of these three outcomes were considered quite positive and one quite negative, although there was much more variation with respect to evaluation of the negative outcome. Most participants agreed that observing and learning about wildlife and experiencing excitement were desirable outcomes, but not everybody thought that seeing wounded or dead animals was necessarily undesirable.

One way to determine the impact of the salient beliefs on the overall attitude is to examine the mean $b \times e$ products in Column 5 of Table 3.3. There it can be seen that most beliefs made a positive contribution to attitudes toward hunting. The four beliefs with the strongest positive impact on attitudes all linked hunting to positively valued outcomes: observing and learning about wildlife, creating or maintaining significant relations with friends and family, experiencing excitement, and relaxing and relieving stress. Interestingly, the beliefs linking hunting to negative or neutral outcomes (i.e., seeing wounded or dead animals; getting dirty, wet, or cold; and feeling tired and exhausted) made the smallest contributions to the attitude toward hunting. It should again be pointed out that this finding is not necessarily generalizable to other behaviors. For example, in research concerning the determinants of attitudes toward consistent condom use, beliefs linking condom use to such negative outcomes as reduced sexual pleasure, a lack of trust, and reduced intimacy usually make large contributions to the overall attitude toward condom use (see, e.g., Kasprzyk & Montaño, 2007; von Haeften & Kenski, 2001).

To return to the hunting example, it is also important to note that, despite the fact that most beliefs contributed to a positive attitude toward hunting, this set of beliefs suggests that, on average, people essentially held neutral attitudes toward hunting. That is, the mean expectancy-value summation across all participants, which could range from –108 to +108, was only 25.20. Consistent with this, the mean direct attitude score also indicated that, on average, attitudes toward hunting in this population were neutral (Mean = –0.035 on a scale ranging from –3 to +3). Once again, however, the standard deviations of both the belief composite and the direct attitude measure were quite large, indicating that, within this population, there was considerable variation in attitudes toward hunting. Thus, it is instructive to consider how much of this variation can be explained by particular beliefs and their evaluative aspects.

The last column in Table 3.3 presents the correlations between each of the $b \times e$ products and the direct measure of attitude toward hunting. It can be seen that each of the beliefs linking hunting to positive outcomes helped to explain variation in attitude (r ranged from .50 to .68). That is, in each case, the stronger people's beliefs that hunting leads to these positive outcomes, the more favorable their attitude. In marked contrast, although two of the three $b \times e$ products for negative outcomes were significantly related to attitudes toward hunting, they each accounted for very little variation (r ranged from .03 to .26).[14]

Our discussion suggests that a given belief's contribution to the overall attitude, and its ability to account for variation in the attitude, can be discerned by examining the value of the $b \times e$ product and its correlation with the overall attitude. It has sometimes been proposed (e.g., Cooper, Burgoon, & Roter, 2001) that a better way of identifying the relative contributions of different beliefs is to regress the overall attitude on all belief-by-evaluation products and to use the regression coefficients as estimates of each belief's importance as a determinant of attitude. It should be realized, however, that the regression coefficients in such an analysis represent the *unique* variance in attitudes explained by each of the beliefs. When two beliefs are highly correlated with each other, only one will receive a high regression weight, and the other would thus be regarded as unimportant. From a psychological perspective, this conclusion will often be invalid.

To illustrate this point, we performed a regression analysis on the data in the hunting study. Such an analysis assigns regression coefficients to the $b \times e$ products in a way that assures the best possible prediction of the overall attitude. In the hunting data, the multiple correlation was found to be .72, which is only slightly higher than the .69 correlation between the sum of the products ($\Sigma b_i e_i$) and the direct measure of attitude toward hunting. In other words, at least in this particular data set, little was gained by treating each $b \times e$ product as an independent predictor of attitude.

Table 3.4 shows the standardized regression coefficients for each of the 12 $b \times e$ products. It can be seen that only one of the positive beliefs—the belief that hunting leads to excitement—carried a significant regression weight. The $b \times e$ product for this outcome had the highest zero-order correlation with the direct attitude ($r = .68$; Table 3.3), and it also correlated highly with the $b \times e$ products for the other positive outcomes. As a result, none of the other positive $b \times e$ products had a significant regression coefficient. It would be unreasonable to conclude, however, that the other beliefs were irrelevant or that considering the other beliefs did not add important information to our understanding of the attitude. For example, although the belief that hunting leads to excitement had a correlation of .92 with the belief that hunting helps to create or maintain significant relationships with family and friends, these two beliefs are substantively very different. Disregarding the second belief because it did not have a significant regression coefficient would be a mistake. It is for this reason that we examine the zero-order correlations between the $b \times e$ products and the overall attitude rather than the regression coefficients.

Note also that in the regression analysis, seeing wounded or dead animals and feeling tired and exhausted had significant regression coefficients and would thus be considered important determinants of attitude toward hunting. This contrasts with the conclusions we derived by considering the

TABLE 3.4 Hunting Beliefs and Attitudes: Standardized Regression Coefficients for Prediction of Attitude From Belief x Evaluation Products ($N = 329$)

Behavioral belief	Regression coefficient
Viewing scenery and enjoying nature	.06
Observing and learning about wildlife	.00
Feeling tired and exhausted	−.13*
Creating or maintaining significant relationships with family or friends	.09
Relaxing and relieving stress	.06
Getting exercise and staying in shape	−.11
Feeling a sense of competence	−.14
Experiencing solitude, time to think	.15
Getting dirty, wet, or cold	−.04
Feeling a sense of belonging and familiarity with nature	.03
Experiencing excitement	.68*
Seeing wounded or dead animals	.22*

*Significant at $p < .01$.

mean $b \times e$ products and the correlations of these products with the overall attitude. We saw that neither of these beliefs made much of a contribution to the attitude, nor did they account for much variance in the attitude scores. We thus strongly discourage use of regression analysis to identify important salient beliefs or to explain the determinants of an attitude.

☐ Summary and Conclusions

Consistent with most contemporary views, we defined attitude as a latent disposition to respond with some degree of favorableness or unfavorableness to a psychological object. An attitude's essential characteristic, therefore, is its bipolar evaluative dimension. In the context of our reasoned action approach, the evaluation of interest is the attitude toward personally performing a particular behavior. We discussed the logic of Thurstone and Likert scaling, two well-known belief-based methods of attitude measurement, but we noted that most research conducted in the context of our theory relies on the semantic differential to obtain a relatively direct measure of attitude toward a behavior. Research has shown that although the bipolar evaluative adjective scales comprising the semantic differential measure of attitude can be divided into experiential and instrumental categories, at a higher level of abstraction these two categories nevertheless comprise a single evaluative factor. In addition, some investigators have viewed experiential evaluative responses as the affective component of attitude, but we have argued that the term *affect* should be used to refer to a separate response system with a somatic component characterized by some degree of arousal. While attitudes are always directed toward some object, affect includes generalized mood states without a well-defined object of reference (sadness vs. happiness) as well as qualitatively different emotions (e.g., anger, fear, pride) with clear evaluative implications.

Our approach to the formation of attitudes relies on the expectancy-value model, which assumes that attitudes are formed spontaneously and inevitably as we form beliefs about an object. In the case of a behavior, these beliefs are mainly concerned with the behavior's likely consequences. The salient beliefs that are assumed to determine attitudes toward a behavior can be elicited in a free-response format, and a set of modal salient beliefs can be constructed by identifying the beliefs most frequently emitted by a random sample from the research population. According to the model, each belief links the behavior to an outcome, and the outcome's positive or negative valence contributes to the attitude in direct proportion to the perceived probability that the behavior will produce the outcome in question (i.e., the strength of the belief). The belief strength × evaluation products are summed across all salient outcomes to produce an overall expectancy-value index. We reviewed evidence showing that such an expectancy-value index correlates well with a direct attitude measure. We noted that the measure of belief strength can be scored in either a bipolar or unipolar fashion. Although in the past we have recommended bipolar scoring, and although in general bipolar scoring leads to better prediction of attitude than does unipolar scoring, we now recognize that, particularly when respondents disagree that a behavior will lead to a negative outcome, care must be taken to ensure that bipolar scaling is appropriate.

We also noted that several investigators have challenged the basic logic of multiplying belief strength by outcome evaluation, and we demonstrated that this challenge was without merit. We showed that what has often been taken as empirical support for these challenges is largely based on inappropriate methodology (i.e., hierarchical regression). When properly studied, there is strong support for multiplying belief strengths by outcome evaluations. In addition, we also showed that although expectancy-value indices based on salient beliefs or beliefs that respondents rate as important lead to better predictions of attitude than expectancy value indices based on nonsalient or unimportant beliefs, little is to be gained by adding a measure of importance to the expectancy-value formulation.

☐ Notes

1. We shall see herein that this procedure is used to meet the criterion of internal consistency in Likert's (1932) attitude scaling method.
2. Although essential to the construction of a valid Thurstone scale, the criterion of irrelevance has rarely been applied. To apply it, a preliminary attitude score can be computed on the basis of the items that have met the criterion of ambiguity. More recently, the development of item response theory (see Hambleton, Swaminathan, & Roger, 1991; Reise, Ainsworth, & Haviland, 2005) has provided more sophisticated ways of testing the operating characteristics or tracelines of attitudinal items.
3. Earlier we suggested that this criterion can also be used to select adjective pairs for inclusion on an evaluative semantic differential.
4. Note that the term *Likert scale* refers to a multi-item attitude scale derived by means of the summated ratings procedure developed by Likert. No single item constitutes a Likert scale or a Likert-type scale. Furthermore, the response format for items on a Likert scale can take various forms. It can contain fewer or more than five response alternatives, and labels other than *strongly agree–strongly disagree* can be used.
5. The concept of accessibility implies only that people can easily become aware of accessible beliefs, not that they are aware of them at all times.
6. It is possible to find in the literature two views of the ways accessible beliefs function to determine attitudes (see Fabrigar, MacDonald, & Wegener, 2005). According to one view, as new attitudes are formed they are stored in memory, and the stored evaluation is automatically activated or retrieved when a person is confronted with the attitude object. The second view assumes that attitudes are temporary constructions derived from accessible information about the attitude object every time it is needed (e.g., Schwarz, 2000). There is little empirical evidence to prefer one interpretation over the other, and the practical implications of accepting one view rather than the other are not readily apparent.
7. It should be recalled that nonsalient beliefs can serve as indicators of attitude, and we would therefore expect that a measure based on such beliefs will correlate with a direct attitude measure. In fact, standard attitude scaling methods, such as Thurstone and Likert scaling, rely on largely nonsalient beliefs. However, we saw that for such beliefs to be good indicators of attitude, they must be carefully selected to be relevant for the attitude in question. In the Petkova, Ajzen, and Driver (1995) study, the nonsalient beliefs were not so selected, which may explain why they did not predict the direct attitude as well as did the salient beliefs which, on theoretical grounds, are assumed to be relevant for the attitude.

8. It is also consistent with balance theory (Heider, 1958) where, in a triadic configuration, two positive links or two negative links imply that the third link should be positive for balance to be obtained. Similarly, one positive and one negative link imply a negative third link (see Fishbein & Ajzen, 1975). Thus, for example, if P does not believe that O has a positive attribute, balance is obtained if P dislikes O. Similarly, if P does not believe that O has a negative attribute, balance results if P likes O.

9. More sophisticated "optimal scaling" procedures are available to decide how to best score belief scales (see Ajzen, 1991; Holbrook, 1977; Schmidt, 1973).

10. Some investigators (e.g., Sheth & Talarzyk, 1972) have measured outcome importance in place of outcome evaluation. This is clearly inappropriate because outcomes rated as important can be valued positively as well as negatively.

11. In at least one investigation (van der Pligt & de Vries, 1998a) relatively low correlations were observed. This investigation again dealt with cigarette smoking and included a set of 15 beliefs concerning the consequences of this behavior. Apparently, participants were not asked to rate the importance of each outcome but merely to select the three most important outcomes. This is therefore a binary measure, that is, a given outcome either was or was not selected as important. Given that many outcomes were selected by only a small proportion of participants, correlations of this measure with any other variable will tend to be low. Indeed, the investigators reported that across outcomes, importance correlated on average .14 with evaluative polarity and .21 with belief polarity. However, given the problematic nature of the importance measure, these modest correlations cannot be taken as evidence for the independent influence of belief importance on attitudes.

12. Note that this is exactly the procedure employed in Likert scaling, which also involves a multiplication of belief strength and attribute or outcome evaluation (see Fishbein & Ajzen, 1975; Green, 1954).

13. The actual scale used in the study was an 11-point scale, but for purposes of comparison with the outcome evaluation measure, we recoded it into a 7-point scale.

14. It is also possible to examine the correlation between belief strength and attitude and between outcome evaluation and attitude. Because outcome evaluations in this particular study were almost uniformly positive, belief strength correlated well with the direct attitude measure for most beliefs whereas outcome evaluation did not.

4

Perceived Norms and Their Determinants

There is general agreement that the social environment can exert strong influence on people's intentions and actions. This influence is captured most frequently in the concept of *social norm*, a central construct in the theorizing of sociologists and other social scientists. Generally speaking, social norms refer to what is acceptable or permissible behavior in a group or society. Divergent theoretical perspectives emphasize different aspects of the normative construct. Rational choice theorists (see Boudon, 2003) assume that human behavior is usually guided by self-interest and view social norms as placing limits on such behavior. From this perspective, the major function of norms is to ensure that behavior serves not only the interests of the individual but also of the larger social system. It is thus rational for people to conform to social norms because violations are punished. In the symbolic interactionist tradition (Blumer, 1969; Goffman, 1958) people are thought to look for meaning in their social interactions. Norms provide meaning by structuring the situation and offering guidelines regarding appropriate or inappropriate behavior. Finally, a third perspective, sometimes referred to as social behaviorism, defines norms entirely in terms of behavioral regularities (see Karlson, 1992). In this view, people are guided by the patterns of behavior common in their social environments. In sum, norms have been conceptualized as strict rules, as general guidelines, or simply as empirical regularities.

☐ Perceived Social Pressure

In our reasoned action framework, norms are more narrowly defined and are focused on the performance of a particular behavior. That is, we view norms as perceived social pressure to perform (or not to perform) a given behavior. This perceived norm—together with attitude toward the behavior and perceived behavioral control—determines the intention to perform the behavior in question. Other things equal, the stronger the perceived social pressure, the more likely it is that an intention to perform the behavior will be formed.

Compliance With Perceived Social Pressure

It is instructive to consider why perceived social pressure may influence intentions and behavior. One way to approach this issue is in terms of the five bases of social power identified by French and Raven (1959). Based on their analysis it may be suggested that others can exert influence on our behavior because they possess one or more types of power:

1. *Reward power*: We may comply with perceived social pressure because the social agent exerting the pressure is thought to have the power to reward desired behavior.
2. *Coercive power*: Conversely, the social agent may be able to mete out punishment for noncompliance.
3. *Legitimate power*: Compliance with perceived social pressure may be based on the belief that the social agent has the right to prescribe behavior due to his or her role or position in a particular group, network, or society at large.
4. *Expert power*: We may comply with perceived social pressure because of the social agent's knowledge, expertise, skills, or abilities.
5. *Referent power*: Compliance with perceived social pressure may derive from a sense of identification with the social agent; that is, people may comply because they want to be like the agent.

There is an assumption inherent in much theorizing that social norms have no influence on behavior unless they are accompanied by sanctions (see, e.g., Bandura, 1997). In French and Raven's (1959) analysis, however, only reward and coercive power involve sanctions to encourage compliance or prevent noncompliance. The other three bases of power produce compliance without using rewards for normative behavior or punishment for violations of social norms. Our reasoned action approach is in agreement with the French and Raven analysis in that we too assume that perceived social pressure can influence behavior even when no rewards or punishments are anticipated.

Injunctive Versus Descriptive Norms

In our initial formulation of the reasoned action approach, we introduced the concept of *subjective norm*, defined as an individual's perception that most people who are important to her think she should (or should not) perform a particular behavior. In both the theories of reasoned action and planned behavior (Ajzen, 1991; Ajzen & Fishbein, 1980; Fishbein & Ajzen, 1975), the term *subjective norm* referred to a specific behavioral prescription or proscription attributed to a generalized social agent. It was a person's perception that important others prescribe, desire, or expect the performance or nonperformance of a specific behavior. We used the term *subjective* norm because this perception may or may not reflect what most important others actually think should be done.

It has become clear, however, that normative prescriptions represent only one source of perceived normative pressure. In addition to believing that particular individuals or groups do or do not want us to perform a given behavior, we may also experience normative pressure because we believe that important others are themselves performing or not performing the behavior in question. The common request to "Do as I say, not as I do" reflects the recognition that both types of normative pressure can influence behavior. These two types of norms have been termed *injunctive* and *descriptive* (see Cialdini, Reno, & Kallgren, 1990). Injunctive norms refer to perceptions concerning what should or ought to be done with respect to performing a given behavior, whereas descriptive norms refer to perceptions that others are or are not performing the behavior in question. In contrast to our original use of the term subjective norm, which referred only to injunctive norms, the normative component in the Integrative Model (Fishbein, 2000) and in our current theoretical framework captures the total social pressure experienced with respect to a given behavior. It is assumed that this perception incorporates and integrates both the desires and the actions of important referent individuals and groups.

Interestingly, all five of French and Raven's (1959) bases of power are relevant for explaining the influence of injunctive norms, whereas only expert and referent power appear to provide bases for the operation of descriptive norms. People may be motivated to behave in accordance with what they believe others think they should do (injunctive norms) because the social agent has the power to reward or punish them, because the agent has the right to request it, because the agent is an expert, or because they want to be like the agent. The operation of reward, coercive, and legitimate power all imply that the social agent expects a particular kind of behavior; that is, it implies an injunctive norm. Expert and referent power can also serve as a basis for compliance with descriptive norms. That is, people may model their behavior on those of others because they view these others as experts or because they want to be like them. Descriptive norms are less likely to derive their influence from reward, coercive, or legitimate power because the observation that others do or do not perform a behavior does not necessarily imply that these others have the power to reward or punish us or that they can legitimately expect us to behave as they do.

The work of Cialdini (2001; Kallgren, Reno, & Cialdini, 2000; Reno, Cialdini, & Kallgren, 1993) suggests further that descriptive norms can influence behavior by providing evidence as to what will likely be effective and adaptive action. If most others are performing a given behavior, people may well assume that it is a sensible thing to do under the circumstances. Of course, this would be especially true if these others are experts with respect to the behavior in question. By simply registering what most others are doing in a particular situation and by imitating their actions one can usually choose efficiently and well. Cialdini argued that imitating the actions of others offers an information-processing advantage and a decision-making shortcut when choosing how to behave in a given situation.

Cialdini's (2001) view implies that in addition to the direct effect of descriptive norms on intentions described earlier, descriptive norms can also have indirect effects. We often have information about the behavior of others that goes beyond simply registering what they are doing. First, we may note that their behavior is rewarded or punished by others, and this information can influence attitudes toward the behavior as well as lead to the inference that the behavior is prescribed or proscribed (injunctive norm). Second, we may learn that the behavior leads to other positive or negative outcomes, again affecting attitudes, and third, we may learn that certain resources are required and certain barriers have to be overcome to perform the behavior. The latter would influence perceptions of behavioral control. In other words, descriptive norms can affect intentions directly or indirectly by influencing attitudes, injunctive norms, and perceived behavioral control.

In this chapter we first discuss the concept of injunctive norm as defined and applied in the theories of reasoned action and planned behavior. After examining how these norms are measured, we consider the role of injunctive normative beliefs as determinants of injunctive norms and address conceptual and methodological issues related to these determinants. Motivation to comply with the perceived prescriptions of important social referents has proven to be a particularly problematic construct, and we reconsider its role in our conceptual framework. We then turn to a discussion of how the concept of descriptive norm can be incorporated in our theory as part of perceived social pressure to engage in a behavior. We will see that the addition of descriptive norms may help to explain why subjective norms typically make only a relatively small independent contribution to the prediction of intentions and actions. To avoid confusion, we use the term *injunctive norms* when dealing only with perceptions of what others think we should do and the term *descriptive norms* when referring to the perceived behavior of others. We use the terms *perceived norm* or *perceived social pressure* to refer to the overall normative influence derived from perceived injunctive and descriptive norms.

Injunctive Norms

Like other constructs in our model of behavioral prediction, injunctive norms are focused on a given action. To predict intention and behavior, the measure of injunctive norm, like the measure of attitude, has to correspond to, or be compatible with, the measures of intention and behavior in terms of the action, target, context, and time elements. For example, if we were interested in measuring a woman's injunctive norm with respect to getting a mammogram in the next 2 weeks, we could ask a question such as the following:
Most people who are important to me think

I should |___|___|___|___|___|___|___| I should not

get a mammogram in the next 2 weeks.
Alternatively (or in addition) we could ask questions such as the following:
Most people who are important to me want me to get a mammogram in the next 2 weeks.

Agree |___|___|___|___|___|___|___| Disagree

Most people whose opinions I value think that it is

Appropriate |___|___|___|___|___|___|___| Inappropriate

for me to get a mammogram in the next 2 weeks.
Most people whom I respect and admire would

support |___|___|___|___|___|___|___| oppose

my getting a mammogram in the next 2 weeks.[1]
   Clearly, like other latent constructs, there are many possible indicators of an injunctive norm. Note that each of the previous examples focuses on the prescriptions of a generalized social agent (e.g., most people who are important to me, people whose opinions I value). That is, they are beliefs about what a generalized normative referent views as appropriate (or inappropriate) behavior and about what that generalized referent thinks

should or ought to be done. It is important to recognize that although measures of injunctive norms are obtained at an individual level (i.e., they are measures of an individual's perceptions of important others' prescriptions), the injunctive norm often concerns a behavioral rule or prescription that applies equally to all members of a population or to a subset of the population who are in a particular role, position, or social environment. Indeed, for many behaviors, injunctive norms will be the same for different individuals so long as these individuals occupy the same role or social position. For example, there is general agreement that people should wash their hands after going to the bathroom, but this norm is often violated. And in a college setting, students know that they are expected to attend their classes regularly, but many students don't. Thus, for at least some behaviors, although there may be considerable variance in intentions and behavior, injunctive norms may have very little, if any, variance. Under these circumstances, it is clear that the injunctive norm will not be correlated with the behavior, but it is not clear that the norm is having no impact on the behavior. It is possible that the injunctive norm has about the same impact on the behavior of every individual, but it cannot account for observed *differences* among individuals in their intentions or behaviors. In other words, the norm may be affecting the behavioral mean but not its variance. This discussion raises the more general question about reliance on covariation between predictor and criterion to infer the predictor's importance as a determinant of intentions or behavior. We return to this issue in Chapter 6.

Determinants of Injunctive Norms

Normative Beliefs

In our theory, just as attitudes are assumed to be based on a set of salient behavioral beliefs, injunctive norms are said to derive from a set of salient injunctive normative beliefs. These injunctive normative beliefs are beliefs that a particular referent individual or group thinks I should or should not perform the behavior in question. Injunctive normative beliefs are thus similar to injunctive norms, except that they involve specific referent individuals or groups rather than a generalized social agent. Our reasoned action approach suggests that, in forming an injunctive norm, the normative prescriptions of various individuals and groups are taken into account. Clearly, not every possible referent will be relevant or important for a given behavior. Similar to attitude formation, it is assumed that only salient or readily accessible referents influence the person's injunctive norm. As in the case of behavioral beliefs, we can elicit a person's salient normative referents in a free-response format. For example, with respect to getting a mammogram in the next 2 weeks, respondents could be asked to list referents in response to the following:

> If you considered getting a mammogram in the next 2 weeks, there might be individuals or groups who would think you should or should not perform this behavior. If any such individuals or groups come to mind when you think about getting a mammogram in the next two weeks, please list them below.

Alternatively, respondents could be asked to answer a series of questions such as the following:

1. Please list all people or groups who would approve of your getting, or who would encourage you to get, a mammogram in the next 2 weeks.
2. Please list all people or groups who would disapprove of your getting, or who would discourage you from getting, a mammogram in the next 2 weeks.
3. Please list any other people or groups you might want to talk to if you were trying to decide whether or not to have a mammogram in the next 2 weeks.

In formulating these open-ended elicitation questions, it is again essential to ensure compatibility in behavioral elements. That is, the behavior defined in the injunctive norm should be exactly replicated in eliciting salient referents. For example, if the injunctive norm is concerned with whether important others think I should wear jeans at work, then relevant referents should be elicited with respect to my wearing jeans at work and not with respect to my wearing jeans in general or my wearing jeans at home. Clearly, different referents may be salient when a given action is considered in different contexts. Similarly, variations in the action, target, or time elements of a behavior may also change the salience or accessibility of referent individuals or groups.

Suppose we are trying to understand the injunctive norm of a woman who is contemplating having a child in the next 12 months. Table 4.1 shows a hypothetical set of referents listed by the woman in response to normative elicitation questions. It can be seen that the woman listed six referents: her husband, priest, mother, best female friend, sister, and doctor. Given this information, we can now measure the woman's injunctive normative beliefs about each referent by using the same scale format previously used to measure the injunctive norm. For example, the woman's injunctive normative belief about the prescriptions of her husband could be measured as follows:

My husband thinks that

  I should |___|___|___|___|___|___|___| I should not

have a child in the next 12 months.

TABLE 4.1 Hypothetical Example of a Woman's Injunctive Normative Beliefs About Having a Child in the Next 12 Months

Normative referent	Belief strength (b)	Motivation to comply (m)	b × m
Husband	−3	+3	−9
Priest	+2	+1	+2
Mother	+3	+1	+3
Best female friend	−2	+2	−4
Sister	+1	0	0
Doctor	0	+3	0
$N_I \propto \Sigma n_i m_i$			−8

Responses to this scale could be scored from +3 (*I should*) to −3 (*I should not*). Column 1 of Table 4.1 shows the woman's hypothetical normative beliefs for her six salient referents. As can be seen, she believes her husband and best female friend feel strongly that she should not have a child in the next 12 months, whereas her mother and priest feel strongly that she should. The remaining two referents are seen as relatively neutral in regard to this behavior.

It is important to recognize that normative beliefs are quite different from behavioral beliefs or outcome expectancies. A statement such as, "My having a child in the next 12 months would please my mother" does not represent a normative belief. Instead, it is a behavioral belief (or outcome expectancy) because it associates performing the behavior with a certain outcome (pleasing my mother) and is thus expected to influence the woman's attitude toward having a child in the next 12 months. Although behavioral beliefs that focus on social outcomes may also have an indirect influence on the corresponding normative belief, this need not be the case. This distinction between normative beliefs and what Bandura (1997) has called social outcome expectancies (i.e., behavioral beliefs) may appear somewhat arbitrary, yet there are many cases where a person holds one type of belief but not the other. For example, I may believe that buying my wife flowers will please her without believing that she thinks I should buy her flowers. In fact, one reason that buying flowers may please my wife is that this behavior was neither expected nor prescribed. Conversely, I may believe that my wife thinks I should tell the truth without believing that "my telling the truth will please my wife."

Of course, there are also instances where believing that others think one should perform a behavior will be accompanied by the belief that performing the behavior will please those others. For example, a woman may believe that her husband feels very strongly that she should not abort an unwanted pregnancy. As a result, she may also form the belief that he would be pleased if she did not, in fact, have an abortion.

Motivation to Comply

According to our original reasoned action framework, knowing peoples' beliefs about the prescriptions of their salient referents was not sufficient to predict or understand their injunctive norms. Although people may believe that a particular individual or group thinks they should (or should not) perform a given behavior, they may not care what that referent prescribes. We assumed that knowing what a referent prescribes may put little or no pressure on a person to carry out that behavior unless that person is motivated to comply with the referent in question. Thus, we argued that it was also necessary to assess motivation to comply with each salient referent. Specifically, according to the original formulation of our reasoned action approach, an injunctive norm is based on the total set of salient injunctive normative beliefs, each weighted by motivation to comply with the referent. This is shown in Equation 4.1, where N_I is the injunctive norm, n_i is the injunctive normative belief about referent i, m_i is the motivation to comply with referent i, and the sum is over the total number of salient referents:

$$N_I \propto \Sigma n_i m_i \qquad (4.1)$$

This model implies that there is no necessary relation between any single normative belief (weighted or unweighted) and the injunctive norm. In fact, as can be seen in Table 4.1, although only two of the six normative beliefs are negative, the overall injunctive norm is predicted to be negative. By the same token, if a given normative belief were to change, this does not mean that a change in the injunctive norm would have to follow. As in the case of attitudes, a normative belief concerning the prescription of one salient referent could be replaced by another concerning the prescription of a different referent, but the strength of the two normative beliefs (and motivations to comply) might be the same. Similarly, a change in one salient normative belief could be canceled by an opposite change in another salient normative belief. It should also be evident that two people with the same set of relevant referents may have different injunctive norms and that people with very different sets of relevant referents may have the same injunctive norm.

Regarding the measurement of motivation to comply with a given referent, we recommended assessing the construct at the level of the referent in general rather than with respect to the referent's prescription concerning the particular behavior of interest. To return to our example of the woman

who is contemplating having a child in the next 12 months, motivation to comply with each of her salient referents could be assessed as follows:
In general,

I want to do |___|___|___|___|___|___|___| I don't want to do

what my doctor thinks I should do.
Another possible format would be the following:
In general, I want to do what my doctor thinks I should do.

strongly agree |___|___|___|___|___|___|___| strongly disagree

We recommended staying at the general level of motivation to comply with a particular referent because once we have assessed a person's normative belief and behavioral intention, a behavior-specific measure of motivation to comply becomes redundant, adding no unique information. Consider a woman who has a strong intention to have a child in the next 12 months. If she believes that her husband supports her and thinks she should have a child, we can be sure that, if asked, she would indicate a strong motivation to comply with her husband when it comes to having a child in the next 12 months. Similarly, if she thought that her husband was opposed to her having a child, she would indicate that she is not motivated to comply with her husband *with respect to this particular behavior*. No new information is gained by asking the behavior-specific motivation to comply question. It is mainly for this reason that we recommended measuring motivation to comply at the general level. In addition, we also felt that a measure of general motivation to comply would provide information about a referent's overall power to influence a broad range of behaviors. However, because a given referent's power base is likely to vary from domain to domain, it may be preferable to assess domain-specific motivation to comply. For example, physicians have expertise in the health domain but not necessarily in such domains as entertainment or cooking. We might thus be motivated to comply with physicians only when it comes to our health, and asking about general motivation to comply might underestimate their influence on our behavior in the health domain. A measure of motivation to comply might therefore better be formulated as follows:
When it comes to family planning,

I want to do |___|___|___|___|___|___|___| I don't want to do

what my doctor thinks I should do.
In Column 2 of Table 4.1 it can be seen that our hypothetical woman shows considerable variation in her motivations to comply with her various referents in the domain of family planning. While she is strongly motivated to comply with her husband and her doctor, she is not at all motivated to comply with her sister. According to our theory, injunctive

norms can be predicted from the index we obtain if we multiply normative belief strength by the corresponding motivations to comply and then sum the products. We assumed that by taking motivation to comply into account, we would ensure that important referents are given proportionately more weight in the prediction of the injunctive norm. Because people have little or no motivation to comply with an unimportant referent, the weighted sum of normative beliefs should correspond to the belief concerning the prescriptions of most important others (i.e., the injunctive norm).

Note that whereas normative beliefs are measured on bipolar scales, motivation to comply is measured on a unipolar scale. It should be clear that when people say that they don't want to do what a certain referent prescribes, this does not mean that they necessarily want to do the opposite. For example, if my coworker thinks that I should not drink alcohol and if, in the health domain, I am not motivated to do what my coworker thinks I should do, this does not mean that I will feel social pressure to drink. It just means that the coworker's proscription does not weigh very heavily as a determinant of my injunctive norm with respect to my drinking.[2]

These computations are illustrated in Column 3 of Table 4.1. It can be seen that the woman's injunctive norm is predicted to be somewhat negative (–8). That is, we would predict that she would have a relatively weak injunctive norm to the effect that most of her important others think she should not have a child in the next 12 months.

Modal Normative Beliefs

Our discussion thus far has dealt only with predicting a person's injunctive norm from the personal injunctive normative beliefs and motivations to comply that are based on the referents the person listed in response to open-ended elicitation questions. As in the case of behavioral beliefs, it will often be useful to construct a standard set of *modal* salient normative beliefs. This can be done by asking a representative sample of the population under study to list the people or groups who would approve or disapprove of their performing the behavior in question. To obtain a list of salient referents, we select the most frequently mentioned individuals or groups. In the final standard questionnaire we assess normative beliefs and motivation to comply with respect to each of these modal salient referents.

Table 4.2 shows the salient normative referents of adolescents aged 14 to 16 with respect to engaging in sexual intercourse in the next 12 months (Fishbein, Bleakley, Hennessy & Jordan, in preparation). It can be seen in Column 1 that the most frequently mentioned referents relevant to this behavior were the adolescents' family and friends, including their romantic partners if they had one. The mean normative belief strength with

TABLE 4.2 Normative Beliefs and Their Correlations With Injunctive Norms (N_I) Regarding Sexual Intercourse

Salient referents	Strength of normative belief (n)		Motivation to comply (m)		$n \times m$		Correlation	
	M	(SD)	M	(SD)	M	(SD)	$n \times m$ with N_I	n with N_I
Mother	−2.27	(1.34)	4.37	(1.65)	−9.98	(7.58)	.38	.38
Father	−2.00	(1.63)	4.07	(1.87)	−8.25	(8.22)	.32	.40
Friends	−0.06	(2.01)	4.16	(1.73)	−0.02	(9.27)	.43	.44
Best friend	−0.33	(2.09)	4.87	(1.75)	−2.64	(10.90)	.43	.47
Partner	0.54	(2.03)	4.46	(1.83)	3.71	(9.98)	.20	.23
Grandmother	−1.94	(1.49)	4.27	(1.94)	−8.43	(8.25)	.28	.29
Brother	−1.19	(1.96)	3.64	(1.92)	−4.21	(8.43)	.31	.40
Sister	−1.42	(1.65)	3.79	(1.96)	−5.52	(7.94)	.40	.45

Note. Strength of normative belief scored −3 to +3; motivation to comply 1 to 7.
Source: Fishbein, Bleakley, Hennessy & Jordan, in preparation (with permission).

respect to each referent is shown in Column 1, where it can be seen that, on average, participants believed that their social referents were opposed to their engaging in sexual intercourse. The only exception is the romantic partner who, perhaps not surprisingly, was perceived to be somewhat in favor of their having sex.

Columns 3 and 4 of the table present the means and standard deviations of motivation to comply with each normative referent, measured on a unipolar scale scored from 1 to 7. It is evident that, on average, participants were most strongly motivated to comply with their best friends and romantic partners and least with their brothers and sisters. The perceived social pressure exerted by the different referents is indicated by the product of normative belief (n_i) times motivation to comply (m_i). In Column 5 it can be seen that, with the exception of the respondent's romantic partner, all normative referents exerted normative pressure not to engage in sexual intercourse.

To determine the influence of each normative referent on the injunctive norm, the $n \times m$ product for each referent was correlated with a direct measure of this norm. These correlations are displayed in Column 7 of Table 4.2. All correlations were statistically significant, ranging from .20 for romantic partner to .43 for best friend and other friends. Furthermore, consistent with the model shown in Equation 4.1, the direct measure of injunctive norm had a significant correlation of .48 with the sum of the $n \times m$ products.

Issues Related to Normative Beliefs and Motivation to Comply

When a modal salient set of referents is identified for a population, one or more of the referents included in the set may not be relevant for a given respondent. For example, for most behaviors, one or more of the following are almost always among the most frequently listed referents: husband, wife, spouse, brother, and sister. However, not every respondent will have a spouse or a sibling. Thus, in assessing normative beliefs (and motivations to comply) with a standardized questionnaire, it is important to provide the respondent with a "not applicable" alternative. Different respondents may therefore have different numbers of salient referents, and we must decide whether to add or to average the $n \times m$ products in arriving at the belief composite. The model shown in Equation 4.1 suggests a summation over the products. This implies that a person who experiences social pressure from, say, six normative referents will, with all else being equal, hold a stronger injunctive norm than a person who experiences social pressure from only two or three referents. In retrospect, a closer look at the way the injunctive norm was defined and measured indicates that computing the mean of the $n \times m$ products may actually be more appropriate. That is, if injunctive norms are defined as what most of my important others think I should do, then it does not matter how many important others are involved. Irrespective of the number of referents considered, if most of these referents are perceived to exert pressure to perform or not perform a behavior, participants would be expected to reply in the same way to the direct measure of injunctive norm. For this to be reflected in the belief-based measure, the mean of the belief × motivation products should be computed rather than the sum of these products. Clearly, however, this issue is important primarily when many participants in a study lack one or more of the salient referents. In most cases, the results obtained by summing or averaging the $n \times m$ products will make little difference. Thus, for example, in the sexual intercourse study discussed earlier (Fishbein et al., in preparation), we saw that the index based on the sum of the products correlated .48 with the direct measure of the injunctive norm. When the products were averaged, the correlation was .50.

The Role of Motivation to Comply

While there is considerable empirical evidence to support the hypothesis that injunctive norms can be predicted from a consideration of the person's salient injunctive normative beliefs, the evidence concerning the role of motivation to comply is far less compelling. Indeed, research has shown that multiplying injunctive normative beliefs by motivation to comply usually adds little or nothing to the prediction of injunctive norms (e.g., Budd, North, & Spencer, 1984; Montaño, Thompson, Taylor, & Mahloch, 1997; Sayeed et al., 2005). For example, in a study concerned with women's intentions to get a mammogram (Montaño et al., 1997), normative beliefs and motivations to comply were assessed with respect to doctor, family, friends, people in the news, and others in the medical community. In addition, a single item was used to assess injunctive norms directly. The correlation between the sum of the normative beliefs and the injunctive norm was .67, compared to a correlation of .61 when the norms were weighted by motivations to comply. Similar results were obtained in a study of seat belt use among college students (Budd et al., 1984). Normative beliefs regarding five social referents either were or were not multiplied by motivation to comply with these referents. A direct measure of injunctive norm with respect to wearing a seat belt on long journeys correlated .78 with the belief-based measure when motivation to comply was taken into account and .81 when it was omitted.

This pattern of findings is also apparent in the data on sexual intercourse presented in Table 4.2. In the last column of the table it can be seen that without taking motivation to comply into account, the correlations between normative beliefs and injunctive norm ranged from .23 for romantic partner to .47 for best friend. These correlations are just as high or even slightly higher than the correlations obtained when normative beliefs were weighted by motivation to comply (Column 7 in Table 4.2). Similarly, we reported above a correlation of .50 between the direct measure of injunctive norm and the mean of the normative belief x motivation to comply products. Without motivation to comply (i.e., when the normative beliefs were averaged without weighting them by motivation to comply), the comparable correlation was .53.

In sum, there is considerable evidence that injunctive normative beliefs provide the cognitive foundation for injunctive norms. In contrast, based on the kinds of findings just reviewed we must conclude that, despite the construct's intuitive appeal, motivation to comply appears to contribute little to the prediction of injunctive norms. One possible explanation is that salient normative referents represent important individuals and groups with respect to the behavior of interest and that most people are, at least to some extent, motivated to comply with these important others. Obtaining an independent measure of this motivation may therefore provide little unique information, although it can add error variance and thus even reduce correlations with a direct measure of injunctive norm. Future efforts should perhaps be directed at finding other ways of measuring motivation to comply or at finding new ways of weighting normative beliefs to improve the prediction of injunctive norms and thereby help to increase our understanding of the underlying determinants.

Descriptive Norms

As noted previously, our earlier work focused exclusively on injunctive norms, but it has become increasingly clear that this is not the only type of normative influence on an individual's behavior. As was recognized in the integrative model, a second major source of perceived social pressure is descriptive norms, that is, norms based on perceptions of what other people are doing. The interest in descriptive norms is not new. It is very common for investigators to ask their respondents how many of their friends, peers, or classmates perform such behaviors as smoking cigarettes, using drugs, drinking alcohol, and using condoms. Most of this research is done with young people and is concerned with risky behaviors of this kind (see, e.g., Hawkins & Catalano, 1992; Sayeed et al., 2005). This is done under the assumption that peer pressure is an important determinant of behavior. Although measures of the frequency with which a behavior is performed by a particular peer group can be of interest in their own right, they may not be appropriate measures of descriptive norms in the context of our reasoned action framework. For one, measures that focus on a specific peer group may fail to capture the influence of other normative referents, and they do not provide a direct measure of the overall descriptive norm.

Second, we are often interested in predicting behavior within a given time frame. The perceived frequency with which peers perform the behavior often lacks compatibility in that it does not specify a particular time element. In the following section we consider how we might assess descriptive norms in the context of our reasoned action framework.

Measuring Descriptive Norms

Only a relatively small number of studies to date have assessed descriptive norms in the context of our model of behavioral prediction and questions remain concerning the proper operationalization of this construct. We will address two major issues: identification of an appropriate generalized social agent and the question of compatibility, particularly compatibility in terms of the time element.

Earlier we saw that injunctive norms can be assessed by asking respondents to indicate whether a generalized social agent such as their important others think they should or should not perform a behavior of interest. In an analogous fashion, we can try to think of a generalized social agent whose behavior serves as the basis for the descriptive norm. Thus, we might develop items such as the following:

1. Most people who are important to me

   do |___|___|___|___|___|___|___| do not

   perform behavior X.

2. How many of the people whom you respect and admire perform behavior X?

   Very few |___|___|___|___|___|___|___|Virtually all

Note, however, that unlike injunctive norms where important others or people you respect and admire are appropriate generalized agents for all behaviors, it may not be appropriate for all of one's important or respected others to perform (or not to perform) a particular behavior. For example, consider a woman's intention to get a pelvic examination in the next 2 weeks. It should be obvious that although male referents will often be included among a woman's important or respected others, this behavior is irrelevant for men. Thus, at least for some behaviors, asking whether most important or respected others perform the behavior may underestimate the normative pressure exerted by the descriptive norm.

To remedy this situation we could develop alternative indicators of descriptive norms that define the generalized agent in other ways. Thus, respondents could be asked to respond to items such as the following:

1. Most people like me perform behavior X

   Always |____|____|____|____|____|____|____| Never

2. How many people similar to you perform behavior X?

   Virtually none |____|____|____|____|____|____|____| Almost all

It is up to the investigator to formulate items that specify a generalized social agent appropriate for the behavior of interest. Of course, as in the case of injunctive norms, the indicators used to assess descriptive norms have to be validated in pilot work.

Compatibility

In our way of thinking about descriptive norms, we assume that a person's own behavior is influenced by the perceived behavior of others, be it their past behavior, their current behavior, or their anticipated future behavior. Depending on the nature of the behavior under investigation, people may rely on one or more of these sources of information in forming their descriptive norms. In our discussions of our reasoned action approach, we have repeatedly stressed the importance of maintaining strict compatibility between measures in terms of target, action, context, and time elements. When it comes to descriptive norms, however, this requirement is problematic. Consider a study designed to predict whether people will get tested for HIV in the next 30 days. We can assess injunctive norms (as well as attitudes, perceptions of control, and intentions) that exhibit perfect correspondence with this behavioral criterion. For example, to assess injunctive norms, we can ask our respondents whether most of their important others think they should or should not get tested for HIV in the next 30 days. To obtain a measure of descriptive norm that is compatible with the behavior we could ask whether most people like the respondent *will* be tested for HIV in the next 30 days. However, many people like the respondent may have been recently tested for HIV and would therefore not be expected to be tested again in the next 30 days, suggesting, incorrectly, that the respondent experiences little or no social pressure to perform this behavior. On the other hand, if we decided to ask whether most people like the respondent have been tested for HIV in the past 30 days, we may again underestimate perceived social pressure if many have been tested more than 30 days ago or if the respondent expects that they will get the test in the next 30 days. To avoid these problems, one possible approach would be to formulate the question as follows:

How many of the people you respect and admire have gotten an HIV test in the past or will get an HIV test in the next 30 days?

Virtually none |___|___|___|___|___|___|___| Almost all

For other kinds of behavior, however, different questions may be more appropriate. Suppose we are trying to predict whether people will smoke marijuana in the next 30 days. We could again ask how many of their important others have smoked marijuana in the past or will do so in the next 30 days. However, it is possible that important others have performed this behavior in the distant past but no longer do so. In this case, we may want to limit the time frame for past behavior also to 30 days. Still other behaviors lie in the future and it would make no sense to ask about past behavior at all. If we want to predict whether people will go to see a particular newly released movie in the next 2 weeks, we could simply ask them how many people who are important to them or who are like them will see the movie in the next 2 weeks. In short, it is again up to the investigator to formulate items appropriate to the behavior of interest and to validate their measure in the formative stages of the research.

Descriptive Normative Beliefs

Analogous to our theorizing regarding the determinants of injunctive norms, we assume that the perceived behaviors of particular individuals or groups serve as the cognitive foundation for descriptive norms. Consider, for example, students' regular class attendance. To elicit salient descriptive referents regarding this behavior, we might pose a question such as the following:

> Sometimes, when we are not sure what to do, we look to see what others are doing. When it comes to attending your classes on a regular basis, list the individuals or groups whose behavior you might look to for guidance.

As in the case of injunctive normative beliefs, we can either consider a participant's personal descriptive referents or we can construct a modal set of salient referents by selecting the individuals and groups listed most frequently by a representative sample of respondents. Imagine that the referents emitted in the elicitation were best friend, other friends, classmates, and students at the college in general. With respect to each of these referents, we can then assess descriptive normative beliefs, using one or more of the following formats:

1. My best friend regularly attends classes.

   Agree |___|___|___|___|___|___|___| Disagree

2. How many of your classmates regularly attend their classes?

____ None
____ Very few
____ Some
____ Most
____ Almost all
____ All

3. What percentage of students at your college regularly attend their classes?

Please enter a number between 0% and 100%.

_____ %

To summarize briefly, it should be possible to assess descriptive norms directly by means of different indicators dealing with the perceived behavior of a generalized social agent such as important, esteemed, or similar referents. In addition, it should also be possible to elicit salient referents and then to assess descriptive normative beliefs with respect to these referents. These normative beliefs can then be summed (or averaged) to derive a descriptive normative belief composite, which would be expected to correlate with the direct measure of the descriptive norm. Preliminary evidence in support of this expectation comes from the study of sexual intercourse among adolescent boys and girls referred to previously (Fishbein et al., in preparation). In this study, a direct measure of descriptive norm was obtained as follows: Most people like me

have not had |____|____|____|____|____|____|____| have had sexual intercourse.

In addition, participants were asked to indicate how many of their male friends, female friends, males their age, and females their age have ever had sexual intercourse. These ratings were obtained on a five-point scale labeled *none, a few, about half, most,* and *all.* The sum of these descriptive normative beliefs was found to have a significant correlation of .53 with the direct measure of the descriptive norm.

Identifying With Normative Referents

Just as we originally assumed that injunctive normative beliefs should be weighted by motivation to comply with a given referent, so too it may perhaps be suggested that descriptive normative beliefs be given weights to take into account the possibility that the perceived behavior of some referents has a greater influence on the formation of a descriptive norm than does the behavior of other referents. This might be done by assessing a person's identification with the different referent individuals or groups, multiplying the measures of descriptive normative beliefs regarding given referents by the corresponding identity measures, and then summing the normative belief by identity products. To the best of our knowledge no empirical research to date has performed this test. However, our earlier discussion regarding the role of motivation to comply suggests that such an attempt to weight descriptive normative beliefs by a measure of identification with the referent may do little to improve prediction of the overall descriptive norm.

Indirect support for this expectation can be found in studies that have used measures of group identity as moderators of the relation between descriptive normative beliefs and behavioral intentions or actual behavior. For example, Rimal and Real (2003) attempted to predict self-reported alcohol consumption among college students from descriptive normative beliefs regarding their fellow students and the interaction between these beliefs and identification with this referent. Group identity was assessed by asking participants how much they aspired to be like most students and how similar they thought they were to this reference group. Neither of these measures was found to have a significant moderating effect on the relation between the descriptive norm and drinking behavior. In a subsequent study on alcohol consumption (Rimal & Real, 2005), significant moderating effects were obtained, but their contributions to the prediction of behavior were minimal. The interaction between descriptive norm and desire to be like the referent (i.e., aspiration) increased explained variance in intentions by 0.6%, and for similarity the increase was 0.5%. These effects were found to be significant mainly because of the large sample size ($N = 1,352$). Similarly disappointing findings were reported in studies dealing with intentions to use contraceptives among Ethiopian adolescents (Fekadu & Kraft, 2002) and with practicing yoga among college students in the United States (Rimal, Lapinski, Cook, & Real, 2005).[3]

Correlations Between Injunctive and Descriptive Norms

Thus far, we have separately considered injunctive and descriptive norms. From a reasoned action perspective, however, we are interested in the higher-order construct of social norm or perceived social pressure. It should be recognized that descriptive and injunctive norms can coexist and can either be congruent with each other or be contradictory. For example, parents who are smokers often tell their children that they should not smoke. A number of studies in recent years have assessed both types of norms and have reported the correlations between them (McMillan & Conner, 2003; Rivis & Sheeran, 2003; Smith-McLallen & Fishbein, 2008, 2009).

To illustrate, consider a study among college students concerning their use of LSD, amphetamines, cannabis, and ecstasy (McMillan & Conner, 2003). Injunctive and descriptive normative beliefs were assessed with respect to partners, best friends, other friends, family, and health experts. For example, the following item was used to measure injunctive normative beliefs regarding use of each of the four drugs in relation to the participant's best friend: "My best friend thinks I should not or should use this drug." Responses were provided on a seven-point scale ranging from −3 (*should not*) to +3 (*should*). In addition, motivation to comply with each of the referents was assessed. A sample item is, "With regards to using this drug, I want to do what my best friend thinks I should." The motivation to comply items were rated on a seven-point scale ranging from 1 (*strongly disagree*) to 7 (*strongly agree*). The belief strength and motivation to comply measures were multiplied, and the mean of the products was computed across referents to provide an overall index of injunctive normative beliefs.

Descriptive normative beliefs were assessed with respect to the same referent individuals and groups. With respect to best friend and partner, the participants were asked to respond to the following item: "Please indicate, by ticking the box beside each drug, which drugs your partner uses." The item was scored either 0 (*does not use this drug*) or 1 (*uses this drug*). A different item was used to assess descriptive normative beliefs regarding other friends, family, and health experts: "Please indicate, by ticking the appropriate box, how many (if any) of the people in your family use each drug." Responses were scored on a six-point scale ranging from 1 (*none*) to 6 (*all*). The scores on each item were standardized and then averaged to yield an overall index of descriptive normative beliefs.

The reported correlations between the injunctive and descriptive normative belief indices were .47 for use of LSD, .53 for use of ecstasy, .54 for use of amphetamines, and .65 for use of marijuana. A correlation of similar magnitude ($r = .42$) between a direct measure of injunctive norm and a descriptive normative belief index was reported by Povey, Conner, Sparks, James, and Shepherd (2000) in relation to healthy eating.

In a study dealing with cancer patients' information-seeking behaviors, Smith-McLallen, Fishbein & Hornik (under review) used direct items to assess perceived injunctive and descriptive norms. Respondents were asked to indicate their degree of agreement with the following two items: "Most people who are important to me think I should actively seek information about issues related to my cancer from a source other than [my] doctor in the next 12 months" (injunctive norm) and "Most people like me (e.g., other cancer patients) actively seek information about issues related to their cancer from a source other than their doctors" (descriptive norm). The correlation between these two measures was .53.

Another study by Smith-McLallen and Fishbein (2008) also obtained direct measures of descriptive as well as injunctive norms. This study was concerned with three cancer screening behaviors (getting a colonoscopy, getting a mammogram, testing for prostate-specific antigen [PSA] in the blood) and three lifestyle behaviors (eating fruits and vegetables, exercising, dieting to lose weight). All six injunctive norms were assessed with respect to "people most important to you," and the same generalized agent served as the referent for the descriptive norms concerning the three lifestyle behaviors. Because this particular generalized referent was not appropriate for the screening behaviors, the generalized agent for these behaviors was, "people most similar to you." The correlations between injunctive and descriptive norms ranged from .46 to .54 for the screening behaviors and from .25 to .46 for the lifestyle behaviors. These findings suggest that it is not unreasonable to combine measures of injunctive and descriptive norms to arrive at a single measure of perceived norm or perceived normative pressure. Consistent with this argument, in the Fishbein et al. (in preparation) study of adolescent sexual behavior, three items were used to directly assess the social norm: Most people who are important to me think I should have sex in the next 12 months; Most people like me have had sex; and most people like me will have sex in the next 12 months. For these three normative items, coefficient alpha = .75. In Chapter 6, we address the question of whether, compared with separate measures of injunctive and descriptive norms, the use of a single normative pressure measure increases or decreases the predictive power of our model of behavioral prediction.

At this point in time, however, it is worth considering whether a direct measure of perceived social norms can be predicted from an index of underlying normative beliefs. Recall that, in the study by Fishbein et al. (in preparation), the injunctive norm was predicted from an index of injunctive normative beliefs with ($r = .48$) or without ($r = .50$) weighting by motivation to comply, and the descriptive norm was predicted from an index of descriptive normative beliefs ($r = .52$). A critical question is whether the measure of social norm can be predicted from a single index comprised of both descriptive and injunctive normative beliefs. Consistent with predictions based on our reasoned action framework, the correlation of the combined normative belief index with the direct measure of normative pressure was .65.

These findings suggest that just as instrumental and experiential evaluations reflect different aspects of attitude, injunctive and descriptive norms may reflect different aspects of perceived social pressure. At the same time, the significant correlations between injunctive and descriptive norms suggest that it is possible to obtain an overall index of perceived social pressure by combining measures of injunctive and descriptive norms. In other words, a hierarchical model can describe the nature of perceived social pressure, where injunctive and descriptive norms are first-order factors and the overall perceived social norm is the higher second-order construct (see Hagger & Chatzisarantis, 2005). Thus, just as we saw in Chapter 3 that good measures of attitude toward a behavior will usually contain both instrumental and experiential items, good measures of perceived social pressure will usually contain items assessing descriptive as well as injunctive norms. It is therefore important to include measures of both injunctive and descriptive norms in the pilot phase of research with our theory.

☐ Discussion and Conclusions

In this chapter we examined the role of perceived social norms in the context of our reasoned action approach. We drew a distinction between perceived injunctive norms that reflect what important others think we should do and perceived descriptive norms that reflect what we believe others have done, are doing, or are likely to do. Whereas standard validated procedures are available to measure injunctive norms associated with a generalized social agent as well as injunctive normative beliefs associated with specific referents, questions remain about how to best assess descriptive norms and descriptive normative beliefs. The identification of a generalized social agent for the assessment of descriptive norms, as well as issues of compatibility in time elements between a measure of descriptive norm and the behavior under investigation were seen to be particularly problematic. We showed that the nature of the behavior will usually determine what kinds of items can be used to assess the overall descriptive norm directly and to asses the descriptive normative beliefs associated with different social referents. The increasing number of studies that include measures of descriptive norms will provide information that will allow us to validate alternative measurement approaches.

According to the initial formulation of our reasoned action approach, we assumed that people's behavior was likely to be affected by normative beliefs to the extent that they are motivated to comply with the social referent. Thus, in the case of injunctive normative beliefs, we recommended assessing motivation to comply with the referent. In a similar fashion, it seems reasonable to assume that the influence of descriptive normative beliefs may depend on the person's identification with the social referent. Although intuitively reasonable, empirical evidence to date has provided little support for the importance of motivation to comply or of group identification.

Although many questions still remain about how to best integrate descriptive norms into our model of behavioral prediction, at this point in time we would recommend a measure of social norms that incorporates both injunctive and descriptive norms. Moreover, we would recommend identifying a salient set of descriptive and injunctive normative beliefs that can be combined to arrive at an index of normative beliefs that determines the social norm. Support for this position is presented in Chapter 6, when we consider the predictive validity of our model for the prediction of behavior.

As a final note we would like to make it clear that in this chapter we have focused on social norms and normative beliefs as defined within our reasoned action framework. Some investigators have been interested in other kinds of normative constructs, such as moral norms and partner norms. We consider these constructs as well other possible additions to the theory in Chapter 9.

☐ Notes

1. Some investigators have also assessed motivation to comply with the generalized agent (e.g., my most important others). In our earlier writings we assumed that people would be motivated to comply with their important others, and we argued that it was therefore unnecessary to measure motivation to comply with a generalized social agent. Consistent with this assumption, measures of motivation to comply with important others have been found to contribute little to the prediction or understanding of intentions and behavior (Budd, 1986; Sayeed, Fishbein, Hornik, Cappella, & Ahern, 2005). Thus, unless it can be shown that for a given behavior there is a reasonable amount of variation in motivation to comply with important others, we would continue to argue that it is not necessary to measure motivation to comply at this level.

2. As in the case of behavioral beliefs and outcome evaluations, it is possible to use an empirical criterion to decide how to score normative belief and motivation to comply measures. In our experience, bipolar scoring of normative belief and unipolar scoring of motivation to comply tend to produce the best correlation with a direct measure of the overall injunctive norm.

3. In a study on binge drinking among Australian college students, Johnston and White (2003) reported a significant moderating effect of identification with friends and peers at the university on the relation between normative beliefs regarding this referent and behavioral intentions. The interaction accounted for an additional 3% of the variance. However, the measure of normative beliefs in this study contained items that assessed injunctive as well as descriptive norms.

Perceived Behavioral Control and Its Determinants

There is general agreement that individual differences in perceived control play an important role in human functioning (see Baltes & Baltes, 1986; Fiske & Taylor, 1991; Lefcourt, 1981, 1983; Rodin, 1986; Strickland, 1989; Thompson & Spacapan, 1991). Indeed, as a possible explanation of behavior, the construct of control rivals the attitude construct in popularity. Unfortunately, the terms used to identify and define control constructs vary greatly across investigators. Rodin (1990) observed that "the construct has been called by many different things, including, besides control, self-directedness, choice, decision freedom, agency, mastery, autonomy, self-efficacy, and self-determination" (p. 1). Thompson and Spacapan (1991) reached a similar conclusion: "Perceptions of control, locus of control, self-efficacy, helplessness, powerlessness, judgments of contingency, control ideology—there is no shortage of terms that fall under the rubric of 'control'" (p. 7). In a review of the literature, Skinner (1996) identified no fewer than 100 control-related constructs and definitions. Some of these constructs include the term *control*, as in personal control, sense of control, locus of control, outcome control, and action control. Others such as *efficacy, agency, mastery, effectance,* and *autonomy* do not explicitly refer to control but address similar or identical issues.

It is not our goal to bring order to this profusion of conceptualizations.[1] Suffice it to say that the various concepts tend to describe perceived control as a general sense of personal competence or perceived ability to influence events (e.g., Burger, 1989; Rodin, 1990). In many of these conceptions, perceived control is akin to a personality disposition that does not vary as a function of the behavior under consideration: High perceived control represents a fundamental expectation that internal factors, such as competence, willpower, and determination, are responsible for behaviors,

153

outcomes, and events in a person's life. It is assumed that people vary in the extent to which they adhere to this expectation and that increased perceived control is associated with improved health and well-being, as well as greater success in life (Skinner, 1996). Extending this line of reasoning, Rotter (1966) proposed that people may attribute outcomes in their lives to external as well as internal factors. This distinction drew attention to individual differences in perceived *locus of control*, that is, the extent to which people view events in their lives as controlled by external factors (e.g., luck, other people, circumstances) as opposed to internal factors (e.g., skills and abilities, motivation). Like the general sense of personal competence or perceived control, perceived locus of control was assumed to hold across all behaviors, outcomes, and events.

Such generalized perceptions of control over events in one's life are not of central concern for our purposes. They are considered background factors and their place in our theoretical framework is considered in Chapter 7. In this chapter we discuss the definition and measurement of perceived behavioral control as well as its determinants. In the process, it will become clear how this construct, which plays a central role in our reasoned action model, differs from other control-related conceptualizations.

☐ Defining and Measuring Perceived Behavioral Control

In Chapter 2 we discussed actual behavioral control, which is often difficult to measure, and we contrasted it with perceived behavioral control, the construct of interest for our purposes. We also drew a distinction between internal and external control factors. We now consider some of these issues in greater detail.

Definition of Perceived Behavioral Control

In the preceding two chapters we discussed attitudes toward performing a behavior and perceived norms, two major determinants of intentions and actions. Within our conceptual framework, however, having a favorable attitude and perceiving social pressure may not be sufficient for the formation of an intention to perform a behavior. In addition to attitudes and perceived norms, intentions are also influenced by perceived control over performance of the behavior. As we saw in Chapter 2, perceived behavioral control is defined as the extent to which people believe that they are capable of performing a given behavior, that they have control over its performance. Perceived behavioral control is assumed to take into account the availability of information, skills, opportunities, and other resources required to perform the behavior as well as possible barriers or obstacles that may have to be overcome. Assuming that attitudes and perceptions of social pressure support performance of the behavior, the greater the perceived behavioral control the stronger should be the intention to perform the behavior in question. Perhaps more important, if people believe that they do not have control over performance of a behavior, they may not form strong behavioral intentions to perform it even if they hold positive attitudes and perceive strong social pressure to do so.

Self-Efficacy

This view of perceived behavioral control is by no means new or unique to our theoretical framework. Indeed, it owes considerable debt to Bandura's (1977, 1989, 1997) concept of *self-efficacy*, which carries the major explanatory burden in his social cognitive theory. Social cognitive theory deals with the cognitive regulation of motivation, affect, and action. In his early writings, Bandura (1991, p. 257) defined perceived self-efficacy as "...people's beliefs about their capabilities to exercise control over their own level of functioning and over events that affect their lives." In his more recent publications (e.g., Bandura, 1995, 1997, 1998) he has clarified and refined the construct, emphasizing that self-efficacy is not a context-free global disposition but that, instead, it "should be measured in terms of particularized judgments of capability that may vary across realms of activity, under different levels of task demand within a given activity domain, and under different situational circumstances" (Bandura, 1997, p. 42). Thus, "perceived self-efficacy refers to beliefs in one's capabilities to organize and execute the courses of action required to produce given attainments" (p. 3). It can be seen that our definition of perceived behavioral control as "the extent to which people believe that they are capable of, or have control over, performing a given behavior" is very similar to Bandura's conception of self-efficacy.

Measuring Perceived Behavioral Control

As is true of other constructs in our theory, perceived behavioral control must be conceptualized and assessed in accordance with the principle of compatibility such that it involves the same target, action, context, and time elements as the behavioral criterion. Like attitude and perceived norm, perceived behavioral control can be measured by asking direct questions about capability to perform a behavior. In addition, we can also measure people's beliefs about the likelihood that specific factors that may interfere with or facilitate performance of the behavior will be present when they try to perform the behavior in question. These control beliefs are assumed to determine perceptions of behavioral control and should therefore correlate with a direct measure.

A variety of direct questions can be used to assess respondents' perceptions of control. These questions have to reflect aspects of the construct consistent with its definition as the perceived capability of performing a behavior. For example, if we were interested in assessing people's perceptions of control over smoking cessation, we might ask one or more of the following questions.

1. If I really wanted to I could stop smoking in the next 6 months.

   Extremely likely | ___ | ___ | ___ | ___ | ___ | ___ | ___ | Extremely unlikely

2. My stopping smoking in the next 6 months is

   not at all up to me | ___ | ___ | ___ | ___ | ___ | ___ | ___ | completely up to me.

3. I have complete control over my stopping smoking in the next 6 months.

   Strongly agree | ___ | ___ | ___ | ___ | ___ | ___ | ___ | Strongly disagree

Table 5.1 displays the items that were used in a number of studies, together with the reported reliabilities (usually alpha coefficients) of the composite scores. Clearly, there is considerable commonality in the items employed, all focusing on a person's perceived ability to carry out a given course of action. In the set of studies shown in Table 5.1, the internal consistencies or reliabilities of the direct measures were quite high, ranging from .61 to .90.

Self-Efficacy Measures

Despite the theoretical similarity between perceived behavioral control and Bandura's concept of self-efficacy, operations designed to assess self-efficacy can take a very different form. The recommended methodology (see Bandura, 1997, pp. 42–46) for measuring perceived self-efficacy requires individuals to respond to a number of items on which they rate the certainty that they can perform the behavior of interest under varying circumstances and levels of task demand. It is suggested that these ratings be obtained on a 10-point scale (from 0 to 100 in 10-unit intervals or from 1 to 10 in 1-unit intervals), but investigators often use fewer response levels in their research (e.g., Betz, Hammond, & Multon, 2005). The mean response over all items serves as a measure of perceived self-efficacy with respect to the behavior of interest.

TABLE 5.1 Direct Measures of Perceived Behavioral Control

Source	Behavior	Items used	Reliability
Sheeran & Orbell (1999b), Study 2	Taking a multivitamin pill every day for the next 3 weeks	For me to ... would be very easy–very difficult If I want to I will easily be able to ... The number of external influences that may prevent me from ... How much control do you think you have over your ability to ...	.90
Courneya, Bobick, and Schinke (1999), Study 1	Participating in regular physical exercise	For me to ... is extremely difficult–extremely easy How much control do you have over ... If I wanted to I could easily ...	.81
Conner and McMillan (1999)	Using cannabis/ marijuana in the next 3 months	For me ... would be difficult–easy How much control do you think you have over ... How much do you feel that whether ... is beyond your control If I wanted to, I could easily ...	.90
Conner, Sheeran, Norman, and Armitage (2000)	Attending a health screening — measured on two occasions	... would be difficult–easy I could easily ... if I wanted to How much control have you over ...	.61, .74
Netemeyer, Burton, and Johnston (1991), Study 1	Voting in the October 24 governor's election primary	For me to ... is difficult–easy If I wanted to I could easily ... How much control do you have over whether you do or do not ... It is mostly up to me whether ...	.76
Godin et al. (1996)	Using a condom each time I have sexual intercourse with a new partner in the next 3 months — 3 samples	For me ... would be very difficult–very easy If I wanted to I would make sure ... I feel I would be capable of convincing my new partner to ...	.79, .63, .83

Consider again the issue of smoking cessation. In a recent Internet-based study of this behavior (Christie & Etter, 2005), participants were instructed as follows:

> The following are some situations in which certain people might be tempted to smoke. Please indicate whether you are sure that you could *refrain* from smoking in each situation.

Table 5.2 shows the 12 situations included in the self-efficacy scale. It can be seen that each item describes a possible barrier to smoking cessation (e.g., when I am with smokers, after a meal). Participants were asked to indicate how certain they were that they could overcome the barrier on the following five-point scale:

_____ Not at all sure _____ Not very sure _____ More or less sure

_____ Fairly sure _____ Absolutely sure

A score for perceived self-efficacy with respect to smoking cessation was derived by computing the average response to the 12 items. This score represents the participant's perceived ability to persist and overcome possible barriers and thus achieve the goal of smoking cessation. Similar to a measure of perceived behavioral control over smoking cessation, the higher the self-efficacy score, the more certain participants were that they could refrain from smoking (even under a variety of difficult circumstances). Thus, although the two types of measures are quite different on the surface, they appear to assess the same underlying construct.

Not all self-efficacy measures focus on performing a single behavior under a variety of circumstances. Self-efficacy has also been assessed with respect to behavioral categories or goals. In these cases, a typical self-efficacy scale asks people how certain they are that they could perform various behaviors in the category or perform behaviors that are necessary for goal achievement. Here it is assumed that the different behaviors vary in their degree of difficulty. To illustrate, in a study among American high school students (Zimmerman, Bandura, & Martinez-Pons, 1992), a set of 11 items was used to assess perceived self-efficacy with respect to self-regulated learning. Among the items on the scale were "finish homework assignments by deadlines," "study when there are other interesting things to do," "take class notes of class instruction," and "participate in class discussions." For each item the students were asked to rate how well they thought they could perform the indicated behavior on a seven-point scale ranging from 1 (*not well at all*) through 3 (*not too well*) and 5 (*pretty well*) to 7 (*very well*). The mean score over the 11 items was taken as a measure of perceived self-efficacy in the domain of academic functioning; this measure of self-efficacy had an alpha reliability coefficient of .87.

TABLE 5.2 A Measure of Perceived Self-Efficacy With Respect to Smoking Cessation

The following are some situations in which certain people might be tempted to smoke. Please indicate whether you are sure that you could refrain from smoking in each situation.

__ Not at all sure __ Not very sure __ More or less sure __ Fairly sure __ Absolutely sure

1. When I feel very anxious
2. When I am angry
3. When I am with smokers
4. When having coffee or tea
5. When having a drink with friends
6. When I feel the urge to smoke
7. After a meal
8. When I feel depressed
9. When drinking beer, wine or other spirits
10. When celebrating something
11. When I feel nervous
12. When I want to think about a difficult problem

Source: Christie, D. H., & Etter, J.-F. o., *Addictive Behaviors*, 30, 981–988, 2005 (with permission).

Note that in contrast to the first self-efficacy measure, which focused on overcoming barriers that could prevent performance of a given behavior, this instrument is composed of items that are each very similar to a direct measure of perceived control over a single behavior. Irrespective of whether such an item is labeled a measure of self-efficacy or a measure of perceived behavioral control, participants are simply asked to indicate how certain they are that they can perform each of the behaviors in a behavioral category. We conclude that perceptions of behavioral control or self-efficacy expectations with respect to a given behavior can be assessed in two ways: by specifying a behavior and possible barriers or by directly asking about control over performance of the behavior. Both measures can be extended to assess perceived control or self-efficacy with respect to a behavioral category or to goal attainment. For example, as we just saw, we can directly ask about control over the performance of each of a set of behaviors that comprise a behavioral category or over a set of behaviors that are relevant for attainment of a goal. Alternatively, we can define a behavioral category or specify a goal and identify barriers to engaging in that category (e.g., "How certain are you that you could study even if ...") or to goal attainment (e.g., "How certain are you that you could get an A on your exam even if..."). No matter which operations are employed, it would appear that the resulting measure reflects the same underlying construct, namely, the perceived ability to perform a particular behavior, to engage in a category of behaviors, or to reach a certain goal.

Self-Efficacy Versus Perceived Behavioral Control

Several investigators have questioned the unitary conception of perceived behavioral control and have argued that there are important differences between self-efficacy expectations and perceived control. Terry
and O'Leary (1995) attempted to demonstrate these differences in a study
concerned with the prediction of regular physical exercise. They considered two subsets of items. One subset consisted of three seven-point
items that Terry and O'Leary thought were indicators of perceived self-
efficacy. Among those were, "For me to exercise for at least 20 minutes
three times per week for the next fortnight will be" *very easy* (1) to *very
difficult* (7), and "If I wanted to it would be easy for me to exercise for at
least 20 minutes three times per week for the next fortnight" (*strongly
disagree* (1) to *strongly agree* (7)). The second subset was composed of four
items that they thought assessed perceived behavioral control. Examples
are, "How much control do you have over whether you exercise for at
least 20 minutes three times per week for the next fortnight?" (*no control*
(1) to *complete control* (7)), and "I feel in complete control of whether I exercise for at least 20 minutes three times per week for the next fortnight"
(*completely false* (1) to *completely true* (7)). Structural equation modeling
confirmed the predicted two-factor structure: A model that contained
two separate latent variables provided a significantly better fit to the data
than did a model that combined the seven indicators into a single latent
variable. The sets of items comprising the two constructs each had high
internal consistency (alpha = .80 for "self-efficacy" items and alpha = .85
for "control" items).

It is not at all clear, however, why Terry and O'Leary (1995) decided
that items concerned with the perceived ease or difficulty of performing
a behavior are indicators of self-efficacy. This interpretation is inconsistent with Bandura's (1977) conceptualization of the self-efficacy construct.
According to Bandura, "... highly self-efficacious individuals may view
certain undertakings as inherently difficult but believe firmly that they
can succeed through ingenuity and perseverant effort" (p. 127). Thus, the
ability to perform easy behaviors or overcome low barriers is not considered an indication of high self-efficacy. To have self-efficacy, people must
believe that they can perform the behavior even in the face of difficult
obstacles. Recognizing this inconsistency, Armitage and Conner (1999b; see
also Armitage & Conner, 2001) decided to assess self-efficacy by means of
items that did not directly refer to the ease or difficulty of performing the
behavior. In their study of intentions to eat a low-fat diet, a questionnaire
containing eight perceived behavioral control items was administered
twice, separated by 3 months. Principal components factor analysis followed by orthogonal rotation revealed the two factors shown in Table 5.3.
Looking at the bold-faced factor loadings, it can be seen that the first factor

TABLE 5.3 Factor Loadings of Perceived Behavioral Control Items

Items	Time 1		Time 2	
	Factor 1	Factor 2	Factor 1	Factor 2
I believe I have the ability to eat a low-fat diet.	.73	.17	.80	.14
To what extent do you see yourself as capable of eating a low-fat diet?	.80	.16	.81	.25
How confident are you that you will be able to eat a low-fat diet?	.83	.20	.84	.18
If it were entirely up to me, I am confident that I would be able to eat a low-fat diet.	.83	.07	.82	.22
Whether or not I eat a low-fat diet is entirely up to me.	−.01	.73	.14	.75
How much personal control do you feel you have over eating a low-fat diet?	.28	.76	.36	.74
There are likely to be plenty of opportunities for me to eat a low-fat diet.	.26	.59	.36	.60
How much do you feel that eating a low-fat diet is beyond your control?	.09	.76	.04	.74

Source: Armitage, C. J., & Conner, M., *British Journal of Social Psychology, 38,* 35–54, 1999 (with permission).

is represented by items that inquire into the participant's ability to eat a low-fat diet, whereas the items on the second factor directly refer to control over this behavior. Alpha coefficients of the factor-based scores were satisfactory at both times, ranging from .70 to .87. Consistent with Terry and O'Leary's interpretation of two different control constructs, Armitage and Conner concluded that the first factor reflected self-efficacy and the second factor reflected perceived behavioral control. Similar results were reported in a second study by Armitage and Conner (1999a) concerning the same behavior.

It is again not clear why Armitage and Conner (1999b) decided that their first factor reflects self-efficacy and the second perceived control. While the results of factor-analytic studies suggest that it is possible to distinguish between two different aspects of perceived behavioral control, we see no theoretical basis for calling one factor self-efficacy and the other factor control. As we have tried to show, from a theoretical perspective self-efficacy and perceived behavioral control are virtually identical. Both refer to a person's perceived capability to perform a certain behavior or attain a certain goal, and both can be assessed by items that deal with ability to perform the behavior or attain the goal (under circumstances that vary in difficulty) as well as by items that have to do with control over performance of the behavior or over goal attainment. Nevertheless, in a number of subsequent studies, investigators have followed in the footsteps of Terry and O'Leary (1995) and of Armitage and Conner (1999b) and have argued that the two factors emerging in factor analyses of control-related items represent two theoretically different constructs: self-efficacy and perceived behavioral control. These studies have dealt with physical exercise (Kraft, Rise, Sutton, & Røysamb, 2005), academic performance (Manstead & van Eekelen, 1998), breast self-examination (Norman & Hoyle, 2004), eating fruits and vegetables and low-fat foods (Povey, Conner, Sparks, James, & Shepherd, 2000), red meat consumption (Sparks, Guthrie, & Shepherd, 1997), and use of alcohol and cannabis (Armitage, Conner, Loach, & Willetts, 1999). We offer an alternative interpretation of the two-factor structure, after first considering questions related to the perceived ease or difficulty of performing a behavior.

Perceived Ease or Difficulty of Behavioral Performance

Rather than asserting a difference between self-efficacy items and perceived control items, Trafimow, Sheeran, Conner, and Finlay (2002) proposed a distinction between items that assess the perceived difficulty of performing a behavior and control over its performance. In a series of studies, they showed that items measuring perceived difficulty are indeed empirically distinct from items measuring perceived control. For example, in one of their studies the investigators asked participants in three different conditions of the experiment to imagine that there was a 0%, 50%, or 98% chance that a 10 km race would be cancelled due to rain. The investigators then assessed perceived control and perceived ease/difficulty of completing the race. The perceived control item was, "How much would completing the race be under your control?" Responses were provided on a four-point scale that ranged from 0 (*not at all under my control*) to 3 (*extremely under my control*). For perceived difficulty, participants were asked, "How much would completing the race be easy to do?" and the response scale ranged from 0 (*not at all easy*) to 3 (*extremely easy*). Consistent with the idea that perceived control and perceived difficulty are not necessarily the same, the study revealed a significant effect of the manipulated chance of rain on perceived control over completing the race but not on perceived ease of completing it. (The investigators did not report the correlation between the two measures.)

However, an earlier investigation of reducing red meat consumption (Sparks et al., 1997) raises questions about the distinction between perceived control and perceived difficulty as well. These investigators started with a set of 25 perceived behavioral control items culled from published research. Seven items made explicit reference to difficulty, seven made reference to control, and the remaining items made no explicit reference to either of these constructs (e.g., "It is up to me whether or not I reduce the amount of red meat"). Cronbach's alpha for the total set of items was .93, indicating very high internal consistency. Nevertheless, a principal components factor analysis revealed five dimensions of perceived behavioral control. Because the investigators were interested in the distinction between difficulty and control, they focused on the first two factors. The five items with high loadings on the first but not the second factor were selected as measures of perceived difficulty, whereas those with high loadings on the second but not the first factor served as measures of perceived control. The reliabilities of these measures were .90 and .83.[2] However, examination of the factor loadings for the full set of 25 items raises doubts about the proper interpretation of the two factors. For example, some items referring explicitly to control (e.g., "I have complete control over reducing the amount of red meat I eat from now on") had higher loadings on the difficulty factor than on the control factor. Similarly, the item with the highest loading on the first (difficulty) factor ("I could successfully reduce the amount of red meat that I eat from now on") seems to have very little to do with, and certainly does not explicitly refer to, difficulty.

In factor analyses of perceived behavioral control items, the items that refer to the perceived ease or difficulty of performing a behavior have tended to load on a factor that most often has been labeled *self-efficacy*. For example, Manstead and van Eekelen (1998) asked high school students to respond to a questionnaire concerning the goal of attaining at least a 7 (out of 10) in upcoming exams in history, English, and physics classes. The questionnaire included six items designed to distinguish between self-efficacy and perceived behavioral control. The first two items were designed to measure perceived behavioral control: "Whether or not I attain at least a 7 for [course] in the upcoming exam is completely up to me" (*agree–disagree*); and "How much control do you have over whether you attain at least a 7 for [course] in the upcoming exam?" (*none–complete*). The next three items were designed to measure self-efficacy: "I am certain that I can attain at least a 7 for [course] in the upcoming exam" (*completely disagree–completely agree*); "How confident are you that you will attain at least a 7 for [course] in the upcoming exam?" (*very little–a great deal*); and "There is a lot that I can do to be sure of attaining at least a 7 for [course] in the upcoming exam" (*completely disagree–completely agree*). The sixth and final item was included to explore whether easy–difficult type items were a better measure of self-efficacy or of perceived control: "Attaining at least a 7 for [course] in the upcoming exam is for me..." (*very difficult– very easy*).

A principal components analysis followed by oblique rotation revealed two correlated factors. The first factor was composed of the *easy–difficult* item and two of the three "efficacy" items (i.e., confident I can and certain I can). The remaining "efficacy" item loaded on a second factor with the two "control" items. The first factor (containing the *easy–difficult* item) was labeled *self-efficacy* whereas the second factor was labeled *perceived control*.

The finding that the *easy–difficult* item was highly correlated with items reflecting confidence in one's ability to perform the behavior is not surprising. It stands to reason that people who believe that it would be easy for them to perform a given behavior will also think that they can do it and, conversely, that people who judge that performing the behavior would be difficult are more likely to believe that they may not be able to perform the behavior. However, as we pointed out earlier, according to Bandura (1997) believing that one can perform easy behaviors has little to do with self-efficacy. Indeed, it is only when people believe that they can perform difficult behaviors or that they can perform a behavior under challenging circumstances that they are likely to develop a sense of self-efficacy. It is for this reason that investigators who are trying to distinguish between self-efficacy and control need to pay special attention to the proper role of *easy–difficult* items. Clearly, neither Terry and O'Leary's (1995) inclusion of only easy–difficult items in their measure of "self-efficacy" nor Armitage and Conner's (1999a) decision to explicitly exclude *easy–difficult* items from their measure can contribute to our understanding of the role of perceived difficulty in the measurement of perceived control.

When we attempt to develop a direct measure of perceived behavioral control, we must make sure not only that the items selected have high internal consistency but also that these items possess discriminant validity. In the context of our reasoned action approach, this means that items designed to assess perceived behavioral control should correlate more highly with each other than with items designed to assess attitudes or perceived norms. What's more, it is possible that items shown to have good convergent and discriminant validity for one behavior may lack these types of validity with respect to another behavior. This is analogous to the concept-scale interactions we discussed in Chapter 3 in relation to direct measures of attitude.

Items referring to the ease or difficulty of performing a behavior appear to be particularly vulnerable to this type of interaction. Such items are included in most direct measures of perceived behavioral control, perhaps because in early presentations of the theory of planned behavior, Ajzen (1985, 1988; Ajzen & Madden, 1986) described perceived behavioral control as the perceived ease or difficulty of performing a behavior. In retrospect, it now seems clear that an *easy–difficult* item is not necessarily a good indicator of perceived behavioral control. Whether it is or is not a valid indicator is an empirical question. Its validity should be tested in formative research before it, or any other item, is used to directly assess perceived behavioral control. Indeed, although in some applications items referring to ease or difficulty of performing a behavior are found to be good indicators of overall perceived behavioral control (Table 5.1; see also Trafimow & Duran, 1998), in others they are found to correlate more strongly with the experiential aspect of attitude than with other control items (Kraft et al., 2005; Leach, Hennessy, & Fishbein, 1999; Yzer, Hennessy, & Fishbein, 2004).

For example, Yzer et al. (2004), investigated marijuana use among 570 middle and high school students (mean age = 15). The behavior was defined as "your using marijuana nearly every month for the next 12 months." Perceived difficulty of performing this behavior was measured on a seven-point *difficult–easy* scale. Two seven-point scales with endpoints labeled *"not under my control–under my control"* and *"not up to me–up to me"* were used to assess perceived behavioral control. Attitude was measured with both instrumental and experiential semantic differential items. The instrumental evaluative items were *bad–good, foolish–wise, harmful–beneficial, dumb–smart, unhealthy–healthy,* and *unnecessary–necessary,* and the experiential evaluative items were *stressful–relaxed, unenjoyable–enjoyable,* and *unpleasant–pleasant.*

A series of structural equation analyses indicated that, prior to considering the role of perceived difficulty, the best fitting baseline model was one in which attitude and perceived control were identified as separate constructs, with the attitude being best viewed as a higher-order construct involving an experiential and an instrumental dimension. A further series of analyses tested to see whether the *easy–difficult* item was best viewed as an indicator of perceived control, of the higher-order attitude construct, of the experiential aspect of attitude, or of the instrumental aspect of attitude. Consistent with earlier findings (Leach et al., 1999), these analyses indicated that *easy–difficult* was best viewed as an indicator of the experiential aspect of attitude. Thus, as suggested earlier, the use of easy–difficult items to measure perceived control can be problematic, and such items should be used only with caution.

Capacity Versus Autonomy: A Hierarchical Model of Perceived Control

We have tried to show that although there is good empirical evidence that items meant to assess perceived behavioral control can be separated into two factors, identifying them as self-efficacy expectations and perceived control is misleading and unjustified (see Ajzen, 2002a). Table 5.4 displays the kinds of items that have been found to load on the two factors in different studies. Items on the first factor refer primarily to the ability to perform a behavior, that is, to the belief that one can, is able to, or is capable

TABLE 5.4 Two Factors of Perceived Behavioral Control Items

Factor 1

For me to perform behavior x would be... (*very easy–very difficult*).

If I wanted to, I could easily perform behavior x. (*strongly agree–strongly disagree*)

I am certain that I can perform behavior x. (*completely disagree–completely agree*)

I believe I have the ability to perform behavior x. (*definitely do–definitely do not*)

To what extent do you see yourself as capable of performing behavior x? (*very capable–very incapable*)

How confident are you that you will be able to perform behavior x? (*very sure–very unsure*)

Factor 2

How much control do you have over whether you perform behavior x? (*no control–complete control*)

I feel in complete control over whether I perform behavior x. (*completely false–completely true*)

Whether or not I perform behavior x is completely up to me. (*disagree–agree*)

How much do you feel that performing behavior x is beyond your control? (*not at all–very much*)

It is mostly up to me whether or not I perform behavior x. (*strongly agree–strongly disagree*)

The number of events outside my control which could prevent me from performing behavior x are ... (*numerous–very few*).

of, performing the behavior. Judgments of the perceived ease or difficulty of performing the behavior also tend to load on this factor. The items on the second factor deal mainly with degree of control over performing the behavior. Also included on this factor are judgments that performance of the behavior is "up to me." We believe that these two factors are best labeled *capacity* and *autonomy* and that they represent two aspects of perceived behavioral control (and of self-efficacy), not separate indicators of self-efficacy versus perceived control. In fact, from our perspective, trying to distinguish empirically between self-efficacy and perceived control is problematic in principle. We have argued that, theoretically, perceived self-efficacy and perceived behavioral control refer to the same latent construct, namely, to perceived ability to perform a given behavior or to carry out a certain course of action. If perceived self-efficacy and perceived behavioral control are indeed synonymous, it will not be possible to develop indicators that empirically distinguish between them.

To recapitulate, perceived behavioral control or self-efficacy refers to the perceived ability to carry out a certain course of action. In standard measures of perceived self-efficacy, respondents are asked to estimate their ability to perform a behavior under various circumstances, and the mean of their estimates serves as a measure of self-efficacy. In our reasoned action framework, perceived behavioral control is usually assessed by means of various direct questions that probe for ability to perform the behavior. Research has shown that items of this kind tend to fall into two categories, which we have termed *perceived capacity* and *perceived autonomy*. However, these two control factors are found to be correlated, and measures that combine both types of items can have high internal consistency. Thus, similar to the measurement of attitudes by means of instrumental and experiential evaluative items and to the measurement of perceived norms by means of injunctive and descriptive items, a comprehensive measure of perceived behavioral control can be obtained by including items representing both capacity and autonomy. A hierarchical model in which capacity and autonomy constitute first-order factors and perceived behavioral control a second-order factor perhaps best represents this component in our model of behavioral prediction (Ajzen, 2002a; Hagger & Chatzisarantis, 2005).

Empirical evidence regarding the internal consistency of various items designed to assess perceived behavioral control confirm this point of view. We saw earlier (Table 5.1) that measures of perceived behavioral control composed of both capacity and autonomy items had high internal consistency even when these items loaded on separate factors. In line with this finding, a meta-analysis of 90 studies that used multi-item scales to assess perceived behavioral control reported the average alpha coefficient to be about .65 (Cheung & Chan, 2000).

Finally, we should also note a methodological problem related to the effort to distinguish between perceived self-efficacy and perceived control. It can be seen in Table 5.4 that items associated with Factor 1 (capacity) usually have a single behavioral focus, whereas items associated with Factor 2 (autonomy) often involve a behavioral comparison. For example, the items "For me to perform behavior x would be easy–difficult" and "If I wanted to I could easily perform behavior x" are focused exclusively on performance of the behavior in question. In contrast, such items as "How much control do you have over whether you perform or do not perform behavior x?" and "Whether or not I perform behavior x is completely up to me" ask the respondent to consider the issue of control in relation to both performing the behavior and not performing the behavior. To illustrate the importance of this distinction, consider cigarette smoking. Heavy smokers may well agree that if they wanted to they could easily smoke, but they may at the same time realize that whether they do or do not smoke is not completely up to them. This difference in focus on one or both sides of a behavior could, by itself, account for the observed two-factor structure of perceived behavioral control items.

Internal Versus External Sources of Control

The argument that perceived self-efficacy differs substantively from perceived control derives in part from the distinction between internal and external sources of control (see Ajzen, 2002a). As we noted in Chapter 2, some control factors, including skills and willpower, are internal to the individual whereas other factors, such as task demands and the actions of other people, are located externally. Terry and O'Leary (1995; see also & Conner, 1999a; Manstead & van Eekelen, 1998) maintained that self-efficacy is related primarily to internal factors (capability) whereas perceived control is a function of external factors (e.g., other people and events that can interfere with performance of the behavior). According to this view, people are assumed to have a high sense of self-efficacy in relation to performing a behavior if they believe that they possess the qualities and attributes that will allow them to successfully carry out the behavior. In a similar fashion, they are assumed to have a high sense of perceived control if they believe that there are no external obstacles or barriers to prevent them from performing the behavior. However, it could just as easily have been argued that people have a strong sense of self-efficacy when they believe they can overcome obstacles and barriers, and that they have a strong sense of perceived control when they believe that they have the necessary skills and abilities to successfully carry out the behavior in question.

It is interesting to note that there is no indication in Bandura's (1997) theorizing that self-efficacy beliefs are restricted to internal factors (see Bandura, 1997 for an in-depth discussion of perceived self-efficacy). This is confirmed by examining items used in work with the self-efficacy construct. For example, in a study dealing with employment and housing (Epel, Bandura, & Zimbardo, 1999), homeless people were asked to rate, on a nine-point scale, the strength of their beliefs that they can construct a résumé, impress employers and rental agents, and get others to help them—all factors that could influence their ability to obtain employment or housing.[3] Clearly, the ability to construct a résumé and to impress others can be considered internal factors, but receiving help from others is usually classified as an external factor.[4]

More important, a moment's reflection reveals that perceived control over a behavior (or self-efficacy) is independent of the internal or external locus of the factors responsible for our perceived ability or lack of ability to perform it. Capacity and autonomy are *conceptually* independent of whether a control factor is internal or external. I may believe that I am able (i.e., that I have the capacity) to eat a low-fat diet because I have familiarized myself with the fat contents of various foods (an internal factor) or because low-fat foods are readily available (an external factor). Similarly,

I may believe that I have limited autonomy in relation to eating a low-fat diet because I have little willpower (an internal factor) or because the dining hall where I have most of my meals provides no information about the fat content of the food that is served (an external factor). Most likely, both perceived capacity and perceived autonomy with respect to performing a behavior reflect beliefs about the presence of internal as well as external factors that may facilitate or impede performance of a behavior. To complicate matters, the same variable—for example, ability, an internal factor—can be viewed by some people as malleable and potentially under volitional control and by other people as immutable and hence not amenable to control (Dweck & Leggett, 1988; Hong, Chiu, Dweck, Lin, & Wan, 1999).

Consistent with this line of reasoning, perceived behavioral control in our reasoned action approach refers to people's general expectations regarding the degree to which they are capable of performing a given behavior, the extent to which they have the requisite resources and believe they can overcome whatever obstacles they may encounter. Whether these resources and obstacles are internal or external to the person is immaterial. Our theoretical framework is concerned only with the extent to which control factors are believed to be present and are perceived to facilitate or impede performance of the behavior under consideration. When people believe that they have the required resources and opportunities (e.g., skills, time, money, cooperation by others) and that the obstacles they are likely to encounter are few and manageable, they should have confidence in their ability to perform the behavior and thus exhibit a high degree of perceived behavioral control (or self-efficacy). Conversely, when they believe that they lack requisite resources or that they are likely to encounter serious obstacles, they should have less confidence in their ability to perform the behavior and hence hold a relatively low level of perceived behavioral control (or self-efficacy).

To be sure, it is conceivable that respondents confronted with questions about their ability to perform a behavior (capacity items) consider mainly internal rather than external factors and that beliefs about external factors are more readily accessible when respondents ponder whether performance of the behavior is under their control or is completely up to them (autonomy questions). Whether this is in fact the case is, however, an empirical question and cannot be taken for granted. We consider this question next, after discussing the measurement of control beliefs.

☐ Control Beliefs

We have repeatedly noted that many different factors—some internal, others external—determine the degree of control a person has over performance of a behavior. Readily accessible beliefs regarding these control factors are assumed to determine the overall level of perceived behavioral control. These salient control beliefs, like salient behavioral and normative beliefs, may be based in part on past experience with the behavior, but they will usually also be influenced by second-hand information, by observation of the experiences of acquaintances and friends, and by other factors that increase or reduce perceived ability to perform the behavior in question. The more of the required resources and opportunities individuals think they possess, and the fewer obstacles or impediments they anticipate, the greater should be their perceived control over their performance of the behavior. Just as behavioral beliefs concerning consequences of a behavior are viewed as determining attitudes, and normative beliefs regarding the prescriptions and behaviors of specific referents are viewed as determining perceived normative pressure, so too are beliefs about resources and opportunities viewed as underlying perceived behavioral control.

In their totality, control beliefs lead to the perception that one has or does not have the ability to carry out the behavior (i.e., perceived behavioral control). Equation 5.1 shows the relation between control beliefs and perceived behavioral control in symbolic form. In this equation, PBC is perceived behavioral control; c_i is the belief that control factor i will be present; p_i is the power of factor i to facilitate or impede performance of the behavior; and the sum is over the number of salient control beliefs.

$$PBC \propto \Sigma c_i p_i \qquad (5.1)$$

Analogous to the identification of salient behavioral and normative beliefs, salient control beliefs can be elicited by asking participants to list the factors they believe would enable them to perform the behavior as well as the factors that are likely to impede its performance. These factors constitute the individual's control beliefs. For example, suppose we are interested in predicting regular class attendance among female college students. We could ask a female student to list the factors that would enable her to attend class regularly in the course of the current semester and the factors that might interfere with or prevent performance of this behavior. Assume that the five control factors shown in Table 5.5 were emitted in response to these questions.

TABLE 5.5 Belief-Based Measure of Perceived Behavioral Control (PBC): Hypothetical Example of a Student's Salient Control Beliefs

Control factor	Belief strength (c)	Power (p)	c × p
Having reliable transportation	7	+1	+7
Conflicting events	2	–3	–6
Getting enough sleep	4	+1	+4
Being sick	1	–2	–2
Upsetting personal problems	3	0	0
$PBC \propto \Sigma c_i p_i$			+3

Note: Belief strength on a scale of 1 to 7; power on a scale of –3 to +3.

To obtain quantitative data regarding control beliefs, the participant is asked to respond to two questions with respect to each control factor, one to assess control belief strength and the other to measure the factor's power to facilitate or impede behavioral performance. Belief strength could be measured as follows:

1. How likely is it that you will have reliable transportation this semester?

   Extremely unlikely |___|___|___|___|___|___|___| Extremely likely

Alternatively, the belief strength question might take the following form:

2. I will have reliable transportation this semester.

   Agree |___|___|___|___|___|___|___| Disagree

To assess the power of this factor, we could ask questions such as the following:

1. My having reliable transportation this semester would make it

   easier |___|___|___|___|___|___|___| more difficult for me to
   attend class regularly.

2. My having reliable transportation this semester would facilitate my ability to attend class regularly.

   Agree |___|___|___|___|___|___|___|Disagree

In the hypothetical example in Table 5.5 control belief strength is scored in a unipolar fashion (from 1 to 7) and power of the control factor in a bipolar fashion (from -3 to $+3$). It can be seen that the student thought it highly unlikely that there would be events to conflict with her class schedule or that she would get sick. Further, she considered it highly likely that she would have reliable transportation and only slightly likely that she would have upsetting personal problems. Finally, she was unsure whether she would be able to get enough sleep in the course of the semester.

Consistent with the model shown in Equation 5.1, a composite of control beliefs is obtained by multiplying the strength of each control belief by its perceived power and then summing the product terms across all control beliefs. The products of belief strength and perceived power for our hypothetical student are displayed in the last column of Table 5.5. It can be seen that control beliefs regarding the possibility of conflicting events and being sick lowered overall perceived behavioral control and that the availability of reliable transportation and getting enough sleep strengthened the sense of perceived control. The composite index of control beliefs took the value of $+3$ (on a possible -35 to $+35$ scale), indicating a very modest level of perceived control over attending class regularly.

In Table 5.5, control belief strength was scored in a unipolar fashion, from 1 to 7, and perceived power in a bipolar fashion, from -3 to $+3$. However, it would also be possible to use a bipolar scoring scheme for the strength of the control beliefs. As in the case of behavioral beliefs (see Chapter 3), the control belief that a potential barrier (e.g., $p = -2$) is highly unlikely to be present ($c = -3$) may well raise the overall level of perceived control. It is therefore suggested that, as in the case of behavioral beliefs, an analysis be performed prior to computing the product terms to determine the best scoring scheme (unipolar or bipolar) for the belief strength scale.[5]

Control Beliefs and Perceived Behavioral Control

A set of *modal* salient control beliefs can be constructed by eliciting control factors in a representative sample of respondents and by selecting the most frequently mentioned factors. Note that, as in the case of behavioral and normative beliefs, we would not expect high internal consistency among salient control beliefs. It stands to reason that people will associate facilitating as well as impeding factors with the performance of many behaviors. Although investigators have frequently measured control beliefs, in only a few published studies thus far have they tried to secure measures of both control belief strength and the power of control factors. One exception is the study on eating a low-fat diet referred to earlier (Armitage & Conner, 1999a). In this study, seven modal salient control beliefs were identified in a pilot study. The control factors most frequently listed by the participants dealt largely with obstacles to maintaining a low-fat diet: that doing so is time-consuming, expensive, and inconvenient; that it requires strong motivation and knowledge of the fat contents of various foods; that low-fat foods must be readily available; and that high-fat foods pose temptation. Participants were asked to indicate, on seven-point scales, the frequency with which each of the control factors will be present (*never* to *frequently*) and the extent to which its presence would make successful performance of the behavior more or less likely (*less likely–more likely*). Note that although the first measure assesses control belief strength, the second measure is best viewed as a conditional intention, not a measure of perceived power. To assess perceived power we would have to ask about the extent to which the presence of the control factor would facilitate or impede performance of the behavior. Unfortunately, most attempts to measure perceived power have used the conditional intention measure.[6]

We saw earlier that it is possible to obtain a direct measure of perceived behavioral control by asking people whether they believe that they are capable of performing a behavior of interest, whether they believe that doing so is completely under their control, and so forth. According to our model of behavioral prediction, composite measures of control beliefs, representing the determinants of perceived behavioral control, should correlate with such direct measures. Empirical research provides good evidence for this expectation. For example, in an analysis of 16 of their own studies, Gagné and Godin (2000) reported correlations ranging from .24 to .72, with a median correlation of .57. Another estimate of the magnitude of this correlation across different studies is available in a meta-analysis of 18 data sets (Armitage & Conner, 2001). The mean correlation between a direct measure of perceived behavioral control and a belief composite was found to be .52. However, it is not clear in how many of these studies the composite control belief measure included an assessment of perceived power. Moreover, even when perceived power was assessed, it is not clear whether this variable was assessed appropriately or, as previously described, as a measure of a conditional intention.

Table 5.6 illustrates the correlations between control beliefs and perceived behavioral control obtained in an investigation of mountain climbing and other leisure activities in a college student population (Ajzen & Driver, 1991). Perceived behavioral control over mountain climbing was assessed by means of two questions, each with a seven-point response scale: (1) For me to engage in mountain climbing is ... (*difficult–easy*); (2) I believe I have the resources required to go mountain climbing (*false–true*). The mean response to these two questions served as a direct measure of perceived behavioral control, with an internal consistency coefficient alpha of .67.

Four factors that could facilitate or interfere with mountain climbing had been identified in a pilot study and are shown in Table 5.6: having good weather for mountain climbing, not having proper equipment, living near mountains, and lacking skills and knowledge for mountain climbing. To

TABLE 5.6 Mean Control Beliefs, Perceived Power, and Correlation of Belief Strength by Power Products With Perceived Behavioral Control (PBC) Over Mountain Climbing

Control belief	Strength of control belief (c)		Power (p)		c × p		Correlation
	M	(SD)	M	(SD)	M	(SD)	c × p with PBC
Good weather for mountain climbing	0.07	(2.21)	2.26	(1.45)	0.12	(4.08)	.39**
Lacking proper equipment	2.14	(1.60)	-2.08	(1.61)	-5.14	(5.23)	.56**
Living near mountains	-0.01	(2.41)	2.18	(1.40)	-0.12	(6.29)	.17*
Lacking appropriate skills and knowledge	1.44	(2.02)	-2.22	(1.24)	(-3.93)	-3.93	.66**

Note. Strength of control belief and perceived power can range from −2 to +2.
*p < .05; **p < .01.

Source: Ajzen, I., & Driver, B. L., Leisure Sciences, 13, 185–204, 1991 (with permission).

assess control belief strength, participants were asked to rate each control factor on a seven-point *true–false* scale (e.g., "I live near mountains"; *true–false*). A seven-point response scale was also used to obtain a measure of each control factor's perceived power. For example, with respect to living near mountains, participants were asked, "Living near mountains makes mountain climbing..." (*easier–more difficult*).

Four products of control belief strength times perceived power were computed and summed to produce a composite index of control beliefs (Equation 5.1). An optimal scaling analysis (see Chapter 3) showed that bipolar scoring of both belief strength and perceived power measures was superior to unipolar scoring. Both measures were therefore scored in bipolar fashion, from –3 to +3. In accordance with the model displayed in Equation 5.1, the summative $c \times p$ index was found to have a correlation of .65 with the direct measure of perceived behavioral control. We can thus proceed to examine the effects of individual control beliefs on the overall sense of perceived behavioral control.

The first two columns in Table 5.2 show the means (and standard deviations) for control belief strength. It can be seen that, on average, the college student participants believed that they did not have the proper equipment for mountain climbing and that they lacked appropriate skills and knowledge. They neither agreed nor disagreed with respect to having good weather and living near mountains.

The means (and standard deviations) of the perceived power measure are displayed in the next two columns. There it can be seen that good weather and living near mountains were perceived as facilitating mountain climbing, whereas lacking proper equipment or appropriate skills and knowledge were believed to impede this behavior.

The means (and standard deviations) of the products of belief strength and perceived power are shown in Columns 5 and 6 of Table 5.6, and in the last column we see the correlations of these products with the direct measure of perceived behavioral control. These correlations are all statistically significant. Consideration of the salient control beliefs can therefore help us explain the participants' level of perceived behavioral control. The greatest impact on perceived control was exerted by the extent to which participants thought they lacked the proper equipment, skills, and knowledge for mountain climbing. The smallest, though still highly significant, impact was due to beliefs about the weather and its effects on mountain climbing.

In sum, we have seen that salient control beliefs can help explain people's general perceptions of control over a behavior. Control belief strength, together with the control factors' perceived power to facilitate or hinder performance of the behavior, can raise or lower a person's sense of perceived behavioral control, and in their totality, salient control beliefs can account for considerable variance in this sense of self-efficacy.

Internal Versus External Control Factors Reconsidered

We can now return to the suggestion that perceived capacity reflects internal control factors whereas perceived autonomy reflects external factors. Consistent with this suggestion, we conceded the possibility that internal beliefs may be more readily accessible when respondents judge their capacity to perform a behavior and that beliefs about external factors may be more readily accessible when they confront autonomy questions. However, we also argued that there was no good a priori reason to expect this to be the case, that this proposition can only be tested empirically. Of the studies reviewed earlier that tried to distinguish between capacity ("self-efficacy") and autonomy ("control"), only two (Armitage & Conner, 1999b; Armitage et al., 1999) examined the relation of specific control beliefs to separate measures of these two components, and the results failed to support expectations. Armitage and Conner (1999b) identified seven control beliefs with respect to eating a low-fat diet and used these to predict capacity and autonomy by means of multiple regression. Some of the beliefs seemed to tap internal factors (e.g., "To eat a low-fat diet requires willpower") and others external factors (e.g., "Eating a low-fat diet costs too much money"). Still other beliefs would be difficult to classify. For example, the belief that "eating a low-fat diet is inconvenient" may refer to an internal disinclination to prepare low-fat foods or to external lack of availability. Similarly, "I don't always know which foods are low in fat" may reflect a failure to obtain the needed information (internal) or the information's unavailability (external). As might be expected, therefore, the results of the study were difficult to interpret. In general, there was considerable overlap between control beliefs that predicted capacity and autonomy. Two beliefs considered to reflect internal factors ("I do not have enough time to eat a low-fat diet" and "I have always eaten a low-fat diet") had significant regression weights in the prediction of capacity as well as autonomy, and examination of the zero-order correlations revealed significant associations between all seven beliefs and each of the two control factors.

Similarly disconfirming findings were reported by Armitage et al. (1999) in a study of alcohol and cannabis use among college students. After structural equation analysis had confirmed the capacity and autonomy factors of perceived behavioral control, scores for each factor were correlated with three control beliefs in the case of alcohol consumption and four control beliefs with respect to cannabis use. In the words of the investigators, "There were no discernable patterns of control beliefs that specifically predicted [autonomy] and not [capacity], suggesting no generalizable model for explaining perceived control" (p. 312).

Clearly, then, there is no empirical evidence at this point to support the proposition that perceived capacity represents beliefs about the operation of internal factors or that perceived autonomy represents beliefs about the effects of external factors.

☐ Summary and Conclusions

In this chapter we defined perceived behavioral control as the extent to which people believe that they are capable of performing a given behavior or attaining a certain goal. Conceptually, perceived behavioral control is equivalent to Bandura's (1989) self-efficacy expectation although different operations are typically employed when these constructs are assessed in empirical research. We saw that, like self-efficacy, perceived behavioral control reflects both internal and external factors that may facilitate or impede performance of a given behavior. Factor analyses of items used to assess perceived control have revealed two subcomponents that we have termed *capacity* and *autonomy*. Theoretical considerations as well as empirical research indicate that these components should not be equated with self-efficacy versus perceived control. A hierarchical model in which capacity and autonomy represent two subcomponents of a higher-order control factor seems to best represent the nature of perceived behavioral control. We also noted that there is no empirical support for the idea that one of the two components reflects beliefs about internal control factors and the other beliefs about external control factors.

By eliciting readily accessible beliefs about factors that can impede or facilitate performance of a behavior under investigation we can obtain substantive information about the determinants of perceived behavioral control. Analogous to the expectancy-value model of attitudes, our model of the relation between control beliefs and overall perceived behavioral control involves two considerations related to control beliefs: the likelihood that a given control factor will be present (control belief strength) and the extent to which its presence would facilitate or impede performance of the behavior (power of the control factor). Measures of these two aspects are multiplied, and the sum of the products provides a control belief index that is found to be highly correlated with a direct measure of perceived control. In addition, the correlation of each product with the direct measure of perceived behavioral control provides an indication of the control factor's contribution to a person's overall sense of control over the behavior.

☐ Notes

1. Interested readers are directed to Skinner's (1996) excellent review.
2. The fact that the overall scale, which included items of both types, had a high degree of internal consistency suggests that notwithstanding the results of the factor analysis, it is possible to combine both types of items into a single scale.
3. Note that this measure of self-efficacy asks participants to indicate whether they can perform different behaviors in the service of attaining a certain goal, not whether they can perform a given behavior under a variety of difficult circumstances.
4. Respondents were asked about their ability to attain control over the external factor. Thus, although receiving help from others is an external factor whose presence would facilitate performance of the behavior, the crucial issue for perceived control over the behavior is whether people believe that it is within their power to secure the needed help.
5. In a meta-analysis of 16 of their own data sets, Gagné and Godin (2000) found that unipolar scoring of control belief strength produced somewhat higher correlations with a direct measure of perceived behavioral control than did bipolar scoring, whereas it made little difference whether perceived power was scored in a unipolar or bipolar fashion. Unfortunately, as will be discussed later in the text, the perceived power measure in these 16 studies actually assessed conditional intentions.
6. This may explain why the measure of perceived power in these studies is usually found to correlate very highly with a measure of intention.

6 CHAPTER

Attitudes, Norms, and Control as Predictors of Intentions and Behavior

In the previous three chapters we defined and described attitudes, perceived social norms, and perceived behavioral control, and we discussed the role of beliefs as a foundation for these three constructs. We saw that by carefully eliciting and measuring salient behavioral, normative, and control beliefs about a behavior of interest we gain useful information about its likely determinants. In the present chapter we take this approach one step further by examining the postulated relations between attitudes, perceived social norms, and perceptions of behavioral control on one hand and intentions on the other. According to our reasoned action framework, attitudinal, normative, and control considerations determine a person's intentions. This is true irrespective of whether we are interested in the intention to perform a single behavior, to engage in a behavioral category, or to achieve some goal. To illustrate, by measuring corresponding attitudes, perceived norms, and perceived behavioral control, we should be able to predict intentions to jog 2 miles a day (a single behavior), to exercise every day (a behavioral category), or to lose weight (an outcome or goal). Although, as we saw in Chapter 2, intentions to engage in a behavioral category or to achieve a behavioral goal often have less predictive validity than intentions to perform a specific behavior, the predictive validity of a given intention should have no effect on our ability to predict the intention itself. Our theory should be as capable of predicting intentions to reach a goal as it is of predicting intentions to perform a specific behavior or to engage in a behavioral category. As long as our measures of attitudes, perceived norms, and perceived control are fully compatible with the intention under consideration, these measures should provide accurate prediction of the behavioral intention.

The relative contribution of attitudes, perceived norms, and perceived behavioral control to the prediction of intentions is expected to vary from one person to another, from one group of individuals to another, and from one behavior to another. The intentions of some individuals, or populations, may be affected mostly by attitudes and less so by perceived norms and perceived control, whereas other individuals or populations may be affected more by normative than attitudinal or control considerations. Still others may be guided mostly by their perceptions of control over performance of the behavior. In a similar manner, one type of behavior may be more under the influence of attitudinal than normative or control factors, whereas other behaviors may show a different pattern of influence. Thus, working out on a treadmill could show a different pattern of influence than using illegal drugs or taking public transportation to work. Moreover, it should be recalled that behaviors are defined in terms of four elements: action, target, context, and time. The relative importance of attitudes, perceived norms, and perceived control can be affected not only by the nature of the action but also by target, context and time. For example, the pattern of influence could change as we try to predict intentions to ride the bus to work versus riding the train to work (change in target element) or riding the bus to a baseball game (change in context element).

It is important to note that, in some instances, one or even two of the three basic determinants of intention may not carry a statistically significant weight in the prediction of intentions. Far from posing a problem for the theory, even such extreme variations in the contributions of the three components are to be expected. All they suggest is that for some individuals, populations, or behaviors, one or another of the three potential determinants of intentions is largely irrelevant (see Ajzen & Fishbein, 2004). Thus, a behavior may be guided primarily by attitudinal considerations (i.e., by beliefs about the behavior's likely consequences and the evaluations of these consequences), and normative or control considerations may be largely irrelevant. Another behavior may also show little or no normative influence but a strong effect of both attitudinal and control considerations. This is important information about the behavior's determinants and can guide the development of interventions designed to produce behavioral change (see Chapter 10); it should not, as has sometimes been argued (e.g., Ogden, 2003), be taken as evidence against the theory. Of course, if intentions could not be predicted from any combination of the three components, this would constitute evidence against the theory's validity, at least with respect to the particular behavior under investigation and within the population studied.

☐ Separate Effects of Attitudes, Norms, and Control on Intentions

Before testing our model of behavioral prediction as a whole, we examine how well each of its three major components correlates with behavioral intentions. Generally speaking, we would expect that people's intentions to perform a behavior will strengthen to the extent that they hold favorable attitudes toward the behavior and feel social pressure to perform it. Perceived behavioral control, however, is expected to *moderate* the effects of attitudes and social norms on intentions, just as it was expected to moderate the influence of intentions on behavior (see Chapter 2). That is, we would not necessarily expect a strong direct correlation between perceived behavioral control and intention. The fact that I am capable of performing a behavior does not necessarily imply that I will intend to do so (see Eagly & Chaiken, 1993). Although, as we shall see later, there is some evidence for the moderating role of perceived behavioral control (see Yzer, 2007), the amount of additional variance explained by the interaction between perceived behavioral control and attitude, and by the interaction between perceived control and perceived norm, is generally quite low. However, this research has usually relied on hierarchical regression analyses, and we discussed the problems associated with such tests of moderation in Chapters 2 and 3. In any event, the vast majority of studies that have been conducted within our reasoned action framework have used attitudes, perceived norms, and perceptions of control as independent predictors of intentions.

Several meta-analyses of the empirical literature have provided evidence to show that intentions can be predicted with considerable accuracy from measures of attitudes toward the behavior, perceived norms, and perceived behavioral control (Albarracín, Johnson, Fishbein, & Muellerleile, 2001; Armitage & Conner, 2001; Godin & Kok, 1996; Hagger, Chatzisarantis, & Biddle, 2002; Sheeran & Taylor, 1999; Sheppard, Hartwick, & Warshaw, 1988; van den Putte, 1993). For a wide array of behaviors, across the different meta-analyses, the mean correlations of attitudes with intentions range from .45 to .60. For the prediction of intentions from perceived social norms, the mean correlations range from .34 to .42, and for the prediction of intention from perceived behavioral control, the range is .35 to .46.

Note that meta-analyses of this kind tend to include all relevant studies and usually do not try to account for the reliability or validity of the predictor and criterion measures. We consider some of these measurement issues next. In most past research, the attitude measures typically contained both instrumental and experiential items, and perceived behavioral control was usually assessed by means of capacity as well as autonomy items. The measures of perceived social norm, however, mostly consisted of injunctive normative items because most studies to date have been based on the theories of planned behavior or reasoned action and neither of these theories identifies descriptive norms as an important determinant of intention and behavior.

It is worth noting that the identification of separate instrumental and experiential aspects of attitude and the identification of separate capacity and autonomy aspects of perceived control came after the fact as a result of factor analyses of items used to directly measure these constructs. In marked contrast, there were strong a priori theoretical grounds for including descriptive as well as injunctive norms in our measure of social norm. Thus, it is important to ask whether a single measure of perceived social pressure (i.e., of the social norm), provides as good as, or a better prediction of, intention as does a model that treats injunctive and descriptive norms as separate predictors.

An answer to this question can be found in several investigations that have examined the roles of descriptive as well as injunctive norms. In a meta-analysis of 21 such studies dealing with diverse behaviors, Rivis and Sheeran (2003) found that measures of injunctive and descriptive norms correlated significantly with each other (mean $r = .38$), and both had significant correlations with intentions (mean $r = .44$ and .46, respectively). A secondary analysis of the data presented in the Rivis and Sheeran article shows that taken together the two normative measures produce a mean multiple correlation of .54 with intentions. More important from our perspective, a few studies have combined measures of descriptive and injunctive norms into a single score representing overall normative pressure. Albarracín, Fishbein, and Middlestadt (1998) measured injunctive and descriptive norms with regard to condom use and found that both were correlated with intentions to use condoms ($r = .45$ and .44, respectively). When the two measures were combined, the single perceived norm construct had an even stronger correlation ($r = .61$) with intentions. Similar results were reported by Rhodes and Courneya (2003a) with respect to exercise intentions and by Sayeed, Fishbein, Hornik, Cappella, and Ahern (2005) for the prediction of drug use intentions.

However, the most direct test of the utility of a single normative measure is one that compares the predictive validity of a single measure of perceived social pressure with the predictive validity of a model in which intention is regressed on separate measures of injunctive and descriptive norms. The study by Smith-McLallen & Fishbein (2008) discussed in Chapter 4 addressed this issue. Recall that in this study a national sample of respondents 50 years of age and older were asked to indicate their intentions to engage in three lifestyle behaviors (i.e., eat fruits and vegetables, exercise, diet to lose weight) and three cancer-screening behaviors (i.e., get a colonoscopy, a mammogram, or a prostate-specific antigen [PSA] test). For five of these six behaviors (women were not asked about the PSA test and men were not asked about mammograms), respondents indicated their intentions to perform the behavior as well as their perception that most important others thought they should or should not perform the behavior and their perceptions that most important others engage in the three lifestyle behaviors or that "most people like me" engage in the three screening behaviors. A measure of perceived social pressure was computed by summing the two normative items. Table 6.1 shows the zero-order and multiple correlations for each of the six behaviors. It can be seen that the single perceived social pressure score did almost as well as the multiple correlation.

Very similar results were found in the study by Fishbein et al. (in preparation) concerning adolescents intentions to engage in sexual intercourse in the next 12 months. Here, the measure of social norm was based on three items:

1. Most people who are important to me think I should have sexual intercourse in the next 12 months.
2. Most people like me have had sexual intercourse.
3. Most people like me will have sexual intercourse in the next 12 months.

The first item was taken as a measure of injunctive norm, and the average of the last two comprised a measure of descriptive norm. Regressing the intention on the injunctive and descriptive norm resulted in a multiple correlation of .61, which was identical to the zero-order correlation with the combined perceived normative pressure measure. Thus, consistent with

TABLE 6.1 Prediction of Intentions From Separate Measures of Injunctive and Descriptive Norms and From Overall Perceived Norm

Behavior	Injunctive and descriptive norms (R)	Overall perceived norm (r)
Colonoscopy	.67	.64
Mammogram	.54	.52
Prostate-specific antigen (PSA)	.67	.63
Eat fruits and vegetables	.54	.54
Exercise	.39	.38
Diet	.57	.54

Source: From Smith-McLallen, A., & Fishbein, M., *Psychology, Health & Medicine*, 2008 (with permission).

our conclusions in Chapter 4, like measures of attitude and perceived control, it is possible to identify a single social norm construct that incorporates both injunctive and descriptive aspects of perceived normative pressure.

☐ Combined Effects of Attitudes, Norms, and Control on Intentions

Based on the discussions in the preceding chapters, we can now outline the methods and procedures that would be required to predict and explain a behavior of interest within our theoretical framework. As a first step, we would conduct formative research to elicit salient behavioral, normative, and control beliefs, and we would usually construct sets of modal salient beliefs common in the research population. Second, in the same pilot phase, we would also select items to directly assess attitudes, perceived norms, perceptions of behavioral control, and intentions. The information obtained in the pilot work is then used to construct a standard questionnaire, which is administered to a new sample of participants. At a later point in time, the participants' behavior is recorded. The data obtained can be submitted to a variety of statistical procedures to test the adequacy of the theoretical model and to explore the determinants of intentions and behavior on a substantive level.

In Chapter 2 we reviewed evidence to show that intentions, properly assessed, are usually good predictors of behavior and that, at least under some circumstances (e.g., when actual control is relatively low), perceived behavioral control can further improve behavioral prediction. In Chapters 3, 4, and 5 we saw that salient behavioral, normative, and control beliefs can be used to predict and explain, respectively, attitudes, perceived norms, and perceptions of behavioral control. We now move one step further by considering the extent to which attitudes, perceived norms, and perceived control predict intentions. For this test, we should not use the belief-based indices that are assumed to serve as the determinants of the three predictors. Instead, we need valid (direct) measures of attitudes, perceived norms, perceived control, and intentions. These measures are typically obtained by means of standard scaling procedures, such as Likert scaling or the semantic differential, to ensure that the items on the final instrument are good indicators of the underlying constructs. Moreover, for a direct test of the model, each of the three proximal predictors (i.e., attitudes, norms, and perceived control) should be considered a unitary construct. Each construct may be assessed by multiple indicators, especially if we want to conduct structural equation modeling, but for the prediction of intentions we would normally not break attitudes up into experiential and instrumental evaluations, or perceived norms into injunctive and descriptive norms, or perceived behavioral control into capacity and autonomy.

Support for treating the three predictors as unitary factors can be found in a study on leisure time physical activity and dieting by Hagger and Chatzisarantis (2005). University students and employees completed questionnaires that measured their attitudes, perceived norms, perceived control, and intentions with respect to either physical activity or dieting. The questionnaire assessed instrumental as well as experiential aspects of attitude, injunctive as well as descriptive components of social influence, and the capacity and autonomy aspects of perceived behavioral control. Two weeks later, the participants provided self-reports of their dieting or physical activity behaviors. Confirmatory factor analyses corroborated the validity of the distinctions between the two components of each of the theory's three major predictors. That is, a model that treated the two aspects of each predictor as separate factors was superior to a model that treated the two aspects as a single factor. However, a structural equation analysis provided support for the hierarchical view advocated in Chapters 3, 4, and 5. A model that entered experiential and instrumental attitudes, injunctive and descriptive norms, and capacity and autonomy as six separate factors performed no better than a model in which these subcomponents were treated as indicators of the higher-order constructs of attitude, perceived social norm, and perceived behavioral control.

Illustrative Evidence for Predictive Validity

Even though virtually hundreds of studies have tested variations of our theory, we were able to find only relatively few that contained all of the elements required for a complete and valid test, as previously outlined. In many studies one or more of the predictors (attitudes, perceived norms, and perceived behavioral control) were assessed not by means of standard measurement procedures but only by means of belief-based indices. This begs the question as to whether these indices actually capture the determinants of the construct. As we noted in Chapters 3, 4, and 5, standard procedures are required to ensure valid measures of attitudes, perceived norms, and perceptions of control. Belief-based indices are best considered measures of the determinants of these constructs; their validity must be confirmed by showing that they are predictive of a standard, validated measure of the relevant construct. Also, relatively few studies to date have measured descriptive norms, and when these norms were assessed, investigators often used injunctive and descriptive norms as separate predictors of intentions rather than treating them as possible indicators of a single underlying construct. The same is true for measures of capacity and autonomy; these measures are also often entered separately into the prediction equation. This is less often the case with respect to experiential and instrumental aspects of attitude. Here, investigators usually combine the two types of items into a single attitude measure. Additional complications arise when investigators include other variables they deem relevant in the prediction equation, a practice that can make it difficult to evaluate the predictive validity of our basic model of behavioral prediction.

Nevertheless, in our review of the literature we were able to identify a number of studies in very different behavioral domains that came close to what would be required for a valid test of our reasoned action framework. In each of these studies, the investigators used what have become standard measures of the framework's variables. With these standard instruments, attitudes toward the behavior are assessed by means of an evaluative semantic differential, perceived social norms by items that directly ask what important others think one should do or what these important others are doing,[1] and perceived behavioral control by inquiring whether the behavior is under the participants' control or the extent to which the participants believe that they are capable of performing the behavior. The criterion measure of intention is obtained by asking people how likely it is that they will, intend to, or plan to perform the behavior under consideration. In the studies we examined, a simple statistical method was used to test the model, namely, multiple linear regression. In this method, the measure of intention is regressed on attitudes, perceived norms, and perceived control, resulting in a multiple correlation that, when squared, indicates how much variance in intentions is accounted for by a simultaneous consideration of all three predictors. The analysis also provides regression weights that reflect the independent contribution of attitudes, norms, and perceived control to the prediction of intentions.

Consider, for example, a study on leisure time physical activity among individuals with spinal cord injury (Latimer & Martin Ginis, 2005b). The investigators used two seven-point scales to directly assess intentions, asking participants whether they intend to and whether they will try to "do at least 30 minutes of leisure time physical activity on most days in the next week." The sum of the responses to the two questions served as the measure of intention. (The correlation between the two items was not reported.) Note that this criterion refers to a behavioral category, not a single action. Attitudes toward engaging in this behavioral category (i.e., toward "participating in leisure time physical activity on most days in the next week") were assessed by means of a six-item evaluative semantic differential that contained three experiential adjective pairs (e.g., *relaxing–stressful*) and three instrumental adjective pairs (e.g., *valuable–worthless*). Consistent with the requirement that the items assess the same underlying evaluative attitude, the internal consistency coefficient alpha for the six-item scale was .84. Two items assessed perceived norms directly by asking participants whether most people who were important to them thought they should engage in the specified physical activity and whether these important others would approve of their participating. Note that, in keeping with our earlier version of the theory, these two items assessed injunctive norms; no measure of descriptive norms was obtained. Again, the correlation between the two normative items was not reported, but they were summed to yield a measure of perceived normative pressure. Finally, to assess perceived behavioral control, the investigators started with Armitage and Conner's (1999) seven control items. These items assessed the capacity factor (e.g., "How confident are you that you will be able to participate in leisure time physical activity ..."; *very unsure–very sure*) as well as the autonomy factor (e.g., "Whether or not I participate in leisure time physical activity ... is entirely up to me"; *agree–disagree*). A factor analysis revealed the two expected factors, but two of the seven items loaded on both factors. After eliminating these items, a second factor analysis of the remaining five items resulted in a one-factor solution with high internal consistency (alpha = .85). Thus, although the investigators started out with a two-factor conception of perceived behavioral control, their final measure of this construct—like their measures of attitudes, injunctive norms, and intentions—was a unitary score representing the higher-level construct as a whole.

Consistent with our reasoned action approach, intentions were predicted with a high degree of accuracy. As can be seen in the first row of Table 6.2, the multiple correlation was .78, indicating that attitudes, injunctive norms, and perceptions of behavioral control simultaneously accounted for 61% of the variance in intentions to engage in leisure time physical activity.[2] It can also be seen that each of the three predictors in the model was found to correlate significantly with intentions. These correlations were .58 for attitudes, .48 for injunctive norms, and .66 for perceived behavioral control. Even though all three correlations were quite high and statistically significant, the regression coefficients obtained in the multiple regression analysis showed that perceived control made a larger independent contribution to the prediction of intentions (beta = .46) than did either attitudes (beta = .29) or injunctive norms (beta = .27). Nevertheless, the regression coefficients were statistically significant for all three predictors.

Studying a very different behavior, Armitage, Norman, and Conner (2002) examined the determinants of college students' intentions to drive after drinking alcohol. A questionnaire contained direct measures of this intention as well as direct measures of attitudes toward the behavior, injunctive norms, and perceptions of behavioral control. Three seven-point scales were used to assess intentions. Respondents indicated the extent to which they *definitely do not–definitely do* intend to, expect they will, and want to "drive after drinking alcohol." The alpha coefficient

TABLE 6.2 Prediction of Intentions From Attitudes, Perceived Social Norm (PSN), and Perceived Behavioral Control (PBC): Sample Studies

Intention	Population	Attitude		PSN		PBC		Multiple R
		r	β	r	β	r	β	
Leisure time physical activity (Latimer & Martin Ginis, 2005b)	Individuals with spinal cord injury	.58	.29	.48	.27	.66	.47	.78[a]
Driving after drinking alcohol (Armitage, Norman, & Conner, 2002)	College students	.71	.34	.71	.41	.64	.23	.82[a]
Completing the current school year (Davis, Ajzen, Saunders, & Williams, 2002)	Inner city high-school students	.47	.22	.47	.28	.62	.44	.71
Applying for a promotion (Giles & Larmour, 2000)	Employees in an unspecified organization	.66	.15[a]	.60	.16[a]	.87	.70[a]	.90[a]
Using ecstasy (Orbell, Blair, Sherlock, & Conner, 2001)	Unspecified adults	.75	.44	.69	.24	.58	.34	.88
Consuming soft drinks (Kassem & Lee, 2004)	High-school students	.72	.52	.42	.19	.54	.28	.78
Using condoms (Villarruel, Jemmott, Jemmott, & Ronis, 2004)	Latino adolescents	.63	.26	.67	.36	.59	.34	.77
Breast cancer screening (Drossaert, Boer, & Seydel, 2003)	Women in a Dutch breast cancer screening program	.60	.42	.20	.09	.49	.29	.70
Donating blood (Giles & Cairns, 1995)	College students	.55	.25	.22	.11	.73	.61	.78
Recycling of waste paper (Cheung, Chan, & Wong, 1999)[b]	College students	.66	.43	.52	.27	.57	.21	.74
Quit smoking (Godin, Valois, Lepage, & Desharnais, 1992)[c]	Smokers	.31	.22	.12*	.17*	.52	.55	.62
Eating a healthy diet (Hagger, Chatzisarantis, & Harris, 2006)	College students	.70	.55	.50	.21	.42	.22	.77[a]

Notes: r = correlation coefficient, β = standardized regression coefficient, R = multiple correlation. * Not significant, all other coefficients are significant at $p < .05$. [a] Computed on the basis of correlations reported in the article. [b] We are grateful to Darius Chan for providing the correlation coefficients. [c] We are grateful to Gaston Godin for providing the correlation coefficients.

indicated a high degree of internal consistency,[3] and the scores for the three items were combined to produce a measure of intention. Attitudes were assessed by means of a four-item semantic differential scale. The adjective pairs on this scale were *foolish–wise, harmful–beneficial, bad–good,* and *undesirable–desirable.* Note that these adjectives are all of an instrumental rather than of an experiential nature. The internal consistency among these items was again high,[4] and the mean response was used as a measure of attitude. Two items measured perceived social pressure: "People who are important to me want me to drive after drinking alcohol" (*strongly agree–strongly disagree*) and "People who are important to me think *I should not–I should* drive after drinking alcohol." The correlation between these two items was .62, and a measure of injunctive norms was obtained by computing the average response. Finally, perceived behavioral control was assessed by means of three seven-point items that asked participants whether they thought they had the ability to drive after drinking alcohol (*definitely do not–definitely do*), to what extent they saw themselves as being capable of driving after drinking alcohol (*very incapable–very capable*), and how confident they were that they will be able to drive after drinking alcohol (*not very confident–very confident*). The three items had high internal consistency,[5] and the average score was used as a measure of perceived behavioral control. Note that just as the attitude measure was largely instrumental in nature and the measure of perceived social pressure addressed only the injunctive and not the descriptive norm, the measure of perceived behavioral control dealt only with perceived capacity to perform the behavior and not with autonomy.

Despite these potential limitations, the results of the study (second row of Table 6.2) were strongly supportive of the theory. The multiple correlation for the prediction of intentions from instrumental attitudes, injunctive norms, and perceived capacity was .82, accounting for 67% of the variance in intentions.[6] As in the physical activity study by Latimer and Martin Gines (2005b), intentions correlated significantly with attitudes ($r = .71$), perceived norms ($r = .71$), and perceived behavioral control ($r = .64$). In this case, however, the highest regression weight was associated with the subjective norm (beta = .41), followed by attitude (beta = .34) and perceived control (beta = .23). All three coefficients were statistically significant, indicating that each factor contributed independently to the prediction of intentions.

Results of several additional studies are shown in the remainder of Table 6.2. The intentions considered cover a wide range of behavioral domains, from drug use and smoking to engaging in physical activity, breast cancer screening, using condoms, and driving after drinking alcohol. It can be seen in the last column that in virtually every case intentions were predicted with a high degree of accuracy from a simultaneous consideration of attitudes, perceived norms, and perceived behavioral control.

The multiple correlations ranged from .62 to .88, indicating that the three predictors explained between 39% and 77% of the variance in intentions. It is instructive to compare these multiple correlations with the general pattern of findings as reflected in meta-analyses of research based on our reasoned action approach. In meta-analytic reviews covering a broad range of different behaviors (Armitage & Conner, 2001; Cheung & Chan, 2000; Notani, 1998; Rivis & Sheeran, 2003; Schulze & Wittmann, 2003), attitudes, perceived norms, and perceived behavioral control produced mean multiple correlations with intentions that ranged from .59 to .66. Meta-analyses have also been conducted in two specific behavioral domains: condom use and physical exercise. In the area of condom use, the predictive validity of the model, as indicated by mean multiple correlations, was .71 (Albarracín et al., 2001) and .65 (Sheeran & Taylor, 1999). For physical activity, the average multiple correlations were .55 (Downs & Hausenblas, 2005) and .67 (Hagger et al., 2002). The results of these various meta-analyses show somewhat lower multiple correlations than those displayed in Table 6.2. Perhaps the simplest explanation for the difference is the fact that the sample of studies selected for inclusion in our table had what appeared to be good direct measures of the three predictors and of intentions that evidenced a high degree of correspondence. This confirms the importance of developing valid direct measures of each of the theory's components.

Variations in Regression Coefficients

Notwithstanding the high multiple correlations displayed in Table 6.1, the results also show—as we would expect—considerable variation in the relative contributions of attitudes, perceived norms, and perceived behavioral control to the prediction of intentions. Although our theory makes no specific predictions concerning the relative weights of the three components, we do expect these weights to vary across behaviors and across individuals or populations. In the great majority of applications, the relative weights of the three components are estimated empirically by means of multiple regression or structural equation analyses without prior hypotheses about the relative importance of the different components. However, it may be possible to make predictions on an intuitive basis or on the basis of other theories relevant to the behavior of interest. For example, it has sometimes been suggested that attitudes will be more important than perceived norms for individuals low as opposed to high in self-monitoring tendency (see Ajzen, Timko, & White, 1982), and the same pattern has also been predicted for comparisons of individualistic versus collectivistic cultures (Ybarra & Trafimow, 1998). By the same token, it could be predicted that leisure behaviors, such as going to a movie, will be largely under the influence of attitudes, whereas behaviors that affect other people (e.g., littering) will show a stronger influence of perceived norms. Still other behaviors that involve serious potential barriers to their execution, such as quitting smoking cigarettes, may be expected to show evidence of the importance of perceived behavioral control.

Some of the patterns of influence displayed in Table 6.2 may appear counterintuitive. However, closer inspection of the population and behavior reveals possible reasons for the obtained patterns. For example, as a general rule, attitudes tend to account for more variance in intentions to engage in physical activity than do either perceived norms or perceived behavioral control (see Hagger et al., 2002). The study by Latimer and Martin Ginis (2005b) in the first row of Table 6.2 showed a different pattern, with perceived control explaining more unique variance in intentions than either attitudes or injunctive norms. Recall, however, that the participants in this study were individuals with spinal cord injury, and it stands to reason that for this population issues of control take on special importance.

Or consider the study on breast cancer screening by Drossaert, Boer, and Seydel (2003). Health screening decisions, such as getting a mammogram or a colonoscopy, are strongly influenced by perceived social pressure and less so by attitudes and perceptions of control (Smith-McLellen & Fishbein, 2008). This may be due to the fact that intentions to undergo a screening are often prompted by a doctor's recommendation, thus producing perceived social pressure. In contrast, the women in the Drossaert et al. study could get a periodic mammogram as part of an ongoing screening program in the Netherlands. The behavior of these women thus had to be largely self-motivated, and, consistent with this, their personal attitudes toward getting a mammogram were better predictors of intentions than were injunctive norms or perceptions of behavioral control. Interestingly, breast self-examinations to detect possible cancer have been shown to be best predicted by perceived behavioral control (Norman & Hoyle, 2004), perhaps due to the fact that many women doubt their ability to accurately detect possible warning signs on their own.

Meaning of Regression Coefficients

In our discussion thus far we have assumed that regression coefficients reflect the independent contributions of attitudes, perceived norms, and perceived behavioral control to the prediction of intentions. We now need to consider the substantive meaning of differences between regression weights. According to the most common interpretation, a predictor's regression coefficient reflects its relative importance as a *determinant* of intentions. For example, when it is found that attitude has a higher regression coefficient in the prediction of intentions than perceived norm or perceived control, it can reasonably be argued that attitudinal considerations outweigh normative and control considerations as causal factors influencing intentions.[7] However, we must exercise caution in our interpretation of low regression coefficients because their proper interpretation depends on the reason for the observed low regression weights.

Clearly, a low regression coefficient will be obtained when there is little or no correlation between a predictor and the intention. In most instances, this is an indication that the predictor is not an important determinant of intentions. An exception to this rule may occur when the low correlation is due to little or no variance in the predictor variable. In Chapter 4 we pointed out that measures of injunctive norms sometimes have little or no variance because there is widespread agreement as to what important others think one should do. For example, smokers know that most important others think they should not smoke in smoke-free environments like restaurants and office buildings. This injunctive norm may well be an important determinant of intentions not to smoke in these environments, but because it is the same for all individuals, its influence is not reflected in the correlation with intentions.

In other instances a predictor with a relatively low regression coefficient may nevertheless have a high zero-order correlation with intentions. In Table 6.2, for example, perceived control over driving after drinking alcohol (Row 2) had a substantial zero-order correlation with intention ($r = .64$) but a relatively low regression coefficient (beta = .23). Similarly, attitudes toward applying for a promotion (Row 4) correlated highly ($r = .66$) with intentions but had a regression weight of only .16. The reason for the disparity in the magnitude of correlation and regression coefficients is that the predictors are intercorrelated. Thus, for example, attitude can correlate highly with intentions, but it will get a relatively low regression weight if it also correlates highly with perceived social norm or perceived control and if it has a lower correlation with intention (even slightly lower) than either of the latter variables In this case, attitude may still be an important determinant of intention despite its relatively low regression coefficient.

In conclusion, a high regression coefficient generally implies that the predictor in question is an important determinant of intentions, but a low regression coefficient cannot necessarily be interpreted as evidence that a predictor variable is unimportant. If the predictor has a high zero-order correlation with intention, it is likely to have at least some influence on that intention. In contrast, when a low regression weight is accompanied by a low correlation, this can usually be interpreted as an indication that the variable in question plays little or no role in determining the intention. One possible exception occurs when scores on the predictor variable have a highly restricted range. The importance of these issues will become apparent in our discussion of interventions designed to change intentions and behavior in Chapter 10.

Systematic Comparisons of Regression Weights

The studies summarized in Table 6.2 reveal considerable variation across different behavioral domains in the relative contributions of attitudes, perceptions of social norms, and perceived control to the prediction of intentions. Unfortunately, it is not clear whether the observed patterns are due to the particular behaviors that were investigated or to other differences between studies, such as the research population or the particular measures used to assess the theory's constructs. However, similar variations in patterns of influence are also evident when intentions to perform different kinds of behaviors are predicted in the context of a single study using the same participants and measuring instruments. Table 6.3 presents data from a study by Sheeran, Trafimow, Finlay, and Norman (2002) in which attitudes, injunctive norms, and perceptions of control were used to predict intentions to perform 30 different behaviors. We show the results for eight of these behaviors selected for illustrative purposes.

It can be seen that there was considerable variation in the regression weights associated with the three predictors and that with respect to three of the behaviors, one of the variables did not contribute significantly to the prediction of intentions. Nevertheless, the multiple correlations in the last column show that even in these instances, intentions were predicted quite well by a simultaneous consideration of all three components. The table has been arranged such that the first two behaviors (avoiding eating meat, going to a night club) are primarily under the control of attitudinal

TABLE 6.3 Prediction of Intentions From Attitudes, Injunctive Norm, and Perceived Behavioral Control: Regression Coefficients and Multiple Correlations

| | Regression coefficients | | | |
Intention	Attitude	Injunctive norm	Perceived behavioral control	R
Avoid eating meat	.60	.11*	.18	.77
Go to a night club	.49	.29	.18	.75
Take vitamin pills	.21	.46	.13	.62
Go home (e.g., visit parents)	.10*	.37	.32	.59
Get at least 7 hours sleep	.11*	.31	.47	.57
Avoid smoking cigarettes	.14	.22	.46	.65
Engage in exercise	.37	.30	.36	.73
Go out for a meal	.18	.34	.24	.57

Source: Sheeran, P., Trafimow, D., Finlay, K. A., & Norman, P., *British Journal of Social Psychology, 41*, 253–270, 2002 (with permission).
* Not significant, all other coefficients are significant at $p < .05$.

considerations, followed by two behaviors (taking vitamin pills, visiting parents) that are mainly influenced by injunctive norms, followed, in turn, by two behaviors (getting at least 7 hours of sleep, avoiding smoking cigarettes) for which perceived behavioral control carries most weight. The last two behaviors (engaging in exercise, going out for a meal) are included to show that some behaviors may be strongly influenced by all three components.

Clearly, then, regression weights associated with attitudes, norms, and perceived control can vary considerably from one behavior to another. By the same token, these weights can also differ from one population to another. For example, the influence of gender on the relative contributions of attitudes, norms, and perceived control can be seen in a study of condom use among multipartner heterosexual individuals (von Haeften & Kenski, 2001). Although the multiple correlation between intentions to use condoms for vaginal sex with main partners and attitudes, injunctive norms, and the autonomy aspect of control was highly significant and quite similar for both men ($R = .71$) and women ($R = .77$), control considerations contributed significantly to the prediction of this intention for women (beta = .20) but not for men (beta = −.05).[8] This finding is hardly surprising in light of the fact that in the case of condom use, behavioral control is more of an issue for women than for men.

Gender differences in the relative weights of attitudes, norms, and perceived control were also found with respect to intentions to eat sweet snack foods (Grogan, Bell, & Conner, 1997). Women's intentions to eat such foods were influenced by their attitudes toward this behavior as well as their injunctive norms, whereas men's intentions were determined only by their attitudes. This finding suggests that, when it comes to eating snacks, normative considerations play a more important role for women than for men.

Differences in regression weights due to ethnicity were reported in a study of regular marijuana use among Black and White adolescents (Yzer, Fishbein, & Cappella, 2007). For African American females, perceived norms (beta = .48) and attitudes (beta = .36) but not perceived control (beta = .06) were found to be significant predictors of intentions to use marijuana regularly. The multiple correlation in this subsample was .71. For White females, the multiple correlation was similar ($R = 77$), but in this subsample the regression coefficients for all three predictors were significant. In addition, attitudes carried more weight than norms (beta = .51 and .30), and both of these regression weights were higher than the weight for perceived behavioral control (beta = −.11). Another example of ethnic differences comes from a comparison of native Dutch citizens and a sample composed of various minorities living in the Netherlands (van Hooft, Born, Taris, & van der Flier, 2004). Intentions to seek a new job in the next 4 months were completely under normative control in the minorities sample but primarily under attitudinal control in the Dutch sample.

Individual Differences

If we carry the comparison between different subgroups to its logical conclusion, we can propose that individuals may differ from one another in the extent to which their intentions are influenced by attitudes, perceived social norms, and perceived behavioral control. Several investigators (Finlay, Trafimow, & Jones, 1997; Finlay, Trafimow, & Moroi, 1999; Johnston, White, & Norman, 2004; Sheeran, Norman, & Orbell, 1999; Sheeran et al., 2002; Trafimow & Finlay, 1996) have tested this idea by means of a procedure originally proposed by Carlson (1969). In the Carlson study, 30 behaviors were selected, and, with respect to each behavior, participants were asked to indicate their intentions, attitudes, and perceived norms.[9] For each participant, a within-subjects analysis was performed. That is across the 30 behaviors, intentions were regressed on attitudes and perceived norms, and thus for each participant, regression weights for attitudes and perceived norms were obtained. These regression coefficients were then used to identify individuals whose intentions, across different kinds of behaviors, were primarily under the control of one or another of the predictor variables. In most studies using this within-subjects approach, only attitudes and injunctive norms have been used to predict intentions. Attitudes received a higher regression weight than norms for 70% to 80% of the participants (see Finlay et al., 1997; Johnston et al., 2004; Trafimow & Finlay, 1996); for the remaining 20% to 30%, the normative component had a higher regression coefficient than the attitudinal component.

For example, in the study by Trafimow & Finlay (1996), single items were used to assess attitudes, injunctive norms, and intentions with respect to each of 30 behaviors. On the basis of within-subjects regressions, participants were divided into two groups: those whose intentions were primarily determined by attitudes (79%); and those whose intentions were primarily determined by injunctive norms (21%). Within each of these groups, each of the 30 behavioral intentions was then predicted separately, resulting in regression coefficients for attitude and injunctive norm with respect to each behavior. Consider, for example, "volunteering my time to helping others." In the total sample, the intention to perform this behavior was predicted quite accurately ($R = .69$), with attitude receiving much more weight (beta = .63) than the injunctive norm (beta = .15). In the attitudinally controlled sample, the multiple correlation was .74, and attitudes were the only significant predictor of intentions (beta = .72); the regression coefficient for the injunctive norm was not significant (beta = .06). The pattern of results was very different for the normatively controlled subsample. Once again, the multiple correlation was quite high ($R = .71$), indicating good overall prediction of intentions, but now only injunctive norms carried a significant regression weight (beta = .63 vs. .13 for attitudes). We selected this behavior to illustrate that the relative importance of the attitudinal and normative predictors can differ drastically from one group of individuals to another. Although the dramatic reversal in the relative importance of attitudes and injunctive norms was rare, the regression weights for attitudes were always higher in the attitudinal than in the normative subgroup, and the regression weights for norms were always higher in the normative than in the attitudinal subgroup. Similar patterns of results were also reported by Finlay et al. (1997, 1999), Finlay et al. and Johnston et al. (2004) in the domain of health behaviors.

These findings confirm the proposition that a given behavior may be primarily under the influence of attitudes for some people and primarily under the influence of normative considerations for others. In a similar manner, it has been argued (Sheeran et al., 2002) that perceived behavioral control can be a more important determinant of intentions for some individuals than for others. To demonstrate this, Sheeren and his associates regressed intentions on perceived control as well as on attitudes and injunctive norms. Based on within-subjects correlations across 30 behaviors, participants were classified into two groups: individuals whose intentions were influenced primarily by attitudinal or normative considerations (75%); and those whose intentions were influenced primarily by perceived behavioral control (25%). Each of the different behavioral intentions was then predicted from attitudes, injunctive norms, and perceived behavioral control separately within each of the two groups.

To illustrate the impact of individual differences in the relative importance of perceived behavioral control, consider the intention to eat fruit. In the total sample of participants, attitudes and perceived behavioral control had the same regression coefficient (.38), whereas the effect of injunctive norms was not significant (beta = .08). The multiple correlation was .69. Considering only participants whose intentions were primarily determined by attitudes or injunctive norms, the regression coefficient for norms continued to be nonsignificant (beta = .06), whereas the coefficient for attitude went up to .42 and the coefficient for perceived control went down to .30. The multiple correlation for the prediction of intentions in this subsample was .66. In contrast, for participants whose intentions overall were largely determined by perceptions of control, the regression coefficient of perceived behavioral control in the prediction of intentions to eat fruit went up to .62, whereas attitudes and norms had regression coefficients of .25 and .03, respectively, with a multiple correlation of .77. Thus, among participants whose intentions across different behaviors were primarily influenced by attitudes or injunctive norms, the intention to eat fruit was largely determined by attitudes, whereas among participants whose intentions were generally influenced by perceived behavioral control, the intention to eat fruit was in fact largely determined by this factor.

Testing Hypotheses About Regression Weights

Up to this point we have simply tried to show that in the prediction of intentions, the regression weights of attitudes, norms, and control can vary as a function of the behavior and of the population or individual under consideration. As a general rule, we interpret these variations as reflective of differences in the relative importance of the three predictors. Notwithstanding the issues we discussed earlier regarding the meaning of low regression coefficients, we saw that the patterns of regression weights reported in various investigations—although not necessarily predicted— are usually quite reasonable and can help to explain the behavior under consideration. Thus, for example, although we would not necessarily have predicted that women's intentions to perform breast self-examinations are strongly affected by perceived behavioral control, in retrospect this finding makes perfectly good sense if we assume that women's intentions to perform such self-examinations take into account their perceived ability to detect abnormalities.

More persuasive evidence that the regression coefficients do indeed reflect the relative importance of the three predictors would be obtained if we could develop and test a priori hypotheses about the patterns of regression coefficients to be expected. We want to emphasize that there is nothing in our reasoned action approach that would lead us to expect any particular pattern of regression coefficients. It is up to the investigator to generate hypotheses regarding the relative importance of the three predictors. These hypotheses can best be developed by considering theories concerning the behavior in question or by examining available information about the behavioral domain.

Correlational Evidence

One approach taken by investigators is to measure properties of the individual, whether personality characteristics or other factors, that would be expected to influence the relative importance of attitudes, norms, and perceived control as predictors of behavioral intentions. For example, Trafimow and Finlay (1996) hypothesized that a high score on a measure of the collective self predisposes individuals to be sensitive to normative considerations in the formation of their intentions. Compared with people with a weak collective self, people who have a strong collective self should be more likely to behave in accordance with the opinions of those who are important to them. Recall that these investigators estimated the relative importance of attitudes and injunctive norms as determinants of intentions for a given individual by computing within-subject regressions across a set of behaviors. Consistent with their hypothesis, Trafimow and Finlay found that the stronger one's collective self, the greater the relative importance placed on the injunctive norm (i.e., the higher the individual-level normative regression coefficient). The correlation between the measure of collective self and the relative importance of injunctive norms was .24.

In contrast to this approach, which relies on within-subjects analyses across behaviors, most investigators measure a given individual difference variable and examine the extent to which it moderates the effects of attitudes, perceived norms, and perceived behavioral control on intentions to perform a given behavior. For example, it has been suggested that generalized fear of negative evaluation raises the extent to which perceived social norms predict behavioral intentions (Latimer & Martin Ginis, 2005a). The investigators used a 12-item scale to assess fearfulness associated with receiving disapproval and criticism from others. In addition, they measured attitudes, perceived norms, perceived behavioral control, and intentions with respect to engaging in physical activity. Consistent with expectations, the measure of injunctive norm was a significant predictor of exercise intentions (beta = .22) only for the subset of individuals with a high fear of negative evaluation from others. The injunctive norm did not significantly affect exercise intentions (beta = .01) in the subset of individuals with a low fear of evaluation from others.

Among other individual difference variables that have been proposed to moderate the influence of attitudes, social norms, and perceived control on intentions are self-monitoring and socal identification with a social group. Individuals high in self-monitoring are assumed to be "highly sensitive to social and interpersonal cues of situationally appropriate performances," whereas individuals low in this tendency are thought to "display expressive behavior that truly reflects their own attitudes, traits, feelings, and other current inner states" (Gangestad & Snyder, 1985, p. 322). This conception of self-monitoring implies that perceived norms are more important factors for people high rather than low in self-monitoring tendency whereas attitudes are more important factors for people who are low rather than high in self-monitoring. Some empirical support for this hypothesis has been reported (e.g., Hillhouse, Turrisi, & Kastner, 2000; Prislin & Kovrlija, 1992); however, it has also been found that the moderating effect of self-monitoring is obtained only for individuals who are high in private self-consciousness (Miller & Grush, 1986), and some studies have failed to find any moderating effect of self-monitoring (e.g., Ajzen et al., 1982).

With regard to social identification, it has been suggested (Terry & Hogg, 1996; Terry, Hogg, & White, 1999) that the more people that identify with a given referent group, the more the perceived norms of that group will influence behavioral intentions.[10] This hypothesis was confirmed in relation to the prediction of intentions to use condoms and to engage in sun-protective actions (Terry & Hogg, 1996), as well as intentions to recycle household waste (Terry et al., 19999). However, a study on intentions to use contraception among sexually active adolescents in Ethiopia (Fekadu & Kraft, 2002) failed to replicate these findings.

In sum, it is possible to generate hypotheses concerning the likely influence of personality or other individual difference factors on the relative importance of attitudes, perceived social norms, and perceptions of behavioral control. It seems reasonable to propose that people who tend to monitor their behavior in terms of the social environment, who come from collectivistic societies, who fear evaluation by others, or who identify closely with a reference group will be more influenced by normative considerations than will be individuals who don't have these characteristics. While not part of our reasoned action framework, hypotheses of this kind can augment our theory and help to further our understanding of factors that influence intentions and behavior. Unfortunately, research that has relied on measures of individual difference variables as possible moderators has, at best, yielded mixed results. Perhaps a more promising approach to understanding the basis for variations in the relative weights of attitudes, norms, and perceived control is an experimental one in which we try to influence the relative weights of one or more of the three components by manipulating potential moderating factors.

Experimental Evidence

Some evidence that the relative contributions of attitudes and norms can be manipulated experimentally was reported by Ajzen and Fishbein (1970). Pairs of college students played two Prisoner's Dilemma games. These games present the players with two options, one cooperative and the other competitive. On every trial of the game, each player can choose either the cooperative option or the competitive option. The number of points earned by each player depends upon their combined decisions; the consequences of the different combinations of choices are shown to them in a payoff matrix. Mutual cooperation produces better outcomes for both players than mutual competition, but most points are earned by choosing the competitive option when the other player chooses to cooperate. In this case, competitive players win more points than they would by cooperating while the cooperative player loses points. Each player thus faces a dilemma between cooperation for a modest payoff and competition for a possibly larger gain.

Following eight practice trials, the participants completed a questionnaire that assessed their attitudes toward choosing the cooperative strategy, their normative beliefs as to what the other player thought they should do, and their intentions to choose the cooperative strategy in a series of 10 subsequent trials. To manipulate the relative importance of attitudinal and normative considerations, participants in different conditions of the experiment played the games under either cooperative, individualistic, or competitive motivational orientations. In the cooperative orientation condition they were told that the goal of the game was for the two players to jointly accumulate as many points as possible. In the competitive condition they were told that the goal was for them to win more points than the other player, and in the individualistic orientation they were told to win as many points as possible, irrespective of the other person's fate. The multiple correlations for the prediction of intentions from attitudes and normative beliefs were very high for both Prisoner's Dilemma games under all three motivational orientations, ranging from .63 to .92. More important, the regression analyses showed that, as predicted, under a cooperative orientation normative considerations accounted for a much greater proportion of variance in behavioral intentions than did attitudes (beta = .71 vs. .23 and .54 vs. .24 in the two games), whereas the reverse was true under competitive motivational instructions (beta = .33 vs. .69 and .30 vs. .67). In the individualistic condition, injunctive norms carried more weight in Game 1 (beta = .55 vs. .35), but norms and attitudes were equally important as determinants of intention in game 2 (beta = .43 vs. .42).

Armitage, Conner, and Norman (1999) reasoned that mood could have an effect on the relative importance of attitudes and subjective norms as predictors of intentions. Specifically, one of the hypotheses they entertained on the basis of prior research was the prediction that a negative mood state leads to more in-depth processing of a behavior's likely consequences (i.e., attitudes) whereas a positive mood predisposes people to be attuned to more "superficial" or "peripheral" considerations, such as perceived norms. Participants in one of their two studies were asked to respond to a list of 20 self-referent mood statements designed to induce either a positive mood (e.g., "People really seem to like me") or a negative mood (e.g., "I have very little to look forward to"). Following this mood induction, the participants completed a questionnaire that assessed their attitudes toward using condoms, their perception of the injunctive norms regarding condom use, and their intentions to use condoms. The results showed that intentions were predicted quite well in both mood conditions (R = .53 and .51 for positive and negative mood), but as expected, the regression coefficients showed a greater influence of norms than of attitudes under positive mood (beta = .51 and .06, respectively), whereas under negative mood the reverse pattern was obtained (beta = .14 and .45, respectively).

Finally, Ybarra and Trafimow (1998) hypothesized that when a person's private self is made more accessible in memory, attitudes should have a greater impact on the formation of a behavioral intention than should injunctive norms. In contrast, when the collective self is primed, injunctive norms should have a greater impact than attitudes. The investigators reported support for this hypothesis in a series of three experiments. To illustrate, in the first experiment participants were primed to make either the private self or the public self more accessible. In the private self condition, they were asked to think about what made them different from their family and friends, whereas in the collective self condition they were asked to think about what they have in common with their family and friends. Following this, they participated in an ostensibly unrelated study in which they were asked to indicate their attitudes, perceived injunctive norms, and intentions toward using condoms. Overall, for participants in both experimental conditions, intentions to use condoms were accurately predicted from attitudes and norms ($R = .68$ in the private self condition and $R = .71$ in the collective self condition). Consistent with expectations, however, the intentions of participants who were primed with the private self were more affected by attitudes (beta = .54) than by injunctive norms (beta = .23). In contrast, the pattern was reversed in the collective self condition, with injunctive norms accounting for more variance in intentions (beta = .53) than attitudes (beta = .29). The other two studies in this series of investigations produced very similar results using different priming procedures.

To summarize briefly, the results of investigations using correlational and experimental methods have provided evidence for the proposition that the nature of the behavior as well as differences associated with the research population or the individual can influence the relative importance of attitudes, perceived norms, and perceptions of control for the prediction of intentions. The patterns of observed differences in regression weights that have been obtained in correlational studies tend to be intuitively reasonable, and predictable differences in regression weights have been obtained by experimentally manipulating features of the situation.

☐ Mediating Processes

According to our model of behavioral prediction, attitudes and subjective norms can influence behavior only indirectly by their effects on intentions. The effect of perceived control on behavior is more complex. Theoretically, it can influence behavior in two ways. First, it can moderate the effects of attitudes and of perceived norms on intentions and through intentions it can influence behavior. Second, it can directly moderate the effect of intentions on behavior. However, in Chapter 2 and earlier in this chapter we noted that most investigators treat perceived control as a separate independent predictor of both intentions and behavior. Thus, perceived control is expected to influence behavior indirectly via intentions and, as a proxy of actual control, to also have a direct link to behavior. In a simple method often used to test the predicted mediating effects of intentions, behavior is regressed on all antecedents: intentions, attitudes, perceived behavioral control, and perceived norms.[11] The correlation and regression coefficients are then examined for evidence of mediation. According to our reasoned action framework, only intention and perhaps perceived control should carry significant regression weights in the prediction of behavior since the influence of attitudes and norms should be mediated by intention.

Consider, for example, a study of breast self-examination (BSE) conducted by Norman and Hoyle (2004). Female employees of a telecommunications company completed a questionnaire with respect to performing breast self-examinations and 4 weeks later reported whether they had performed BSE in the previous month. Attitude had a correlation of .43 with self-reported BSE, injunctive norm a correlation of .35, and perceived control a correlation of .51; all three correlations were highly significant. However, in a secondary analysis of the data, only attitude and perception of control carried significant regression weights in the prediction of behavior. The investigators performed a hierarchical regression analysis in which they predicted BSE behavior from the three model components as well as intention. It was found that only intention contributed significantly to the prediction of BSE behavior, indicating that the significant effects of attitudes and perceptions of control on behavior that were found earlier were mediated by intentions.

In a study of drivers' compliance with speed limits (Elliott, Armitage, & Baughan, 2003), perceived behavioral control retained a direct effect on behavior after controlling for intentions. Participants completed a questionnaire that included measures of intention, attitude, injunctive norms, and perceived control with respect to staying within speed limits in built-up areas in the next 3 months. After 3 months, the participants reported whether they had stayed within speed limits in built-up areas in the past 3 months. Zero-order correlations for the prediction of behavior from attitudes, injunctive norms, and perceived control were all highly significant ($r = .34$, .37, and .64, respectively). However, a secondary analysis of the data showed that only perceived behavioral control made a significant contribution to the prediction of behavior. A regression analysis showed that this effect remained significant even after controlling for intentions, confirming the theory's assumption that perceived control can have a direct as well as an indirect effect on behavior.

The results of these and other studies (e.g., Hausenblas & Downs, 2004; Latimer & Martin Ginis, 2005b; Orbell, Blair, Sherlock, & Conner, 2001) support our theory by showing that the effects of attitudes and perceived norms on behavior are mediated by intentions, whereas perceived behavioral control can have both mediated and direct effects.

☐ From Beliefs to Behavior

In Chapter 2 we showed that behavior can be predicted from intentions to perform the behavior and perceptions of control over its performance. The next three chapters dealt with the different kinds of considerations or beliefs that, in the final analysis, are assumed to determine intentions and actions. In Chapter 3 we examined the effects of behavioral beliefs on attitudes; in Chapter 4 we discussed normative beliefs and their effects on perceived norms; and in Chapter 5 we dealt with control beliefs and their effects on perceived behavioral control. In the current chapter we have shown that, in combination, attitudes, perceived norms, and perceptions of control afford good prediction of intentions and that the relative weights of these components vary in meaningful ways from behavior to behavior and from population to population. Finally, we reviewed some evidence for the proposition that attitudes and perceived norms affect behavior indirectly through their influence on intentions whereas perceived behavioral control can have mediated as well as direct effects on behavior.

In the present section we try to combine all of these elements to present a full picture of our reasoned action approach. From our perspective, behavior is ultimately determined by the readily accessible or salient beliefs people have about their performing the behavior in question. Three broad classes of beliefs are distinguished:

1. Beliefs that performing a given behavior will lead to positively or negatively valued outcomes (behavioral beliefs or outcome expectancies).
2. Beliefs that certain referent individuals or groups support or oppose performance of the behavior or are themselves performing the behavior (normative beliefs).
3. Beliefs that certain personal or situational factors that can facilitate or inhibit performance of the behavior are likely (or unlikely) to be present (control beliefs).

We have repeatedly emphasized that the best way to identify the behavioral, normative, and control beliefs that are salient in a given population is to elicit them from a representative sample of the population in question (see also Middlestadt, Bhattacharyya, Rosenbaum, & Fishbein, 1996). Indeed, formative elicitation research is a central feature of our approach.

Although we conceive of behavioral, normative, and control beliefs as distinct categories, it is important to recognize that there is likely to be overlap among these categories. Consider, for example, regular physical exercise. One commonly held behavioral belief about engaging in regular exercise is that this behavior is time-consuming. At the same time, many people also tend to hold the control belief that they don't have enough time to exercise. Similarly, if I believe that my sister wants me to buy her a present for her birthday (normative belief), I may also believe that doing so will please her (behavioral belief). To the extent that there is overlap of this kind among behavioral, normative, and control beliefs, we would expect attitudes, perceived normative pressure, and perceptions of control to also correlate with each other. As a general rule, people who are important to me will encourage me to perform behaviors that produce positive outcomes and to avoid behaviors that are likely to lead to negative outcomes. Likewise, I am unlikely to form positive attitudes toward performing behaviors that I know are not under my control, and important others would not expect me to perform them. Thus, although the three components are conceptually distinct, empirically they are likely to exhibit some degree of interdependence.

Mediated Effects of Beliefs

It is at the level of beliefs that we obtain substantive information about the considerations that lead people to perform, or not to perform, a given behavior. By examining salient behavioral, normative, and control beliefs we gain insight into the factors that produce favorable or unfavorable attitudes toward a behavior, that generate perceived social pressure to engage or not to engage in the behavior, and that lead to a sense of control over performance of the behavior. The effect of salient beliefs on intentions is assumed to be mediated by these broad dispositions. Thus, in accordance with the expectancy-value model described in Chapter 3, the summed products of behavioral beliefs × outcome evaluations ($\Sigma b_i e_i$) is expected to correlate with intention, but its effect on intention is assumed to be mediated by the overall attitude toward the behavior that is assessed directly by means of a standard attitude scaling method. In a similar fashion, the composite of normative beliefs × motivation to comply ($\Sigma n_i m_i$) described in Chapter 4 should affect intentions indirectly through its influence on perceived norm. And the index of control beliefs × perceived power of the control factors ($\Sigma c_i p_i$) discussed in Chapter 5 is expected to have an indirect effect on intentions via the general construct of perceived behavioral control.

Consider, for example, a study of glass recycling conducted in Germany (Lüdemann, 1997). In this study, behavioral, normative, and control beliefs as well as attitudes, injunctive norms, perceptions of behavioral control, and intentions were assessed with respect to this behavior.[12] A secondary analysis of the published data showed that, consistent with expectations, attitudes correlated significantly with a summative index of behavioral beliefs (r = .60); injunctive norms had a correlation of .59 with an injunctive normative belief index; and perceived behavioral control correlated .63 with an index of control beliefs. Using the three belief indices to predict intentions resulted in a multiple correlation of .73. However, direct measures of attitudes, injunctive norms, and perceptions of control produced a multiple correlation of .78 with intentions. More important, adding behavioral, normative, and control beliefs to the regression equation that contained the direct measures increased the explained variance in intentions by only 2%.

Similar results were obtained in a study of adolescent sexual behavior (Fishbein et al., in preparation). Composite indices of behavioral, normative, and control beliefs about engaging in sexual intercourse in the next 12 months correlated quite highly with the corresponding direct measures of attitude (r = .71), perceived norm (r = .67), and perceived behavioral control (r = .47). Predicting intentions to engage in sexual intercourse from the three direct measures resulted in a multiple correlation of .74, and adding the three belief composites to the prediction equation increased the explained variance in intentions by about 2%. Because the sample was quite large (N = 543), this increase was statistically significant.

A final example is provided by the study on hunting behavior (Hrubes, Ajzen, & Daigle, 2001) discussed in Chapter 3. There we saw that attitudes toward hunting correlated strongly with the behavioral belief × outcome evaluation composite (r = .76). The study also obtained high correlations between injunctive norms and the index of normative beliefs (r = .74) and between perceived behavioral control and a composite measure of control beliefs (r = .72). The multiple correlation for the prediction of intentions from the three belief indices was .89, a highly significant coefficient. However, when intentions were predicted from the direct measures of attitudes, injunctive norms, and perceptions of control, the multiple correlation was .93, and this correlation stayed virtually unchanged when the three belief composites were added to the regression equation.

In short, the results of different investigations show that the effects of behavioral, normative, and control beliefs on intentions and behavior are generally mediated, respectively, by attitudes toward the behavior, perceived norms, and perceived control over the behavior.

The Explanatory Value of Beliefs

The work we have reviewed in this and in previous chapters has shown that, consistent with our reasoned action approach, beliefs influence attitudes, perceived norms, and perceived behavioral control, and as a result of these influences they indirectly affect intentions and behavior. This suggests that to fully understand why people do or do not perform a behavior of interest we must examine the underlying behavioral, normative, and control beliefs. In Chapters 3, 4, and 5 we discussed how these different types of beliefs can help to explain prevailing attitudes, perceived norms, and perceptions of control. In the present section we try to show how beliefs can be used to explain differences in intentions and actions. Toward this aim, we divide the sample into participants who perform the behavior of interest, or who intend to perform it, and those who do not. We can then compare the mean beliefs in the two subsamples. In addition, we also report correlations for the total sample between individual beliefs and measures of intentions or behavior. The stronger the correlation, the more the belief in question discriminates between those who do and do not perform (or intend to perform) the behavior in question.

Illustrations

Of the multitude of studies conducted in the context of our theory, only a minority have assessed beliefs; most rely on direct measures of the three major components to predict intentions and behavior. Even when investigators do assess beliefs, some consider only one or another of the three types of beliefs or, for various reasons, decide not to measure outcome evaluations, motivation to comply with normative referents, or the perceived power of control factors. As a result, there are only a small number of studies that contain a complete set of beliefs that can be examined in relation to intentions and actions.

Mountain Climbing

One study that obtained a full set of behavioral, normative, and control belief measures was mentioned in Chapter 5. It had to do with five different outdoor leisure activities (Ajzen & Driver, 1991). We illustrate how beliefs can be used to explain such behaviors by examining one of the activities, mountain climbing. College students completed a questionnaire with respect to mountain climbing and, 1 year later, they reported, on a six-point scale from *never – more than 20 times*, the frequency with which they had engaged in this behavior during the preceding 12 months. Consistent with our model of behavioral prediction, intentions and perceived behavioral control significantly predicted mountain climbing behavior with a multiple correlation of .69. Intentions, in turn, were predicted from attitudes toward mountain climbing, injunctive norms, and perceptions of control ($R = .72$). Although all three components correlated significantly with mountain climbing intentions, the regression analysis showed that perceived control was the most important determinant (beta = .52, $p < .01$), followed by subjective norm (beta = .18, $p < .05$); the regression coefficient for attitude was not significant (beta = .12).

Table 6.4 shows the influence of control beliefs on mountain climbing behavior. As mentioned in Chapter 5, an elicitation study had identified four potential control factors: having good weather for mountain climbing, not having proper equipment, living near mountains, and lacking skills and knowledge for mountain climbing. With respect to each factor, participants indicated, on seven-point scales, whether the factor was true for them (e.g., "I don't have the proper equipment for mountain climbing"; *true–false*) and whether the factor's presence would making mountain climbing easier or more difficult. The first question assessed the strength of the control belief (c) and the second the factor's perceived power (p) to facilitate or inhibit performance of the behavior. Scores on the two items were multiplied,[13] and the correlation of the product with mountain climbing behavior is displayed in Column 1 of Table 6.4.

It can be seen that the $c \times p$ products associated with lacking proper equipment and lacking appropriate skills and knowledge predicted the frequency with which the participants went mountain climbing; the weather and proximity to mountains were largely irrelevant. To examine these effects more closely, the sample of students was divided into participants who had gone mountain climbing at least once (41.8%) during the preceding 12 months and those who had not. Columns 2 and 3 of Table 6.4 show the

TABLE 6.4 Correlations of Control Belief (c) × Perceived Power (p) Products With Mountain Climbing Behavior, and Mean Belief Strength and Perceived Power of College Student Mountain Climbers and Nonclimbers

Control factor	Correlation c_ip_i – behavior	Mean belief strength Climbers	Nonclimbers	Mean perceived power Climbers	Nonclimbers
Good weather for climbing	.14	0.61	−0.32*	2.36	2.18
Lacking proper equipment	.46**	1.34	2.71**	−1.64	−2.40**
Living near mountains	.02	0.36	−0.27	1.80	2.45**
Lacking skills and knowledge	.49**	0.10	2.40**	−2.07	−2.33**

Source: Ajzen, I., & Driver, B. L., *Leisure Sciences, 13*, 185–204, 1991 (with permission)
Note: Belief strength and perceived power can range from −3 to +3.
* $p < .05$.
** $p < .01$.

mean control belief strength for climbers and nonclimbers, and Columns 4 and 5 show the mean power of the control factors for these two subgroups.

The results indicate that, in comparison with nonclimbers, climbers were somewhat more likely to believe that they could climb in an area with good weather, but there was little difference between the groups in the perceived power of this factor to facilitate or inhibit mountain climbing; both groups believed that good weather would make mountain climbing easier. Similarly, there was little difference in perceived living distance from mountains, but nonclimbers more than climbers thought that living near mountains would make mountain climbing easier.

More marked differences were observed with respect to the possession of proper equipment and appropriate skills and knowledge. In this college student sample, most students believed that they lacked proper equipment to go mountain climbing, but mountain climbers were significantly less likely to believe that this was the case than were nonclimbers. Moreover, although climbers as well as nonclimbers believed that lacking proper equipment would make mountain climbing more difficult, nonclimbers held this belief more strongly. Finally, the two groups agreed that lacking appropriate skill and knowledge would make mountain climbing more difficult, but climbers agreed only slightly that they lacked the appropriate skills and knowledge to go mountain climbing, whereas nonclimbers strongly believed that they did not have the appropriate skills or knowledge.

This pattern of results helps to identify the factors that can facilitate or interfere with mountain climbing. Possession of proper equipment and of appropriate skills and knowledge were viewed as important prerequisites. Participants who strongly believed that they lacked these prerequisites were unlikely to go mountain climbing. Indeed, the correlations in Column 1 of Table 6.4 indicate that both beliefs contributed significantly to the decision to go mountain climbing. Having good weather and living near mountains were also salient factors, but these considerations did not distinguish clearly between climbers and nonclimbers, and the correlations in Column 1 show that neither control belief contributed significantly to the mountain climbing decision.

Comparable analyses with respect to the effects of normative beliefs on mountain climbing behavior are displayed in Table 6.5. Salient normative referents identified in the pilot study were friends, parents, boyfriend/girlfriend, brothers/sisters, and other family members. Normative beliefs strength (n) and motivation to comply (m) were assessed with respect to each of these referents. For example, participants were asked to rate, on seven-point scales, "If I went mountain climbing my friends would" (7–1, *approve–disapprove*), and "I care whether my friends approve or disapprove of my recreational activities" (1–7, *not at all–very much*). Note that motivation to comply was assessed with respect to normative expectations in the

TABLE 6.5 Correlations of Injunctive Normative Belief × Motivation to Comply Products With Mountain Climbing Behavior, and Mean Belief Strength and Motivation to Comply of College Student Mountain Climbers and Nonclimbers

Injunctive normative referents	Correlation $n_i m_i$–intention	Mean belief strength		Mean motivation to comply	
		Intenders	Nonintenders	Intenders	Nonintenders
Friends	.20*	6.00	5.32**	5.36	5.41
Parents	.32**	5.28	3.99**	5.02	4.62
Boyfriend/ girlfriend	.30*	5.72	4.82**	4.44	4.24
Brothers/ sisters	.26**	5.78	4.95**	5.40	5.45
Other family	.29**	5.44	4.61**	5.72	5.55

Source: Ajzen, I., & Driver, B. L., *Leisure Sciences, 13*, 185–204, 1991 (with permission).
Note: Belief strength and motivation to comply can range from 1 to 7.
* $p < .05$.
** $p < .01$.

general domain of recreational activities, not with respect to the specific behavior of mountain climbing. Normative belief strength and motivation to comply were multiplied, and the resulting products were correlated with reported mountain climbing frequency. The results are shown in the first column of Table 6.5.

It can be seen that all five $n \times m$ products correlated significantly with mountain climbing, suggesting that each referent exerted some influence on the behavior. Comparing the means for climbers and nonclimber shown in Columns 2 through 5 we can see that there was little difference between the groups in terms of their motivations to comply with the five referents. In contrast, there were significant differences between climbers and nonclimbers in belief strength. Generally speaking, the more that participants believed that a referent approved of their going mountain climbing, the more likely they were to engage in this behavior.

Finally, Table 6.6 displays the effects of behavioral beliefs on mountain climbing behavior. Even though attitude did not carry a significant weight in the regression equation, attitudes did have a strong zero-order correlation with intentions ($r = .50$, $p < .01$). Thus, as discussed earlier in this chapter, under these circumstances it is worth examining the underlying behavioral beliefs. In the pilot study seven modal salient outcomes of mountain climbing had been identified: improved physical fitness; developing experience and skills; endangering your life; experiencing nature and the outdoors; a sense of accomplishment; physical injury (pulled

TABLE 6.6 Correlations of Behavioral Belief (b) x Outcome Evaluation (e) Products With Mountain Climbing Behavior, and Mean Belief Strength and Outcome Evaluation of College Student Mountain Climbers and Nonclimbers

Behavioral belief	Correlation $b_i e_i$ – behavior	Mean belief strength		Mean evaluation	
		Climbers	Nonclimbers	Climbers	Nonclimbers
Improve physical fitness	.22**	2.13	1.73*	2.89	2.72*
Develop experience and skills	.21*	2.30	1.95*	2.70	2.64
Endanger your life	.39**	0.16	1.16**	-2.36	-2.20
Experience nature and outdoors	.26**	2.74	1.56	2.69	2.27**
Get a sense of accomplishment	.22**	2.66	2.48*	2.82	2.73
Get physical injury	.07	0.07	0.56*	-2.11	-1.96
Be tired and exhausted	.30**	1.37	1.13	-0.36	-0.72

Source: Aizen, I., & Driver, B. L., *Leisure Sciences, 13,* 185–204, 1991 (with permission).
Note: Belief strength and outcome evaluations can range from –3 to +3.
* $p < .05$.
** $p < .01$.

muscles, broken bones); and being tired and exhausted. Behavioral belief strength (b) and outcome evaluations (e) were assessed on seven-point scales, such as "Mountain climbing improves physical fitness" (*likely–unlikely*) and "Improved physical fitness is" (*harmful–beneficial*). Belief strength and outcome evaluation, each scored in bipolar fashion, were multiplied, and the individual products were correlated with mountain climbing behavior; the results are shown in Column 1 of Table 6.6.

Except for the belief that mountain climbing may lead to physical injury, all $b \times e$ products significantly correlated with behavior. The strongest effect was due to the belief that mountain climbing endangers your life. As might be expected, the less people believed that this negative outcome would occur, the more likely they were to go mountain climbing. In addition, beliefs about mountain climbing leading to being tired and exhausted and experiencing nature and the outdoors also strongly influenced the behavior. More detailed information is obtained by comparing the belief strength and outcome evaluations of participants who did and did not participate in mountain climbing. Generally speaking, these comparisons show that the more people believed that mountain climbing would produce positive outcomes, and the less they believed that it would produce negative outcomes, the more likely they were to go mountain climbing. For example, the stronger the belief that mountain climbing improves physical fitness without endangering one's life, the more likely was performance of this behavior.

There were few significant differences in outcome evaluations between climbers and nonclimbers. All participants placed positive value on such outcomes as improved physical fitness and developing experience and skills but negative value on endangering their lives and suffering physical injury. However, climbers valued improved physical fitness and experiencing nature and the outdoors significantly more positively than did nonclimbers.

In conclusion, examination of behavioral, normative, and control beliefs with respect to mountain climbing provides us with a detailed picture of this behavior's determinants. Among the important considerations that predispose mountain climbing are having proper equipment and requisite skills and knowledge, support of such important referents as parents and boyfriend or girlfriend, and beliefs that mountain climbing improves physical fitness and permits experiencing nature and the outdoors without endangering one's life.

Sexual Intercourse Among Adolescents

As another example, consider the study mentioned earlier (Fishbein et al., in preparation) concerning the intentions of adolescents to have sexual intercourse in the next 12 months. Approximately equal numbers of Black and White males and females between the ages of 14 and 16 completed an online survey with respect to this behavior. Recall that there was a strong multiple correlation for the prediction of intentions ($R = .74$), and although all three predictors made significant contributions, attitudes had the highest regression weight (beta = .67), followed by perceived norms (beta = .30), and finally perceived behavioral control (beta = .10). Consequently, we first consider the effects of behavioral beliefs on intentions to have sexual intercourse.

A set of 13 modal salient outcomes of engaging in sex in the next 12 months had been identified in a pilot study. These outcomes are shown in Table 6.7. Because it could be assumed that people would generally agree on the valence of these outcomes, and to reduce the burden on

TABLE 6.7 Correlations of Behavioral Beliefs With Intentions and Mean Belief Strength of High-School Students Who Intend and Do Not Intend to Have Sexual Intercourse

Behavioral belief	Correlation with intention	Mean belief strength	
		Intenders	Nonintenders
If I have sexual intercourse in the next 12 months, it would ...			
give me pleasure	.53	2.28	0.34
get me or my partner pregnant	−.17	−1.60	−0.87
increase the quality of my relationship with my partner	.45	0.93	−0.76
give me an STD	−.34	−2.01	−0.76
give me HIV/AIDS	−.35	−2.23	−0.92
please my partner	.39	2.30	0.95
make my parents mad	−.19	0.79	1.52
make my friends think badly of me	−.36	−2.26	−1.06
increase feelings of intimacy between me and my partner	.32	1.56	0.42
make me feel as though someone had taken advantage of me	−.43	−2.45	−0.97
gain the respect of my friends	.15	−0.99	−1.33*
make me feel good about myself	.40	0.38	−1.02
hurt my relationship with my boyfriend/girlfriend	−.31	−1.93	−0.79

Source: Fishbein, M., Bleakley, A., Hennessy, M., & Jordan, A. *Predicting adolescent sexual behavior: Applying the reasoned action approach.* Unpublished manuscript, in preparation (with permission).

Notes: All correlations are significant ($p < .05$). Belief strength can range from −3 to +3.
*Difference between intenders and nonintenders not significant; all other differences $p < .05$.

respondents in an online survey, outcome evaluations were not measured but were instead assigned a value of +1 or –1. For example, "giving me pleasure" and "pleasing my partner" were considered positive outcomes, whereas "getting a sexually transmitted disease (STD)" and "hurting the relationship with my partner" were assumed to be negative outcomes. The only exception was the outcome of getting me or my partner pregnant. Because it was not clear whether a given participant would evaluate this outcome positively or negatively, a measure of outcome evaluation was obtained. This measure was then used to assign a value of +1 or –1 to the outcome.[14]

The first column in Table 6.7 presents the correlations between the strength of each behavioral belief and intentions to have sex. Although some of the correlations are quite low, because of the large sample size (N = 543), all correlations are statistically significant. Using the magnitude of the correlation as a measure of a belief's influence on intentions, four positive beliefs were of particular importance: "having sex would give me pleasure, would increase the quality of my relationship with my partner, would make me feel good about myself, and would please my partner." The more strongly people held these belief, the more they intended to have sex. Among the negative beliefs, the four most important outcomes had to do with "making me feel as though someone had taken advantage of me," "making my friends think badly of me," "giving me an STD," and "giving me HIV/AIDS." Agreement with these beliefs correlated negatively with intentions to have sex.

To compare the beliefs of participants who intended to have sexual intercourse in the next 12 months with those who did not, the sample was divided at the midpoint of the intention scale. Participants with scores above 4 on the seven-point scale were treated as intenders, whereas participants with scores of 4 or lower were treated as nonintenders. The mean behavioral beliefs for the two subgroups are shown in Columns 2 and 3 of Table 6.7. The first thing to note is that most differences were differences in degree rather than in kind. That is, participants in both group tended to agree that certain outcomes were likely to happen and that other outcomes were unlikely to occur. For example, participants in both subgroups agreed that having sex would please their partners, but intenders held this belief more strongly than did nonintenders. Similarly, both groups disbelieved that having sex would get them or their partner pregnant, but intenders were more certain that this would not happen than nonintenders.

There were, however, two instances in which intenders and nonintenders held substantively different beliefs. Whereas intenders thought that having sex would make them feel good about themselves and would increase the quality of their relationships with their partners, nonintenders disagreed that these outcomes would result from having sex.

In this study, descriptive as well as injunctive normative beliefs were assessed. Normative referents had been identified in formative research. Injunctive normative beliefs (n) as well as motivations to comply (m) were measured with respect to each of the eight referents shown in Table 6.8, whereas descriptive normative beliefs were obtained with respect to the four referents shown in Table 6.9. For the eight injunctive normative beliefs, products of belief strength and motivation to comply were computed, and these $n \times m$ products were correlated with intentions to have sex in the next 12 months. As can be seen in the first Column of Table 6.8, each of the eight normative referents significantly influenced intentions to have sex. Generally speaking, the influence of friends (friends, best friend, boyfriend or girlfriend) was more pronounced than was the influence of family (mother, father, grandmother, brother(s), sister(s)). Inspection of Columns 2 and 3 shows that intenders and nonintenders alike recognized that their family members thought they should not engage in sex, but nonintenders held these beliefs more strongly than did intenders. However, when it came to friends, intenders and nonintenders held very different normative beliefs. Intenders

TABLE 6.8 Correlations of Injunctive Normative Belief x Motivation to Comply Products With Intentions and Mean Belief Strength and Motivation to Comply of High School Students Who Intend and Do Not Intend to Have Sexual Intercourse

Injunctive normative referents	Correlation $n_i m_i$-intention	Mean belief strength		Mean motivation to comply	
		Intenders	Nonintenders	Intenders	Nonintenders
Mother	.30	−1.80	−2.52	4.08	4.52
Father	.29	−1.42	−2.30	3.81	4.18*
Friends	.48	1.17	−0.68	4.09	4.19*
Best friend	.49	0.95	−0.97	4.81	4.90*
Boyfriend/ girlfriend	.48	1.58	−0.25	4.79	4.25
Grandmother	.20	−1.54	−2.14	4.14	4.33*
Brother(s)	.34	−0.17	−1.65	3.60	3.67*
Sister(s)	.37	−0.64	−1.82	3.48	3.94

Source: Fishbein, M., Bleakley, A., Hennessy, M., & Jordan, A., *Predicting adolescent sexual behavior: Applying the reasoned action approach*. Unpublished manuscript, in preparation (with permission).

Notes: All correlations are significant ($p < .05$). Belief strength can range from −3 to +3, motivation to comply from 1 to 7.
*Difference between intenders and nonintenders not significant; all other differences $p < .05$.

TABLE 6.9 Correlations of Descriptive Normative Beliefs With Intentions and Mean Belief Strength of High School Students Who Intend and Do Not Intend to Have Sexual Intercourse

Descriptive normative referents	Correlation with intentions	Mean belief strength	
		Intenders	Nonintenders
Female friends	.45	3.18	2.20
Male friends	.37	3.49	2.52
Females my age	.33	3.30	2.66
Males my age	.28	3.48	2.81

Source: Fishbein, M., Bleakley, A., Hennessy, M. & Jordan, A. *Predicting adolescent sexual behavior: Applying the reasoned action approach.* Unpublished manuscript, in preparation (with permission).

Notes: All correlations and differences between intenders and non-intenders are significant ($p < .05$). Belief strength can range from 1 to 5.
* Not significant; all other differences $p < .05$.

believed that their friends thought they should have sex, whereas nonintenders believed that their friends thought they should not have sex.

Looking at Columns 4 and 5 of Table 6.8 we see that, with only one exception, intenders were less motivated to comply with their referents than were nonintenders, although only the differences with respect to mothers and sisters reached statistical significance. One possible explanation for this finding is that young adolescents who intend to engage in sexual intercourse are rebellious and therefore not particularly motivated to comply with normative referents. The one exception occurred in relation to one's boyfriend or girlfriend. In this case, intenders had significantly stronger motivations to comply than did nonintenders.

Looking at the correlations between descriptive normative beliefs and intentions in Table 6.9, it can be seen that the perceived behavior of friends and other peers also significantly affected intentions to have sex. The more strongly the adolescents believed that others their age perform this behavior, the more they themselves intended to do so. It can also be seen that the descriptive norms of friends had a stronger influence on intentions to have sex than had the perceived behavior of other same-age peers. The data in Columns 2 and 3 suggest that more male than female adolescents are believed to be sexually active. The differences between intenders and nonintenders were consistent with the correlations: Participants who intended to have sex believed that more of their friends and peers are having sex than did nonintenders.

Finally, we turn to control beliefs to find out what kinds of factors adolescents think facilitate or interfere with having sexual intercourse. The pilot study had identified 10 salient control factors, which are shown in Table 6.10. The assessment of control beliefs in this study relied on the approach suggested by Bandura (1997) to measure self-efficacy beliefs (see Chapter 5). Participants were asked to indicate how certain they were that they could have sexual intercourse in the next 12 months under conditions specified by the different control factors. For example, with respect to the first control factor, they rated, on a seven-point scale that ranged from *I am certain I could not* to *I am certain I could,* how certain they were that they could have sex in the next 12 months even if they didn't have a regular partner. These beliefs were found to correlate significantly with intentions to have sex, as can be seen in the first column of Table 6.10. Generally speaking, the more the adolescents believed that they could overcome potential barriers to having sex, the more they intended to engage in sexual intercourse. The most important control factor was associated with their perception that they could have sex if their partner wanted to have sex. This belief had a correlation of .60 with intentions, a finding consistent with the commonsense notion that an important prerequisite for having sexual intercourse is the cooperation of a willing partner.

TABLE 6.10 Correlations of Control Beliefs With Intentions and Mean Belief Strength of High School Students Who Intend and Do Not Intend to Have Sexual Intercourse

Control belief	Correlation with intention	Mean belief strength	
		Intenders	Nonintenders
How certain are you that you could have sexual intercourse even if ...			
you didn't have a regular partner	.38	0.71	−0.95
your partner didn't want to	.36	−0.25	−1.59
you didn't have a place to be alone	.20	−1.50	−2.21
you didn't have condoms or birth control available	.20	−1.50	−2.21
your parents would be mad	.49	1.00	−1.16
your boyfriend/girlfriend wanted to	.60	2.31	−0.34
you had been drinking or using drugs	.25	0.18	−0.96
you are feeling lonely and depressed	.34	0.26	−1.24
it went against your personal beliefs	.31	−0.20	−1.53
it went against your religion	.39	0.65	−1.14

Source: Fishbein, M., Bleakley, A., Hennessy, M., & Jordan, A. *Predicting adolescent sexual behavior: Applying the reasoned action approach.* Unpublished manuscript, in preparation (with permission).

Notes: Belief strength can range from −3 to +3. All correlations and differences between intenders and nonintenders are significant ($p < .05$).

Looking at the comparisons between participants who intended to have sex and those who did not, we find that nonintenders believed that they would not be able to have sex under any of the specified conditions, even when they thought that their partners wanted to have sex (see Column 3). In contrast, the intenders were quite confident that they could have sexual intercourse under 6 of the 10 conditions. They were most certain that they could have sex if their partners wanted to, and they felt strongly that they could not have sex if a condom or birth control was unavailable. They also had low efficacy beliefs when their partners did not want to have sex, when they didn't have a place to be alone, and when they felt that having sex was against their personal beliefs.

☐ Summary and Conclusions

In this chapter we reviewed empirical evidence that lends support to the general structure of our reasoned action approach. We saw that by examining salient behavioral, normative, and control beliefs elicited from the research population we can gain a good understanding of the different types of consideration that guide intentions and behavior. In other words, it appears that people's intentions and consequent behavior can ultimately be traced to the subjectively held information they have about the likely consequences of the behavior, about the prescriptions, proscriptions or behaviors of normative referents, and about facilitators and barriers to behavioral performance. Consistent with our theory, research has shown that these effects of beliefs on intentions are mediated by more general dispositions: attitude toward the behavior in the case of behavioral beliefs, perceived norms in the case of normative beliefs, and perceived behavioral control in the case of control beliefs. Thus, the formation of beliefs about a behavior's likely consequences and the evaluations of these consequences spontaneously produce an overall positive or negative evaluation of the behavior. This attitude is usually activated automatically and can thus influence the intention to engage in the behavior. In a similar fashion, formation of normative beliefs produces a general perceived norm, and formation of control beliefs results in a general sense of perceived control, both of which can also exert an effect on intentions.

Also consistent with our reasoned action approach, attitudes and perceived norms are usually found to influence behavior indirectly by way of intentions, whereas perceived control can have both a direct effect on behavior and an effect that is mediated by intentions. Finally, we saw that the relative contributions of attitudinal, normative, and control considerations to the prediction of intentions exhibit reasonable patterns. Under certain conditions, attitudes tend to carry more weight than perceived norms or perceived control whereas under other conditions, perceived control or perceived social norms may become more important. Similarly, whereas the behavior of some individuals is influenced more by normative than attitudinal considerations, the behavior of other individuals is influenced primarily by attitudinal factors.

In short, as stipulated in our model of behavioral prediction, the research we have reviewed in this chapter provides support for a chain of effects from behavioral, normative, and control beliefs through attitudes, norms, and perceived control, through intentions to behavior. Of course, this chain of effects need not stop with performance of the behavior. When a behavior is carried out, it can result in unanticipated positive or negative consequences, it can elicit favorable or unfavorable reactions from others, and it can reveal unanticipated difficulties or facilitating factors. This feedback is likely to change the person's behavioral, normative, and control beliefs and thus affect future intentions and actions.

It is important to recognize that the research we have reviewed is correlational in nature and thus cannot provide strong evidence in support of the postulated causal links. It is conceivable, for example, that in a process of rationalization, attitudes influence behavioral beliefs or a general sense of self-efficacy influences control beliefs. Thus, people who are inclined to engage in a particular behavior for whatever reasons may rationalize their decision by coming to believe that the likely consequences justify it, that others support it, and that they have the capacity to successfully carry it out. People's tendencies to engage in such processes have been well documented (see, e.g., Abelson et al., 1968), but our reasoned action approach focuses on the prospective causal links from beliefs to behavior. We reconsider the issue of causality in Chapter 9, and in Chapters 10 and 11 we review experimental evidence in support of the causal links postulated in our theory.

☐ Notes

1. Unfortunately, as mentioned above, most published research has assessed only injunctive norms.
2. The original analysis entered severity of injury as a control variable prior to the TPB predictors. The results reported here are based on a secondary analysis of the correlational data presented in the published paper, which considered only the basic variables in the theory. However, the results reported here are virtually identical to the results of the original analysis.
3. The study examined intentions to engage in several different behaviors, and only the range of alpha coefficients was reported. The lowest value in the range was .90.
4. The lowest alpha coefficient for all behaviors considered was .85.

5. The coefficient alpha was at least .81.
6. Here, too, we performed a secondary analysis of the data because demographic variables and measures of multidimensional health locus of control were entered into the regression equation prior to the variables comprising our model of behavioral prediction.
7. This proposition rests on the assumption that the three predictors are assessed with equal reliability. Low reliability will tend to reduce a predictor's correlation with intention and therefore will adversely affect its regression coefficient.
8. These results were obtained in a secondary analysis of the correlational data presented in von Haeften and Kenski (2001, Table 2).
9. The measure of perceived norm in these studies was a measure of the injunctive norm.
10. Note that this hypothesis concerns the moderating effect of identification with a given normative referent on the influence of that group's perceived norm on intentions, not its moderating effect on the influence of perceived social pressure in general.
11. Sometimes, the analysis is done in two steps, where behavior is regressed on intention and perceived control in the first step and attitudes and perceived norms in the second step. The regression coefficients obtained in the final step are examined for evidence of mediation.
12. The TPB variables were assessed with respect to recycling of glass and with respect to disposing of glass in the trash. Differences between the two measures were used in the analyses.
13. As mentioned in Chapter 5, bipolar scoring was used for control belief strength and perceived power.
14. These values were used to compute the composite of behavioral beliefs that are assumed to serve as the determinants of the attitude toward the behavior.

CHAPTER

Background Factors and Origins of Beliefs

According to our reasoned action approach, the psychological foundation for human action can be found in behavioral, normative, and control beliefs. In the present chapter we examine the origins of these beliefs in an effort to deepen our understanding of the determinants of human social behavior. We first discuss some of the psychological processes whereby beliefs are formed and then turn to the influence of personal, social, and environmental factors on behavioral, normative, and control beliefs.

☐ Belief Formation

We define beliefs as subjective probabilities. Behavioral beliefs involve the subjective probability that performing a behavior leads to a certain outcome. Injunctive normative beliefs are subjective probabilities that particular referents prescribe or proscribe performance of a behavior, whereas descriptive normative beliefs are subjective probabilities that particular referents are or are not performing the behavior. Finally, control beliefs involve the subjective probabilities that particular factors that can facilitate or impede performance of the behavior will be present.

Observational Beliefs

One obvious source of information on which beliefs can be based is direct observation. In the case of behavioral beliefs, people may notice that when they perform a given behavior, certain outcomes are likely to follow.

Similarly, injunctive normative beliefs can be formed by way of direct observation if a referent explicitly tells a person what the person should do, and descriptive normative beliefs can be formed by observing what a referent actually does. Finally, people can also learn about the presence of control factors through direct observation when, while trying to perform a behavior, they encounter barriers or facilitating factors.

To take a concrete example, people may find out that smoking marijuana makes them drowsy (behavioral belief), they may have been explicitly told by their parents not to smoke marijuana (injunctive normative belief), they may have seen their best friend smoke marijuana (descriptive normative belief), and they may have been offered marijuana at a party (control belief). These direct experiences associated with performance of a behavior result in the formation of *observational beliefs* about the behavior. Because the validity of one's own senses is rarely questioned, these observational beliefs are—at least initially—held with very high probability. Over time, forgetting or encountering contradictory information can reduce the strength of some of these beliefs.

Informational Beliefs

Many beliefs are formed not on the basis of direct observation but by accepting information provided by an outside source. Such sources include television and radio, the Internet, newspapers, books, magazines, lecturers, friends, relatives, and coworkers. For example, we may see an advertisement that Viagra alleviates erectile dysfunction. Based on this information, we may form the behavioral belief that "my using Viagra will alleviate my erectile dysfunction." By the same token, we may read in *Newsweek* that 73.4% of women over 40 regularly get a mammogram and form a corresponding descriptive normative belief. An informational control belief may be formed when we learn from a friend that a certain doctor's office accepts Medicare. If we are on Medicare ourselves, the belief that the doctor's office accepts Medicare constitutes a facilitating factor.

Inferential Beliefs

People can form beliefs that go beyond direct observation or information from outside sources by means of various inference processes. One possibility is for inferences to be based on observational beliefs. For example, if I observe the outcomes produced by another person's behavior, I may infer that the same outcomes would occur if I performed the behavior. Similarly, if I observe that my own behavior produces a certain outcome, I may infer that other related outcomes are also likely to occur. For example, if I discover that regular exercise has lowered my blood pressure, I may infer that regular exercise will increase my life expectancy. Inferential belief formation can also occur with respect to normative beliefs. My belief that my parents are religious conservatives may lead me to infer that they think I should not drink, use drugs, or have premarital sexual relations. The formation of inferential control beliefs is evident when my belief that I have limited time for one leisure activity leads me to expect that I will also have limited time for other leisure activities.

To recapitulate, three different processes underlie belief formation. First, behavioral, normative, and control beliefs can be established on the basis of direct observation (observational beliefs). Second, they can be established by accepting information that is provided by an outside source (informational beliefs). Finally, behavioral, normative, and control beliefs can be formed through a process of inference that relies on other beliefs relevant to the behavior under consideration (inferential beliefs). For a more detailed discussion of these three types of belief formation processes, see Fishbein and Ajzen (1975, Chapter 5).

☐ The Nature of Beliefs

Whether based on direct observation, outside information, or inference processes, we assume that once beliefs related to a particular behavior have been formed, they provide the basis for attitudes, subjective norms, and perceptions of control, which, in turn, lead to intentions and actions. It is important to note that, within our reasoned action framework, we do *not* assume that people are rational but only that their actions follow reasonably from their beliefs. Given that beliefs are often based on information provided by others and on fallible inference processes, behavioral, normative, and control beliefs need not be veridical. They can be inaccurate, biased to conform with preconceptions or motives, or they may represent rationalizations, wishful thinking, or other irrational processes. Nevertheless, the beliefs people hold constitute the information they have about a behavior, and because they naively assume that their beliefs are valid (Ross & Ward, 1996), they act upon them.

To take an extreme example, paranoid schizophrenics may hear voices warning them that others are out to harm them. If they act on these warnings, their behavior may be considered "irrational," but it follows reasonably from the beliefs they formed on the basis of the voices they heard. More commonly, people's cognitive processes, predispositions, and desires can bias their interpretation of available information (see Nisbett & Ross, 1980), leading to the formation of inaccurate beliefs that then provide the basis for action. For example, it has been argued that the decision to go to war in Iraq was based on a biased reading of intelligence information, a bias occasioned by the U.S. administration's desire to change the regime in Iraq.

Of course, people can also behave in apparently irrational ways not because they suffer from mental illness or have preexisting biases but because they rely on inaccurate information. For example, many Americans approved of the invasion of Iraq because they were led to believe that Saddam Hussein had weapons of mass destruction and that there was a connection between Iraq and the attack on the United States on September 11, 2001. We return to the question of irrationality in the context of our reasoned action approach in Chapter 10.

☐ Differences in Beliefs: The Role of Background Factors

We assume that beliefs are not innate but instead are acquired in daily encounters with the real world. Observed differences in beliefs must therefore be the result of differential learning experiences. The kinds of experiences people have are likely to vary as a function of personal characteristics (e.g., personality, temperament, intelligence, values), social and cultural factors (e.g., ethnicity, race, religion, education), and exposure to media and other sources of information. In Chapter 1 we saw that many investigators have used *background factors* of this type to explain behavior in a variety of domains. We also pointed out, however, that the number of background factors that could be considered is virtually unlimited. Our reasoned action approach does not identify the kinds of background factors that should be considered in relation to a particular behavior. However, it does suggest that we may want to consider a background factor only if we have reason to believe that people who vary in terms of that factor may have been exposed to different experiences and thus may have formed different behavior-relevant beliefs. Our task is aided by the availability of theories and research findings in many different behavioral domains that point to the importance of particular kinds of background factors. Thus, we saw in Chapter 1 that party identification, a background variable, is a good predictor of voting choice in presidential elections. Similarly, health disparities have been reported as a function of ethnicity, and sensation seeking has been found to predict risk-taking behaviors among adolescents.

In the present chapter we examine the value as well as the limitations of these kinds of factors in our attempts to explain human social behavior. We argue that people who come from different backgrounds with varying personal experiences can form different beliefs with respect to one behavior but the same or very similar beliefs with respect to another. For example, the experiences of men and women growing up in our society may lead them to form different beliefs regarding their ability to drive after drinking but the same beliefs when it comes to the value of attending college. If this were the case, it would not be surprising to find a greater proportion of male than female drunk drivers but no differences in the proportion of men and women who apply to college.

These considerations imply that a given background factor will be associated with the performance of a behavior only to the extent that the background factor is related to the behavioral, normative, or control beliefs that serve as the determinants of the behavior under consideration.[1] Individuals who differ in terms of demographic characteristics, exposure to information, knowledge, or personality traits may well differ in the beliefs they hold with respect to specific behaviors. When this is the case, they would also be expected to exhibit differences in the likelihood that they would perform those behaviors. By the same token, however, when the behavior-relevant beliefs are unrelated to a particular background factor, the factor in question is not expected to influence the behavior.

Demographic Variables

Irrespective of the behavior under investigation, most studies gather, among other things, information about demographic characteristics of the research population. Most commonly assessed are gender, race or ethnicity, age, education, and income, social class, or other indicators of socioeconomic status. Segmenting the population along these dimensions allows investigators to determine whether the prevalence of the behavior under study varies across subgroups. Information about differential prevalence rates can be very useful for identifying important social indicators such as disparities in the use of health protective measures; rates of victimization, drug abuse, teenage pregnancy, and divorce; and differential income levels and consumption patterns. This information can then also be used to help guide allocation of resources to populations at risk or to assist in the development and marketing of commercial products. When demographic differences are found, they can stimulate the exploration of possible reasons for the observed differences.

There is a great deal of evidence that behavioral differences are indeed associated with demographic characteristics in a wide variety of domains. For example, in the domain of political behavior, women—compared with men—are more likely not only to participate in presidential elections but also to vote for the Democratic rather than the Republican candidate. In the 2004 presidential election, for example, 60.1% of voting-age women and 56.3% of voting-age men reported voting in the election (MacManus, 2006). Among the women, 51% voted for John Kerry, the Democratic candidate, whereas 55% of the men voted to reelect the incumbent Republican President, George W. Bush (Carol, 2006).

Gender differences are also found in many other domains, but gender is not always associated with differences in behavior. For example, survey statistics for 2005 show that among high school students, approximately equal percentages of girls and boys reported smoking cigarettes (Johnston, O'Malley, Bachman, & Schulenberg, 2006). Further, in both groups, smoking during the past 30 days increased with the student's grade level, from 9.3% among 8th graders to 23.2% among 12th graders. On the other hand, within this same population, heroine use, which stayed constant at 0.5%, did not increase as a function of age (or grade level).

Similarly discordant patterns of findings are observed with respect to racial, ethnic, socioeconomic, and other demographic differences. Consider, for instance, statistics in the health domain. In comparison with White Americans, African Americans are more likely to get tested for HIV/AIDS, but they are less likely to get influenza or pneumococcal vaccines (Centers for Disease Control & Prevention, 2000). With respect to smoking and engaging in physical activity to lose weight or to prevent weight gain, no meaningful differences are found between Black and White adults (Centers for Disease Control & Prevention, 2004). Similarly, level of education is sometimes found to be related to health-protective behaviors, but at other times it is not. For example, among American adults age 50 or over, 37% of college graduates—but only 21% of those with less than high school education—have had a sigmoidoscopy in the past 5 years or a colonoscopy in the past 10 years (Wee, McCarthy, & Phillips, 2005). On the other hand, education was found to be unrelated to physical activity in a population with chronic kidney disease (Eng & Martin Ginis, 2007).

In sum, many behaviors are found to be associated with one or more demographic characteristics. However, as might perhaps be expected, a demographic variable that is found to be related to one behavior may show no relation to another, and observed patterns of differences not only can vary from one population to another but also can change over time. For example, the so-called gender gap in voting preferences mentioned earlier is a relatively recent phenomenon. Prior to the 1980 presidential election, a higher percentage of women than men tended to vote for Republican presidential candidates, but as we saw already, women are now more likely than men to vote for Democratic presidential candidates.

Within our reasoned action framework, complex patterns of association between demographic characteristics and various behaviors are not unexpected because we assume that different segments of the population will behave in different ways only to the extent that their past experiences have led them to form different behavioral, normative, or control beliefs.

If a demographic characteristic is found to have an effect on a behavior of interest, we would expect this effect to be mediated by the theory's proximal variables. Thus, if we control for behavioral intentions and perceived behavioral control, we would expect the relation between the background factor and behavior to be greatly reduced and usually to become nonsignificant. Similarly, if the factor is found to be related to the intention to perform a behavior, the strength of this association should be significantly reduced or eliminated if attitudes, norms, and perceived control are held constant. Next, we provide illustrations of these effects with respect to two background factors: gender and ethnicity.

Gender

Consider the study on hunting behavior (Hrubes, Ajzen, & Daigle, 2001) mentioned in Chapters 3 and 6. A reanalysis of the data from this study showed that gender (a background factor) had a significant effect on hunting behavior. As would perhaps be expected, men were much more likely to go hunting than were women (Table 7.1). Specifically, men reported having gone hunting an average of 13.04 times during the past year compared with an average of less than once ($M = 0.61$) for women, producing a point-biserial correlation of .28 ($p < .001$) between gender and hunting behavior (Table 7.2). The results of the study can help explain the reason for this relationship. As can be seen in Table 7.2, hunting behavior was primarily determined by intentions to go hunting ($r = .57$); perceived behavioral control, although also significantly correlated with behavior ($r = .46$), did not improve prediction over and above intentions.

TABLE 7.1 Means and Standard Deviations for Reasoned Action Constructs Applied to Hunting: Differences Between Men and Women

Construct	Men		Women	
	Mean	SD	Mean	SD
Behavior frequency	13.04	21.43	0.61	3.38
Intention	0.53	2.87	−2.60	1.43
Perceived control	1.28	2.19	−1.19	2.13
Attitude	1.00	2.49	−2.06	1.64
Perceived norm	0.61	2.43	−1.92	1.49

Source: Reanalysis of data from Hrubes, D., Ajzen, I., & Daigle, J., Leisure Sciences, 23, 165–178, 2001 (with permission).

Notes: Constructs are scored from −3 to +3. All mean differences between men and women are statistically significant at $p < .01$.

TABLE 7.2 Effects of Gender on Hunting Behavior and Hunting Intentions: Results of Hierarchical Multiple Regression

Step	Predictor	r	β	R	r	β	R
	Hunting Behavior						
1	Intention	.57	.54		.57	.54	
	Perceived behavioral control	.46	.04*	.57	.46	.04*	
2	Gender				.28	.02*	.57
	Hunting Intention						
1	Attitude	.91	.51		.91	.51	
	Injunctive norm	.89	.38		.89	.38	
	Perceived behavioral control	.76	.08	.93	.76	.08	
2	Gender				.46	.02*	.93

Source: Reanalysis of data from Hrubes, D., Ajzen, I., & Daigle, J., Leisure Sciences, 23, 165–178, 2001 (with permission).
Note: r = correlation coefficient. β = regression coefficient. R = multiple correlation.
*Not significant. All other coefficients significant at $p < .05$.

From the perspective of our theory of behavioral prediction, the effect of gender on hunting behavior must be attributed to gender differences in the behavior's immediate antecedents: primarily intentions and, to some extent, perceptions of behavioral control. Consistent with this argument, men had positive intentions to go hunting in the next 12 months ($M = 0.53$), whereas women had strong negative intentions ($M = -2.61$). The men also believed that they had significantly more control over this behavior ($M = 1.29$) than did women ($M = -1.19$). Importantly, when gender was added to the equation on the second step of the hierarchical regression analysis, it did not significantly improve prediction of hunting behavior. This finding suggests that the effect of gender on hunting behavior was indeed mediated by intentions and perceptions of control. As shown in Table 7.2, the initial multiple correlation of .57 was unaffected by the addition of gender to the prediction equation.

The results of our reanalysis can also explain the observed gender differences in hunting intentions. As can be seen in Table 7.2, in the total sample, intentions were predicted with considerable accuracy ($R = .93$) from attitudes, injunctive norms, and perceptions of behavioral control. Although all three zero-order correlations were quite high, the regression coefficients indicate that intentions to go hunting were primarily determined by attitudes toward this behavior. To influence intentions, therefore, gender must have had an effect on one or more of these variables, and especially on attitudes. The data in Table 7.1 confirm this expectation. In comparison with women, not only did men believe, as we saw previously, that they had more behavioral control over hunting; they also held more positive attitudes toward hunting, and they also perceived more social pressure to go hunting. Because of these effects, gender was found to correlate strongly with intentions to go hunting in the next 12 months ($r = .46$; Table 7.2). But again, when gender was added to the regression equation after attitudes, injunctive norms, and perceived control were taken into account, it failed to improve prediction of intention. As can be seen in Table 7.2, the multiple correlation for the prediction of intentions remained at .93.

Gender-Related Beliefs

To fully understand the reasons why men are more likely to go hunting than women, we must examine their underlying beliefs. Because attitude was the most important predictor of hunting intentions, we would expect major gender differences in the behavioral beliefs that serve as the determinants of the attitude. Table 7.3 shows the 12 most frequently mentioned outcomes of hunting that were elicited in a pilot study. In Chapter 3 we saw that, in their totality, these salient behavioral beliefs correlated highly

TABLE 7.3 Mean Belief Strength and Mean Outcome Evaluations for Behavioral Beliefs About Hunting: Differences Between Men and Women

Behavioral beliefs	Belief strength		Outcome evaluation	
	Men	Women	Men	Women
Viewing scenery and enjoying nature	1.65	−0.40*	2.64	2.77
Observing and learning about wildlife	1.83	0.48*	2.42	2.20
Feeling tired and exhausted	0.22	−0.58*	0.01	−0.03
Creating or maintaining significant relationships with family or friends	1.10	−0.79*	2.64	2.77
Relaxing and relieving stress	1.39	−1.00*	1.66	2.77
Getting exercise and staying in shape	1.34	−0.48*	2.55	2.79*
Feeling a sense of competence	1.19	−0.56*	2.39	2.67*
Experiencing solitude, time to think	1.70	−0.08*	2.52	2.65
Getting dirty, wet, or cold	1.49	0.68*	−.03	0.06
Feeling a sense of belonging and familiarity with nature	1.35	−0.23*	2.41	2.58
Experiencing excitement	1.86	0.04*	2.45	2.28
Seeing wounded or dead animals	1.31	1.59	−1.15	−1.89*

Source: Reanalysis of data from Hrubes, D., Ajzen, I., & Daigle, J., *Leisure Sciences, 23,* 165–178, 2001 (with permission).
Note: Belief strength and outcome evaluation scored from −3 to +3.
* Difference between men and women significant at $p < .05$.

with a direct measure of attitude toward hunting ($r = .73$), and by examining the strength of the different beliefs as well as the associated outcome evaluations we were able to discern their effects on the overall attitude. The results displayed in Table 7.3 permit us to compare men and women in terms of the outcomes they associate with hunting, and, by doing so, we gain insight into the reasons for their differential hunting behavior. It can be seen that there were relatively few significant gender differences with respect to outcome evaluations. Most of the salient outcomes of hunting—whether viewing scenery and enjoying nature, observing and learning about wildlife, or experiencing solitude and time to think—were judged to be highly favorable by both men and women. The only exceptions occurred with respect to getting exercise and staying in shape, feeling a sense of competence, and seeing wounded and dead animals. In comparison with women, men considered these outcomes to be more positive or less negative.

The major differences between men and women had to do with their subjective probabilities that hunting would produce the various outcomes. Generally speaking, women were much less likely than men to believe that hunting leads to favorable outcomes. For example, they thought it much less likely that hunting allows you to view scenery and enjoy nature, relax and relieve stress, or feel a sense of belonging and familiarity with nature. Only with respect to the likelihood of seeing wounded or dead animals was there no gender difference.

In sum, this set of findings regarding behavioral beliefs about hunting can help explain why men were much more likely to go hunting than were women. For reasons not explored in this study, men by and large believed more strongly than women that going hunting leads to positive outcomes. Consequently, they held more favorable attitudes toward hunting, and, because attitudes were the primary determinants of hunting intentions, men also held stronger intentions to engage in this behavior and actually went hunting more frequently.

Ethnicity

In the Annenberg Sex and Media Study (see, e.g., Bleakley et al., 2009, in press; Fishbein et. al., in preparation; Hennessy, M., Bleakley, A., Fishbein, M. & Jordan, A., in press), ethnic differences in adolescent sexual behavior could also be explained by reference to underlying beliefs. It has consistently been found that, in comparison with their White peers, Black adolescents are more likely to be sexually active (see Mosher, Shandra, & Jones, 2005; Silver & Bauman, 2006). In the present study, the correlation between ethnicity and intentions to have sex in the next 12 months was .20 ($p < 01$), indicating that, consistent with the usually observed difference in behavior, Black adolescents held less negative intentions toward having sex. The mean intention for Blacks, on a –3 to +3 scale, was –0.38 compared with a mean of –1.27 for Whites.

To explain the differences in intentions, we first look at the regression of intentions on attitudes, perceived norms, and perceived behavioral control. The results displayed in Table 7.4 show that, for the total sample, intentions to have sex in the next 12 months were predicted with considerable accuracy ($R = .72$) from our theory's three components. The addition of ethnicity on the second step of the regression analysis had no appreciable impact, explaining no additional variance in intentions. Thus, the effect of ethnicity on intentions to be sexually active was fully mediated by the theory's predictors.

In Table 7.5 we see that the difference in intentions between Black and White adolescents was reflected, as expected, in their attitudes, perceived

TABLE 7.4 Hierarchical Regression of Intentions to Have Sex on Reasoned Action Constructs and on Ethnicity (White vs. Black)

Step	Predictor	r	b	R	r	b	R
1	Attitude	.70	.53		.70	.53	
	Perceived social pressure	.59	.22		.59	.23	
	Perceived behavioral control	.41	.06*	.72	.41	.05*	
2	Ethnicity				.20	.01*	.72

Source: Fishbein, M., Bleakley, A., Hennessy, M., & Jordan, A. *Predicting adolescent sexual behavior: Applying the reasoned action approach*. Unpublished manuscript, in preparation (with permission).
*Not significant. All other coefficients significant at $p < .05$.

TABLE 7.5 Means and Standard Deviations for Reasoned Action Constructs Applied to Having Sex: Differences Between Black and White Adolescents

	Blacks (N = 228)		Whites (N = 222)	
Construct	Mean	SD	Mean	SD
Intention	–0.38	2.41	–1.27	2.00
Attitude	0.35	1.89	–0.39	1.70
Perceived social norm	0.06	1.67	–0.84	1.67
Perceived behavioral control	1.63	1.46	0.89	1.82

Source: Fishbein, M., Bleakley, A., Hennessy, M., & Jordan, A. *Predicting adolescent sexual behavior: Applying the reasoned action approach*. Unpublished manuscript, in preparation (with permission).
Notes: Constructs are scored from –3 to +3. All mean differences between Blacks and Whites are statistically significant at $p < .01$.

norms, and perceived behavioral control. On average, Black teenagers held more favorable attitudes toward having sexual intercourse in the next 12 months, perceived more social pressure to have sex, and believed that they had more control over whether they did or did not engage in this behavior.

Ethnicity-Related Beliefs

Returning to Table 7.4, it can be seen that although attitude had the highest regression coefficient in the prediction of intentions (beta = .53), the regression coefficient of perceived norm was also strong and highly significant (beta = .22). Because we focused on attitudes and behavioral beliefs in our discussion of hunting behavior, for purposes of illustration we now consider perceived norms and the underlying normative beliefs. In the present study, injunctive as well as descriptive normative beliefs were assessed, and as we saw in Chapter 4, when the two types of normative beliefs were combined into a single normative belief index the correlation between the index and the direct measure of perceived norm was .65 ($p < .01$).

The descriptive and injunctive normative beliefs of the Black and White adolescents are displayed in Table 7.6. Descriptive norms were assessed on a five-point response scale that ranged from *none have had sex* (1) to *all have had sex* (5). It can be seen that in comparison with White participants, Black adolescents were significantly more likely to believe that their male and female friends as well as males and females their own age have had sex. Injunctive norms were assessed with respect to eight salient referents: mother, father, partner, friends, best friend, grandmother, brother, sister. Participants were asked to rate, on a seven-point scale, their belief that each referent thought they *should not have sex* (–3) or *should have sex* (+3). As can be seen in the bottom part of Table 7.6, Black and White adolescents alike believed that members of their family (mother, father, grandmother, brother, sister) generally disapproved of their engaging in sexual intercourse, and there were no significant differences between Whites and Blacks in the perceived disapproval of female family members. In contrast, White adolescents perceived significantly more disapproval than their Black counterparts from male family members. The most important differences, however, had to do with normative beliefs concerning friends and partners. Whereas African American adolescents believed that their friends and partners thought they should be sexually active, White adolescents were more likely to believe that these referents would disapprove.

The observed differences between Black and White teenagers in descriptive and injunctive normative beliefs help to explain the ethnic differences in intentions to engage in sexual intercourse and the ethnic differences in

TABLE 7.6 Mean Belief Strength for Normative Beliefs About Having Sex: Differences Between Black and White Adolescents

Normative referents	Blacks (N=228)		Whites (N = 222)	
	Mean	SD	Mean	SD
Descriptive				
Female friends	2.79	1.19	2.15	0.87
Male friends	3.30	1.39	2.26	1.02
Females my age	3.17	2.08	2.55	0.87
Males my age	3.45	1.19	2.57	0.98
Injunctive				
Mother	−2.16	1.46	−2.38*	1.24
Father	−1.77	1.79	−2.26	1.34
Friends	0.36	2.07	−0.42	1.91
Best friend	0.00	2.15	−0.73	1.95
Partner	0.88	1.93	−0.01	1.98
Grandmother	−1.94	1.53	−1.47*	1.50
Brother	−0.92	2.15	−1.47	1.59
Sister	−1.42	1.75	−1.44*	1.48

Source: Fishbein, M., Bleakley, A., Hennessy, M., & Jordan, A. *Predicting adolescent sexual behavior: Applying the reasoned action approach.* Unpublished manuscript, in preparation (with permission).

Note: Descriptive normative beliefs are scored from 1 to 5, injunctive normative beliefs from −3 to +3.

* Mean difference between Blacks and Whites not significant. All other mean differences are significant at $p < .05$.

actual sexual behavior. Note, however, that the present study also revealed important differences in behavioral and control beliefs, and these beliefs must also be considered for a more complete explanation of differences in sexual behavior between White and Black adolescents.

In conclusion, demographic characteristics, such as gender, age, ethnicity, and socioeconomic status, are often found to be associated with differences in behavior. It is generally recognized, of course, that variations in demographic characteristics do not *cause* differences in behavior. Demographic variables segment the population along certain dimensions and reveal differences in behavior among different subgroups, but by themselves they cannot explain these differences. Nevertheless, by exploring why behavior differs among segments of the population, we can deepen our understanding of a behavior's underlying determinants. The research described in this section showed how this can be done in the context of our theory of behavioral prediction. The most valuable substantive information is obtained by comparing the beliefs of the different segments of the population that are found to behave in different ways. Such a comparison does not provide information as to why individuals with different demographic characteristics hold different beliefs, but once we have identified the beliefs on which they differ, we can understand the differences in their behavior.

Further Evidence for the Mediated Effect of Demographic Variables

Most studies conducted in the context of our reasoned action approach collect demographic information about the participants. In some of these studies, the information is used only to describe the sample characteristics (e.g., Courneya, Friedenreich, Arthur, & Bobick, 1999). In other studies, it is used to segment the population to compare demographic subgroups that differ in behavior in terms of their behavior-relevant beliefs, attitudes, and intentions. For example, based on knowledge that younger people and males are more likely to be involved in traffic accidents than older people and females, Parker, Manstead, Stradling, and Reason (1992) compared beliefs, attitudes, injunctive norms, and intentions among these subgroups with respect to drunk driving, speeding, close following, and dangerous overtaking. Consistent with our reasoned action approach, they found significant difference between men and women and between young and old on all four of these variables.

In a minority of studies, investigators explicitly test the proposition that the effects of demographic characteristics are mediated by the theoretical determinants of intentions and behavior (Armitage, Norman, & Conner, 2002; Christian & Armitage, 2002; Elliott, Armitage, & Baughan, 2003; Jennings-Dozier, 1999; Robinson & Smith, 2002; Tolma, Reininger, Ureda, & Evans, 2003; Willemsen, de Vries, van Breukelen, & Oldenburg, 1996). This is typically done by means of multiple regression analyses in which the demographic variables of interest are regressed on intentions or behavior together with measures of the theory's predictors (attitudes, perceived social norms, and perceived behavioral control). If, in the final equation, a demographic variable is found to retain a significant regression coefficient, its effect is deemed not to have been fully mediated by the theory.

The results of these studies by and large provide good evidence for mediation. Consider, for example, a study that, among other things, investigated the effects of age on three risk-taking behaviors: condom use, binge drinking, and drunk driving (Armitage et al., 2002). Age was found to be negatively related to intentions to always use condoms ($r = -.43$, p

< .01), positively related to intentions to drive after drinking alcohol (r = .27, p < .01), and unrelated to intentions to get very drunk at least twice in the next week, that is, binge drinking (r = –.09, n.s.). Regression analyses showed that the significant effects of age on intentions to use condoms and to drive after drinking were virtually eliminated once attitudes, subjective norms, and perceived behavioral control were taken into account. For condom use, the beta coefficient of age declined from –.43 to –.08, and for driving after drinking it declined from .27 to –.06. The final regression coefficients were not statistically significant.

Armitage et al. (2000) also conducted a similar analysis with respect to the effects of gender. Men and women were found to differ significantly only with respect to intentions to drive after drinking (r = –.30, p < .01); there were no significant correlations between gender and condom use or binge drinking. In a regression analysis it was found that, once attitudes, perceived norms, and perceived control were taken into account, the effect of gender on intentions to drive after drinking declined significantly. The regression coefficient for gender went from –.31 (p < .01) to –.13 (p < .05). The fact that the regression coefficient remained significant indicates that the effect of gender on intentions to drive after drinking was only partially mediated by the direct measures of attitude, subjective norm, and perceived behavioral control.

To summarize briefly, empirical research within our reasoned action framework has shown that demographic characteristics such as age, gender, and ethnicity tend to influence intentions and behavior indirectly. A number of studies have revealed that differences in intentions associated with variation in demographic characteristics of a population are eliminated or greatly reduced when attitudes, perceived norms, and perceived behavioral control are taken into account. Similarly, differences in behavior associated with variation in demographic characteristics are eliminated or greatly reduced when intentions and perceived control are taken into account. However, although there are only a few studies that have provided relevant data, the most interesting substantive information about the role of demographic characteristics is obtained by examining the underlying behavioral, normative, and control beliefs. Demographic characteristics segment the population into subgroups with very different life experiences. As a result, members of the various subgroups are likely to form very different beliefs relevant to a given behavior. We have illustrated this by showing that gender differences in hunting can be attributed, among other things, to the fact that men and women hold very different beliefs about the likely outcomes of this behavior and by showing that differences in sexual behavior between White and Black teenagers can be attributed, among other things, to their divergent perceptions of social pressure from normative referents.

Personal Dispositions

As noted earlier, demographic characteristics, such as age, ethnicity, and gender, by themselves do not provide an explanation for observed differences in behavior. In contrast, personal dispositions such as self-esteem, sensation seeking, religiosity, intelligence, locus of control, or conservatism–liberalism hold out promise of providing psychologically meaningful explanations of behavior. Indeed, as we saw in Chapter 1, when investigators try to understand the determinants of a certain behavior, they often focus on broad dispositions or individual difference variables that appear relevant for the behavior in question. The personality trait of conscientiousness, for example, could be invoked to explain differences in tardiness; sensation seeking to account for risk-taking behavior; authoritarianism to explain punitive child-rearing practices; prejudice to deal with the problem of discrimination; party identification to account for voting choice; and job satisfaction to explain absenteeism.

Our review in Chapter 1 of research on voting, organizational behavior, and racial discrimination revealed the limitations of this approach. Broad dispositional variables are predictive of some behaviors but not of others, and they generally can explain only a relatively small proportion of variance in any given behavior. Thus, we saw that although party identification is found to be predictive of voting choice, it cannot be used to explain voting participation; job satisfaction is generally a poor predictor of job performance, voluntary turnover, absenteeism, and tardiness; and correlations between prejudice and discriminatory behaviors are found to be quite low.

Other examples abound. Self-esteem stands out as a potentially important determinant of health-related behaviors. Generally speaking, low self-esteem is often expected to predispose such detrimental health behaviors as smoking, drug and alcohol abuse, and unsafe sex. However, a recent review of the literature (Baumeister, Campbell, Krueger, & Vohs, 2003; see also Dawes, 1994) found little evidence for these expectations. "Most studies on self-esteem and smoking have failed to find any significant relationship, even with very large samples and the correspondingly high statistical power.... Large, longitudinal investigations have tended to yield no relationship between self-esteem and either drinking in general or heavy, problem drinking in particular. Self-esteem does not appear to prevent early sexual activity or teen pregnancy" (Baumeister et al., p. 35).

In sum, broad personal dispositions are of limited predictive utility in relation to any particular behavior. Although there are exceptions to the rule (e.g., party identification as a predictor of voting choice), broad dispositions are not found to correlate consistently with specific behaviors. Moreover, even when significant correlations are obtained, they tend to be of rather low magnitude (Ajzen, 2005; Mischel, 1968). Nevertheless, there are at least three reasons that we should continue to investigate these types of dispositions. First, as we will see in the next chapter, broad dispositions can account for general patterns of behavior even if they don't predict any particular action. Second, they can help to explain some of the beliefs people hold with respect to a given behavior. Finally, we will see in Chapter 10 that broad personal dispositions can provide valuable information about effective strategies for behavior change interventions.

Effects of Personal Dispositions on Beliefs

In the present section we consider the possibility that differences in beliefs may be related to personality traits and other broad dispositions. A personal disposition is of interest to the extent that it correlates significantly with the behavior under investigation. According to our model of behavioral prediction, this correlation can be explained by the effects of the disposition on the ultimate determinants of the behavior, i.e., on the underlying behavioral, normative, and control beliefs. Examining differences in beliefs associated with the personal disposition can thus help further our understanding of the behavior's determinants. Consider, for example, the personality trait of introversion–extroversion. It stands to reason that extroverted and introverted individuals may have very different experiences in the same social setting. They may be exposed to different kinds of information as they interact with others, and they may use this information in different ways. As a result, they are likely to form very different behavioral, normative, and control beliefs with respect to attending a party or other social events.

By the same token, extroverts and introverts may also form different beliefs about performing other kinds of behaviors, although we would not expect them to hold different beliefs with respect to all behaviors. Consider, for example, the finding that extroverts tend to exercise (e.g., Rhodes & Courneya, 2003b) and volunteer (Carlo, Okun, Knight, & de Guzman, 2005) more frequently than introverts. By examining the behavioral, normative, and control beliefs of these two types of individuals we may be able to gain a better understanding of how this personality trait affects exercising or volunteering. However, like other broad personality dispositions, extroversion is often unrelated to the performance of specific behaviors. To illustrate, in one study (Britt & Garrity, 2006) extroversion did not predict such unsafe driving practices as tailgating and cutting off other cars, whereas in another (Hewlett & Smith, 2006) it failed to predict daily caffeine consumption. Comparing the beliefs of extroverted and introverted individuals could provide useful information to explain why this personality variable is not related to unsafe driving and caffeine consumption behaviors. First, it is possible that the two types of individuals hold essentially the same behavioral, normative, and control beliefs about the behavior of interest. Second, although introverts and extroverts may differ in some beliefs, these differences could be counterbalanced by differences in other beliefs. For example, introverts may believe that one positive outcome is likely and another is unlikely, whereas the reverse may be true for extroverts. The net influence of these behavioral beliefs on attitudes toward unsafe driving or daily caffeine consumption would thus be about the same for the two types of individuals. Third, recall that attitudes, perceived norms, and perceived control are based on *sets* of salient beliefs. Differences between introverts and extroverts on one or two beliefs may not be sufficient to produce significant differences in attitudes, perceived norms, or perceptions of control. Fourth, even if introverts and extroverts differ in, say, their attitudes, this difference would not be expected to influence intentions and behavior if the behavior was largely determined by perceived norms or perceived control. Finally, even if introverts and extroverts are found to differ in their intentions to perform the behavior, they may show no differences in behavior if those who intend to perform it fail to do so perhaps because of environmental constraints.

Clearly, by placing introversion–extroversion or any other dispositional variable in the context of our model of behavioral prediction we gain a great deal of additional information about its role as a determinant of behavior. We learn not only whether the dispositional factor produces differences in behavior but also why the disposition predicts or fails to predict the behavior of interest. Our reasoned action approach posits a causal chain from beliefs through attitudes, norms, and perceived control, to intentions and behavior. We can trace the influence of a dispositional variable along this chain of effects to see how it influences behavior or where in the chain the influence breaks down. Also, studying a personal disposition in the context of our theory permits us to test the proposition that the disposition's effect on intentions and behavior is mediated by the theory's predictors.

In a number of recent studies, investigators have examined the predictive validity of personality traits in the context of our reasoned action approach. These studies have focused primarily on our theory's ability to mediate the effects of personality on behavior and have not examined the influence of personality traits on underlying beliefs. Much of this research has been conducted by Kerry Courneya and his associates in relation to exercise behavior (Courneya, Bobick, & Schinke, 1999; Courneya et al., 2004; Rhodes & Courneya, 2003b; Rhodes, Courneya, & Jones, 2002, 2004). The investigators typically assess the Big Five personality traits: openness, conscientiousness, extroversion, agreeableness, and neuroticism (see Costa & McCrae, 1985) as well as attitudes, norms, perceived control, and intentions with respect to exercising. In addition, they obtain information about the participants' exercise behavior. In an early investigation (Courneya et al., 1999, Study 1), neuroticism, conscientiousness, and extroversion were found to correlate significantly with exercise intentions and behavior, whereas openness and agreeableness did not. Hierarchical regression analyses revealed that the effects of neuroticism and conscientiousness were completely mediated by attitudes, perceived norms, and perceived control. The effects of extroversion on intentions and behavior were mostly mediated by these constructs, but the results also revealed a significant albeit small direct effect.

In subsequent research (Rhodes & Courneya, 2003b; Rhodes et al., 2002; see also Rhodes et al., 2004) the investigators discovered that only the activity subscale of the extroversion trait was significantly related to exercise intentions and behavior; the positive affect and sociability subdimensions were largely irrelevant. Again, however, as in the case of the overall extroversion trait, the activity subscale's effect on intentions and actions was largely but not completely mediated by attitudes, perceived norms, and perceived behavioral control.[2]

Interestingly, and in contrast with the results of the studies reviewed thus far, another investigation in this research program (Courneya et al., 2004) found that none of the Big Five personality traits—including extroversion—had a significant effect on exercise intentions or behavior. To add to the complexity, Conner and Abraham (2001, Study 2) also reported a study in which extroversion failed to correlate with exercise intentions and behavior, but as in the Courneya et al. (1999) study, exercise intentions and behavior correlated significantly with conscientiousness. The effect of conscientiousness on intentions was completely mediated by attitudes, norms and perceived control, but the effects of conscientiousness on behavior was only partially mediated by intentions and perceived control.

In sum, as is true of other types of background factors, there is some inconsistency in the effects of the Big Five personality traits on intentions and behavior. With respect to exercise, openness and agreeableness appear to be largely irrelevant, and the effects of neuroticism, conscientiousness, and extroversion have been inconsistent across studies. When these traits are found to correlate with intentions and behavior, their effects are found to be largely, although not always completely, mediated by attitudes, perceived norms, and perceptions of behavioral control. When direct (i.e., unmediated) effects of personality and other individual difference variables on intentions or behavior are found, this is often interpreted to mean that the theory's variables are not sufficient to predict and explain the behavior of interest (see Conner & Armitage, 1998). We consider the question of our theory's sufficiency in Chapter 9.

Personal Dispositions and Beliefs

Although the studies reviewed herein suggest that broad personal dispositions tend to have primarily indirect effects on intentions and behavior, they did not provide information about the effects of such variables on underlying beliefs. We can draw on data from the study on adolescent sexual behavior mentioned earlier (Fishbein et al., in preparation) to illustrate how this might be done. In addition to examining ethnic differences, the study also dealt with *sensation seeking*, an individual difference variable that has often been found to predict such adolescent risk-taking behaviors as drinking, using drugs, and having sexual intercourse. Although correlations can be fairly low, adolescents and young adults high in sensation seeking tend to be significantly more likely to engage in risk-taking behaviors than those low in sensation seeking. In this study, male and female Black and White adolescents aged 14 to 16 completed a baseline questionnaire that measured intentions, attitudes, perceived norms, and perceived behavioral control in relation to having sex in the next 12 months, as well as the sensation-seeking disposition.

Consistent with expectations, the measure of sensation seeking correlated significantly with intentions to have sexual intercourse in the next 12 months ($r = .23$, $p < .01$). In addition, sensation seeking also correlated significantly with attitudes toward having sex in the next 12 months ($r = .20$, $p < .01$), with perceived social pressure to have sex ($r = .14$, $p < .01$), and with perceived behavioral control ($r = .10$, $p < .05$). The results showed that intentions could be predicted with considerable accuracy from attitudes, perceived norms, and perceptions of control; the multiple correlation was .74. When sensation seeking was added to the prediction equation, a small but statistically significant increase in explained variance was observed. The multiple correlation increased to .75. Thus, we again find that the effect of a personal disposition—sensation seeking—on intentions is mediated almost completely by the theory's constructs.

To get a better understanding of the relation between sensation seeking and intentions, we compared the behavioral, normative, and control beliefs of individuals high and low in sensation seeking. Significant mean differences were obtained with respect to 5 of 14 behavioral beliefs, all 4 descriptive normative beliefs, 4 of 8 injunctive normative beliefs, and 8 of 10 control beliefs. Examination of the significant differences revealed that, in comparison with low sensation seekers, high sensation seekers saw more advantages and fewer disadvantages to having sex in the next 12 months, they believed that more of their friends and people their age were engaging in sexual intercourse, they believed that their friends and siblings were more likely to approve (or less likely to disapprove) of their having sex, and they were less likely to believe that such potential barriers as not having a regular partner or sex being against their religion would inhibit their ability to have sex. This pattern of differences would lead us to expect that high sensation seekers will be more inclined to engage in sexual intercourse than individuals low on this dimension, and these differential inclinations indeed found expression in different attitudes, perceived norms, perceptions of control, and intentions. These findings have important implications for our understanding of the role of sensation seeking in relation to sexual behavior among adolescents.

To recapitulate, our discussion of personality and other broad dispositions as background factors has shown how consideration of these kinds of factors can expand our understanding of individual differences in behavior. We have argued that, like demographic characteristics, personal dispositions can influence the behavioral, normative, and control beliefs people hold about a behavior. By examining the effects of a given personal disposition on these beliefs, we can begin to understand why the disposition makes a difference in some behaviors but not others. We can trace the disposition's influence from beliefs through attitudes, perceived norm, and perceived control to intentions and ultimately to behavior.

Other Background Factors

Many background factors in addition to demographic characteristics and personal dispositions have been studied in attempts to predict and understand social behavior. Among these factors are mood and emotions as well as intelligence and knowledge. These are clearly individual level variables. Some social scientists, especially sociologists, have argued for the importance of social structure variables as determinants of behavior. We next briefly consider both individual and structural level background factors.

Knowledge

Investigators are often interested in the accuracy of people's information in a certain domain. For one, there is general agreement that greater knowledge allows people to make more informed decisions in line with their personal preferences. For example, the more knowledgeable we are about the candidates in an election, the better able we are to vote for candidates who will represent our interests and pursue policies we support. Similarly, it is assumed that the more knowledge we have about cancer or some other illness, the better able we are to choose a course of treatment that is most appropriate for us. In these latter cases there is often no one correct decision; accurate information simply allows people to choose a course of action that will best serve their personal interests.

Sometimes, however, it is assumed not only that knowledge permits choice of a preferred course of action but also that a decision based on accurate information is likely to be the "correct" decision. This can perhaps be seen most clearly in the health domain. For example, after the cause of AIDS was identified in the early 1980s, an effort was made to inform the public about the AIDS virus and the ways it is transmitted.

This was done under the assumption that a well-informed public would engage in safer sex and drug use behaviors and, conversely, that people who lack accurate information would fail to take proper precautions. In short, investigators make the assumption that unsafe health behavior is due to a lack of relevant knowledge and that if people had more accurate information they would engage in recommended health practices.

To test whether accurate information results in appropriate decisions and actions it is possible to create a knowledge test and to correlate the respondents' accuracy scores with their intentions or actions. Items on such tests make assertions about the issue of interest, and respondents are asked to indicate whether they believe that the assertions are true or false. For example, a 40-item test developed to assess knowledge about breast cancer (Misovich, Martinez, Fisher, Bryan, & Catapano, 2003) includes items such as the following:

- Benign breast lumps do not turn into cancer.
- For every 20 women, 1 will develop breast cancer in her lifetime.
- A lumpectomy involves the removal of the woman's entire breast.
- Less than half of all breast cancers occur in women over 50 years old.

An accuracy score is computed by counting the number of correct responses.[3] Knowledge surveys of this kind can be of interest in their own right. In the health domain, knowledge tests can be used to evaluate the effectiveness of health education brochures and other health promotion materials. Similarly, in the political domain, accuracy of people's information can be used as an indicator of exposure to mass media news coverage, and it can also serve as an indicator of interest and involvement in the political process (see, e.g., Price & Zaller, 1993).

However, as we have noted, researchers in the health domain often assume that the greater the accuracy of a person's information concerning a given illness or course of treatment, the more likely it is that the person will adopt appropriate health-protective behaviors. As reasonable as this may appear, the empirical evidence provides minimal support for this hypothesis. For example, in a meta-analysis of seven data sets on the prediction of condom use intentions (Sheeran & Taylor, 1999), the correlations of general AIDS knowledge and intentions to use condoms ranged from .17 to .56., with a mean weighted correlation of .21. In most of these studies the relationship was weak and nonsignificant. More importantly, general AIDS knowledge did not account for much variance in actual condom use behavior (e.g., Ananth & Koopman, 2003). Similarly, disappointing results have been reported with respect to the relation between knowledge about colorectal cancer screening and actually getting a screening examination (Guerra, Dominguez, & Shea, 2005), knowledge about breast cancer and performing breast self-examinations (Schlueter, 1982), and knowledge about diabetes and compliance with a diabetes control regimen (Spirito, Ruggiero, Duckworth, & Low, 1993) as well as with a host of other health-related behaviors.

Knowledge, Motivation, and Behavior

Many investigators realize that knowledge is but one factor that may influence the decision to perform a particular behavior. Specifically, it has been argued that knowledge is a necessary but not a sufficient condition for the behavior to be performed (DiClemente, 1989; Fisher & Fisher, 1992). Consistent with this point of view, the information-motivation-behavioral skills (IMB) model (Fisher & Fisher, 1992, 2000) positions knowledge in the broader context of a general theory for the prediction of health-related behavior. According to this model, "Information that is directly relevant to a particular health domain is an initial prerequisite for enacting a health behavior" (Misovich et al., 2003, p. 777). However, personal and social motivation to engage in the behavior, as well as objective skills for performing the behavior and a sense of self-efficacy for doing so, are also considered to be crucial determinants.

The IMB model has been applied to the prediction of such health behaviors as safer sex practices and breast self-examination. This research has consistently shown that knowledge is not directly related to behavior. Instead, it is related to motivational factors (e.g., beliefs, attitudes, perceived norms and perceived control) and behavioral skills, which, in turn predict actual behavior (Fisher & Fisher, 1992; Fisher, Fisher, Williams, & Malloy, 1994; Misovich et al., 2003). Similarly, in accordance with the AIDS risk reduction model (Catania, Kegeles, & Coates, 1990), it has been found that knowledge regarding AIDS transmission routes, symptoms, and outcomes had no direct effect on behavior but instead influenced perceived risk of infection, which in turn affected safer sex intentions and actions. In neither research program, therefore, did inclusion of a measure of information or knowledge improve prediction of behavior.

Other attempts to incorporate knowledge in more general models of health behavior have also met with very little success. For example, knowledge about osteoporosis among young women has been studied in the context of the health belief model (Silver Wallace, 2002) and Bandura's social cognitive theory (Ievers-Landis et al., 2003). In both of these studies, accuracy of information about osteoporosis was found to be largely unrelated to exercising and calcium intake, two recommended preventive behaviors.[4] According to Silver Wallace, "Knowledge has been consistently shown to be noninfluential in predicting behavior" (p. 170).

In some ways, these results are typical of findings regarding the effects of other kinds of background factors on behavior. Knowledge does not consistently influence behavior, and when it does, the effect of general knowledge on behavior tends to be small and mediated by more proximal antecedents of the behavior. It may be argued, however, that knowledge differs in important ways from other kinds of background factors. Knowledge tests are designed to assess the information people have about a certain topic. When respondents agree or disagree with knowledge items, they essentially express their beliefs with respect to the topic in question. Within the context of our reasoned action approach, beliefs reflect the information people have about a given issue or behavior. It may therefore appear that measures of knowledge, which are essentially measures of beliefs, should be related to behavioral performance. There are, however, several problems with this line of reasoning.

First, many belief statements in knowledge tests are not concerned with the behavior of interest but deal with general knowledge in a given domain. For example, the items on the knowledge test regarding breast self-examination shown earlier deal not with the behavior of performing breast-self examinations but with such questions as to whether benign breast lumps turn into cancer and what proportion of breast cancers occur in women over 50 years of age. The assumption is made that accurate information about breast cancer and how it develops will lead to the formation of appropriate beliefs about preventive courses of action, including breast self-examination. This assumption is of questionable validity. In the context of our theory, the beliefs relevant for predicting and understanding breast-self examination are beliefs about positive and negative consequences of this behavior (behavioral beliefs), beliefs about the normative expectations and the actual behaviors of important others, and beliefs concerning factors that may facilitate or impede performing breast self-examinations (control beliefs). There is no reason to assume that general information about breast cancer will necessarily influence the formation of these kinds of beliefs. From our perspective, general beliefs about breast cancer rates or about the significance of finding lumps in the breast are best considered background factors that may or may not influence behavioral, normative, or control beliefs.

Moreover, even when a knowledge test does contain some behavior-relevant statements (e.g., consistent condom use will prevent AIDS; breast self-examination increases the likelihood of early detection of breast cancer), these statements do not necessarily represent *salient* beliefs about the behavior. Instead, they are statements made up by investigators in accordance with their assumptions about what people should know with respect to a topic like diabetes, AIDS, breast cancer, osteoporosis, or political candidates. Some of the statements reflect what is considered to be accurate information about the topic, and others are assertions that are considered to be inaccurate; however, they do not necessarily represent the respondents' readily accessible salient beliefs with respect to the behavior.

Finally, responses to items on a knowledge test are scored for their accuracy, not for whether they encourage or discourage performance of the behavior. Even if the items on a knowledge test were concerned with salient behavior-relevant beliefs, once responses are scored for accuracy they can no longer be expected to predict behavior. For example, a woman who wrongly assumes that a breast self-examination can distinguish between benign cysts and malignant tumors would receive a low score on a knowledge test, but this inaccurate belief may well encourage her to perform the behavior.

The finding that scores on knowledge tests usually fail to predict behavior has often been interpreted to imply that accurate knowledge in and of itself is not sufficient to predict or explain behavioral performance. By extension, this has further been viewed as an indication that providing new (accurate) information, by itself, will produce little or no change in behavior. Our analysis, however, leads to a very different conclusion. As we will see in Chapters 10 and 11, it is indeed possible to change behavior by providing people with behavior-relevant information. In terms of predicting and understanding performance of a behavior, we have seen in previous chapters that intentions and behaviors follow reasonably from the beliefs people have about performing the behaviors in question. Whether these beliefs are accurate or inaccurate, biased or unbiased, rational or irrational is of no consequence for the prediction and explanation of the behavior; what matters is the content of the beliefs. Beliefs that performing the behavior will lead to positive outcomes, that important others support its performance or perform it themselves, and beliefs that facilitating factors will be present or that potential barriers can be overcome should all increase the likelihood that the behavior will be performed. Conversely, beliefs that performing the behavior will produce negative outcomes, that others disapprove of its performance or are themselves not performing it, and beliefs that potential barriers make performance of the behavior difficult should all reduce the likelihood that the behavior will be performed. This is true whether the behavioral, normative, and control beliefs are accurate or inaccurate.

In sum, knowledge tests mainly assess the accuracy of general information about a broad topic or domain, not about the performance of any particular behavior in that domain. Like any other background factor, such information can influence intentions and behavior indirectly by influencing behavioral, normative, or control beliefs with respect to the behavior in question. Earlier we encountered evidence for such mediating processes when we saw that the effect of knowledge on breast self-examinations was mediated by behavioral skills or self-efficacy beliefs (e.g., Fisher et al., 1994). Similarly, in the study by Ievers-Landis et al. (2003) mentioned earlier, the effect of information accuracy on behaviors designed to prevent osteoporosis was mediated by perceived risk of developing this condition.

Generally speaking, the higher the accuracy of people's information with respect to a disease or medical condition, the more likely it is that they will appreciate the dangers posed by the disease. Moreover, and more important, they may also form the behavioral belief that performing a recommended behavior will reduce the risk of developing the condition; the normative beliefs that their doctors, spouses, and other important referents think they should perform the behavior; and perhaps also control beliefs to the effect that certain facilitators will be present that will help them perform the behavior. However, accuracy of information about a medical condition will often have little effect on behavioral performance. For example, compared with women who are poorly informed about breast cancer, women who are well informed may be more likely to believe that performing breast self-examinations will increase the chances of early detection, but they may be less likely to believe that they can accurately detect suspicious lumps. In this case, considering only these two beliefs in isolation, accuracy of information about breast cancer would have no appreciable net effect on breast self-examination behavior. It is perhaps for this reason that research has found at best modest relations between knowledge and behavior.

Affect: Moods and Emotions

The effect of mood and emotion on behavior is another area of great interest to theorists and practitioners alike. In Chapter 3 we discussed the distinction between affect and evaluation or attitude. We saw that attitudes contain both instrumental and experiential aspects. The experiential component is represented by such adjective pairs as *pleasant–unpleasant*, *boring–interesting, enjoyable–unenjoyable*, and *comfortable–uncomfortable*. We have maintained, however, that these kinds of judgments are evaluative in nature and do not represent affective or emotional states. We saw in Chapter 3 that affect includes generalized mood states without a clearly defined object of reference (e.g., sadness vs. happiness) as well as such qualitatively different emotions as anger, fear, and pride. Like attitudes, affective states have an evaluative dimension, that is, a degree of positive or negative valence, but in addition, they also contain an element of arousal, that is, a degree of activation or deactivation. Thus, anger is an unpleasant emotion with a high degree of activation, whereas feeling relaxed is a pleasant emotion at a relatively low level of activation.

When considering the effects of affect on behavior, it is important to distinguish between moods or emotions that are independent of any particular behavior and moods or emotions tied to the performance of the particular behavior under consideration. Various experiences can make us feel happy or sad, and it has been assumed that these moods can influence our attitudes and behaviors (see Clore & Schnall, 2005). Moods and emotions can, however, also be tied to the performance of a particular behavior as when we feel anxious about going to the dentist, fearful about flying, or proud about our decision to quit smoking.

Generalized Moods and Emotions

Within the framework of our reasoned action approach, such generalized moods as happiness and sadness can have a strong impact on intentions and behaviors, but like other background factors, this influence is assumed to be indirect. It is well known that general moods can have systematic effects on beliefs and evaluations: People in a positive mood tend to evaluate events more favorably and to judge favorable events as more likely to occur than people in a negative mood (e.g., Forgas, Bower, & Krantz, 1984; Johnson & Tversky, 1983; Schaller & Cialdini, 1990). Such effects are likely to influence behavioral beliefs, such that pleasant affective states would make favorable outcomes appear more likely and the outcomes themselves more positive, whereas unpleasant states would increase the likelihood and negative valence of undesirable outcomes.

Moreover, general affect can also influence the kinds of behavioral beliefs that are readily accessible in memory (Clark & Waddell, 1983; Goldstein, Wall, McKee, & Hinson, 2004; McKee, Wall, Hinson, Goldstein, & Bissonnette, 2003). For example, McKee et al. (2003) conducted a study on the effects of mood on beliefs about smoking cigarettes among female college students who were smokers or former smokers. Using a standard musical mood induction procedure, positive and negative moods were produced by exposing participants to a 10-minute segment of either pleasant or unpleasant music. In a control condition, no music was played. Using a free-response belief elicitation method, participants then responded to the stem, "When I smoke cigarettes I expect to..." The first response elicited was classified into one of three categories, two of which referred to positive beliefs about smoking (e.g., be sociable, relieve stress) and one to negative beliefs about smoking (e.g., cough, smell terrible). As expected, compared with participants in the negative mood condition, participants in the positive mood condition were more likely to emit favorable beliefs about smoking and less likely to emit unfavorable beliefs.

In a similar fashion, different normative referents may become readily accessible under pleasant as opposed to unpleasant affective states, and it is also possible that moods influence motivation to comply with salient referents. Finally, generalized moods may also influence the salience of control factors as well as overall perceptions of control such that we are more likely to believe that we are capable of performing a particular behavior in a happy as opposed to a sad mood.

The same arguments can be made for the effects of more specific emotions, such as anger, fear, or pride. Once an emotion of this kind has been aroused, it may influence beliefs about a variety of different behaviors (see Nabi, 2003). Consider, for example, an individual who is angry or proud because of something that happened at work and is then confronted with an opportunity to help another person. It is conceivable that the negative emotion of anger makes more readily accessible certain negative beliefs about helping another person (e.g., being inconvenienced), whereas the positive emotion of pride increases the salience of positive beliefs. As a result, the individual would be less likely to offer assistance when feeling angry as opposed to proud.

In sum, generalized moods and emotions are considered background factors in our model of behavioral prediction. Like other background factors they can influence behavioral, normative, and control beliefs and thus affect intentions and actions indirectly. However, like other background factors, moods and emotions do not always influence beliefs relevant to a given behavior, and even when they do influence certain beliefs, the effects may not be strong enough to affect attitudes, perceived norms, or perceptions of behavioral control. We would thus expect only relatively weak and inconsistent effects of generalized moods and emotions on intentions and behavior. To the best of our knowledge, this issue has not yet been systematically investigated.

Behavior-Specific Emotions

Emotions can be associated with a particular behavior in at least two different ways. First, people may anticipate that certain emotional consequences would follow if they performed a certain behavior. Thus, they may believe that quitting cigarettes would make them feel proud, that engaging in unprotected sexual intercourse would make them feel anxious or guilty, or that they would feel regret if they ate junk food or used drugs or alcohol (see Cappella, 2007; Conner & Sparks, 2005; Richard, van der Pligt, & de Vries, 1995). In Bandura's (1997) social cognitive theory, anticipated emotions of this kind are considered self-evaluative outcome expectancies; they are viewed as being similar in status to physical and social outcome expectancies. From our reasoned action perspective, anticipated affective reactions are beliefs about the likely consequences of performing a behavior, and they are no different from other behavioral beliefs. To the extent that people anticipate positive affective consequences, their attitudes toward the behavior should become more favorable, and, to the extent that they anticipate negative affective consequences, their attitudes should become more unfavorable.

Some investigators, however, have pointed out that elicitation of salient beliefs in a free-response format usually does not produce anticipated emotional reactions as likely consequences of a behavior (see, e.g., Abraham & Sheeran, 2003; Conner & Abraham, 2001). They have thus argued that anticipated emotions are different in kind from a behavior's other anticipated consequences and that they therefore can explain additional variance in intentions and behavior, variance not accounted for by behavioral beliefs, attitudes, or any of the other variables contained in our theory. We consider this issue in our discussion of the theory's sufficiency in Chapter 9.

The second way emotions may become relevant for a particular behavior is related to the fact that individuals may experience certain emotions when they actually engage in a behavior or when they think about performing the behavior. Consider first emotions aroused by thinking about behavioral performance. Some people experience an intense emotion of fear when they think of flying, of going to the dentist, or of being in enclosed spaces. Similarly, the thought of attending a daughter's wedding or running in the Boston marathon may produce feelings of great joy or elation. Like the effects of generalized moods and emotions, these emotional reactions that accompany contemplation of the behavior are likely to influence behavioral, normative, and control beliefs. Fear and anxiety may lead to more negative beliefs about the behavior, whereas joy and happiness may lead to more favorable beliefs about the behavior. The emotions that are experienced when contemplating performance of a behavior are thus again best viewed as background factors that may or may not have an effect on intentions and subsequent behavior.

In sum, the possible effects of emotions discussed thus far can easily be encompassed within the context of our reasoned action approach. Moods and emotions can be considered background factors whose effects on behavior are mediated by behavioral, normative, and control Beliefs, and anticipated affect can be viewed as a particular type of behavioral belief. Emotions, however, can also arise during actual performance of a behavior. It has sometimes been argued that when these emotions are particularly intense, the logic of reasoned action no longer applies. People may then be "overcome by emotion" and no longer act in a way that follows reasonably from their behavioral, normative, and control beliefs. Thus, people may "strike out" in anger, get "caught up in the heat of the moment" and engage in unprotected sex, or panic under fire. We consider these kinds of issues in Chapter 9.

Social Environment

Whereas psychologists and other behavioral scientists tend to focus on individuals and what motivates their behavior, sociologists and other social scientists usually emphasize the importance of the social environment as a determinant of human action. Features of the social environment include population density; prevalence of such institutions as hospitals, libraries, churches, schools, and playgrounds; neighborhood quality as reflected in crime rates, drug use, and air quality; and other factors such as the availability of child care and public transportation. When a community contains strong social networks that enable individuals to draw on the community's resources, the community is said to have a high level of social capital (Portes, 1998). Social indicators reveal the advantages of living in such communities. Among other things educational achievement and income tend to be relatively high, whereas unemployment, teen pregnancy, crime, and drug use are relatively low. Some of the reported relationships between social capital and specific social indicators are remarkably strong. For example, a state-level measure of social capital had correlations of −.50 with AIDS case rates and −.78 with teen pregnancy rates (see Holtgrave, 2007). In another line of research, however, a state-level measure of social capital was found to be largely unrelated to economic output and unemployment, although it did predict economic equality and employment stability (Casey & Christ, 2005).

Clearly, we can learn a great deal about important societal forces by studying social phenomena at an aggregate level. At the same time, we have seen that an individual level analysis with its emphasis on beliefs, attitudes, and intentions can also provide considerable insight into the determinants of human social behavior. It is therefore unfortunate that there has been relatively little communication between investigators working at these two levels of analysis. Researchers in the psychological tradition could benefit from paying more attention to social structure variables, and those working in the sociological tradition could benefit from learning about the individual-level mechanisms that mediate the phenomena they observe at the societal level.

We believe that our reasoned action approach can provide a useful bridge between the aggregate and individual levels of analysis. On one hand, our theory focuses on the proximal antecedents of individual behaviors, but on the other it also can be used to study the role of broad structural variables such as neighborhood quality, social capital, and availability of medical and social services. Within our theory, these latter structural variables serve as the background in which individual level variables are embedded. To illustrate, imagine that research with aggregate level variables has found a strong relation between social capital and mental health and that we want to get a better understanding of this relationship by applying our reasoned action approach. We would start out by considering the behaviors that are likely to promote mental health, and we would try to identify which of these behaviors may be affected by social capital. Because social capital refers to the extent of people's involvement in community networks and their trust in the community, we might hypothesize that social support is an important mediating factor. A high level of social capital should permit people to request and receive assistance in times of crisis, and this may in turn promote mental health. Consequently, we could focus our attention on the behavior of seeking social support when needed.

To conduct our research, we would develop a questionnaire that would include measures of behavioral, normative, and control beliefs with respect to seeking social support; attitudes, perceived norms, and perceived control with respect to this behavior; intentions to seek social support; and a measure of actual support seeking behavior. We would also need to secure valid measures of social capital and of the participant's level of mental health. Social capital would have to be assessed at the individual level so that we could examine its correlations with our theory's constructs and with the mental health outcome measure. Several individual-level measures of social capital have indeed been developed and used in social capital research (e.g., Fitzpatrick, Piko, Wright, & LaGory, 2005; Steptoe & Feldman, 2001). Like other background factors that are found to influence behavior or the attainment of behavioral goals, the individual-level measure of social capital would be expected to correlate with some of the beliefs people hold with respect to seeking social support, and these effects of social capital could help to explain why social capital is related to behavior and to the outcome criterion.

Note that a relation between social structure variables and behaviors or outcome measures observed at the aggregate level may or may not obtain at the individual level. We saw earlier, for example, that the greater a state's social capital, the lower the percentage of teenagers in the state who become pregnant in a given year ($r = -.78$; Holtgrave, 2007). It would be unusual to find a correlation of this magnitude at the individual level. Nevertheless, whenever a significant relation is obtained, it is possible to examine the effects of the social structure variable on behavioral, normative, and control beliefs and thereby gain a better understanding of the role it plays as a determinant of behavior or of a behavioral outcome such as teen pregnancy.

In sum, we have seen that people's behavior and various outcome indicators can vary greatly as a function of the social environment. To elucidate the psychological mechanisms that mediate the relations between social structure variables and behavior we have proposed the use of our model of behavioral prediction as a bridge between aggregate and individual-level analyses. This can be done by assessing structural variables, such as social capital, at the individual level and examining the relations of the obtained scores with the constructs in our theoretical model. It is worth noting, however, that the translation of aggregate level structural variables to the level of the individual can change their meaning. For example, a community's crime rate can be assessed objectively by counting the number of incidents in different crime categories and combining them into an overall index. To translate this variable to the individual level, we might ask people how many incidents in the different crime categories they believe occur in their community and then aggregate their responses across categories. Although perhaps of interest in its own right, this index of *perceived* crime may be an over- or underestimate of the actual crime rate in the community, and its relation to behavior or to such indicators as unemployment or drug use may tell us little about the importance of the community's actual crime rate.

To circumvent this problem, we could try to apply the reasoned action approach in a different manner. Instead of reducing social structure variables to the level of the individual, we could aggregate the individual level variables. For example, we could compute, for each unit of analysis (e.g., the state), the means for each of the theory's constructs—or the percentage of people who respond positively or negatively with respect to each construct—and then correlate these aggregate measures with the unit-level social structure variable. Of course, this begs the question as to whether the theory's individual-level variables change their meaning in the process of translation to the aggregate level. Relations observed at the individual level could change drastically at the aggregate level. For instance, the average attitude toward seeking psychological counseling may differ little across states and thus show only low correlations with intentions to seek counseling. In contrast, there may be considerable variance among individuals in their attitudes toward this behavior, and at this level, attitudes may be found to be an important predictor of intentions.

☐ Summary and Conclusions

Many studies in the social and behavioral sciences provide information about differences in behavior due to social structure variables, demographic characteristics, or personal attributes. Data of this kind can be very helpful in identifying variability in behavior across different segments of the population. However, at least at the level of the individual, relations between background factors of this kind and behavior tend to be rather weak and inconsistent across behaviors and populations. We have tried to show how a reasoned action approach can provide a useful tool for researching the role of background factors. By including them in the context of our theory we can trace the extent to which they influence behavioral, normative, and control beliefs with respect to the particular behavior under investigation. Unfortunately, relatively few studies have looked at background variables in relation to these behavior-relevant beliefs. This is unfortunate for at least three reasons. First, as we have tried to show in this chapter, by examining the effects of a background factor on beliefs we can explain why the factor in question does or does not influence a particular behavior in a given population. Second, and equally important, by studying the effects of background factors on beliefs about a behavior of interest we gain insight into the possible origins of the beliefs that serve as the cognitive foundation for the behavior. Finally, by treating structural, demographic, or personal characteristics as background factors that can influence beliefs about a behavior of interest, we can accommodate disparate explanatory constructs in a consistent theoretical framework for the prediction of human social behavior.

☐ Notes

1. We saw in Chapter 6 that demographic, personal, and other background factors can also influence behavior by affecting the relative importance of a behavior's determinants. Thus, background factors can influence the relative weights of intentions and perceptions of control as determinants of behavior, and they can affect how much weight is associated with attitude, perceived norms, and perceived control as determinants of intentions.
2. In these studies, the zero-order correlations of intentions and behavior with any of the other four personality traits were not reported.
3. Actually, in the breast cancer knowledge test, responses are obtained on a five-point *strongly disagree–strongly agree* scale. Agreements with correct assertions and disagreements with incorrect assertions receive high scores.
4. In the Ievers-Landis et al. (2003) study, knowledge about physical exercise predicted calcium intake, but it had no significant effect on exercising.

General Attitudes and the Prediction of Behavior[1]

As we noted in Chapter 3, more than any other construct, attitude occupies a central role in social psychological theory and research. In the early days of attitude research, most investigators accepted as a given that human behavior is guided by social attitudes. In fact, the field of social psychology was originally defined as the scientific study of attitudes (Thomas & Znaniecki, 1918; Watson, 1925) because it was assumed that attitude was the key to understanding human behavior. Early work with the attitude construct gave no reason to doubt this assumption. Applying newly developed methods to assess attitudes, it was shown that groups known to differ in their patterns of behavior in a given domain also held correspondingly different attitudes. Thus, for example, divinity students were found to hold more favorable attitudes toward the church than other college students (Thurstone & Chave, 1929); military training groups, veterans, and conservative political groups had more favorable attitudes toward war than labor groups and professional men (Stagner, 1942); and businessmen were found to be more opposed to the prohibition of alcohol than were Methodists (Smith, 1932; see also Bird, 1940). Indeed, in his influential early review of the attitude literature, Allport (1935) stated that "the concept of attitude is probably the most distinctive and indispensable concept in contemporary American social psychology. No other term appears more frequently in experimental and theoretical literature... This ... concept has been so widely adopted that it has virtually established itself as the keystone in the edifice of American social psychology" (p. 784).

In light of the fact that attitude was considered the most important explanatory construct in social psychology, it is surprising to note that by the late 1960s, fewer than 50 studies had been published in which investigators tried to use measures of attitude to predict actual behavior. In a provocative and highly influential review of this literature, Wicker (1969) reached the following pessimistic conclusions regarding the strength of the attitude–behavior relation: "Taken as a whole, these studies suggest that it is considerably more likely that attitudes will be unrelated or only slightly related to overt behaviors than that attitudes will be closely related to actions. Product–moment correlation coefficients relating the two kinds of responses are rarely above .30, and often are near zero" (p. 65). Based on this empirical evidence, he questioned the existence of attitudes, or at least the relevance of attitudes to behavior: "The present review provides little evidence to support the postulated existence of stable, underlying attitudes within the individual which influence both his verbal expressions and his actions" (p. 75).

From the perspective of our approach, low attitude–behavior relations are neither unexpected, nor do they imply that attitudes are irrelevant for the prediction of behavior. In early research on the attitude–behavior relation, investigators were by and large concerned with broad social issues such as racial integration and discrimination, aggression, conformity, authoritarianism, religiosity, labor–management relations, and so forth. They felt that behaviors in these domains were reflections of broad underlying attitudes. Thus, racial discrimination was assumed to reflect prejudicial attitudes toward racial or ethnic minorities, pro-social behavior was explained by reference to altruistic attitudes, and adherence to religious traditions was assumed to be a reflection of favorable attitudes toward religion and the church. The first step, typically, was to develop an instrument, or select an existing instrument, that would assess attitudes presumed to be relevant to the domain of interest. Investigators then tended to select a single behavior that they could readily observe and that they believed would be indicative of behavior in the domain of interest. In retrospect, there is reason to doubt that the particular behaviors selected—or for that matter any single behavior—could be representative of the broad behavioral domains under investigation. For example, as we saw in Chapter 1, in studies on racial prejudice and discrimination, investigators often measured attitudes of White participants toward African Americans and then assumed that these general attitudes would predict whether participants would sign a petition to extend library hours after watching a Black or White confederate sign or refuse to sign the petition (Himelstein & Moore, 1963); whether, when given a choice, prejudiced participants would prefer to take a break with White rather than Black individuals (Rokeach & Mezei, 1966); or whether participants would agree to have their pictures taken with a Black person of the opposite sex and to release these pictures for a variety of purposes (De Fleur & Westie, 1958; Linn, 1965). Given the idiosyncratic and nonrepresentative nature of the behavioral criteria it is hardly surprising that investigations of this kind obtained virtually no evidence for a relation between attitudes and behavior. It would be far-fetched to conclude, however, that these negative findings can tell us anything about the predictive validity of attitudes in general.

In Chapter 2 we pointed out that a behavior is defined in terms of four elements: the action, the target at which the action is directed, the context in which it occurs, and the time of its occurrence. To have good predictive validity the attitude measure would have to be fully compatible with the behavior of interest; that is, the measure of attitude would have to evaluate performing the same action, with respect to the same target, context, and time as these elements had been defined in the behavioral criterion. General attitudes, however, are focused solely on the target element; they do not specify a particular action, context, or time. For example, attitudes toward gays or lesbians, toward the church, the press, political candidates, and immigrants define the target that is being evaluated, but the other elements are left unspecified. As such they are broad dispositions to respond favorably or unfavorably with respect to the target in question. According to the principle of compatibility, we should not expect such broad attitudes to be good predictors of specific behaviors. Instead, the principle of compatibility suggests that the appropriate behavioral criterion for a broad attitude is a measure of behavior that is also defined only in terms of the target element. In other words, the behavioral criterion would have to be an aggregated measure of behavior that generalizes across action, context, and time elements (Fishbein & Ajzen, 1974). Because general attitudes continue to play a central role in many explanations of behavior, we examine them in more detail. We first briefly consider the role of general attitudes as predictors of broad behavioral patterns, but our primary focus is on the relation between general attitudes and specific behaviors.

☐ General Attitudes and Behavioral Patterns

When Thurstone (1931) developed his attitude scaling technique he wrote, "It is quite conceivable that two men may have the same degree or intensity of affect favorable toward a psychological object and that their attitudes would be described in this sense as identical but ... that their overt actions would take quite different forms which have one thing in common, namely, that they are about equally favorable toward the object" (pp. 261–262). Thus, in his initial introduction of a standardized attitude measurement instrument, Thurstone made it clear that people who hold the same general attitude can behave in different ways. Consider, for example, two individuals with equally favorable attitudes toward the church. One may express this favorableness by giving money to the church and the other by contributing time. Conversely, starting from the behavioral side of the equation, one person may be observed to donate money to the church whereas another may not do so, yet both may hold the same attitude toward the church. It is simply that the second person expresses his or her attitude differently, perhaps by organizing a church picnic.

In short, we cannot expect strong relations between general attitudes toward an object and any given behavior directed at that object. However, when the behavioral criterion is broadly representative of the behavioral domain rather than a single arbitrarily selected action, strong relations between attitudes and behavior are observed. For example, in a study of religiosity (Fishbein & Ajzen, 1974) five different attitude measurement procedures (Thurstone, Likert, Guttman, semantic differential, and self-report scales) were used to assess general attitudes toward religion. The five measures of attitudes toward religion correlated highly with each other. In addition, participants in the study were asked to indicate whether they did or did not perform each of a set of 100 behaviors that were assumed to be relevant to religiosity. Among these behaviors were "pray before or after meals," "refuse to state a religious preference during university registration," and "date a person against parents' wishes." Whereas the general attitude toward religion measures were typically poor predictors of any one of the individual behaviors, they showed strong correlations with an aggregate measure across all 100 behaviors, a measure designed to reflect the general pattern of religious behavior. Specifically, the average correlations between the five general attitude measures and each of the 100 single behaviors ranged from .12 to .15. In contrast, the correlations of the five general attitudes with the aggregate measure of behavior ranged from .61 to .71. Similar results showing that attitudes were better predictors of aggregate behavioral measures than of single behaviors were reported for abortion activism (Werner, 1978) and for protection of the environment (Weigel & Newman, 1976).

Findings of this kind have done much to dispel the concern that general attitudes toward objects are unrelated to overt action. We now understand that such attitudes can predict behavior, but only if the measure of behavior is broadly representative of the attitude domain.[2] Individual behaviors performed in a particular context tend to be influenced not only by general attitudes but also by a wide range of additional factors. By incorporating a large number of behaviors relevant to the domain of interest within a criterion measure, the influence of these additional factors is essentially eliminated, leaving a relatively pure index of the evaluative behavioral disposition. Described in this manner, it may appear that the advantage of aggregation is simply to increase the reliability of the behavioral measure. However, identification of a set of behaviors that have evaluative implications and are broadly representative of the domain under investigation not only increases the measure's reliability but also ensures that the behavioral criterion has construct validity. For example, to obtain a measure of discrimination against a group of people such as the mentally ill, any single behavior—even if reliably assessed—cannot capture the broad meaning of discrimination. To obtain a measure of discrimination against the mentally ill that is not only reliable but also valid, we must consider a variety of behaviors, each of which reflects some degree of favorableness or unfavorableness with respect to the mentally ill.

Social scientists study a wide range of social issues and problems including racism and sexism, lack of political participation, aggression, and altruism. To investigate important phenomena of this kind it is perfectly reasonable to focus on broad behavioral dispositions like general attitudes and personality characteristics as explanatory constructs. However, our discussion should make it clear that when this is done, it is incumbent on the investigator to obtain an appropriate measure of the phenomenon at the behavioral level. Whether it is aggression or altruism, discrimination or political participation, one or two haphazardly chosen behaviors cannot capture these broad behavioral domains. Only a carefully selected set of behaviors broadly representative of the domain in question can do justice to these complex social issues. When general attitudes fail to predict behavior in research on these broad classes of behavior or behavioral categories, the fault usually lies not with the attitude measure but rather with the poor, unrepresentative measure of behavior.

☐ General Attitudes and Specific Behaviors

Investigators, however, are often not interested in broad societal phenomena but are concerned with predicting and understanding performance of particular behaviors, perhaps hiring a member of a minority group or renting an apartment to the mentally ill. Many examples are found in the health domain where investigators have a substantive interest in understanding and influencing such behaviors and behavioral categories as using condoms to prevent AIDS and other sexually transmitted diseases, cigarette smoking, breast self-examination, exercising, or eating a low-fat diet. Similarly, in the domain of environmental protection, investigators are concerned with such behaviors or behavioral categories as recycling of glass, plastic, and paper, conserving water, or reducing the consumption of energy. In the context of our reasoned action approach, general attitudes—like any other background variable—can influence specific behaviors of this kind by affecting the behavioral, normative, or control beliefs concerning the behavior in question. For example, in comparison with people with positive attitudes toward an outgroup, people who hold negative attitudes toward the outgroup may be more likely to believe that hiring a member of that group would lead to negative outcomes such as conflicts in the workplace. As a result, they might hold more negative attitudes toward hiring a member of the outgroup, and thus they may neither intend to nor actually hire an outgroup member. In this case, we would observe a correlation between general attitudes toward the outgroup and a specific behavior, that is, hiring an outgroup member. However, it is also possible that people with different attitudes toward an outgroup hold very similar beliefs about the likely consequences of hiring a member of that group. In that case, we may observe little relation between general attitudes toward the outgroup and hiring decisions.

In our reasoned action approach we start from the behavior and look for the behavior's proximal antecedents: intentions; attitudes toward the behavior, perceived norms, and perceived behavioral control; as well as the underlying behavioral, normative, and control beliefs. In this approach, general attitudes are considered a background factor that may or may not influence any particular behavior. By way of contrast, many social psychologists take as their starting point the accepted central importance of general attitudes and assume that measures of such attitudes will serve to predict and explain any behavior directed at the attitude object. When confronted with inconsistent and low relations between general attitudes and specific behaviors, many investigators persist in their assumption that general attitudes serve a central explanatory function and look for factors or conditions that influence the extent to which such attitudes are likely to predict overt behavior. In the next section we examine some of the attempts that have been made to forge connections between general attitudes and the performance of specific behaviors.

Attitude Strength

It is an article of faith in psychology that human behavior is complex and, therefore, very difficult to explain and predict. In line with this reasoning investigators have proposed that general attitudes can have a strong impact on behavior but that this is to be expected only under certain conditions or for certain types of individuals. In other words, the degree of attitude–behavior consistency is assumed to be moderated by factors related to the person performing the behavior, to the situation in which it is performed, or to characteristics of the attitude itself (for reviews see Ajzen, 2005; Sherman & Fazio, 1983).

In reviewing this body of research, it is our impression that the strength with which an attitude is held emerges as a particularly important moderating factor. Clearly, the more positive or negative one's attitude, the more likely it is that one would behave in accordance with that attitude. However, in recent years, the concept of attitude strength has become much more complex. Generally speaking, strong attitudes are assumed to involve issues of personal relevance and are held with great conviction or certainty. As a result, they are also assumed to be persistent over time and resistant to attack, to impact perceptions and judgments, and—most important for present purposes—to guide overt behavior (Krosnick & Petty, 1995). This contrasts with weakly held attitudes that are expected to have lower predictive validity. However, there is considerable disagreement regarding the definition and measurement of attitude strength. In the first systematic review of the relevant literature, Raden (1985) noted that although attitude strength had been frequently discussed, it "has generally not been defined with any precision and it does not appear to have any agreed-upon meaning for attitude researchers" (p. 312). As we mentioned in Chapter 3, contemporary usage of the term *attitude strength* has expanded to include, in addition to attitudinal extremity, such aspects as confidence in one's attitude, involvement with the attitude object, direct experience with the attitude object, its centrality or importance, attitudinal ambivalence, the attitude's accessibility in memory, and its temporal stability (see Krosnick, Boninger, Chuang, Berent, & Carnot, 1993; Krosnick & Petty, 1995; Raden, 1985).

It can be seen that some of these attitudinal aspects are best conceptualized as antecedents of attitude strength whereas others are best conceptualized as consequences of attitude strength. For example, among the likely antecedents of attitude strength are involvement and personal relevance, attitudinal ambivalence, and direct experience with the attitude object. In contrast, an attitude's accessibility in memory, its temporal stability, and its resistance to persuasion are potential consequences of attitude strength. However, if attitude strength is viewed as a latent, hypothetical construct, then all of these aspects of attitude could serve as manifest indicators of attitude strength. Consistent with this idea, different indicators of attitude strength tend to correlate with each other although the correlations are often relatively low (Krosnick & Petty, 1995; Raden, 1985). Despite the low correlations among different indicators, however, empirical research has shown that attitude strength—no matter how it is assessed—tends to moderate the attitude–behavior relation as expected. That is, strongly held attitudes generally predict behavior better than weakly held attitudes.

An early indication that strongly held attitudes are better predictors of behavior than weakly held attitudes can be found in a study by Sample and Warland (1973), who examined the extent to which confidence in an attitudinal position moderates the attitude–behavior relation. As noted already, a measure of confidence can be viewed as an indicator of attitude strength. Attitudes of college students toward student government were assessed by means of a 15-item Likert scale. After indicating the extent to which they agreed or disagreed with each of 15 items the participants were asked to read each item again and to now rate, on a five-point scale, how certain they were with respect to the response they had given to the item. The Likert scale assessed attitudes toward student government along a single bipolar evaluative dimension. It was assumed, however, that participants at any given position on that evaluative dimension could differ in terms of how strongly they held their attitudes. The confidence ratings were designed to assess this aspect of the attitude. Based on the sum of these certainty ratings, participants were divided into low and high confidence groups. After dividing the participants into these two subgroups, the investigators were able to compute separate correlations between attitudes and behavior for people with relatively strong attitudes (i.e., the high confidence group) and for people with relatively weak attitudes (the low confidence group). Specifically, attitudes toward student government were used to predict participation in undergraduate student elections, ascertained from voting records. The correlation between attitudes and voting was .26 for the total sample, .10 for respondents with low confidence in their attitudes, but .47 for respondents with high confidence. The results thus demonstrate the moderating effect of confidence in one's attitude on the attitude–behavior correlation.

Other investigators, using alternative indicators of attitude strength, have also found higher predictive validity for strongly as opposed to weakly held attitudes. For example, in a study on the effect of vested interest (Sivacek & Crano, 1982, second study), college students completed a scale designed to assess their attitudes toward instituting a comprehensive exam at their university as a prerequisite for graduation. Vested interest in the topic was measured by asking participants to rate the extent to which the proposed exam would affect them personally. The behavior recorded was whether or not participants (1) signed a petition opposing the proposed exam; (2) whether or not they volunteered to help with such tasks as distribute petitions and write letters to newspapers; and (3) the number of hours of help they pledged. In addition, an aggregate measure of behavior was obtained by constructing a scale on the basis of these three types of action. For the total sample of participants, attitude–behavior correlations ranged from .34 to .43 for the three individual actions, whereas a correlation of .60 was obtained with respect to the prediction of the behavioral aggregate. This again demonstrates the importance, discussed earlier, of aggregation to achieve strong attitude–behavior correlations. As to the effect of vested interest, the correlations between attitudes and single actions ranged from .24 to .42 for participants who fell in the lowest third of the vested interest distribution and from .60 to .74 for participants in the highest third. Using the behavioral aggregate score, the comparable correlations were .53 and .82, respectively.

Also consistent with the idea that strong attitudes are better predictors of behavior than weak attitudes is the finding that attitudes based on direct experience are more predictive of subsequent behavior than are attitudes based on secondhand information (Fazio & Zanna, 1981). To illustrate, in one of a series of studies in this research program (Regan & Fazio, 1977), the correlation between attitudes and behavior was examined with respect to five types of intellectual puzzles. In the secondhand information condition of the experiment, participants were given a description of each puzzle type and were shown previously solved examples of the puzzles. By way of contrast, in the direct experience condition participants were given an opportunity to work on each of the five puzzle types. Expressed interest in each puzzle type served as a measure of attitude, and behavior (order and proportion of each puzzle type attempted) was assessed during a 15-minute free-play period. Correlations between attitudes and the two measures of behavior were .51 and .54 in the direct experience condition and .22 and .20 in the indirect experience condition. Because attitudes based on direct experience are held with greater confidence than attitudes based on secondhand information (see Fazio & Zanna, 1981), findings of this kind have been interpreted as support for the moderating role of attitude strength.

In conclusion, even though work on attitude strength has clearly shown that this variable moderates the attitude–behavior relation as expected, it must be realized that this success is a mixed blessing. On the one hand, work on attitude strength has provided information about the processes whereby attitudes guide behavior, and it may thus help us design interventions to increase the likelihood that people will act in accordance with their attitudes. For example, we may be able to strengthen attitude-behavior relations by highlighting the personal relevance of an issue or by encouraging individuals to obtain direct experience with the attitude object or to think carefully about it.[3] On the other hand, when we demonstrate the moderating effect of attitude strength, we not only identify a subset of individuals for whom attitudes are relatively good predictors of behavior (i.e., individuals with strong attitudes), but we also identify subsets of individuals for whom attitudes are at best poor predictors of behavior (i.e., individuals with relatively weak attitudes). Measurement of attitude strength does therefore not provide a general solution to the prediction of specific actions from general attitudes (see Ajzen, 2005).

Fazio's MODE Model

The most sophisticated attempt to deal with the processes whereby general attitudes may influence performance of specific behaviors can be found in Fazio's (1986; 1990a; 1995; Fazio & Towles-Schwen, 1999) MODE model. A schematic representation of the model is shown in Figure 8.1. Building on past work concerning the effects of attitudes on perceptions and judgments (see Eagly, 1998, for a review), the model assumes that general attitudes can influence or bias perception and judgments of information relevant to the attitude object, a bias that is presumed to be congruent

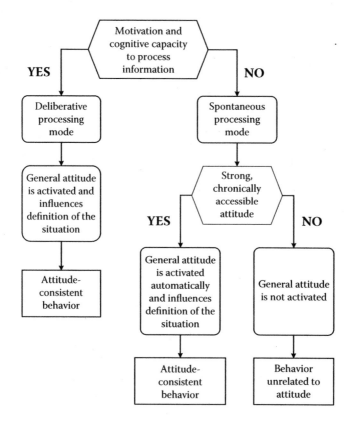

FIGURE 8.1   Fazio's MODE model.

with the valence of the attitude. However, for this bias to occur the attitude must first be "activated." Consistent with the logic of other dual-mode processing theories (see Chaiken & Trope, 1999), the MODE model posits that attitudes can be activated in one of two ways: in a controlled or deliberative fashion and in an automatic or spontaneous fashion. The acronym MODE is used to suggest that "*m*otivation and *o*pportunity act as *de*terminants of spontaneous versus deliberative attitude-to-behavior processes" (Fazio, 1995, p. 257). When people are sufficiently motivated and have the cognitive capacity to do so, they can retrieve or construct their attitudes toward an object in an effortful manner. When motivation or cognitive capacity is low, attitudes can become available only if they are automatically activated. According to the MODE model, such automatic or spontaneous activation is reserved for strong attitudes. Specifically, within the MODE framework, attitude is defined as a learned association in memory between an object and a positive or negative evaluation of that object, and attitude strength is equivalent to the strength of this association (Fazio,

1990a). Thus, automatic attitude activation occurs when a strong link has been established in memory between the attitude object and a positive or negative evaluation. The degree of accessibility (i.e., attitude strength) is usually operationalized by measuring the latency of responses to attitudinal questions: the faster the response, the more accessible, and thus the stronger, the attitude is assumed to be (e.g., Fazio, Sanbonmatsu, Powell, & Kardes, 1986; Fazio & Williams, 1986; see also Fazio, 1990a). The stronger the attitude, the more likely it is that it will be automatically activated, be chronically accessible from memory, and hence be available to guide behavior.

As noted earlier, according to the MODE model, individuals who hold favorable attitudes are likely to notice, attend to, and process primarily the object's positive attributes, whereas individuals with unfavorable attitudes toward the object are likely to direct attention to its negative qualities. These perceptions of the object (and relevant contextual elements, such as social norms) influence the person's "definition of the event," possibly directing attention to positive or negative consequences of performing the behavior in line with the positive or negative evaluation of the object. Consistent with an expectancy-value model of attitude (see Chapter 3), this process is expected to influence the person's attitude toward the behavior and thus to guide behavior in accordance with the valence of the general attitude. Importantly, however, this automatic biasing effect increases with the strength of the attitude, that is, with its accessibility. As a result, readily accessible attitudes are more likely than relatively inaccessible attitudes to bias the definition of the event, to influence attitudes toward possible behaviors in the situation and hence to guide performance of specific behaviors with respect to the attitude object.[4]

Empirical Support for the MODE Model

The MODE model has obvious implications for the prediction of specific behaviors from general attitudes. Consistent with work on attitude strength previously discussed, attitudes that are readily accessible from memory (i.e., strong attitudes) should be better predictors of specific behaviors than less accessible attitudes. This effect of accessibility should be particularly pronounced in the spontaneous processing mode because in this mode people lack the motivation or cognitive capacity to effortfully retrieve their attitudes. Highly accessible attitudes will be automatically activated and will be available to guide behavior, but less accessible attitudes will not be activated and behavior will be determined not by general attitudes but by other factors in the situation. In the deliberative processing mode even relatively inaccessible attitudes can be effortfully retrieved, and thus they can still have an effect on behavior.

Some of the findings regarding attitude strength reviewed earlier can now be reinterpreted in terms of attitude accessibility. For example, there is evidence that vested interest and involvement, as well as direct experience of interacting with the attitude object, tend to produce readily accessible attitudes, as indicated by low latency of responses to attitudinal questions (see Fazio, 1995). And as we saw earlier, consistent with the MODE model, high vested interest and direct experience do indeed produce stronger attitude–behavior relations than do low vested interest or secondhand information.

Studies that were designed to directly test the MODE model's predictions concerning the attitude-to-behavior process (Berger & Mitchell, 1989; Fazio, Chen, McDonel, & Sherman, 1982; Fazio, Powell, & Williams, 1989; Fazio & Williams, 1986; Kokkinaki & Lunt, 1997) have focused on behavior in the deliberative processing mode. The results of these studies are also generally consistent with the model. For example, Fazio and Williams (1986) predicted voting choice in the 1984 presidential election from attitudes toward the two major candidates (Ronald Reagan and Walter Mondale) assessed several months earlier. In addition to attitude valence, the investigators also assessed the accessibility of these attitudes by asking participants to respond as quickly as possible to the attitude questions and recording response latencies. As hypothesized, prediction of voting choice was significantly better for participants with relatively accessible (low latency) attitudes toward the candidates than for participants with relatively inaccessible attitudes. Similar results were obtained for the prediction of choice among intellectual puzzles from attitudes toward the puzzles (Fazio et al., 1982, Experiment 4) and for prediction of product selection from attitudes toward the products (Berger & Mitchell, 1989; Fazio et al., 1989; Kokkinaki & Lunt, 1997).

Issues Related to the MODE Model

The MODE model provides an elegant account of the processes and conditions under which general attitudes toward objects will or will not influence the performance of specific behaviors. Nevertheless, several important issues have been raised in regard to this approach. First, the assumption that only strong attitudes are activated automatically in the presence of the attitude object has been challenged in priming research, where it was found that all attitudes are activated automatically, irrespective of their strength or accessibility (Bargh, Chaiken, Govender, & Pratto, 1992; Bargh, Chaiken, Raymond, & Hymes, 1996).[5] In a rebuttal to the conclusion that all attitudes are activated automatically, Fazio (1993, 2001) reexamined the priming results and concluded that they are not inconsistent with the idea that highly accessible attitudes are more likely to be automatically activated. In any event, the MODE model's basic implication for attitude-behavior consistency does not depend on the assumption that only strong attitudes are automatically activated. All we need to assume is that readily accessible or strong attitudes are more likely than less accessible attitudes to bias perceptions and judgments. As a result, they should also predict behavior better than weak attitudes.

Nevertheless, if the findings of Bargh and his associates (1992, 1996) are accepted at face value, at least one prediction derived from the MODE model would no longer apply. The model predicts that the moderating effect of accessibility is stronger in the spontaneous than in the delib-erative processing mode. If it is true, however, that highly accessible as well as relatively less accessible attitudes are automatically activated, this would imply that we should not expect any differences between the spon-taneous and deliberative modes because weak as well as strong attitudes would be automatically activated in both modes of operation. To the best of our knowledge, these conflicting hypotheses have not been submitted to empirical test. As noted earlier, the moderating effect of attitude acces-sibility on the attitude–behavior relation has been studied only in the con-text of deliberative behavior, not in the spontaneous mode of operation.

The MODE model has served as an integrative framework for the diversity of attitude strength dimensions. As we noted earlier, many of the attitude strength factors that have been found to moderate the atti-tude–behavior relation have also been shown to influence the attitude's accessibility in memory. However, it has also been suggested that attitude accessibility is not necessarily the crucial moderating variable. Instead, it might be the certainty with which the attitude is held, its subjective importance, its extremity, or its temporal stability, all factors that tend to be correlated with accessibility (see Eagly & Chaiken, 1998). To test which of the different aspects of attitude strength is the crucial explanatory fac-tor requires simultaneous assessment of the proposed alternatives. We are aware of only one study (Doll & Ajzen, 1992) that has attempted such a comparison. This study provided support for the moderating role of atti-tude stability rather than attitude accessibility. Compared with second-hand information, direct experience with different video games was, as in previous research, found to raise the accessibility of attitudes toward playing those games, but it also increased the temporal stability of the attitudes. The stronger attitude–behavior relation following direct as opposed to indirect experience could be better explained by the greater stability of the attitudes than by their higher level of accessibility.

Finally, as Eagly and Chaiken (1993) noted, the processes linking gen-eral attitudes to specific behaviors in the MODE model are spelled out in greater detail for the deliberative than for the spontaneous processing mode. It is assumed that in the deliberative mode general attitudes, if they are sufficiently strong, color the perceived consequences of the behavior and thus influence attitudes toward the behavior. They may also affect normative and control beliefs and thereby influence perceived norms and perceptions of control. It is for these reasons that general attitudes are related to performance of the specific behavior itself. It may be argued that similar processes occur under conditions of low motivation or low cognitive capacity, that is, in the spontaneous processing mode. Although Fazio (1990a) assumed that in the spontaneous processing mode, "individuals will not be sufficiently motivated to deliberate and construct an attitude toward the behavior" (p. 93), it has been suggested that such attitudes can occur spontaneously without much cognitive effort (see Ajzen & Fishbein, 2000; Eagly & Chaiken, 1998). The effect of general attitudes on specific behaviors, in deliberative as well as spontaneous processing contexts, may therefore be mediated by their effects on behavioral, normative, and control beliefs.

Implications of the MODE Model

Research on attitude strength has shown that general attitudes are better predictors of specific behaviors when these attitudes are relatively strong rather than weak. The MODE model has further helped to clarify the processes involved by pointing to the important role of the attitude's accessibility in memory. In this model, highly accessible attitudes are assumed to bias perceptions and judgments, resulting in a favorable or unfavorable definition of the event. When considering the performance of any particular behavior with respect to the attitude object, the definition of the event guides the person's behavior in such a way as to make it consistent with the valence of the general attitude. More specifically, we saw that strongly held general attitudes may predict specific behaviors because they can lead to the formation of behavioral, normative, and control beliefs that are consistent with the positive or negative definition of the event. It is important to realize, however, that from the perspective of our reasoned action approach there is no necessary relation between general attitudes and behavioral, normative, or control beliefs with respect to a given behavior. In some instances, even a strongly held general attitude toward an object may influence only a few of the underlying beliefs about the behavior, too few to make much of a difference in attitudes toward the behavior, in perceived norms, or in perceived behavioral control. When this is the case, we would expect little or no relation between the general attitude and behavioral intentions or actual behavior. It also follows that, in this case, attitude accessibility would not moderate the attitude–behavior relation; neither accessible (strong) nor inaccessible (weak) attitudes would predict the specific behavior very well.

Past research on the relation between general attitudes and specific behaviors tends to bear out this line of reasoning. As we noted in Chapter 1 and earlier in the present chapter, investigators have reported little success when trying to use measures of general attitudes to predict such specific behaviors as job absence and turnover, various interactions with African Americans, participation in civil rights activities, and attendance of labor union meetings (see Wicker, 1969). Any model dealing with the influence of general attitudes on specific behaviors should be able to account for these negative findings. According to the MODE model, the observed low attitude–behavior correlations imply that participants in the various studies held relatively weak attitudes, too weak to influence their definition of the event and guide their behavior—even if these attitudes were activated. Without further evidence, this supposition cannot be completely discounted, but it seems reasonable to assume that people hold fairly strong attitudes toward their jobs, their labor unions, members of minority groups, and civil rights. Strong attitudes of this kind should be chronically accessible and thus available to guide behavior. However, in actuality, even under these ideal conditions from the MODE model perspective, the observed correlations between broad attitudes and specific behaviors are found to be disappointingly low. Thus, neither the general notion of attitude strength nor the more detailed account contained in the MODE model can provide a satisfactory explanation of the relation between general attitudes and the performance of specific behaviors.

☐ Implicit Versus Explicit Attitudes

In this section we consider one other line of work that has a bearing on the prediction of behavior from general attitudes, namely, work on implicit versus explicit attitude measures. Implicit attitude measurement represents one of the major recent developments in attitude research and, in particular, in research on prejudice and discrimination (see Chapter 1). Implicit attitude measures are designed in part to overcome social desirability biases inherent in explicit measures and in part to enable assessment of subtle attitudes of which respondents may not be fully aware. It is argued that even though they may not be consciously endorsed, culturally pervasive stereotypes (often acquired passively in the process of socialization or by observing certain groups and social roles that co-occur repeatedly) can, without a person's knowledge, influence behavior. Several investigators therefore turned to implicit measures of attitude because they believed that implicit measures are capable of circumventing these problems by providing information about beliefs and attitudes that individuals are unwilling or unable to self-report.

Unfortunately, as described in Chapter 1, implicit measures are not found to be better predictors of prejudicial (or other) behaviors than are explicit measures. There are several possible explanations for the lack of success of implicit measures. First, as discussed earlier in this chapter, because of a lack of compatibility in action, context, and time elements, broad dispositions such as general attitudes toward targets—whether measured implicitly or explicitly and even when internally consistent and valid—will not be very good predictors of any specific behavior directed at that target.

Second, just as people may be unwilling to express prejudicial, socially undesirable, or politically incorrect responses on a questionnaire, so too may they be unwilling to publicly engage in discriminatory, socially unacceptable, or politically incorrect behaviors. Given that people who are unwilling to show their prejudice on a pencil-and-paper attitude measure may also be unlikely to show their prejudice behaviorally, implicit measures of one's "true" or "hidden" attitude will usually be poor predictors of discriminatory and other socially undesirable behaviors that are under one's volitional control. Indeed, in recognition of this problem, researchers in this area generally agree that implicit measures should best predict behaviors that are not consciously monitored or that are difficult to control and that they should be less predictive of behaviors that are under conscious control. Conversely, there is also general agreement that explicit measures of attitude will best predict behaviors that are under volitional control but will be poor predictors of spontaneously emitted reactions that are not consciously monitored (see, e.g., Dovidio, Brigham, Johnson & Gaertner, 1996). Unfortunately, even though there is some limited support for the superiority of explicit measures with controlled behaviors and implicit measures with spontaneous reactions (see Chapter 1), neither implicit nor explicit measures of attitudes toward a target are found to be very good predictors of specific behaviors; correlations rarely exceed .30.

In addition, a meta-analysis of research with the implicit association test (IAT) (Greenwald, Poehlman, Uhlmann, & Banaji, in press) provided only very limited support for the distinct roles of implicit and explicit attitude measures. Our previous discussion suggests that the more people are motivated to conceal their true attitudes because of social desirability concerns, the weaker should be the correlations between *explicit* measures of attitude and actual behavior. At the same time, the more control they have over the behavior that is to be predicted, the stronger should be the correlations between *explicit* measures of attitude and actual behavior. The opposite pattern is expected with respect to *implicit* attitude measures. That is, the predictive validity of *implicit* measures should be better for behaviors in socially sensitive domains and for behaviors that are not consciously controlled. To test these hypotheses, Greenwald et al. rated the attitudes assessed in the different studies for their likelihood of eliciting self-presentation concerns. Similarly, the behaviors were rated for their degree of controllability. The moderating effects of these factors were examined across 86 independent samples reported in 61 studies. As expected, the more controllable the behavior, the stronger the predictive validity of explicit attitude measures ($r = .28$). Also consistent with expectations, the more socially sensitive the attitude domain, the weaker was the predictive validity of explicit attitude measures ($r = -.36$). However, contrary to what might be expected, there were no significant effects of either of these variables on the correlations between implicit measures of attitude and the performance of specific behaviors.

The distinction between implicit and explicit measures of attitude suggests one other possibility for improving behavioral prediction. It has often been reported that implicit attitude measures correlate only weakly with explicit measures of the same attitude (see, e.g., Cunningham, Preacher, & Banaji, 2001; Fazio & Olson, 2003; Karpinski & Hilton, 2001; Neumann, Hülsenbeck, & Seibt, 2004). These findings suggest that implicit and explicit methods may serve to assess two distinctly different attitudes (Wilson, Lindsey, & Schooler, 2000) and that prediction of behavior could perhaps be improved by considering implicit and explicit measures simultaneously. However, examination of empirical studies that have assessed the same attitude by implicit and explicit means provides no support for this proposition. Zero-order correlations reveal that, in most cases, only one attitude type correlates significantly with behavior. Sometimes explicit attitudes are significant predictors and implicit attitudes are not (e.g., Asendorpf, Banse, & Muecke, 2002; Bosson, Swann, & Pennebaker, 2000; Wiers, Van Woerden, Smulders, & De Jong, 2002), whereas in other instances implicit attitudes are significant predictors of behavior and explicit attitudes are not (e.g., Egloff & Schmukle, 2002; Hugenberg & Bodenhausen, 2003). As might therefore be expected, in these cases multiple regression analyses show that only one of the two measures makes a significant contribution to the prediction of behavior. To be sure, a few studies have found significant zero-order correlations for both implicit and explicit attitudes (e.g., Czopp, Monteith, Zimmerman, & Lynam, 2004; Maison, Greenwald, & Bruin, 2004, Study 3; Teachman & Woody, 2003). Even here, however, inclusion of both measures in a regression analysis produced only a relatively small improvement in predictive validity. For example, in the Czopp et al. (2004) study, prediction of condom use went from a correlation of .31 when only an explicit attitude measure was used to a correlation of .35 when an implicit measure was added to the prediction equation, a statistically significant but relatively small increase of 2% in explained variance. Clearly, although our understanding of sensitive beliefs and attitudes such as stereotypes and prejudice may eventually benefit from the measurement of implicit as well as explicit attitudes (for reviews see Blair, 2001; Fiske, 1998), the inclusion of both types of measures does not guarantee better behavioral prediction.

Interpreting Implicit Attitude Measures

There is considerable disagreement about exactly what is being assessed by means of the IAT, evaluative priming, or other implicit measurement techniques (see Fazio & Olson, 2003). For example, it is not clear whether these techniques are truly assessing attitudes or whether they assess some other construct such as the strength of well-learned culturally pervasive associations. To illustrate, in early Western movies, Hopalong Cassidy, Gene Autry, and Roy Rogers always wore white hats whereas villains always wore black. Thus, when people taking the IAT respond faster to "white/good" and "black/bad" combinations than to "white/bad" and "black/good" combinations, it is not at all clear that this is truly an indication of a prejudicial attitude toward African Americans.

As we noted previously, early research provided little evidence for a relation between explicit measures of prejudice and specific (controlled) behaviors with respect to members of the ethnic or racial group in question (see Ajzen & Fishbein, 1977; Wicker, 1969). This same disconnect has been the focus of researchers interested in the changing nature of prejudice. It is perhaps in part because of the failures of general measures of prejudice to predict specific discriminatory actions that investigators turned to implicit measures. It was quickly recognized, however, that implicit attitude measures may not be able to predict overt behaviors over which people have volitional control. Note that if this is indeed the case, it undermines the initial rationale for replacing explicit with implicit measures of prejudice. If implicit measures cannot be expected to predict controlled behavior any better than explicit measures, the implicit measures would have no advantage in this regard. Unfortunately, as we already noted, there is little support for the expectation that implicit attitudes provide good prediction even of spontaneous, noncontrolled behaviors.

Although the assessment of implicit attitudes appears to have little utility for the prediction of specific behaviors, it may be worthwhile to consider how such measures might fit into our theoretical framework. First and foremost, since implicit measures are measures of general attitude toward an object, we would not expect very high correlations with any single behavior irrespective of whether that behavior was or was not under an individual's control. However, just as we saw earlier that explicit attitude measures tend to be good predictors of (controllable) behavioral patterns (i.e., multiple-act criteria), it is possible that implicit attitudes would also be good predictors of multiple-act criteria composed of spontaneous, noncontrolled behaviors. Theoretically then, it is possible to provide a more realistic test of the hypothesis that explicit attitudes influence patterns of controllable but not of spontaneous behaviors while implicit attitudes influence patterns of spontaneous but not of controllable behaviors. If, as previously suggested, such spontaneous behaviors are important cues to prejudice that impact upon race relations, it would clearly be important to try to change implicit as well as explicit measures of racial stereotypes and attitudes.

We believe, however, that the real test of the utility of implicit measures will come when investigators start to assess behaviors that are directly compatible with their attitude measures. In accordance with the principle of compatibility discussed in Chapter 2, to predict specific behaviors we should use implicit measurement techniques to assess attitudes toward performing these same specific behaviors rather than to assess general attitudes toward targets, and we should use implicit measures of general attitudes to predict performance of behavioral aggregates that are compatible with these broad attitudinal dispositions. As we have repeatedly noted, within our reasoned action framework, strong attitude–behavior correlations can be expected only under conditions of strict compatibility.

☐ General Attitudes as Background Factors

In the framework of our reasoned action approach, when predicting specific behaviors, the effects of general attitudes, if any, are assumed to be mediated by more proximal behavior-specific dispositions: behavioral, normative, and control beliefs; attitudes toward the behavior, perceived norms, and perceived behavioral control; and intentions to perform the behavior. In our discussion of Fazio's (1990a) MODE model we saw that, at least in the deliberative mode of operation, people's general attitudes are assumed to influence their beliefs about the likely consequences of a behavior directed at the attitude object, and perhaps also normative and control beliefs with respect to performance of the behavior. These ideas are clearly consistent with our view of general attitudes as background factors. Our model, however, does not assume a necessary link between general attitudes and specific behaviors, but when such a link is found, it is expected to be mediated by the behavior's proximal determinants.

In Chapter 7 we showed how demographic variables, personality traits, and other kinds of background factors can influence behavior via their effects on the behavior's proximal determinants. In this section we briefly consider evidence that general attitudes may also be considered a background factor whose effect on specific behaviors is mediated by the predictors in our model of behavioral prediction. Our review of the literature revealed only a few studies that directly tested this idea, and these studies appear to provide tentative support. For example, in a study of recycling behavior (Valle, Rebelo, Reis, & Menezes, 2005) the investigators assessed general attitudes toward protection of the environment as well as attitudes, injunctive norms, and perceived control with respect to recycling. Although the investigators did not measure intentions to recycle, they did obtain a self-report of recycling behavior. Consistent with our theory, the effect of general environmental attitudes on recycling behavior was mediated by attitudes toward recycling and by perceived behavioral control.

In a study conducted in Taiwan (Chiou, Huang, & Chuang, 2005), an attempt was made to predict intentions to purchase CDs of a well-known Taiwanese pop music group ("F4"). The investigators assessed attitudes toward the group, attitudes toward their music, as well as attitudes, injunctive norms, perceived behavioral control, and intentions to purchase F4 CDs. In comparison with participants with relatively unfavorable attitudes toward F4, participants with relatively favorable attitudes held more positive attitudes toward the music and also more favorable attitudes toward purchasing the group's CDs, more favorable perceived norms, greater perceptions of control, and stronger purchase intentions. The study also provided some evidence that the effect of attitude toward the group's music on purchase intentions was mediated by attitudes toward this behavior.

A better illustration of the processes whereby general attitudes may come to exert an effect on specific behavior can be found in a study of voting behavior (Kenski & Fishbein, 2005). As we saw in Chapter 1, unlike most other general attitudes toward objects, attitudes toward candidates, at least in the United States, are consistently found to be good predictors of voting choice. The typical correlation between attitudes toward a candidate and voting for that candidate is around .50. If it can be shown that our theory's predictors can account for these relatively high correlations, this would provide strong support for our treatment of general attitudes as a background factor.

The data reported here are part of a study of the U.S. 2000 presidential election, which focused on choice between the two major candidates, George W. Bush and Al Gore. We report data only with respect to voting for Bush, but essentially the same results were obtained with respect to voting for Gore. In a telephone interview prior to the election the following variables, among others, were assessed:

- Evaluations of eight possible outcomes of electing George W. Bush (e.g., making it harder for a woman to get an abortion; allowing workers to invest some of their social security contributions in the stock market; see Table 8.1 for the list of outcomes).

TABLE 8.1 Mean Belief Strength and Mean Outcome Evaluations for Behavioral Beliefs About Voting for George W. Bush in the 2000 U.S. Presidential Election: Differences Between Voters With Favorable (Bush+) and Unfavorable (Bush–) Attitudes Toward Bush

Behavioral beliefs	Belief strength		Outcome evaluation	
	Bush+	Bush–	Bush+	Bush–
Making it harder for a woman to get an abortion	0.28	0.52	0.13	–0.62*
Requiring a license to buy a handgun	–0.30	–0.42	0.05	1.06*
Banning soft-money campaign contributions	0.04	–0.61*	0.52	0.91*
Using government money to help parents send children to private schools	0.68	0.55	0.24	–0.47*
Allowing workers to invest social security contributions in the stock market	0.89	0.55*	0.81	–0.09*
Covering medical prescriptions under Medicare	0.70	–0.08*	0.10	0.22
Having a more liberal Supreme Court	–0.96	–0.78	–0.73	0.31*
Allowing the death penalty for some crimes	0.94	0.84	1.08	0.66

Source: Reanalysis of data from Kenski, K., & Fishbein, M., *Journal of Applied Social Psychology, 35*, 487–507, 2005 (with permission).

Note: Belief strength and outcome evaluation scored from –2 to +2.
* Difference between Bush+ and Bush– significant at $p < .05$.

- The perceived likelihood that voting for Bush will lead to each of the eight outcomes.
- Attitudes toward voting for Bush.
- Injunctive norms with respect to this behavior.
- Intentions to vote for Bush.
- Attitudes toward the candidate George W. Bush.

Participants were recontacted after the election and were asked to report for whom they had voted. The analyses reported here are based on the 324 respondents—approximately equal numbers of registered Democrats, Republicans, and Independents—who reported casting a presidential ballot in the election.

From the perspective of our reasoned action model, voting for a given candidate should be a function of intentions to vote for the candidate and of perceived behavioral control. However, the choice to vote for one candidate rather than another is always under the individual's control, and it is for this reason that perceived behavioral control was not assessed in this study.[6] Consistent with expectations, the intention to vote for Bush correlated .82 with the actual vote. Also, intentions to vote for Bush were predicted accurately from attitudes and injunctive norms concerning this behavior ($R = .77$). Attitude toward voting for Bush was clearly the more important predictor of intention, with a regression coefficient of .66. The regression coefficient for perceived norm, although also significant, was only .16. Finally, consistent with the expectancy-value model of attitude, there was a strong correlation ($r = .60$) between attitudes toward voting for Bush and the sum of the products involving beliefs about the consequences of voting for Bush and the evaluations of those consequences.

Clearly, these findings provide strong support for our reasoned action approach. However, consistent with prior research on voting choice, there was a substantial correlation ($r = .59$) between general attitudes toward George W. Bush and whether the participants cast their votes for this candidate. To gain a better understanding of the reasons for this correlation, we divided the sample into participants with favorable attitudes toward Bush ($N = 157$) and participants with neutral or negative attitudes ($N = 172$). As can be seen in Table 8.2, fully 77% of the participants with favorable attitudes toward Bush reported voting for him as compared with only 20% of participants with neutral or unfavorable attitudes. The same pattern was also evident with respect to the proximal variables in our model of behavioral prediction. Thus, in comparison with participants with relatively unfavorable attitudes toward Bush, participants with positive attitudes had stronger intentions to vote for this candidate, held

TABLE 8.2 Means and Standard Deviations for Reasoned Action Constructs Applied to Voting in the 2000 U.S. Presidential Election: Differences Between Participants With Favorable and Unfavorable Attitudes Toward George W. Bush

| | Attitude Toward Bush | | | |
| | Favorable | | Unfavorable | |
	Mean	SD	Mean	SD
Proportion voting for Bush	0.77	0.40	0.20	0.42
Proportion intending to vote for Bush	0.83	0.31	0.20	0.36
Attitude toward voting for Bush	1.25	0.82	−0.76	1.11
Perceived norm about voting for Bush	0.89	1.14	−0.64	1.34

Source: Reanalysis of data from Kenski, K., & Fishbein, M., *Journal of Applied Social Psychology, 35*, 487–507, 2005 (with permission).

Notes: Voting behavior and intention are proportions; attitude and perceived norm are scored from −2 to +2. All mean differences between participants with favorable and unfavorable attitudes toward Bush are statistically significant at $p < .01$.

more favorable attitudes toward voting for him, and perceived stronger normative pressure to vote for him.

These findings imply that the strong correlation between attitudes toward Bush and voting choice may be due to the effects of the general attitudes on the behavior-relevant beliefs, attitudes, and intentions. Consistent with this argument, when attitude toward the candidate was added to the regression equations, it had no effect at all on the prediction of voting behavior and only a very small effect on the prediction of intentions. Specifically, when voting for Bush was regressed on intentions and on attitudes toward the candidate, the multiple correlation was the same ($R = .82$) as the zero-order correlation between voting intentions and behavior. For the prediction of intentions, when attitudes toward Bush were added to the prediction equation over and above attitudes toward voting for Bush and subjective norms, the multiple correlation increased from .77 to .78, an increase that, although statistically significant, accounted for less than 2% of the variance. In short, these regression analyses confirmed that the variables in our reasoned action approach mediated the effects of general attitudes on voting choice.

The most detailed information as to why voting behavior could be predicted from general attitudes toward the candidate can be obtained by examining the effects of these attitudes on beliefs about the consequences of voting for the candidate. The results displayed in Table 8.1 permit us to compare the behavioral beliefs of participants with favorable and unfavorable attitudes toward George Bush. It can be seen that significant differences between these two groups were related primarily to outcome evaluations rather than to the beliefs that voting for Bush would lead to the outcomes in question. It is perhaps not surprising that voters with positive and negative attitudes toward Bush generally agreed that certain policies were likely to be enacted if he were elected. They differed primarily in their evaluations of these policies, and the differences were in the expected direction. Examination of the differences in outcome evaluations shows, for example, that compared with participants with neutral or negative attitudes, participants with positive attitudes toward George Bush assigned more favorable evaluations to making it harder for a woman to get an abortion, to using government money to send children to private schools, and to allowing the death penalty for some crimes, and they assigned less favorable evaluations to requiring a license for a person to buy a handgun and to having a more liberal Supreme Court. Clearly, these effects can explain the observed differences in attitudes toward voting for George Bush, and given the strong influence of these attitudes on intentions, they also explain the differences in voting intentions and behavior.

☐ Summary and Conclusions

General attitudes toward institutions, groups of people, policies, and other broad psychological objects are a central explanatory construct in theories and research on human social behavior. Evidence for the importance of these kinds of attitudes initially emerged in demonstrations that groups known to differ in their patterns of behavior toward a given psychological object also differ in their general attitudes toward that object. For example, members of the military and of pacifist organizations behave in very different ways when it comes to matters of war and peace, and they also hold very different attitudes in this domain. Similarly, research has shown that measures of general attitudes, such as attitudes toward the church or religion, predict broad patterns or aggregates of religious behaviors. Work on general attitudes toward psychological objects can therefore provide very useful information. It can help us understand broad behavioral patterns, and it can perhaps also provide a basis for changing such patterns of behavior. Thus, if we could reduce prejudice toward a certain outgroup, we may observe a corresponding reduction in the overall level of discriminatory behavior directed at the group in question.

However, we should not expect that a change in general attitudes toward an out-group will have much of an impact on any particular behavior, such as hiring decisions. Empirical research has shown repeatedly that the relation between general attitudes and specific behaviors tends to be very low. It is for this reason that our reasoned action approach focuses on a particular behavior of interest and identifies the proximal determinants of that behavior. Nevertheless, general attitudes do have a place in our conceptual framework: They are viewed as background factors that can help explain differences in behavior-specific beliefs, attitudes, and intentions. This view provides a bridge to investigators who are interested in the processes that link broad attitudes to the performance of specific behaviors. For example, it is quite consistent with the MODE model's suggestion that general attitudes can influence the definition of the situation and thus can affect the beliefs people hold about performing a particular behavior (see Fazio, 1990a).

Clearly, then, general attitudes can influence particular behaviors directed at the attitude object, but such effects are expected only if the general attitudes influence proximal determinants of the behaviors under consideration. This implies that there is no necessary link between a general attitude and any particular behavior. From our reasoned action perspective, therefore, a good understanding as to why people perform or fail to perform a particular behavior can be obtained only by examining the behavior's proximal antecedents, and the most detailed account is provided by measuring the underlying behavioral, normative, and control beliefs. By the same token, we will see in Chapter 10 that, to be effective, communications and interventions designed to change a particular behavior should be directed at the proximal determinants of the behavior in question.

□ Notes

1. Some sections of this chapter first appeared in Ajzen and Fishbein (2005).
2. The same argument can be made with respect to personality characteristics and other broad behavioral dispositions (Ajzen, 2005; Jaccard, 1974). Personality traits usually do not correlate well with individual behaviors, but they are found to correlate highly with an index of behaviors broadly indicative of, or relevant to, the behavioral disposition under investigation.
3. This does not mean that strengthening an attitude will increase the likelihood that the behavior will be performed. Rather, when a positive attitude is strengthened, the behavior becomes more likely, but when a negative attitude is strengthened, performance of the behavior becomes less likely.
4. In his more recent theorizing, Fazio (e.g., Fazio & Dunton, 1997; Fazio & Towles-Schwen, 1999) has suggested that deliberation permits other motives such as fear of invalidity or motivation to control seemingly prejudiced reactions to override the expression of even strong, chronically accessible attitudes, thus depressing the observed attitude–behavior relation. We will return to this issues in our discussion of implicit versus explicit attitudes.
5. Similarly, work with the semantic differential on the measurement of meaning (Osgood, Suci, & Tannenbaum, 1957) has shown that attitude or evaluation is the most important aspect of any concept's connotative meaning, and just as the denotative meaning of a concept with which a person is familiar is activated automatically, so too is its evaluative meaning.
6. In contrast, whether a person does or does not participate in an election may well be influenced by control beliefs.

Challenges to the Reasoned Action Approach

In previous chapters we reviewed various aspects of our reasoned action approach to the prediction and understanding of human social behavior. Since its inception more than 40 years ago, this approach has generated a substantial body of literature that includes literally hundreds of empirical studies applying it to a multitude of behavioral domains. Notwithstanding its popularity, however, our approach is not without its critics, and it faces a number of challenges. Some researchers accept the theory's basic premises but question its sufficiency, whereas others reject the theory as an adequate explanation of human social behavior. In this chapter, we address both of these concerns.

☐ The Question of Sufficiency

According to our model of behavioral prediction, we should be able to predict performance of any behavior from intentions to perform the behavior and from perceived behavioral control. Intentions, in turn, should be predictable from attitude toward the behavior, perceived norm, and perceived behavioral control. Consideration of additional variables should not improve prediction of either intention or behavior. This is known as the theory's sufficiency assumption. In previous chapters we saw that our theory does indeed permit quite accurate prediction of behavior. Nevertheless, it has been proposed that the constructs contained in the theory may not be sufficient to fully explain people's intentions and actions (see Conner & Armitage, 1998). Indeed, one of the most frequently addressed questions in research with our model has to do with the prospect of increasing the amount of explained variance in intentions or behavior by adding one or more predictors.

In earlier treatments of the theories of reasoned action, planned behavior, and the integrative model (Ajzen, 1991; Ajzen & Fishbein, 1980; Fishbein, 2000; Fishbein & Ajzen, 1975), the possibility of adding more predictors was explicitly left open. In fact, the theory of planned behavior was developed in this fashion by adding perceived behavioral control to the original theory of reasoned action, and the integrative model continued this tradition by adding descriptive norms to the theory of planned behavior. However, for the sake of parsimony, additional predictors should be proposed and added to the theory with caution, and only after careful deliberation and empirical exploration. Because this is an issue of obvious concern to many investigators, we briefly describe some of the criteria that, in our opinion, should be met by any proposed addition.[1] First, like the theory's existing predictors (attitude toward the behavior, perceived norm, perceived behavioral control, and intention), the proposed variable should be behavior-specific, conforming to the principle of compatibility. That is, it should be possible to define and measure the proposed factor in terms of the target, action, context, and time elements that describe the behavioral criterion. Second, it should be possible to conceive of the proposed variable as a causal factor determining intention and action. This implies that a change in the proposed variable can be expected to produce a change in intention or behavior. Third, the proposed addition should be conceptually independent of the theory's existing predictors rather than be redundant with them. Fourth, the factor considered should potentially be applicable to a wide range of behaviors studied by social scientists. Finally, the proposed variable should consistently improve prediction of intentions or behavior if it is to be made part of the theory. In the present section we consider the major proposed additions to the theory that may be able to meet these criteria. Before doing so, however, we consider a few methodological concerns.

The Limits of Predictive Validity

In previous chapters we saw that when our reasoned action approach is applied with methodological rigor, it affords considerable predictive validity. Thus, in Chapter 6 we discussed a number of studies in different behavioral domains in which attitudes, perceived norms, and perceptions of behavioral control accounted for large proportions of variance in intentions (Table 6.1). Similarly, evidence that behavior can be predicted quite well from intentions and perceptions of control was presented in Chapter 2. In our experience, when proper care is taken to ensure that measures of the theory's constructs comply with the principle of compatibility and that these measures are reliable and have convergent and discriminant validity, our theory can account for about 50% to 60% of the observed variance in intentions and for about 30% to 40% of the variance in behavior. The lower predictive validity in the case of behavior may be attributable, among other things, to the fact that intentions can change prior to the opportunity to perform the behavior. In addition, it can sometimes be difficult to carry out an intended action (see Chapter 2).

When considering the question of sufficiency, it is instructive to ask how much additional variance in intentions and actions can potentially be explained by including additional predictors in the theory. At first glance, it might appear that we could account, at most, for an additional 40% of the variance in intentions and an additional 60% of the variance in behavior. However, it must be realized that even when predictor and criterion variables are carefully assessed, they contain random error of measurement. Well-constructed measures of attitudes, perceived norms, perceptions of control, intentions, and behavior rarely exhibit reliabilities (internal consistencies) in excess of .75 or .80. The amount of nonrandom variance is computed by squaring these values. Thus, even well-constructed measures contain only about 55% to 65% of meaningful variance. Predictions of intentions and behavior are attenuated as a result of this lack of perfect reliability. Thus, the results of successful research within our reasoned action framework tend to approach the theoretical limits of predictive validity. Nevertheless, there is potential room for improvement.

Of course, not all studies conducted in the context of our theory have obtained measures with highly desirable psychometric properties. When the measures of the theory's components are relatively poor, predictive validity tends to decline. For example, in some instances the theory's three components have been reported to account for as little as 10% of the variance in intentions. When this is the case, additional predictors— especially if validly assessed—may well account for additional variance in intentions, but it would be inappropriate to take this as evidence for the theory's insufficiency. With better measures of the theory's basic constructs, the additional factors might not contribute unique variance. The question of sufficiency is thus best examined in the context of studies that have secured good measures of the theory's major components.

The Normative Component

Investigators have considered a number of possible additions to our model of behavioral prediction. Some of the proposed additions focus on the model's normative component, and, as we saw in Chapter 4, we have expanded the normative component in our model to include perceptions of descriptive as well as injunctive norms. Rather than viewing descriptive norms as a fourth, independent predictor of intentions, we view descriptive norms as one aspect of the more general construct of perceived social pressure or social norm. In a different vein, several investigators (Corby, Jamner, & Wolitski, 1996; Jamner, Wolitski, Corby, & Fishbein, 1998; Nucifora, Kashima, & Gallois, 1993) interested in HIV prevention have assigned a special role to the normative expectations of one's sex or drug use partner (partner norm), separate from other normative beliefs or direct measures of perceived norms. Other theorists have proposed adding the concept of moral norm (e.g., Beck & Ajzen, 1991; Gorsuch & Ortberg, 1983; Harrison, 1995; Manstead, 2000; Warburton & Terry, 2000; Zuckerman & Reis, 1978). When partner norms or moral norms have been included as additional predictors in our theory, they have generally been found to increase the proportion of explained variance in intentions. Note, however, that in contrast to descriptive norms, which are of potential importance for virtually any kind of behavior, partner norms or moral norms are meaningful only in relation to certain classes of behavior, that is, in relation to behaviors that involve a sex or drug partner in the case of partner norms and behaviors that have a moral dimension in the case of moral norms. Indeed, to the best of our knowledge, partner norms have been given the status of a separate component only in sexually transmitted disease (STD) and HIV research, and most of the studies that have shown an added (residual) effect for moral norm have dealt with behaviors that have a clear moral dimension, such as shoplifting, cheating, and lying (Beck & Ajzen); returning an erroneous tax refund to the Internal Revenue Service (IRS) or, for seminary students, taking a job that requires working on Sundays (Gorsuch & Ortberg, 1983); volunteering to work in a homeless shelter (Harrison, 1995) or volunteering to provide other community services (Warburton & Terry, 2000); and donating blood (Zuckerman & Reis, 1978).

When dealing with these kinds of behaviors it is clearly warranted to obtain a measure of partner norm or moral norm to see if it adds to the prediction of intention or behavior. However, it should be clear that these factors fail to meet our fourth criterion for permanent expansion of the theory, the criterion that the proposed variables be relevant beyond a limited range of behaviors. Moreover, although partner norms and moral norms are usually treated as additional independent predictors of behavior, they, like the descriptive norm, may best be viewed as representing additional aspects of the overall social norm. That is, it seems reasonable to assume that multiple factors may contribute to the perceived normative pressure to perform or not perform a given behavior. This would suggest that, when appropriate for the behavior under investigation, formative research using a reasoned action approach should consider moral or partner norms in addition to injunctive and descriptive norms in the development of direct measures of the social norm. To the best of our knowledge, this has not yet been done.

Another kind of normative concept, *personal norm*, may appear to hold out more promise for permanent inclusion as an independent predictor in our theoretical model. This concept refers to people's judgments as to whether they themselves (as opposed to important others) think they should or should not perform a given behavior. As such, personal norms could potentially be relevant for many different kinds of behavior. However, even though investigators sometimes use the term *personal norm* in their research, they often define and measure this concept in terms of moral rather than personal norms (see, e.g., Kaiser, Hübner, & Bogner, 2005; Parker, Manstead, & Stradling, 1995). Even when personal norms are assessed by asking participants whether they themselves think they should perform a behavior, the responses are likely to be spontaneously influenced by all relevant information—that is, by their beliefs about the behavior's likely consequences, what they believe important others think they should do or what these important others themselves do, as well as potential barriers and facilitating factors. In other words, the concept of personal norm is very similar to the concept of intention and it is likely influenced by the same kinds of factors (Fishbein & Ajzen, 1975).[2]

In sum, the proposed additions of partner norm, moral norm, and personal norm are basically meant to expand and clarify the nature of normative influence in the context of our reasoned action framework. Our discussion suggests that the special status accorded to partner norms and moral norms can be of utility in relation to certain kinds of behavior. However, we believe that these constructs are better viewed as additional contributors to the construct of social norm than as independent predictors of behavioral intentions or behavior. The concept of personal norms, however, is perhaps best viewed as equivalent to behavioral intentions.

Although considerations regarding the normative component have played a role in the sufficiency controversy, most challenges have focused on three other potential candidates for inclusion in our theory: self-identity, anticipated affect, and past behavior.

The Role of Past Behavior

Past Behavior and the Prediction of Future Behavior[3]

It is well known that past behavior can be a very good predictor of future action. Of greater importance, the relation between prior and later behavior is often not fully mediated by the predictors in our reasoned action approach (Ajzen, 1991; Albarracín, Johnson, Fishbein, & Muellerleile, 2001; Bagozzi, 1981; Bentler & Speckart, 1979; Fredricks & Dossett, 1983;

for reviews, see Conner & Armitage, 1998; Ouellette & Wood, 1998). For example, in a study of exercise behavior (Norman & Smith, 1995), undergraduate college students completed a questionnaire on two occasions, 6 months apart. A secondary analysis of the data showed that, without past exercise, intentions and perceived control measured at time 1 accounted for 27% of the variance in exercise behavior as measured at time 2. Adding past exercise behavior to the time 1 prediction equation raised the proportion of explained variance to 47%, a highly significant increase.

Based on findings of this kind, some investigators have suggested that past behavior be added as a predictor to our theory. It should be clear, however, that past behavior does not meet the criterion of causality. Unlike attitude, perceived norm, perceived behavioral control, and intention, frequency of past behavior cannot readily be used to explain performance of later action. To argue that we behave the way we do now because we performed the behavior in the past begs the question as to why we previously behaved that way. In fact, investigators who have proposed the addition of past behavior have usually done so under the assumption that the frequency with which a behavior has been performed in the past can be used as an indicator of *habit strength*. With repeated performance, behavior is said to habituate, and it is habit strength—rather than past performance frequency as such— that is assumed to influence later action (see Aarts, Verplanken, & van Knippenberg, 1998; Ouellette & Wood, 1998; Triandis, 1977). In other words, with repeated performance, behavior is assumed to come under the direct control of stimulus cues, bypassing intentions and perceptions of behavioral control.

We saw in Chapter 2, however, that there is little empirical support for the hypothesis that intentions decline in predictive validity as behavior becomes routine or habitual. Instead, at least two reasons may be suggested for the unmediated, direct impact of past on future behavior in the context of our theory (see Ajzen, 2002b). The first reason is methodological, having to do with the measures of intention and behavior. Whereas behavior at two points in time is most often assessed in terms of frequency of performance, measures of intention most often rely on assessments of the likelihood or subjective probability that one will perform the behavior in question. For example, in the exercise domain, investigators typically ask participants how often they have exercised regularly in a given period of time to assess prior as well as subsequent behavior. In contrast, intentions may be assessed by items that ask about the likelihood that the participants will exercise regularly in the specified period of time. There is thus greater scale compatibility between measures of past and future behavior than between measures of intention and either past or future behavior (Courneya & McAuley, 1993). The greater shared method variance between measures of past and later behavior may be at least in part responsible for the direct, residual effect of past behavior on future behavior. We discussed the problem of scale incompatibility in Chapter 2.

Beyond scale compatibility, the residual effect of past on future behavior may also be due to the possibility that intentions undergo change as people try to implement an intended action. For instance, if, in the course of executing an intended behavior, people encounter unanticipated consequences or difficulties, they may revert to their original pattern of behavior, thus lending predictive validity to prior behavior (see Ajzen, 2002b, for a discussion). To illustrate, consider a person who has not exercised regularly in the past but who forms the intention to do so in the future. Initial attempts to carry out this intention may reveal that this behavior is more difficult or less beneficial than anticipated. As a result, attitudes and perceptions of control may change, and the person may abandon the plan, no longer intending to exercise. The previously measured intention would fail to predict the person's actual behavior, but a measure of prior behavior would afford accurate prediction. If a sufficient number of participants in a study changed their intentions in this manner, the relation between past and later behavior would not be fully mediated by the original intention.

Past Behavior and the Prediction of Intentions

The previous discussion provides a possible explanation for the residual effect of past on future behavior. It has also been reported, however, that frequency of past behavior accounts for appreciable variance in *intentions* even after controlling for attitudes, norms, and perceived control. These findings cannot be attributed to either scale incompatibility or to changes in intentions.[4] Some relevant research is summarized in Table 9.1.

Consider the study of exercise behavior by Abraham and Sheeran (2003) in which college students indicated their intentions to exercise at least six times over the next 2 weeks as well as their corresponding attitudes, injunctive norms, and perceived control with respect to this behavior. In addition, as a measure of past behavior, they were asked, "How many days did you exercise in the last 2 weeks?" Then 2 weeks later they reported on their actual behavior by responding to the following question: "How often did you exercise in the last 2 weeks?" Note that the measure of later behavior had good scale compatibility with the measure of prior behavior but not with the measures of the variables in our theory. As might therefore be expected, past behavior was found to have a large residual effect on later behavior after controlling for intentions and perceived control. In a secondary analysis of the data, the multiple correlation for the prediction of behavior from intentions and perceptions of control went from .60 without past behavior to .73 when past behavior was included in the prediction equation.

TABLE 9.1 Residual Effects of Past Behavior (PB) on Intentions After Controlling for TPB Variables

Study	TPB variables		TPB variables + PB		Increase in explained variance
	R	R^2	R	R^2	
Single study: Exercising (Abraham & Sheeran, 2003)	.705	.497	.763	.582	8.5%
Single study: Household recycling (Terry, Hogg, & White, 1999)	.649	.421	.718	.515	9.5%
Meta-analysis: Condom use (Albarracín, Johnson, Fishbein, & Muellerleile, 2001)	.643	.402	.707	.499	9.7%
Meta-analysis: Multiple behaviors (Sandberg & Conner, 2005)	.544	.296	.625	.391	9.6%
Meta-analysis: Multiple behaviors (Rise, Sheeran, & Skalle, 2006)	.583	.340	.686	.470	12.6%

Note: R = multiple correlation for prediction of intentions; R^2 = amount of explained variance in the prediction of intentions.

More importantly for present purposes, past exercise behavior also had a residual effect on *intentions* to exercise in the future. Attitudes, injunctive norms, and perceived control jointly had a multiple correlation of .64 with intentions to exercise in the next 2 weeks. Because the amount of explained variance in intentions is equal to the square of this correlation, the theory accounted for approximately 41% of the variance in intentions. By comparison, the correlation between past behavior and exercise intentions was .61; that is, past behavior accounted for 37% of the variance in the intention to exercise. Moreover, when past behavior was added to the prediction equation, it raised the multiple correlation significantly, from .64 to .72. Thus, taking past exercise behavior into account increased the explained variance in exercise intentions from 41% to 51% (the square of .72).

Very similar results were obtained in a study of household recycling by Terry, Hogg, and White (1999). In this case, attitudes, perceived norms, and perceived control accounted for 42% of the variance in intentions to recycle household waste in the next 2 weeks. When self-reported past recycling participation was added to the prediction equation, the explained variance in intentions increased to 51.5%, an increase of 9.5%.

This pattern of findings is confirmed by three meta-analyses of research using a reasoned action approach that also included measures of past behavior. One meta-analysis (Albarracín et al., 2001) focused on condom use, whereas the other two (Rise, Sheeran, & Skalle, 2006; Sandberg & Conner, 2005) included studies on a broad range of behaviors, such as exercising, eating a low-fat diet, giving money to charity, smoking initiation, engaging in casual sex, obtaining genetic screening, and playing the lottery. In the analysis by Albarracín et al., attitudes, perceived norms, and perceived control accounted, on average, for approximately 40% of the variance in intentions to use condoms. By adding past behavior to the prediction equation, an additional 9.7% of the variance could be explained, resulting in a final R^2 of about .50. In the Sandberg and Conner meta-analysis, the three proximal predictors of intention had a mean multiple correlation of .54 (30% explained variance) with intentions to perform various behaviors. This multiple correlation increased to .63 when past behavior was added to the prediction equation, raising explained variance in intentions by 9.6%. Finally, in the Rise et al. meta-analysis, the addition of past behavior raised prediction of intentions from a mean multiple correlation of .58 to .69, a 13% increase in explained variance (Table 9.1).[5]

In summary, including past behavior as an additional predictor has consistently been found to produce a substantial increase in the amount of explained variance in later behavior as well as in behavioral intentions. The former finding is not necessarily problematic from the perspective of our reasoned action approach because it can be explained by reference to issues of scale compatibility and changes in intentions over time. In contrast, the finding that past behavior consistently accounts for approximately an additional 10% of the variance in *intentions* raises important questions about sufficiency of the predictor variables in our theory. According to our theory, valid measures of attitudes, perceived norms, and perceived control should permit us to account for all or most of the meaningful variance in behavioral intentions (the sufficiency assumption). As is true of any other variable not contained in the theory, the effect of past behavior on intentions should be mediated by the theory's three major predictors. The residual, nonmediated effect of past behavior on intentions thus violates the sufficiency assumption. It shows that intentions and past behavior have some variance in common that is not shared by attitudes, perceived norms, and perceptions of control. In other words, the theory's three major predictors can explain variance in past behavior as well as in current intentions, but past behavior and intentions also share common variance that is not explained by the theory's predictors.

The Residual Effect of Past Behavior on Intentions

One interpretation of the finding that the effect of past behavior on intentions is not fully mediated by attitudes, perceived norms, and perceived control is that the sufficiency assumption is invalid. In other words, intentions may be determined not only by attitudes, norms, and perceived control but also by one or more additional variables, and these additional variables are captured, at least in part, by measures of past behavior. This explanation implies that if we could identify and assess these additional variables, then the direct residual effect of past behavior on intentions would disappear. It is conceivable that the two most frequently proposed additions to the theory—self-identity and anticipated affect—constitute the missing components. We now review research regarding these variables and then consider the extent to which they can account for the residual effect of past behavior on intentions.

Self-Identity

The interest in self-identity is related at least in part to the finding that, in the context of our reasoned action approach, measures of perceived norm often account for less variance in intentions than might intuitively be expected (see Chapter 4). It has been suggested (e.g., Armitage & Conner, 1999) that "the normative component ... should be extended to encapsulate more complex facets of normative conduct" (p. 262; see also Terry & Hogg, 1996). Self-identity has been considered as one possible extension. Relying on ideas derived from role theory (Biddle, 1979; Biddle & Thomas, 1966) and social identity theory (Turner, 1991; Turner, Hogg, Oakes, Reicher, & Wetherell, 1987), a number of investigators have proposed that people's self-concepts can influence their intentions and actions. The social roles of a mother or father, a student or professor, a nurse or physician normatively entail performance of certain kinds of behaviors. Similarly, social categories can be defined by behavior, such as the categories of smokers, shoppers, or exercisers. Some investigators (e.g., Armitage & Conner, 1999; Charng, Piliavin, & Callero, 1988; Sparks & Shepherd, 1992) have argued that people who identify with a certain role or social category are expected to perform, and are more likely to perform, behaviors consistent with that role or category than individuals whose self-concepts do not identify them with the role or category in question. Several tests of this assumption have been conducted in the context of our reasoned action approach. The critical question in these studies is whether adding a measure of self-identity improves prediction of intentions or behavior after controlling for the theory's standard components.

   In our discussion of the normative component in Chapter 4 we saw that degree of identification with a group can influence the relative importance of perceived norms (Terry & Hogg, 1996). In other words, self-identification with a group can serve as a *moderator* of the relation between perceived norm and behavioral intention such that the normative component becomes increasingly important as identity with the group goes up. Recent work on self-identity, however, has viewed this factor not as a moderating variable but as a direct influence on intentions, in parallel with attitudes, perceived norms, and perceived behavioral control. The results of empirical research appear to be quite consistent with this latter point of view. When measures of self-identity are added to our model of behavioral prediction they often explain additional variance in intentions (see, e.g., Armitage & Conner, 1999; Conner & McMillan, 1999; Sparks & Shepherd, 1992). In a meta-analysis of 24 data sets from studies concerning the prediction of intentions (Rise, Sheeran, & Skalle, 2006), inclusion of self-identity raised explained variance by 13 percentage points. Based solely on the theory's three basic antecedents of intention (i.e., attitudes, perceived norms, and perceived control), the multiple correlation for the prediction of intentions was .58, and this correlation increased to .68 with the addition of self-identity on the second step of a hierarchical regression analysis.

Parenthetically, when it comes to the prediction of behavior, measures of self-identity sometimes also make an independent contribution, but the contribution tends to be much smaller and in most cases it is nonsignificant. For example, to predict frequency of marijuana use, Conner and McMillan (1999) assessed intentions to use marijuana in the next 3 months as well as perceptions of control with respect to this behavior. A multiple correlation of .85 was obtained for the prediction of behavior. The investigators also assessed self-identity as a marijuana user, but this measure failed to explain any additional variance in marijuana use.

Measures of Self-Identity

To better understand the role of self-identity within our reasoned action framework, it is instructive to examine how this concept has been operationalized. In what was probably the first study of self-identity in the context of our theory, Charng, Piliavin, and Pallero (1988) assessed the extent to which participants identified themselves as blood donors by asking them to respond, on a nine-point *agree–disagree* scale, to the following five items:

- Blood donation is something I rarely even think about. (Reverse scored)
- I would feel at a loss if I were forced to give up donating blood.
- I really do not have a clear feeling about blood donation. (Reverse scored)
- For me, being a blood donor means more than just donating blood.
- Blood donation is an important part of who I am.

In another study conducted a few years later, Sparks and Shepherd (1992) used the following two items, followed by *agree–disagree* scales, to assess self-identity with respect to green consumerism:

- I think of myself as a green consumer.
- I think of myself as someone who is very concerned about green issues.

Most subsequent investigators have fashioned their measures of self-identity after the items used in these two studies. A question can be raised, however, as to whether items of this kind really assess "self-identity." In fact, none of the studies we have seen provide independent evidence for construct validity. To our eyes, many of the items used to assess self-identity appear to capture the extent to which performance of a given behavior (or class of behaviors) is important or essential to the participant (e.g., "I would feel at a loss if I were forced to give up blood donation"). Other items appear to have more to do with descriptive norms than with the self-concept. For example, many investigators would consider "drinking alcohol is a normal part of everyday life" (Conner, Warren, Close, & Sparks, 1999, Study 1 and Study 3) a measure of descriptive norm. Finally, some items appear to address the participant's self-concept more directly, but they do so by inquiring into the person's actual behavior. Consider, for example, such items as, "I think of myself as a cannabis user" (Conner & McMillan, 1999) and "Would you classify yourself as a non-drinker, a light drinker, a moderate drinker, or a heavy drinker?" (Conner et al., 1999, Study 2). These items clearly reflect self-reports of current behavior.

The significance of any observed relation between self-identity and intentions or behavior depends on the way self-identity is assessed. When importance items are used, the measure of self-identity basically assesses the extent to which a person values performance of the behavior. Thus, it may be conceptually similar to attitude toward the behavior but as an alternative attitude measure may capture aspects of attitude not represented in the traditional semantic differential instrument, and, thus, this enriched attitude measure may add to the prediction of intentions. Although we are unaware of any empirical tests, this implies that if importance scales were included in the semantic differential measure of attitude, obtaining a separate measure of self-identity by means of importance items would be of little value. (Semantic differential scales to capture this dimension might be formulated as follows: "For me to perform the behavior is *important–unimportant, essential–not essential, significant–insignificant*.")

When the items that are used to assess self-identity refer to descriptive norms, we would expect self-identity to improve prediction of intentions only if the measure of perceived norm was based solely on injunctive norms and did not include items referring to descriptive norms. Again, to the best of our knowledge, this hypothesis has not been subjected to empirical test.

Finally, when self-identity items represent self-reports of current behavior, we return full circle to the prediction of intentions or behavior from past behavior. As shown already, adding a measure of past behavior to the prediction equation tends to account for additional variance in intentions and behavior over and above the influence of attitudes, norms, and perceived control. A measure of self-identity that merely captures past behavior thus provides no new insights.

From a conceptual perspective, then, the way self-identity has been assessed in research with our reasoned action approach is problematic. For one thing, it is not at all clear that the measures used have much to do with self-identity in that they do not really address a person's identification with a social group or with a social role. Moreover, some measures of self-identity overlap with the attitudinal and normative components of our theory, whereas others reflect a person's past behavior. Overall, then, although measures of self-identity tend to account for additional variance in intentions, we see little value in pursuing self-identity, as it is currently operationalized, as an independent determinant of intention in our model of behavioral prediction.

Self-Identity and the Effects of Past Behavior on Intentions

We began our discussion of self-identity in the context of trying to explain the residual impact of past behavior on intentions. We considered the possibility that self-identity is one of the missing components in the theory and that if it were included in the prediction equation (in addition to attitudes, perceived norms, and perceived control), the direct effect of past behavior on intentions would be greatly reduced or eliminated. The meta-analysis of 24 data sets by Rise et al. (2006) discussed earlier provides relevant data. In a secondary analysis of the mean correlations, we first regressed intentions on attitudes, perceived norms, and perceived control. This resulted in a multiple correlation of .58. On the second step, we added self-identity to the prediction equation, which raised the multiple correlation to .68, for an increase of 12% in explained variance ($.68^2 - .58^2 = .46 - .34 = .12$). Finally, on the third step we entered past behavior and found that it continued to exert a strong independent effect, accounting for an additional 7% of the variance in intentions.[6] The final multiple correlation in the prediction of intentions was .73. Clearly, then, the direct effect of past behavior on intentions cannot be attributed to a failure to include self-identity (as currently operationalized) in our model of behavioral prediction.

Anticipated Affect

If self-identity cannot account for the direct, unmediated relation between past behavior and intentions, perhaps this relation can be attributed to the role of anticipated affect—another frequently proposed addition to our reasoned action approach. We saw previously that, for the most part, interest in self-identity grew out of concern with the theory's normative component. In contrast, work on anticipated affect was stimulated in part by interest in the nature of the attitudinal component. As we see later in this chapter, a major criticism of our approach is the concern that reasoned action models are too rational, not taking sufficient account of affective or emotional reactions (Conner & Armitage, 1998; Rapaport & Orbell, 2000; Richard, de Vries, & van der Pligt, 1998). In Chapter 7 we discussed the role of affect and emotions in the context of our theory. We showed that general affective states, such as sadness or happiness, as well as such specific emotions as pride or anger can be considered background factors that influence beliefs and evaluations. They can thus have an indirect effect on intentions and behavior, mediated by the theory's components. However, work on anticipated affect goes further by assuming that anticipated affective reactions have a direct effect on intentions and actions.

Consider, for example, a study by Abraham and Sheeran (2003) in which the investigators attempted to predict how often college students exercise in the course of a 2-week period. They assessed intentions to exercise at least six times in the next 2 weeks as well as attitudes, injunctive norms, and perceived behavioral control with respect to this behavior. In addition, they used two items to assess anticipated regret. Specifically, participants indicated the extent to which they would feel regret and the extent to which they would feel upset if they did not exercise at least six times in the next 2 weeks. The intention to exercise had a multiple correlation of .64 with attitudes, perceived norms, and perceived behavioral control, and the multiple correlation for the prediction of behavior from intentions and perceptions of control was .60. When anticipated regret was added to the prediction equations, both multiple correlations increased significantly to .71 and .63, respectively. In terms of explained variance (R^2), these improvements in prediction represent a 10% increase in the case of intentions and a 4% increase in the case of behavior.

These results are quite representative of the general pattern of findings regarding the effects of anticipated affect. A relevant meta-analysis of 19 studies with 24 data sets covering a broad range of behaviors was reported by Sandberg and Conner (2008). As is usually found to be the case, the variables in our reasoned action approach enabled quite accurate prediction of intentions (mean $R = .54$) and behavior (mean $R = .41$). However, the inclusion of anticipated affect accounted for an additional

7% of the variance in intentions and for an additional 1% of the variance in behavior (both changes in explained variance were statistically significant). Note that these findings are quite similar to the results of the meta-analyses concerning the effect of self-identity discussed earlier.

Measures of Anticipated Affect

To interpret the significance of these findings we took a closer look at the kinds of measures used to assess anticipated affect. Influenced by research on decision making (e.g., Janis & Mann, 1977; Luce & Raiffa, 1957), some investigators focus almost exclusively on the dimension of anticipated regret (e.g., Abraham, Henderson, & Der, 2004; Frost, Myers, & Newman, 2001; Sheeran & Orbell, 1999). This is illustrated by the Abraham and Sheeran (2003) study on physical exercise previously described. In this study, participants indicated how much they would regret and be upset by not exercising regularly. Most studies in this domain, however, have assessed a range of anticipated affective reactions in addition to regret, reactions such as feeling worried and tense (Conner & Abraham, 2001); exhilarated (Conner, Smith, & McMillan, 2003); sad, sorry, and proud (Conner, Sandberg, McMillan, & Higgins, 2006); and satisfied and relaxed (Conner, Graham, & Moore, 1999).

Note that, from our reasoned action perspective, these measures of anticipated affect are best viewed as assessing beliefs about possible outcomes of performing a given behavior. In Bandura's (1997) terms, they would be considered self-standard outcome expectancies. Although these anticipated outcomes are of an affective nature, it is important to recognize that they do not necessarily represent salient outcomes. In most studies, the anticipated outcomes considerd are not elicited in a free-response format during formative research. Instead, the investigators select a few possible affective reactions and ask participants to rate the likelihood that they would experience each of these reactions if they performed the behavior of interest. These responses are then aggregated to obtain a measure of anticipated affect. As such, measures of anticipated affect can be considered partial (and nonvalidated) estimates of attitude toward a behavior based on beliefs about some of the behavior's possible affective outcomes.

Perhaps more interesting, however, is another feature of these measures found in many studies. Whereas the standard variables in our theory are assessed with respect to performing the behavior of interest, anticipated affective reactions are often measured in relation to *not* performing the behavior. One illustration of this can again be found in the Abraham and Sheeran (2003) study. Here, participants expressed their attitudes, perceived norms, perceived control, and intentions with regard to exercising on a regular basis in the next 2 weeks, but they were asked how much they would regret it and how upset they would be if they did *not* exercise regularly in the next 2 weeks. Or, to give another example, Conner et al. (1999) described different hypothetical scenarios involving sexual intercourse (after drinking alcohol vs. drinking nonalcoholic beverages and sex with a stranger vs. sex with a long-standing partner). They then assessed the variables in our model with respect to using a condom in the situation described, but to measure anticipated affect, they asked participants to indicate how likely it was that if they did *not* use a condom, they would feel regret, worried, satisfied, and relaxed.

In at least one study (Moan, Rise, & Andersen, 2005), the variables in our theoretical approach were assessed in relation to *not* performing a behavior (not smoking indoors when your children are present), whereas anticipated affect was assessed with respect to performing the behavior (smoking indoors in the presence of your children). Specifically, the investigators derived separate measures of anticipated positive affect (e.g., satisfied, calm, pleased, relaxed) and anticipated negative affect (e.g., regret, apprehension, anxiety, shame, guilt, anger, fear) in relation to the behavior of smoking (rather than of not smoking) indoors in the presence of one's children.

An important implication of these differences in measurement procedures is the fact that, although not always explicitly acknowledged, every behavior involves a choice among alternative courses of action even if the only alternative is to not perform the behavior in question. A number of investigators have suggested that prediction of intentions and behavior could be improved if attitudes, norms, and perceived control with respect to each of the alternative courses of action were taken into account (see Ajzen & Fishbein, 1969; Davidson & Morrison, 1983; Jaccard, 1981; Letirand & Delhomme, 2005). Clear support for this view can be found in a study by Ajzen and Fishbein (1969). College students were asked to consider eight activities they could perform on a Friday night (e.g., going to a party, going to a concert, playing poker, reading a mystery novel). Among other things, they expressed their attitudes with respect to performing each of these activities. In addition, all 28 possible combinations of activities were created, and participants were asked to express the likelihood that they would perform one or the other of the paired activities. For example, they were asked to express their choice intentions with respect to going to a party versus playing poker on the following bipolar scale:

On a Friday night

I would go to a party |___|___|___|___|___|___|___| I would play poker

can't decide

This choice intention was predicted in two ways. First, an attempt was made to predict it from each of the individual attitudes toward the two alternative activities (e.g., from the attitude toward going to a party). Second, the difference between the two attitudes was computed, and this differential attitude was used to predict the choice intention. In all but 2 of the 28 choice dilemmas, the differential attitude predicted choice intentions better (mean $r = .61$) than did either of the individual attitudes (mean $r = .42$).

These findings may help explain the direct effect of anticipated affect on behavioral intentions. Remember that measures of anticipated affect have to do with outcome expectancies and thus may represent at least a partial measure of attitude toward a behavior. It follows that studies on anticipated affect tend to obtain two attitude measures: an attitude toward performing the behavior and an attitude toward not performing the behavior. And, as we just saw, taking into account both attitudes affords better prediction of intentions than considering either attitude alone. This could explain the finding that adding a measure of anticipated affect to the prediction equation tends to increase the explained variance in intentions, over and above the prediction obtained on the basis of the standard constructs in our theory. Thus, the observed increment in predictive validity may have little to do with anticipated affect as such but more with the fact that attitudes toward both performance and nonperformance of the behavior are being taken into account.

Some support for this argument comes from a study on anticipated regret (Conner et al., 2003) in which the variables in our theory and anticipated affect addressed the same behavior. In this study concerned with speeding in a hypothetical situation the investigators measured participants' attitudes and intentions with respect to speeding in that situation, as well as anticipated affect based on questions about feelings of regret and exhilaration if they did speed. Recall that in studies that assessed attitudes toward performing a behavior and anticipated regret with respect to *not* performing it (or vice versa), the addition of anticipated affect to the model increased the explained variance in intentions by about 8% to 10%. In contrast, in the current study where attitudes and anticipated affect were concerned with the same behavior, the addition of anticipated affect did not produce a significant increase in explained variance. In the only other study (O'Connor & Armitage, 2003) we were able to find where anticipated affect and attitudes were measured with respect to the same behavior (harming oneself), very similar findings were obtained. That is, the addition of anticipated affect did not improve prediction of intentions to do harm to oneself.

In sum, when investigators obtain what are essentially two measures of the same attitude, having the second measure adds little or no predictive validity. In contrast, when the second attitude is concerned with an alternative behavioral option (e.g., with not performing as opposed to performing the behavior), taking this attitude into account can help to improve prediction of intentions. The reason for this is that very different beliefs may underlie attitudes toward performance and nonperformance of a given behavior. For example, smokers are known to hold very different behavioral beliefs about continuing to smoke and about quitting (see Fishbein, 1980). Exploring these different sets of beliefs—and the resultant attitudes—can sometimes provide useful information that is not available when only one behavioral alternative is considered. In fact, we would expect that, just as in the case of attitudes, predictive accuracy will increase if we assess normative pressure to perform as well as to not perform a behavior and if we assess perceptions of control with respect to these two behavioral alternatives.

Although the consideration of behavioral alternatives may be useful and even necessary in some situations, note that doing so comes at considerable cost. If we were to assess all constructs in our theory with respect to two or more behavioral alternatives, the questionnaire could become excessively long, and even if participants were willing to complete it, measurement reliability might suffer. This should therefore be done only when it is well justified from a conceptual or practical perspective. For example, for a complete understanding of voting choices in a given election, investigators typically assess beliefs and attitudes with respect to each of the major candidates and not just with respect to one of the candidates. In contrast, attempts to predict participation in an election usually focus on beliefs and attitudes only with respect to the behavioral alternative of casting a vote. As we saw in Chapter 1, prediction of participation in elections has been much less successful than prediction of voting choice. It is conceivable that the additional assessment of people's beliefs and attitudes with respect to *not* participating in the election would improve prediction.

Anticipated Affect and the Effects of Past Behavior on Intentions

Recall that one of the reasons for examining the role of anticipated affect was to see if it could help explain the direct effect of past behavior on intentions. In other words, it is possible that the effect of past behavior on intentions would be mediated by the components of our theory if anticipated affect were included as an additional predictor in our model of behavioral prediction. The empirical evidence does not support this expectation. For example, in the study by Abraham and Sheeran (2003) on physical exercise described earlier, a hierarchical regression analysis produced the following results. When attitudes, injunctive norms, and perceptions of control were entered on the first step, a multiple correlation of .64 was obtained for the prediction of intentions. As described earlier, when anticipated regret with respect to *not* exercising was entered on the second step, explained variance in intentions increased by 10% to produce a multiple correlation of .71. Finally, adding past exercise behavior to the prediction equation increased explained variance in intentions significantly by another 6%, and the final multiple correlation was .75.

A comparable hierarchical regression analysis was reported by Sandberg and Conner (2008) in their meta-analytic review of research on anticipated affect. In this analysis based on 19 data sets, past behavior contributed 6% of additional variance after the variables in our model and anticipated affect were taken into consideration. Clearly, then, like self-identity, anticipated affect cannot explain the residual effect of past behavior on intentions once attitudes, perceived norms, and perceived control have been taken into account.

One other possibility can be explored, namely, that adding both self-identity and anticipated affect to the regression equation could eliminate the direct effect of past behavior on intentions. We are aware of only one study (Jackson, Smith, & Conner, 2003) that has examined this possibility. The investigators in this study predicted intentions to engage in physical activity (and actual physical activity behavior) among university employees. In addition to attitudes, injunctive norms, perceptions of control, and intentions with respect to this behavior, the investigators also assessed anticipated affect, self-identity, moral norms, and past physical activity behavior. The results showed that even after taking into account self-identity, anticipated affect, and moral norms, in addition to attitude, perceived norms, and perceived control, past behavior continued to make a significant contribution to the prediction of physical activity intentions.

In sum, we saw that existing measures of self-identity do not appear to contribute to our understanding of behavior by providing new insights that are not already available in our theory's primary constructs. Similarly, it would appear that the role of anticipated affect may have more to do with assessing attitudes toward behavioral alternatives than with anticipated affective reactions as such. Moreover, even though self-identity and anticipated affect often account for additional variance in intentions, their inclusion in the prediction equation does not eliminate the residual effect of past behavior on intentions. At this point we have no ready explanation for this residual effect. It is conceivable that there are other important and as yet unidentified variables that mediate the effect of past behavior on intentions, that is, that the model in its present form is not sufficient. Alternatively, it is also possible that past behavior actually does have a direct, unmediated causal effect on intentions in ways that we don't yet understand. One of the remaining challenges for investigators interested in working with our reasoned action approach is to explain the causal mechanism whereby past behavior has its effect on intentions.

☐ The Question of Rationality

Investigators interested in the sufficiency of our reasoned action approach generally accept its basic premises but ask whether prediction can be improved by expanding the model to include additional predictors. By way of contrast, some investigators have questioned the reasoned action framework on theoretical grounds, criticizing it for being too rational and deliberative, for failing to take adequate account of emotions, and for being applicable only to Western culture. We now consider each of these issues in turn.

Deliberative Versus Spontaneous Action

The concern with rationality is stimulated in part by the development of dual-mode processing models in cognitive and social psychology and in research on human judgment and decision making. Generally speaking, these models contrast deliberative, systematic, higher-level processing of information with more intuitive, spontaneous, or heuristic ways of making judgments and reaching decisions. We discussed one such model, Fazio's (1990) MODE model of the processes whereby general attitudes may influence specific behaviors, in Chapter 8. Many more models of this kind have been proposed (see Chaiken & Trope, 1999). Some theorists (e.g., Gibbons, Gerrard, Blanton, & Russell, 1998; Reyna & Farley, 2006) have criticized cognitive approaches, such as our theory, on the grounds that these approaches are too rational, focusing on the deliberative mode of operation to the exclusion of an intuitive or spontaneous mode.

According to Reyna and Farley (2006), for example, "Major explanatory models of risky decision making can be roughly divided into (a) those, including health-belief models and the theory of planned behavior, that adhere to a 'rational' behavioral decision-making framework that stresses deliberate, quantitative trading off of risks and benefits; and (b) those that emphasize nondeliberative reaction to the perceived gists or prototypes in the immediate decision environment" (p. 1). Similarly, Gibbons et al. (1998) have insisted that "not all behaviors are logical or rational…. It would be hard to argue that behaviors that impair one's health or well being, such as having sex without contraception when pregnancy is not desired or drunk driving, are either goal-directed or rational…. Nonetheless, these behaviors are common, especially among young persons" (p. 1164). And consistent with this, Reyna and Farley suggest that "the older models of deliberative decision making (resulting in behavioral intentions and planned behaviors) fail to account for a substantial amount of adolescent risk taking, which is spontaneous, reactive, and impulsive" (p. 6).

These quotes illustrate two basic misconceptions regarding our reasoned action approach. First, the theorists assume that some behaviors are inherently irrational, and, because they believe that our theory presumes rationality on the part of the actor, they claim that our theory cannot account for the behaviors in question. We take issue with this argument on both theoretical and empirical grounds. As we have repeatedly tried to make clear (see Ajzen & Fishbein, 1980, 2000, 2005; see also Chapter 3), there is nothing in our theory to suggest that people are rational or that they behave in a rational manner. We assume that in the course of their lives people form various kinds of behavioral, normative, and control beliefs. Many of these beliefs are based on direct experience and conform reasonably well to reality, but some are inaccurate and misrepresent the true state of affairs; some are derived by way of deliberative inference processes and others by way of intuition; some are based on logical trains of thought, and some are biased by wishful thinking or other self-serving motives. Whatever the origin of their beliefs, however, we assume that people's attitudes, perceptions of normative pressure, perceptions of behavioral control, and ultimately their intentions follow spontaneously and inevitably from their beliefs. It is only in this sense that behavior is considered to be reasoned.

The argument that our approach cannot deal with irrational behavior can also be challenged from an empirical perspective. In fact, whether a behavior is considered rational or irrational depends on the definition of rationality and, in any event, is irrelevant for our purposes; we should be able to predict and explain virtually any behavior on the basis of our theory. The empirical evidence reviewed throughout this book strongly supports this argument. Our model of behavioral prediction has been shown to be valid in many different contexts. Some of the behaviors that have been predicted involve considerable risk and may appear to be irrational, such as exceeding the speed limit, smoking cigarettes, or having sex without a condom. Even the performance of addictive behaviors has been studied quite successfully within this theoretical framework. Consider, for example, use of illicit drugs and alcohol consumption. In a study of these behaviors among college students (Armitage, Conner, Loach, & Willetts, 1999), self-reported frequency of cannabis use and of alcohol consumption were well predicted from intentions assessed 1 week earlier. The study also provided evidence to show that these intentions could be predicted from attitudes, perceived norms, and perceptions of behavioral control, which, in turn, could be explained by examining the underlying behavioral, normative, and control beliefs.

The second misconception concerning our theory is related to the argument that performance of many behaviors, particularly among adolescents, is nonintentional, representing instead an intuitive reaction to the situation. According to this perspective, a theory that stipulates intentions as the proximal antecedent of behavior, cannot account for actions of this kind. It is true of course that people may enter a situation without intending to perform a certain behavior yet performance of that behavior may occur once they are in the situation. Thus, a teenager who had not considered smoking marijuana at a party may do so when it is offered to her. This event, however, is quite consistent with our theory. We would argue that when confronted with the offer to smoke marijuana, certain beliefs and attitudes regarding this behavior are activated automatically, resulting in the spontaneous formation of an intention, and it is this spontaneous intention that accounts for the behavior. Although we are not aware of direct empirical tests concerning this hypothesis, it may be possible to study automatic activation of intentions with suitable reaction time measures.

The suggestion that behavior is often nonintentional, merely an intuitive reaction to the situation, has actually been submitted to empirical test (see Chapter 2). Recall that according to Gibbons and his associates (e.g., Gibbons, Gerrard, Cleveland, Wills, & Brody, 2004), the nonintentional or irrational aspects of behavior can be captured by a measure of willingness (rather than intention) to perform a behavior. However, as we noted in Chapter 2, their measure of willingness appears to have little to do with irrationality or intuitive reactions to a situation. For example, in one of three studies by Gibbons et al. (1998), willingness to engage in unprotected sex was assessed by asking participants to "imagine being with their boyfriend or girlfriend who wanted to have sex but with no birth control available" and to indicate how likely it was that they would do each of the following: have sex but use withdrawal, not have sex, and have sex without any birth control. Responses to the second option were reverse-scored, and the average of the three items served as an index of willingness to engage in unprotected sex. As the investigators expected, this measure slightly but significantly improved prediction of reported sexual activity over and above the prediction afforded by a measure of the likelihood that one would engage in unprotected sex.

Note first that the willingness index in this study was based on the average of three intention items. As such, it is difficult to see why this measure is considered anything but a measure of intention or why it should be able to predict nonintentional behavior. Moreover, the finding that the willingness index improved prediction of behavior may have nothing to do with its ability to assess readiness to engage in an unintended action but instead may reflect the fact that the index took into account intentions to engage in unprotected sex as well as the alternative intention not to engage in this behavior. As we saw earlier in our discussion of anticipated affect, this alone could account for the slightly improved prediction of behavior.

To summarize briefly, contrary to common misconceptions, our reasoned action approach does not assume rationality. In our theory, people do not have to review their beliefs prior to the performance of every behavior, do not have to engage in elaborate deliberations or mental calculations to arrive at their attitudes, perceived norms, or perceptions of control, and do not have to form a conscious intention to engage in the behavior. Instead, these dispositions can be activated automatically without much cognitive effort and can direct behavior spontaneously without conscious awareness of their influence. The theory is capable of dealing with many different kinds of behavior, including behaviors that might be considered irrational or spontaneously activated by situational cues. Our theory is thus not inconsistent with the dual-mode processing perspective in that it allows for operation in a deliberative mode as well as operation in a more spontaneous, intuitive mode (see Ajzen & Sexton, 1999).

Limiting Conditions

The context in which individuals find themselves can have powerful effects on their behavior. This recognition is perhaps one of the most important contributions of social psychology to our understanding of human social behavior. Well-known illustrations of the power of the context can be found in Milgram's (1963) studies of obedience and Zimbardo's (Haney, Banks, & Zimbardo, 1973) work on the decisive effects of role assignment in an experimental prison environment. Some of the issues raised in relation to reasoned action models have to do with their ability to account for behavior that is under the influence of powerful contextual factors. In addition, theorists have also questioned the ability of our approach to deal with powerful causes of behavior internal to the individual, such as addictions and phobias or other strong emotions. The present section addresses these kinds of issues.

Note first that our theory is far from oblivious to the importance of the behavioral context. Because we recognize that the context has a powerful influence on behavior, we include it as one of the elements that define the behavior. Indeed, in Chapter 2 we made it clear that, in our framework, an action performed in one context is considered to be a different behavior than the same action performed in a different context. Nevertheless, some investigators have questioned our theory's ability to explain behavior in certain contexts or under certain kinds of circumstances. Many of these concerns have to do with situations that involve strong emotions, phobias, or addictions. It is often asserted that under the influence of strong emotions or cravings, behavior is irrational rather than reasoned. In other words, people's behavior is said to be no longer guided by considerations about the behavior's consequences or by normative and control considerations. Thus, it is argued, our model of behavioral prediction, with its emphasis on beliefs and their role as the basic determinants of intentions and actions, is irrelevant for behavior that is performed in the presence of strong emotions or addictive cravings.

Before discussing the relevance of our model for behaviors under these kinds of circumstances, it is important to realize that the concern is not with the theory's ability to predict and explain behavioral intentions. Even people who are addicted to alcohol or have a fear of heights are likely to have behavioral intentions relevant to these states. Thus, people who are addicted to alcohol may intend to avoid drinking at a party, and people with acrophobia may intend to avoid high places. As with any other intention, our theory should be able to predict these kinds of intentions by reference to attitudes, perceived norms, and perceived behavioral control, and it should be possible to explain the intentions in terms of the underlying behavioral, normative, and control beliefs. The question, therefore, is not the theory's ability to account for intentions to perform problematic kinds of behavior. Instead, it is the much more fundamental question as to whether intentions can be considered to be the determinants of certain types of behavior.

Uncontrollable Behaviors and Behaviors Outside of Awareness

There are certain kinds of behavior over which people have limited control or that they perform outside of awareness. Among the behaviors that are usually beyond one's control are ticks and reflexes, whereas such nonverbal reactions as facial expressions, eye contact, tone of voice, and speed of walking represent behaviors that are typically performed outside of awareness. It is probably true that a reasoned action framework is largely irrelevant for the former kinds of behaviors. Ticks, stuttering, eye blinks, and other reflexes occur involuntarily and are very difficult to control. Clearly, beliefs, attitudes, and intentions are not particularly useful explanatory constructs for these kinds of behavioral responses.

It is worth noting, however, that many behaviors that are usually performed outside of awareness can be brought under volitional control. Our reasoned action approach could therefore in principle be applied to behaviors of this kind. For example, people can form intentions to maintain eye contact in interaction with another person, to smile, to speak softly, or to walk slowly. In most situations, however, people do not intend to exercise control over these behaviors, and our theory would again be irrelevant. Of course, our theory was never meant to deal with behaviors that occur outside of awareness. As we noted in Chapter 8, behaviors of this kind can have important implications, especially in interpersonal relationships where nonverbal behaviors can signal prejudice, friendship, or other beliefs and attitudes. Our theory, however, was developed to deal with socially relevant behaviors that are considered to be important in their own right, such as drinking, sexual intercourse, exercising, voting, job performance, cancer screening, and smoking. And it is in fact with respect to these kinds of behaviors that the theory has found its major applications.

In conclusion, it should be clear that our reasoned action approach is not designed to account for every observable response. It cannot explain why people have ticks or why they stutter, nor is it particularly useful for understanding nonverbal behaviors that occur outside of awareness.

Addictive Behaviors

A frequent challenge to our theory has to do with addictions. People can become addicted to alcohol, nicotine, heroin, and other substances as well as to specific behaviors such as gambling and running. It is usually assumed that once an addiction takes hold, it exercises control over the behavior and intentions and cognitive factors then become largely irrelevant.[7] Thus, when people are addicted to alcohol, their drinking behavior is assumed to be a function of their addiction and to be independent of their intentions. Their beliefs about drinking may lead them to form negative attitudes toward drinking and, consequently, to form an intention to not drink, but these processes are deemed largely irrelevant, and they are expected to have little effect on actual drinking behavior.

Just as our theory was not designed to explain ticks and other involuntary responses, it was also not designed to explain addictions. It cannot explain who will become addicted to a certain substance or behavior or why some people become addicted and others don't. Nevertheless, we would expect that the theory will help us to predict and understand drinking, smoking, using drugs, gambling, and other addictive behaviors. From our perspective, people perform these kinds of behaviors because they intend to do so, and these intentions can be explained by reference to underlying beliefs, attitudes, perceived norms, and perceptions of control. And, in fact, the empirical evidence strongly supports this view. We have, in previous chapters, had occasion to refer to some of the relevant research. Among other things the theory has been successfully applied to the prediction and explanation of smoking and smoking cessation (e.g., Conner et al., 2006; Higgins & Conner, 2003; Hill, Boudreau, Amyot, Dery, & Godin, 1997), drinking alcohol (e.g., Norman, Bennett, & Lewis, 1998; Rise & Wilhelmsen, 1998; Wall, Hinson, & McKee, 1998), use of marijuana and other drugs (e.g., Armitage et al., 1999; Conner & McMillan, 1999; McMillan & Conner, 2003), as well as gambling behavior (e.g., Sheeran &

Orbell, 1999; Walker, Courneya, & Deng, 2006). Clearly, these and other findings indicate that a reasoned action approach can account for a variety of risk-taking behaviors.

However, our theory is probably not applicable to the small proportion of the population who become physiologically or neurologically addicted to the extent that they no longer have control over the behavior under consideration. Even for such heavily addicted individuals, however, our theory should allow us to predict *intentions* to continue or to stop engaging in the addictive behaviors. Indeed, people's knowledge of their addiction can serve as a background factor that influences their beliefs about performing the addictive behavior and about ceasing to engage in it, but addicted individuals may find cessation impossible because they lack the actual control to do so. Moreover, if they form an intention to quit and try to do so, they will generally experience painful physiological and psychological withdrawal symptoms, and, as a result, they may change their beliefs, attitudes, and intentions and, at least for the moment, decide not to try to quit. This possible change in intentions as a function of experiences in the behavioral situation is discussed in the next section. As we saw already, however, the vast majority of the population who are not seriously addicted can, and usually do, act on their intentions to perform or not perform health-risk behaviors.

Strong Emotions and Intoxication

The final challenge to be discussed in relation to a reasoned action approach is the frequently heard argument that strong emotions and intoxication with drugs or alcohol can overpower reason and lead to unintended behavior. This implies that our theory is unsuitable for the prediction and explanation of behaviors performed under strong emotions or when people are intoxicated or under the influence of drugs. We disagree with this assertion and believe that our theory is, in principle, applicable to behavior under these circumstances. At the same time, however, we recognize that these kinds of situations raise important methodological and theoretical issues.

Strong Emotions

Let us first consider what is probably the most intense and extreme form of emotional arousal, a phobic reaction such as fear of flying (aerophobia), fear of closed spaces (claustrophobia), or fear of heights (acrophobia). As in the case of physiological addictions, our reasoned action approach does not presume to explain the origin of phobias or to predict who will experience a phobic reaction. Moreover, people who experience an intense phobic reaction have little or no control over their behavior or their bodily reactions, and thus our theory is largely irrelevant.

Interestingly, however, knowledge of one's phobia can act as a background factor that is likely to influence beliefs about phobia-relevant behaviors. A strong fear of flying, for example, can produce beliefs that getting on an airplane will result in various negative affective reactions, such as breaking out in a cold sweat, being nauseous, throwing up, or crying. This would of course also influence the person's attitude toward getting on an airplane and would lead to an intention to avoid doing so. Our theoretical framework can thus help us understand at least some of the behaviors of phobic individuals by taking into account the kinds of beliefs they are likely to form.

Sexual Arousal, Intoxication, and Drug Effects

There is a great deal of interest in the effects of sexual arousal and of being under the influence of alcohol and drugs on risk-taking behavior, in particular on engaging in unprotected sex. As we saw in Chapters 2 and 6, there is strong support for the ability of our theory to predict condom use in a variety of different contexts and for various populations. Clearly, these findings belie the claim that sexual arousal overwhelms reasoning and leads to unintended risk-taking behavior.

Nevertheless, it has often been argued that "in the heat of the moment" people will engage in unprotected sex if condoms are not available despite their previously stated intentions to the contrary (see Gold, 1993, 2000). Although there is relatively little empirical evidence to support this claim, there is no reason to doubt that such unintended risk-taking behavior does indeed occur. In Chapter 2 we considered a possible reason for this gap between intentions and behavior. There we noted that people often find it very difficult to anticipate what they will think and how they will feel in a certain situation. The beliefs about a behavior that are readily accessible when filling out a questionnaire or responding to questions in an interview can differ greatly from the beliefs that are activated in the behavioral situation, particularly when the behavioral situation is novel or unique. As a result, intentions expressed prior to entering the behavioral situation may fail to predict actual behavior. In principle, if we could assess our theory's constructs in the behavioral context, responses would be more realistic and more predictive of behavior in that context. Of course, this is rarely if ever possible in practice.

It stands to reason, however, that people who have had direct experience in the situation of interest will develop more realistic expectations regarding the beliefs and feelings they are likely to experience in that situation. As a result, their intentions should be more predictive of their behavior in the situation than the intentions of less experienced individuals. Although not focused on intentions, the research on the role of direct experience discussed in Chapter 8 provides some support for these ideas.

The same arguments concerning the importance of presenting as realistic a scenario as possible when assessing the constructs in our model of behavioral prediction can also be made with respect to the effects of alcohol intoxication and being high on drugs. The factors people consider when they are sober may differ considerably from those they focus on when they are intoxicated or high. Alcohol consumption has been shown to decrease the likelihood of condom use during casual sex (MacDonald, Zanna, & Fong, 1996), a finding interpreted as consistent with alcohol myopia (Steele & Josephs, 1990)—the tendency for alcohol intoxication to decrease cognitive capacity so that people are likely to attend only to the most salient situational cues. Interestingly, alcohol intoxication is also found to increase measured *intentions* to engage in unprotected sex (MacDonald et al.). Nevertheless, because we usually assess attitudes and intentions when respondents are sober, our measures may not permit very accurate prediction of behavior performed while intoxicated or high on drugs.

Cross-Cultural Applications

Related to the question of rationality is the argument that our reasoned action approach does not apply to non-Western cultures. It is assumed that unlike Western cultures, in which decisions tend to be made by individuals in a more or less rational manner, in non-Western contexts decisions are group-based and influenced by social factors that may not coincide with individual beliefs and preferences. For these reasons it is assumed that models developed and tested in individualistic Western countries cannot be used to explain the behavior of people in non-Western, collectivistic cultures and, therefore, that cognitive models like our reasoned action approach cannot be used to inform the design of interventions in those cultures (e.g., Airhihenbuwa & Obregon, 2000; Eaton, Flisher, & Aaro, 2003). In a strong rebuttal of this critique, Kasprzyk and Montaño (2007) presented data from a study they conducted in Zimbabwe, where they showed that our reasoned action approach could be used very effectively to predict men's intentions to use condoms with a variety of different partners: spouse, steady partner, casual partner, and commercial sex worker. Comparable with the results obtained in the United States and in other Western countries, multiple correlations for the prediction of intentions from attitudes, perceived norms, and perceptions of control ranged from .53 to .73 across the different partners. Moreover, Kasprzyk and Montaño also showed that it was possible to explain condom use intentions by examining the behavioral, normative, and control beliefs underlying this behavior.

In fact, it is difficult to see how an argument could be made that our theory is limited to a particular culture (see Fishbein, 2000). When properly applied, the theory requires that behavioral, normative, and control beliefs be elicited in the population of interest. This implies that we take the perspective of the culture into account. It is to be expected that the salient beliefs identified with respect to a given behavior differ from culture to culture. However, there is every reason to believe that attitudes, perceived norms, and perceptions of behavioral control will follow reasonably and spontaneously from these beliefs in non-Western cultures just as they do in Western societies. Indeed, it is condescending to presume that non-Western people are somehow less capable of using the information available to them than are people in Western countries. The differences we can expect to find have to do with the contents of people's beliefs and with the weights they place on attitudinal, normative, and control considerations and not with the processes whereby beliefs are formed, the ways these beliefs influence attitudes, perceived norms, and perceived control, or the processes whereby these factors guide intentions and behavior. Thus, for example, it is very likely that the behavior of buying a cell phone is perceived to have very different consequences in a developing African country than in the United States or Western Europe, and this may produce very different attitudes toward this behavior in the different countries. By the same token, normative and control beliefs are also likely to vary across these different cultures. In addition, as we noted in Chapter 4, perceived social norms may have a greater impact in collectivistic than in individualistic cultures. However, once beliefs have been elicited and the constructs of our model of behavioral prediction have been validly assessed, we believe that it becomes possible to predict and explain intentions and behavior irrespective of the cultural context.[8]

☐ Methodological Issues

Several concerns of a methodological nature have been raised in relation to work within our reasoned action approach. These concerns can be divided into two categories: issues related to the validity of assessing our theory's constructs with a questionnaire and the logic of testing causal effects by means of correlational data.

Validity of Questionnaire Measures

When participants respond to a questionnaire based on our reasoned action approach they are essentially asked to think about a behavior that is of interest to the investigator and to consider its likely consequences, the normative expectations and behaviors of important others, and potential facilitating factors and barriers to performance of the behavior. It is possible that these processes change the dynamics of the situation in important ways.

Accessibility of Beliefs

Responding to the questionnaire can lead participants to consider behavior-relevant issues that might not have been salient prior to responding to the questionnaire. Of particular importance from a theoretical perspective is the possibility that responding to the questionnaire will make salient certain behavioral, normative, and control beliefs that would otherwise not have been accessible. It has been argued (e.g., Feldman & Lynch, 1988; Ogden, 2003) that processes of this kind may create or change attitudes, perceived norms, perceptions of control, and intentions rather than permitting the questionnaire to merely measure these constructs. This is clearly a legitimate concern, but it applies to all questionnaire studies, not just to surveys conducted in the context of our reasoned action approach (see Schwarz, Groves, & Schuman, 1998). There is always a possibility that our measurement instruments will influence the phenomena we are studying. However, it should be recalled that the modal salient behavioral, normative, and control beliefs that comprise a questionnaire based on our theoretical approach are supposed to have been elicited in formative research in a free-response format. If this procedure is followed, it lowers the risk that the assessment itself will create or change the cognitions of interest.

Consistency Bias

A related issue has to do with potential effects of assessing beliefs, attitudes, perceived norms, perceptions of control, and intentions on correlations among the theory's components. Underlying this concern is the assumption that the questionnaire encourages a certain kind of response bias. Specifically, it has been argued that self-presentational concerns may lead participants to strive to create a degree of consistency among the theory's components that did not exist prior to completing the questionnaire (Budd, 1987). This could happen if participants, in an attempt to appear consistent, brought later responses in line with responses they provided earlier in the questionnaire. A bias of this kind would tend to produce overestimates of correlations among the theory's components. Budd further suggested that this response bias would occur only when the relationships among the theory's components are apparent to the participants.

To test this hypothesis, Budd (1987) constructed a questionnaire based on our reasoned action approach with respect to three behaviors: smoking cigarettes, brushing teeth at least three times a day, and exercising for 20 minutes or more at a time. With respect to each of these behaviors, the questionnaire measured attitudes, injunctive norms, and intentions as well as behavioral beliefs and outcome evaluations and injunctive norma- tive beliefs and motivation to comply. Attitudes were measured by means of four evaluative semantic differential scales and norms and intentions apparently by means of one item each; the number of behavioral and nor- mative beliefs included in the questionnaire was not reported. Thus, it is not clear how many responses in total were provided by the participants. Two versions of the questionnaire were created, and each version was administered to a sample of college students. In the thematic version, the three behaviors were presented in separate sections, with items assessing a given construct appearing consecutively. The order of the three behav- iors was counterbalanced. In the random version of the questionnaire, the items assessing different constructs in relation to the different behav- iors were all presented in random order such that there was no relation between any two consecutive items.

The results of the study revealed a major effect of thematic versus ran- dom item ordering. There were strong and significant correlations among the theory's components in the thematic version (ranging from .36 to .82 across the three behaviors) but very weak and mostly nonsignificant cor- relations (ranging from .02 to .41) in the random version. It was also dis- covered, however, that the random version of the questionnaire produced much less reliable (internally consistent) measures of attitudes than did the thematic version. The respective alpha coefficients across the three behaviors ranged from .47 to .52 in the random version versus .78 to .84 in the thematic version.[9] Budd (1987) conceded that the results of his study could be due to this difference in measurement reliability rather than dif- ferences in response bias. Furthermore, he acknowledged an additional possible explanation of his results, namely, that the thematic question- naire may have "encouraged the subjects to think more deeply about their attitude and to access an attitude schema that enabled them to report their attitude in a more consistent and accurate way" (p. 105).[10] To put it dif- ferently, the nonsystematic presentation of items in the random version of the questionnaire may have been confusing to the participants, mak- ing it difficult for them to think carefully about the issues and to report their beliefs, attitudes, injunctive norms, and intentions accurately. This problem may have been exacerbated by the fact that not only were items assessing different constructs presented in random order but also that these items dealt with three different behaviors.

Some empirical support for these ideas can be found in a study by Armitage and Conner (1999) that dealt with eating a low-fat diet. They administered a questionnaire containing multi-item measures of attitude, perceived injunctive norm, perceived behavioral control, and intention to eat a low-fat diet over the next month to a sample from the general population. The questionnaire also assessed self-identity and included a 20-item social desirability scale. In a thematic version of the questionnaire, the multiple items assessing a given construct were presented together in blocks, whereas in a second version all items were presented in completely random order.

Contrary to the results reported by Budd (1987), only minor differences were observed between the thematic and random versions of the questionnaire. The internal consistency coefficients alpha for the different constructs were high in both versions. In fact, these coefficients tended to be somewhat higher in the random version (ranging from .67 for perceived norm to .93 for intention) than in the thematic version (.65 to .88). More importantly, there was also no advantage to the thematic version in terms of predictive validity. If anything, the random version permitted a somewhat better prediction than the thematic version. In the random version, the prediction of intentions from attitudes, norms, and control resulted in a multiple correlation of .86 compared with a multiple correlation of .80 in the thematic version.

It would seem reasonable to attribute the contradictory findings to the fact that whereas Budd's (1987) questionnaires dealt with three different behaviors (all intermixed in the random version), the questionnaire used in the Armitage and Conner (1999) study addressed only one behavior. However, results similar to Armitage and Conner's findings emerged in another study that dealt with multiple behaviors (Ellen & Madden, 1990). In the first of two experiments, Ellen and Madden compared a standard, paper-and-pencil questionnaire with two computer-administered versions. With respect to each of 12 common behaviors (e.g., going to a movie, exercising, going to a party), attitudes, injunctive norms, and intentions were assessed by means of two items each, for a total of 72 items. In the paper-and-pencil questionnaire as well as in one of the two computer-administered surveys, the items were presented in thematic order and separately for each behavior. In the second computer version, the 72 items were presented in random order. Because paper-and-pencil questionnaires permit respondents to see all items for a given behavior at the same time, the investigators expected this format to yield the highest correlations among the theory's components. With respect to the computer-administered versions, random presentation was expected to produce lower correlations among components than thematic presentation. Contrary to these hypotheses, the two computer-administered surveys produced higher correlations than did the paper-and-pencil questionnaire, and as in the Armitage and Conner study, the random version had a slight advantage over the thematic version. The mean multiple correlations for the prediction of intentions from attitudes and injunctive norms were .40 for the paper-and-pencil format and .63 and .69, respectively, for the thematic and random versions of the computer-administered survey.

The second experiment reported by Ellen and Madden (1990) showed that the relatively high correlations obtained with random item presentation is not a result of the fact that items were administered by computer. This experiment added a random paper-and-pencil version to the three previous administration formats, but the questionnaire dealt with only two behaviors: donating blood and exercising. Beliefs, attitudes, and intentions with respect to these behaviors were assessed. Administration format had no significant effect on correlations among the variables for blood donation, but with respect to exercising, the two random-order presentations (paper-and-pencil and computer-administered) produced significantly higher correlations (ranging from .51 to .79) than the two thematic presentations (correlations ranging from .20 to .64).

In conclusion, whereas in Budd's (1987) experiment, thematic presentation of items yielded higher correlations among the theory's measures than did random presentation, two subsequent experiments (Armitage & Conner, 1999; Ellen & Madden, 1990) failed to replicate these findings. These latter studies showed not only that random item presentation does not necessarily interfere with high correlations among the variables comprising our model of behavioral prediction but also that random presentation can even increase the strength of these correlations. Clearly, more research is needed to determine how much, if any, of the observed correlations among the components of our reasoned action approach is due to the actual associations among the constructs and how much may be due to participants' attempts to appear internally consistent.

The Effect of Measuring Intentions

It is a well-known phenomenon that the proportion of people who intend to engage in socially desirable behaviors is greater than the proportion of people who actually do and that the proportion of people who intend to perform socially undesirable behaviors is smaller than the proportion who actually engage in such behaviors. Sherman (1980) referred to these discrepancies as errors of prediction. According to Sherman, prediction errors are indicated when the self-predictions (i.e., intentions) made by one group of people are different from the actual behavior observed in another comparable group. The question of interest is what happens when the behavior of people who previously expressed their intentions is compared with the behavior of people who were not asked to express their intentions? Sherman hypothesized that once intentions are expressed, "They might well lead to a set of inferences, expectations, and cognitive representations of events, so that subsequent behavior is consistent with the (mis) predictions" (p. 213). In other words, social desirability tendencies may lead people to express intentions to perform socially desirable behaviors (e.g., exercise regularly) and not to perform socially undesirable or embarrassing behaviors (e.g., get drunk at a party). Then, once the intention to perform a behavior is expressed, it may induce some people who would otherwise not have done so to act in accordance with their intentions.

Sherman (1980) performed three experiments to test this hypothesis: one involving a socially undesirable behavior (writing a counterattitudinal essay); one an embarrassing behavior (singing the "Star Spangled Banner" over the telephone); and one a socially desirable behavior (volunteering 3 hours to collect money for the American Cancer Society). In each experiment, two conditions were created: one in which participants expressed their intentions before they were given an opportunity to perform the behavior; and a control group in which intentions were not assessed prior to observation of the behavior. For example, in the first experiment female college students living in dormitories were asked to indicate whether they would be willing to write (contrary to their own position on the issue) an essay opposing open visitation by members of the opposite sex. They were told that they were in no way making a commitment to write the essay but were merely providing anonymous information about what they would do if asked. Then, 2 weeks later, a different experimenter approached the participants and asked them to actually write the essay. In the control condition, participants were directly approached with the request to write the essay.

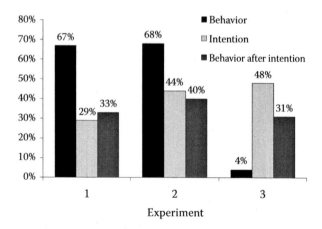

FIGURE 9.1 Effect of expressing an intention on later behavior. Experiment 1 involved writing a counterattitudinal essay, Experiment 2 involved singing over the telephone, and Experiment 3 involved volunteering to collect money for the American Cancer Society (from Sherman, 1980).

As can be seen in Figure 9.1 (first two bars in each set), consistent with expectations, the proportion of participants in the control conditions who agreed to write the counterattitudinal essay and to sing the "Star Spangled Banner" over the telephone was significantly larger than the proportion of participants in the experimental conditions who thought they would agree (i.e., intended) to perform these behaviors. The reverse pattern was observed for the socially desirable behavior of agreeing to collect money for the American Cancer Society. Here, in the experimental condition, a large proportion of the participants expressed an intention to volunteer, but in the control condition, very few actually did.

Examining the third bar of data from each experiment, it can be seen that after expressing intentions, actual behavior came very close to intended actions in the first two experiments that dealt with undesirable behaviors. In the third experiment, a gap remained between favorable intentions to collect money for the American Cancer Society and actual volunteering even among participants who first expressed their intentions. In the experimental group, 48% indicated that they would volunteer, but only 31% actually did. Nevertheless, this 31% is considerably closer to the percentage intending to do so than to the percentage of volunteers in the control condition.

Subsequent research has corroborated and extended these findings to other behavioral domains. Thus, expressing intentions to register and intentions to vote in the 1984 U.S. presidential election was found to increase actual registration and participation in the election (Greenwald, Carnot, Beach, & Young, 1987); indicating intentions to floss one's teeth, to avoid fatty foods, and to read for pleasure increased the likelihood that these behaviors would be performed (Levav & Fitzsimons, 2006); expressing intentions to donate blood increased registrations at blood drives and actual blood donations (Godin, Sheeran, Conner, & Germain, 2008); and even with respect to the purchase of such expensive products as automobiles and personal computers, expressing a buying intention increased actual purchase behavior (Morwitz, Johnson, & Schmittlein, 1993).

It thus seems clear that asking people to estimate their future behavior (i.e., to express their behavioral intentions) can have a considerable impact on their subsequent behavior. Note, however, that these findings do not question the predictive validity of intentions; as we have noted repeatedly in previous chapters, the correlations between measured intentions and actual behavior are quite high. Indeed, the data presented by Sherman (1980) permitted a secondary analysis that showed intention–behavior correlations of considerable magnitude, ranging from .59 for volunteering to collect money for the American Cancer Society to .85 for writing a counterattitudinal essay. Because we do not have direct access to people's intentions, we do not know whether observed intention–behavior correlations are higher (or lower) than they would have been had we not asked our participants to express their intentions. All we can say with confidence is that, of all the measures available to social scientists, behavioral intentions are generally found to be the best predictors of actual behavior.

Correlational Data and Causal Effects

Our model of behavioral prediction describes a chain of causal effects in which behavioral, normative, and control beliefs are the fundamental building blocks that determine attitudes, perceived social norms, and perceptions of behavioral control. These three factors produce behavioral intentions, and the intentions (moderated by control) lead to behavior. Most tests and applications of the theory, however, have been correlational in nature. Although, as we have seen, empirical findings are consistent with the theory, correlational data cannot establish causal effects in a definitive way. In the next two chapters of this book we consider behavioral intervention studies conducted in the context of our theory. These studies can provide stronger evidence regarding the postulated causal effects. In these studies, attempts are made to change behavioral, normative, or control beliefs, and the effects of such changes in beliefs are examined further down the causal chain through attitudes, perceived norms, and perceived control to intentions and behavior. In the present section we briefly consider research suggestive of the proposition that beliefs can influence attitudes and evidence showing that changes in intentions are reflected in actual behavior.

Persuasive Communication

In our approach, salient beliefs provide the informational foundation for attitudes, perceived norms, and perceived behavioral control and, thus, ultimately for intentions and actual behavior. Beliefs reflect the information people have relevant to the behavior of interest, whether that information is accurate or not. It follows that if we expose people to new information, and this new information is accepted, existing beliefs will change or new beliefs will be formed. Thus, exposure to new information about the possible consequences of engaging in a behavior may be expected to produce changes in people's attitudes toward performing that behavior, changes consistent with the nature of the new information.

Over the past 60 years, a vast body of research on the effects of persuasive communication has validated this expectation. Persuasive communications present arguments in favor of (or against) a certain position on an issue, arguments usually bolstered by supportive evidence (see Fishbein & Ajzen, 1975, 1981). Although questions remain regarding the factors that make a persuasive message more or less effective, there can be no doubt that exposure to such a message often produces changes in beliefs and attitudes. Compared with a no-message control group, participants who receive a persuasive message usually change their attitudes in the advocated direction (for reviews, see Eagly & Chaiken, 1993; McGuire, 1985; Petty & Cacioppo, 1986). The finding that providing new information can change attitudes provides at least indirect evidence for the idea that beliefs—which represent a person's information about the attitude—provide the basis for attitudes toward the object.

Changing Intentions

At the other end of the causal chain, there is growing evidence to show that intentions not only predict behavior but also actually have a causal impact on behavior. Webb and Sheeran (2006) reported a meta-analysis of 47 intervention studies in which the experimental treatment had produced a significant change in intentions. In these studies, the investigators also observed subsequent behavior. Webb and Sheeran found that, on average, the interventions had produced medium to large changes in intentions (mean $d = 0.66$) and that these changes in intentions resulted in small to medium changes in behavior (mean $d = 0.36$).

☐ Summary and Conclusions

In this chapter we considered a number of issues and concerns raised in relation to our reasoned action approach. One of the most frequently addressed questions has to do with the sufficiency of our theory. Many investigators have proposed expanding the theory in the expectation that adding more variables will improve prediction of intentions and behavior. The fact that past behavior is consistently found to have a residual effect on intentions after controlling for attitudes, perceived norms, and perceived control lends credence to the proposition that other possible determinants of intention may be missing from our model. Among the most frequently studied potential additions are self-identity and anticipated affect. However, measures of self-identity tend to reflect attitudes, perceived norms, and past behavior, and measures of anticipated affect address attitudes toward alternatives to the behavior under investigation. Because both constructs, as currently assessed, overlap considerably with existing predictors in our theory, they fail to meet one of our criteria for the inclusion of new variables, namely, that the proposed addition be conceptually independent of the theory's existing predictors, rather than be redundant with them. Furthermore, neither the inclusion of self-identity nor the inclusion of anticipated affect is found to eliminate the residual effect of past behavior on intentions.

Contrary to a common misperception, our reasoned action approach assumes neither rationality on the part of an actor nor extensive deliberation in the formation of attitudes, perceived norms, perceptions of control, and intentions. As we noted in Chapters 1 and 3, and indeed throughout this volume, we only assume that intentions and actions follow consistently (reasonably) from behavioral, normative, and control beliefs, which form an informational foundation for behavior. Our model of behavioral prediction is capable of dealing with spontaneously performed behaviors as well as with deliberative behavior. The former is likely when a behavior has become routine and the latter when the behavior is fairly novel or complex. However, in either case, we assume that performance of the behavior is preceded by activation of an intention, even if this activation occurs below conscious awareness.

Nevertheless, there are limits to the theory's realm of applicability. Our theory does not—nor was it ever meant to—apply to behaviors over which people have no control (e.g., reflexes) or that occur outside of awareness (e.g., facial expressions or bodily postures). The latter, however, can often be brought under conscious control, and in those cases our theory may apply. We recognize that there are important differences between the (hypothetical) context in which the theory's constructs are typically assessed and the (real) context in which behavior occurs. The effects of strong emotions, addictions, or sexual arousal in a real context is often not anticipated when people express their beliefs, attitudes, and intentions on a questionnaire. It follows that, under these circumstances, the predictive validity of intentions may be reduced.

Finally, this chapter dealt with several methodological concerns. Some of these concerns have to do with use of a questionnaire, and they thus apply to other questionnaire research as well. We saw that, at least at present, there is little evidence for a bias on the part of respondents to make their answers internally consistent. Random item presentation tends to produce responses that are as internally consistent as is thematic presentation. On the other hand, assessing intentions is found to increase the likelihood that people will act in accordance with their expressed intentions. In any event, intentions—as assessed in work based on our reasoned action approach—are found to be good predictors of behavior. Moreover, when intentions change as a result of an intervention, the change is also reflected in actual behavior, a finding that lends support to the assumption that intentions have a causal effect on behavior. Interventions designed to change behavior in the context of our theory are the topic of the next two chapters.

☐ Notes

1. See also O'Keefe (2002, p. 127) for a discussion of criteria for inclusion of additional variables in the theories of reasoned action and planned behavior.
2. It is for this reason that Fishbein and Ajzen (1975) decided to drop the personal norm construct from the original theory of reasoned action.
3. Parts of this section are adapted from Ajzen and Fishbein (2005).
4. In some studies, intentions—but not attitudes, norms, or perceived control—are assessed in terms of frequency or quantity, just as are reports of past and later behavior. When this is the case, scale compatibility can explain at least some of the added predictive value of past behavior on intention. However, many studies do not suffer from this problem, and the residual effect of past behavior on intentions in these studies cannot be attributed to issues of scale compatibility.
5. As is usually the case, these two meta-analyses included studies that varied in the quality of their measures and in the extent to which measurement compatibility was maintained. The inclusion of studies with problematic measures can reduce the mean predictive validity.
6. Self-identity partially mediated the effect of past behavior on intention. It reduced the original 13% of variance explained by past behavior (Table 9.1) to 7%.
7. Note the similarity between this argument and the account of habitual behavior discussed in Chapter 2.
8. This is not meant to minimize the potential difficulties of measuring the theory's constructs in a developing country where access to parts of the population may be difficult and where illiteracy rates may be relatively high. We are here discussing the applicability in principle of the reasoned action approach to non-Western cultures.
9. See Lam, Green, and Bordignon (2002) for similar findings.
10. In support of this possibility, Frantom, Green, and Lam (2002) found that thematic grouping of items tends to produce higher-quality data than random presentation.

Changing Behavior

Theoretical Considerations

Our reasoned action framework stipulates a causal sequence of events describing the processes that determine human social behavior. The sequence begins with the formation of behavioral, normative, and control beliefs regarding a particular behavior of interest. These beliefs constitute the person's available behavior-relevant information. To the extent that the beliefs are readily accessible, they lead to the spontaneous formation of an attitude toward the behavior, to perceived social pressure to perform or not to perform the behavior, and to a sense of self-efficacy or perceived behavioral control in relation to performing the behavior. The intention to engage in the behavior, or to refrain from doing so, emerges spontaneously from these general dispositions when performance of the behavior is at issue. Finally, to the extent that the individual has sufficient volitional control over the behavior, the intention is carried out.

We saw in previous chapters how this conceptual framework can be used to predict and explain intentions and behavior. By identifying and measuring the beliefs that are salient in the population we gain insight into the important considerations that guide people's decisions and actions. Knowledge regarding the behavioral beliefs people hold provides the basis for understanding attitudes toward the behavior, information about normative beliefs helps explain perceived norms, and inspection of control beliefs leads to an understanding of perceived behavioral control. It should also be evident that this approach has important implications for interventions that are designed to change intentions and behavior. Generally speaking, our model of behavioral prediction suggests that influencing intentions and behavior requires changes in the relevant salient behavioral, normative, or control beliefs. By identifying the behavioral, normative, and control beliefs that serve as the underlying determinants of a behavior we also gain important information about the kinds of beliefs that would have to be changed to effect a change in intentions and behavior. In fact, providing this kind of information is arguably the single most important contribution of our approach to the problem of effective behavior change interventions.

As a conceptual framework for behavior change interventions, our theory has a number of distinct characteristics. First and foremost is its clear focus on the determinants of a particular behavior that is to be changed. Different behaviors are based on different sets of salient beliefs, and different behaviors thus call for different interventions. Second, the theory assumes that a relatively small number of variables are sufficient to understand and change any socially significant behavior. Specifically, the major determinants that must be considered are attitude toward the behavior, perceived social norm, and perceived behavioral control—and their underlying cognitive foundations as reflected in behavioral, normative, and control beliefs. Although, as we saw in the previous chapter, there are other variables such as moral norms, self-identity, and anticipated affect that may help to explain a given behavior, we believe that if we can bring about change in one or more of the theory's three major components, we should observe changes in intentions and, in the presence of adequate volitional control, changes in behavior as well. Third, because beliefs represent the information people have about a behavior, providing new information can change these beliefs and thus be an effective way of changing intentions and actions. Finally, our approach provides a set of proven methods and procedures for measuring the theory's component variables and for identifying the kinds of factors that have to be changed to effect behavior change. These methods therefore also provide a means for evaluating the effectiveness of a behavior change intervention.

☐ Specifying Intervention Goals

Generally speaking, the goal of any intervention is to alleviate a social problem that has been identified in a given population or segment of the population, be the problem economic, educational, or health-related in nature. The problem and population provide the basic parameters for the intervention. Because many social problems are caused, at least in part, by human behavior, the focus naturally turns to attempts to change behavior. Specifically, it becomes necessary to identify those behaviors that, if changed, would produce the desired outcome. It is therefore essential to clearly identify the behavior that is to be changed. Consider, for example, a researcher interested in reducing the incidence of colon cancer. Knowing that colonoscopy is an effective tool not only for the diagnosis but also for the prevention of colon cancer (by identifying and removing precancerous polyps), the researcher may decide to design an intervention to increase the likelihood that people in the relevant age group will obtain a colonoscopy at recommended time intervals. In other instances, the desired effect of an intervention is not to produce a new behavior but, instead, to reinforce existing behavior. Thus, investigators interested in reducing lung cancer rates may decide on an intervention that is designed to prevent young nonsmokers from starting to smoke.

To reiterate, most interventions implemented by social scientists are designed to change behaviors. In many cases it is assumed that a change in these behaviors will help to alleviate a perceived social problem. But even if successful, there is no guarantee that changes in behavior produced by an intervention will lead to the desired outcome. Consider, for instance, the growing obesity problem in the United States, especially among children and adolescents. It is generally agreed that one of the factors contributing to the obesity epidemic is a sedentary lifestyle. An intervention may therefore be designed to get young people to engage in regular physical exercise. However, even if the intervention is successful in getting more young people to exercise, it would not necessarily reduce obesity in this population. For example, increased physical activity may raise food intake, an effect that negates the benefits of exercise. In other words, weight loss is influenced by a number of different variables including physical activity, diet, use of appetite suppressants, as well as constitutional factors. Disregarding constitutional factors, interventions rarely if ever can address all behaviors that may have a causal effect on the outcome of interest, and their success, therefore, cannot be guaranteed. It is up to the investigator to use all available information to identify the most important behaviors that need to be changed. Once this is done, our theory can help design interventions to change the behaviors thus selected, but it cannot assure attainment of the desired outcome.

Defining the Behavior to Be Changed

Behaviors Versus Goals

The previous discussion is closely related to the distinction we drew in Chapter 2 between behaviors and goals. There we saw that goal attainment depends not only on the behaviors performed by an individual but also on other factors that may not be under the individual's volitional control. A student may study hard by attending classes regularly, taking careful notes, reading all course assignments, preparing papers, and taking exams, yet still not attain a high grade because this outcome also depends on the instructor's teaching ability, quality of the exams, and other factors beyond the student's control. An intervention can target the relevant behaviors (e.g., it can be designed to increase studying), but, as we noted already, even if it successfully increases studying behaviors, it cannot ensure goal attainment.

It may appear that an intervention strategy could be adopted that directly targets the intention to attain a behavioral goal. Thus, we could design an intervention to change intentions to lose weight under the assumption that formation of this intention will lead people to change their behavior in such a way that they will lose weight. We noted in earlier chapters that our reasoned action approach can help to predict and explain any intention, not only intentions to perform specific behaviors but also intentions to attain goals. However, as a general rule, the link between behavioral intentions and behavior is stronger than the link between goal intentions and goal attainment. As an intervention strategy, therefore, we recommend targeting behaviors rather than goals.

Single Behaviors Versus Behavioral Categories

In Chapter 2 we also drew a distinction between specific behaviors and behavioral categories such as exercising, dieting, and studying. Recall that a behavior is defined in terms of its target, action, context, and time elements. A behavioral category differs from a specific behavior in that its action element is generalized to include an array of different behaviors that comprise or define the behavioral category in question. Thus, the behavioral category "exercising" includes running, swimming, riding a bicycle, walking on a treadmill, climbing stairs, and a multitude of other physical activities. As in the case of a single behavior, we can also define target, context, and time elements of the behavioral category. For example, we might be interested in exercising (action) in a gym (target) with a friend (context) for at least 30 minutes three times a week (time).

Just as it possible to target an intervention at a single behavior, the intervention can also be designed to change intentions to engage in a behavioral category. However, when the intention to perform a behavioral category is modified, it is not clear which of the behaviors that comprise the category will change. Thus, it makes sense to direct an intervention at intentions to perform a behavioral category only if we don't care which particular behavior within the category is affected. In the exercise domain, for example, the criterion might be defined as exercising vigorously three times a week for at least 20 minutes at a time. Whether the exercise consists of jogging, biking, or climbing stairs may be of no interest to the investigator because each of these behaviors is considered to be sufficient to bring about the desired health benefits. For other behavioral categories, a single behavior within the category may not be sufficient, and the intervention may have to be designed to affect multiple behaviors. For example, in the case of studying, we may want students to engage not in a single behavior, such as reading assigned materials, but in many different studying behaviors, including reading assigned materials, writing papers, and attending lectures. Changing the intention to study, although it may change one or two behaviors in the behavioral category, may not be sufficient to bring about the ultimate goal of improving the student's grades. With these types of behavioral categories it may be necessary to identify a few critical behaviors and to target those in the intervention instead of targeting the intention to perform the behavioral category as a whole.

Similarly, if our interest is in a particular kind of behavior, say attending lectures, then targeting the behavioral category (i.e., targeting the intention to study), even if successful, cannot guarantee change in the desired lecture attending behavior. To increase the likelihood that students will attend their classes regularly we should try to increase their intentions to engage in this particular behavior.

Intention Versus Implementation

Once the behavior or behavioral category has been clearly identified we can begin to make plans for the behavior change intervention. Behavior change interventions are based on the assumption that a substantial proportion of the target population is not performing a recommended behavior or is performing a behavior that is putting them or others at risk for negative outcomes. Obviously, we should first verify this assumption. As part of this process of verification, we may discover that the problematic behavior is prevalent in only certain segments of the population, a finding that can help to refine the definition of the target population.

Assuming that a substantial proportion of the target population indeed fails to perform the desired behavior, our theoretical perspective suggests that this may occur for two reasons. First, people may not intend to perform the behavior, and second, they may have the intention to perform it but fail to carry out their intentions. According to Gollwitzer (1990, 1999), when people do not yet intend to perform a desired behavior but consider doing so, they are in a deliberative mind-set in which they seek information about the feasibility and desirability of the contemplated behavior. Once they have decided to perform the behavior and thus have the appropriate intention they are said to be in an implemental mind-set where they focus on information relevant to the implementation of the intention, that is, on where, when, and how to act on the intention. As we shall see next, very different intervention strategies are required depending on whether the appropriate intention has or has not already been formed.

☐ Designing an Intervention

We are now ready to consider the various steps involved in designing a behavior change intervention. The first step, as noted earlier, is to decide which behavior is to be changed or reinforced and to delimit the target population of interest. We discuss the design of an intervention in terms of getting people to perform a recommended behavior they currently do not perform, but the same considerations apply to stopping an undesirable behavior or reinforcing an existing behavior.

Formative Research

As we saw earlier in this chapter, interventions are usually initiated to alleviate serious social problems, whether related to education, health, unemployment, or other concerns. If successful, interventions not only make a contribution to individual well-being but, in the long term, also can save money and allow us to reallocate resources to the solution of other problems. We should thus be willing to invest the time and effort required to design an effective intervention. Just as we would not think of developing and administering a new drug without exhaustive testing and follow-up evaluation, we should not be designing and implementing behavior change interventions without careful development and evaluation. In fact, in our view, a poorly designed intervention not only squanders scarce resources but may be worse than no intervention at all. On the following pages we describe stages in the preparation, implementation, and evaluation of a behavior change intervention. This process will appear to many to be more onerous and time-consuming than it actually is, but from our perspective, it is time and effort well spent. Careful preparation and development of the intervention will greatly increase its chances of success.

First Phase

Once the behavior to be addressed has been identified and clearly defined, it is necessary to perform basic formative research in preparation for the intervention. In the initial phase we elicit salient behavioral, normative, and control beliefs and directly assess attitudes, perceived norms, perceived behavioral control, and intentions. In addition, we also obtain self-reports of past behavior and demographic information. It is extremely important that the pilot sample be representative of the research population. If the population contains distinct segments with potentially different beliefs and attitudes regarding the behavior of interest, these segments must be adequately represented in the pilot sample. Thus, we may have to ensure that the pilot sample includes both men and women, representatives of relevant ethnic groups, young and old, and so forth. For a highly homogenous population, a pilot sample of about 30 individuals will usually be sufficient, but for a more heterogeneous population, a larger sample will be required. As a rule of thumb, we try to include about 15 to 20 participants from each major subgroup. The demographic data collected in the questionnaire can help us verify representativeness.

This initial phase of the formative research contains qualitative as well as quantitative components. First and foremost, we use the qualitative component to identify the salient behavioral, normative, and control beliefs about performing the behavior of interest, beliefs that are common in the target population. As described in Chapters 3, 4, and 5, we obtain this information by asking participants to do the following:

- List what they believe to be the advantages and disadvantages of performing the behavior of interest.
- Indicate who would approve and who would disapprove of their performing the behavior as well as their beliefs as to who does and who does not perform the behavior.
- List the factors that would make it easier or more difficult for them to perform the behavior.

Content analyses of these open-ended responses allow us to construct lists of modal salient behavioral, normative, and control beliefs.

We use the quantitative component of the pilot study to provide information about several important theoretical issues. First, we use it to measure the prevalence of the behavior in the population. If prevalence of the desired behavior is high, then it becomes clear that an inappropriate behavior has been selected, one that does not have to be changed. Second, we ask whether people intend to perform the behavior and how much control they perceive they have over performing the behavior. The answer to the first question determines whether the intervention should be designed to change existing intentions and to produce new intentions or to help people act on existing intentions. In many instances, both types of interventions are needed for different segments of the target population, a point to which we return next. We can also examine the relation between intention and past behavior as well as the extent to which this relation is moderated by perceived behavioral control. As we saw in Chapter 9, past behavior is usually highly correlated with future behavior and can therefore be used as a proxy for likely future behavior. The measures of intention and perceived control permit us to obtain at least a rough estimate of our ability to predict the behavior of interest. If intentions and perceived control cannot account for much of the variance in past behavior, they are unlikely to predict future behavior. There would thus be no point in trying to change either of these factors.

Third, in addition to intentions and perceived behavioral control we assess people's attitudes and perceived norms. By regressing intentions on the direct measures of attitudes, perceived norms, and perceived control we get a preliminary estimate of how well intentions can be predicted. Here, too, if intentions cannot be predicted from the theory's three components, it would be useless to design an intervention to change one or more of the components. In addition, the regression analysis also yields an initial estimate of the relative importance of the theory's three predictors. As we shall see next, this estimate is needed to determine which component to target in the intervention.

By including multiple items for each construct, we can take advantage of the pilot data to refine our direct measures of attitude, perceived norm, perceived control, and intention to ensure that each of these measures has internal consistency and discriminant validity. In addition, the pilot study can be used to develop measures of background variables the investigator may be interested in and to obtain an initial test of their relevance. Thus, if self-esteem is thought to be an important factor in the behavioral domain under investigation, a self-esteem scale might be included in the pilot questionnaire. The data obtained can be used to refine the self-esteem scale to arrive at a set of items with high internal consistency, and correlations can be computed between self-esteem scores and measures of the constructs in our theory. In particular, it would be important to show that self-esteem does indeed correlate with intentions and past behavior. If it does not, self-esteem can be dismissed as a relevant background factor.

Finally, the initial pilot study also allows us to identify problems in scale formats, item wording, and so on and to deal with several more practical issues such as how to gain access to members of the population and how to best communicate information to them. For example, the pilot study should allow us to answer questions such as the following:

- Can we approach individuals directly by telephone, or would it be better to go through community organizations?
- Do members of the target population know how to use a computer?
- Do they watch television and can thus be exposed to public service announcements?
- Do they have means of transportation to come to a data collection center, or do interviewers have to go to their homes?

The effectiveness of many interventions depends in part on securing the cooperation and involvement of the target population. Some investigators have gone so far as to argue that community participation and community mobilization are essential prerequisites for successful behavior change interventions (e.g., Swartz & Kagee, 2006; Whitehead, Kriel, & Richter, 2005). The initial formative research can begin to establish connections to the community and to provide answers to very important logistical questions. Although these types of pragmatic issues are clearly important in the development of an intervention, our discussion focuses primarily on the intervention implications of our reasoned action approach.

Second Phase

Once the initial phase of formative research has been completed, a questionnaire designed to measure the constructs in our model of behavioral prediction (including background factors) can be constructed. The construction of such a questionnaire—although it must be carefully planned and executed—follows a standard procedure that is neither very difficult nor very time-consuming (see Appendix). The first pilot study will have produced a set of validated items for obtaining direct measures of attitude, perceived norms, perceptions of control, and intentions; as well as lists of modal salient behavioral, normative, and control beliefs. In the next phase of the development of an intervention, we administer the closed questionnaire developed on the basis of the initial elicitation phase. This questionnaire contains direct measures of the theory's constructs, and, in addition, it obtains quantitative belief measures. Specifically, we use it to assess the strength of the beliefs that the behavior will produce certain outcomes and the evaluations of these outcomes, the strength of descriptive and injunctive normative beliefs and motivations to comply with salient referents, as well as control beliefs and the perceived power of salient control factors to facilitate or interfere with performance of the behavior. These data allow us to validate the results of the initial small pilot study to make sure that there is indeed a low prevalence of the behavior in the population, to determine whether the problem is lack of intention or inability to act on the intention, to show that we can predict current behavior from intention and perceived control, and to confirm the initial estimates regarding the relative importance of attitudes, norms, and perceived control in the prediction of intentions.[1]

In addition, and more important, this phase of the research allows us to make sure that attitudes, perceived norms, and perceived behavioral control are, as expected, related to the salient beliefs identified in the initial phase. In the case of attitudes, we correlate the summed products of behavioral beliefs times outcome evaluations with the direct attitude measure (see Chapter 3). In a parallel fashion, we compute indices of normative beliefs and of control beliefs and correlate these indices with direct measures of perceived social norms and perceived behavioral control, respectively. For the normative component, we multiply injunctive normative beliefs by motivation to comply with the referent and descriptive normative beliefs by identification with the referent.[2] The summation of all product terms, injunctive and descriptive, is expected to correlate with a direct measure of overall perceived social pressure to engage in the behavior (see Chapter 4). For perceived behavioral control, we obtain quantitative measures of control belief strength and the power of the control factors to facilitate or impede behavioral performance. These measures tell us how likely people believe it is that the salient control factors will be present when they try to perform the behavior and the extent to which their presence would facilitate or impede performance of the behavior. The summed products of these two measures provide a control belief index that should correlate with the direct measure of perceived behavioral control (see Chapter 5). Low correlations would be a warning sign, indicating that changes in the identified beliefs will have relatively little impact on the component we are trying to change.[3] Unless problems are encountered that require substantive changes in the survey instrument, the questionnaire administered in the second pilot study can also provide baseline data for the evaluation of the intervention's effectiveness.

Actual Control

Thus far we have dealt only with the factors that are typically assessed within our reasoned action framework to predict and understand intentions and behaviors. When it comes to designing a behavior change intervention, however, one other factor takes on particular importance. In addition to *perceived* behavioral control and its underlying control beliefs, it is often necessary to obtain information about people's *actual* control over the behavior. Unfortunately, as mentioned in Chapter 2, no standard procedures for assessing actual control are available and it is in fact quite difficult to know what internal and external control factors would have to be considered. For example, it is far from self-evident what skills and abilities are needed to use condoms with a new or occasional partner. Nevertheless, it is not unreasonable to assume that among these skills are knowing where and how to acquire condoms, how to communicate and negotiate with one's partner about condom use, and how to correctly use condoms.

We have argued that to the extent that people's control beliefs and overall perceptions of control are veridical, these perceptions can be used as a proxy for actual control. The salient control factors elicited in the first pilot study can thus serve as a starting point for identifying potential issues of control. However, to the extent possible, we should also try to establish whether these factors constitute actual (real) barriers or facilitating factors. For example, imagine that lack of public transportation is one of the salient factors mentioned in the first pilot study as a possible barrier to getting a colonoscopy. We can try to establish if this is a realistic concern by checking with the transportation authorities on the kinds of public transportation available in the area. This would provide a measure of actual control with respect to this particular factor. In addition, we would also need to ascertain whether it is true that lack of public transportation actually interferes with getting to the doctor's office or hospital (i.e., whether it is a realistic barrier). To do this, we can use the phase 2 questionnaire to ask participants whether they can obtain alternative transportation, perhaps from a friend who owns a car and whether they could afford to hire a taxi. We can also go beyond the questionnaire to inquire in the community whether local organizations provide transportation for purposes of medical treatment or screening, such as getting a colonoscopy. If public transportation is indeed unavailable, we could try to pressure the regional transportation authority to extend service to the neighborhood. Alternatively, we could contact nongovernmental organizations to determine whether they are willing to provide transportation or to pay for taxi service to the local hospital.

Or, to take another example, suppose that a frequently mentioned facilitating factor in applying for a job is ability to prepare a résumé. To determine the extent to which participants possess this skill, we could design a short test that requires them to list their highest level of education, their last job held, to give one or two references, and to provide information on how they themselves can be contacted (e.g., phone number, address, contact person). If a large proportion of the respondents have difficulty passing this test, we know that the intervention should include relevant skills training in how to prepare a résumé.

Beyond examining the extent to which perceived barriers and facilitators are realistic, the investigator should also consider potential control factors that were not elicited in the first pilot phase. Participants may not be aware of the existence of certain barriers or facilitating factors, whether internal or external. Identification of these factors relies on the investigator's knowledge and experience as well as on familiarity with the behavior and population of interest.

In short, in addition to providing a test of the predictive validity of our reasoned action approach, we use the second phase of the formative research to identify internal and external control factors that may actually facilitate or impede behavioral performance. These factors can then be addressed in the intervention.

Changing Intentions

Suppose the formative research revealed that a large proportion of the population does not intend to perform the recommended behavior. The behavioral intervention, therefore, may be designed to change the intentions of these individuals. According to our reasoned action approach, we can do this only by changing attitudes, perceived norms, or perceived control. Because beliefs provide the basis for these factors, the intervention must target the beliefs that underlie the component we wish to change. Thus, to change attitudes toward the behavior, we must change the value of the set of behavioral beliefs salient in the population of interest; to change perceived norm we must change the value of the set of salient normative beliefs; and to change perceived behavioral control, we must address the value of the set of underlying control beliefs.

The major purpose of the second phase of the formative research in this case is to prepare the basis for the behavioral intervention by identifying the specific behavioral, normative, and control beliefs that have to be targeted to bring about changes in intentions. Before we can select the beliefs, however, we must decide which of the three determinants of intention (i.e., attitude, perceived norm, and perceived control) should be addressed. We may be able to eliminate from consideration one or another of the three components by examining its mean and standard deviation. For example, if most people have a very positive attitude toward the behavior, little can be gained by designing an intervention to make attitudes more favorable. The same consideration applies to perceived norm and perceived control.

We saw in previous chapters that all three components tend to correlate with intentions, but their relative importance varies as a function of the behavior and the population under consideration. It stands to reason that, all else being equal, an intervention will be most effective if it targets the component that carries most of the weight in predicting intentions. This is an important consideration because different types of interventions will be needed if the decision is made to change attitudes than if the decision is made to change perceived norms or perceived behavioral control. If a component correlates highly with the intention and carries a significant regression weight, it is a good candidate for change.[4] As we shall see next, however, all other things are usually not equal, and the relative weights of the three predictors are only one criterion for deciding which of the three components should be addressed.

At this point we have made an initial selection of one or more of the theory's major components to target in the intervention with the aim of changing intentions. We now need to identify the underlying beliefs that, if changed, are likely to have a strong impact on the targeted component. Having established that the direct measures can be predicted from the relevant belief indices we can turn to selecting the specific beliefs that are to be targeted. One obvious consideration in selecting the beliefs to be changed has to do with ceiling or floor effects. If most people already strongly agree with a particular belief, there is little we can do to strengthen it further, and if most people strongly disagree, we cannot weaken it any further. This parallels the considerations we discussed in terms of selecting which of the three components to target.

The second consideration has to do with a given belief's explanatory power. As we saw in Chapter 6, the data obtained in this second phase of the formative research can be used to identify beliefs that discriminate between individuals who perform the behavior (or intend to perform it) and individuals who do not. For example, we may find that the behavioral beliefs that getting a colonoscopy is painful and that it is embarrassing are held much more strongly by people who do not intend to undergo the procedure than by people who do. We can identify the most discriminating behavioral beliefs by examining the correlation between each belief by evaluation ($b \times e$) product and our measure of intention. Similar analyses can be conducted to identify the most discriminating normative and control beliefs. The stronger the correlation, the more likely it is that changing the belief will result in changes in intentions.[5]

Note that in the case of behavioral beliefs, the intervention can be designed to change either the strength of the belief or the evaluation of the outcome. Consider, for example, the belief that my voting for a certain presidential candidate will lead to an improved economy. Under the assumption that people are in favor of an improved economy, we could try to make attitudes more favorable by raising the perceived likelihood that voting for the candidate will indeed produce this outcome. Another salient belief may link voting for the candidate to an increase in the defense budget. If most people believe that voting for the candidate will indeed produce this outcome, attitudes toward voting for the candidate could be made more favorable by raising people's evaluations of an increased defense budget. As a general rule, it is usually more difficult to change outcome evaluations (which are themselves attitudes based on many beliefs) than it is to change the strength of a single belief.

The same kinds of considerations apply to changing perceived norms and perceptions of behavioral control. In the case of injunctive norms we can target either the strength of the normative belief regarding a given referent or motivation to comply with that referent, and in the case of descriptive norms, we can again target the strength of the normative belief or identification with the referent. Finally, for perceived behavioral control the intervention can be targeted at the strength of the belief that a given control factor will be present or at the perceived power of the control factor to facilitate or impede behavioral performance.

A third consideration for selecting beliefs to target is more subjective, involving a judgment as to whether it will be possible to change the particular belief under consideration (Hornik & Wolf, 1999). As a general rule, beliefs based on personal experience are often much more difficult to change than beliefs based on secondhand information or beliefs inferred from other available information. (See Chapter 3 for a discussion of the differences between these types of beliefs.) For example, in research on condom use it has been found that one of the highly accessible beliefs about using a condom is that doing so reduces sexual pleasure. If this belief is based on sufficient personal experience, it would be very difficult if not impossible to change it by means of a persuasive communication. (Nor could we easily change a person's negative evaluation of reducing sexual pleasure.)

An additional important consideration is that attitudes, norms, and perceived control can be influenced not only by changing existing salient beliefs but also, and sometimes more easily, by making new beliefs salient. In other words, we can provide people with information that will lead them to form new behavioral, normative, or control beliefs in support of the recommended behavior.

Whether we change existing beliefs or make new beliefs salient, it is important to realize that changing or adding one or two beliefs may not be sufficient to produce a change in attitude, perceived social norm, or perceived control. One possible reason for this is that changing one belief may produce unintended changes in other salient beliefs or make new beliefs salient. These changes could counteract the effects of any change in the targeted belief. We consider this potential impact effect in our discussion of persuasive communication. Only when there is a substantial shift in the summative indices of behavioral, normative, or control beliefs can we expect a change in the targeted component. This implies that, whenever possible, our intervention should be designed to change multiple beliefs rather than only one or two.

In conclusion, we have reviewed three criteria for selecting salient beliefs to be targeted in an intervention that is designed to change intentions (and behavior):

1. Absence of a ceiling or floor effect; that is, there should be enough room for change in the belief to occur.
2. Strong association between the belief and intention.[6]
3. The extent to which change in the belief is judged feasible.

In addition, we also considered the possibility of identifying new beliefs that could be made salient or of increasing the salience of existing beliefs.

Acting on Intentions

When people fail to perform a recommended behavior, the typical reaction of many professionals is that people don't have all the relevant information (see Chapter 7) or that they have the "wrong attitude." Given this assumption, most interventions are designed to provide appropriate knowledge or to influence attitudes, and more often than not, these kinds of interventions fail. Our model of behavioral prediction suggests at least one possible explanation for such failures. If people already intend to perform the behavior in question but are not acting on those intentions, they already have the "right attitude." A measure of intention prior to development of the intervention would have revealed the futility of trying to change attitudes and intentions. In our theory, failure to carry out an intended action has a number of possible causes related to issues of perceived and actual control over performance of the behavior. This can be seen by considering, for those who don't act on their intentions, the four possible combinations of low and high perceived control and low and high actual control, as displayed in Table 10.1.

When perceived control and actual control are high, people have the skills, abilities, willpower, and other internal factors required to perform the behavior and they can effectively deal with potential external barriers, can obtain needed cooperation of others, and have the money, time, and other requisite resources. Moreover, in this case their *beliefs* about these control factors also support a high level of perceived behavioral control. Given the intention to perform the behavior and the high levels of perceived and actual control, we would expect to find few if any individuals in this cell of the table; that is, under these conditions we would expect most people to act on their intentions and perform the behavior.

When actual and perceived control are both low—that is, when people accurately perceive that they don't have much control—it is hardly surprising that they don't perform the behavior. To help these individuals carry out their intentions, we must identify the critical internal and external control factors that prevent them from performing the behavior and design an intervention to deal with these factors. Thus, we may have to offer skills training, teach people how to avoid or get around obstacles to performance of the behavior, or conduct social engineering to remove external barriers. As we will see next, different types of interventions will be required to deal with different kinds of control issues. By raising actual behavioral control we will usually also influence corresponding perceptions of control.

The remaining two cells in Table 10.1 represent combinations in which people's perceptions of control are not veridical. When they believe that

TABLE 10.1 Implications of Perceived and Actual Control for Behavior-Change Interventions When People Fail to Act on Their Intentions

	High Actual Control	Low Actual Control
High perceived control	Behavior is likely to be performed. No intervention required.	Provide skills or remove barriers to actual control.
Low perceived control	Raise perceived control to bring it in line with actual control.	Provide skills or remove barriers to actual control and raise perceived control.

they have more control than they actually have, we again need to work on providing needed resources and removing barriers to performance of the behavior. When actual control is high but people don't realize that they can perform the behavior, changes in control beliefs can bring their perceived control in line with their high actual control.

Clearly, then, an intervention to help people act on their intentions is focused on perceived and actual control over performance of the behavior. Take first the question of actual control. We have drawn a distinction between internal control factors (e.g., skills and abilities) and external control factors (e.g., bureaucratic barriers or lack of social support). One way to look at the issue is to assume that an intended behavior will be carried out only if the person's skills, abilities, and other internal resources are sufficient to overcome any external barriers that may be encountered. When internal control is not sufficient to overcome external impediments, an intervention may be designed either to raise the level of internal control or to remove some of the external barriers. As we shall see, different strategies can be used to improve skills and abilities, and different kinds of social engineering can help overcome external barriers.

Turning to perceived control, the elicitation of salient beliefs in the first pilot study provides initial information about control factors that are perceived to be capable of facilitating or inhibiting performance of the behavior. In the second pilot study we obtain quantitative measures of control belief strength (c) and the perceived power (p) of these factors. By looking at the mean $c \times p$ products, we can identify the particular skills and abilities or external impediments that are perceived to present a problem and that can be targeted in an intervention.

In conclusion, at the end of the second phase of formative research we should have available the information needed to design both an intervention to change intentions and an intervention to help people act on their intentions. In the former case, we will have identified the component or components that are to be targeted and the underlying beliefs that should be changed for maximum impact on intentions. In the latter case, we will have identified the control beliefs as well as the actual internal and external control factors that need to be changed to help people carry out their intentions.[7]

☐ Intervention Strategies Designed to Change Intentions

We first discuss interventions whose primary purpose is to change the intentions of individuals who currently do not intend to perform the desired behavior. It is important to realize that identification of the factors that can be targeted in an intervention to make it maximally effective is really all that our reasoned action framework can offer. It has little to say about the means, strategies, or techniques that can be used to bring about desired changes in the identified factors (Fishbein & Ajzen, 2005; Hobbis & Sutton, 2005). Nevertheless, our approach can help investigators avoid certain pitfalls that often undermine an intervention's effectiveness. First, the theory draws attention to the importance of attacking the relevant behavioral, normative, or control beliefs. The beliefs that provide the foundation for the behavior of interest may be termed *primary beliefs* (see Fishbein & Ajzen, 1981). An intervention may be effective in changing certain beliefs, but if these are not primary beliefs the intervention may have little effect on intentions and behavior. Consider, for example, the large number of interventions that attempt to provide people with accurate information in a given domain. As we saw in Chapter 7, the amount of knowledge a person has with respect to a given domain is often largely unrelated to performance of a given behavior within that domain. Thus, even if people exposed to the intervention acquire more accurate information, if this information does not change their primary behavioral, normative, or control beliefs in the desired direction, a change in intentions and behavior cannot be expected.

A second caveat has to do with possible *impact effects* of the intervention. Whereas an intervention may indeed change some of the targeted primary beliefs, it may at the same time produce changes in other, nontargeted primary beliefs. If these impact effects are in the desired direction, they would tend to reinforce the effect of the intervention. However, if the impact effects are contrary to the recommended behavior, they will counteract and undermine the intervention's effectiveness. Consider, for example, an intervention that is designed to get people to believe that obtaining a colonoscopy will prevent colon cancer. A change in this behavioral belief could at the same time also produce the belief that most people are getting colonoscopies, a descriptive normative belief that would support performance of the behavior. Alternatively, however, the intervention may produce a negative impact effect if the descriptive normative belief formed is that few important referents get a colonoscopy. Even though not targeted in the intervention, formation of this descriptive normative belief would tend to work against the intervention.

In the remainder of this section we consider some of the alternative intervention strategies that have been employed to change intentions and behavior. We can maximize the chances of a successful intervention by combining these strategies with insights derived from our reasoned action approach.

Persuasive Communication

Intervention strategies designed to change behavioral intentions can take many different forms. They range from one-on-one encounters, as in the case of a counseling or therapy session, through group discussions and workshops, to mass media campaigns, such as public service announcements. Individuals subjected to an intervention are exposed to new information or experiences that may change some of their behavior-relevant beliefs and, as a result, affect their intentions and behavior. However, the effectiveness of an intervention is not guaranteed. If it is found to influence behavior, its effects should be traceable to changes in primary beliefs. If the intervention fails to produce the desired behavior change, then our theory of behavioral prediction can, as we shall see next, help to identify the reasons for the failure.

Perhaps the most widespread intervention strategy relies on a persuasive message to communicate relevant information to the target population. The message can be brief or lengthy, and it can be presented in print, audio, audiovisual, or interactive format. A main advantage of the persuasive communication strategy compared with other kinds of strategies is that it can be used to reach a wide audience at relatively low cost. From our perspective, it is critical that the information contained in the message be directed at changing the primary beliefs identified during formative research. Unfortunately, there are no general guidelines to tell us what kinds of information should be included in the message to maximize the likelihood that the desired changes in primary beliefs will be produced. Thus, is it more effective to simply make the assertion that the primary belief is true or false, or is it always better to include supportive evidence? Should the supportive evidence be in the form of empirical data, or should it be some form of logical argument? How should the statements in the message be phrased? What grammatical forms should they take? And so on and so forth. Although much has been written under the rubric of rhetoric about how to construct effective arguments (see Toulmin, 1958), there is very little empirically validated theory or set of principles to help us answer questions of this kind.

The Hovland Approach

Research on communication and persuasion has, however, produced a number of other general principles that may help us produce an effective persuasive communication. Much of this research leaves it up to the investigator to construct a message and asks what factors will make the message *as constructed* more or less effective. Scientific work on persuasive communication began during World War II in an attempt to determine the effects of war-time propaganda (Hovland, Lumsdaine, & Sheffield,

1949). This was followed by a period of intense experimental research at Yale University in the 1950s and 1960s conducted by Carl Hovland and his associates (Hovland, Janis, & Kelley, 1953; Sherif & Hovland, 1961). These investigators assumed that for a message to be persuasive it has to be attended to, comprehended, and accepted. Their research focused on a variety of variables that may influence these processes and hence determine the amount of persuasion. These variables were classified as source factors (e.g., the communicator's credibility or attractiveness), message factors (e.g., emotional vs. rational appeals, order of argument presentation), and receiver factors (e.g., the receiver's self-esteem or intelligence).

Surprisingly, the investigators in this research tradition had little real interest in the content of the message. Even when message factors were studied, these factors had to do with general features of the message, such as the order in which arguments were presented or whether a conclusion was explicitly drawn or left implicit, not with the substantive arguments contained in the message. In addition, investigators in this tradition did not pay much attention to the distinctions among beliefs, attitudes, intentions, and behavior. They assumed that the same factors would influence a message's effectiveness irrespective of the nature of the variable they were trying to change. As a result, they were also not concerned with the relations between the substantive arguments contained in the message and the targeted variable (Fishbein & Ajzen, 1975). Hovland and his associates (e.g., Hovland, Janis, & Kelley, 1953) thus provided no guidance regarding the kinds of information that would have to be included in the message to produce the desired change in a given dependent variable. To put this in the context of a behavioral intervention, a message created in the Hovland tradition may contain arguments that do not deal directly with the primary beliefs that determine the behavior. From our perspective, such a message will often not be very effective and may even be counterproductive.

What's more, although the program of research initiated by the Hovland group (e.g., Hovland, Janis, & Kelley, 1953) was extremely prolific and highly influential, this approach produced very few generalizable conclusions. Perhaps the most replicated finding concerns the role of communicator credibility. As a general rule, a message attributed to a highly credible communicator (i.e., to a source with high expertise and trustworthiness) tends to be more persuasive than the same message attributed to a less credible communicator (see Pornpitakpan, 2004, for a review of the relevant research). But even this intuitively plausible conclusion has to be qualified, because the degree of source credibility does not always influence a message's effectiveness. Among other things it has been found that communicator credibility is of little importance when the message contains strong arguments (McCroskey, 1970), and high credibility can sometimes even be counterproductive (Pornpitakpan, 2004). The other factors examined in the Hovland tradition, whether related to the source, the receiver, or the message, produced largely inconsistent findings in terms of their effects on a message's persuasiveness (Eagly & Himmerlfarb, 1974; Fishbein & Ajzen, 1975).

The main implication for interventions that can be derived from this line of research, therefore, is that once we have constructed a persuasive communication, it will usually be to our advantage to attribute it to a source who, in our target population, is considered to have a high level of expertise regarding the behavior of interest and to be trustworthy.

The Elaboration Likelihood Model

Stimulated in part by a desire to account for the inconsistent pattern of findings generated by research in the Hovland tradition, Petty and Cacioppo (1986; see also Petty and Wegener, 1999) began a program of research in the 1980s that led to the development of the Elaboration Likelihood Model (ELM), without doubt the most influential contemporary framework for work on persuasive communication. Like Chaiken's (1980) contemporaneous heuristic/systematic model, the ELM is a dual-mode processing theory that distinguishes between a central (or systematic) and a peripheral (or heuristic) mode of processing the information contained in a persuasive message. When receivers process the information carefully and elaborate on it, they are said to operate in the central mode. Alternatively, they may pay little attention to the arguments contained in the message and rely instead on relatively simple cues or heuristics, such as communicator credibility or the number of arguments provided, to decide whether to accept or reject the advocated position. Similar to the logic of Fazio's (1990) MODE model, another dual-mode processing theory discussed in Chapter 8, people will tend to process the message centrally when two conditions are met. First, the receiver must be motivated to carefully scrutinize the message arguments. This is likely to be the case, for example, when the topic of the message is of personal relevance to the receiver. Second, the receiver must have the cognitive capacity to carefully process the information contained in the message. The ability to scrutinize message arguments can be undermined by distraction and enhanced by repeated exposure to the message.

When receivers of a message are operating in the central mode and are carefully scrutinizing the arguments contained in the message, the effectiveness of the message will largely be determined by the quality of these arguments. A message containing strong arguments in support of the advocated position is expected to be met with positive reactions, to produce changes in cognitive structure (i.e., in beliefs regarding the topic of the message), and hence to get receivers to change their opinions in the advocated direction. A message containing weak arguments is expected to be counterargued, not to produce changes in cognitive structure, and thus to have little effect on the receiver's opinion regarding the issue.

When receivers are operating in the peripheral mode, the nature and quality of arguments contained in the message are relatively unimportant. Here, the presence of peripheral cues, such as the communicator's high versus low credibility or pleasant versus unpleasant mannerisms, can determine the extent to which receivers change their opinions in the advocated direction.

The ELM thus suggests that fundamental change in beliefs and attitudes will occur primarily in the central mode where message information is systematically processed. The change produced by the message under these conditions is expected to be well grounded in underlying beliefs, to persist over time, to be resistant to counterpropaganda, and to influence later behavior. In contrast, change based on peripheral cues is thought to be relatively superficial, to be short-lived, and hence to be less likely to have an impact on later behavior.

The logic of the ELM provides several general guidelines for construction of an intervention. It suggests that to produce lasting changes in beliefs and to influence behavior we should ensure that participants in the intervention are operating in the central mode. That is, we should try to make the message personally relevant to them and thus to motivate them to process the content of the message. Moreover, we should enable them to process the message arguments carefully by creating conditions that minimize distraction and by using easily understandable language, repeating arguments, and so forth. Of course, it must be remembered that a strategy of this kind will be effective only if the message contains strong, persuasive arguments in support of the behavior we are trying to promote. If the arguments are relatively weak, careful scrutiny of the arguments will lead to counterarguing and rejection of the message.

To summarize briefly, the work initiated by Hovland and further developed and refined by Petty and Cacioppo (1986) in their Elaboration Likelihood Model directs our attention to a number of variables and processes important for understanding persuasive communication. To appreciate the contributions of this work we must consider the central question that was raised and how it was answered. Essentially, investigators in this tradition took as a given that exposure to a persuasive communication can bring about change in beliefs and attitudes. They had relatively little interest in the nature of the arguments contained in the message or in how these arguments relate to the targeted variable. The primary question of interest to them had to do with the factors and processes that make a message as constructed more or less effective. In the work stimulated by Hovland's approach, this question was addressed by examining the effects of various source, message, and receiver factors. For the most part, these kinds of factors were thought to have main effects on persuasion. Thus, it was expected that if the message is attributed to a credible or attractive communicator it is more effective than if the same message is attributed to a less credible or less attractive communicator or that receivers with low self-esteem would change more in response to the message than receivers with high self-esteem. Even with respect to message factors, the interest was not in the content of the message but mainly in its structure, that is, in the way the same material was presented. For example, experiments were conducted to test whether order of presentation made a difference and whether drawing an explicit conclusion was more or less effective than leaving it implicit. Similarly, major variations in message content (e.g., high-fear vs. low-fear appeals or one-sided vs. two-sided messages) were concerned with meta-features of the persuasive communication rather than with the nature or types of substantive arguments contained in the message.

In the Hovland approach, the effects of source, receiver, and message characteristics on opinion change were assumed to be mediated by attention, comprehension, and acceptance of the message. A more sophisticated analysis of the mediating processes was offered by McGuire (1968), who recognized that certain factors can have contradictory effects on different mediators. Thus, attention to and comprehension of a message (or, in McGuire's terms, reception of the message) can increase as a function of the receiver's intelligence but at the same time acceptance of the message (or yielding to it) may decline with degree of intelligence. As a result, because opinion change is a joint function of reception and yielding, we may observe a curvilinear inverted U-shape relation between intelligence and opinion change, with most change occurring among receivers at intermediate levels of intelligence.

The question as to what makes a message as constructed more or less effective was answered in a different way in the Elaboration Likelihood Model. In the Hovland approach the persuasion process was likened to a learning situation in which the message would be effective only if it was attended to, comprehended, and retained. In contrast, the ELM viewed the receivers as actively engaged in the persuasion process, capable of critically evaluating the arguments presented and generating their own thoughts about the message. The effect of the message is largely dependent on the extent to which the receivers engage in these activities—that is, the degree to which they operate in the central as opposed to the peripheral processing mode. Perhaps the most important contribution of the ELM was its recognition that mode of processing interacts with argument quality to produce changes in beliefs and attitudes. Specifically, argument quality influences the amount of change primarily when the message is centrally processed. Under these conditions, a strong message will have a much greater persuasive impact than will a weak message. Argument quality has much less of an effect when receivers operate in the peripheral processing mode because in this mode they don't carefully scrutinize the arguments in the message. The ELM made it clear that variables such as communicator credibility become particularly important when information is processed peripherally rather than centrally. In addition to stressing the importance of these interactions, the ELM identified the conditions under which receivers are likely to operate in the central or peripheral processing modes. For example, when receivers are distracted they are likely to process information peripherally, and when the message is personally relevant to them they are likely to engage in central processing.

Argument Quality

Although work with the Elaboration Likelihood Model drew attention to the importance of high quality or strong arguments under central processing conditions, the theory was not designed to tell us what makes a particular argument strong or why one argument is stronger or more effective than another. Argument quality was generally "treated as an expedient methodological tool rather than a conceptually meaningful construct" (Areni, 2003, p. 349). From a practical perspective, selection of strong arguments to include in a message is perhaps the most important aspect of a behavior change intervention. Generally speaking, it is up to investigators to use their own intuition and knowledge of the behavior under consideration to construct effective arguments. Of course, reliance on intuition can be misleading and can generate a message that is ineffective or one that produces less change in behavior than would be obtained by means of a stronger message.

Petty and Cacioppo (1979) recognized the importance of argument quality and acknowledged that little research has been done to identify the specific attributes that make some arguments persuasive and others less so. In their own work they also decided to forego systematic investigation of this issue. Instead they used empirical criteria to define argument strength. Specifically, Petty and Cacioppo recommended that investigators formulate a large number of potential arguments and then ask a sample of respondents to rate each argument for its quality or persuasiveness (see Updegraff, Sherman, Luyster, & Mann, 2007, for an example). Strong and weak messages are constructed by selecting arguments with high versus low mean persuasiveness ratings. Each message is given to a new sample of respondents who are instructed to think about it and evaluate it carefully. Consistent with the cognitive response approach to persuasion (see Petty, Ostrom, & Brock, 1981), the participants are then asked to list the thoughts elicited by the message. These thoughts are coded as to whether they are favorable, unfavorable, or neutral with respect to the advocated position. A strong message is expected to elicit predominantly favorable thoughts, whereas a weak message should elicit mainly unfavorable thoughts. In some cases (e.g., Petty & Cacioppo, 1979) the thought-listing procedure is employed to select individual arguments. Specifically, participants are asked to consider an argument and list the thoughts that are elicited by it. An argument is considered to be strong to the extent that positive thoughts outweigh negative thoughts.

Unfortunately, a moment's reflection reveals that this approach is unlikely to produce valid estimates of argument strength. It stands to reason that people's own attitudes will tend to bias their judgments of a statement's plausibility or persuasiveness. In fact, based on the assumption that "a statement will be considered a more plausible or effective argument by subjects who agree with the position which the statement supports than by subjects who disagree with that position" (Waly & Cook, 1965, p. 646), Waly and Cook devised an indirect attitude measure that relies on effectiveness judgments of attitude-relevant arguments. Recall that in the standard Likert scaling procedure (see Chapter 3) participants indicate their agreement with belief statements on a *strongly disagree* to *strongly agree* scale. In an attempt to disguise the purpose of the instrument and thus to minimize possible social desirability biases, Waly and Cook asked participants to indicate whether the belief statements were or were not persuasive under the assumption that there is a strong correspondence between degree of agreement with an item and judgment of its effectiveness. Thus, reliance on judgments of effectiveness or quality is likely to produce arguments or messages that support the respondents' own beliefs rather than a strong argument or message that can change the beliefs of a person who disagrees with the advocated position.

Similarly, a potential problem of the thought-listing method has to do with the fact that an argument will tend to elicit few negative thoughts (and many positive thoughts) among participants who agree with it and few positive thoughts (and many negative thoughts) among individuals who disagree with it. In other words, as in the case of direct quality or effectiveness ratings, the respondents' own position on the issue addressed by the argument can bias the nature of their cognitive responses. We might be misled to conclude that we have a strong argument to include in our message only because the majority of participants in our sample happened to agree with it. It is perhaps possible to mitigate this bias by sampling only participants who disagree with our arguments or by asking participants to not simply list their thoughts but to list both positive and negative thoughts in response to the argument. Whether either of these modifications would actually improve our ability to identify strong arguments is an empirical question.

In conclusion, we don't at this point have a good, validated method to assess an argument's strength or quality. The best investigators can do when designing an intervention is to formulate arguments that appear to provide strong support for the desired behavior and perhaps compare their own intuitions against those of a group of respondents for purposes of consensual validation. However, the ultimate test as to whether a strong message has indeed been created is found in its effectiveness at changing the beliefs that were targeted in the intervention.

Acceptance, Yielding, and Impact Effects

We have seen that the communication and persuasion literature does not provide clear guidance regarding the kinds of arguments to be included in a message or how message arguments should be structured. As noted before, our reasoned action approach is also very limited in the guidance it can provide. Nevertheless, it sets some general parameters within which an effective message must operate. Our approach requires that the behavior of interest be clearly defined and that the message be directed at changing the primary behavioral, normative, or control beliefs identified in formative research as important determinants of that behavior. At a minimum, the message will have to include statements representing one or more of these primary beliefs. For example, suppose that the intervention is designed to get people who are about to turn 50 to obtain a colonoscopy and pilot work has identified the following four primary beliefs as targets for the intervention.

- My getting a colonoscopy in the next 2 months would be embarrassing.
- My getting a colonoscopy in the next 2 months would be painful.
- My doctor thinks I should get a colonoscopy in the next 2 months.
- My health insurance won't cover my getting a colonoscopy in the next 2 months.

A bare-bones message might simply present statements corresponding to each of these four beliefs. Thus, the message might simply state, "Your getting a colonoscopy in the next 2 months will be neither embarrassing nor painful; it is recommended by your doctor, and there are ways to have the costs of a colonoscopy paid for even if you don't have health insurance coverage."

Note, first, that these arguments are formulated at a personal level, not a general level. Clearly, a person may agree that doctors think people over 50 should get a colonoscopy yet not believe that "my doctor thinks that I should get a colonoscopy" in the next 2 months. Second, the statements formulated should be truthful for ethical and practical reasons. It would obviously be unethical to mislead people, and it could also be counter-productive. For example, people may accept our claim that the cost of a colonoscopy can be covered by noninsurance sources, but if they discover this to be false, it will undermine the effectiveness of the intervention.

Perhaps more important, simply making an assertion or argument will often not be sufficient to bring about change in a primary belief. As indicated earlier, we have no way of knowing in advance how strong a given argument is and which, if any, of our arguments would produce a change in the corresponding primary belief. To increase the likelihood that people will accept the arguments, the message will usually contain supportive information in the form of additional arguments or empirical evidence. For example, to try to convince people that their getting a colonoscopy would not be painful, we could tell them that the procedure is performed under general anesthesia and that they will be asleep throughout the examination.

Perhaps the most important contribution of our approach to the development of an effective intervention is that it tells us which beliefs should be changed. If we succeed in changing the primary beliefs selected in the pilot work, there is a good chance that the message will have the desired impact on the behavior. In the absence of this conceptual framework, messages are often formulated with an emphasis on the quality of the arguments they contain, without due attention to the relation between those arguments and the target behavior. For example, a message could be constructed that contains strong arguments about colonoscopies, perhaps indicating that this method can be used to prevent colon cancer by removing precancerous polyps or that this method can lead to early detection and treatment of colon cancer, which can increase life expectancy and quality of life. Even though these arguments may be quite effective in creating favorable attitudes toward colonoscopies as a medical procedure, they may do little to influence people's attitudes toward the behavior of their personally getting a colonoscopy. In other words, if the arguments contained in a message are not directly tied to the behavior of interest, the message is unlikely to be effective. This could also explain why messages that increase people's perception that they are at risk for a certain disease or condition typically do not lead them to adopt a particular recommended action (see, e.g., Fishbein, 2003; Gerrard, Gibbons, & Bushman, 1996). The perception that I am at risk for contracting colon cancer, for example, may have little effect on the primary beliefs that determine my decision to get a colonoscopy. Our approach provides general guidance concerning the content of the message in that it specifies the particular primary beliefs that must be addressed if the message is to be successful at changing a behavior.

The effects of a message on primary beliefs can be analyzed in terms of three kinds of processes (Fishbein & Ajzen, 1981): *acceptance, yielding,* and *impact.* Receivers of the message can be said to *accept* an argument targeting a particular primary belief to the extent that they agree with it. Thus, to return to the previous example, if—after exposure to the message—participants disagree that getting a colonoscopy in the next 2 months would be embarrassing, they have accepted the argument directed at this primary belief. A first step in testing the intervention's effectiveness, therefore, involves assessment of the extent to which the participants accept the major arguments contained in the message. This can be done using the same kinds of scales we have recommended for the assessment of beliefs strength, as in the following example:

My getting a colonoscopy in the next 2 months would be embarrassing.

unlikely |___|___|___|___|___|___|___| likely

However, evidence that the message's major arguments have been accepted is not sufficient to conclude that the message has produced a *change* in people's beliefs. If they already agreed with an argument before they were exposed to the message, acceptance of the argument does not reflect a change. Only by comparing acceptance of an argument after exposure to the message with acceptance prior to exposure or with acceptance by participants in an appropriate control group who did not receive the message can we be sure that a change has indeed occurred. A change in acceptance of a major message argument directed at a primary belief is termed *yielding*. To be sure, the major arguments are formulated such that they diverge from the initial primary beliefs. Thus, whereas participants may initially believe that getting a colonoscopy is embarrassing, the major argument corresponding to this belief asserts that it is not embarrassing. If participants accept this argument, they must have changed their primary beliefs. In other words, because of the way the primary beliefs were selected to permit room for change, and because of the way the message argument attacking the belief is formulated, acceptance of the argument will usually reflect a change in the corresponding belief. Nevertheless, it is incumbent on the investigator to make sure that the observed acceptance does indeed indicate a change (i.e., yielding).

Acceptance and yielding represent the intended message effects. We want participants to accept the major arguments contained in the message and to change their corresponding primary beliefs. As noted earlier, however, a message may also have unintended effects that go beyond the information contained in the message. Most important, the message may influence primary beliefs that were not targeted. These kinds of changes are termed *impact effects*. To illustrate, suppose that participants accept the major arguments about getting a colonoscopy contained in the message and that this acceptance reflects yielding to the arguments because it represents a change in the corresponding primary beliefs. At the same time they may come to form new beliefs or change existing beliefs not mentioned in the message, perhaps that their getting a colonoscopy will produce long-lasting discomfort, that their friends don't get colonoscopies, that it will interfere with their work, that it will make them appear old and frail. These impact effects involve either unanticipated creation of new salient beliefs or changes in existing salient beliefs, both of which may well influence attitudes, perceived norms, and perceptions of control in an undesired direction, thus undermining the effectiveness of the intervention.

In fact, it must be recalled that attitudes, perceived norms, and perceptions of control are based on sets of underlying behavioral, normative, and control beliefs, respectively. The summative index of behavioral belief strength multiplied by outcome evaluations provides the basis for attitudes, the summative index of normative belief strength times motivation to comply or identification with referents provides the basis for perceived normative pressure, and the summative index of control beliefs multiplied by the perceived power of the control factors is the basis for perceived behavioral control. We expect a change in attitudes, perceived norms, and perceptions of control only to the extent that the respective summative indices change. It follows that even if we have evidence that a message has produced the desired changes in two or three primary beliefs, this may not be sufficient to produce a significant change in the total belief indices, and the message may therefore not have a significant impact on attitudes, perceived norms, or perceived control. Furthermore, unanticipated impact effects on unmentioned primary beliefs will also influence the summative belief index and may strengthen or weaken the overall effect of the message.

Message Content

We have discussed a number of general principles for designing a persuasive communication, some emerging from theory and research on attitude change and some derived from our own conceptual framework. We are still left, however, with questions concerning the structure of the message. What kinds of arguments are likely to be effective? How should these arguments be formulated? What should be the relations among the arguments contained in the message? Very little empirical research has addressed these kinds of issues.

As indicated earlier, many ideas relevant to these questions have been of major concern in the study of rhetoric. Rhetoric is the use of language to produce certain effects. Interest in rhetoric has a long tradition going back to ancient Greece. Philosophers and linguists have invested a great deal of time and effort analyzing the components and structure of language in an effort to identify linguistic tools for effective communication and persuasive impact (see Brandt, 1970, for a review and discussion). Among the many devices considered are use of metaphors and similes, logical reasoning, examples, analogies, and rhetorical questions. Much of this work, however, is nonempirical. One notable exception is research comparing messages that include metaphors with messages that use only literal text (see, e.g., Ottati, Rhoads, & Graesser, 1999). For a variety of reasons, it is usually assumed that use of metaphors will increase a message's persuasive impact. A meta-analytic review of this literature, however, provided little support for this proposition (Sopory & Dillard, 2002).

Logical Syllogisms

One line of research that may help to structure a message has to do with the logical organization of, and relations among, arguments and supportive evidence (Areni, 2003; McGuire, 1960; Toulmin, 1958; Wyer, 1970b). It is possible to define the major arguments presented in a message as the conclusions we would like participants to reach and the evidence as premises leading up to these conclusions. The logic of drawing valid conclusions from certain premises has occupied philosophers for a long time. This logic is perhaps best captured in syllogistic reasoning. A syllogism consists of three belief statement or propositions, one a major premise, the second a minor premise, and the third a conclusion. Generally speaking, these propositions are related in such a fashion that, given the validity of the major and minor premises, the conclusion must also be true. Consider, for example, the following premises:

1. All American citizens over the age of 21 have the right to drink alcohol.
2. Jane Doe is an American citizen over the age of 21.

If these two premises are true, it follows logically that Jane Doe has the right to drink alcohol.

We could try to build this type of logic into a persuasive message. To return to the colonoscopy example, we could treat the belief that my getting a colonoscopy will not be painful as the desired conclusion. A logical syllogism to promote this conclusion might take the following form:

Major premise: All people who are anesthetized feel no pain.
Minor premise: If you were to have a colonoscopy, you would be anesthetized.
Conclusion: If you were to have a colonoscopy you would feel no pain.

We could build this syllogism into our message. However, it is an empirical question whether this way of organizing major arguments and supportive evidence is more or less effective than any other kind or argumentation.

Framing

Another general principle that may help us formulate arguments in a message has to do with the way the arguments are framed. According to prospect theory (Kahneman & Tversky, 1979), people are willing to take a chance if it could help them avoid a bad outcome, but they are unwilling to take a chance if it involves risking a good outcome. Moreover, prospect theory made it clear that it is possible to frame a decision situation in either a positive (gain) frame or a negative (loss) frame. For example, in one of their experiments, Tversky and Kahneman (1981, p. 453) posed the following decision dilemma in a positive (lives to be saved) frame.

Imagine that the United States is preparing for the outbreak of an unusual Asian disease, which is expected to kill 600 people. Two alternative programs to combat the disease have been proposed. Assume that the exact scientific estimates of the consequences of the programs are as follows:

> If Program A is adopted, 200 people will be saved. (72%)
> If Program B is adopted, there is 1/3 probability that 600 people will be saved and 2/3 probability that no people will be saved. (28%)

The values in parentheses show the percentage of participants who chose each option. Consistent with prospect theory, most people opted to save 200 people for sure rather than risk losing everybody.

Compare these findings with those when the same decision dilemma was formulated in the following negative (lives to be lost) frame:

> If Program C is adopted, 400 people will die. (22%)
> If Program D is adopted, there is 1/3 probability that nobody will die and 2/3 probability that 600 people will die. (78%)

Again consistent with the theory, in this case most people chose to take a chance of saving everybody rather than condemning 400 people to certain death. Although the decisions made by the participants in the two frames appear intuitively to be eminently reasonable, it must be realized that the decision dilemmas in the two framing conditions are logically equivalent. That is, saving 200 out of 600 people (Program A) is identical to losing 400 out of the 600 people (Program C). Similarly, a 1/3 probability of saving all 600 people is the same as a 2/3 probability of saving nobody. The beauty of Tversky and Kahneman's (1981) experiment is the demonstration that the way the dilemma is framed has a dramatic impact on the decision. They interpreted the different results in the two framing conditions as risk aversion in the case of a positive frame and risk seeking in the case of a negative frame.

Salovey, Rothman, and their associates (e.g., Apanovitch, McCarthy, & Salovey, 2003; Banks, Salovey, Greener, & Rothman, 1995; Rothman, Salovey, Antone, & Keough, 1993) tried to apply ideas derived from prospect theory to persuasion in the health domain (for reviews, see Rothman, Bartels, Wlaschin, & Salovey, 2006; Rothman & Salovey, 1997). They divided health-related behaviors into those that involve protection or prevention and are relatively risk free and those that involve diagnosis or screening, which involve a degree of risk or uncertainty in that they could lead to the detection of a serious condition. Examples of protective behaviors are using a condom and using a sunscreen, whereas examples of screening behaviors are getting a mammogram or being tested for HIV. Drawing an analogy to prospect theory, Rothman and Salovey predicted that a gain-framed message is more effective in changing protective behaviors, whereas a loss-framed message is more effective for changing screening behaviors.

The results of empirical research provide some support for this hypothesis; however, the support is not unequivocal, and mixed findings are often reported. For example, in one experiment in this research program (Rothman et al., 1993), the results supported the hypotheses for women but not for men. Consistent with expectations, among the women, a negatively framed message produced more screening for skin cancer (a "risky" screening behavior) than a positively framed message, whereas the positively framed message produced more requests for suntan lotion with a high skin protective factor (a "risk-free" protection behavior) than did the negatively framed message. Framing made little difference among the men. Rothman et al. suggested that this gender difference might be due to the fact that women were more concerned about the risk of skin cancer than were men.

A later study by Banks et al. (1995) also produced what can, at best, be considered mixed results. In this study, Banks et al. examined the effects of message framing on, among other things, women's attitudes toward breast cancer and mammography, on risk perception, on intentions to get a mammogram, and on actually getting screened for breast cancer in the following 12 months. Two versions of a message containing six major arguments were created: one formulated in a gain frame, and the other in a loss frame. For example, one argument in the gain frame indicated that detecting breast cancer early can save your life. The equivalent argument in the loss frame indicated that failing to detect breast cancer early can cost you your life. Because getting a mammogram may be considered risky in the sense that it may reveal a tumor, the loss-framed message was expected to be more effective than the gain-framed message. The results revealed no differences in attitudes, risk perception, and intentions, but there was a marginally significant advantage for the loss frame in terms of actual behavior.

Although it would be premature to make recommendations for interventions based on findings regarding the effects of framing, this work illustrates how theory and research have the potential to help establish guidelines for the formulation of effective arguments.

Other Influence Strategies

Many efforts at behavior change rely on persuasive communication as a component of the intervention but also include additional components that involve a variety of other influence strategies. In contrast to persuasive communications, which expose individuals to a message provided by the communicator, most alternative strategies require active participation on the part of the individual. Among these strategies are group discussions (e.g., Prislin, Jordan, Worchel, Semmer, & Shebilske, 1996), role playing (e.g., St. Onge, 1995), mental simulation (Taylor & Pham, 1996, 1998), and successive approximation (e.g., Wheeler & Hess, 1976). In addition, modeling (observing another person's behavior; e.g., Bandura & Barab, 1973) and self-modeling (observing one's own videotaped behavior; Dowrick, 1999) are also common intervention strategies. Many of these strategies were developed by clinical psychologists to help their patients overcome phobias, stuttering, pathological shyness, and other problems that interfere with daily functioning. They can, however, be adapted for interventions that are designed to change intentions and behaviors of any kind.

From the perspective of our reasoned action framework, the success of these kinds of intervention strategies depends on the extent to which they succeed in changing the primary beliefs that serve as the fundamental determinants of the target behavior. We noted earlier that persuasive communications are often designed without much attention to the contents of the message or to the way in which the arguments contained in the message relate to the behavior that is being targeted. In the same vein, active participation strategies as well as modeling are often implemented without a clear understanding of the primary beliefs that are to be changed, and many of these efforts therefore fail to reach their full potential or even result in failure. In contrast, when active participation strategies target primary beliefs identified in pilot work, they are found to be quite effective. A good example is provided by the program of research conducted by John and Loretta Jemmott (Jemmott et al., 1999; see also Jemmott & Jemmott, 2007). in their attempts to reduce risky sexual behavior among African American adolescents. This work is discussed in Chapter 11.

To summarize briefly, in the previous sections we discussed intervention strategies that can be used to bring about change in intentions and behavior. Persuasive communication is undoubtedly the most versatile and frequently employed strategy, but other strategies also provide important intervention tools. It is up to the investigator to decide which strategy, or combination of strategies, to employ. The decision will depend in part on the nature of the behavior and the population and on the resources available. In the following sections we deal with strategies that are appropriate for individuals who already intend to perform the behavior of interest but for one reason or another fail to act on their intentions.

Stages of Change

A crucial consideration in our approach to interventions is whether people do or do not have the intention to engage in the behavior under consideration. Different interventions are required to change people's intentions as opposed to helping people act on their existing intentions. Other theories, however, suggest that in the process of changing their behavior, people go through a series of stages (Kübler-Ross, 1969; Lippke & Ziegelmann, 2006; Prochaska, DiClemente, & Norcross, 1992; Schwarzer, 2008). The best-known and most widely used of these stage theories is Prochaska, DiClemente and Norcross's (1992) transtheoretical model (see also Prochaska & DiCemente 1983, and Prochaska & Norcross, 2002). According to this model, behavior change involves five stages: *precontemplation, contemplation, preparation, action,* and *maintenance*. In the precontemplation stage, people have no intention of changing their behavior in the foreseeable future. In the contemplation stage, they have formed an intention to perform the behavior in the foreseeable future but have not yet acted upon their intention. When they reach the preparation stage, people begin to perform the behavior but not consistently. When they start to engage in the behavior consistently they are said to be in the action stage. Finally, after performing the behavior consistently for an extended period of time, usually at least 6 months, they are considered to be in the maintenance stage.

The model was developed in the context of changing such problematic behaviors as smoking, drinking, or drug use. Initially, Prochaska and DiClemente conceptualized change as a linear progression through the five stages, but they soon recognized that linear progression is a relatively rare phenomenon with the problematic behaviors they were investigating. People can relapse at any stage to an earlier stage and thus may cycle repeatedly through stages in the sequence (see Prochaska et al., 1992; Prochaska & Norcross, 2002).

In the transtheoretical model of change it is assumed that different processes are involved in the transition from one stage to the next and that therefore different intervention strategies are required at different points in the sequence (Prochaska et al., 1992). For example, one of the processes assumed to be involved in the transition from precontemplation to contemplation is a cognitive or experiential process called consciousness raising. To engage this process, people in the precontemplation stage can be encouraged to seek and attend to information about the benefits and difficulties of changing the behavior in question. A behavioral process—counterconditioning—is implicated in the transition from the action stage to the maintenance stage. Counterconditioning involves finding alternative activities to prevent relapse. For instance, in the case of quitting smoking, when tempted to smoke, people in the action stage may be encouraged to engage in physical activity or find other things to do with their hands. Generally speaking, the transtheoretical model suggests that cognitive strategies are effective in the early stages (precontemplation to preparation), whereas behavioral strategies are needed to move people from preparation to action and maintenance.

Finally, as the transtheoretical model developed, two critical mediating variables were incorporated: decisional balance (the pros and cons of changing behavior), and self-efficacy (confidence in the ability to change). The different processes that produce transition from one stage to the next are assumed to influence the perceived balance of pros and cons and perceived self-efficacy. Behavior change is expected only when the perceived pros outweigh the perceived cons and when people believe that they have the ability to change their behavior (see Prochaska & DiClemente, 1984).

To summarize briefly, in the transtheoretical model it is assumed that behavior change involves a sequence of discrete stages, that qualitatively different processes are implicated in the transition from one stage to the next at different points in the sequence, and that the effects of these processes are mediated by decisional balance and self-efficacy. More than anything else, this model made it clear that behavior change is not an all-or-none phenomenon but instead involves a series of steps or stages and that different strategies may be required to move people from one stage to the next at different points in the sequence.

The logic of this analysis is consistent with our earlier distinction between individuals who have no intention to engage in a desired behavior and individuals who have formed the intention but are not acting on it. Of course, we don't need a complex stage model to realize that different intervention strategies are required for these two types of individuals: one strategy to change intentions and another to help people act on their intentions. However, the transtheoretical model goes beyond this distinction between intenders and nonintenders to describe a sequence of five discrete stages and a complex set of processes associated with stage transitions. Unfortunately, the stages comprising this model do not necessarily address some critical questions that, from our theoretical perspective, would have to be answered prior to developing an intervention. For example, beyond the fundamental division between individuals who intend to perform a desired behavior and individuals who do not, we would want to know the following. First, for individuals who do not intend to perform the behavior, is this because they have given little thought to it or because they have thought long and hard and decided not to? Clearly, we would need different types of interventions to bring about change in these two cases. Second, for individuals who intend to perform the behavior but have not acted on the intention, is this because they haven't had an appropriate opportunity, because they didn't act even though they had the opportunity, or because they attempted to act on their intentions but were unsuccessful? Once again, different types of interventions would be required for these different cases.

Not only does the transtheoretical model fail to make these kinds of distinctions, but there is also little empirical evidence to show that the different assumed processes are important at only certain transition points. Although some processes seem to be more important at certain stages than at others, the data suggest that all processes can influence behavior change to some degree throughout the sequential stages of change (Prochaska & DiClemente, 1983). Indeed, assuming that a certain process is relevant for change at only one transition point can be misleading and counterproductive. Consider, for example, the process called self-liberation, which essentially requires people to tell themselves that they can perform the behavior if they really want to. Note, first, that this is little more than an indication of self-efficacy or perceived behavioral control.[8] According to Prochaska and DiClemente, the process of self-liberation is important primarily in the transition from preparation to action (Prochaska et al., 1992), and interventions encouraging self-liberation will therefore only be effective at the preparation stage. We have seen, however, that perceived behavioral control is an important determinant of intentions as well as of behavior. To produce an intention to engage in the behavior, it may therefore be necessary to target perceived behavioral control, that is, to encourage self-liberation, at the precontemplation stage. For certain behaviors, people are unlikely to reach the preparation stage (which is defined in terms of the intention to perform the behavior and some prior attempts to do so) unless they have a sufficient level of perceived control (i.e., of "self-liberation"). To illustrate, among African Americans, intentions to get a colonoscopy or other kind of cancer screening are primarily determined by perceived behavioral control (Smith-McLallen & Fishbein, 2009). To get individuals in this population to form an intention to get a colonoscopy, for example, it would be necessary to increase their level of perceived control or self-efficacy. Thus, we might try to increase the likelihood that people will tell themselves that they can perform the behavior. That is, we might try to invoke the self-liberation process. Without some intervention to increase their perceived control, they many never form the desired intention and hence never reach the preparation stage.

Stages of Change and the Reasoned Action Approach

Questions regarding the transtheoretical model of change have also been raised in the context of research within our reasoned action framework. A stage model becomes interesting when movements from one discrete stage to the next are accompanied by sudden changes in behavior or its social-psychological determinants. For example, if attitudes toward the behavior were found to be relatively unchanged from precontemplation to contemplation but to become much more favorable once individuals move into the preparation stage, the radical change in attitudes could be explained by the unique processes assumed to be active in the transition from contemplation to preparation. However, if changes in attitudes are gradual across the whole sequence of stages, there is no justification for assuming that different processes are involved at different transition points. In fact, in this case it is not even clear whether we need to break the sequence into discrete stages.

Several empirical studies have shown a continuous pattern of change in attitudes, perceived norms, perceived control, and intentions across the five stages of change specified by the transtheoretical model (Armitage & Arden, 2002; Armitage, Povey, & Arden, 2003; Courneya, 1995; de Vries & Backbier, 1994; Malotte et al., 2000). Generally speaking, the biggest changes in these variables tend to occur between precontemplation and contemplation, followed by smaller changes in movements from contemplation to preparation to action, and relatively little change from action to maintenance. In other words, as attitudes, perceived norms, perceived control, and intentions become increasingly favorable, people move from one stage to the next, until they begin to perform the behavior on a regular basis. Few additional changes are observed as they maintain the new behavior over time. Examination of decisional balance scores shows a corresponding pattern of change. It is generally found that, at the precontemplation stage, the number of perceived cons exceeds the number of perceived pros. By the time people reach the preparation stage, the decisional balance has changed to an advantage for the pros over the cons; the crossover tends to occur at the contemplation stage. Because the balance of pros and cons is closely related to people's attitudes, this suggests that as attitudes change from unfavorable to favorable, people tend to move into the contemplation stage. Taken together, the findings of the different studies imply that attitudes, perceived norms, perceptions of control, and intentions change gradually in the process of behavior change, and there is little evidence for a discrete sequence of steps.

☐ Strategies for Helping People Act on Their Intentions

From our perspective, then, the important distinction is between individuals who do not currently intend to perform a desired behavior and individuals who do intend to perform it but don't act on their intentions. Earlier in this chapter we argued that failure to carry out an existing intention is usually due to low actual or perceived control over the behavior. Thus, individuals may lack the skills, abilities, or information needed to carry out an intended behavior, or they may believe that they lack these requisite resources. In addition, external barriers may prevent them from enacting their intentions, or they may perceive external barriers which they are unable to overcome. We have seen that many of these perceived and actual control issues can be identified during formative research. The intervention is designed to help people overcome actual and perceived lack of control and to take advantage of facilitating internal and external control factors.

The same strategies used to influence people's intentions can also be adopted in interventions designed to help people act on their intentions. For example, pamphlets are often used to impart information on how to perform breast or testicular self-examinations, how to stop smoking, how to avoid drunk driving, and so forth. This strategy is directed at individuals who already intend to perform these behaviors but are not sure how to do it or have found it difficult to carry out their intentions. Like other persuasive messages, those designed to help people act on their intentions often take the form of written communications that usually contain drawings or pictures to illustrate proper procedures. Similarly, when using a modeling strategy, individuals observe how another person performs the behavior, and in this way they can acquire the necessary skills. Alternatively, participatory techniques such as role playing and simulation can be used to help individuals practice the intended behavior. All of these strategies can change perceived behavioral control and, to some extent, can help increase actual control over behavioral performance. In addition, it may also be necessary to engage in a measure of social engineering to remove external barriers and to provide individuals with the means to successfully carry out their intentions.

Implementation Intentions and Commitment

As we saw in Chapter 2, when asked to explain why they failed to act on their intentions, people often mention that they simply forgot or that it slipped their minds (Orbell, Hodgkins, & Sheeran, 1997; Sheeran & Orbell, 1999). In those instances, a very effective means for closing the intention–behavior gap is to prompt people to form an implementation intention (Gollwitzer, 1999). Simply asking people when, where, and how they will carry out their intentions greatly increases the likelihood that they will do so. The beneficial effects of implementation intentions have been found with respect to such normal, everyday activities as completing a project during Christmas vacation (Gollwitzer & Brandstätter, 1997), taking a daily vitamin C pill (Sheeran & Orbell, 1999), and eating healthy food (Verplanken & Faes, 1999), as well as for disagreeable tasks, such as performing a breast self-examination (Orbell et al., 1997) and resuming functional activities following surgery (Orbell & Sheeran, 2000). Formulating an implementation intention has been found to be of particular benefit for individuals with severe cognitive deficits, such as drug addicts undergoing withdrawal and schizophrenic patients (Gollwitzer & Brandstätter, 1997).

According to Gollwitzer (1999; Gollwitzer & Schaal, 1998), implementation intentions are effective because they allow people to delegate control of their goal-directed behaviors to the stimulus situation.[9] Formulation of an implementation intention is assumed to activate the mental representation of a specified situation and make it chronically accessible. Consistent with this assumption, implementation intentions are found to enhance vigilance for relevant situational cues, which are well remembered and easily detected (Aarts, Dijksterhuis, & Midden, 1999; Gollwitzer, 1996; Orbell et al., 1997). As a result, when the situational cues are encountered, initiation of the goal-directed action is expected to be swift and efficient and to require no conscious intent, the hallmarks of automaticity (Bargh, 1996).

Perhaps consistent with this account, implementation intentions may be effective because they improve memory for the behavioral intention. By specifying where, when, and how the behavior will be performed, implementation intentions provide a number of specific cues that can enhance recall of the intention and thus make it more likely that the intention will be carried out. Alternatively, it is possible to attribute the effectiveness of implementation intentions to a sense of commitment they engender. When people state explicitly—and publicly—that they will perform a behavior in a certain situation and at a certain point in time, they arguably make a commitment to carry out their intentions. And there is considerable evidence that making a commitment can greatly increase the likelihood that people will perform the behavior to which they have committed themselves (Boyce & Geller, 2000; Braver, 1996; Cialdini, 2001;

Kiesler, 1971). Consistent with this interpretation, asking people to make an explicit commitment to return a brief survey concerning TV newscasts was found to be just as effective in helping them carry out their intentions as was asking them to form an implementation intention (Ajzen, Czasch, & Flood, in press). In fact, making a commitment was sufficient to produce a high rate of return, and adding an implementation intention did not further increase intention–consistent behavior.

To recapitulate, we have reviewed a variety of strategies that can be used to bring about changes in intentions as well to help people act on their intentions. These strategies include persuasive communications, group discussions, role playing, simulations, modeling, as well as the use of implementation intentions and commitment. Our reasoned action approach provides information about the behavioral, normative, or control beliefs that need to be targeted in an intervention, but it does not tell us which of these strategies will be effective in bringing about the desired changes. It is up to the investigator to select the strategy or combination of strategies to use in an intervention. Of course, there is no guarantee that the intervention, even if carefully planned, will have the desired impact. In fact, it can even be counterproductive, perhaps reinforcing performance of undesirable behaviors. It is therefore incumbent on the investigator to conduct a careful pretest of the intervention to make sure that it has the potential to produce the desired change and that it does not have undesirable side effects.

☐ Evaluating Intervention Effects

It should be clear by now that our model of behavioral prediction can serve not only to gain an understanding of a behavior's determinants and to design an intervention guided by that understanding but it also can be used as a conceptual and methodological framework for evaluating the effectiveness of the intervention. Use of our approach to assess an intervention's impact has the potential to provide two important kinds of information. When the intervention is found to be effective in producing behavior change, the theory permits us to trace the intervention's impact by way of the behavior's psychological antecedents. This opens the way to making improvements in the design and delivery of the intervention and thus to enhancing its future effectiveness. When the intervention fails to produce changes in behavior, we can use information provided by the theory to identify the reasons for the failure. With this information in hand, we can redesign the intervention to overcome its deficiencies.

It is important to realize that the methods and procedures developed in the context of our reasoned action approach can be used to evaluate the effectiveness of any behavior change intervention, whether the design of that intervention was or was not guided by our theory. If the intervention was targeted at a given behavior we can administer a questionnaire to assess the extent to which it influenced salient behavior-relevant beliefs, attitudes toward the behavior, perceived norms, perceived behavioral control, and intentions.[10]

Ideally, an experimental or quasi-experimental design is employed for evaluation purposes. In these designs an intervention group is compared with a suitable control group that is not exposed to the intervention of interest (see Rossi, Lipsey, & Freeman, 2004). In the case of a true experimental design, participants are assigned at random into intervention and control groups. When this is impossible for practical reasons, we can employ a quasi-experimental design in which we forgo random assignment and compare preexisting groups, one of which is exposed to the intervention and one of which is not. In either case, a questionnaire assessing the constructs in our theory is administered in both groups, and behavior is assessed after the intervention. The information thus obtained allows us to examine the influence of the intervention on salient behavioral, normative, and control beliefs; to trace changes in these beliefs to changes in attitudes, perceived norms, and perceived behavioral control; and to trace changes in these factors to changes in intentions and, ultimately, to changes in behavior.

Diagnosing Success and Failure

At the risk of repeating ourselves we briefly summarize some of the information we can obtain by using our theoretical framework to diagnose the reasons for the intervention's success or failure. In the case of an intervention designed to change intentions, we start out by examining the particular primary beliefs that the intervention was designed to change. If these primary beliefs in the intervention group are significantly different from the beliefs in the control group and the difference is in the desired direction, we can say that the intervention accomplished its immediate goals. Conversely, if there are no significant differences in primary beliefs then the intervention failed and cannot be expected to lead to behavior change. However, the observed changes in primary beliefs may be insufficient to bringing about changes in attitudes, perceived norms, or perceived control. This could occur if an insufficient number of primary beliefs changed in the desired direction or if unanticipated impact effects on other primary beliefs produced countervailing changes in the opposite direction. Careful examination of changes in salient primary beliefs can reveal why the intervention did or did not produce changes in one or more of the three major determinants of intentions. This information can be very helpful for designing more effective future interventions.

Significant effects in one or more of the theory's three major components should be accompanied by changes in intentions. If intentions failed to change, we can explore the reasons for this failure. It is possible that the component addressed was not an important determinant of intentions. This may well be the case when the intervention was designed without proper pilot testing to determine which of the three components accounts for most of the variance in intentions.

Finally, the evaluation will also examine the extent to which changes in intentions are reflected in actual behavior. A breakdown at this stage can occur, for example, if unanticipated issues of control prevented many people from carrying out their newly formed intentions. Exploration of this possibility may require postintervention interviews with the participants to identify the problems they encountered when they tried to implement their intentions.

Our reasoned action approach can also be used to evaluate the effectiveness of an intervention designed to help people carry out existing intentions. Here, the focus is usually on control beliefs and actual control. If the intervention changed the targeted control beliefs and increased perceived and actual behavioral control, it should have enabled people to act on their intentions. The evaluation should assess whether these changes in control beliefs and perceived control did indeed occur, and, if not, it should provide information to help in the design of a more effective intervention.

It is also worth noting that our theoretical framework can help to evaluate interventions that attempt to change a particular behavior by targeting what we have called background factors such as self-esteem or racial prejudice. For example, there is evidence to show that, under certain conditions, contact between members of different racial or ethnic groups tends to reduce prejudice toward the outgroup (see Pettigrew & Tropp, 2006, for a review). It is assumed that such changes in attitudes will be accompanied by changes in a variety of interracial behaviors, perhaps—among other things—reducing biases in hiring decisions. A questionnaire administered after the intervention can assess the participants' attitudes toward the outgroup as well as their behavioral, normative, and control beliefs about hiring a member of the outgroup and their attitudes, perceived norms, perceived behavioral control, and intentions with respect to this behavior. Even if contact with members of the outgroup is found to reduce prejudice, the relatively low correlation usually found between general attitudes of this kind, and specific behaviors (see Chapter 8) suggests that the reduction in prejudice may not be accompanied by a greater readiness to hire a member of the outgroup. Evaluation of the intervention within our conceptual framework allows us to determine why the change in prejudice did not produce a change in the particular behavior or, if it did, to trace the effect to the behavior's more proximal antecedents.

☐ Targeting and Tailoring an Intervention

Many investigators have argued that different interventions may be required for different segments of the population (see IOM, 2002). Designing interventions appropriate for a particular population segment is known as *targeting*. Most commonly, the population is segmented on the basis of demographic characteristics such as ethnicity, gender, age, or religion. However, segmentation may also be based on differences in personality traits, values, or lifestyles. For example, different approaches may be adopted for soccer moms as opposed to Nascar fans, for conservatives versus liberals, for regular churchgoers versus people who rarely attend church services. In early work, targeting was concerned primarily with demographic features of the targeted population. For example, when trying to change the behavior of Black as opposed to White teenagers, the intervention might employ a Black rather than a White, Hispanic, or Asian communicator. Similarly, the channel of communication could be targeted to different population segments such that ceratin radio stations might be used to present messages to Black teenagers whereas other stations might be used to expose White teenagers to the message. More recently, targeting has also started to be concerned with the content of the information that is being communicated to make sure that the content is relevant for each identified segment of the population.

When carried to the extreme, targeting can be reduced to the level of the individual, an approach known as *tailoring* (for reviews, see Hawkins, Kreuter, Resnicow, Fishbein, & Dijkstra, 2008; Noar, Benac, & Harris, 2007). In tailoring, information about particular individuals is used to modify the intervention for maximum effect. Specifically, different elements of the intervention are combined in various ways to respond to the participant's unique personal characteristics or beliefs. For example, different information may be provided to respondents holding different beliefs, and a young female who holds a given belief may receive different information from an older female who holds the same belief. To achieve this level of specificity requires an interactive framework in which elements of the intervention are selected in a way that takes into account the participant's responses to prior elements. Tailored interventions are often administered on a computer or over the Internet.

Although targeting and tailoring can be concerned with various aspects of the intervention, from our theoretical perspective the crucial question has to do with the extent to which targeted or tailored interventions are designed to change the primary beliefs that determine the behavior of interest. When the intervention is targeted at one or more segments of the population, the primary beliefs are the salient behavioral, normative, and control beliefs that are most common in the identified segments. Because modal salient beliefs can differ greatly from one population segment to another, targeted interventions designed to change the same behavior in these different segments will usually have to address different beliefs.

From our perspective, tailoring an intervention to particular individuals involves identifying the individual's personal salient beliefs and then designing the intervention to change those particular beliefs. Because different individuals will hold different salient behavioral, normative, and control beliefs, no two interventions will be exactly alike. Tailoring aims to attain an optimal fit between the intervention and the individual whose behavior is to be changed. It is often assumed that this strategy is more effective than targeting, in which the same intervention is administered to everybody in a relatively homogenous population. Unfortunately, very few, if any, studies have directly compared the effectiveness of a tailored communication with a similarly constructed targeted communication. Most studies have simply tried to show that a tailored communication can be effective by comparing it with a control group that receives either no information or a standard informational brochure. The jury is therefore still out as to the relative effectiveness of tailored versus targeted approaches. Moreover, even if it is found that a tailored message is somewhat more effective than a targeted message, it is not clear that this benefit outweighs the higher cost of tailored interventions.

☐ Searching for the Magic Bullet: Behavioral Aggregates

Thus far in this chapter we have considered primarily interventions that target one particular behavior. This approach is sometimes questioned because it requires that we develop different interventions for different behaviors. Because we presumably have neither the resources nor the time to change one behavior at a time, this approach is viewed as inefficient. One might argue that, instead, we should design an intervention in such a way that it would change an array of different behaviors that are viewed as interrelated. For example, it is often assumed that adolescents who drink alcohol are also likely to use drugs, smoke cigarettes, engage in sexual intercourse, drop out of school, get involved in neighborhood fights, and so forth. Similarly, it can perhaps be assumed that students who fail to do their reading assignments also fail to hand in papers on time, do not attend lectures regularly, fail to use online resources, and so on. Ideally, an intervention would be capable of addressing all such interrelated behaviors in one fell swoop.

From our perspective, this search for a magic bullet—although understandable—is fraught with difficulties. To be sure, the different behaviors that are to be changed may be considered to belong to the same behavioral category and we have seen that interventions can indeed be targeted at a behavioral category. An intervention directed at a behavioral category would attempt to change intentions to engage in that category by addressing the behavioral, normative, or control beliefs that ultimately determine this intention. When applied to a heterogeneous set of behaviors, however, such an approach is problematic. First, we have seen that even if the intervention changed intentions to engage in a behavioral category, there is no guarantee that any particular behavior in the category will be performed. Second, and more important, we have made it clear that behavioral categories must be clearly defined such that it becomes possible in an intervention to target the intention to engage in the category. Thus, we can define what we mean by exercising, studying, or political participation and then design interventions to change people's intentions to engage in these behavioral categories. In contrast, it is not clear what intention would have to be changed to bring about changes in such disparate behaviors as drinking, using drugs, engaging in sexual intercourse, dropping out of school, and joining neighborhood gangs. In other words, although it could be argued that these are all problem behaviors, it is not at all clear that the different behaviors can meaningfully be considered part of a single category of behaviors that can be addressed and influenced by the same intention.

Indeed, the strategies usually suggested to bring about change in such heterogeneous sets of behaviors take a very different approach. These strategies are designed to change broad behavioral dispositions deemed relevant for the set of behaviors in question. For example, adolescent drug and alcohol use, smoking, sexual intercourse, and so forth are often attributed to low self-esteem (see Baumeister, Campbell, Krueger, & Vohs, 2003; Dawes, 1994). It might therefore be proposed that the behavior change intervention be designed to raise adolescents' self-esteem under the assumption that this would cut down on the whole range of problem behaviors. Similarly, it is frequently suggested that a broad range of discriminatory behaviors in medical treatment, housing, employment, education, and so forth could be greatly reduced by eliminating prejudice based on race, ethnicity, sexual preference, or gender.

This kind of approach has merit under certain conditions and for certain purposes. It is well known that different behaviors in a given behavioral domain can be aggregated to produce a measure of the general behavioral tendency free of the unique features of any given behavior (see Ajzen, 2005; Fishbein & Ajzen, 1974). The only prerequisite for aggregation is that the different behaviors do indeed have something in common, that is, that they correlate with each other, even if only to a low degree. The principle of compatibility discussed in previous chapters suggests that such a broad behavioral aggregate will exhibit a strong correlation with a general attitude or other general disposition relevant for the behaviors that comprise the aggregate. Thus, in Chapter 8 we described a study (Fishbein & Ajzen, 1974) in which general attitudes toward religion were shown to correlate strongly with a broad aggregate of behaviors in this domain.

Before we decide to target an intervention at a broad disposition, such as self-esteem or prejudice, we should of course verify that the disposition in question does indeed correlate strongly with the aggregate of behaviors we are trying to change. In Chapter 8 we presented some evidence that prejudice does indeed correlate well with aggregates of discriminatory behaviors, despite the fact that its correlations with single behaviors tend to be rather low. The case for targeting self-esteem to reduce problem behaviors among adolescents is much more difficult to make. Self-esteem is found to be virtually unrelated to most problem behaviors (Baumeister et al., 2003), and there is no reason to expect that self-esteem would predict an aggregate of such behaviors. An intervention designed to raise self-esteem, even if successful, is therefore unlikely to reduce problem behaviors among adolescents.

In addition to the requirement of a strong correlation between the disposition that is targeted and the behavioral aggregate that is to be changed, we must also ensure that the observed correlation reflects a causal effect of the disposition on the behavior. Again, in the case of prejudice, this appears to be a reasonable expectation. Most investigators would agree that prejudice can have a causal effect on discriminatory behavior. In the case of self-esteem, however, the direction of causal influence has not been clearly established. In fact, it can be argued convincingly that staying in school, resisting drugs, avoiding fights, and so forth raise self-esteem rather than the other way around (Dawes, 1994). If this is indeed the case, then a change in self-esteem, even if self-esteem did correlate with an aggregate of these kinds of problem behaviors, would do little to produce behavior change.

Finally, it must be realized that, as in the case of behavioral categories, change in a behavioral aggregate does not ensure change in any particular behavior. For example, even if we succeeded in reducing prejudice, this may have little or no impact on discriminatory hiring practices. As we noted in Chapter 2, our theory was developed to help us predict and explain single behaviors because policy makers and organizations as well as researchers are most often interested in such single behaviors rather than in general patterns or aggregates of behavior. Nevertheless, if one is satisfied with achieving changes in broad behavioral patterns, then a focus on general dispositions can provide a useful approach for an intervention.

☐ Ethical Concerns

One remaining issue needs to be addressed in relation to behavior change interventions. Many people seem to believe that it is acceptable to provide individuals with information that will allow them to reach an informed decision but that it is unethical to provide information designed to persuade them to adopt a behavior that is deemed desirable or to discontinue an undesirable behavior. Although this is certainly a valid concern, it should be realized that social agents exert influence on people's behavior all the time. Legislation is passed to regulate smoking and to increase seatbelt use; physicians instruct their patients to exercise or diet or to adhere to a medical regimen; police departments implement programs to reduce drug use and gang violence among adolescents; governmental and nongovernmental agencies exhort people to be screened for or to get vaccinated to prevent various diseases. Behavior change interventions are simply part of these kinds of efforts.

Of course, we have an obligation to ensure that the information provided in an intervention is as accurate as possible, based on the latest scientific knowledge. Even when accurate, however, it should be clear that if the information provided produces a change in people's beliefs, persuasion has taken place whether we intended it or not. In other words, it is impossible to provide information about a behavior that doesn't have the potential to persuade. At the same time, it is important to remember that people are free to accept or reject the information provided in an intervention. Moreover, we must also be concerned with the ethical implications of not intervening to change behaviors that are known to be detrimental to the individual's well-being or to the well-being of others or society as a whole. For example, it can be argued that our knowledge about the detrimental effects of smoking imposes on us a moral responsibility to try to reduce smoking. Thus, although it is important to be aware of the ethical implications of behavior change interventions, we believe that with respect to many behaviors, persuasive attempts should not, on an a priori basis, be considered unethical and that the potential benefits to the individual or society must be taken into account.

☐ Summary and Conclusions

By providing an understanding of a behavior's determinants, our model of behavioral prediction also offers a framework for designing behavior change interventions and for evaluating their effectiveness. In this chapter we discussed the implications of our approach. We noted that although it is possible to consider change along a continuum of stages, the most important distinction is between interventions designed to get people to form an intention to engage in a desired behavior (or to stop performing an undesirable behavior) and interventions designed to help people act on an existing intention. In the former case, pilot work is required to identify the salient behavioral, normative, and control beliefs that provide the basis for the intention that is to be changed, and this information should then be used to design an intervention that targets these primary beliefs. Formative research should also provide information about the relative importance of attitudes, perceived norms, and perceived control as determinants of intentions, and this information should further guide the selection of primary beliefs to be targeted.

Selection of appropriate primary beliefs is perhaps our theory's most important contribution to behavior change interventions. The theory offers little guidance as to the specific strategies that will most effectively bring about the desired changes in behavioral, normative, or control beliefs. Such guidance must come from outside our theory. Research on persuasive communication—by far the most popular strategy for changing beliefs, attitudes, and intentions—has revealed that a message is likely to be more effective if it comes from a credible source, if it contains strong arguments, and if the receivers pay careful attention to these strong arguments. However, we also noted that little is known about the factors that make for a strong argument or about the best way to structure a message. From the perspective of our reasoned action approach, the important point to remember is that persuasive communications, or any other intervention strategy designed to change an intention, must be directed at the primary beliefs that have been identified as the basic determinants of the particular intention under consideration.

When people are known to have the appropriate intentions but fail to act on them, formative research is required to identify the reasons for the failure. Sometimes it may be sufficient to remind people, to get them to form an implementation intention, or to motivate them to carry out their intentions by asking them to make an explicit commitment. At other times, however, formative research may identify internal or external control factors that prevent people from carrying out their intentions. In those instances, the intervention will have to provide people with the necessary skills and resources to overcome internal or external obstacles.

☐ Notes

1. Even though the initial pilot phase may have suggested that we can safely disregard one of the three components because it did not correlate with intentions, the need to validate this tentative initial finding means that we nevertheless should include measures of this component and of its underlying beliefs in the second pilot questionnaire.

2. In Chapter 4 we noted, however, that motivation to comply usually does not add much to the predictive validity of injunctive norms and that identification with a referent may also be of limited value for the predictive validity of descriptive norms.

3. A low correlation may be taken as an indication that aspects of the theory dealing with the relations between beliefs on one hand and attitudes, norms, and perceived control on the other do not hold in this particular case (i.e., for this behavior in this population). Alternatively, it may be an indication that we have not identified all important salient beliefs in the pilot study or that we don't have valid direct measures of the theory's three major components.

4. Consistent with our discussion in Chapter 6, if the nonsignificant regression coefficient is due to problems of multicollinearity, the component is worth considering so long as the zero-order correlation is relatively high and significant. It must also be realized, however, that use of regression coefficients to estimate a component's relative importance rests on the assumption that the three components are assessed with equal reliability or that unreliability has been taken into account.

5. From a theoretical perspective, to produce a change in one of the theory's components we should look at the correlations between beliefs and a direct measure of the component in question. However, because our ultimate aim is to influence intentions, the belief–intention correlation is of greater practical significance.

6. Recall that we examine the correlation between product terms and intentions, not between belief strength and intentions.

7. We should at this stage also have set the parameters on various logistical considerations such as how to sample and gain access to the target population and the channels of communication that are most likely to reach the population.

8. Self-liberation is considered a process that moves people from the preparation stage to the action stage by influencing either decisional balance or self-efficacy. It is not clear why two measures of basically the same construct (i.e., self-liberation/self-efficacy) play such different roles in the transtheoretical model.

9. Implementation intentions can also transfer control over a behavior to internal cues, such as moods or emotions (Gollwitzer, personal communication).

10. At the very least, we would want to assess attitudes, norms, perceived control, and intentions directly without necessarily going to the level of salient beliefs.

Changing Behavior

Sample Interventions

In light of the fact that literally hundreds of studies have been conducted to apply and test our model of behavioral prediction, it is surprising how few of these studies have used the model as a basis for developing and evaluating behavior change interventions (Murphy & Brubaker, 1990). Moreover, even when a research project is thought to constitute a test of an intervention based on our theory, the intervention often fails to meet the requirements described in Chapter 10. Consider, for example, Hardeman et al.'s (2002) narrative review of 30 published articles describing 24 separate studies that they considered to be explicit applications of our reasoned action approach to an intervention or its evaluation. Of the 24 studies reviewed, four did not involve an intervention and hence are largely irrelevant for present purposes. For instance, one of the studies reviewed (Babrow, Black, & Tiffany, 1990) used our model to predict intentions to participate in a smoking cessation program, but no attempt was made to influence the strength of these intentions. In another study (Estabrooks & Carron, 1998), our reasoned action approach was used to predict attendance in an exercise program and to compare the relative importance of capability and autonomy aspects of perceived behavioral control. Again, no attempt was made to change attendance intentions or behavior.

Two other studies reviewed by Hardeman at al. (2002) included an intervention component, but neither the design of the intervention nor its evaluation was grounded in our reasoned action approach (see Anderson et al., 1998; Bowen, 1996). More common, however, were studies that used measures of our theory's constructs to evaluate an existing intervention even though the intervention itself was not designed on the basis of the theory (e.g., Beale & Manstead, 1991; Orbell, Hodgkins, & Sheeran, 1997; Sheeran & Orbell, 1999; Van Ryn & Vinokur, 1992).

A good illustration of how the theory can be used for evaluation purposes is provided by Van Ryn and Vinokur's (1992) program to help unemployed individuals find a job. The behavior change intervention in this program consisted of an 8-hour workshop conducted over a 2-week period. Because the volunteer participants already held positive attitudes and perceived social pressure with respect to looking hard for a job, the workshop focused primarily on increasing the participants' sense of self-efficacy by helping them to develop job-search skills and inoculating them against setbacks. Although the workshop had been carefully developed and pretested over a period of time, the focus of the workshop was not based on our reasoned action approach. For example, in the developmental stage, no attempt had been made to elicit control beliefs, and thus the issues addressed in the workshop were not necessarily directed at salient control beliefs. Nevertheless, our model was used to evaluate the success of the intervention. A questionnaire assessing attitude, injunctive norm, perceived control, and intention with respect to looking for a job was administered prior to the intervention as well as 1 month and 4 months after the intervention. The behavioral criterion was an index of 10 self-reported job-search behaviors that included reading job listings in newspapers and other publications, checking with employment agencies, using or sending out a résumé, and filling out application forms. At 1-month follow-up, intentions to try hard to look for a job were predicted well ($R = .80$) from corresponding attitudes, injunctive norms, and perceptions of control, and the multiple correlation for the prediction of behavior from intentions and perceptions of control was .72. More importantly, compared with a control group of unemployed individuals who did not participate in the workshop, the workshop participants reported a higher level of postworkshop job-search behavior, and this effect of the intervention was found to be mediated by perceived behavioral control. Specifically, the workshop gave people a greater sense of self-efficacy related to looking for a job, and this change in self-efficacy influenced their job-seeking behavior both directly and indirectly by its effects on intentions. It was also reported that the intervention raised reemployment significantly more among participants in the workshop than among members of the control group.

Only six (Brubaker & Fowler, 1990; Jemmott, Jemmott, & Fong, 1998; Murphy & Brubaker, 1990; Parker, Stradling, & Manstead, 1996; Rodgers & Brawley, 1993; Sanderson & Jemmott, 1996) of the 24 studies reviewed by Hardeman et al. (2002) appear to have made full use of our reasoned action approach to both design the intervention and to evaluate its effectiveness. But two of these six studies are problematic. As we mentioned throughout the previous chapters, an essential requirement in any application of our theory is strict compatibility among all measures. Unfortunately, the studies by Parker et al. (1996) and Rodgers and Brawley (1993) were compromised by a lack of compatibility in their measures. Consider the Rodgers and Brawley study. Participants in a weight-loss program that met once a week for 10 weeks completed a questionnaire with respect to changing their eating and physical activity behaviors. Among other things, participants expressed their intentions to adopt healthier eating habits on a daily basis over the next 4 weeks as well as their intentions to participate in physical activity about two times per week over the next 4 weeks. Unfortunately, the behavioral criterion in this study was incompatible with the measures obtained in the questionnaire. Rather than measuring the participants' eating and exercise behaviors, the behavioral criterion categorized participants into those who had stayed and those who had dropped out of the 10-week program. Clearly, the action, context, and time elements of the intention differed greatly from these elements in the measure of behavior. Dropping out of a weight-loss program cannot be considered to be equivalent either to eating a healthy diet or to engaging in physical activity.

Though cautioning that it is difficult to draw strong inferences on the basis of a small number of studies that "were often of poor design" (p. 149), Hardeman et al. (2002) concluded that interventions based on our reasoned action approach generally have only small effects on intentions and behavior. However, if we consider only the four studies in the Hardeman et al. review that actually used our approach to design as well as to evaluate an intervention and that were careful to observe the principle of compatibility (Brubaker & Fowler, 1990; Jemmott et al., 1998; Murphy & Brubaker, 1990; Sanderson & Jemmott, 1996), the interventions are found to have had strong effects on the targeted theoretical components and on actual behavior.

In the years since the Hardeman et al. (2002) review of the literature, other studies appropriately applying our reasoned action approach have started to appear with increasing frequency (see, e.g., Rutter & Quine, 2002). In the present chapter we illustrate how our approach can be used effectively in intervention research by reviewing a few of the studies that have applied the theory systematically to the design and evaluation of an intervention. Most of these intervention studies attempted to change intentions and corresponding behaviors, but we also describe interventions designed to help people act on their intentions.

☐ Interventions Designed to Change Intentions

Testicular Self-Examination

We previously suggested that properly designed interventions grounded in our model of behavioral prediction can have a marked impact. A good case in point are two studies (Brubaker & Fowler, 1990; Murphy & Brubaker, 1990) designed to get men to perform testicular self-examinations (TSE). To illustrate, in the experimental condition of the Murphy and Brubaker study, high school students enrolled in a family planning or health class were exposed to a 12-minute videotaped presentation developed on the basis of our theory. Relying on information from prior research regarding TSE, the persuasive communication discussed the advantages of performing TSE and countered any potential negative aspects of the procedure. In addition, the message emphasized that parents, physicians, and peers support TSE, and it demonstrated the steps involved in performing TSE and the ease with which it could be mastered. Thus, the persuasive message attempted to change attitudes by targeting behavioral beliefs, perceived injunctive norms by targeting injunctive normative beliefs, and perceived behavioral control by targeting control beliefs.

Two additional conditions were created in the experiment. In an information condition the students were exposed to an audiovisual presentation (i.e., slides accompanied by a sound track) that provided information about testicular and other forms of cancer. It did not address the behavior of interest itself; that is, it did not discuss the consequences of performing TSE, did not mention normative expectations of important others, did not deal with issues of behavioral control, and did not explicitly recommend performing testicular self-examinations. Finally, in a control condition participants read a pamphlet containing information about health in general that did not mention testicular cancer or TSE.

A questionnaire administered prior to the intervention assessed knowledge about TSE and whether participants had performed the procedure in the past. Immediately after the intervention a questionnaire was administered that assessed intentions to perform TSE over the next month and included direct measures of attitudes, norms, and perceptions of control with respect to this behavior. In addition, the questionnaire also assessed six behavioral beliefs and their outcome evaluations and three normative beliefs and motivation to comply with the normative referents; it did not assess control beliefs. A 1-month follow-up questionnaire assessed participants' performance of TSE in the preceding month, and it reassessed

TSE knowledge, attitudes, perceived norms, and perceptions of control, as well as intentions to perform TSE in the following month.

A multiple regression analysis on the immediate posttest data showed that intentions could be predicted from attitudes, perceived norms, and perceived control ($R = .59$) and that only the attitude component contributed significantly to the prediction. Moreover, an index of behavioral beliefs ($\Sigma b_i e_i$) correlated significantly with the direct attitude measure ($r = .59$), and an index of normative beliefs ($\Sigma n_i m_i$) correlated significantly with the direct measure of perceived norm ($r = .63$).

Prior to the intervention 24% of the participants had heard of testicular self-examination and only 5% had ever performed TSE. There were no pre-existing differences between the experimental conditions in this regard. But 1 month after the intervention 42% in the theory-based intervention condition reported having performed TSE in the preceding month compared with 23% in the information and 6% in the control conditions. These large differences were statistically significant. Similar differences were observed at the immediate follow-up in intentions to perform TSE and in attitudes toward this behavior. There were no significant differences in direct measures of perceived norms and perceived behavioral control. Examination of changes in targeted beliefs showed significant differences between conditions in some of the behavioral and normative beliefs. Specifically, compared with the control group, participants exposed to the theory-based intervention were more likely to believe that performing TSE helps detect cancer and does not take too much time and that their doctors and parents think they should perform TSE. Participants in the information condition fell between the theory-based and control conditions on these belief measures.

Using Public Transportation

Another well-designed intervention grounded in our reasoned action approach was reported by Bamberg (2006). This intervention, conducted in Germany, was designed to promote use of public transportation and was based on the expectation that geographical relocation may present a good opportunity to effect change. Residents of other towns and cities who planned to move to Stuttgart, a city of about 600,000 inhabitants, within 6 months were recruited and assigned at random into intervention and control groups.

The intervention was developed on the basis of information obtained in prior research that had used our theory to predict and understand the use of public transportation (see, e.g., Bamberg, Ajzen, & Schmidt, 2003; Bamberg & Schmidt, 1993). Participants in the intervention condition received an official welcome letter from the local transportation authority accompanied by an invitation to test their services by means of a 1-day free pass valid for all public transportation in the city. In addition, the mailed package contained information about the public transportation system as well as a map and tailored information about routes and schedules for reaching various areas and facilities from the participant's place of residence. Participants in the control group did not receive this mailing.

Two items each were used to assess attitudes, perceived injunctive norms, perceptions of control, and intentions with respect to using public transportation for daily trips from participants' place of residence.[1] In addition, participants were asked to keep a diary of their travels on a particular preselected day. These measures were obtained both prior to, and following, the move to Stuttgart and the intervention.

A secondary analysis of the data obtained prior to the move[2] showed that intentions to use public transportation could, as expected, be predicted from attitudes, injunctive norms, and perceptions of control regarding this behavior. The multiple correlation for the prediction of intentions was .85. All three components were found to make significant contributions to the prediction. Intentions and perceptions of control, in turn, permitted quite accurate predictions of behavior. The multiple correlation was .79, and, although intention was the more important of the two predictors, both had significant effects on behavior.

Regarding changes in behavior and its antecedents in the control condition, the data indicated that the geographic relocation by itself had only small and often nonsignificant effects. Attitudes toward using public transportation became somewhat more favorable, as did perceived norms and perceptions of control; however, there was no significant change in intentions, nor did actual use of public transportation change significantly. Prior to the move 18% of the participants in the control group reported using public transportation on the selected day, and after the move 25% reported doing so. These findings contrast sharply with the results for the intervention condition. The combination of moving to a new city and receiving the free trial pass and accompanying information had strong and significant effects on attitudes, injunctive norms, and perceptions of control. In addition, the intervention strengthened intentions to use public transportation, and it more than doubled actual use, raising the percentage of participants using public transportation from 18% to 47%.

HIV/AIDS Prevention

Our reasoned action approach has probably been used most frequently to design and evaluate interventions in the area of HIV/AIDS prevention. We saw in previous chapters that a large number of studies based on our approach have been conducted to predict and understand the use of condoms to prevent HIV/AIDS and other sexually transmitted diseases (see Albarracín, Johnson, Fishbein, & Muellerleile, 2001). This work has shown that, with very few exceptions, the same salient normative and control beliefs tend to emerge across different populations and behaviors. Salient normative referents usually include parents, sex partner, friends, health professionals, and religious authorities; and the salient control factors are related primarily to the availability of condoms and to the partner's willingness to use condoms.

In contrast, behavioral beliefs often differ depending on the sex partner and the type of sex involved. Thus, for example, salient behavioral beliefs about using condoms for vaginal sex tend to differ from salient behavioral beliefs about using condoms for anal sex. Among the beliefs common to these two behaviors are the beliefs that using a condom will prevent sexually transmitted diseases and that this behavior will reduce sexual pleasure. However, in the case of vaginal sex, people also tend to believe that using condoms will prevent pregnancy, but this is obviously not an issue in the case of anal sex. In the latter case, issues of cleanliness become more salient. In the same way, issues of fidelity (or the lack thereof) are more salient when using a condom with a regular than with a casual partner.

Of the studies in this domain that have relied on our approach, most have merely tried to predict condom use intentions and behavior, but several behavior change interventions have also been reported. A good illustration can be found in the program of intervention research conducted by John and Loretta Jemmott and their associates (e.g., Jemmott, Jemmott, & Fong, 1992; Jemmott, Jemmott, Braverman, & Fong, 2005; Jemmott, Jemmott, Fong, & McCaffree, 1999; Jemmott et al., 1998; see Jemmott & Jemmott, 2007, for a review). This research is designed to reduce risky sexual behavior primarily among African American adolescents. The investigators begin with formative research to identify salient behavioral, normative, and control beliefs about safer sex practices, such as condom use and abstinence. In the formative research attitudes and perceptions of behavioral control are generally found to have strong effects on intentions and behavior. The interventions are therefore designed primarily to "change behavioral beliefs about the consequences of protective and risky sexual behaviors and control beliefs about factors that would facilitate or thwart adolescents' performance of such behaviors" (p. 248). To the extent that changes in these factors are brought about, we should observe changes in intentions and actual behavior.

Generally speaking, interventions in this program include a series of interactions with adolescents designed to change their attitudes and perceptions of control with respect to abstaining from sexual activity or using condoms by attacking specific beliefs that were determined to be important in formative research. Our theoretical framework is then also used in the evaluation phase of the investigation. In most of the studies the intervention program consists of several modules, usually lasting about 50 minutes, each of which contains a number of developmentally appropriate activities. Culturally relevant videos depict adolescents in various realistic situations that invoke thoughts and feelings about HIV infection, AIDS, and sexual risk behaviors while highlighting prevention skills. These videos, as well as group discussions, deal with the consequences of condom use for AIDS prevention and sexual enjoyment. The participants also engage in role playing in which they observe, analyze, and practice negotiating abstinence or condom use in a variety of situations. In addition, the intervention encourages the adolescents to make proud and responsible decisions to protect themselves and their community.

Consider, for example, the study by Jemmott et al. (1998) in which 6th- and 7th-grade adolescents were exposed either to an intervention designed to encourage abstinence from sexual activity, an intervention to encourage condom use for safer sex, or a control intervention dealing with general matters of health. The interventions consisted of eight 1-hour modules, four administered on each of two consecutive Saturdays. The abstinence intervention, in addition to increasing knowledge, was designed to strengthen behavioral beliefs supporting abstinence and to increase self-efficacy and behavioral skills. Specifically, the intervention attempted to strengthen the behavioral beliefs that abstinence can prevent pregnancy and contraction of sexually transmitted infections, including HIV, as well as the belief that abstinence can foster attainment of personal goals. In addition, the intervention was meant to produce a sense of self-efficacy and provide skills to resist pressure to have sexual intercourse and to negotiate abstinence.

The safer-sex intervention, while mentioning that abstinence is preferred, emphasized that if participants do engage in sexual intercourse, it is important that they use condoms to prevent pregnancy and sexually transmitted diseases. In addition, the intervention was designed to allay concerns that using condoms reduces sexual pleasure and to increase self-efficacy and skills regarding the proper use of condoms and the ability to negotiate condom use with a sex partner.

Participants in the control group were exposed to a similarly structured intervention as in the two experimental groups, but theirs was a general health promotion program that focused not on AIDS and sexual behavior but on behaviors that put people at risk of cardiovascular disease, stroke, and certain types of cancer.

Questionnaires were administered prior to the intervention, immediately after its completion, and at 3-, 6-, and 12-month follow-ups. The questionnaires assessed sexual behavior and condom use during the preceding 3 months, as well as a number of behavioral and control beliefs. The behavioral beliefs were primarily concerned with the utility of using condoms and of practicing sexual abstinence to prevent pregnancy and various STDs, the impact of condom use on sexual pleasure, and the effect of abstinence on career goal attainment. Control beliefs focused on availability of condoms, condom use skills, impulse control, and negotiation skills. In addition to assessing beliefs, the questionnaire also measured attitudes and intentions with respect to having sex in the next 3 months as well as perceived self-efficacy and intentions in relation to condom use.

Immediately after the intervention, several of the behavioral and control beliefs were found to have changed in the advocated direction. All behavioral and control beliefs regarding abstinence were significantly more supportive of this behavior in the abstinence intervention than in the control condition. Not surprisingly, among those exposed to the abstinence intervention, attitudes toward engaging in sexual intercourse as well as intentions to have sex in the next 3 months became more negative. With respect to condom use, all behavioral beliefs in the safer-sex intervention changed in support of this behavior as did beliefs about condom availability and impulse control. Unfortunately, no direct measure of attitude toward using condoms was obtained, but as would be expected, changes in the control beliefs led to a significant increase in perceived self-efficacy. Despite the changes in behavioral beliefs and perceived control, there was no significant difference between safer sex and control participants in their intentions to use condoms.

Nevertheless, the behavior reported at the 3-month follow-up was largely consistent with the observed changes in beliefs. Compared with the control condition, the abstinence intervention significantly reduced sexual activity. Whereas 21.5% of those in the control condition engaged in sex in the previous 3 months, only 12.5% of those exposed to the abstinence intervention did so. Interestingly, the safer-sex intervention also tended to reduce sexual activity, with only 16.6% of participants in this condition engaging in sexual intercourse. The differences between this group and the other two groups were, however, not statistically significant. More important, the safer-sex intervention significantly increased consistent condom use as reported 3 months after the intervention. Whereas 36.1% of the participants in the control condition (and 38.1% of those in the abstinence condition) reported consistent condom use during the past 3 months, this behavior was reported by 65.6% of those exposed to the safer-sex intervention. Without further reinforcement, however, these effects had largely dissipated 6 months after the intervention.

The AIDS Community Demonstration Projects

Perhaps the most elaborate behavior change intervention program conducted to date in the framework of our reasoned action approach is the AIDS Community Demonstration Project (ACDP) (CDC, 1999; Corby & Wolitski, 1997; Fishbein et al., 1997) initiated by the Centers for Disease Control and

Prevention. The major purpose of the intervention was to increase consistent condom use and consistent needle sterilization to reduce HIV infections in high-risk communities. The project involved five U.S. cities: Dallas, Denver, Long Beach, New York City, and Seattle. The at-risk populations of interest were men who have sex with men but do not identify themselves as being gay, injecting drug users, female sex partners of male injecting drug users, female sex workers, and youth in high-risk situations. Within each of the participating cities, the ACDP intervention was directed at one to three of these groups (see O'Reilly & Higgins, 1991).

Depending on the risk population being considered, one or more of the following behaviors were addressed:

- Consistent condom use for vaginal sex with a main partner.
- Consistent condom use for vaginal sex with an occasional partner.
- Consistent condom use for anal sex with a main partner.
- Consistent condom use for anal sex with an occasional partner.
- Consistent use of bleach to clean needles, syringes, and other drug injection equipment.

Altogether, interventions were implemented in 10 different high-risk communities, and reports of risk behavior in those communities were compared with similar data obtained in 10 matched control communities that were not exposed to the intervention. To evaluate the effect of the intervention, 10 cross-sectional waves of anonymous field interviews were conducted in each of the 10 intervention and 10 control communities from February 1991 through June 1994. The first two waves were completed before the implementation of intervention activities and the remainder over the 32-month intervention period.

Although the basic protocol of the intervention was the same in each community, each project implemented the protocol in accordance with the specific local circumstances and population. The central element of the intervention consisted of role model stories that were distributed to members of the intervention communities in community newsletters or other small media materials such as pamphlets, flyers, or baseball cards. Based on the data from the field interviews, the role model stories were directed at either attitudes, perceived norms, or perceived control with respect to one of the risk behaviors relevant to the population being considered. The role model stories were drawn from interviews with members of the target population and contained authentic stories about a community member's beliefs or attitudes associated with his or her attempts to change one of the population-appropriate HIV-related risk behaviors.

The materials also contained basic AIDS information, instructions on the use of condoms, and free condoms. Brochures for the injecting drug use communities additionally contained information about needle sterilization and free bleach kits. Community volunteers were recruited to distribute the small media materials and were trained to engage community members in conversation during distribution. They directed the community members to specific role model stories, discussed stories that had been distributed earlier, and supported and reinforced any indication of positive change.

As indicated previously, questionnaires were administered cross-sectionally by an independent group of trained interviewers to random samples of community members at two time periods before the intervention (the baseline assessment) and then two or three times a year over the next 32 months for a total of eight additional administrations. Among other things the questionnaire asked participants to indicate whether they had been exposed to ACDP AIDS-related information as well as to report their performance of each of the five behaviors of interest in the past 3 months. The questionnaires administered in each wave contained, among other things, direct measures of attitudes, perceived norms, perceived control, and intentions with respect to each behavior the participants could have performed. For example, only those who had anal sex with a regular partner were asked about always using a condom for anal sex with their regular partner, and only those who had shared drugs were asked about always using bleach to clean their injection equipment. Attitudes toward consistently engaging in the relevant behavior from now on were assessed on three seven-point bipolar adjective scales (*good–bad, pleasant–unpleasant, wise–foolish*). Two items assessed perceived normative pressure. With respect to one of the behaviors, for example, participants were asked:

1. "Would you say that most of the people who are important to you think you should or should not use a condom every time you have vaginal sex with an occasional partner?"(*should–should not*)
2. "How many of the people you know use a condom every time they have vaginal sex with an occasional partner?" (*all or almost all–none or almost none*).

To measure perceived behavioral control, participants were asked to respond to the following question: "If you wanted to use a condom every time you had vaginal sex with an occasional partner, how sure are you that you could?" The seven-point response scale ranged from *I am extremely sure I could not* to *I am extremely sure I could*. Finally, intentions were assessed by asking, "How likely do you think it is that from now on you will use a condom every time you have vaginal sex with an occasional partner?" Responses were provided on a seven-point *extremely sure I will–extremely sure I won't* scale.

In the final four data collection phases participants could volunteer to complete a second questionnaire that assessed behavioral and normative beliefs, again with respect to each behavior they could have performed. These beliefs had been identified in elicitation studies conducted prior to the intervention. About 80% of the participants agreed to take this second questionnaire.

The most complete test of the predictive validity of our model can be obtained by examining the data collected in the later phases that included measures of behavioral and normative beliefs. Regression analyses revealed a good fit between model and data. Consider, for example, men's intentions to always use condoms for vaginal sex with their main partners from now on. In the seventh data collection phase, attitudes, perceived norms, and self-efficacy predicted these intentions with a multiple correlation of .78, and the intention had a correlation of .73 with self-reported behavior. Furthermore, the index of behavioral beliefs correlated .83 with the direct attitude measure, and the index of normative beliefs correlated .50 with the direct measure of perceived normative pressure (see Fishbein et al., 1997). Highly significant multiple correlations were also found with respect to the other four risk behaviors.

Perhaps of greater interest, the ACDP intervention had a significant impact on the behavior of participants interviewed in the intervention communities. For example, prior to the intervention 27.4% of the participants in the control communities and 24.6% of participants in the intervention communities reported that they always used condoms for vaginal sex with their occasional or casual partners. By the final wave of the intervention there was no appreciable change in the control communities but a significant increase to 33.4% in the intervention communities. The difference between the changes in control and intervention communities (9.2%) was statistically significant. With respect to condom use with one's main partner, there was little consistent condom use at baseline (prior to the intervention only 8.5% of those in the intervention communities and only 9.1% in the control communities were always using condoms with their main partners). Although there were significant increases in consistent condom use with one's main partner in both intervention and control communities, there was, once again, more change in the intervention than in the control communities. Whereas consistent condom use with main partners increased to 17.0% of the population in the intervention communities ($p < .001$), it increased only to 13.4% ($p < .05$) of the population in the control communities, but this difference between the changes in control and intervention communities (4.2%) was not statistically significant.

The major dependent variable in the study, however, was a measure of where an individual was on a stage of change continuum. Following Prochaska and DiClemente (1983; see also Harlow et al., 1999; Schnell, Galavotti, Fishbein, & Chan, 1996), stage of change for a given behavior was defined by a five-point ordinal scale ranging from precontemplation to maintenance (see Chapter 10). The stages of change for condom use were defined as follows:

1 = Precontemplation: has no intention to always use condoms in the future.

2 = Contemplation: does not use condoms but intends to begin using them every time in the future.

3 = Preparation: almost always or sometimes uses condoms and intends to use condoms every time in the future.

4 = Action: has used condoms every time for less than 6 months.

5 = Maintenance: has used condoms every time for 6 or more months.

Consistent with expectations, the behavior change intervention was found to have significantly moved people along the stages of change continuum of condom use with respect to both main and occasional partners. With respect to consistently using condoms with occasional partners, the intervention communities' mean location on the stages of change continuum increased from 2.76 to 3.18 ($p < .001$) while there was no significant change in mean stage of change within the control communities (baseline mean = 2.82, final wave mean = 2.90). More important, the change in the intervention communities was significantly greater than the change in the control communities. The intervention also significantly advanced the stage of change for condom use with one's main partner.

According to our theory, to produce these advances along the stages of change continuum the intervention should have led to changes in underlying beliefs, which in turn should have led to changes in condom use attitudes, perceived normative pressure, or perceived control. Moreover, changes in one or more of these central components of the theory should have led to changes in intention and behavior (and thus also to changes in stage of change). Somewhat surprisingly, with respect to using condoms consistently with either main partners or occasional partners there was little differential change between intervention and control communities in either attitudes or perceived norms. Perceived self-efficacy, however, increased significantly in the intervention communities as did intentions to use condoms consistently with respect to both types of partner (Yzer, 2007; Yzer, Fishbein, & Hennessy, 2008), and each of these changes was significantly greater than the changes that occurred in the control communities. The significant changes in self-efficacy and intentions can thus explain the changes in condom use and stage of change. The intervention seems to have increased people's confidence that they could use condoms consistently with their main and their occasional partners, and these changes produced corresponding increases in intentions and behavior. The effects of the intervention were even more pronounced when only those individuals in the community who were actually exposed to the intervention were included in the analyses (see Fishbein et al., 1997).

With respect to using bleach to disinfect needles, the rate at which this behavior was performed actually declined significantly in the control communities but not in the intervention communities. Within the control communities, use of bleach decreased from 16.1% to 5.9% of the population ($p < .01$), whereas in the intervention communities the reduction was from 26.6% to 22.9% (ns). The difference between the two change scores was not significant. When all participants in the intervention group were considered, similar nonsignificant findings were obtained with respect to movement on the stage of change continuum. Although there was a slight increase in mean stage of change in the intervention communities (from 2.91 to 2.99) and a slight decrease in the mean stage of change in the control communities (from 2.51 to 2.41), these intervention versus control changes were not significantly different. However, when only participants who reported exposure to the intervention were considered, those who were exposed to the intervention changed significantly more on the stage of change continuum than did the participants in the control communities.

In sum, the AIDS Community Demonstration Projects demonstrate the effectiveness of a behavior change intervention based on our model of behavioral prediction. It illustrates how the same basic strategy can be applied to different behaviors in different populations. Of course, it is necessary to conduct formative research to make sure that the intervention is targeted at salient beliefs relevant for the behavior and population in question. Our conceptual framework can then be used to develop materials and procedures for the intervention and to evaluate its effectiveness at various stages.

Project RESPECT

Project RESPECT was also a multisite intervention program supported by the Centers for Disease Control and Prevention (Kamb, Dillon, Fishbein, & Willis, 1996; Kamb et al., 1998). It was a randomized controlled trial designed to prevent the spread of HIV/AIDS by encouraging people to use condoms consistently. Project RESPECT was conducted in sexually transmitted disease (STD) clinics that were located in Denver, Long Beach, Baltimore, San Francisco, and Newark. Men and women from diverse ethnic groups who engaged in a variety of sexually related AIDS risk behaviors participated in the study.

Participants were assigned at random to one of three individual face-to-face prevention strategies: two experimental interventions and a control condition. One intervention program consisted of brief counseling involving two 20-minute sessions 10 days apart, and the second was an enhanced counseling program involving four sessions over a 2-week period (an initial 20-minute session and three additional 60-minute sessions, 4, 10, and 14 days after the initial session). Participants in the control (or educational) condition received general information about HIV/AIDS and its prevention in two didactic 5-minute sessions that were also 10 days apart. All participants were tested for HIV in the first session, and the results of the test were discussed in the session that occurred 10 days later. Only HIV-negative individuals were retained in the study; HIV-positive patients were referred to HIV services for care and treatment.

In the brief counseling intervention, the participants' AIDS-related risk behaviors were discussed; possible barriers to consistent condom use were identified; they were encouraged to take steps to begin using condoms with their main and occasional partners; and—if they failed to attain the goals set in the first session—reasons for the failure were discussed in the second session. The enhanced counseling intervention was developed in accordance with our theoretical framework. The initial 20-minute session was identical to the first session in the brief counseling condition, involving a discussion of AIDS-related risk behaviors and encouragement and plans to take concrete steps toward consistent condom use. Each of the three subsequent 60-minute sessions attempted to change one of our theory's main components. One session tried to make attitudes toward consistent condom use more favorable by discussing the consequences of this behavior, reinforcing supportive beliefs and countering negative beliefs brought up in the discussion. Another session dealt with normative beliefs. It pointed to changes in the community in support of condom use (e.g., the opening of condom stores) and tried to convince participants that important referents approve of consistent condom use. The third session addressed factors that could prevent or facilitate consistent condom use and tried to provide participants with the resources and skills needed to perform this behavior.

A questionnaire was administered prior to the intervention and immediately following the intervention. In addition, participants in all three conditions were scheduled for follow-up visits 3, 6, 9, and 12 months after the intervention.[3] At baseline, 6, and 12 months a complete STD physical examination was performed. The questionnaire, administered prior to the intervention, immediately after the intervention, and at each follow-up visit, contained measures of the basic constructs in our theory with respect to consistent condom use for vaginal sex with main or occasional partners. The first part of the questionnaire obtained information about the participants' sex partners and sexual behavior in the past 3 months. In the remainder of the questionnaire, men were asked to express their beliefs, attitudes, perceived norms, perceptions of control, and intentions with respect to consistent condom use, whereas women answered the same questions in relation to getting their partners to use condoms consistently.

Attitudes were assessed by means of a seven-item evaluative semantic differential scale. Two items were used to assess perceived social pressure: one an injunctive norm; the other a descriptive norm. For example, in relation to sex with the main partner, the injunctive norm question for male respondents was formulated as follows: "Do most people who are important to you think you *should–should not* always use a condom for vaginal sex with a main partner?" The descriptive norm question was, "How many of the men you know use a condom every time they have vaginal sex with their main partners?" To assess perceived behavioral control, male participants were asked, "How sure are you that you can use a condom every time you have vaginal sex with your main partner?" Intentions were assessed by asking respondents how likely it was that, from now on, for at least the next 3 months, they will use a condom every time they have vaginal sex with their main partner.

In addition to these direct measures of attitude, perceived norm, perceived control, and intention, the questionnaire also assessed salient behavioral and normative beliefs as well as perceived barriers with respect to consistent condom use. The beliefs and perceived barriers had earlier been elicited as part of the formative research conducted in preparation for the intervention.

Consistent with expectations, intentions to use condoms for vaginal sex with both main and occasional partners predicted actual condom use behavior significantly for both men and women. For example, considering only participants in the control group, the correlation coefficients between baseline intentions to always use condoms for vaginal sex with one's main partner and self-reported condom use 3 months later were .45 ($p < .001$) for men and .42 ($p < .001$) for women. These intentions were predicted with considerable accuracy from attitudes, perceived norms, and perceived control. Again considering only the control group, the multiple correlation for predicting men's intentions to always use a condom for vaginal sex with their main partner was .59, whereas the multiple correlation for women was .64. Interestingly, although all three of the theory's components were significant predictors of the men's intentions (the regression coefficients were .33, .23, and .18, all $p < .001$, for attitudes, perceived control, and perceived norms, respectively), only attitudes and perceived control appeared to be important determinants for women; the regression coefficients were .42 ($p < .001$), .26 ($p < .001$), and .05 (ns) for attitudes, perceived control, and perceived norms, respectively. Thus, consistent with the findings of Sheeran, Abraham, and Orbell (1999), though perceived norms had a small but significant influence on men's intentions to use condoms with their main partners, they had little influence on women's condom use intentions vis-à-vis their main partners.

Most importantly, both path analyses (Rhodes, Stein, Fishbein, Goldstein, & Rotheram-Borus, 2007) and growth curve analyses (Fishbein, Hennessy et al., 2001) provided strong evidence that the interventions produced significant changes in condom use behavior. Whereas both enhanced and brief counseling increased women's use of condoms with their main partners, only enhanced counseling increased the frequency with which men used a condom with their main partner. More specifically, 3 months following the intervention, condoms were used 60% of the time by the main partner of a woman in enhanced counseling and 56% of the time by main partners of women in brief counseling. In contrast, condoms were used only 51% of the time by main partners of women in the educational control condition (all differences are significant at the .001 level). For men the corresponding percentages were 56%, 45%, and 46%.

Why were both interventions successful for women but only the enhanced intervention was successful for men? The answer is relatively straightforward. While both enhanced and brief counseling changed women's behavioral and control beliefs (and thus their attitudes, perceptions of control, and their intentions), only enhanced counseling changed men's behavioral and control beliefs; brief counseling had virtually no effect on the men's beliefs. Interestingly, although one whole session of enhanced counseling was developed to change normative beliefs, neither the enhanced nor the brief counseling intervention was successful in changing normative beliefs or perceived normative pressure. Unexpectedly, the relative importance of norms as determinants of intentions did increase following the intervention.

To summarize briefly, compared with the educational intervention, both brief and enhanced counseling increased the attitudes and self-efficacy of women. For men, only enhanced counseling produced significant changes in these two determinants of intention. Thus, for increasing condom use, both counseling interventions seemed to be effective for women, but only the more intensive counseling was effective for men.

Validity of Self-Reported Behavior and Use of Biological Outcome Measures

It is important to mention that the primary outcome measure in Project RESPECT was not condom use but incidence of new STDs. In comparison with the didactic educational intervention, both brief and enhanced counseling significantly reduced STD incidence, but there was no significant difference in STD reduction between the two counseling conditions. Thus, the finding that enhanced counseling led to greater condom use than brief counseling was largely ignored, and it was assumed that brief counseling was as effective as enhanced counseling in preventing HIV. "The finding that the 4-session enhanced counseling and the much shorter 2-session brief counseling had equivalent STD reduction was surprising and is good news for public health programs" (Kamb et al., 1998, p. 1166).

Actually, this finding is not as surprising as might at first appear because the experiment was underpowered to detect small but meaningful differences in STD incidence rates between conditions. More important, the willingness to dismiss the behavioral findings reflects a general distrust of self-reports and of their utility as outcome measures for evaluating the efficacy of behavioral interventions, particularly in the area of HIV prevention. For example, Zenilman et al. (1995) investigated the relationship between STD clinic patients' self-reported condom use and STD incidence. Patients coming to an STD clinic in Baltimore who agreed to participate in the study were examined for STDs upon entry and approximately 3 months later. At the time of the follow-up exam, participants were asked to report the number of times they had had sex in the past month and the number of times they had used a condom while having sex. Incident (new) STD rates were compared for those who reported 100% condom use and those who reported occasional use or no use of condoms. Zenilman et al. found no significant relationship between self-reported condom use and incident STDs for male and female clients. Based on this finding, they questioned the veracity of the self-reports, and they suggested that intervention studies using self-reported condom use as the primary outcome measure were at best suspect and at worst invalid. Similar concerns have been expressed in relation to Project RESPECT data by Peterman et al. (2000).

Clearly, if people reporting 100% condom use are as likely (or more likely) to acquire STDs than those who report never or occasionally using condoms, it would seem reasonable to conclude that these self-reports cannot be trusted. Unfortunately, such a view fails to recognize the complex relationship between behavioral and biological measures. Although we briefly touched on questions of the validity of self-reports and on the differences between behaviors and outcomes in Chapter 2, we have not considered these questions in any detail. Since we have argued for the utility of self-report measures, we now try to demonstrate that not only are behavioral self-report data such as those presented by Zenilman et al. (1995) valid but, more important, when they are taken in conjunction with other behavioral data, self-reports also can provide important insights into the relations between biological and behavioral outcomes (see also Pequegnat et al, 2000; Fishbein & Jarvis, 2000).

Because the validity of self-reports of condom use have been questioned repeatedly, we use these self-reports to illustrate the role of behavior change as a factor influencing a biological outcome—in this case a measure of STD incidence. To understand how behavior change can influence STD incidence it is important to consider May and Anderson's (1987) model of the reproductive rate for STDs (including HIV):

$$R_0 = \beta c D \tag{11.1}$$

R_0 is the reproductive rate of infection, "typically interpreted as the expected total number of secondary infections arising from a single primary infection early in the epidemic when virtually all individuals are susceptible" (Pinkerton & Abramson, 1994, p. 373). When the reproductive rate is greater than 1, the epidemic is growing; when R_o is less than one, the epidemic is dying out; and when R_o equals 1, the epidemic is in a state of equilibrium.

β is transmission efficiency, or the ease with which an infected person can transmit the disease to an uninfected partner.

c is the rate of partner exchange.

D is the length of time a person is infectious.

Note that each of the parameters on the right side of Equation 11.1 (β, c, and D) can be influenced by behavior or behavior change. For example, transmission efficiency (β) can be reduced by increasing condom use or by delaying the onset of sexual activity; the rate of partner exchange (c) can be influenced by decreasing the number of partners; and the length of time a person is infectious (D) can be influenced by increasing the likelihood that the person will seek care at the first sign of symptoms or by increasing the likelihood that the person will participate in screening programs or get regular health checkups.

The impact on the reproductive rate of a given change in any one parameter will depend on the values of the other two parameters. For example, if we increase condom use to reduce transmission efficiency and thus to lower the reproductive rate of HIV, the impact of such an increase in condom use would depend on both the prevalence of the disease and the sexual mixing patterns in the population. Clearly, if there is no disease in the population, increases in condom use (or decreases in transmission efficiency) will not affect the spread of the disease. In contrast, an increase in condom use among those members of the population who are most likely to transmit or acquire an STD can, depending on prevalence of the disease in the population, have a big impact on the epidemic (see Reiss & Leik, 1989).

To complicate matters further, it must also be recognized that changes in one parameter may directly or indirectly influence one of the other parameters. For example, an intervention program that successfully increased condom use could also lead to an increase in number of partners (perhaps because now people feel somewhat safer). If this were in fact the case, an increase in condom use would not necessarily lead to a decrease in the reproductive rate of STDs. In other words, the impact on STD incidence of a given increase (or decrease) in condom use will differ depending on the values of the other parameters in the model. In addition, condom use behaviors are very different with partners one perceives as "safe" than they are with partners one perceives as "risky." For example, one is much more likely to use condoms with occasional or casual partners than with one's spouse or main partner (see Peterman et al., 2000).

Clearly, we cannot expect to find a simple linear relation between increases in condom use and lower STD incidence. Moreover, many factors beyond condom use may influence transmission efficiency. For example, the degree of infectivity of the donor, characteristics of the host, and the type and frequency of sexual practices all influence transmission efficiency, and variations in these factors will also influence the nature of the relation between increased condom use and STD incidence.[4]

In addition to the issues already mentioned, different STDs have very different transmissibility rates, and condoms are not equally effective in preventing all STDs. Although correct and consistent condom use can prevent HIV, gonorrhea, syphilis, and probably chlamydia, condoms are less effective in interrupting transmission of herpes and genital warts (Cates & Holmes, 1996). Thus, although it is always better to use a condom than not, the impact of condom use is expected to vary by disease. Finally, it should also be noted that it is possible to acquire an STD even with consistent condom use because consistent condom use is not necessarily *correct* condom use. As Warner and his colleagues (Warner, Clay-Warner, Boles, & Williamson, 1998; Warner et al., 2008) have noted, incorrect condom use and condom use errors occur with surprisingly high frequencies. In addition, at least some "new" or incident infections may be "old" STDs that initially went undetected or that did not respond to treatment.

Based on the theoretical transmission model previously described, Fishbein & Jarvis (2000) hypothesized that condom use will have little or no relationship to STD incidence among those with low-risk partners and that correct and consistent condom use will significantly reduce STD incidence among those with high-risk partners. These hypotheses are strongly supported by the data from Project RESPECT, despite an apparent paradox: An initial look at the data suggested that consistent condom users are *more* likely to contract a new STD than are those who never use a condom. Specifically, of the 2,799 participants in Project RESPECT, 17.2% reported always using a condom, 8.9% reported never using a condom, and the remaining 73.9% reported sometime use. Overall, 16.1% of the participants acquired a new STD during the 12 months of the study period. Consistent with the earlier findings of Zenilman et al. (1995), always-users were not significantly less likely to acquire an STD (14.9%) than sometimes-users (16.8%). Even more striking was the finding that, although not statistically significant, never-users were the least likely to acquire an STD over the 12-month period (12.0%). The question to be addressed is whether, as Zenilman et al. suggested, these data indicate a lack of veracity on the part of respondents or whether these data simply indicate the complexity of the relationship between condom use and incident STD.

The finding that consistent use of condoms is insufficient to reduce the likelihood of STD incidence is really not surprising given that correct as well as consistent condom use is necessary for disease prevention. As

noted previously, there is a surprisingly large amount of incorrect condom use. In the present sample, the most frequently reported error was
that of condom breakage (36.2%) followed by initially putting the condom
on backward and then flipping it over to put it on correctly (34.2%). Also
prevalent were the errors of starting but not finishing intercourse with
a condom (32.7%) and, conversely, not starting but finishing intercourse
with a condom (22.8%). Having a condom fall off during intercourse was
also reported with high frequency (27.7%). Overall, fully 70% of always-
users and 76% of sometime-users reported using condoms incorrectly at
least once during the past 12 months.

Given these high frequencies of incorrect condom use, even among
those who used them consistently, a new user category was developed:
people who both always used condoms and reported making no condom
errors during the year. People in this category should have a lower rate of
STD acquisition than always-users who used condoms incorrectly or than
sometimes-users. Consistent with this expectation, correct and consistent
condom use did lower STD incidence. Among the always-users who were
not error-free, consistent condom use was no better at reducing STDs than
was sometime use (16.7% vs. 16.8%). However, always-users who used condoms consistently and correctly were significantly less likely to acquire an
STD (6.9%) than either of the other two groups.

While these findings are encouraging, they still do not explain why
those who reported *never* using condoms during sex had lower incidence
rates over the 12-month period than always-users who made errors or
sometime-users. Even if one supposes that condom use is entirely ineffective in reducing STD transmission, this would not account for non-
use being associated with a *reduction* in STD acquisition. Such a finding
could be explained, however, if, compared with the other condom use
groups, nonusers were disproportionately represented by individuals
at low risk. For example, if the never-users were more likely to be in a
mutually monogamous relationship or less likely to have new or casual
partners, then this low-risk behavioral profile, rather than lack of condom
use, could account for their lower rate of STD acquisition. To examine this
possibility, all participants were categorized as being either at high or
low actual or perceived risk to acquire STDs over the course of the year.
Participants were considered at high *actual* risk if they had one or more
casual partners over the 12-month study, had one or more new partners
over the 12-month study, or believed that their main partner had other sex
partners. Accordingly, actual risk was scored as low if the participants
had no casual partners and no new partners and if they did not report that
their main partner had other partners during the year. The second variable, *perceived* risk, was based on a question asking participants at baseline
to indicate "how likely it would be that they would contract HIV if they
were to have sex with their partner if they did not use a condom." The

question was asked separately for main and casual partners, if applicable. Note that this is not a general measure of perceived risk but a behavioral belief about the consequences of not using a condom. For respondents with both main and casual partners, the two responses were averaged to obtain a single index of perceived risk ranging from 1 (low) to 7 (high). Perceived risk was scored as high if the participants score was higher than 4 and as low if their score was equal to or less than 4.

To obtain an overall measure of risk, participants were categorized as having a high-risk profile if they scored high in both actual and perceived risk ($n = 978$) and as having a low-risk profile if they scored low in both ($n = 521$). Participants scoring high on one dimension and low on the other were classified as having a moderate-risk profile ($n = 1277$). Consistent with expectations, STD clinic clients who never used condoms were significantly more likely to have a low-risk profile (45.2%) and significantly less likely to have a high-risk profile (18.4%) than members of any other group (sometime-users: 16.4% low risk and 35.2% high risk; always-users with errors: 14.4% low, 46.0% high; and always-users without errors: 17.2% low and 36.8% high). In sum, it appears that the low rate of STD incidence among those who never used condoms reflects the fact that most of these individuals were having sex with partners who were unlikely to be infected.

The effects of condom use and risk profile on STD incidence are summarized in Figure 11.1. The figure presents the rate of STD acquisition as a function of risk profile for all four condom use groups (i.e., correct and consistent; consistent with errors; occasional; never). It can be seen that a low-risk profile was associated with a low rate of STD acquisition in all four groups (no significant differences between groups). Further, those clients with moderately high or high-risk profiles had a greater rate of STD acquisition in every group except one: always-users who made no errors. Consistent with expectations, then, at-risk individuals who consistently and correctly used condoms significantly reduced their likelihood of acquiring an STD.

To summarize, a careful theoretical analysis shows that there is no reason to expect a simple relationship between a self-reported behavior and a biological outcome measure. The impact of performing a given behavior (or a category of behaviors) on a biological outcome (or any other outcome for that matter) will almost always depend on many other factors. Thus, although people may honestly report engaging in some behavior, they may still fail to successfully reach some biological goal. Just as one can honestly report consistent condom use and still acquire an STD, so too can one honestly report dieting or exercising yet neither lose weight nor reduce one's likelihood of getting cancer or heart disease. Unfortunately, findings like these have often led investigators to question the veracity of self-reports. What we have tried to show is that a more detailed analysis of the data, based on an understanding of the

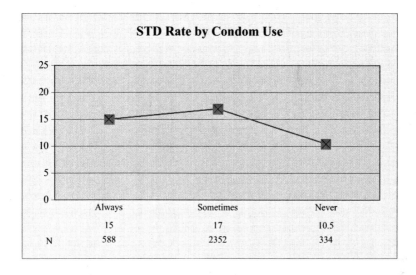

(a)

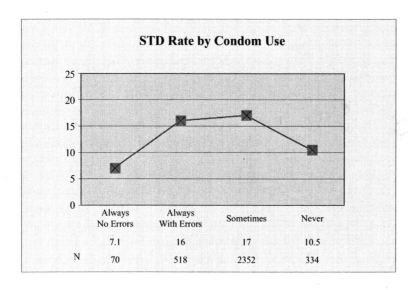

(b)

FIGURE 11.1   STD incidence as a function of condom use and risk profile in Project RESPECT.

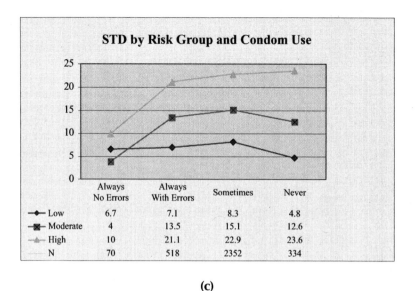

(c)

FIGURE 11.1   (continued)

theoretical relationships between the behavioral and biological outcome measures, may support the validity of self-reports, and, more important, also that this type of analysis may shed light on potentially critical issues that will have to be taken into account in designing interventions. In the domain of HIV/AIDS, the previously described analysis indicates that HIV prevention interventions should not be directed at simply increasing consistent condom use but at increasing *correct and consistent* condom use. As we have tried to show throughout this book, this change, like any other change in the definition of the behavioral criterion, may have important theoretical and methodological implications. Although we would recommend always obtaining both behavioral and biological outcome measures whenever this is feasible, we have tried to make it clear that behavioral self-reports can provide important evidence for the effectiveness of interventions designed to affect health outcomes, even in the absence of biological measures.

☐ Interventions Designed to Help People Act on Their Intentions

Up to this point we have considered attempts to influence people's behavior by changing their intentions. In fact, in most situations, the problem of getting people to engage in a recommended behavior derives from the fact that they have little or no intention to do so, and it is difficult to change their attitudes, perception of social norms, or perceptions of behavioral control. However, there are cases where individuals already intend to perform the desired behavior or where it is relatively easy to get them to form such intentions. The problem in these instances is more one of helping people carry out their intentions than it is to strengthen or otherwise modify their intentions.

When individuals intend to perform a particular behavior and have actual control over doing so, their failure to act on their intentions is often due either to forgetting or to procrastination (see Chapter 2). If the behavior must be performed on or before a particular date, as is the case for, say, buying a lottery ticket, doing so can easily "slip one's mind," and the opportunity is lost. Similarly, people may procrastinate and delay performing an unappealing task until it is too late. Students who intend to write an optional term paper to improve their grades, for example, may keep putting it off until it is too late and the deadline has passed. As we saw in Chapter 10, these kinds of problems can often be overcome by asking people to form an implementation intention or to develop a plan that specifies when, where, and how they will perform the behavior in question (Gollwitzer, 1996, 1999).

Sheeran and Orbell (Orbell et al., 1997; Sheeran & Orbell, 1999b, 2000b; Sheeran & Silverman, 2003) have conducted a number of studies in the context of our reasoned action approach that have taken advantage of implementation intentions to increase the likelihood that an intended behavior will be carried out. In these investigations, a questionnaire assessing attitudes, injunctive norms, perceived control, and intentions was administered to all participants prior to asking those in the intervention condition to formulate an implementation intention. A measure of behavior was obtained at a later point in time. It was expected that participants who intended to perform the behavior would be more likely to do so if they were in the intervention rather than in the control condition.

In the first of this series of studies (Orbell et al., 1997), female students and administrators at a university in the United Kingdom served as participants. The behavior of interest was performing breast self-examinations (BSE). The participants first completed a questionnaire with respect to performing BSE in the next month. The questionnaire included direct measures of attitudes, perceived injunctive norms, perceptions of control, and intentions with respect to performing this behavior. At the end of the questionnaire one half of the participants were asked to write down, first, where they would perform BSE in the next month and, second, at what time of day they would perform BSE. This served as the implementation intention intervention. Then, 1 month later participants again filled out the same questionnaire. In addition, they were asked to report whether they had performed BSE in the preceding month and, if so, how often they had done so.

The results of this study showed, first, that prior to the intervention there were no significant differences between the intervention and control groups in terms of any of the constructs in our model of behavioral prediction. Second, the intervention was found to have a profound impact on subsequent behavior. Whereas only 14% of the women in the control group reported having performed breast self-examinations in the preceding month, 64% of the women who had formed an implementation intention did so. This effect is even more pronounced if we consider only those women who intended to perform BSE. A woman was classified as holding the intention to perform BSE if her responses on all three items used to assess intention were above the midpoint of the seven-point scale. Among these women, everybody in the implementation intention group (100%) reported performing BSE compared with 53% in the control group.

Similar results were reported by Sheeran and Orbell (2000b) in a study on cervical cancer screening in which 92% of the participants with an implementation intention were found to perform the screening compared with 69% without it. And, in a study concerning a very different behavior (Sheeran & Silverman, 2003), 36% of the university employee participants attended a fire training course after forming an implementation intention compared with only 14% who attended the course if they had not formed an implementation intention.[5]

These findings demonstrate that forming an implementation intention can greatly increase the likelihood that people will act on their existing intentions. That is, implementation intentions are found to moderate the effect of favorable intentions on behavior. However, it is conceivable that implementation intentions also have a more direct effect on behavior. Asking individuals who do not currently intend to engage in a given behavior to form an implementation intention may, at least for some participants, produce an intention to perform the behavior and, for this reason, may increase the proportion of individuals who do so. This possibility could have been examined in the Orbell et al. (1997) study, in which a second questionnaire was administered following the intervention. Unfortunately, the investigators did not report whether the intervention had an effect on any of the variables assessed in the second questionnaire.

Some relevant information comes from the study by Ajzen, Czasch, and Flood (in press), which was mentioned briefly in Chapter 10. In this study college students were asked to watch and rate two TV newscasts on their own and to return the ratings to the experimenters. The manipulation of implementation intention came prior to assessment of the variables in our theory. After describing the task, participants in the implementation intention condition were asked to write down where and when they would watch the newscasts as well as to indicate in which campus mailbox they would deposit their rating forms. Participants in the control condition were not asked to form an implementation intention. All participants then completed a questionnaire that assessed their attitudes, injunctive norms, perceptions of control, and intentions with respect to performing the requested task.

Examination of the mean scores revealed no significant differences between experimental and control conditions. Attitudes, norms, perceptions of control, and intentions were thus unaffected by formation of an implementation intention. However, this result must be interpreted with caution because the mean scores on all measures were uniformly high. Because performing the task was part of an experiment for which participants received academic credit, virtually everybody intended to do it. This may have created a ceiling effect, preventing any further change in intentions that might otherwise have been produced by formation of an implementation intention.

The formation of the implementation intention was found to significantly increase the number of participants who carried out their intentions. Whereas in the control group only 12% of the participants completed the task, after forming an implementation intention, 58% did so. An explicit commitment to complete the task was found to have a similar effect. Some of the participants in the study were asked to sign a form on which they committed themselves to watch the newscasts and return their ratings to the experimenter, without indicating when and where they would do so (i.e., without forming an implementation intention). Making the commitment again had no significant effect on any of the constructs in our model, but it raised to 61% the proportion of participants who acted on their intentions to complete the task.

☐ Summary and Conclusions

This chapter described a few sample interventions conducted in the framework of our reasoned action approach. We saw that behavior change interventions can be quite effective when they are designed carefully in accordance with the principles discussed in Chapter 10. Specifically, to influence individuals who currently do not intend to perform a desired behavior requires formative research to identify the primary behavioral, normative, and control beliefs that are then targeted in the intervention. We have reviewed research showing that changes in these beliefs are reflected in the corresponding attitudes, perceived norms, or perceptions of control, and these changes in turn impact intentions and actions. We have also reviewed research that addressed two important issues: the veracity of self-reports and the relationship between behavioral and biological outcome measures in intervention research. We saw that we should not expect a simple linear relation between self-reported behavior and biological outcomes, and, therefore, the failure to find such a relationship should not be taken as evidence for the invalidity of behavioral self-reports. Moreover, we tried to show that by taking the complexity of the relationship between behavioral and biological outcome measures into account, one can, in fact, validate self-report measures and gain important insights into the conditions under which a change in behavior will have an impact on a biological outcome measure.

Rather than being concerned with changing intentions to bring about behavior change, some interventions are confronted with an alternative task. They deal with individuals who already have the intention to perform a recommended behavior and also have control over its performance—yet fail to act on their intentions. In these instances, inducing them to form an implementation intention—that is, to consider where, when, and how they will carry out their intentions—or getting them to make a public commitment to perform the behavior in question can be a very effective intervention strategy.

☐ Notes

1. The same measures were also obtained with respect to using a car for daily trips, but the main focus was on use of public transportation. The questionnaire also assessed behavioral, normative, and control beliefs, but no results regarding these variables were reported.
2. These secondary analyses are based on correlations among latent variables. We would like to thank Sebastian Bamberg for providing the correlation matrix.
3. The experiment contained a second control condition. Participants in this condition attended the two 5-minute information sessions, but they were not scheduled for follow-up visits.
4. These same conclusions follow from other models of STD transmission, such as Reiss & Leik's (1989) model of the probability of being infected.
5. This study also contained an intervention in the form of a persuasive message designed to change intentions to attend the fire preparation course, but this intervention was found to have no significant effect on any of the variables in our theory or on actual attendance.

Conclusion

☐ Retrospective

Our reasoned action approach to the prediction and change of human social behavior and its attendant methodology have been in the making for over 45 years. Growing out of work on an expectancy-value model of attitude (Fishbein, 1963), the original formulation (Fishbein, 1967a) of a reasoned action approach was an adaptation of Dulany's (1968) verbal learning theory of propositional control. According to Dulany, people's intentions to give specific verbal responses (or classes of responses) in a verbal learning experiment were a function of their "hypotheses of the distribution of reinforcement" and their "behavioral hypotheses." That is, the more they believed that emitting a particular response would lead to positive reinforcement (or would enable them to avoid negative reinforcement) (i.e., the hypothesis of the distribution of reinforcement) and the more they believed that the experimenter thought they should, or wanted them to, emit a given response (i.e., the behavioral hypothesis) and the more they were motivated to comply with the experimenter, the more likely they would be to form an intention to, and to actually emit, the verbal response (or class of responses) in question.

By recognizing that the hypothesis of the distribution of reinforcement represented one of many possible beliefs about the consequences of performing a behavior, Dulany's (1968) first component was translated as the person's attitude toward performing a behavior, an attitude that is based on the person's beliefs that performing the behavior would lead to positive or negative outcomes. Similarly, by recognizing that people often take into account the desires and expectations of relevant others in deciding whether to perform a given behavior, the second component in Dulany's theory was translated into an index representing the amount of normative pressure that is felt with respect to performing or not performing the behavior in question. Thus, the original formulation of our model of behavioral prediction suggested that intentions were the immediate determinants of behavior and that intentions were themselves a function of attitudes toward performing the behavior (based on underlying beliefs and their evaluative aspects) and on perceptions of what specific referent others thought one should or should not do and motivation to comply with those referents. The realization that behavior could be quite accurately predicted from intentions and the shift from general attitudes toward objects or institutions to attitudes toward personally performing a behavior were important turning points in theorizing about the attitude–behavior relation. In the current book we have described the continuing development of our ideas about the determinants of social behavior, and we have discussed the implications of our approach for the development and evaluation of interventions designed to change behavior.

A great deal of research has been guided by our reasoned action approach. This research, by us and others, has led to various modifications, additions, and refinements to our theory. Nevertheless, the theory's basic assumptions have stood the test of time. We believe that our theory provides a coherent framework for understanding social behavior and for designing behavior change interventions. Although we recognize that people do not necessarily act in a rational manner and that they may base their decisions on incomplete and inaccurate information, we nevertheless assume that their behavior follows reasonably, consistently, and often automatically, from the information available to them, that is, from their behavior-relevant beliefs. Aspects of this process can occur below conscious awareness, especially for well-practiced routine behaviors, but we believe that most human behavior of interest is rarely if ever completely automatic. We have tried to show that, even when activated by environmental cues, behavior is best viewed as mediated and controlled by a set of cognitive and evaluative antecedents that serve as the behavior's proximal determinants.

Stated briefly, according to our model of behavioral prediction, human social behavior is ultimately guided by considerations regarding a behavior's likely consequences (*behavioral beliefs*), by perceived demands of the social environment (*normative beliefs*), and by one's perceptions of barriers and facilitators that may be present when attempting to perform a behavior (*control beliefs*). Individuals who believe that their performing the behavior of interest produces mainly favorable consequences automatically and spontaneously develop a positive *attitude toward the behavior*, whereas individuals who believe that performance of the behavior leads to mainly negative outcomes develop a negative attitude toward the behavior. By the same token, individuals who believe that important others with whom they are motivated to comply think they should perform the behavior, and that these important others themselves engage in the behavior, are likely to perceive social pressure to perform the behavior; that is, their *perceived social norm* supports behavioral performance. Conversely, when important others are thought to discourage performance of the behavior, or are themselves not performing it, individuals will perceive social pressure to not engage in the behavior. Finally, individuals who believe that more facilitators than barriers will be present when they attempt to perform the behavior and who also believe that they can overcome the potential obstacles that are likely to be present will develop a sense of *perceived behavioral control* or self-efficacy in relation to the behavior. On the other hand, when individuals believe that they lack the requisite resources or that they cannot overcome potential barriers, they will perceive low control over the behavior. In combination, attitudes toward the behavior, perceived norms, and perceptions of control produce an *intention* to perform (or not to perform) the behavior, and this intention is carried out to the extent that the person actually has control over the behavior.

Beliefs thus provide the foundation for intentions and actions. However, the behavioral, normative, and control beliefs that are readily accessible in relation to a given behavior can differ from person to person, from one group or culture to another, and they can change over time. The fact that beliefs can vary across individuals, populations, and over time helps to explain the influence of various *background factors* on behavior. It is well known that the culture in which we grow up has a profound influence on our beliefs in such areas as politics, religion, health, and economics, as well as on our general understanding of people and the world. It should come as no surprise, therefore, that behavior often differs from one culture to another. By examining the behavioral, normative, and control beliefs salient in cultures or subcultures that differ in a behavior of interest we gain a better understanding of the reasons for the observed differences.

The same logic applies to such demographic characteristics as age, gender, level of education, and socioeconomic status. Individuals who differ in any of these characteristics are likely to have been exposed to different experiences in their lives and, as a result, may have formed different beliefs in relation to a behavior of interest. To the extent that they differ in their behavioral, normative, or control beliefs, they would also be expected to form different intentions and to behave in different ways. Again, by measuring these beliefs we gain increased understanding of the ways demographic characteristics produce differences in intentions and actions.

Finally, personal variables, such as intelligence, personality traits, self-esteem, and global attitudes toward objects, issues, and events, can also predispose individuals to form different behavioral, normative, and control beliefs with respect to the behavior under investigation. We have seen that these beliefs—and the attitudes, perceived norms, and perceptions of control they produce—mediate the effects of personal variables on intentions and actions. Our reasoned action approach can thus help explain the ways personal factors lead to differences in overt behavior.

However, it is also true that differences in cultural, demographic, and personal variables are often not associated with behavioral differences. Our theory would suggest several possible reasons. First, with respect to the behavior of interest these kinds of variables may not lead to significantly different behavioral, normative, and control beliefs. Second, the differences that do exist may be insufficient to generate different attitudes, perceived norms, or perceptions of control. Finally, even if a given background factor is associated with a significant difference in one of the theory's components, the background factors will be unrelated to the behavior if that component itself is unrelated to the intention and therefore to the behavior.

Incorporation of background factors permits our theory to provide an integrative framework for much research in the social and behavioral sciences. Work in many domains tends to focus on demographic variables, on situational and cultural factors, and on personal characteristics. These different lines of research have provided valuable information and considerable insight into factors relevant to behavior in one domain or another. At the same time, however, the focus on what we have termed *background factors* has led to a profusion of constructs and theories. Some of these background factors (e.g., demographic characteristics and broad personality traits) can be considered with respect to virtually any behavior; others (e.g., job satisfaction, prejudice, party identification, health locus of control) are limited to a particular behavioral domain. Moreover, and perhaps most important, broad background factors are usually found to account for only a small proportion of the variance in behavior. Our model of behavioral prediction complements these efforts by offering a single conceptual framework that can be applied to any behavior of interest, whether in the domain of politics, economics, health, or religion. In this framework, background factors take their rightful place as possible antecedents or explanations for differences in beliefs that are then reflected in different intentions and actions. We have seen that applications of this kind have met with considerable success in predicting and explaining many different kinds of social behavior and in accounting for the role of various personal, cultural, and demographic variables.

We believe that the popularity of our theoretical framework derives from several important characteristics. First, and foremost, is its wide applicability. Short of strong addictions, involuntary reflexes, and expressive reactions below conscious awareness, almost any social behavior should be predictable in the context of our theory if reliable and valid measures of the theory's constructs are obtained. Second, our theory is parsimonious in that it postulates only three major determinants of intentions and actions: attitudes, perceived norms, and perceived control. These determinants are intuitively reasonable and conform to major theoretical constructs that have proved their utility over the years. Attitudes, representing personal preferences, play a major role in social psychological theories; norms serve as a central explanatory construct in sociological theorizing; and perceived control or self-efficacy is a fundamental construct in clinical psychology. Although our theory is, in principle, open to the inclusion of additional predictors, we should weigh any proposed addition against the advantages of parsimony. Certainly, we would not support additions that greatly overlap with one or more of the constructs already contained in our model.

Finally, work with our reasoned action model has produced a tried and tested set of methods and measurement procedures that have become standard in most applications. Belief elicitation in pilot work is followed by construction of a set of modal salient beliefs. In the main study, a standard questionnaire is administered that, in addition to assessing salient beliefs, also obtains direct measures of attitude toward the behavior, perceived normative pressure, perceived behavioral control, and intention. Behavior, often in the form of self-reports, is measured either concurrently or at a later point in time. Instructions for developing such a questionnaire, and a sample questionnaire, are provided in the Appendix. The availability of this structured set of procedures greatly facilitates application of our approach to novel domains.[1]

☐ Future Directions

As popular and successful as our approach has proven to be, questions remain, and several issues are yet to be resolved. Some of the questions have to do with the theory's three major components. Items designed to assess attitudes toward a behavior are usually found to form two clusters or factors. These factors are often labeled cognitive and affective components of attitude, but we have argued that both factors are evaluative in nature and have suggested use of the terms *instrumental* and *experiential*. Instrumental aspects are revealed in ratings of the extent to which performing the behavior is useful or rewarding, whereas experiential aspects are indicated by ratings of the behavior as pleasurable or boring. Because both factors are evaluative in nature we believe they are best viewed as representing subordinate dimensions of a superordinate attitude toward the behavior. We also noted a possible alternative interpretation, however.

In the health domain, behaviors such as exercising, maintaining a healthy diet, and going to the dentist are deemed good or wise in an instrumental sense yet are experienced as unpleasant. In the case of other behaviors, such as smoking cigarettes, the instrumental aspect is negative whereas the experiential aspect is positive. In other words, we often find that one attitudinal aspect is positive whereas the other is negative, and this alone could account for the emergence of two evaluative factors; that is, we may simply be distinguishing between positive and negative evaluations. Empirical research is needed to determine the appropriate interpretation of the two-factor structure of attitude toward a behavior.

A similar issue arises in relation to perceived behavioral control. Factor analyses of control items used to obtain direct measures of this construct usually also identify two factors. One factor, often termed *self-efficacy*, contains such items as, "I have the necessary skills and abilities to perform the behavior" and "I can perform the behavior if I want to." The second factor, usually termed *perceived control*, is characterized by such items as, "Whether I do or do not perform the behavior is completely up to me" and "Whether or not I perform the behavior is entirely under my control." Calling one factor self-efficacy and the other perceived control carries with it the implication that self-efficacy and perceived behavioral control are fundamentally different constructs. Indeed, some investigators have argued that self-efficacy reflects internal control factors and perceived control reflects external control factors. We saw, however, that the empirical evidence does not support this interpretation. We pointed out that from a theoretical perspective self-efficacy and perceived behavioral control are virtually identical, and we offered *capacity* and *autonomy* as descriptively more appropriate terms for the two factors. Furthermore, just as the two-factor attitude structure may be a methodological artifact, we identified a possible methodological interpretation of the two-factor control structure. Capacity items ask respondents to rate the extent to which they have the ability or are capable of performing a given behavior. These items thus focus attention on the particular behavior under investigation. Autonomy items, on the other hand, usually ask participants to consider the extent to which performance or nonperformance of the behavior is under their control or is up to them. The focus here is on control over performance as well as nonperformance of the behavior. This methodological difference by itself may be sufficient to produce the two-factor structure of control items. This idea could be tested empirically by using the same format in phrasing the autonomy and capability items.

Another issue related to the control construct concerns both the theoretical and methodological role of perceived difficulty. From a theoretical perspective, Bandura (1977, 1997) has argued that individuals do not develop a sense of self-efficacy by performing easy, nonchallenging behaviors; instead, their sense of self-efficacy depends on their perception that they can perform the behavior even under difficult and challenging conditions. Research has shown, however, that *easy–difficult* items often serve to define (or load highly on) the capacity factor. Thus, whereas a high score on this aspect of perceived control implies a belief in the availability of necessary skills and abilities to perform easy behaviors, a low score suggests a belief in the absence of the skills and abilities to perform difficult behaviors. From a theoretical perspective, it makes little sense to conclude that people have self-efficacy or perceived control if they think they have the skills and abilities to perform easy but not difficult behaviors. To complicate matters further, items addressing the ease or difficulty of performing a behavior are often more highly correlated with the experiential aspect of attitudes than with either the capacity or autonomy aspect of perceived control. Clearly, therefore, such items should be used with caution and only after their validity as a measure of perceived behavioral control has been established.

Another set of questions about the perceived behavioral control construct has to do with the measurement of control beliefs and the relations between these beliefs and a direct measure of perceived control. Given how often our theory has been tested, it is surprising how few studies have elicited and assessed control beliefs and perceived power. Moreover, as was pointed out in Chapter 5, most attempts to investigate the strength of the relationship between direct measures of perceived control and a belief-based index of its determinants have either failed to measure perceived power or have measured it incorrectly. Thus, there are very limited data concerning this aspect of our model of behavioral prediction. Clearly, more work is needed to explore ways to assess control beliefs and to validate the obtained belief indices by examining their correlations with direct measures of perceived behavioral control.

Our theory's normative component raises still other kinds of concerns. We are interested in people's perception of the overall social pressure exerted on them to perform or not to perform a given behavior. We have come to recognize that this perceived social pressure should take into account descriptive as well as injunctive norms. We have also come to recognize that, at least for certain behaviors, moral norms may also contribute to the amount of normative pressure one feels to perform or not perform a given behavior. Whereas much work has been done to explore the nature of injunctive norms, descriptive norms are a relatively recent addition to our theory, and thus we are still exploring the best way to obtain direct measures of the normative component. Though it is certainly possible to obtain direct measures of injunctive and descriptive norms, we saw in Chapter 4 that identifying a generalized social agent for the assessment of descriptive norms is often difficult. When we assess injunctive norms directly we can define the generalized social agent as "most people who are important to me" or "most people whom I respect and admire."

We saw, however, that these kinds of generalized social agents are often inappropriate if we want to obtain a direct measure of descriptive norm. Additionally, when we measure injunctive norms, compatibility with the behavior never poses a serious issue: We can make sure that our injunctive norm measure involves the same target, action, context, and time elements as the behavior. In contrast, it can be difficult to define the time element of a descriptive norm measure such that it corresponds to the time element of the behavior. For example, although descriptive norms are theoretically based on the perceived behavior of others, when assessing such norms, it is not clear under what circumstances it is appropriate to ask about the past, the present, or the likely future behavior of important referent individuals or groups. Thus, just as more work is needed on the development of a direct measure of perceived control, so too is more work needed on the development of a direct measure of perceived social pressure.

In addition, although it stands to reason that not all injunctive normative beliefs are equally important determinants of injunctive norms, the notion of motivation to comply has plagued the theory from its inception. Empirically, weighting injunctive normative beliefs by motivation to comply tends to add little to the prediction of injunctive norms. We have always found this surprising given that the mean motivation to comply scores obtained in most studies vary across referents and these variations generally appear to make very good sense. For example, when it comes to sexual behavior young adolescents are most motivated to comply with their best friend and are least motivated to comply with their siblings. Despite these meaningful mean differences, motivation to comply has contributed neither to the prediction of social norms nor to the prediction of intentions and behavior. Although it seems reasonable to assume that the prescriptions and proscriptions of some referents carry more weight than those of others, it is possible that high motivation to comply is essentially a given when we deal with important referent individuals or groups. It is also possible that there are limitations to the current conceptualization or operationalization of this construct.

Just as it makes sense to assume that we pay more attention to the wishes and expectations of some referents than others, it also makes sense to assume that the behavior of some referents has a bigger impact on our own behavior than does the behavior of other referents. We have suggested that it may be possible to use a measure of identification with each referent group to improve prediction of the descriptive norm from an index of normative beliefs. There is, however, very little empirical evidence to support this suggestion. In fact, even less is known about how to weight the relative importance of descriptive normative beliefs than about how to weight the relative importance of injunctive normative beliefs. Clearly, at this point in time, the weighting of injunctive normative beliefs by motivation to comply and the weighting of descriptive normative beliefs by identification with the referent remain open questions.

Finally, questions remain with regard to the extent to which skills and abilities and environmental factors moderate the intention–behavior relationship. To be sure, intentions are usually very good predictors of behavior, and there is convincing evidence that intentions have a causal impact on behavior: When intentions are modified, changes in behavior are seen to follow (Webb & Sheeran, 2006). Nevertheless, according to our theory people can carry out their intentions only to the extent that they have the requisite skills and resources and there are no environmental constraints preventing behavioral performance. In other words, we believe that people can carry out their intentions only to the extent that they have actual control over their performance of the behavior in question. It is therefore important to have valid measures of actual behavioral control available. In practice, perceptions of control are usually taken as a proxy for actual control under the assumption that perceived control reflects actual control reasonably well. However, in many instances this assumption may be unfounded, thus impairing the model's predictive validity. Clearly, more attention must be given to the problem of measuring actual control over performance of the behavior under investigation. We need to develop ways of identifying the resources, skills, and abilities required to perform a given behavior and of assessing the extent to which individuals possess these skills and abilities. By the same token, we must be able to identify potential barriers to, and facilitators of, the behavior's performance and measure the extent to which such barriers and facilitators are present when opportunities to perform the behavior arise. In addition, we also need to develop measures of the extent to which individuals are capable of taking advantage of facilitators and of overcoming or circumventing barriers. Also, it is not clear under what conditions perceived behavioral control is sufficiently realistic to be used as a proxy for actual control and under what conditions reliance on perceived control would be misleading.

Many investigators have turned to our theory because they wanted to gain a better understanding of the factors that determine a particular behavior that is of interest to them. From a practical perspective, application of our reasoned action approach to a behavior of interest can indeed provide insight into why people do or do not perform the behavior in question. Moreover, there is value in the accumulation of such studies in that they provide a basis for meta-analyses and other attempts to derive general conclusions about the theory's predictive validity and about the relative weights of the three components. These types of research syntheses also allow us to look for variables that moderate the strength of the relations among the theory's constructs.

Some investigators go beyond simply testing the validity of our model of behavioral prediction by proposing the inclusion of additional factors that they believe could improve the theory's predictive validity. Among the most frequently proposed additions are self-identity, anticipated affect, and past behavior. Challenging our theory's sufficiency assumption, adding these factors to our model tends to improve prediction of intentions and behavior, thus raising a number of interesting conceptual issues. Although we could not find a good explanation for the residual effect of past behavior on intentions, we concluded that the increase in explained variance due to self-identity and anticipated affect can be accommodated within the context of our theory. We tried to show how measures of self-identity could best be viewed as capturing aspects of attitude toward the behavior, descriptive norm, and current or past behavior. To the extent that measures of self-identity provide some assessment of past or current behavior or capture aspects of attitudes and perceived social pressure that are not already being measured (e.g., they essentially assess the descriptive norm in a study where only the injunctive norm has been measured), our reasoned action approach would expect them to account for additional variance in behavior.

The explanation of the residual effect of anticipated affect is quite different. Here we tried to demonstrate that in those studies where anticipated affect has made what appears to be an independent contribution to the prediction of intention and behavior, the measures of anticipated affect focused not on performing the behavior of interest but, instead, on *not* performing the behavior. The additional variance accounted for by anticipated affect can thus be explained as just another indication that a consideration of both performance and nonperformance of a behavior leads to better prediction than a consideration of only one or the other.

Our inability to find an explanation for the residual effect of past behavior on intention can be taken as an indication that the theory's constructs are insufficient to account for all meaningful variance in intentions and, therefore, that one or more additional predictors are probably needed. The fact that neither the inclusion of self-identity nor of anticipated affect eliminated the direct effect of past behavior on intentions can be viewed as further evidence that they do not represent new explanatory variables that should be added to our model.

Clearly, in an effort to obtain a full understanding of behavioral determinants, it is reasonable to look for variables in addition to attitudes, perceived norms, and perceptions of control that can theoretically influence intentions and behavior. From our perspective, like the theory's existing predictors, the proposed variables should be behavior-specific, conforming to the principle of compatibility.

☐ Changing Behavior

We have tried to show that our model of behavioral prediction has important implications for behavior change interventions. According to our theoretical framework, prior to developing an intervention, we must first determine whether the intervention should be directed at influencing intentions or at helping people act on the intentions they already hold. Attempts to change behavior may have to influence people's behavioral intentions, and they may also have to ensure that people have the skills, social support, and other resources needed to perform the behavior and to overcome potential obstacles. With respect to changing intentions the theory can help guide the investigator by identifying the behavioral, normative, or control beliefs to be targeted in the intervention. Similarly, when it comes to helping people act on their intentions, the theory can help to identify the important control factors that should be addressed. Research conducted in the context of our theory has been much more concerned with behavioral prediction than with behavioral change. Indeed, there is a stark contrast between the large number of studies that have applied the theory to predict a multitude of different behaviors and the relatively small number that have used the theory as a framework for developing and evaluating behavior change interventions. Among the latter, most have focused on changing intentions (and thus behavior) with less attention being paid to helping people act on those intentions. In many published papers investigators report the results of a correlational study showing that intentions and behavior in a given domain are well predicted and explained by the theory's constructs. They will then often note the utility of the obtained information for interventions designed to change the intention and behavior in question. The interventions themselves, however, are typically left for an unspecified future date or for others to carry out. Needed at this point are more investigations that use our theory to design and evaluate behavior change interventions.

According to our model of behavioral prediction, the chain of events that ultimately produces behavior modification begins with changes in behavioral, normative, or control beliefs. Although we can identify the particular beliefs that should be targeted in an intervention, our theory tells us little about how to bring about changes in those beliefs. The information we do have about this question comes largely from research on persuasive communication. According to the Elaboration Likelihood Model (ELM) and other dual-mode processing models, to bring about fundamental change in people's attitudes—change that will persist over time and guide behavior—it is necessary to construct strong arguments and to make sure that receivers of the message are motivated and able to process the message carefully. In our discussion of behavior change interventions in Chapter 10 we offered some general guidelines for designing an effective intervention, but to some extent these guidelines were based more on conjecture than on sound theory or empirical evidence. Among other things, research is needed to establish whether interventions are indeed most effective when they target beliefs underlying the component that carries the most weight in the prediction of intentions. Similarly, should the intervention target only the beliefs that underlie the most important component, or should it target all the beliefs that are significantly correlated with the intention? To a certain extent, intervention research is still in its infancy, and there are a large number of critical questions about intervention and message design that are waiting to be addressed.

Once individuals have formed the intention to perform a behavior of interest, further issues arise as we try to help them act on their intentions. Most prominent, as noted previously, is the question of control. We must develop a better understanding of how to provide people with the skills and resources needed to perform the behavior and to overcome potential barriers. In addition, even when all the necessary skills and resources are in place, people often fail to carry out their intentions. More research is needed to further our understanding of the best ways to help people act on their intentions. For example, what are the factors that prevent procrastination or the failure of prospective memory?

☐ Final Comment

The three basic components of our theoretical framework—attitudes, perceived social norms, and perceived behavioral control—when considered simultaneously, are found to account for a considerable proportion of the nonrandom variance in intentions, and intentions and perceived control are found to explain a sizable proportion of the variance in behaviors. This is true across a wide variety of behaviors in many different behavioral domains. Within particular behavioral domains, investigators have tried to identify other kinds of predictor variables relevant to the domain in question. These efforts have typically focused on demographic characteristics, personality variables, attitudes toward objects, and other broad dispositions. We have viewed these variables as background factors. Being very general, these kinds of factors tend to have only a relatively small effect on any particular behavior. Nevertheless, on occasion, background factors are identified that correlate strongly with the behavior of interest. As we saw in Chapter 1, prejudicial attitudes toward an outgroup are usually a relatively poor predictor of any particular behavior toward members of the outgroup, but party identification tends to predict voting choice quite well. Yet even when a background factor is found to correlate significantly with a particular behavior, its inclusion in a regression equation—together with attitudes toward the behavior, perceived social norms, and perceived control—accounts for very little if any additional variance in intentions or behavior. This does not imply, of course, that general dispositions and other background factors are irrelevant. It simply means that even though these kinds of factors can provide important information about the origins of differences in behavior, their effects tend to be mediated by the more proximal predictors of intentions and behavior in our theoretical model. This also implies that our theory can help explain why a given background factor does or does not influence the particular behavior under investigation. Thus, if gender is found to be related to a given behavior, we should, according to our theoretical framework, be able to identify specific behavioral, normative, or control beliefs on which there are significant differences between men and women. The fact that the effects of background variables on intentions and behavior are almost always indirect (i.e., mediated) rather than direct also implies that if our goal is to bring about change in a particular behavior, our best strategy is not to try to influence broad background factors but, rather, to target the intervention at behavior-relevant beliefs, attitudes, and intentions. In the first chapter of this book we suggested that our reasoned action approach not only could help us predict and explain human social behavior but also could serve as a unifying framework to incorporate the great variety of constructs that have been used to predict and explain behavior in different domains. We hope that this book has illustrated how our approach can serve this unifying function and that investigators in different areas of research will be encouraged to move toward a common theoretical framework.

☐ Notes

1. At the same time, however, it must be noted that reliance on a single set of measurement procedures can limit the generalizability of our findings. Use of alternative approaches to the measurement of the theory's constructs should therefore not be discouraged.

REFERENCES

Aarts, H., & Dijksterhuis, A. (2000). Habits as knowledge structures: Automaticity in goal-directed behavior. *Journal of Personality and Social Psychology, 78*, 53–63.

Aarts, H., Dijksterhuis, A., & Midden, C. (1999). To plan or not to plan? Goal achievement of interrupting the performance of mundane behaviors. *European Journal of Social Psychology, 29*, 971–979.

Aarts, H., Verplanken, B., & van Knippenberg, A. (1998). Predicting behavior from actions in the past: Repeated decision making or a matter of habit? *Journal of Applied Social Psychology, 28*, 1355–1374.

Abelson, R. P., Aronson, E., McGuire, W. J., Newcomb, T. M., Rosenberg, M. J., & Tannenbaum, P. H. (1968). *Theories of cognitive consistency: a sourcebook.* Chicago: Rand-McNally.

Abraham, C., Henderson, M., & Der, G. (2004). Cognitive impact of a research-based school sex education programme. *Psychology & Health, 19*, 689–703.

Abraham, C., & Sheeran, P. (2003). Acting on intentions: The role of anticipated regret. *British Journal of Social Psychology, 42*, 495–511.

Airhihenbuwa, C. O., & Obregon, R. (2000). A critical assessment of theories/models used in health communication for HIV/AIDS. *Journal of Health Communication, 5*, 5–15.

Ajzen, I. (1985). From intentions to actions: A theory of planned behavior. In J. Kuhl & J. Beckman (Eds.), *Action-control: From cognition to behavior* (pp. 11–39). Heidelberg, Germany: Springer.

Ajzen, I. (1988). *Attitudes, personality, and behavior.* Chicago: Dorsey Press.

Ajzen, I. (1991). The theory of planned behavior. *Organizational Behavior and Human Decision Processes, 50*, 179–211.

Ajzen, I. (2002a). Perceived behavioral control, self-efficacy, locus of control, and the theory of planned behavior. *Journal of Applied Social Psychology, 32*, 665–683.

Ajzen, I. (2002b). Residual effects of past on later behavior: Habituation and reasoned action perspectives. *Personality and Social Psychology Review, 6*, 107–122.

Ajzen, I. (2005). *Attitudes, personality, and behavior* (2nd ed.). Maidenhead, England: Open University Press.

Ajzen, I., Brown, T. C., & Carvajal, F. (2004). Explaining the discrepancy between intentions and actions: The case of hypothetical bias in contingent valuation. *Personality and Social Psychology Bulletin, 30*, 1108–1121.

Ajzen, I., Czasch, C., & Flood, M. G. (in press). From intentions to behavior: Implementation intention, commitment, and conscientiousness. *Journal of Applied Social Psychology.*

Ajzen, I., Darroch, R. K., Fishbein, M., & Hornik, J. A. (1970). Looking backward revisited: A reply to Deutscher. *The American Sociologist, 5*, 267–273.

Ajzen, I., & Driver, B. L. (1991). Prediction of leisure participation from behavioral, normative, and control beliefs: An application of the theory of planned behavior. *Leisure Sciences, 13*, 185–204.

Ajzen, I., & Driver, B. L. (1992). Application of the theory of planned behavior to leisure choice. *Journal of Leisure Research, 24*, 207–224.

411

Ajzen, I., & Fishbein, M. (1969). The prediction of behavioral intentions in a choice situation. *Journal of Experimental Social Psychology, 5,* 400–416.

Ajzen, I., & Fishbein, M. (1970). The prediction of behavior from attitudinal and normative variables. *Journal of Experimental Social Psychology, 6,* 466–487.

Ajzen, I., & Fishbein, M. (1977). Attitude-behavior relations: A theoretical analysis and review of empirical research. *Psychological Bulletin, 84,* 888–918.

Ajzen, I., & Fishbein, M. (1980). *Understanding attitudes and predicting social behavior.* Englewood Cliffs, NJ: Prentice-Hall.

Ajzen, I., & Fishbein, M. (2000). Attitudes and the attitude-behavior relation: Reasoned and automatic processes. In W. Stroebe & M. Hewstone (Eds.), *European review of social psychology* (Vol. 11, pp. 1–33). Chichester, England: Wiley.

Ajzen, I., & Fishbein, M. (2004). Questions raised by a reasoned action approach: Comment on Ogden (2003). *Health Psychology, 23,* 431–443.

Ajzen, I., & Fishbein, M. (2005). The influence of attitudes on behavior. In D. Albarracín, B. T. Johnson, & M. P. Zanna (Eds.), *The handbook of attitudes* (pp. 173–221). Mahwah, NJ: Lawrence Erlbaum Associates.

Ajzen, I., & Fishbein, M. (2008). Scaling and testing multiplicative combinations in the expectancy-value model of attitudes. *Journal of Applied Social Psychology 33,* 2222–2247.

Ajzen, I., & Madden, T. J. (1986). Prediction of goal-directed behavior: Attitudes, intentions, and perceived behavioral control. *Journal of Experimental Social Psychology, 22,* 453–474.

Ajzen, I., & Sexton, J. (1999). Depth of processing, belief congruence, and attitude-behavior correspondence. In S. Chaiken & Y. Trope (Eds.), *Dual-process theories in social psychology* (pp. 117–138). New York: Guilford.

Ajzen, I., Timko, C., & White, J. B. (1982). Self-monitoring and the attitude-behavior relation. *Journal of Personality and Social Psychology, 42,* 426–435.

Albarracín, D., Fishbein, M., & Middlestadt, S. (1998). Generalizing behavioral findings across times, samples, and measures: A study of condom use. *Journal of Applied Social Psychology, 28,* 657–674.

Albarracín, D., Johnson, B. T., Fishbein, M., & Muellerleile, P. A. (2001). Theories of reasoned action and planned behavior as models of condom use: A meta-analysis. *Psychological Bulletin, 127,* 142–161.

Albarracín, D., & Wyer, R. S., Jr. (2000). The cognitive impact of past behavior: Influences on beliefs, attitudes, and future behavioral decisions. *Journal of Personality and Social Psychology, 79,* 5–22.

Allport, G. W. (1935). Attitudes. In C. Murchison (Ed.), *Handbook of social psychology* (pp. 798–844). Worcester, MA: Clark University Press.

Allport, G. W. (1954). *The nature of prejudice.* Oxford, England: Addison-Wesley.

Ananth, P., & Koopman, C. (2003). HIV/AIDS knowledge, beliefs, and behavior among women of childbearing age in India. *AIDS Education and Prevention, 15,* 529–546.

Anderson, A. S., Cox, D. N., McKellar, S., Reynolds, J., Lean, M. E. J., & Mela, D. J. (1998). Take five, a nutrition education intervention to increase fruit and vegetable intake: Impact on attitudes towards dietary change. *British Journal of Nutrition, 80,* 133–140.

Anderson, J. E., Anjani, C., & Mosher, W. D. (2005). *HIV testing in the United States, 2002. Advance data from vital and health statistics,* No.363. Centers for Disease Control and Prevention, U.S. Department of Health and Human Services.

Apanovitch, A. M., McCarthy, D., & Salovey, P. (2003). Using message framing to motivate HIV testing among low-income, ethnic minority women. *Health Psychology, 22,* 60–67.

Areni, C. S. (2003). The effects of structural and grammatical variables on persuasion: An elaboration likelihood model perspective. *Psychology & Marketing, 20,* 349–375.

Armitage, C. J., & Arden, M. A. (2002). Exploring discontinuity patterns in the transtheoretical model: An application of the theory of planned behavior. *British Journal of Health Psychology, 7,* 89–103.

Armitage, C. J., & Conner, M. (1999a). Distinguishing perceptions of control from self-efficacy: Predicting consumption of a low-fat diet using the theory of planned behavior. *Journal of Applied Social Psychology, 29,* 72–90.

Armitage, C. J., & Conner, M. (1999b). Predictive validity of the theory of planned behaviour: The role of questionnaire format and social desirability. *Journal of Community and Applied Social Psychology, 9,* 261–272.

Armitage, C. J., & Conner, M. (1999c). The theory of planned behaviour: Assessment of predictive validity and "perceived control." *British Journal of Social Psychology, 38,* 35–54.

Armitage, C. J., & Conner, M. (2000). Attitudinal ambivalence: A test of three key hypotheses. *Personality & Social Psychology Bulletin, 26,* 1421–1432.

Armitage, C. J., & Conner, M. (2001). Efficacy of the theory of planned behavior: A meta-analytic review. *British Journal of Social Psychology, 40,* 471–499.

Armitage, C. J., Conner, M., Loach, J., & Willetts, D. (1999). Different perceptions of control: Applying an extended theory of planned behavior to legal and illegal drug use. *Basic and Applied Social Psychology, 21,* 301–316.

Armitage, C. J., Conner, M., & Norman, P. (1999). Differential effects of mood on information processing: Evidence from the theories of reasoned action and planned behaviour. *European Journal of Social Psychology, 29,* 419–433.

Armitage, C. J., Norman, P., & Conner, M. (2002). Can the Theory of Planned Behaviour mediate the effects of age, gender and multidimensional health locus of control? *British Journal of Health Psychology, 7,* 299–316.

Armitage, C. J., Povey, R., & Arden, M. A. (2003). Evidence for discontinuity patterns across the stages of change: A role for attitudinal ambivalence. *Psychology & Health, 18,* 373–386.

Asendorpf, J. B., Banse, R., & Muecke, D. (2002). Double dissociation between implicit and explicit personality self-concept: The case of shy behavior. *Journal of Personality & Social Psychology, 83,* 380–393.

Babrow, A. S., Black, D. R., & Tiffany, S. T. (1990). Beliefs, attitudes, intentions, and a smoking-cessation program: A planned behavior analysis of communication campaign development. *Health Communication, 2,* 145–163.

Bagozzi, R. P. (1981). Attitudes, intentions, and behavior: A test of some key hypotheses. *Journal of Personality and Social Psychology, 41,* 607–627.

Bagozzi, R. P. (1984). Expectancy-value attitude models: An analysis of critical measurement issues. *International Journal of Research in Marketing, 1,* 295–310.

Bagozzi, R. P., Lee, K.-H., & Van Loo, M. F. (2001). Decisions to donate bone marrow: The role of attitudes and subjective norms across cultures. *Psychology & Health, 16,* 29–56.

Bagozzi, R. P., & Warshaw, P. R. (1990). Trying to consume. *Journal of Consumer Research, 17,* 127–140.

Baltes, M. M., & Baltes, P. B. (Eds.). (1986). *The psychology of control and aging.* Hillsdale, NJ: Lawrence Erlbaum Associates.

Bamberg, S. (2006). Is a residential relocation a good opportunity to change people's travel behavior?: Results from a theory-driven intervention study. *Environment and Behavior, 38,* 820–840.

Bamberg, S., Ajzen, I., & Schmidt, P. (2003). Choice of travel mode in the theory of planned behavior: The roles of past behavior, habit, and reasoned action. *Basic and Applied Social Psychology, 25,* 175–188.

Bamberg, S., & Schmidt, P. (1993). Choosing between means of transportation: An application of the theory of planned behavior. *Zeitschrift für Sozialpsychologie, 24,* 25–37.

Bandura, A. (1977). Self-efficacy: Toward a unifying theory of behavioral change. *Psychological Review, 84,* 191–215.

Bandura, A. (1986). *Social foundations of thought and action: A social cognitive theory.* Englewood Cliffs, NJ: Prentice-Hall, Inc.

Bandura, A. (1989). Human agency in social cognitive theory. *American Psychologist, 44,* 1175–1184.

Bandura, A. (1991). Social cognitive theory of self-regulation. *Organizational Behavior and Human Decision Processes, 50,* 248–287.

Bandura, A. (1995). Exercise of personal and collective efficacy in changing societies. In A. Bandura (Ed.), *Self-efficacy in changing societies* (pp. 1–45). Cambridge, England: Cambridge University Press.

Bandura, A. (1997). *Self-efficacy: The exercise of control.* New York: Freeman.

Bandura, A. (1998). Health promotion from the perspective of social cognitive theory. *Psychology and Health, 13,* 623–649.

Bandura, A., & Barab, P. G. (1973). Processes governing disinhibitory effects through symbolic modeling. *Journal of Abnormal Psychology, 82,* 1–9.

Banks, S. M., Salovey, P., Greener, S., & Rothman, A. J. (1995). The effects of message framing on mammography utilization. *Health Psychology, 14,* 178–184.

Bargh, J. A. (1996). Automaticity in social psychology. In E. T. Higgins & A. W. Kruglanski (Eds.), *Social psychology: Handbook of basic principles.* (pp. 169–183). New York: Guilford Press.

Bargh, J. A., Chaiken, S., Govender, R., & Pratto, F. (1992). The generality of the automatic attitude activation effect. *Journal of Personality and Social Psychology, 62,* 893–912.

Bargh, J. A., Chaiken, S., Raymond, P., & Hymes, C. (1996). The automatic evaluation effect: Unconditional automatic attitude activation with a pronunciation task. *Journal of Experimental Social Psychology, 32,* 104–128.

Bassili, J. N. (1995). Response latency and the accessibility of voting intentions: What contributes to accessibility and how it affects vote choice. *Personality and Social Psychology Bulletin, 21,* 686–695.

Baumeister, R. F., Campbell, J. D., Krueger, J. I., & Vohs, K. D. (2003). Does high self-esteem cause better performance, interpersonal success, happiness, or healthier lifestyles? *Psychological Science in the Public Interest, 4,* 1–44.

Beale, D. A., & Manstead, A. S. R. (1991). Predicting mothers' intentions to limit frequency of infants' sugar intake: Testing the theory of planned behavior. *Journal of Applied Social Psychology, 21,* 409–431.

Beck, L., & Ajzen, I. (1991). Predicting dishonest actions using the theory of planned behavior. *Journal of Research in Personality, 25,* 285–301.

Bentler, P. M., & Speckart, G. (1979). Models of attitude-behavior relations. *Psychological Review, 86,* 452–464.

Berger, I. E., & Mitchell, A. A. (1989). The effect of advertising on attitude accessibility, attitude confidence, and the attitude-behavior relationship. *Journal of Consumer Research, 16,* 269–279.

Betz, N. E., Hammond, M. S., & Multon, K. D. (2005). Reliability and validity of five-level response continua for the Career Decision Self-Efficacy Scale. *Journal of Career Assessment, 13,* 131–149.

Biddle, B. J. (1979). *Role theory: Expectations, identities, and behavior.* New York: Academic Press.

Biddle, B. J., & Thomas, E. J. (1966). *Role theory: Concepts and research.* New York: John Wiley & Sons.

Bird, C. (1940). *Social psychology.* Englewood Cliffs, NJ: Prentice-Hall.

Birnbaum, D., & Somers, M. J. (1993). Fitting job performance into turnover model: An examination of the form of the job performance-turnover relationship and a path model. *Journal of Management, 19,* 1–11.

Blair, I. V. (2001). Implicit stereotypes and prejudice. In G. B. Moskowitz (Ed.), *Cognitive social psychology: The Princeton Symposium on the Legacy and Future of Social Cognition* (pp. 359–374). Mahwah, NJ: Erlbaum.

Blanton, H., Jaccard, J., Gonzales, P. M., & Christie, C. (2006). Decoding the implicit association test: Implications for criterion prediction. *Journal of Experimental Social Psychology, 42,* 192–212.

Bleakley, A., Hennessy, M., Fishbein, M. & Jordan, A. (2009). How sources of sexual information relate to adolescents' beliefs about sex. *American Journal of Health Behavior, 33*(1), 37-48.

Bleakley, A., Hennessy, M., Fishbein, M. & Jordan, A. (In press). 'It works both ways: The relationship between media sexual content and adolescent sexual behavior. *Media Psychology*

Blumer, H. (1969). *Symbolic interactionism: Perspective and method.* Englewood Cliffs, NJ: Prentice-Hall.

Bosson, J. K., Swann, W. B. J., & Pennebaker, J. W. (2000). Stalking the perfect measure of implicit self-esteem: The blind men and the elephant revisited? *Journal of Personality and Social Psychology, 79,* 631–643.

Boudon, R. (2003). Beyond rational choice theory. *Annual Review of Sociology, 29,* 1–21.

Bowen, A. M. (1996). Predicting increased condom use with main partners: Potential approaches to intervention. *Drugs & Society, 9,* 57–74.

Boyce, T. E., & Geller, E. S. (2000). A community-wide intervention to improve pedestrian safety: Guidelines for institutionalizing large-scale behavior change. *Environment and Behavior, 32,* 502–520.

Brandimante, M., Einstein, G. O., & McDaniel, M. A. (Eds.). (1996). *Prospective memory: Theory and applications.* Mahwah, NJ: Lawrence Erlbaum Associates.

Brandt, W. J. (1970). *The rhetoric of argumentation.* New York: Bobbs-Merrill.

Braver, S. (1996). Social contracts and the provision of public goods. In D. Schroeder (Ed.), *Social dilemmas: Perspectives on individuals and groups* (pp. 69–86). Westport, CT: Praeger.

Brigham, J. C. (1993). College students' racial attitudes. *Journal of Applied Social Psychology, 23,* 1933–1967.

Britt, T. W., & Garrity, M. J. (2006). Attributions and personality as predictors of the road rage response. *British Journal of Social Psychology, 45*, 127–147.

Brubaker, R. G., & Fowler, C. (1990). Encouraging college males to perform testicular self-examination: Evaluation of a persuasive message based on the revised theory of reasoned action. *Journal of Applied Social Psychology, 20*, 1411–1422.

Budd, R. J. (1986). Predicting cigarette use: The need to incorporate measures of salience in the theory of reasoned action. *Journal of Applied Social Psychology, 16*, 663–685.

Budd, R. J. (1987). Response bias and the theory of reasoned action. *Social Cognition, 5*, 95–107.

Budd, R. J., North, D., & Spencer, C. (1984). Understanding seat-belt use: A test of Bentler and Speckart's extension of the "theory of reasoned action." *European Journal of Social Psychology, 14*, 69–78.

Burger, J. M. (1989). Negative reactions to increases in perceived personal control. *Journal of Personality & Social Psychology, 56*, 246–256.

Bushway, S. D., & Piehl, A. M. (2001). Judging judicial discretion: Legal factors and racial discrimination in sentencing. *Law & Society Review, 35*, 733–764.

Campbell, A., Converse, P. E., Miller, W. E., & Stokes, D. E. (1960). *The American voter*. New York: Wiley.

Campbell, A., Gurin, G., & Miller, W. E. (1954). *The voter decides*. Oxford, England: Row, Peterson, and Co.

Campbell, D. T. (1963). Social attitudes and other acquired behavioral dispositions. In S. Koch (Ed.), *Psychology: A study of a science* (Vol. 6, pp. 94–172). New York: McGraw-Hill.

Cappella, J. N. (2007). The role of discrete emotions in the theory of reasoned action and its successors: Quitting smoking in young adults. In I. Ajzen, R. Hornik, & D. Albarracin (Eds.), *Prediction and change of behavior* (pp. 43–51). Mahwah, NJ: Lawrence Erlbaum.

Carlo, G., Okun, M. A., Knight, G. P., & de Guzman, M. R. T. (2005). The interplay of traits and motives on volunteering: Agreeableness, extraversion and prosocial value motivation. *Personality and Individual Differences, 38*, 1293–1305.

Carlson, A. R. (1969). *The relationships between a behavioral intention, attitude toward the behavior and normative beliefs about the behavior*. Unpublished doctoral dissertation, University of Illinois, Chicago.

Carlson, E. R. (1956). Attitude change through modification of attitude structure. *Journal of Abnormal & Social Psychology, 52*, 256–261.

Carlson, K. A., & Tanner, R. J. (2006). *From ideal to real: How prior contemplation of the ideal can undo self-favoritism*. Unpublished manuscript, Faqua School of Business, Duke University, Raleigh, NC.

Carol, S. J. (2006). Voting choices: Meet you at the gender gap. In Carol, S. J. & Fox, R. L. (Eds.), *Gender and elections: Shaping the future of American politics* (pp. 74–96). New York: Cambridge University Press.

Casey, T., & Christ, K. (2005). Social capital and economic performance in the American states. *Social Science Quarterly, 86*, 826–845.

Catania, J. A., Kegeles, S. M., & Coates, T. J. (1990). Towards an understanding of risk behavior: An AIDS risk reduction model (ARRM). *Health Education Quarterly, 17*, 53–72.

Cates, W. Jr., & Holmes, K.K. (1996). Re: Condom efficacy against gonorrhea and nongonococcol urethritis. *American Journal of Epidemiology, 143*, 843–844.

CDC AIDS Community Demonstration Projects Research Group. (1999). Community-level HIV intervention in five cities: Final outcome data from the CDC AIDS Community Demonstration Projects. *American Journal of Public Health, 89*, 336–345.

Centers for Disease Control and Prevention (2000). *CDC surveillance summaries, September 22, 2000.* MMWR 2000; 49 (No. SS-9). U.S. Department of Health and Human Services.

Centers for Disease Control and Prevention (2004). *Behavioral risk factor surveillance system: BRFSS annual survey data 2004.* U.S. Department of Health and Human Services.

Cervone, D. (1989). Effects of envisioning future activities on self-efficacy judgments and motivation: An availability heuristic interpretation. *Cognitive Therapy & Research, 13*, 247–261.

Chaiken, S. (1980). Heuristic versus systematic information processing and the use of source versus message cues in persuasion. *Journal of Personality and Social Psychology, 39*, 752–766.

Chaiken, S., & Trope, Y. (Eds.). (1999). *Dual-process theories in social psychology.* New York: Guilford Press.

Chaiken, S., & Yates, S. (1985). Affective-cognitive consistency and thought-induced attitude polarization. *Journal of Personality & Social Psychology, 49*, 1470–1481.

Charng, H.-W., Piliavin, J. A., & Callero, P. L. (1988). Role identity and reasoned action in the prediction of repeated behavior. *Social Psychology Quarterly, 51*, 303–317.

Chen, K. (1992). *Political alienation and voting turnout in the United States, 1960–1968.* San Francisco, CA: Mellen University Research Press.

Chen, M., & Bargh, J. A. (1999). Consequences of automatic evaluation: Immediate behavioral predispositions to approach or avoid the stimulus. *Personality and Social Psychology Bulletin, 25*, 215–224.

Cheung, S.-F., & Chan, D. K.-S. (2000). The role of perceived behavioral control in predicting human behavior: A meta-analytic review of studies on the theory of planned behavior. Unpublished manuscript, Chinese University of Hong Kong.

Cheung, S.-F., Chan, D. K.-S., & Wong, Z. S.-Y. (1999). Reexamining the theory of planned behavior in understanding wastepaper recycling. *Environment and Behavior, 31*, 587.

Chiou, J.-S., Huang, C.-Y., & Chuang, M.-C. (2005). Antecedents of Taiwanese adolescents' purchase intention toward the merchandise of a celebrity: The moderating effect of celebrity adoration. *Journal of Social Psychology, 145*, 317–332.

Christian, J., & Armitage, C. J. (2002). Attitudes and intentions of homeless people towards service provision in South Wales. *British Journal of Social Psychology, 41*, 219–232.

Christie, D. H., & Etter, J.-F. o. (2005). Validation of English-language versions of three scales measuring attitudes towards smoking, smoking-related self-efficacy and the use of smoking cessation strategies. *Addictive Behaviors, 30*, 981–988.

Cialdini, R. B. (2001). *Influence: Science and practice* (4th ed.). Boston, MA: Allyn & Bacon.

Cialdini, R. B., Reno, R. R., & Kallgren, C. A. (1990). A focus theory of normative conduct: Recycling the concept of norms to reduce littering in public places. *Journal of Personality and Social Psychology, 58,* 1015–1026.

Clark, M. S., & Waddell, B. A. (1983). Effects of moods on thoughts about helping, attraction and information acquisition. *Social Psychology Quarterly, 46,* 31–35.

Clore, G. L., & Schnall, S. (2005). The influence of affect on attitude. In D. Albarracín, B. T. Johnson, & M. P. Zanna (Eds.), *Handbook of attitudes and attitude change: Basic principles* (pp. 437–489). Mahwah, NJ: Lawrence Erlbaum Associates.

Cohen, J., & Cohen, P. (1975). *Applied multiple regression/correlation analysis for the behavioral sciences.* Mahwah, NJ: Lawrence Erlbaum.

Conner, M., & Abraham, C. (2001). Conscientiousness and the theory of planned behavior: Toward a more complete model of the antecedents of intentious behavior. *Personality & Social Psychology Bulletin, 27,* 1547–1561.

Conner, M., & Armitage, C. J. (1998). Extending the theory of planned behavior: A review and avenues for further research. *Journal of Applied Social Psychology, 28,* 1429–1464.

Conner, M., Graham, S., & Moore, B. (1999). Alcohol and intentions to use condoms: Applying the theory of planned behaviour. *Psychology & Health, 14,* 795–812.

Conner, M., & McMillan, B. (1999). Interaction effects in the theory of planned behavior: Studying cannabis use. *British Journal of Social Psychology, 38,* 195–222.

Conner, M., Norman, P., & Bell, R. (2002). The theory of planned behavior and healthy eating. *Health Psychology, 21,* 194–201.

Conner, M., Sandberg, T., McMillan, B., & Higgins, A. (2006). Role of anticipated regret, intentions and intention stability in adolescent smoking initiation. *British Journal of Health Psychology, 11,* 85–101.

Conner, M., Sheeran, P., Norman, P., & Armitage, C. J. (2000). Temporal stability as a moderator of relationships in the Theory of Planned Behaviour. *British Journal of Social Psychology, 39,* 469–493.

Conner, M., Smith, N., & McMillan, B. (2003). Examining normative pressure in the theory of planned behaviour: Impact of gender and passengers on intentions to break the speed limit. *Current Psychology: Developmental, Learning, Personality, Social, 22,* 252–263.

Conner, M., & Sparks, P. (2005). Theory of planned behaviour and health behaviour. In *Predicting health behaviour: Research and practice with social cognition models* (2nd ed., pp. 170–222). Buckingham, England: Open University Press.

Conner, M., Warren, R., Close, S., & Sparks, P. (1999). Alcohol consumption and the theory of planned behavior: An examination of the cognitive mediation of past behavior. *Journal of Applied Social Psychology, 29,* 1676–1704.

Cooke, R., & Sheeran, P. (2004). Moderation of cognition-intention and cognition-behaviour relations: A meta-analysis of properties of variables from the theory of planned behaviour. *British Journal of Social Psychology, 43,* 159–186.

Cooper, C. P., Burgoon, M., & Roter, D. L. (2001). An expectancy-value analysis of viewer interest in television prevention news stories. *Health Communication, 13,* 227–240.

Corby, N. H., Jamner, M. S., & Wolitski, R. J. (1996). Using the Theory of Planned Behavior to predict intention to use condoms among male and female injecting drug users. *Journal of Applied Social Psychology, 26,* 52–75.

Corby, N. H., & Wolitski, R. J. (Eds.). (1997). *Community HIV prevention: The Long Beach AIDS Community Demonstration Project.* Long Beach: California State University Press.

Costa, P. T., Jr., & McCrae, R. R. (1985). *The NEO Personality Inventory manual.* Odessa, FL: Psychological Assessment Resources.

Coulter, K. S., & Punj, G. N. (2004). The Effects of Cognitive Resource Requirements, Availability, and Argument Quality on Brand Attitudes: A Melding of elaboration likelihood and cognitive resource matching theories. *Journal of Advertising, 33,* 53–64.

Courneya, K. S. (1994). Predicting repeated behavior from intention: The issue of scale correspondence. *Journal of Applied Social Psychology, 24,* 580–594.

Courneya, K. S. (1995). Understanding readiness for regular physical activity in older individuals: An application of the theory of planned behavior. *Health Psychology, 14,* 80–87.

Courneya, K. S., Bobick, T. M., & Schinke, R. J. (1999). Does the theory of planned behavior mediate the relation between personality and exercise behavior? *Basic and Applied Social Psychology, 21,* 317–324.

Courneya, K. S., Friedenreich, C. M., Arthur, K., & Bobick, T. M. (1999). Understanding exercise motivation in colorectal cancer patients: A prospective study using the theory of planned behavior. *Rehabilitation Psychology, 44,* 68–84.

Courneya, K. S., Friedenreich, C. M., Quinney, H. A., Fields, A. L. A., Jones, L. W., & Fairey, A. S. (2004). Predictors of adherence and contamination in a randomized trial of exercise in colorectal cancer survivors. *Psycho-Oncology, 13,* 857–866.

Courneya, K. S., & McAuley, E. (1993). Predicting physical activity from intention: Conceptual and methodological issues. *Journal of Sport and Exercise Psychology, 15,* 50–62.

Courneya, K. S., & McAuley, E. (1994). Factors affecting the intention-physical activity relationship: Intention versus expectation and scale correspondence. *Research Quarterly for Exercise and Sport, 65,* 280–285.

Courneya, K. S., & McAuley, E. (1995). Cognitive mediators of the social influence-exercise adherence relationship: A test of the theory of planned behavior. *Journal of Behavioral Medicine, 18,* 499–515.

Crites, S. L., Fabrigar, L. R., & Petty, R. E. (1994). Measuring the affective and cognitive properties of attitudes: Conceptual and methodological issues. *Personality & Social Psychology Bulletin, 20,* 619–634.

Crosby, F., Bromley, S., & Saxe, L. (1980). Recent unobtrusive studies of Black and White discrimination and prejudice: A literature review. *Psychological Bulletin, 87,* 546–563.

Cunningham, W. A., Preacher, K. J., & Banaji, M. R. (2001). Implicit attitude measures: Consistency, stability, and convergent validity. *Psychological Science, 121,* 163–170.

Czopp, A. M., Monteith, M. J., Zimmerman, R. S., & Lynam, D. R. (2004). Implicit attitudes as potential protection from risky sex: Predicting condom use with the IAT. *Basic and Applied Social Psychology, 26,* 227–236.

Daigle, J. J., Hrubes, D., & Ajzen, I. (2002). A comparative study of beliefs, attitudes, and values among hunters, wildlife viewers, and other outdoor recreationists. *Human Dimensions of Wildlife, 7,* 1–19.

Daniels, L. A. (2001). *State of Black America 2000.* New York: National Urban League.

Davidson, A. R., & Morrison, D. M. (1983). Predicting contraceptive behavior from attitudes: A comparison of within- versus across-subjects procedures. *Journal of Personality and Social Psychology, 45,* 997–1009.

Davis, L. E., Ajzen, I., Saunders, J., & Williams, T. (2002). The decision of African American students to complete high school: An application of the theory of planned behavior. *Journal of Educational Psychology, 94,* 810–819.

Dawes, R. M. (1972). *Fundamentals of attitude measurement.* New York: Wiley.

Dawes, R. M. (1994). *House of cards: Psychology and psychotherapy built on myth.* New York: Free Press.

De Fleur, M. L., & Westie, F. R. (1958). Verbal attitudes and overt acts: An experiment on the salience of attitudes. *American Sociological Review, 23,* 667–673.

De Vries, H., & Backbier, E. (1994). Self-efficacy as an important determinant of quitting among pregnant women who smoke: The ø-pattern. *Preventive Medicine, 23,* 167–174.

Devine, P. G. (1989). Stereotypes and prejudice: Their automatic and controlled components. *Journal of Personality & Social Psychology, 56,* 5–18.

Devine, P. G., & Monteith, M. J. (1999). Automaticity and control in stereotyping. In S. Chaiken & Y. Trope (Eds.), *Dual-process theories in social psychology* (pp. 339–360). New York: Guilford Press.

Devine, P. G., Monteith, M. J., Zuwerink, J. R., & Elliot, A. J. (1991). Prejudice with and without compunction. *Journal of Personality & Social Psychology, 60,* 817–830.

DiClemente, R. J. (1989). Prevention of human immunodeficiency virus infection among adolescents: The interplay of health education and public policy in the development and implementation of school-based AIDS education programs. *AIDS Education and Prevention, 1,* 70–78.

Doll, J., & Ajzen, I. (1992). Accessibility and stability of predictors in the theory of planned behavior. *Journal of Personality and Social Psychology, 63,* 754–765.

Doll, J., & Orth, B. (1993). The Fishbein and Ajzen theory of reasoned action applied to contraceptive behavior: Model variants and meaningfulness. *Journal of Applied Social Psychology, 23,* 395–415.

Dovidio, J. F. (2001). On the nature of contemporary prejudice: The third wave. *Journal of Social Issues, 57,* 829–849.

Dovidio, J. F., Brigham, J. C., Johnson, B. T., & Gaertner, S. L. (1996). Stereotyping, prejudice, and discrimination: Another look. In N. Macrae, C. Stangor, & M. Hewstone (Eds.), *Stereotypes and stereotyping* (pp. 276–319). New York: Guilford.

Dovidio, J. F., Evans, N., & Tyler, R. B. (1986). Racial stereotypes: The contents of their cognitive representations. *Journal of Experimental Social Psychology, 22,* 22–37.

Dovidio, J. F., & Gaertner, S. L. (2000). Aversive racism and selection decisions: 1989 and 1999. *Psychological Science, 11,* 315–319.

Dovidio, J. F., Kawakami, K., Johnson, C., Johnson, B., & Howard, A. (1997). On the nature of prejudice: Automatic and controlled processes. *Journal of Experimental Social Psychology, 33,* 510–540.

Downs, D. S., & Hausenblas, H. A. (2005). The theories of reasoned action and planned behavior applied to exercise: A meta-analytic update. *Journal of Physical Activity and Health, 2*, 76–97.

Dowrick, P. W. (1999). A review of self modeling and related interventions. *Applied & Preventive Psychology, 8*, 23–39.

Drossaert, C. H. C., Boer, H., & Seydel, E. R. (2003). Prospective study on the determinants of repeat attendance and attendance patterns in breast cancer screening using the theory of planned behaviour. *Psychology and Health, 18*, 551–564.

Duckett, L., Henly, S., Avery, M., Potter, S., Hills-Bonczyk, S., Hulden, R., et al. (1998). A theory of planned behavior-based structural model for breast-feeding. *Nursing Research, 47*, 325–336.

Dulany, D. E. (1968). Awareness, rules, and propositional control: A confrontation with S-R behavior theory. In D. Hornton & T. Dixon (Eds.), *Verbal behavior and S-R behavior theory* (pp. 340–387). Englewood Cliffs, NJ: Prentice-Hall.

Dweck, C. S., & Leggett, E. L. (1988). A social-cognitive approach to motivation and personality. *Psychological Review, 95*, 256–273.

Dunton, B. C., & Fazio, R. H. (1997). An individual difference measure of motivation to control prejudiced reactions. *Personality & Social Psychology Bulletin, 23*, 316-326.

Eagly, A. H. (1998). Attitudes and the processing of attitude-relevant information. In J. G. Adair & D. Belanger (Eds.), *Advances in psychological science, Vol. 1: Social, personal, and cultural aspects* (pp. 185–201). Hove, England: Psychology Press/Erlbaum (UK) Taylor & Francis.

Eagly, A. H., & Chaiken, S. (1993). *The psychology of attitudes*. Fort Worth, TX: Harcourt Brace.

Eagly, A. H., & Chaiken, S. (1998). Attitude structure and function. In D. T. Gilbert, S. T. Fiske, & G. Lindzey (Eds.), *The handbook of social psychology* (4th ed., Vol. 1, pp. 269–322). New York: McGraw-Hill.

Eagly, A. H., & Chaiken, S. (2005). Attitude research in the 21st century: The current state of knowledge. In D. Albarracín, B. T. Johnson & M. P. Zanna (Eds.), *Handbook of attitudes and attitude change: Basic principles* (pp. 743-767). Mahwah, NJ: Lawrence Erlbaum Associates.

Eagly, A. H., & Himmerlfarb, S. (1974). Current trends in attitude theory and research. In S. Himmelfarb & A. H. Eagly (Eds.), *Readings in attitude change* (pp. 594–610). New York: Wiley.

Eaton, L., Flisher, A. J., & Aaro, L. E. (2003). Unsafe sexual behaviour in South African youth. *Social Science & Medicine, 56*, 149–165.

Egloff, B., & Schmukle, S. C. (2002). Predictive validity of an implicit association test for assessing anxiety. *Journal of Personality and Social Psychology, 83*, 1441–1455.

Ellen, P. S., & Madden, T. J. (1990). The impact of response format on relations among intentions, attitudes, and social norms. *Marketing Letters, 1*, 161–170.

Elliott, M. A., Armitage, C. J., & Baughan, C. J. (2003). Drivers' compliance with speed limits: An application of the theory of planned behavior. *Journal of Applied Psychology, 88*, 964–972.

Ellis, J. (1996). Prospective memory or the realization of delayed intentions: A conceptual framework for research. In M. Brandimante, G. O. Einstein, & M. A. McDaniel (Eds.), *Prospective memory: Theory and applications* (pp. 1–22). Mahwah, NJ: Lawrence Erlbaum Associates.

Eng, J. J., & Martin Ginis, K. A. (2007). Using the theory of planned behavior to predict leisure time physical activity among people with chronic kidney disease. *Rehabilitation Psychology, 52,* 435–442.

Epel, E. S., Bandura, A., & Zimbardo, P. G. (1999). Escaping homelessness: The influences of self-efficacy and time perspective on coping with homelessness. *Journal of Applied Social Psychology, 29,* 575–596.

Epstein, S. (1979). The stability of behavior: I. On predicting most of the people much of the time. *Journal of Personality and Social Psychology, 37,* 1097–1126.

Estabrooks, P., & Carron, A. V. (1998). The conceptualization and effect of control beliefs on exercise attendance in the elderly. *Journal of Aging and Health, 10,* 441–457.

Evans, M. G. (1991). The problem of analyzing multiplicative composites: Interactions revisited. *American Psychologist, 46,* 6–15.

Fabrigar, L. R., MacDonald, T. K., & Wegener, D. T. (2005). The structure of attitudes. In D. Albarracín, B. T. Johnson, & M. P. Zanna (Eds.), *The handbook of attitudes* (pp. 79–124). Mahwah, NJ: Lawrence Erlbaum Associates.

Fazio, R. H. (1986). How do attitudes guide behavior? In R. M. H. Sorrentino & Edward Tory (Eds.), *Handbook of motivation and cognition: Foundations of social behavior* (pp. 204–243). New York: Guilford Press.

Fazio, R. H. (1990a). Multiple processes by which attitudes guide behavior: The MODE model as an integrative framework. In M. P. Zanna (Ed.), *Advances in experimental social psychology* (Vol. 23, pp. 75–109). San Diego, CA: Academic Press.

Fazio, R. H. (1990b). A practical guide to the use of response latency in social psychological research. In C. Hendrick & M. S. Clark (Eds.), *Research methods in personality and social psychology. Review of personality and social psychology, Vol. 11* (pp. 74–97). Newbury Park, CA: Sage.

Fazio, R. H. (1993). Variability in the likelihood of automatic attitude activation: Data reanalysis and commentary on Bargh, Chaiken, Govender, and Pratto (1992). *Journal of Personality & Social Psychology, 64,* 753–758.

Fazio, R. H. (1995). Attitudes as object-evaluation associations: Determinants, consequences, and correlates of attitude accessibility. In R. E. Petty & J. A. Krosnick (Eds.), *Attitude strength: Antecedents and consequences* (pp. 247–282). Mahwah, NJ: Erlbaum.

Fazio, R. H. (2001). On the automatic activation of associated evaluations: An overview. *Cognition & Emotion. Special Issue: Automatic Affective Processing, 15,* 115–141.

Fazio, R. H., Chen, J., McDonel, E. C., & Sherman, S. J. (1982). Attitude accessibility, attitude-behavior consistency, and the strength of the object-evaluation association. *Journal of Experimental Social Psychology, 18,* 339–357.

Fazio, R. H., & Dunton, B. C. (1997). Categorization by race: The impact of automatic and controlled components of racial prejudice. *Journal of Experimental Social Psychology, 33,* 451–470.

Fazio, R. H., Jackson, J. R., Dunton, B. C., & Williams, C. J. (1995). Variability in automatic activation as an unobtrusive measure of racial attitudes: A bona fide pipeline? *Journal of Personality and Social Psychology, 69,* 1013–1027.

Fazio, R. H., & Olson, M. A. (2003). Implicit measures in social cognition research: Their meaning and uses. *Annual Review of Psychology, 54,* 297–327.

Fazio, R. H., Powell, M. C., & Williams, C. J. (1989). The role of attitude accessibility in the attitude-to-behavior process. *Journal of Consumer Research, 16,* 280–288.

Fazio, R. H., Sanbonmatsu, D. M., Powell, M. C., & Kardes, F. R. (1986). On the automatic activation of attitudes. *Journal of Personality & Social Psychology, 50,* 229–238.

Fazio, R. H., & Towles-Schwen, T. (1999). The MODE model of attitude-behavior processes. In S. Chaiken & Y. Trope (Eds.), *Dual-process theories in social psychology* (pp. 97–116). New York: Guilford.

Fazio, R. H., & Williams, C. J. (1986). Attitude accessibility as a moderator of the attitude-perception and attitude-behavior relations: An investigation of the 1984 presidential election. *Journal of Personality and Social Psychology, 51,* 505–514.

Fazio, R. H., & Zanna, M. P. (1981). Direct experience and attitude-behavior consistency. In L. Berkowitz (Ed.), *Advances in experimental social psychology* (Vol. 14, pp. 161–202). New York: Academic Press.

Feather, N. T. (1959). Subjective probability and decision under uncertainty. *Psychological Review, 66,* 150–164.

Feather, N. T. (Ed.). (1982). *Expectations and actions: Expectancy–value models in psychology.* Hillsdale, NJ: Erlbaum.

Fekadu, Z., & Kraft, P. (2002). Expanding the theory of planned behaviour: The role of social norms and group identification. *Journal of Health Psychology, 7,* 33–43.

Feldman, J. M., & Lynch, J. G. (1988). Self-generated validity and other effects of measurement on belief, attitude, intention, and behavior. *Journal of Applied Psychology, 73,* 421–435.

Ferguson, E., & Bibby, P. A. (2002). Predicting future blood donor returns: Past behavior, intentions, and observer effects. *Health Psychology, 21,* 513–518.

Finlay, K. A., Trafimow, D., & Jones, D. (1997). Predicting health behaviors from attitudes and subjective norms: Between-subjects and within-subjects analyses. *Journal of Applied Social Psychology, 27,* 2015–2031.

Finlay, K. A., Trafimow, D., & Moroi, E. (1999). The importance of subjective norms on intentions to perform health behaviors. *Journal of Applied Social Psychology, 29,* 2381–2393.

Fishbein, M. (1963). An investigation of the relationships between beliefs about an object and the attitude toward that object. *Human Relations, 16,* 233–240.

Fishbein, M. (1967a). Attitude and the prediction of behavior. In M. Fishbein (Ed.), *Readings in attitude theory and measurement* (pp. 477–492). New York: Wiley.

Fishbein, M. (1967b). A consideration of beliefs and their role in attitude measurement. In M. Fishbein (Ed.), *Readings in attitude theory and measurement* (pp. 257–266). New York: Wiley.

Fishbein, M. (1980). A theory of reasoned action: Some applications and implications. In H. E. Howe & M. M. Page (Eds.), *1979 Nebraska symposium of motivation* (Vol. 65–116). Lincoln: University of Nebraska Press.

Fishbein, M. (2000). The role of theory in HIV prevention. *AIDS Care, 12*, 273–278.

Fishbein, M. (2003). Understanding of the role of perceived risk in HIV prevention research. In D. Romer (Ed.), *Reducing adolescent risk: Toward an integrated approach* (pp. 49–55). Thousand Oaks, CA: Sage Publications.

Fishbein, M., & Ajzen, I. (1974). Attitudes towards objects as predictors of single and multiple behavioral criteria. *Psychological Review, 81*, 59–74.

Fishbein, M., & Ajzen, I. (1975). *Belief, attitude, intention, and behavior: An introduction to theory and research.* Reading, MA: Addison-Wesley.

Fishbein, M., & Ajzen, I. (1981). Acceptance, yielding, and impact: Cognitive processes in persuasion. In R. E. Petty, T. M. Ostrom, & T. C. Brock (Eds.), *Cognitive responses in persuasion* (pp. 339–359). Hillsdale, NJ: Erlbaum.

Fishbein, M., & Ajzen, I. (2005). Theory-based behavior change interventions: Comments on Hobbis and Sutton. *Journal of Health Psychology, 10*, 27–31.

Fishbein, M., Ajzen, I., & Hinkle, R. (1980). Predicting and understanding voting in American elections: Effects of external variables. In I. Ajzen & M. Fishbein (Eds.), *Understanding attitudes and predicting social behavior* (pp. 173–195). Englewood Cliffs, NJ: Prentice Hall.

Fishbein, M., Bleakley, A., Hennessy, M., & Jordan, A. (in preparation). *Predicting adolescent sexual behavior: Applying the reasoned action approach.*

Fishbein, M., Guenther-Grey, C., Johnson, W., Wolitski, R. J., McAlister, A., Rietmeijer, C. A., et al. (1997). Using a theory-based community intervention to reduce AIDS risk behaviors: The CDC's AIDS community demonstration projects. In M. E. Goldberg, M. Fishbein, & S. Middlestadt (Eds.), *Social marketing: Theoretical and practical perspectives.* (pp. 123–146). Mahwah, NJ: Lawrence Erlbaum Associates.

Fishbein, M., Hennessy, M., Kamb, M., Bolan, G. A., Hoxworth, T., Iatesta, M., et al. (2001). Using intervention theory to model factors influencing behavior change: Project RESPECT. *Evaluation & the Health Professions, 24*, 363–384.

Fishbein, M., & Jarvis, B. (2000). Failure to find a behavioral surrogate for STD incidence—what does it really mean? *Sexually Transmitted Diseases, 27*, 452–455.

Fishbein, M., Triandis, H. C., Kanfer, F. H., Becker, M., Middlestadt, S. E., & Eichler, A. (2001). Factors influencing behavior and behavior change. In A. Baum & T. A. Revenson (Eds.), *Handbook of health psychology.* Mahwah, NJ: Lawrence Erlbaum Associates.

Fisher, J. D., & Fisher, W. A. (1992). Changing AIDS-risk behavior. *Psychological Bulletin, 111*, 455–474.

Fisher, J. D., & Fisher, W. A. (2000). Theoretical approaches to individual-level change in HIV risk behavior. In J. L. Peterson & R. J. DiClemente (Eds.), *Handbook of HIV prevention AIDS prevention and mental health* (pp. 3–55). New York: Kluwer Academic/Plenum Publishers.

Fisher, J. D., Fisher, W. A., Williams, S. S., & Malloy, T. E. (1994). Empirical tests of an information-motivation-behavioral skills model of AIDS-preventive behavior with gay men and heterosexual university students. *Health Psychology, 13*, 238–250.

Fiske, S. T. (1998). Stereotyping, prejudice, and discrimination. In D. T. Gilbert, S. T. Fiske, & L. Gardner (Eds.), *The handbook of social psychology* (4th ed., Vol. 2, pp. 357–411). Boston, MA: McGraw-Hill.

Fiske, S. T., & Taylor, S. E. (1991). *Social cognition* (2nd ed.). New York: McGraw-Hill Book Company.

Fitzpatrick, K. M., Piko, B. F., Wright, D. R., & LaGory, M. (2005). Depressive symptomatology, exposure to violence, and the role of social capital among African American adolescents. *American Journal of Orthopsychiatry, 75,* 262–274.

Forgas, J. P., Bower, G. H., & Krantz, S. E. (1984). The influence of mood on perceptions of social interactions. *Journal of Experimental Social Psychology, 20,* 497–513.

Frantom, C., Green, K. E., & Lam, T. C. M. (2002). Item grouping effects on invariance of attitude items. *Journal of Applied Measurement, 3,* 38–49.

Fredricks, A. J., & Dossett, D. L. (1983). Attitude-behavior relations: A comparison of the Fishbein-Ajzen and the Bentler-Speckart models. *Journal of Personality and Social Psychology, 45,* 501-512.

French, J. R. P. Jr., & Raven, B. (1959). The bases of social power. In D. Cartwright (Ed.), *Studies in social power.* (pp. 150–167). Ann Arbor: University of Michigan Press.

Frost, S., Myers, L. B., & Newman, S. P. (2001). Genetic screening for Alzheimer's disease: What factors predict intentions to take a test? *Behavioral Medicine, 27,* 101–109.

Gaertner, S. L., & Dovidio, J. F. (1986). The aversive form of racism. In J. F. Dovidio & S. L. Gaertner (Eds.), *Prejudice, discrimination, and racism* (pp. 61–89). Orlando, FL: Academic.

Gagné, C., & Godin, G. (2000). The theory of planned behavior: Some measurement issues concerning belief-based variables. *Journal of Applied Social Psychology, 30,* 2173–2193.

Gangestad, S., & Snyder, M. (1985). "To carve nature at its joints": On the existence of discrete classes in personality. *Psychological Review, 92,* 317–349.

Gant, M., & Luttbeg, N. (1991). *American electoral behavior.* Itasca, IL: F.E. Peacock Publishers.

Gerrard, M., Gibbons, F. X., & Bushman, B. J. (1996). Relation between perceived vulnerability to HIV and precautionary sexual behavior. *Psychological Bulletin, 119,* 390–409.

Gibbons, F. X., Gerrard, M., Blanton, H., & Russell, D. W. (1998). Reasoned action and social reaction: Willingness and intention as independent predictors of health risk. *Journal of Personality and Social Psychology, 74,* 1164–1180.

Gibbons, F. X., Gerrard, M., Cleveland, M. J., Wills, T. A., & Brody, G. (2004). Perceived discrimination and substance use in African American parents and their children: A panel study. *Journal of Personality and Social Psychology, 86,* 517–529.

Giles, M., & Cairns, E. (1995). Blood donation and Ajzen's theory of planned behaviour: An examination of perceived behavioural control. *British Journal of Social Psychology, 34,* 173–188.

Giles, M., & Larmour, S. (2000). The theory of planned behavior: A conceptual framework to view the career development of women. *Journal of Applied Social Psychology, 30,* 2137–2157.

Gimpel, J. G., & Schuknecht, J. E. (2003). Political participation and the accessibility of the ballot box. *Political Geography, 22,* 471–488.

Giner-Sorolla, R. (1999). Affect in attitude: Immediate and deliberative perspectives. In S. Chaiken & Y. Trope (Eds.), *Dual-process theories in social psychology* (pp. 441–461). New York: Guilford.

Godin, G., & Kok, G. (1996). The theory of planned behavior: A review of its applications to health-related behaviors. *American Journal of Health Promotion, 11,* 87–98.

Godin, G., Maticka-Tyndale, E., Adrien, A., Manson-Singer, S., Willms, D., & Cappon, P. (1996). Cross-cultural testing of three social cognitive theories: An application to condom use. *Journal of Applied Social Psychology, 26,* 1556–1586.

Godin, G., Sheeran, P., Conner, M., & Germain, M. (2008). Asking questions changes behavior: Mere measurement effects on frequency of blood donation. *Health Psychology, 27,* 179–184.

Godin, G., Valois, P., Lepage, L., & Desharnais, R. (1992). Predictors of smoking behaviour: An application of Ajzen's theory of planned behaviour. *British Journal of Addiction, 87,* 1335–1343.

Godin, G., Valois, P., Shephard, R. J., & Desharnais, R. (1987). Prediction of leisure-time exercise behavior: A path analysis (LISREL V) model. *Journal of Behavioral Medicine, 10,* 145–158.

Goffman, E. (1958). *The presentation of self in everyday life.* Edinburgh: University of Edinburgh.

Gold, R. S. (1993). On the need to mind the gap: On-line versus off-line cognitions underlying sexual risk taking. In D. J. Terry, C. Gallois & M. McCamish (Eds.), *The theory of reasoned action: Its application to AIDS-preventive behavior* (pp. 227–252). Oxford: Pergamon Press.

Gold, R. S. (2000). AIDS education for gay men: Towards a more cognitive approach. *AIDS Care, 12,* 267–272.

Goldstein, A. L., Wall, A.-M., McKee, S. A., & Hinson, R. E. (2004). Accessibility of alcohol expectancies from memory: Impact of mood and motives in college student drinkers. *Journal of Studies on Alcohol, 65,* 95–104.

Gollwitzer, P. M. (1990). Action phases and mind-sets. In E. T. Higgins & R. M. Sorrentino (Eds.), *Handbook of motivation and cognition: Foundations of social behavior, Vol. 2* (pp. 53–92). New York: Guilford Press.

Gollwitzer, P. M. (1996). The volitional benefits of planning. In P. M. Gollwitzer & J. A. Bargh (Eds.), *The psychology of action: Linking cognition and motivation to behavior* (pp. 287–312). New York: Guilford.

Gollwitzer, P. M. (1999). Implementation intentions: Strong effects of simple plans. *American Psychologist, 54,* 493–503.

Gollwitzer, P. M., & Bayer, U. (1999). Deliberative versus implemental mindsets in the control of action. In S. Chaiken & Y. Trope (Eds.), *Dual-process theories in social psychology* (pp. 403–422). New York: Guilford Press.

Gollwitzer, P. M., & Brandstätter, V. (1997). Implementation intentions and effective goal pursuit. *Journal of Personality and Social Psychology, 73,* 186–199.

Gollwitzer, P. M., & Schaal, B. (1998). Metacognition in action: The importance of implementation intentions. *Personality and Social Psychology Review, 2,* 124–136.

Gorsuch, R. L., & Ortberg, J. (1983). Moral obligation and attitudes: Their relation to behavioral intentions. *Journal of Personality and Social Psychology, 44,* 1025–1028.

Goschke, T., & Kuhl, J. (1996). Remembering what to do: Explicit and implicit memory for intentions. In M. Brandimante, G. O. Einstein, & M. A. McDaniel (Eds.), *Prospective memory: Theory and applications* (pp. 53–91). Mahwah, NJ: Lawrence Erlbaum Associates.

Green, B. F. (1954). Attitude measurement. In G. Lindzey (Ed.), *Handbook of social psychology* (Vol. 1, pp. 335–369). Reading, MA: Addison-Wesley.

Greenwald, A. G., Carnot, C. G., Beach, R., & Young, B. (1987). Increasing voting behavior by asking people if they expect to vote. *Journal of Applied Psychology, 72,* 315–318.

Greenwald, A. G., McGhee, D. E., & Schwartz, J. L. K. (1998). Measuring individual differences in implicit cognition: The implicit association test. *Journal of Personality and Social Psychology, 74,* 1464–1480.

Greenwald, A. G., Poehlman, T. A., Uhlmann, E., & Banaji, M. R. (in press). Understanding and using the Implicit Association Test: III. Meta-analysis of predictive validity. *Journal of Personality and Social Psychology.*

Griffeth, R. W., Hom, P. W., & Gaertner, S. (2000). A meta-analysis of antecedents and correlates of employee turnover: Update, moderator tests, and research implications for the next millennium. *Journal of Management, 26,* 463–488.

Grogan, S. C., Bell, R., & Conner, M. (1997). Eating sweet snacks: Gender differences in attitudes and behaviour. *Appetite, 28,* 19–31.

Guerra, C. E., Dominguez, F., & Shea, J. A. (2005). Literacy and knowledge, attitudes, and behavior about colorectal cancer screening. *Journal of Health Communication, 10,* 651–663.

Guttman, L. (1944). A basis for scaling qualitative data. *American Sociological Review, 9,* 139–150.

Hacker, A. (1995). *Two nations: Black and white, separate, hostile, unequal.* New York: Ballantine Books.

Hackett, R. D., & Guion, R. M. (1985). A reevaluation of the absenteeism-job satisfaction relationship. *Organizational Behavior & Human Decision Processes, 35,* 340–381.

Hackman, J. R., & Anderson, L. R. (1968). The strength, relevance, and source of beliefs about an object in Fishbein's attitude theory. *Journal of Social Psychology, 76,* 55–67.

Hagger, M. S., & Chatzisarantis, N. L. D. (2005). First- and higher-order models of attitudes, normative influence, and perceived behavioural control in the theory of planned behaviour. *British Journal of Social Psychology, 44,* 513–535.

Hagger, M. S., Chatzisarantis, N. L. D., & Biddle, S. J. H. (2002). A meta-analytic review of the theories of reasoned action and planned behavior in physical activity: Predictive validity and the contribution of additional variables. *Journal of Sport and Exercise Psychology, 24,* 3–32.

Hagger, M. S., Chatzisarantis, N. L. D., & Harris, J. (2006). From psychological need satisfaction to intentional behavior: Testing a motivational sequence in two behavioral contexts. *Personality and Social Psychology Bulletin, 32,* 131–148.

Hambleton, R. K., Swaminathan, H., & Roger, H. J. (1991). *Fundamentals of item response theory.* Newbury Park, CA: Sage.

Haney, C., Banks, C., & Zimbardo, P. (1973). Interpersonal dynamics in a simulated prison. *International Journal of Criminology & Penology, 1,* 69–97.

Hardeman, W., Johnston, M., Johnston, D. W., Bonetti, D., Wareham, N. J., & Kinmonth, A. L. (2002). Application of the Theory of Planned Behaviour in behaviour change interventions: A systematic review. *Psychology and Health, 17*, 123–158.

Harlow, L. L., Prochaska, J. O., Redding, C. A., Rossi, J. S., Velicer, W. F., Snow, M. G., et al. (1999). Stages of condom use in a high HIV-risk sample. *Psychology & Health, 14*, 143–157.

Harrison, D. A. (1995). Volunteer motivation and attendance decisions: Competitive theory testing in multiple samples from a homeless shelter. *Journal of Applied Psychology, 80*, 371–385.

Hausenblas, H. A., Carron, A. V., & Mack, D. E. (1997). Application of the theories of reasoned action and planned behavior to exercise behavior: A meta-analysis. *Journal of Sport and Exercise Psychology, 19*, 36–51.

Hausenblas, H. A., & Downs, D. S. (2004). Prospective examination of the theory of planned behavior applied to exercise behavior during women's first trimester of pregnancy. *Journal of Reproductive & Infant Psychology, 22*, 199–210.

Hawkins, D. J., & Catalano, R. F. J. (1992). *Communities that care: Action for drug abuse prevention.* San Francisco, CA: Jossey-Bass.

Hawkins, R. P., Kreuter, M., Resnicow, K., Fishbein, M., & Dijkstra, A. (2008). Understanding tailoring in communicating about health. *Health Education Research, 23*, 454–466.

Heider, F. (1958). *The psychology of interpersonal relations.* Oxford, England: Wiley.

Hennessy, M., Bleakley, A., Fishbein, M. & Jordan, A. (in press). Estimating the longitudinal association between adolescent sexual behavior and exposure to sexual media content. *Journal of Sex Research.*

Herek, G. M. (1994). Assessing heterosexuals' attitudes toward lesbians and gay men: A review of empirical research with the ATLG scale. In B. Greene & G. M. Herek (Eds.), *Lesbian and gay psychology: Theory, research, and clinical applications* (pp. 206–228). Newbury Park, CA: Sage Publications, Inc.

Hewlett, P., & Smith, A. (2006). Correlates of daily caffeine consumption. *Appetite, 46*, 97–99.

Hewstone, M., & Young, L. (1988). Expectancy-value models of attitude: Measurement and combination of evaluations and beliefs. *Journal of Applied Social Psychology, 18*, 958–971.

Higgins, A., & Conner, M. (2003). Understanding adolescent smoking: The role of the Theory of Planned Behaviour and implementation intentions. *Psychology, Health & Medicine, 8*, 173–186.

Hill, A. J., Boudreau, F., Amyot, E., Dery, D., & Godin, G. (1997). Predicting the stages of smoking acquisition according to the theory of planned behavior. *Journal of Adolescent Health, 21*, 107–115.

Hillhouse, J. J., Turrisi, R., & Kastner, M. (2000). Modeling tanning salon behavioral tendencies using appearance motivation, self-monitoring and the Theory of Planned Behavior. *Health Education Research, 15*, 405–414.

Himelstein, P., & Moore, J. (1963). Racial attitudes and the action of Negro and white background figures as factors in petition-signing. *Journal of Social Psychology, 61*, 267–272.

Hobbis, I. C. A., & Sutton, S. (2005). Are techniques used in cognitive behaviour therapy applicable to behaviour change interventions based on the theory of planned behaviour? *Journal of Health Psychology, 10*, 7–18.

Holbrook, M. B. (1977). Comparing multiattribute attitude models by optimal scaling. *Journal of Consumer Research, 4,* 165–171.

Holtgrave, D. R. (2007). Applied aspects of health promotion interventions based on theory of reasoned action and theory of planned behavior. In I. Ajzen, R. Hornik & D. Albarracín (Eds.), *Prediction and change of behavior* (Vol. 273–279). Mahwah, NJ: Lawrence Erlbaum.

Hong, Y.-y., Chiu, C.-y., Dweck, C. S., Lin, D. M. S., & Wan, W. (1999). Implicit theories, attributions, and coping: A meaning system approach. *Journal of Personality and Social Psychology, 77,* 588–599.

Hornik, R., Maklan, D., Cadell, D., Barmada, C., Jacobsohn, L., Prado, A., et al. (2002). *Evaluation of the National Youth Anti-Drug Media Campaign: Fifth Semiannual report of findings.* Report prepared for the National Institute on Drug Abuse (Contract No. N01DA-8-5063). Washington, DC: Westat.

Hornik, R., & Wolf, K. D. (1999). Using cross-sectional surveys to plan message strategies. *Social Marketing Quarterly, 5,* 34–41.

Hovland, C. I., Janis, I. L., & Kelley, H. H. (1953). *Communication and persuasion: Psychological studies of opinion change.* New Haven, CT: Yale University Press.

Hovland, C. I., Lumsdaine, A. A., & Sheffield, F. D. (1949). *Experiments on mass communication. (Studies in social psychology in World War II, Vol. 3.):* Princeton, NJ: Princeton University Press.

Hrubes, D., Ajzen, I., & Daigle, J. (2001). Predicting hunting intentions and behavior: An application of the theory of planned behavior. *Leisure Sciences, 23,* 165–178.

Hugenberg, K., & Bodenhausen, G. V. (2003). Facing prejudice: Implicit prejudice and the perception of facial threat. *Psychological Science, 14,* 640–643.

Ievers-Landis, C. E., Burant, C., Drotar, D., Morgan, L., Trapl, E. S., & Kwoh, C. K. (2003). Social support, knowledge, and self-efficacy as correlates of osteoporosis preventive behaviors among preadolescent females. *Journal of Pediatric Psychology, 28,* 335–345.

IOM. (2002). *Speaking of health: Assessing health communication strategies for diverse populations.* Washington, DC: National Academies Press.

Jaccard, J. J. (1974). Predicting social behavior from personality traits. *Journal of Research in Personality, 7,* 358-367.

Jaccard, J. (1981). Attitudes and behavior: Implications of attitudes toward behavioral alternatives. *Journal of Experimental Social Psychology, 17,* 286–307.

Jaccard, J., & Blanton, H. (2005). Origins and structure of behavior: Conceptualizing behavior in attitude research. In D. Albarracín, B. T. Johnson, & M. P. Zanna (Eds.), *Handbook of attitudes and attitude changes* (pp. 125–171). Mahwah, NJ: Lawrence Erlbaum Associates.

Jaccard, J., & Blanton, H. (2007). A theory of implicit reasoned action: The role of implicit and explicit attitudes in the prediction of behavior. In I. Ajzen, D. Albarracín, & R. Hornik (Eds.), *Prediction and change of health behavior: The reasoned action approach* (pp. 69–93). Mahwah, NJ: Lawrence Erlbaum Associates.

Jaccard, J., McDonald, R., Wan, C. K., Dittus, P. J., & Quinlan, S. (2002). The accuracy of self-reports of condom use and sexual behavior. *Journal of Applied Social Psychology, 32,* 1863–1905.

Jackson, C., Smith, R. A., & Conner, M. (2003). Applying an extended version of the theory of planned behaviour to physical activity. *Journal of Sports Science, 21,* 119–133.

Jamner, M. S., Wolitski, R. J., Corby, N. H., & Fishbein, M. (1998). Using the theory of planned behavior to predict intention to use condoms among female sex workers. *Psychology and Health, 13*, 187–205.

Janis, I. L., & Mann, L. (1977). *Decision making: A psychological analysis of conflict, choice, and commitment.* New York: Free Press.

Jemmott, J. B. I., Jemmott, L. S., Braverman, P. K., & Fong, G. T. (2005). HIV/STD risk reduction interventions for African American and Latino adolescent girls at an adolescent medicine clinic: A randomized controlled trial. *Archives of Pediatric and Adolescent Medicine, 159*(5), 440–449.

Jemmott, J. B., Jemmott, L. S., & Fong, G. T. (1992). Reductions in HIV risk-associated sexual behaviors among Black male adolescents: Effects of an AIDS prevention intervention. *American Journal of Public Health, 82*, 372–377.

Jemmott, J. B. I., Jemmott, L. S., & Fong, G. T. (1998). Abstinence and safer sex HIV risk-reduction interventions for African American adolescents. *Journal of the American Medical Association, 279*, 1529–1536.

Jemmott, J. B. I., Jemmott, L. S., Fong, G. T., & McCaffree, K. (1999). Reducing HIV risk-associated sexual behavior among African American adolescents: Testing the generality of intervention effects. *American Journal of Community Psychology, 27*, 161–187.

Jemmott, L. S., & Jemmott, J. B. I. (2007). Applying the theory of reasoned action to HIV risk-reduction behavioral interventions. In I. Ajzen, D. Albarrací, & R. Hornik (Eds.), *Prediction and change of health behavior: Applying the reasoned action approach* (pp. 243–263). Mahwah, NJ: Lawrence Erlbaum Associates.

Jennings-Dozier, K. (1999). Predicting intentions to obtain a Pap smear among African American and Latina women: testing the theory of planned behavior. *Nursing Research, 48*, 198–205.

Johnson, E. J., & Tversky, A. (1983). Affect, generalization, and the perception of risk. *Journal of Personality & Social Psychology, 45*, 20–31.

Johnston, K. L., & White, K. M. (2003). Binge-drinking: A test of the role of group norms in the theory of planned behaviour. *Psychology & Health, 18*, 63–77.

Johnston, K. L., White, K. M., & Norman, P. (2004). An examination of the individual-difference approach to the role of norms in the Theory of Reasoned Action. *Journal of Applied Social Psychology, 34*, 2524–2549.

Johnston, L. D., O'Malley, P. M., Bachman, J. G., & Schulenberg, J. E. (2006). *Monitoring the future: National results on adolescent drug use. Overview of key findings, 2005.* National Institute on Drug Abuse, U.S. Department of Health and Human Services.

Judge, T. A., Thoresen, C. J., Bono, J. E., & Patton, G. K. (2001). The job satisfaction-job performance relationship: A qualitative and quantitative review. *Psychological Bulletin, 127*, 376–407.

Kahneman, D., & Tversky, A. (1979). Prospect theory: An analysis of decision under risk. *Econometrica, 47*, 263–291.

Kaiser, F. G., Hübner, G., & Bogner, F. X. (2005). Contrasting the theory of planned behavior with the value-belief-norm model in explaining conservation behavior. *Journal of Applied Social Psychology, 35*, 2150–2170.

Kallgren, C. A., Reno, R. R., & Cialdini, R. B. (2000). A focus theory of normative conduct: When norms do and do not affect behavior. *Personality and Social Psychology Bulletin, 26*, 1002–1012.

Kamb, M. L., Dillon, B. A., Fishbein, M., & Willis, K. L. (1996). Quality assurance of HIV prevention counseling in a multi-center randomized controlled trial. *Public Health Reports, 111,* 99–107.

Kamb, M. L., Fishbein, M., Douglas, J. M., Rhodes, F., Rogers, J., Bolan, G., et al. (1998). Efficacy of risk-reduction counseling to prevent human immunodeficiency virus and sexually transmitted diseases. *Journal of the American Medical Association, 280,* 1161–1167.

Kaplan, K. J. (1972). On the ambivalence-indifference problem in attitude theory and measurement: A suggested modification of the semantic differential technique. *Psychological Bulletin, 77,* 361–372.

Kaplan, K. J., & Fishbein, M. (1969). The source of beliefs, their saliency, and prediction of attitude. *Journal of Social Psychology, 78,* 63–74.

Karlson, N. (1992). Bringing social norms back in. *Scandinavian Political Studies, 15,* 249–268.

Karpinski, A., & Hilton, J. L. (2001). Attitudes and the Implicit Association Test. *Journal of Personality & Social Psychology, 81,* 774–788.

Kasprzyk, D., & Montaño, D. E. (2007). Application of an integrated behavioral model to understand HIV prevention behavior of high-risk men in rural Zimbabwe. In I. Ajzen, R. Hornik, & D. Albarracín (Eds.), *Prediction and change of behavior: Applying the reasoned action approach* (pp. 149–172). Mahwah, NJ: Lawrence Erlbaum.

Kassem, N. O., & Lee, J. W. (2004). Understanding soft drink consumption among male adolescents using the theory of planned behavior. *Journal of Behavioral Medicine, 27,* 273–296.

Kenski, K., & Fishbein, M. (2005). The predictive benefits of importance: Do issue importance ratings improve the prediction of political attitudes? *Journal of Applied Social Psychology, 35,* 487–507.

Kerner, M. S., & Grossman, A. H. (1998). Attitudinal, social, and practical correlates to fitness behavior: A test of the theory of planned behavior. *Perceptual and Motor Skills, 87,* 1139–1154.

Kiesler, C. A. (1971). *The psychology of commitment: Experiments linking behavior to belief.* San Diego, CA: Academic Press.

Kinicki, A. J., McKee-Ryan, F. M., Schriesheim, C. A., & Carson, K. P. (2002). Assessing the construct validity of the job descriptive index: A review and meta-analysis. *Journal of Applied Psychology, 87,* 14–32.

Kokkinaki, F., & Lunt, P. (1997). The relationship between involvement, attitude accessibility and attitude-behaviour consistency. *British Journal of Social Psychology, 36,* 497–509.

Koslowsky, M., Sagie, A., Krausz, M., & Singer, A. D. (1997). Correlates of employee lateness: Some theoretical considerations. *Journal of Applied Psychology, 82,* 79–88.

Kraft, P., Rise, J., Sutton, S., & Røysamb, E. (2005). Perceived difficulty in the theory of planned behaviour: Perceived behavioural control or affective attitude? *British Journal of Social Psychology, 44,* 479–496.

Krech, D., & Crutchfield, R. S. (1948). *Theory and problems of social psychology.* New York: McGraw-Hill.

Krosnick, J. A., Boninger, D. S., Chuang, Y. C., Berent, M. K., & Carnot, C. G. (1993). Attitude strength: One construct or many related constructs? *Journal of Personality and Social Psychology, 65,* 1132–1151.

Krosnick, J. A., Judd, C. M., & Wittenbrink, B. (2005). The measurement of attitudes. In D. Albarracín, B. T. Johnson, & M. P. Zanna (Eds.), *Handbook of attitudes and attitude change: Basic principles* (pp. 21–76). Mahwah, NJ: Lawrence Erlbaum Associates.

Krosnick, J. A., & Petty, R. E. (1995). Attitude strength: An overview. In R. E. Petty & J. A. Krosnick (Eds.), *Attitude strength: Antecedents and consequences* (pp. 1–24). Mahwah, NJ: Erlbaum.

Kruglanski, A. W., & Stroebe, W. (2005). The influence of beliefs and goals on attitudes: Issues of structure, function, and dynamics. In D. Albarracín, B. T. Johnson, & M. P. Zanna (Eds.), *Handbook of attitudes and attitude change: Basic principles* (pp. 323–368). Mahwah, NJ: Lawrence Erlbaum Associates.

Kübler-Ross, E. (1969). *On death and dying.* New York: McMillan.

Lam, T. C. M., Green, K. E., & Bordignon, C. (2002). Effects of item grouping and position of the "don't know" option on questionnaire response. *Field Methods, 14,* 418–432.

Landrine, H., Klonoff, E. A., & Alcaraz, R. (1997). Racial discrimination in minor's access to tobacco. *Journal of Black Psychology, 23,* 135–147.

Landy, F. J. (1989). *Psychology of work behavior.* Pacific Grove, CA: Brooks/Cole.

Lapham, S. C., C'de Baca, J., Chang, I., Hunt, W. C., & Berger, L. R. (2002). Are drunk-driving offenders referred for screening accurately reporting their drug use? *Drug & Alcohol Dependence, 66,* 243–253.

LaPiere, R. T. (1934). Attitudes vs. actions. *Social Forces, 13,* 230–237.

Latimer, A. E., & Martin Ginis, K. A. (2005a). The importance of subjective norms for people who care what others think of them. *Psychology & Health, 20,* 53–62.

Latimer, A. E., & Martin Ginis, K. A. (2005b). The theory of planned behavior in prediction of leisure time physical activity among individuals with spinal cord injury. *Rehabilitation Psychology, 50,* 389–396.

Lazarsfeld, P. F., Berelson, B., & Gaudet, H. (1944). *The people's choice.* Oxford, England: Duell, Sloan & Pearce.

Leach, M., Hennessy, M., & Fishbein, M. (1999). Perception of easy-difficult: Attitude or self-efficacy? Unpublished manuscript.

Lefcourt, H. M. (1982). *Locus of control: Current trends in theory and research* (2nd ed.). Hillsdale, NJ: Lawrence Erlbaum Associates.

Lefcourt, H. M. (Ed.). (1981). *Research with the locus of control construct. Vol. 1: Assessment methods.* San Diego, CA: Academic Press.

Lefcourt, H. M. (Ed.). (1983). *Research with the locus of control construct. Vol. 2: Developments and social problems.* San Diego, CA: Academic Press.

Letirand, F., & Delhomme, P. (2005). Speed behaviour as a choice between observing and exceeding the speed limit. *Transportation Research Part F: Traffic Psychology and Behaviour, 8,* 481–492.

Levav, J., & Fitzsimons, G. J. (2006). When questions change behavior: The role of ease of representation. *Psychological Science, 17,* 207–213.

Likert, R. (1932). A technique for the measurement of attitudes. *Archives of Psychology, 140,* 5–53.

Linn, L. S. (1965). Verbal attitudes and overt behavior: A study of racial discrimination. *Social Forces, 43,* 353–364.

Lippke, S., & Ziegelmann, J. P. (2006). Understanding and modeling health behavior: The multi-stage model of health behavior change. *Journal of Health Psychology, 11,* 37–50.

Lowe, R., Eves, F., & Carroll, D. (2002). The influence of affective and instrumental beliefs on exercise intentions and behavior: A longitudinal analysis. *Journal of Applied Social Psychology, 32*, 1241–1252.

Luce, R. D., & Raiffa, H. (1957). *Games and decisions: Introduction and critical survey.* New York: Wiley.

Lüdemann, C. (1997). *Rationalität und Umweltverhalten.* Wiesbaden, Germany: Deutscher Universitäts-Verlag.

MacCallum, R. C., & Austin, J. T. (2000). Applications of structural equation modeling in psychological research. *Annual Review of Psychology, 51*, 201–226.

MacDonald, T. K., Zanna, M. P., & Fong, G. T. (1996). Why common sense goes out the window: Effects of alcohol on intentions to use condoms. *Personality and Social Psychology Bulletin, 22*, 763–775.

MacManus, S. A. (2006). Voter Participation and Turnout: It's a New Game. In Carol, S. J. & Fox, R. L. (Eds.), *Gender and elections: shaping the future of American politics* (pp. 43-73). New York: Cambridge University Press.

Madden, T. J., Ellen, P. S., & Ajzen, I. (1992). A comparison of the theory of planned behavior and the theory of reasoned action. *Personality and Social Psychology Bulletin, 18*, 3–9.

Madu, S. N., & Peltzer, K. (2003). Factor structure of condom attitudes among Black South African university students. *Social Behavior & Personality, 31*, 265–274.

Maison, D., Greenwald, A. G., & Bruin, R. H. (2004). Predictive validity of the implicit association test in studies of brands, consumer attitudes, and behavior. *Journal of Consumer Psychology, 14*, 405–415.

Malotte, C. K., Jarvis, B., Fishbein, M., Kamb, M., Iatesta, M., Hoxworth, T., et al. (2000). Stage of change versus an integrated psychosocial theory as a basis for developing effective behaviour change interventions. *AIDS Care, 12*, 357–364.

Mandler, G. (1967). Verbal learning. In T. M. Newcomb (Ed.), *New directions in psychology* (Vol. 3, pp. 1–50). New York: Holt.

Manstead, A. S. R. (2000). The role of moral norm in the attitude-behavior relation. In D. J. Terry & M. A. Hogg (Eds.), *Attitudes, behavior, and social context: The role of norms and group membership. Applied social research* (pp. 11–30). Mahwah, NJ: Lawrence Erlbaum Associates.

Manstead, A. S. R., & van Eekelen, S. A. M. (1998). Distinguishing between perceived behavioral control and self-efficacy in the domain of academic intentions and behaviors. *Journal of Applied Social Psychology, 28*, 1375–1392.

May, R. M., & Anderson, R.M. (1987). Transmission dynamics of HIV infection. *Nature, 326*, 137–142.

McClelland, G. H., & Judd, C. M. (1993). Statistical difficulties of detecting interactions and moderator effects. *Psychological Bulletin, 114*, 376–390.

McConahay, J. B. (1986). Modern racism, ambivalence, and the Modern Racism Scale. In J. F. Dovidio & S. L. Gaertner (Eds.), *Prejudice, discrimination, and racism* (pp. 91–125). San Diego, CA: Academic Press, Inc.

McConahay, J. B., Hardee, B. B., & Batts, V. (1981). Has racism declined in America? It depends on who is asking and what is asked. *Journal of Conflict Resolution, 25*, 563–579.

McCroskey, J. C. (1970). The effects of evidence as an inhibitor of counter persuasion. *Speech Monographs, 37*, 188–194.

McDonald, M. P., & Popkin, S. L. (2001). The myth of the vanishing voter. *American Political Science Review, 95*, 963–974.

McGuire, W. J. (1960). A syllogistic analysis of cognitive relationships. In M. J. Rosenberg, C. I. Hovland, W. J. McGuire, R. P. Abelson, & J. W. Brehm (Eds.), *Attitude organization and change: An analysis of consistency among attitude components* (pp. 65–111). New Haven, CT: Yale University Press.

McGuire, W. J. (1968). Personality and susceptibility to social influence. In E. E. Borgatta & W. W. Lambert (Eds.), *Handbook of personality theory and research* (pp. 1130–1187). Chicago: Rand McNally.

McGuire, W. J. (1969). The nature of attitudes and attitude change. In G. Lindzey & E. Aronson (Eds.), *The handbook of social psychology* (2nd ed., Vol. 3, pp. 136–314). Reading, MA: Addison-Wesley.

McGuire, W. J. (1985). The nature of attitudes and attitude change. In G. Lindzey & E. Aronson (Eds.), *Handbook of social psychology* (3 ed., Vol. 2, pp. 223–346). New York: Random House.

McKee, S. A., Wall, A.-M., Hinson, R. E., Goldstein, A., & Bissonnette, M. (2003). Effects of an implicit mood prime on the accessibility of smoking expectancies in college women. *Psychology of Addictive Behaviors, 17*, 219–225.

McMillan, B., & Conner, M. (2003). Applying an extended version of the theory of planned behavior to illicit drug use among students. *Journal of Applied Social Psychology, 33*, 1662–1683.

McMillan, B., & Conner, M. (2003). Using the theory of planned behaviour to understand alcohol and tobacco use in students. *Psychology, Health & Medicine, 8*, 317–328.

Middlestadt, S., Bhattacharyya, K., Rosenbaum, J., & Fishbein, M. (1996). The use of theory-based semi-structures elicitation questionnaires: Formative research for CDC's prevention marketing initiative. *Public Health Reports, 111* Supplement 1, 18–27.

Milgram, S. (1963). Behavioral study of obedience. *The Journal of Abnormal and Social Psychology, 67*, 371–378.

Miller, G. A. (1956). The magical number seven, plus or minus two: Some limits on our capacity for processing information. *Psychological Review, 63*, 81–97.

Miller, L. E., & Grush, J. E. (1986). Individual differences in attitudinal versus normative determination of behavior. *Journal of Experimental Social Psychology, 22*, 190–202.

Mischel, W. (1968). *Personality and assessment.* New York: Wiley.

Misovich, S. J., Martinez, T., Fisher, J. D., Bryan, A., & Catapano, N. (2003). Predicting breast self-examination: A test of the information-motivation-behavioral skills model. *Journal of Applied Social Psychology, 33*, 775–790.

Moan, I. S., Rise, J., & Andersen, M. (2005). Predicting parents' intentions not to smoke indoors in the presence of their children using an extended version of the theory of planned behaviour. *Psychology & Health, 20*, 353–371.

Montaño, D. E., Thompson, B., Taylor, V. M., & Mahloch, J. (1997). Understanding mammography intention and utilization among women in an inner city public hospital clinic. *Preventive Medicine: An International Journal Devoted to Practice and Theory, 26*, 817–824.

Morwitz, V. G., Johnson, E., & Schmittlein, D. (1993). Does measuring intent change behavior? *Journal of Consumer Research, 20*, 46–61.

Mosher, W., Shandra, A., & Jones, J. (2005). *Sexual behavior and selective health measures: Men and women 15 to 44 years of age, United States, 2002. Advance data from vital and health statistics; no. 362.* Hyattsville, MD: National Center for Health Statistics.

Mummery, W. K., & Wankel, L. M. (1999). Training adherence in adolescent competitive swimmers: An application of the theory of planned behavior. *Journal of Sport and Exercise Psychology, 21*, 313–328.

Murphy, S. T., & Zajonc, R. B. (1993). Affect, cognition, and awareness: Affective priming with optimal and suboptimal stimulus exposures. *Journal of Personality and Social Psychology, 64*, 723–739.

Murphy, W. G., & Brubaker, R. G. (1990). Effects of a brief theory-based intervention on the practice of testicular self-examination by high school males. *Journal of School Health, 60*, 459–462.

Myers, S. L., & Chan, T. (1995). Racial discrimination in housing markets: Accounting for credit risk. *Social Science Quarterly, 76*, 543–561.

Nabi, R. L. (2003). Exploring the framing effects of emotion: Do discrete emotions differentially influence information accessibility, information seeking, and policy preference? *Communication Research, 30*, 224–247.

Netemeyer, R. G., & Burton, S. (1990). Examining the relationships between voting behavior, intention, perceived behavioral control, and expectation. *Journal of Applied Social Psychology, 20*, 661–680.

Netemeyer, R. G., Burton, S., & Johnston, M. (1991). A comparison of two models for the prediction of volitional and goal-directed behaviors: A confirmatory analysis approach. *Social Psychology Quarterly, 54*, 87–100.

Neumann, R., Hülsenbeck, K., & Seibt, B. (2004). Attitudes towards people with AIDS and avoidance behavior: Automatic and reflective bases of behavior. *Journal of Experimental Social Psychology, 40*, 543–550.

Nisbett, R., & Ross, L. (1980). *Human inference: Strategies and shortcomings of social judgment.* Englewood Cliffs, NJ: Prentice-Hall.

Noar, S. M., Benac, C. N., & Harris, M. S. (2007). Does tailoring matter? Meta-analytic review of tailored print health behavior change interventions. *Psychological Bulletin, 133*, 673–693.

Norman, P., Bennett, P., & Lewis, H. (1998). Understanding binge drinking among young people: An application of the Theory of Planned Behaviour. *Health Education Research, 13*, 163–169.

Norman, P., & Hoyle, S. (2004). The theory of planned behavior and breast self-examination: Distinguishing between perceived control and self-efficacy. *Journal of Applied Social Psychology, 34*, 694–708.

Norman, P., & Smith, L. (1995). The theory of planned behaviour and exercise: An investigation into the role of prior behaviour, behavioural intentions and attitude variability. *European Journal of Social Psychology, 25*, 403–415.

Notani, A. S. (1998). Moderators of perceived behavioral control's predictiveness in the theory of planned behavior: A meta-analysis. *Journal of Consumer Psychology, 7*, 247–271.

Nucifora, J., Kashima, Y., & Gallois, C. (1993). Influences on condom use among undergraduates: Testing the theories of reasoned action and planned behaviour. In D. J. Terry & C. Gallois (Eds.), *The theory of reasoned action: Its application to AIDS-preventive behaviour. International series in experimental social psychology, Vol. 28.* (pp. 47–64). Oxford, England: Pergamon Press, Inc.

O'Callaghan, F. V., Chant, D. C., Callan, V. J., & Baglioni, A. (1997). Models of alcohol use by young adults: An examination of various attitude-behavior theories. *Journal of Studies on Alcohol, 58*, 502–507.

O'Connor, R. C., & Armitage, C. J. (2003). Theory of planned behaviour and parasuicide: An exploratory study. *Current Psychology: Developmental, Learning, Personality, Social, 22*, 196–205.

Ogden, J. (2003). Some problems with social cognition models: A pragmatic and conceptual analysis. *Health Psychology, 22*, 424–428.

O'Keefe, D. J. (2002). *Persuasion: Theory and research* (2nd ed.). Thousand Oaks, CA: Sage.

Ones, D. S., Viswesvaran, C., & Schmidt, F. L. (1993). Comprehensive meta-analysis of integrity test validities: Findings and implications for personnel selection and theories of job performance. *Journal of Applied Psychology, 78*, 679–703.

Ones, D. S., Viswesvaran, C., & Schmidt, F. L. (2003). Personality and absenteeism: A meta-analysis of integrity tests. *European Journal of Personality, 17*, S19–S38.

Orbell, S., Blair, C., Sherlock, K., & Conner, M. (2001). The theory of planned behavior and ecstasy use: Roles for habit and perceived control over taking versus obtaining substances. *Journal of Applied Social Psychology, 31*, 31–47.

Orbell, S., Hodgkins, S., & Sheeran, P. (1997). Implementation intentions and the theory of planned behavior. *Personality and Social Psychology Bulletin, 23*, 945–954.

Orbell, S., & Sheeran, P. (2000). Motivational and volitional processes in action initiation: A field study of the role of implementation intentions. *Journal of Applied Social Psychology, 30*, 780–797.

O'Reilly, K., & Higgins, D. L. (1991). AIDS community demonstration projects for HIV prevention among hard-to-reach groups. *Public Health Reports, 106*, 714–720.

Orth, B. (1985). Bedeutsamkeitsanalysen bilinearer Einstellungsmodelle. *Zeitschrift für Sozialpsychologie, 16*, 101–115.

Osgood, C. E., Suci, G. J., & Tannenbaum, P. H. (1957). *The measurement of meaning.* Urbana: University of Illinois Press.

Ottati, V., Rhoads, S., & Graesser, A. C. (1999). The effect of metaphor on processing style in a persuasion task: A motivational resonance model. *Journal of Personality and Social Psychology, 77*, 688–697.

Ouellette, J. A., & Wood, W. (1998). Habit and intention in everyday life: The multiple processes by which past behavior predicts future behavior. *Psychological Bulletin, 124*, 54–74.

Parker, D., Manstead, A. S. R., & Stradling, S. G. (1995). Extending the theory of planned behaviour: The role of personal norm. *British Journal of Social Psychology, 34*, 127–137.

Parker, D., Manstead, A. S. R., Stradling, S. G., & Reason, J. T. (1992). Determinants of intention to commit driving violations. *Accident Analysis and Prevention, 24*, 117–131.

Parker, D., Stradling, S. G., & Manstead, A. S. R. (1996). Modifying beliefs and attitudes to exceeding the speed limit: An intervention study based on the theory of planned behavior. *Journal of Applied Social Psychology, 26*, 1–19.

Peak, H. (1955). Attitude and motivation. In M. R. Jones (Ed.), *Nebraska symposium on motivation* (Vol. 3, pp. 149–188). Lincoln: University of Nebraska Press.

Pequegnat, W., Fishbein, M., Celentano, D., Ehrhardt, A., Garnett, G., Holtgrave, D., et al. (2000). NIMH/APPC work-group on behavioral and biological outcomes in HIV/STD prevention studies: a position statement. *Sexually Transmitted Diseases, 27*, 127–132.

Perugini, M., & Bagozzi, R. P. (2001). The role of desires and anticipated emotions in goal-directed behaviours: Broadening and deepening the theory of planned behaviour. *British Journal of Social Psychology, 40*, 79–98.

Peterman, T. A, Lin, L. S., Newman, D. R., Kamb, M. L., Bolan, G., Zenilman, J., et al., Project RESPECT Study Group. (2000). Does measured behavior reflect STD risk? An analysis of data from a controlled behavioral intervention study. *Sexually Transmitted Diseases, 27*, 446–451.

Petkova, K. G., Ajzen, I., & Driver, B. L. (1995). Salience of anti-abortion beliefs and commitment to an attitudinal position: On the strength, structure, and predictive validity of anti-abortion attitudes. *Journal of Applied Social Psychology, 25*, 463–483.

Petraitis, J., Flay, B. R., & Miller, T. Q. (1995). Reviewing theories of adolescent substance use: Organizing pieces in the puzzle. *Psychological Bulletin, 117*, 67–86.

Pettigrew, T. F., & Tropp, L. R. (2006). A meta-analytic test of intergroup contact theory. *Journal of Personality and Social Psychology, 90*, 751–783.

Petty, R. E., & Cacioppo, J. T. (1979). Issue involvement can increase or decrease persuasion by enhancing message-relevant cognitive responses. *Journal of Personality and Social Psychology, 37*, 1915–1926.

Petty, R. E., & Cacioppo, J. T. (1983). The role of bodily responses in attitude measurement and change. In J. T. Cacioppo & R. E. Petty (Eds.), *Social psychophysiology: A sourcebook* (pp. 51–101). New York: Guilford Press.

Petty, R. E., & Cacioppo, J. T. (1986). *Communication and Persuasion: Central and peripheral routes to attitude change.* New York: Springer Verlag.

Petty, R. E., & Krosnick, J. A. (Eds.). (1995). *Attitude strength: Antecedents and consequences.* Mahwah, NJ: Erlbaum.

Petty, R. E., Ostrom, T. M., & Brock, T. C. (Eds.). (1981). *Cognitive responses in persuasion.* Hillsdale, NJ: Lawrence Erlbaum Associates.

Petty, R. E., & Wegener, D. T. (1999). The elaboration likelihood model: Current status and controversies. In S. Chaiken & Y. Trope (Eds.), *Dual-process theories in social psychology* (pp. 41–72). New York: Guilford Press.

Pinkerton, S. D. & Abramson, P. R. (1994). An alternative model of the reproductive rate of HIV infection: Formulation, evaluation, and implications for risk reduction interventions. *Evaluation Review, 18*, 371-388.

Pornpitakpan, C. (2004). The persuasiveness of source credibility: A critical review of five decades' evidence. *Journal of Applied Social Psychology, 34*, 243–281.

Portes, A. (1998). Social capital: Its origins and applications in modern sociology. *Annual Review of Sociology, 24*, 1–24.

Povey, R., Conner, M., Sparks, P., James, R., & Shepherd, R. (2000). Application of the Theory of Planned Behaviour to two dietary behaviours: Roles of perceived control and self-efficacy. *British Journal of Health Psychology, 5*, 121–139.

Price, V., & Zaller, J. (1933). Who gets the news? Alternative measures of news reception and their implications for research. *Public Opinion Quarterly, 57*(2), 133–164.

Priester, J. R., & Petty, R. E. (1996). The gradual threshold model of ambivalence: Relating the positive and negative bases of attitudes to subjective ambivalence. *Journal of Personality and Social Psychology, 71*, 431–449.

Prislin, R., Jordan, J. A., Worchel, S., Semmer, F. T., & Shebilske, W. L. (1996). Effects of group discussion on acquisition of complex skills. *Human Factors, 38*, 404–416.

Prislin, R., & Kovrlija, N. (1992). Predicting behavior of high and low self-monitors: An application of the theory of planned behavior. *Psychological Reports, 70*, 1131–1138.

Prochaska, J. O., & DiClemente, C. C. (1983). Stages and processes of self-change of smoking: Toward an integrative model of change. *Journal of Consulting and Clinical Psychology, 51*, 390–395.

Prochaska, J. O., & DiClemente, C. C. (1984). *The transtheoretical approach: Crossing traditional boundaries of therapy*. Homewood, IL: Dow Jones-Irwin.

Prochaska, J. O., DiClemente, C. C., & Norcross, J. C. (1992). In search of how people change: Applications to addictive behaviors. *American Psychologist, 47*, 1102–1114.

Prochaska, J. O., & Norcross, J. C. (2002). Stages of change. In J. C. Norcross (Ed.), *Psychotherapy relationships that work: Therapist contributions and responsiveness to patients* (pp. 303–313). Oxford, England: Oxford University Press.

Raden, D. (1985). Strength-related attitude dimensions. *Social Psychology Quarterly, 48*, 312–330.

Randall, D. M., & Wolff, J. A. (1994). The time interval in the intention-behaviour relationship: Meta-analysis. *British Journal of Social Psychology, 33*, 405–418.

Rapaport, P., & Orbell, S. (2000). Augmenting the theory of planned behaviour: Motivation to provide practical assistance and emotional support to parents. *Psychology & Health, 15*, 309–324.

Regan, D. T., & Fazio, R. H. (1977). On the consistency between attitudes and behavior: Look to the method of attitude formation. *Journal of Experimental Social Psychology, 13*, 28–45.

Reise, S. P., Ainsworth, A. T., & Haviland, M. G. (2005). Item Response Theory: Fundamentals, applications, and promise in psychological research. *Current Directions in Psychological Science, 14*, 95–101.

Reiss, I. L., & Leik, R. K. (1989). Evaluating strategies to avoid AIDS: Number of partners vs. use of condoms. *The Journal of Sex Research, 26*, 411–433.

Remington, N. A., Fabrigar, L. R., & Visser, P. S. (2000). Reexamining the circumplex model of affect. *Journal of Personality & Social Psychology, 79*, 286–300.

Reno, R. R., Cialdini, R. B., & Kallgren, C. A. (1993). The transsituational influence of social norms. *Journal of Personality & Social Psychology, 64*, 104–112.

Reyna, V. F., & Farley, F. (2006). Risk and rationality in adolescent decision making: Implications for theory, practice, and public policy. *Psychological Science in the Public Interest, 7*, 1–44.

Rhodes, F., Stein, J. A., Fishbein, M., Goldstein, R. B., & Rotheram-Borus, M. J. (2007). Using theory to understand how interventions work: Project RESPECT, Condom Use, and the Integrative Model. *AIDS and Behavior, 11*, 393–407.

Rhodes, R. E., & Courneya, K. S. (2003a). Investigating multiple components of attitude, subjective norm, and perceived control: An examination of the theory of planned behaviour in the exercise domain. *British Journal of Social Psychology, 42*, 129–146.

Rhodes, R. E., & Courneya, K. S. (2003b). Relationships between personality, an extended theory of planned behaviour model and exercise behaviour. *British Journal of Health Psychology, 8*, 19–36.

Rhodes, R. E., Courneya, K. S., & Jones, L. W. (2002). Personality, the theory of planned behavior, and exercise: A unique role for extroversion's activity facet. *Journal of Applied Social Psychology, 32*, 1721–1736.

Rhodes, R. E., Courneya, K. S., & Jones, L. W. (2004). Personality and social cognitive influences on exercise behavior: Adding the activity trait to the theory of planned behavior. *Psychology of Sport & Exercise, 5*, 243–254.

Richard, R., de Vries, N. K., & van der Pligt, J. (1998). Anticipated regret and precautionary sexual behavior. *Journal of Applied Social Psychology, 28*, 1411–1428.

Richard, R., van der Pligt, J., & de Vries, N. (1995). Anticipated affective reactions and prevention of AIDS. *British Journal of Social Psychology, 34*, 9–21.

Riketta, M. (2000). Discriminative validation of numerical indices of attitude ambivalence. *Current Research in Social Psychology, 5*.

Rimal, R. N., Lapinski, M. K., Cook, R. J., & Real, K. (2005). Moving toward a theory of normative influences: How perceived benefits and similarity moderate the impact of descriptive norms on behaviors. *Journal of Health Communication, 10*, 433–450.

Rimal, R. N., & Real, K. (2003). Understanding the influence of perceived norms on behaviors. *Communication Theory, 13*, 184–203.

Rimal, R. N., & Real, K. (2005). How behaviors are influenced by perceived norms: A test of the theory of normative social behavior. *Communication Research, 32*, 389–414.

Rise, J. (1992). An empirical study of the decision to use condoms among Norwegian adolescents using the theory of reasoned action. *Journal of Community & Applied Social Psychology, 2*, 185–197.

Rise, J., Sheeran, P., & Skalle, S. (2006). *The role of self-identity in the theory of planned behavior: A meta-analysis.* Unpublished manuscript, Norwegian Institute for Alcohol and Drug Abuse, Oslo.

Rise, J., & Wilhelmsen, B. U. (1998). Prediction of adolescents' intention not to drink alcohol: Theory of planned behavior. *American Journal of Health Behavior, 22*, 206–217.

Rivis, A., & Sheeran, P. (2003). Descriptive norms as an additional predictor in the theory of planned behaviour: A meta-analysis. *Current Psychology: Developmental, Learning, Personality, Social, 22*, 218–233.

Rivis, A., & Sheeran, P. (2003). Social influences and the theory of planned behaviour: Evidence for a direct relationship between prototypes and young people's exercise behaviour. *Psychology and Health, 18*, 567–583.

Robinson, R., & Smith, C. (2002). Psychosocial and demographic variables associated with consumer intention to purchase sustainably produced foods as defined by the Midwest Food Alliance. *Journal of Nutrition Education & Behavior, 33*, 316–325.

Rodgers, W. M., & Brawley, L. R. (1993). Using both self-efficacy theory and the theory of planned behavior to discriminate adherers and dropouts from structured programs. *Journal of Applied Sport Psychology, 5*, 195–206.

Rodin, J. (1986). Aging and health: Effects of the sense of control. *Science, 233*, 1271–1276.

Rodin, J. (1990). Control by any other name: Definitions, concepts, and processes. In J. Rodin & C. Schooler (Eds.), *Self-directedness: Cause and effects throughout the life course* (pp. 1–17). Hillsdale, NJ: Lawrence Erlbaum Associates.

Rokeach, M., & Mezei, L. (1966). Race and shared belief as factors in social choice. *Science, 151*, 167–172.

Rosenberg, M. J. (1956). Cognitive structure and attitudinal affect. *Journal of Abnormal and Social Psychology, 53*, 367–372.

Rosenberg, M. J., Hovland, C. I., McGuire, W. J., Abelson, R. P., & Brehm, J. W. (Eds.). (1960). *Attitude organization and change: An analysis of consistency among attitude components*. New Haven, CT: Yale University Press.

Rosenstock, I. M., Strecher, V. J., & Becker, M. H. (1994). The health belief model and HIV risk behavior change. In R. J. DiClemente & J. L. Peterson (Eds.), *Preventing AIDS: Theories and methods of behavioral interventions. AIDS prevention and mental health* (pp. 5–24). New York: Plenum Press.

Ross, L., & Ward, A. (1996). Naive realism in everyday Life: Implications for social conflict and misunderstanding. In T. Brown, E. Reed & E. Turiel (Eds.), *Values and knowledge* (pp. 103–136). Mahwah, NJ: Erlbaum.

Rossi, P. H., Lipsey, M. W., & Freeman, H. E. (2004). *Evaluation: A systematic approach* (7th ed.). Thousand Oaks, CA: Sage.

Rothman, A. J., Bartels, R. D., Wlaschin, J., & Salovey, P. (2006). The Strategic use of gain- and loss-framed messages to promote healthy behavior: How theory can inform practice. *Journal of Communication, 56*, S202–S220.

Rothman, A. J., & Salovey, P. (1997). Shaping perceptions to motivate healthy behavior: The role of message framing. *Psychological Bulletin, 121*, 3–19.

Rothman, A. J., Salovey, P., Antone, C., & Keough, K. (1993). The influence of message framing on intentions to perform health behaviors. *Journal of Experimental Social Psychology, 29*, 408–433.

Rotter, J. B. (1966). Generalized expectancies for internal versus external control of reinforcement. *Psychological Monographs (General and Applied), 80*, 1–28.

Russell, J. A. (1980). A circumplex model of affect. *Journal of Personality & Social Psychology, 39*, 1161–1178.

Rutter, D., & Quine, L. (Eds.). (2002). *Changing health behaviour: Intervention and research with social cognition models*. Buckingham, England: Open University Press.

Salgado, J. (2002). The Big Five personality dimensions and counterproductive behaviors. *International Journal of Selection & Assessment, 10*, 117–125.

Sample, J., & Warland, R. (1973). Attitude and prediction of behavior. *Social Forces, 51*, 292–304.

Sandberg, T., & Conner, M. (2008). Anticipated regret as an additional predictor in the theory of planned behavior: A meta-analysis. *British Journal of Social Psychology, 47*, 589-606.

Sanderson, C. A., & Jemmott, J. B. I. (1996). Moderation and mediation of HIV-prevention interventions: Relationship status, intentions, and condom use among college students. *Journal of Applied Social Psychology, 26*, 2076–2099.

Sanna, L. J., & Schwarz, N. (2004). Integrating temporal biases: The interplay of focal thoughts and accessibility experiences. *Psychological Science, 15*, 474–481.

Sayeed, S., Fishbein, M., Hornik, R., Cappella, J., & Ahern, R. K. (2005). Adolescent marijuana use intentions: Using theory to plan an intervention. *Drugs: Education, Prevention & Policy, 12*, 19–34.

Schaller, M., & Cialdini, R. B. (1990). Happiness, sadness, and helping: A motivational integration. In E. T. Higgins & R. M. Sorrentino (Eds.), *Handbook of motivation and cognition: Foundations of social behavior* (Vol. 2, pp. 265–296). New York: Guilford Press.

Schifter, D. E., & Ajzen, I. (1985). Intention, perceived control, and weight loss: An application of the theory of planned behavior. *Journal of Personality and Social Psychology, 49*, 843–851.

Schlueter, L. A. (1982). Knowledge and beliefs about breast cancer and breast self-examination among athletic and nonathletic women. *Nursing Research, 31*, 348–353.

Schmidt, F. L. (1973). Implications of a measurement problem for expectancy theory research. *Organizational Behavior & Human Performance, 10*, 243–251.

Schnell, D. J., Galavotti, C., Fishbein, M., & Chan, D. K.-S. (1996). Measuring the adoption of consistent use of condoms using the stages of change model. *Public Health Reports, 111*(Supplement 1), 59–68.

Schulze, R., & Wittmann, W. W. (2003). A meta-analysis of the theory of reasoned action and the theory of planned behavior: The principle of compatibility and multidimensionality of beliefs as moderators. In R. Schulze, H. Holling, & D. Böhning (Eds.), *Meta-analysis: New developments and applications in medical and social sciences* (pp. 219–250). Cambridge, MA: Hogrefe & Huber Publishers.

Schuman, H., Steeh, C., Bobo, L., & Krysan, M. (1997). *Racial attitudes in America: Trends and interpretations.* Cambridge, MA: Harvard University Press.

Schütz, H., & Six, B. (1996). How strong is the relationship between prejudice and discrimination? A meta-analytic answer. *International Journal of Intercultural Relations, 20*, 441–462.

Schwarz, N. (2000). Social judgment and attitudes: Warmer, more social, and less conscious. *European Journal of Social Psychology, 30*, 149–176.

Schwarz, N., & Clore, G. L. (1983). Mood, misattribution, and judgments of well-being: Informative and directive functions of affective states. *Journal of Personality and Social Psychology, 45*, 513–523.

Schwarz, N., & Clore, G. L. (1996). Feelings and phenomenal experiences. In E. T. Higgins & A. W. Kruglanski (Eds.), *Social psychology: Handbook of basic principles* (pp. 433–465). New York: Guilford.

Schwarz, N., Groves, R. M., & Schuman, H. (1998). Survey methods. In D. T. Gilbert, S. T. Fiske, & G. Lindzey (Eds.), *Handbook of social psychology* (4th ed., Vol. 1, pp. 143–179). Boston, MA: McGraw-Hill.

Schwarzer, R. (2008). Modeling health behavior change: How to predict and modify the adoption and maintenance of health behaviors. *Applied Psychology: An International Review, 57*, 1–29.

Sears, D. O. (1988). Symbolic racism. In P. A. Katz & D. A. Taylor (Eds.), *Eliminating racism: Profiles in controversy. Perspectives in social psychology* (pp. 53–84). New York: Plenum Press.

Sheeran, P. (2002). Intention-behavior relations: A conceptual and empirical review. In W. Stroebe & M. Hewstone (Eds.), *European review of social psychology* (Vol. 12, pp. 1–36). Chichester, England: Wiley.

Sheeran, P., Abraham, C., & Orbell, S. (1999). Psychosocial correlates of heterosexual condom use: A meta-analysis. *Psychological Bulletin, 125*, 90–132.

Sheeran, P., Norman, P., & Orbell, S. (1999). Evidence that intentions based on attitudes better predict behaviour than intentions based on subjective norms. *European Journal of Social Psychology, 29,* 403–406.

Sheeran, P., & Orbell, S. (1998). Do intentions predict condom use? Meta-analysis and examination of six moderator variables. *British Journal of Social Psychology, 37,* 231–250.

Sheeran, P., & Orbell, S. (1999a). Augmenting the theory of planned behavior: Roles for anticipated regret and descriptive norms. *Journal of Applied Social Psychology, 29,* 2107–2142.

Sheeran, P., & Orbell, S. (1999b). Implementation intentions and repeated behaviour: Augmenting the predictive validity of the theory of planned behaviour. *European Journal of Social Psychology, 29,* 349–369.

Sheeran, P., & Orbell, S. (2000a). Self-schemas and the theory of planned behaviour. *European Journal of Social Psychology, 30,* 533–550.

Sheeran, P., & Orbell, S. (2000b). Using implementation intentions to increase attendance for cervical cancer screening. *Health Psychology, 19,* 283–289.

Sheeran, P., Orbell, S., & Trafimow, D. (1999). Does the temporal stability of behavioral intentions moderate intention-behavior and past behavior-future behavior relations? *Personality and Social Psychology Bulletin, 25,* 721–730.

Sheeran, P., & Silverman, M. (2003). Evaluation of three interventions to promote workplace health and safety: Evidence for the utility of implementation intentions. *Social Science & Medicine, 56,* 2153–2163.

Sheeran, P., & Taylor, S. (1999). Predicting intentions to use condoms: A meta-analysis and comparison of the theories of reasoned action and planned behavior. *Journal of Applied Social Psychology, 29,* 1624–1675.

Sheeran, P., Trafimow, D., Finlay, K. A., & Norman, P. (2002). Evidence that the type of person affects the strength of the perceived behavioural control-intention relationship. *British Journal of Social Psychology, 41,* 253–270.

Sheppard, B. H., Hartwick, J., & Warshaw, P. R. (1988). The theory of reasoned action: A meta-analysis of past research with recommendations for modifications and future research. *Journal of Consumer Research, 15,* 325–342.

Sherif, M., & Hovland, C. I. (1961). *Social judgment: Assimilation and contrast effects in communication and attitude change.* New Haven, CT: Yale University Press.

Sherman, S. J. (1980). On the self-erasing nature of errors of prediction. *Journal of Personality and Social Psychology, 39,* 211–221.

Sherman, S. J., & Fazio, R. H. (1983). Parallels between attitudes and traits as predictors of behavior. *Journal of Personality, 51,* 308–345.

Sheth, J. N., & Talarzyk, W. W. (1972). Perceived instrumentality and value importance as determinants of attitudes. *Journal of Marketing Research, 9,* 6–9.

Silver, E., & Bauman, L. (2006). The association of sexual experience with attitudes, beliefs, and risk behaviors of inner-city adolescents. *Journal of Research on Adolescents, 16,* 29–45.

Silver Wallace, L. (2002). Osteoporosis prevention in college women: Application of the expanded health belief model. *American Journal of Health Behavior, 26,* 163–172.

Sivacek, J., & Crano, W. D. (1982). Vested interest as a moderator of attitude-behavior consistency. *Journal of Personality and Social Psychology, 43,* 210–221.

Skinner, E. A. (1996). A guide to constructs of control. *Journal of Personality & Social Psychology, 71,* 549–570.

Smith, H. N. (1932). A scale for measuring attitudes about prohibition. *Journal of Abnormal & Social Psychology, 26*, 429–437.

Smith, P. C. (1974). The development of a method of measuring job satisfaction: The Cornell studies. In E. A. Fleishman & A. R. Bass (Eds.), *Studies in personnel and industrial psychology* (3rd ed.). Homewood, IL: Dorsey.

Smith, P. C., Kendall, L. M., & Hulin, C. L. (1969). *The measurement of satisfaction in work and retirement: A strategy for the study of attitudes.* Chicago: Rand Mcnally.

Smith-McLallen, A., & Fishbein, M. (2008). Predictors of intentions to perform six cancer-related behaviors: Roles for injunctive and descriptive norms. *Psychology, Health & Medicine, 13*(4), 389-401.

Smith-McLallen, A. & Fishbein, M. (2009). Predicting intentions to engage in cancer prevention and detection behaviors: Examining differences between black and white adults. *Psychology Health & Medicine, 14*(2), 180-189.

Smith-McLallen, A., Fishbein, M., & Hornik, R. (in preparation). Psychosocial determinants of cancer-related information seeking among cancer patients.

Sopory, P., & Dillard, J. P. (2002). The persuasive effects of metaphor: A meta-analysis. *Human Communication Research, 28*, 382–419.

Sparks, P., Guthrie, C. A., & Shepherd, R. (1997). The dimensional structure of the perceived behavioral control construct. *Journal of Applied Social Psychology, 27*, 418–438.

Sparks, P., Hedderley, D., & Shepherd, R. (1991). Expectancy-value models of attitudes: A note on the relationship between theory and methodology. *European Journal of Social Psychology, 21*, 261–271.

Sparks, P., & Shepherd, R. (1992). Self-identity and the theory of planned behavior: Assessing the role of identification with "green consumerism." *Social Psychology Quarterly, 55*, 388–399.

Spirito, A., Ruggiero, L., Duckworth, M., & Low, K. G. (1993). The relationship of diabetes knowledge to regimen compliance and metabolic control during pregnancy. *Psychology & Health, 8*, 345–353.

St. Onge, S. (1995). Modeling and role-playing. In M. Ballou (Ed.), *Psychological interventions: A guide to strategies* (pp. 21–36): Praeger Publishers / Greenwood Publishing Group.

Stagner, R. (1942). Some factors related to attitude toward war, 1938. *Journal of Social Psychology, 16*, 131–142.

Steele, C. M., & Josephs, R. A. (1990). Alcohol myopia: Its prized and dangerous effects. *American Psychologist, 45*, 921–933.

Steptoe, A., & Feldman, P. J. (2001). Neighborhood problems as sources of chronic stress: Development of a measure of neighborhood problems, and associations with socioeconomic status and health. *Annals of Behavioral Medicine, 23*, 177–185.

Strecher, V. J., Champion, V. L., & Rosenstock, I. M. (1997). The health belief model and health behavior. In D. S. Gochman (Ed.), *Handbook of health behavior research 1: Personal and social determinants* (pp. 71–91). New York: Plenum Press.

Strickland, B. R. (1989). Internal-external control expectancies: From contingency to creativity. *American Psychologist, 44*, 1–12.

Sutton, S., McVey, D., & Glanz, A. (1999). A comparative test of the theory of reasoned action and the theory of planned behavior in the prediction of condom use intentions in a national sample of English young people. *Health Psychology, 18*, 72–81.

Swartz, L., & Kagee, A. (2006). Community participation in AIDS vaccine trials: Empowerment or science? *Social Science & Medicine, 63*, 1143–1146.

Talaska, C. A., Fiske, S. T., & Chaiken, S. (2004). *Predicting discrimination: A meta-analysis of the racial attitude-behavior literature.* Unpublished manuscript.

Taylor, S. E., & Pham, L. B. (1996). Mental simulation, motivation, and action. In P. M. Gollwitzer & J. A. Bargh (Eds.), *The psychology of action: Linking cognition and motivation to behavior* (pp. 219–235). New York: Guilford Press.

Taylor, S. E., & Pham, L. B. (1998). The effect of mental simulation on goal-directed performance. *Imagination, Cognition and Personality, 18*, 253–268.

Teachman, B. A., & Woody, S. R. (2003). Automatic processing in spider phobia: Implicit fear associations over the course of treatment. *Journal of Abnormal Psychology, 112*, 100–109.

Terry, D. J., & Hogg, M. A. (1996). Group norms and the attitude-behavior relationship: A role for group identification. *Personality and Social Psychology Bulletin, 22*, 776–793.

Terry, D. J., Hogg, M. A., & White, K. M. (1999). The theory of planned behaviour: Self-identity, social identity and group norms. *British Journal of Social Psychology, 38*, 225–244.

Terry, D. J., & O'Leary, J. E. (1995). The theory of planned behaviour: The effects of perceived behavioural control and self-efficacy. *British Journal of Social Psychology, 34*, 199–220.

Thomas, W. I., & Znaniecki, F. (1918). *The Polish peasant in Europe and America* (Vol. 1). Boston: Badger.

Thompson, M. M., Zanna, M. P., & Griffin, D. W. (1995). Let's not be indifferent about (attitudinal) ambivalence. In R. E. Petty & J. A. Krosnick (Eds.), *Attitude strength: Antecedents and consequences* (pp. 361–386). Mahwah, NJ: Erlbaum.

Thompson, S. C., & Spacapan, S. (1991). Perceptions of control in vulnerable populations. *Journal of Social Issues, 47*, 1–21.

Thurstone, L. (1928). Attitudes can be measured. *American Journal of Sociology, 33*, 529–554.

Thurstone, L. L. (1931). The measurement of social attitudes. *Journal of Abnormal and Social Psychology, 26*, 249–269.

Thurstone, L. L., & Chave, E. J. (1929). *The measurement of attitude: A psychological method and some experiments with a scale for measuring attitude toward the church.* Chicago: University of Chicago Press.

Tolma, E. L., Reininger, B. M., Ureda, J., & Evans, A. (2003). Cognitive motivations associated with screening mammography in Cyprus. *Preventive Medicine, 36*, 363–373.

Toulmin, S. E. (1958). *The uses of argument.* Cambridge, England: Cambridge University Press.

Tourangeau, R., & Yan, T. (2007). Sensitive questions in surveys. *Psychological Bulletin, 133*, 859–883.

Trafimow, D., & Duran, A. (1998). Some tests of the distinction between attitude and perceived behavioural control. *British Journal of Social Psychology, 37*, 1–14.

Trafimow, D., & Finlay, K. A. (1996). The importance of subjective norms for a minority of people: Between-subjects and within-subjects analyses. *Personality and Social Psychology Bulletin, 22*, 820–828.

Trafimow, D., & Finlay, K. (2002). The prediction of attitudes from beliefs and evaluations: The logic of the double negative. *British Journal of Social Psychology, 41*, 77–86.

Trafimow, D., Sheeran, P., Conner, M., & Finlay, K. A. (2002). Evidence that perceived behavioural control is a multidimensional construct: Perceived control and perceived difficulty. *British Journal of Social Psychology, 41*, 101–121.

Triandis, H. C. (1967). Toward an analysis of the components of interpersonal attitudes. In C. W. Sherif & M. Sherif (Eds.), *Attitudes, ego involvement, and change* (pp. 227–270). New York: John Wiley.

Triandis, H. C. (1972). *The analysis of subjective culture.* New York: Wiley.

Triandis, H. C. (1977). *Interpersonal behavior.* Monterey, CA: Brooks/Cole.

Turner, J. C. (1991). *Social influence.* Bristol, England: Open University Press.

Turner, J. C., Hogg, M. A., Oakes, P. J., Reicher, S. D., & Wetherell, M. S. (1987). *Rediscovering the social group: A self-categorization theory.* Oxford, England: Basil Blackwell.

Tversky, A., & Kahneman, D. (1981). The framing of decisions and the psychology of choice. *Science, 211*, 453–458.

Updegraff, J. A., Sherman, D. K., Luyster, F. S., & Mann, T. L. (2007). The effects of message quality and congruency on perceptions of tailored health communications. *Journal of Experimental Social Psychology, 43*, 249–257.

Valle, P. c. O. D., Rebelo, E. n., Reis, E., & Menezes, J. o. (2005). Combining behavioral theories to predict recycling involvement. *Environment and Behavior, 37*, 364–396.

van den Putte, B. (1993). *On the theory of reasoned action.* Unpublished dissertation, University of Amsterdam, The Netherlands.

van der Pligt, J., & de Vries, N. K. (1998a). Belief importance in expectancy-value models of attitudes. *Journal of Applied Social Psychology, 28*, 1339–1354.

van der Pligt, J., & de Vries, N. K. (1998b). Expectancy-value models of health behavior: The role of salience and anticipated regret. *Psychology and Health, 13*, 289–305.

van der Pligt, J., & Eiser, J. R. (1984). Dimensional salience, judgment and attitudes. In J. R. Eiser (Ed.), *Attitudinal judgment* (pp. 43–63). New York: Springer-Verlag.

van Harreveld, F., van der Pligt, J., de Vries, N. K., & Andreas, S. (2000). The structure of attitudes: Attribute importance, accessibility, and judgment. *British Journal of Social Psychology, 39*, 363–380.

van Hooft, E. A. J., Born, M. P., Taris, T. W., & van der Flier, H. (2004). Job search and the theory of planned behavior: Minority-majority group differences in The Netherlands. *Journal of Vocational Behavior, 65*, 366–390.

Van Ryn, M., & Vinokur, A. D. (1992). How did it work? An examination of the mechanisms through which an intervention for the unemployed promoted job-search behavior. *American Journal of Community Psychology, 20*, 577–597.

Verplanken, B., & Faes, S. (1999). Good intentions, bad habits, and effects of forming implementation intentions on healthy eating. *European Journal of Social Psychology, 29*, 591–604.

Villarruel, A. M., Jemmott, J. B. I., Jemmott, L. S., & Ronis, D. L. (2004). Predictors of sexual intercourse and condom use intentions among Spanish-dominant Latino youth: A Test of the Planned Behavior Theory. *Nursing Research, 53,* 172–181.

Viswesvaran, C., & Ones, D. S. (2000). Perspectives on models of job performance. *International Journal of Selection & Assessment, 8,* 216–226.

von Haeften, I., & Kenski, K. (2001). Multi-partnered heterosexuals' condom use for vaginal sex with their main partner as a function of attitude, subjective norm, partner norm, perceived behavioural control and weighted control beliefs. *Psychology, Health & Medicine, 6,* 165–177.

Wagner, G. J., & Rabkin, J. G. (2000). Measuring medication adherence: Are missed doses reported more accurately than perfect adherence? *AIDS Care, 12,* 405–408.

Walker, G. J., Courneya, K. S., & Deng, J. (2006). Ethnicity, gender, and the theory of planned behavior: The case of playing the lottery. *Journal of Leisure Research, 38,* 224–248.

Wall, A. M., Hinson, R. E., & McKee, S. A. (1998). Alcohol outcome expectancies, attitudes toward drinking and the theory of planned behavior. *Journal of Studies on Alcohol, 59,* 409–419.

Waly, P., & Cook, S. W. (1965). Effect of attitude on judgments of plausibility. *Journal of Personality and Social Psychology, 2,* 745–749.

Wambach, K. A. (1997). Breastfeeding intention and outcome: A test of the theory of planned behavior. *Research in Nursing and Health, 20,* 51–59.

Warburton, J., & Terry, D. J. (2000). Volunteer decision making by older people: A test of a revised theory of planned behavior. *Basic and Applied Social Psychology, 22,* 245–257.

Warner, L., Clay-Warner, J., Boles, J., & Williamson, J. (1998). Assessing condom use practices: Implications for evaluating method and user effectiveness. *Sexually Transmitted Diseases, 25,* 273–277.

Warner, L., Newman, D. R., Kamb, M. L., Fishbein, M., Douglas, J. M. Jr., Zenilman, J., et al. (2008). Problems with condom use among patients attending sexually transmitted disease clinics: prevalence, predictors, and relation to incident gonorrhea and chlamydia. *American Journal of Epidemiology, 167,* 341–349.

Warshaw, P. R., & Davis, F. D. (1985). Disentangling behavioral intention and behavioral expectation. *Journal of Experimental Social Psychology, 21,* 213–228.

Watson, D., & Tellegen, A. (1985). Toward a consensual structure of mood. *Psychological Bulletin, 98,* 219-235.

Watson, J. B. (1925). *Behaviorism.* New York: Norton.

Webb, T. L., & Sheeran, P. (2006). Does changing behavioral intentions engender behavior change? A meta-analysis of the experimental evidence. *Psychological Bulletin, 132,* 249–268.

Wee, C. C., McCarthy, E. P., & Phillips, R. S. (2005). Factors associated with colon cancer screening: The role of patient factors and physician counseling. *Preventive Medicine, 41,* 23–29.

Weigel, R. H., & Newman, L. S. (1976). Increasing attitude-behavior correspondence by broadening the scope of the behavioral measure. *Journal of Personality and Social Psychology, 33,* 793–802.

Weinberg, R. S., Gould, D., & Jackson, A. (1979). Expectations and performance: An empirical test of Bandura's self-efficacy theory. *Journal of Sport Psychology, 1*, 320–331.

Werner, P. D. (1978). Personality and attitude-activism correspondence. *Journal of Personality and Social Psychology, 36*, 1375–1390.

Wheeler, M. E., & Hess, K. W. (1976). Treatment of juvenile obesity by successive approximation control of eating. *Journal of Behavior Therapy and Experimental Psychiatry, 7*, 235–241.

Whitehead, K. A., Kriel, A. J., & Richter, L. M. (2005). Barriers to conducting a community mobilization intervention among youth in a rural South African community. *Journal of Community Psychology, 33*, 253–259.

Wicker, A. W. (1969). Attitudes versus actions: The relationship of verbal and overt behavioral responses to attitude objects. *Journal of Social Issues, 25*, 41–78.

Wiers, R. W., Van Woerden, N., Smulders, F. T. Y., & De Jong, P. J. (2002). Implicit and explicit alcohol-related cognitions in heavy and light drinkers. *Journal of Abnormal Psychology, 111*, 648–658.

Wilke, W. H. (1934). An experimental comparison of the speech, the radio, and the printed page as propaganda devices. *Archives of Psychology*, No. 169.

Willemsen, M. C., de Vries, H., van Breukelen, G., & Oldenburg, B. (1996). Determinants of intention to quit smoking among Dutch employees: The influence of the social environment. *Preventive Medicine, 25*, 195–202.

Wilson, P. M., Rodgers, W. M., Blanchard, C. M., & Gessell, J. (2003). The relationship between psychological needs, self-determined motivation, exercise attitudes, and physical fitness. *Journal of Applied Social Psychology, 33*, 2373–2392.

Wilson, T. D., Lindsey, S., & Schooler, T. Y. (2000). A model of dual attitudes. *Psychological Review, 107*, 101–126.

Woodworth, R. S., & Schlosberg, H. (1954). *Experimental psychology*. New York: Holt.

Worthington, R. L., Dillon, F. R., & Becker-Schutte, A. M. (2005). Development, reliability, and validity of the Lesbian, Gay, and Bisexual Knowledge and Attitudes Scale for Heterosexuals (LGB-KASH). *Journal of Counseling Psychology, 52*, 104–118.

Wyer, R. S. (1970a). The prediction of evaluation of social role occupants as a function of the favorableness, relevance and probability associated with attributes of these occupants. *Sociometry, 33*, 79–96.

Wyer, R. S. (1970b). Quantitative prediction of belief and opinion change: A further test of a subjective probability model. *Journal of Personality and Social Psychology, 16*, 559–570.

Yang-Wallentin, F., Schmidt, P., Davidov, E., & Bamberg, S. (2004). Is there any interaction effect between intention and perceived behavioral control? *Methods of Psychological Research Online, 8*, 127–157.

Ybarra, O., & Trafimow, D. (1998). How priming the private self or collective self affects the relative weights of attitudes and subjective norms. *Personality and Social Psychology Bulletin, 24*, 362–370.

Yzer, M. (2007). Perceived control moderates attitudinal and normative effects on intention: I'd like to, but I can't, so I won't. In I. Ajzen, R. Hornik, & D. Albarracín (Eds.), *Prediction and change of behavior: Applying the reasoned action approach* (pp. 111–127). Mahwah, NJ: Lawrence Erlbaum.

Yzer, M., Fishbein, M., & Cappella, J. (2007). Using behavioral theory to investigate routes to persuasion for segmented groups: A case study of adolescent drug use. In M. Hinner (Ed.), *Freiberger Beiträge zur interkulturellen und Wirtschaftskommunikation: A forum for general and intercultural business communication* (Vol. 3). Frankfurt am Main, Germany: Peter Lang.

Yzer, M. C., Fishbein, M., & Hennessy, M. (2008). HIV prevention interventions affect behavior indirectly: Results from the AIDS Community Demonstration Projects. *AIDS Care, 20,* 456–461.

Yzer, M. C., Hennessy, M., & Fishbein, M. (2004). The usefulness of perceived difficulty for health research. *Psychology, Health and Medicine, 9,* 149–162.

Zajonc, R. B. (1954). *Structure of the cognitive field.* Unpublished dissertation, University of Michigan, Ann Arbor.

Zanna, M. P., & Rempel, J. K. (1988). Attitudes: A new look at an old concept. In D. Bar-Tal & A. W. Kruglanski (Eds.), *The social psychology of knowledge* (pp. 315–334). Cambridge, England: Cambridge University Press.

Zenilman, J. M., Weisman, C. S., Rompalo, A. M., Ellish, N., Upchurch, D. M., Hook, E. W. III, et al. (1995). Condom use to prevent incident STDs: The validity of self-reported condom use. *Sexually Transmitted Diseases, 22,* 1–7.

Zimmerman, B. J., Bandura, A., & Martinez-Pons, M. (1992). Self-motivation for academic attainment: The role of self-efficacy beliefs and personal goal setting. *American Educational Research Journal, 29,* 663–676.

Zuckerman, M., & Reis, H. T. (1978). Comparison of three models for predicting altruistic behavior. *Journal of Personality and Social Psychology, 36,* 498–510.

APPENDIX: CONSTRUCTING A REASONED ACTION QUESTIONNAIRE

In Part I of this appendix we describe the steps involved in the construction of a questionnaire to be used in research with our reasoned action model, and in Part II we provide an example of a standard questionnaire.

☐ Part I: Formative Research

Defining the Behavior

Before any work can begin, the behavior of interest must be clearly defined in terms of its target, action, context, and time elements (see Chapter 2).

Example: Physical Activity

We could define exercise behavior as follows (see Terry & O'Leary, 1995): "Exercising for at least 20 minutes, three times per week, for the next 3 months."

Specifying the Research Population

The population of interest to the investigators also must be clearly defined.

Example: Major Heart Surgery Patients

In this example, only individuals who have just undergone major heart surgery would be included in the research population.

Formulating Items for Direct Measures

Three to six items are formulated to assess each of the major constructs in our reasoned action model: attitude, perceived norm, perceived behavioral control, and intention. Seven-point bipolar adjective scales are typically employed. Sample items assessing intention and each aspect of attitude, perceived norm, and perceived control are shown below; additional items and instructions to the participants are shown in the sample questionnaire (Part II). Participants are asked to circle the number that best describes their personal opinions. Note that the items are formulated to be exactly compatible with the behavioral criterion and to be self-directed.

Attitude: Instrumental and Experiential Aspects

My exercising for at least 20 minutes, three times per week, for the next 3 months would be

bad : 1 : 2 : 3 : 4 : 5 : 6 : 7 : good

pleasant : 1 : 2 : 3 : 4 : 5 : 6 : 7 : unpleasant

Perceived Norm: Injunctive and Descriptive Aspects

Most people who are important to me think I should exercise for at least 20 minutes, three times per week, for the next 3 months.

agree : 1 : 2 : 3 : 4 : 5 : 6 : 7 : disagree

Most people like me exercised for at least 20 minutes, three times per week, in the 3 months following their major heart surgery.

unlikely : 1 : 2 : 3 : 4 : 5 : 6 : 7 : likely

Perceived Behavioral Control: Capacity and Autonomy Aspects

I am confident that I can exercise for at least 20 minutes, three times per week, for the next 3 months.

true : 1 : 2 : 3 : 4 : 5 : 6 : 7 : false

My exercising for at least 20 minutes, three times per week, for the next 3 months is up to me.

disagree : 1 : 2 : 3 : 4 : 5 : 6 : 7 : agree

Intention

I intend to exercise for at least 20 minutes, three times per week, for the next 3 months.

likely : 1 : 2 : 3 : 4 : 5 : 6 : 7 : unlikely

Past Behavior

In the past 3 months, I have exercised for at least 20 minutes, three times per week,.

false : 1 : 2 : 3 : 4 : 5 : 6 : 7 : true

(Note that, in the current example, past behavior may not be a good predictor of future behavior because the past behavior would have occurred prior to the heart surgery.)

Administering a Pilot Questionnaire

Eliciting Salient Beliefs

A small sample of individuals representative of the research population (i.e., postoperative cardiac patients) is used to elicit readily accessible behavioral outcomes, normative referents, and control factors. Although the participants can be assembled in groups, the elicitation is done individually in a free-response format.

Instructions: Please take a few minutes to tell us what you think about the possibility of exercising for at least 20 minutes, three times per week, for the next 3 months. There are no right or wrong responses; we are merely interested in your personal opinions. In response to the questions that follow, please list the thoughts that come immediately to mind. Write each thought on a separate line. (Five or six lines are provided for each question.)

Behavioral Outcomes

1. What do you see as the advantages of your exercising for at least 20 minutes, three times per week, for the next 3 months?
2. What do you see as the disadvantages of your exercising for at least 20 minutes, three times per week, for the next 3 months?
3. What else comes to mind when you think about exercising for at least 20 minutes, three times per week, for the next 3 months?

Normative Referents

When it comes to your exercising for at least 20 minutes, three times per week, for the next 3 months, there might be individuals or groups who would think you should or should not perform this behavior.

1. Please list the individuals or groups who would approve or think you should exercise for at least 20 minutes, three times per week, for the next 3 months.
2. Please list the individuals or groups who would disapprove or think you should not exercise for at least 20 minutes, three times per week, for the next 3 months.
3. Sometimes, when we are not sure what to do, we look to see what others are doing. Please list the individuals or groups who, after major heart surgery, are most likely to exercise for at least 20 minutes, three times per week, for the 3 months following surgery.
4. Please list the individuals or groups who, after major heart surgery, are least likely to exercise for at least 20 minutes, three times per week, for the 3 months following surgery.

Control Factors

1. Please list any factors or circumstances that would make it easy or enable you to exercise for at least 20 minutes, three times per week, for the next 3 months.
2. Please list any factors or circumstances that would make it difficult or prevent you from exercising for at least 20 minutes, three times per week, for the next 3 months.

Constructing Sets of Modal Salient Beliefs

A content analysis (see Chapter 3) of the responses to these questions results in lists of modal salient outcomes, referents, and control factors. These lists are used to construct items to be included in the final questionnaire, as described next.

Formulating Direct Measures

The pilot questionnaire, in addition to eliciting salient outcomes, normative referents, and control factors, also includes the items that were formulated to obtain direct measures of attitude toward the behavior, perceived norm, and perceived behavioral control. The data obtained are used to select reliable and valid items for use in the final questionnaire. Each set of items designed to directly assess a given construct should have a high degree of internal consistency (e.g., a high alpha coefficient), and the measures of the different constructs should exhibit discriminant validity. To achieve these aims, one or two items may have to be dropped for each construct. Confirmatory factory analysis is one means of evaluating the quality of the scales to be included.

Finally, the pilot questionnaire also includes measures of any background factors or other variables the investigator believes may be of interest for the behavior under investigation. These could be demographic characteristics (e.g., age, gender, ethnicity, level of education, income), personality characteristics (e.g., conscientiousness), other individual difference variables (e.g., self-esteem, sensation seeking), or social structure variables (e.g., rural vs. urban residence). The results of the pilot study also allow us to evaluate the utility of these background measures: Do the personality and other individual difference measures have high internal consistency? If not, can internal consistency be improved by deleting some of the items? Do any of the background variables correlate with intentions or past behavior? If not, should they be retained in the final questionnaire?

☐ Part II: Preparing a Standard Questionnaire

We are now ready to put together the standard questionnaire to be used in the main study. This questionnaire includes the following elements.

Behavioral Beliefs and Outcome Evaluations

With respect to each salient behavioral outcome, items are formulated to assess the strength of the behavioral belief and the evaluation of the outcome.

Sample Outcome: Faster recovery from my surgery

Behavioral Belief Strength

My exercising for at least 20 minutes, three times per week, for the next 3 months will result in my having a faster recovery from my surgery.

likely : 1 : 2 : 3 : 4 : 5 : 6 : 7 : unlikely

Outcome Evaluation

My having a faster recovery from my surgery is

good : 1 : 2 : 3 : 4 : 5 : 6 : 7 : bad

Injunctive Normative Beliefs and Motivation to Comply

With respect to each salient normative referent, items are formulated to assess the strength of the injunctive normative belief and the motivation to comply with the referent individual or group.

Sample Injunctive Normative Referent: My Doctor

Injunctive Normative Belief Strength

My doctor thinks that

I should : 1 : 2 : 3 : 4 : 5 : 6 : 7 : I should not

exercise for at least 20 minutes, three times per week, for the next 3 months.

Motivation to Comply

When it comes to matters of health, I want to do what my doctor thinks I should do.

agree : 1 : 2 : 3 : 4 : 5 : 6 : 7 : disagree

Descriptive Normative Beliefs and Identification With the Referent

With respect to each relevant salient referent, items are formulated to assess the strength of the descriptive normative belief and the identification with the referent individual or group.

Sample Descriptive Normative Referent: My Friends

Descriptive Normative Belief Strength

Most of my friends who have undergone major heart surgery have exercised for at least 20 minutes, three times per week, for the 3 months following surgery.

false : 1 : 2 : 3 : 4 : 5 : 6 : 7 : true

Identification With the Referent

When it comes to matters of health, how much do you want to be like your friends?

very much : _1_ : _2_ : _3_ : _4_ : _5_ : _6_ : _7_ : not at all

Control Beliefs and Power of Control Factors

With respect to each salient control factor, items are formulated to assess the likelihood that the factor will be present and the factor's power to facilitate or impede performance of the behavior.

Sample Control Factor: Physical Strength

Control Belief Strength

I will have physical strength in the next 3 months.

likely : _1_ : _2_ : _3_ : _4_ : _5_ : _6_ : _7_ : unlikely

Power of control factor

My having physical strength would enable me to exercise for at least 20 minutes, three times per week, for the next 3 months.

disagree : _1_ : _2_ : _3_ : _4_ : _5_ : _6_ : _7_ : agree

Direct Measures

Other elements of the final questionnaire are the direct measures developed on the basis of the pilot data to assess attitudes, perceived norm, perceived behavioral control, and intentions. In addition, the questionnaire will usually also include a measure of past behavior, as described earlier.

Other Measures

The final questionnaire also includes measures of all demographic characteristics, personality variables, and other background factors the investigator decided to retain.

Behavior

Three months following administration of the questionnaire (or another period as defined by the behavioral criterion), the participants are recontacted and asked to report whether they had exercised for at least 20 minutes, three times per week, for the past 3 months.

☐ Sample Standard Questionnaire

It is important to realize that there is no single reasoned-action questionnaire. Each investigation requires construction of a suitable questionnaire. For purposes of illustration, we use "exercising for at least 20 minutes, three times per week, for the next 3 months" as the behavioral criterion, the same behavior we used as an example in Part 1 of this Appendix. We did not elicit salient beliefs before constructing this questionnaire, nor did we validate its direct measures. The items shown are for illustrative purposes only. They are presented in thematic order, not necessarily in the order in which they would appear in an actual questionnaire. These items may not be appropriate for other behaviors, or even for this behavior when applied to a different population or at a different point in time. Formative research is required to construct a questionnaire suitable for the behavior and population of interest. If beliefs are to be assessed, they must be elicited from a representative sample of the research population. Similarly, items designed to directly assess our theory's constructs must be validated prior to construction of the final questionnaire.

The participants are first given general information about the study.

As you may know, physical activity among postoperative patients varies widely. Some patients engage in vigorous exercise during the first 3 months after major heart surgery whereas others do not. The present survey is part of an investigation that tries to discover some of the reasons that patients do or do not engage in physical activity after surgery. Specifically, we are interested in your personal opinions about exercising for at least 20 minutes, three times per week, for the next 3 months. Please read each question carefully, and answer it to the best of your ability. There are no correct or incorrect responses; we are merely interested in your personal point of view.

Thank you for your participation in this study.

Before turning to the actual questionnaire, they are given general instructions on how to use the response scales.

☐ General Instructions

Many questions in this survey make use of rating scales with seven places; you are to circle the number that best describes your opinion. For

example, if you were asked to rate "Drinking wine" on such a scale, the seven places should be interpreted as follows:
Drinking wine is:

good :_1_   :_2_   :_3_   :_4_   :_5_   :_6_   :_7_ : bad

               extremely quite slightly neither   slightly   quite extremely

If you think that drinking wine is *extremely good*, then you would circle the *number 1*.
Drinking wine is:

good : ① : 2 : 3 : 4 : 5 : 6 : 7 : bad

If you think that drinking wine is *quite bad*, then you would circle the *number 6*.
Drinking wine is:

good : 1 : 2 : 3 : 4 : 5 : ⑥ : 7 : bad

If you think that drinking wine is *slightly good*, then you would circle the *number 3*.
Drinking wine is:

good : 1 : 2 : ③ : 4 : 5 : 6 : 7 : bad

If you think that drinking wine is neither good nor bad, then you would circle the *number 4*.
Drinking wine is:

good : 1 : 2 : 3 : ④ : 5 : 6 : 7 : bad

In making your ratings, please remember the following points:

- Be sure to answer all items—do not omit any.
- Never circle more than one number on a single scale.

☐ The Questionnaire

Please answer each of the following questions by circling the number that best describes your opinion. Some of the questions may appear to be similar, but they do address somewhat different issues. Please read each question carefully.

[Outcome Evaluations]

1. My losing weight is

good :_1_ : _2_ : _3_ : _4_ : _5_ : _6_ : _7_ : bad

2. My suffering pain is

   good : 1 : 2 : 3 : 4 : 5 : 6 : 7 : bad

3. My being tired and exhausted is

   good : 1 : 2 : 3 : 4 : 5 : 6 : 7 : bad

4. My building up physical strength is

   good : 1 : 2 : 3 : 4 : 5 : 6 : 7 : bad

5. My hurting myself is

   good : 1 : 2 : 3 : 4 : 5 : 6 : 7 : bad

6. My healing faster is

   good : 1 : 2 : 3 : 4 : 5 : 6 : 7 : bad

[Behavioral Belief Strength]

7. My exercising for at least 20 minutes, three times per week, for the next 3 months will help me lose weight.

   likely : 1 : 2 : 3 : 4 : 5 : 6 : 7 : unlikely

8. If I exercise for at least 20 minutes, three times per week, for the next 3 months I will suffer pain.

   likely : 1 : 2 : 3 : 4 : 5 : 6 : 7 : unlikely

9. If I exercise for at least 20 minutes, three times per week, for the next 3 months I will be tired and exhausted.

   likely : 1 : 2 : 3 : 4 : 5 : 6 : 7 : unlikely

10. If I exercise for at least 20 minutes, three times per week, for the next 3 months I will build up my physical strength.

    likely : 1 : 2 : 3 : 4 : 5 : 6 : 7 : unlikely

11. If I exercise for at least 20 minutes, three times per week, for the next 3 months I will hurt myself.

    likely : 1 : 2 : 3 : 4 : 5 : 6 : 7 : unlikely

12. My exercising for at least 20 minutes, three times per week, for the next 3 months will help me heal faster.

likely : 1 : 2 : 3 : 4 : 5 : 6 : 7 : unlikely

[Motivation to Comply]

13. When it comes to matters of health, I want to do what my spouse or partner thinks I should do.

agree : 1 : 2 : 3 : 4 : 5 : 6 : 7 : disagree

14. When it comes to matters of health, I want to do what my close friends think I should do.

agree : 1 : 2 : 3 : 4 : 5 : 6 : 7 : disagree

15. When it comes to matters of health, I want to do what my doctor thinks I should do.

agree : 1 : 2 : 3 : 4 : 5 : 6 : 7 : disagree

16. When it comes to matters of health, I want to do what my parents think I should do.

agree : 1 : 2 : 3 : 4 : 5 : 6 : 7 : disagree

[Injunctive Belief Strength]

17. My spouse or partner thinks that I should exercise for at least 20 minutes, three times per week, for the next 3 months.

probable : 1 : 2 : 3 : 4 : 5 : 6 : 7 : improbable

18. My close friends think that I should exercise for at least 20 minutes, three times per week, for the next 3 months.

probable : 1 : 2 : 3 : 4 : 5 : 6 : 7 : improbable

19. My doctor thinks that I should exercise for at least 20 minutes, three times per week, for the next 3 months.

probable : 1 : 2 : 3 : 4 : 5 : 6 : 7 : improbable

20. My parents think that I should exercise for at least 20 minutes, three times per week, for the 3 months.

probable : 1 : 2 : 3 : 4 : 5 : 6 : 7 : improbable

[Identification With Referent]

21. When it comes to matters of health, how much do you want to be like your close friends?

    very much : 1 : 2 : 3 : 4 : 5 : 6 : 7 : not at all

22. When it comes to matters of health, how much do you want to be like your parents?

    very much : 1 : 2 : 3 : 4 : 5 : 6 : 7 : not at all

23. When it comes to matters of health, how much do you want to be like your spouse or partner?

    very much : 1 : 2 : 3 : 4 : 5 : 6 : 7 : not at all

[Descriptive Belief Strength]

24. After major surgery, my close friends would exercise for at least 20 minutes, three times per week, for the next 3 months.

    probable : 1 : 2 : 3 : 4 : 5 : 6 : 7 : improbable

25. After major surgery, my parents would exercise for at least 20 minutes, three times per week, for the next 3 months.

    probable : 1 : 2 : 3 : 4 : 5 : 6 : 7 : improbable

26. After major surgery, my spouse or partner would exercise for at least 20 minutes, three times per week, for the next 3 months.

    probable : 1 : 2 : 3 : 4 : 5 : 6 : 7 : improbable

[Power of Control Factors]

27. Having physical strength would enable me to exercise for at least 20 minutes, three times per week, for the next 3 months.

    agree : 1 : 2 : 3 : 4 : 5 : 6 : 7 : disagree

28. Experiencing pain would make it difficult for me to exercise for at least 20 minutes, three times per week, for the next 3 months.

    agree : 1 : 2 : 3 : 4 : 5 : 6 : 7 : disagree

29. Getting physical therapy would enable me to exercise for at least 20 minutes, three times per week, for the next 3 months.

agree : 1 : 2 : 3 : 4 : 5 : 6 : 7 : disagree

30. Having others to exercise with would enable me to exercise for at least 20 minutes, three times per week, for the next 3 months.

agree : 1 : 2 : 3 : 4 : 5 : 6 : 7 : disagree

[Control Belief Strength]

31. I will have physical strength in the next 3 months.

likely : 1 : 2 : 3 : 4 : 5 : 6 : 7 : unlikely

32. I will experience pain in the next 3 months.

likely : 1 : 2 : 3 : 4 : 5 : 6 : 7 : unlikely

33. I will be getting physical therapy in the next 3 months.

likely : 1 : 2 : 3 : 4 : 5 : 6 : 7 : unlikely

34. I will have others to exercise with in the next 3 months.

likely : 1 : 2 : 3 : 4 : 5 : 6 : 7 : unlikely

[Direct Attitude Scales]

35. My exercising for at least 20 minutes, three times per week, for the next 3 months is

good : 1 : 2 : 3 : 4 : 5 : 6 : 7 : bad

36. My exercising for at least 20 minutes, three times per week, for the next 3 months is

unpleasant : 1 : 2 : 3 : 4 : 5 : 6 : 7 : pleasant

37. My exercising for at least 20 minutes, three times per week, for the next 3 months is

harmful : : 1 : 2 : 3 : 4 : 5 : 6 : 7 : beneficial

38. My exercising for at least 20 minutes, three times per week, for the next 3 months is

interesting : 1 : 2 : 3 : 4 : 5 : 6 : 7 : boring

[Direct Perceived Norm Scales]

39. Most people who are important to me think that I should exercise for at least 20 minutes, three times per week, for the next 3 months.

    true : 1 : 2 : 3 : 4 : 5 : 6 : 7 : false

40. Most people whose opinions I value would approve of my exercising for at least 20 minutes, three times per week, for the next 3 months.

    improbable : 1 : 2 : 3 : 4 : 5 : 6 : 7 : probable

41. Most people I respect and admire will exercise for at least 20 minutes, three times per week, in the 3 months following major heart surgery.

    unlikely : 1 : 2 : 3 : 4 : 5 : 6 : 7 : likely

42. Most people like me have exercised for at least 20 minutes, three times per week, in the 3 months following their major heart surgery.

    agree : 1 : 2 : 3 : 4 : 5 : 6 : 7 : disagree

[Direct Perceived Control Scales]

43. I am confident that I can exercise for at least 20 minutes, three times per week, for the next 3 months.

    true : 1 : 2 : 3 : 4 : 5 : 6 : 7 : false

44. My exercising for at least 20 minutes, three times per week, for the next 3 months is completely up to me.

    disagree : 1 : 2 : 3 : 4 : 5 : 6 : 7 : agree

45. If I really wanted to, I could exercise for at least 20 minutes, three times per week, for the next 3 months.

    likely : 1 : 2 : 3 : 4 : 5 : 6 : 7 : unlikely

46. For me to exercise for at least 20 minutes, three times per week, for the next 3 months is under my control.

    not at all : 1 : 2 : 3 : 4 : 5 : 6 : 7 : completely

[Behavioral Intention Scales]

47. I intend to exercise for at least 20 minutes, three times per week, for the next 3 months.

    definitely do : 1 : 2 : 3 : 4 : 5 : 6 : 7 : definitely do not

48. I will exercise for at least 20 minutes, three times per week, for the next 3 months.

    likely : 1 : 2 : 3 : 4 : 5 : 6 : 7 : unlikely

49. I am willing to exercise for at least 20 minutes, three times per week, for the next 3 months.

    false : 1 : 2 : 3 : 4 : 5 : 6 : 7 : true

50. I plan to exercise for at least 20 minutes, three times per week, for the next 3 months.

    agree : 1 : 2 : 3 : 4 : 5 : 6 : 7 : disagree

[Past Behavior and Behavior Assessed 3 Months Later]

51. In the past 3 months, how often have you exercised for at least 20 minutes, three times per week?

    never : 1 : 2 : 3 : 4 : 5 : 6 : 7 : almost always

52. I have exercised for at least 20 minutes, three times per week, in the past 3 months.

    true : 1 : 2 : 3 : 4 : 5 : 6 : 7 : false

SUBJECT INDEX

I

of condom use, 112–113
control, 7
election, 5, 6, 8, 153, 274, 275, 277
health, 392
of hunting, 120, 229, 230
important vs unimportant, 111, 113
internal factors, 154
modal salient, 108, 112, 209, 212, 452
mutual cooperation produces, 199
negative, 20
observational beliefs, 221
performing behavior, 18, 19, 222, 235, 325, 397, 398
positive vs negative, 123–124, 132, 203, 204, 211, 213, 245
predict election, 10, 11
salient beliefs, 122
social, 136
Outgroup
attitude toward, 361, 408
member, 260
nonverbal behaviors, 16
positive vs negative attitudes, 259
prejudice toward, 278
Outside, 222, 223
Outside of awareness, 304
Overt behavior, 14, 60, 261, 400

P

Partisan attitudes, 9–10, 11
Partisan preference, 7
Partner norm, 152, 284, 285
Party identification
background factors, 400, 408
background variable, 234
partisan attitudes, 9–10, 11
personality traits, 236
voting choice, 10, 224, 236
Past behavior
behavioral intentions, 289
criterion of causality, 286
demographic information, 326–327
direct measures of, 451
measure of intention, 50, 327
normative component, 285
and prediction of future behavior, 285–287
and prediction of intentions, 287–288
predictive validity, 406
questionnaire, 463
recall, 51
residual effect of, 406

Past behavior on intentions, 288, 289–290, 293, 319
Past experiences, 24
Past or current behavior, 49
Past vs future behavior, 50–51
Path analyses, 384–385
Pathological shyness, 352
Pattern of beliefs, 23
Pattern of influence, 180
Patterns and attitudes, 255
Payoff matrix, 199
Peer pressure, 143–144
Perceived
autonomy. *See* Perceived autonomy
barrier. *See* Perceived barrier
behavioral control. *See* Perceived behavioral control
consequences. *See* Perceived consequences
control. *See* Perceived control
norms. *See* Perceived norms
Perceived ability, 153, 156, 158
Perceived autonomy, 167, 176, 177
Perceived barrier, 331, 384
Perceived behavior, 145, 146
Perceived behavioral control (PBC). *See also* Self-efficacy
actual control, 405
additive effects of intentions, 66–68
alpha coefficient, 161, 163, 167, 173
and attitudes, 181
autonomy, 185, 189, 369, 402, 450
barriers, 155, 158
and behavior, 21, 65–66, 72, 186, 191
behavioral predictions, 184
behavior variance, 408
beliefs, 169
BSE, 191, 197
capability and autonomy, 185, 369
capacity vs autonomy, 165–167, 450
colonoscopy, 355–356
constructs and definitions, 153–154
control beliefs, 170–172, 172–176, 329
defined, 64, 154–155, 177
determinants of, 71, 153, 173
direct measures of, 403
effects of intentions on behavior, 113
factor analysis, 161–162, 163, 402
and IM study, 19
individual differences, 195–197
influence behavior, 201–202
intention-past behavior relation, 327
and intentions, 181, 196–197, 328
internal consistency (alpha), 164, 187

Recycling behavior
    diverse behavioral domains, 48
    environment, 2, 259, 274
    glass recycling, 204, 219
    high-opportunity activities, 53
    household waste, 199, 288
    prediction of intentions, **188**
Referent
    descriptive normative beliefs, 405
    descriptive norms, 404
    identification with, 330, 348, 368, 460
    injunctive/descriptive norms,
        329–330n2
    injunctive normative beliefs, 454
    injunctive norms, 333
    modal salient set of, 141
    social identification, 198–199
Referent individuals, 135
Referent issues, 141–142
Referent power, 130, 131, 132
Reflexes, 304, 318
Regressing attitudes on belief composites,
    117–118
Regressing attitudes on individual beliefs,
    114–117
Regression analysis
    alcohol, 114
    breast self-examination, 202
    and data collection phase, 380
    demographic variables, 234
    hunting, 124–125
    intention-behavior correlation, 373
    marijuana, 114–115
    subjective norm, 207, 235
    systematic comparisons, 193–195
    valence, 116
Regression coefficients
    and individual differences, 195
    meaning of, 191–192
    multiple regression, 187
    prediction of intentions, 187
    self-identity and anticipated affect,
        299
    systematic comparisons of, 193–197
    variations in, 190–191
Regression equation, 219
Regression weights
    correlational evidence, 197–199
    experimental evidence, 199–201
    intention, 332n4
    multiple regression, 116
    prediction of intentions, 186
    subjective norm, 189
    systematic comparisons of, 193–195

Regret
    anticipated, 294, 295, 297, 298
    feel, 248, 296
Reinforcement, 377, 397
Relative weights, 190
Religion
    attitude measurement, 258
    behavioral patterns, 278
    behavior of interest, 400
    cultural influence, 399
    divinity vs college students attitudes,
        255
    reflection of favorable attitudes, 256
    and segmentation, 362
    and spontaneous behaviors, 16
    voting choice, 9
Religiosity, 236, 256, 258
Religious affiliation, 6, 24
Representativeness, 327
Response bias, 310, 311
Response latency, 40
Restriction of range, 69–71
Retrospective measure of behavior, 49–51
Reward power, 130
Rhetoric, 348
Risk, perceived, **22**, 26, 243, 245, 389, 390
Risk reduction model, 243
Risk-taking behavior
    age, 234–235, 240
    among adolescents, 224
    marijuana, 305
    reasoned action approach, 306
    sensation seeking, 236
    sexual arousal, 307
    smoking cigarettes, 301, 305
Risky decision making, 300–301
Role playing, 17, 352, 359

S

Safer-sex intervention, 1, 376, 377
Salient beliefs, 98–100
    and attitudes, 125, 126, 127, 238
    and behavior, 122–123, 203, 244
    behavioral outcomes, 451
    bipolar evaluative scales, 106, 451–452
    changing existing, 334
    content analysis, 452–453
    cultural influence, 309
    different behaviors, 322, 336
    and direct attitude measure, 122
    eliciting, 109, 248, 451, 456
    expectancy-value model, 105, 119, 120

AUTHOR INDEX